Lecture Notes in Computer Science

Commenced Publication in 1973
Founding and Former Series Editors:
Gerhard Goos, Juris Hartmanis, and Jan van Leeuwen

Gautam Das   Ved P Gulati (Eds.)

Intelligent
Information Technology

7th International Conference on
Information Technology, CIT 2004
Hyderabad, India, December 20-23, 2004
Proceedings

 Springer

Volume Editors

Gautam Das
University of Texas at Arlington
Department of Computer Science and Engineering
Arlington, TX 76019, USA
E-mail: gdas@cse.uta.edu

Ved P. Gulati
Institute for Development and Research in Banking Technology
Castle Hills, Road No. 1, Masab Tank, Hyderabad, 500 057, India
E-mail: vpgulati@idrbt.ac.in

Library of Congress Control Number: 2004116517

CR Subject Classification (1998): F.1-2, C.2, I.2, H.4, D.2, I.4, H.2

ISSN 0302-9743
ISBN 3-540-24126-4 Springer Berlin Heidelberg New York

Springer is a part of Springer Science+Business Media

springeronline.com

© Springer-Verlag Berlin Heidelberg 2004
Printed in Germany

Typesetting: Camera-ready by author, data conversion by Olgun Computergrafik
Printed on acid-free paper   SPIN: 11369288   06/3142   5 4 3 2 1 0

Preface

The 7th International Conference on Information Technology (CIT 2004) was held in Hyderabad, India, during December 20–23, 2004. The CIT 2004 was a forum where researchers from various areas of information technology and its applications could stimulate and exchange ideas on technological advancements.

CIT, organized by the Orissa Information Technology Society (OITS), has emerged as one of the major international conferences in India and is fast becoming the premier forum for the presentation of the latest research and development in the critical area of information technology. The last six conferences attracted reputed researchers from around the world, and CIT 2004 took this trend forward.

This conference focused on the latest research findings on all topics in the area of information technology. Although the natural focus was on computer science issues, research results contributed from management, business and other disciplines formed an integral part.

We received more than 200 papers from over 27 countries in the areas of computational intelligence, neural networks, mobile and ad hoc networks, security, databases, software engineering, signal and image processing, and Internet and WWW-based computing. The programme committee, consisting of eminent researchers, academicians and practitioners, finally selected 43 full papers on the basis of reviewer grades.

This proceedings contains the research papers selected for presentation at the conference and this is the first time that the proceedings have been published in the Lecture Notes in Computer Science (LNCS) series. The poster papers are being printed as a separate conference proceedings.

We would like to thank the CIT 2004 General Chairs Arun K. Pujari and Chitta Baral, and the organizing committee of the 7th International Conference on Information Technology for their support and co-operation. We also thank the invited speakers.

Thanks are also due to the reviewers who very carefully and timely reviewed the papers, the authors who submitted their papers and all the participants of CIT 2004. The process was very systematic and fast, courtesy of Microsoft's Conference Toolkit; our gratitude to them. We also express our sincere thanks to Alfred Hofmann and the staff of Springer for their professional support.

December 2004   Gautam Das and Ved P. Gulati

Organizing Committee

Arun K. Pujari	University of Hyderabad, India
Chakravarthy Bhagvathi	University of Hyderabad, India
Chitta Baral	Arizona State University, USA
Gautam Das	University of Texas at Arlington, USA
Ved P. Gulati	Institute for Development and Research in Banking Technology, Hyderabad, India
Kamalakar Karlapalem	International Institute of Information Technology, Hyderabad, India
P. Radha Krishna	Institute for Development and Research in Banking Technology, Hyderabad, India

Program Committee

Ashutosh Saxena	Institute for Development and Research in Banking Technology, Hyderabad, India
Akshai Aggarwal	University of Windsor, Ontario, Canada
Ambuj Mohanty	Indian Institute of Management, Calcutta, India
Amit Rudra	Curtin University of Technology, Perth, Australia
Anup Kumar	Louisville University, USA
Ankur Teredesai	Rochester Institute Of Technology, Rochester, New York, USA
Arobindo Gupta	Indian Institute of Technology, Kharagpur, India
Atul Negi	University of Hyderabad, India
Basabi Chakraborty	Iwate Prefectural Uni, Iwate, Japan
B.S. Panda	Indian Institute of Technology, Delhi, India
Bhed Bahadur Bista	Iwate Prefectural Univ, Iwate, Japan
Bimal Kumar Roy	Indian Statistical Institute, Kolkata, India
Binoy K. Das	Integrated Test Range, Chandipur, India
Chitta R. Das	Penn State University, USA
D. Misra	New Jersey Institute of Technology, USA
Debasish Chakraborty	Iwate Prefectural Univ, Japan
Dipankar Dasgupta	University of Memphis, USA
Ganapati Panda	National Institute of Technology, Rourkela, India
Giri Kumar Tayi	University at Albany, USA
Goutam Chakraborty	Iwate Prefectural University, Japan
Govinda Rajulu	International Institute of Information Technology, Hyderabad, India
Jay N. Bhuyan	University of Tuskegee, Alabama, USA
Jayaram Pradhan	Berhampur University, India
Joydeep Ghosh	University of Texas, Austin, USA
Kamalakar Karlapalem	International Institute of Information Technology, Hyderabad, India
King-Ip Lin	University of Memphis, USA

Table of Contents

Computational Intelligence

Neural Networks

Communication Networks

Mobile and Adhoc Networks

Security

Database

Software Engineering

Signal and Image Processing

Internet and WWW-Based Computing

An Approach for Conceptual Modeling and Extracting Expressive Semantics from Dance Videos

K. Rajkumar[1], B. Ramadoss[1], and Krishnamurthi Ilango[2]

[1] Department of Computer Applications
National Institute of Technology, Tiruchirappalli 620015, India
{caz0311,brama}@nitt.edu
[2] Department of Computer Science and Engineering
National Institute of Technology, Tiruchirappalli 620015, India
ilango@nitt.edu

Abstract. Due to the high complexity and exponential growth of videos, video data management tasks, such as understanding and annotating semantic content, are very difficult to be accomplished. Dance videos are one such critical domain. Considering the various dance components, understanding their semantic content conceptually, extracting the expressive semantics, annotating them properly and storing the annotations in a suitable medium for future reuse and analysis, are the essential tasks for the next generation dance systems. This paper presents a conceptual multimedia data model based on Protocol Analysis, called Video Semantics Directed Acyclic Graph (VSDAG) model. The expressive semantic content, represented by VSDAG model, is extracted from the video by a unique video annotation system. The generated annotations are stored in a XML compliant structure.

1 Introduction

Multimedia data mining is the process of converting low-level huge volume of multimedia data into high-level knowledge through interactive and iterative steps. Recently, research focus has shifted from multimedia querying and retrieval to discovering novel *patterns*. Especially, *Video Data Mining* provides ample opportunities and is yet to take off as a mainstream active area of research by the data mining community. New methods and techniques need to be developed to mine video sequences.

With the emerging demand on advanced *Decision Support Systems* for multimedia, more and more attention has been devoted to understanding the semantic content, annotating them properly and representing the annotations in a suitable way for future reuse and analysis. Semantics based annotations will break the traditional linear manner of accessing and browsing media and will support vignette-oriented access of audio and video [1, 2]. However, automatic content annotation tools suffer from the semantic gap between user requirements and the shallowness of the content descriptor. This is the crucial obstacle in the content-based retrieval systems.

The nation's cultural wealth depends on its number of classical and folk dances. From generation to generations till today, dance steps were carried out in the natural language of the country verbally and observing the steps performed by the dancer [3]. This requires the dancer or choreographer to be physically present for training his students. India is an ancient country, which is known for its culture, dances and sculptures. Here, *Bharathanatyam*[4,5] is one of the most important classical dances re-

G. Das and V.P. Gulati (Eds.): CIT 2004, LNCS 3356, pp. 1–10, 2004.
© Springer-Verlag Berlin Heidelberg 2004

spected across the globe. Unfortunately Bharathanatyam does not have its dance movements in written form, that is, in *notes* or notations. To learn the dance, the learner has to observe the Guru continuously and emulate the movements for him.

Notational systems are used in almost all fields and are particularly more important in dances for expressing and communicating ideas to the learners of the dance and to the audience viewing it. Also dance notations archive choreography for later stage performance and learning.

Labanotation has been an important tool published by *Rodolph Laban*(1879 – 1958) in order to record and analyze human movements. In Laban Theory, the dance steps are represented using symbols and are available in paper form as diagram [6]. But the problem with Labanotation is that it requires human annotators. There are only very few notators available for this creation process and many other professional performers and choreographers are not able to read the Laban notations in fact. Moreover, some classical dances, like *Bharathanatyam*, contain semantically rich movements portraying all worldly facts, concepts and scenarios and exhibit a very complex grammar without any notations like musical notes. Also, since every dance either classical or folk is unique in its structure, no common form is available for all the dances so that they could be represented using methods like Labanotation or *Benesh* [7].

In this paper, we propose a semantic video data model which models video content in a hierarchy of *Patham* (called song), *Pallavi*, *Anu Pallavi* and *Saranams*, which are the three parts of a *patham*. For every line of *lyrics* of the patham, *peythams* (which are basic steps) and *casual steps* innovated by the dancer on stage, along with *audience's interpretation* are associated. The hierarchical model provides many semantic levels that facilitate the understanding of the video content. We have implemented a video annotation tool to extract the expressive semantics of dance steps from videos, to view them and to store the extracted annotations in *XML*-compliant way [8].

The organization of the paper is as follows: Section 2 discusses the related work on semantic data models. The Video Semantics Directed Acyclic Graph (*VSDAG*) model to conceptually represent the dance steps in the video is presented in Section 3. Section 4 illustrates the design and implementation of the semantic annotation tool. Conclusions are presented in Section 5.

2   Related Work

In the literature, there are numerous research works about modeling and querying the semantic content of videos. Obviously, video can be modeled at different granularities based on low-level features to high-level semantics. Though automatic content description is desirable with low-level features, the quality of generated annotations is inadequate for later query processing and mining.

In [9], the video data model expresses events and concepts of the real world, based on spatio-temporal relationships among salient objects. A set of predicates is defined to describe the relationships of salient objects and *MOQL* (Multimedia Object Query Language) is proposed. In dance domain, dancer is the only single object throughout the video in solo Bharathanatyam dance. Though we can consider human body parts as other objects, spatio-temporal relationships among body parts will not represent any Bharathanatyam step.

In [10], the spatio-temporal model represents events using spatio-temporal attributes of objects and is used for specific domains like sports videos. For example, '*A pass event in a soccer game*' can be modeled easily but not '*Dance event*' in Bharathanatyam because semantics of dance is described at series of levels.

In [11], *ATN* based semantic data model is proposed. The ATN and its sub networks model video data based on *scenes*, *shots* and *key frames*. Spatial and temporal relationships of semantic objects are modeled using *multimedia input strings*. Also, this model records objects like *players*, *ball*, *ground* etc for *soccer* videos as string only, which is not sufficient to model the dance vocabulary.

In [12], a graph based data model represents objects that appear together as a segment. The appearance of a new object forms a new segment. Also, spatio-temporal relationships along with motion vectors are defined. For query processing, *predicate logic* has been applied. Also, [13] extends this model by incorporating not only the appearance of new object, but also the disappearance of an existing object as a new segment. Moreover, this model stores *trajectory* details efficiently without any redundant information. These two models are more suitable for sports and traffic surveillance videos.

In [14], the data model includes *feature-content layer* and *semantic layer*. The feature layer represents low-level visual features and semantic layer represents objects, the video frames containing the objects and objects relationships. The logical segmentation of video is done based on *temporal cohesion* technique, where as we segment the dance video using the accompanying song.

In [21], *VENUS* detects novelty on natural scenes. It applies *outlier analysis* to find abnormal events (called novel events) after extracting low-level features and generating motion maps. It is more suitable for traffic surveillance. But we require a model to understand several high level semantics such as concept, mood, feelings and events, not only outliers.

3   Graph Based Conceptual Modeling

Conceptual modeling is the abstraction of video data into a structure for later querying its contents and mining some interesting hidden patterns. Dance scholars are experts in describing rhythmic motion and steps comprising dance to humans. For conceptual modeling of dance, we want to know how choreographers describe a dance and how such knowledge can be used to archive dance video.

3.1   Segmentation of Dance Videos

In earlier days, video data have been automatically divided based on cinematic features such as *cuts*, *pans* and *zooms* through *image analysis* methods [15]. And some action sequences such as *traffic surveillance actions*, *aerobics* [16,17], *sports actions* [18], *ballet steps* [19] and day-to-day *human activities* are extracted. Fortunately, video data stream provides some more low-level features to help the annotation process. These include *verbal script* of a presenter in news video, *verbal commentary* of sports video, or sound effects in films such as *thrill* or *frighten*. Unfortunately, dance videos do not provide any of these low-level features. Interestingly, it provides various other high level *cues* in order to segment the video streams. They are,

- Accompanying *song*
- Number of dancers on the stage from *single, duet, trio* to *group*
- Dynamics such as *slow, graceful* or *staccato* movements
- Musical score that accompanies

In our work, we have selected *patham* (song) as the basis for segmenting the dance video content.

3.2 Dance Analysis Based on Protocol Analysis

Dance may be analyzed in two ways. *Lay audience* analyzes dance as a sequence of gestures with style and steps that portray everyday movements. But dance expert understands dance through, its *notations, wire-forms* and *verbal accounts*, its *motifs* as well as its *genre and subject matter.*

Protocol Analysis [20] is an effective method in *Cognitive Psychology* that provides *think aloud* verbalization model. The idea is, while the expert is thinking aloud, he will provide us oral information and other thoughts. This is based on the claim, " to produce a verbalization from a thought, first lexical items must be selected for each relation and entity; second, a syntactical form or order of verbalization must be selected". In Protocol Analysis of dance, we perform the following steps

1. Structuring the dance video: This is done with sectioning video by means of patham and its parts such as pallavi, anu pavallai and saranam as well as identifying motifs such as *turning, leaning, stretching, sharing weight* etc and *dynamics.*
2. Describing movement vocabulary: This is done by identifying basic bharathanatyam peythams (steps) such as *samathristy, aalogithathristy* [4] etc by the dance expert.
3. Interpreting dance by audience: Viewers use *linguistic phrases* without any specialist terms.

3.3 The VSDAG Model

Our semantic video model is designed to allow users to navigate its content randomly through its indexing scheme based on the different granularities of the content. The *DAG* can be used to model the semantics of the dance video elegantly.

3.3.1 Video Hierarchy

Based on the segmentation of *Protocol analysis* method, a video can be divided into pathams. A patham is a song for which dance steps will be choreographed and performed. Patham contains pallav*i*, anu pallavi and a sequential collection of saranams. Each part will consist of a set of Lines. Each Line contains a series of peythams and casual steps called motifs. The properties of the video hierarchy are defined below:

- $V = \{ P_1, P_2, ..., P_N \}$, where P_i denotes the ith patham and N is the total number of pathams in this dance video. Let $B(P_1)$ and $E(P_1)$ be the starting and ending times of patham P_1, respectively. The temporal relation $B(P_1) < E(P_1) < B(P_2) < E(P_2) < ....$ is preserved.

- $P_i = \{ PL^i, AP^i, SA^i_1, ..., SA^i_M \}$ where PL^i is the pallavi of P_i, AP^i is the anu pallavi of P_i, $SA^i_{\ j}$ is the jth saranam of P_i and M denotes the total number of saranams in the patham Pi. Then the temporal relation $B(PL^i) < E(PL^i) < B(AP^i) < E(AP^i) < B(SA^i_1) < E(SA^i_1) < ... < B(SA^i_M) < E(SA^i_M)$ holds.

- $PL^i = \{ L^i_1, L^i_2, ..., L^i_p, \}$, where L^i_j denotes the jth Line of pallavi in the ith patham P_i and p represents the total number of Lines. Let $B(L^i_1)$ and $E(L^i_1)$ be the starting and ending times of the first Line of the pallavi in the ith patham P^i respectively and the temporal order $B(L^i_1)<E(L^i_1)<....<B(L^i_p) < E(L^i_p)$ is preserved.

- $AP^i = \{ L^i_1, L^i_2, ..., L^i_q, \}$, where L^i_j denotes the jth Line of anu pallavi in the ith patham P_i and q represents the total number of Lines. The temporal order is preserved similar to the Lines of pallavi.

- $SA^i_j = (L^{i,j}_1, L^{i,j}_2,...., L^{i,j}_r \}$. The component, $L^{i,j}_b$ represents the bth Line of jth saranam in the ith patham P_i and r is the number of Lines in SA^i_j Then the temporal relation $B(L^{i,j}_1) < E(L^{i,j}_1) < ... < B(L^{i,j}_r) < E(L^{i,j}_r)$ holds.

- **Case-A: L^i_j** = { $PY^{i,j}_1$, $PY^{i,j}_2$, ..., $PY^{i,j}_s$, $CS^{i,j}_1$, $CS^{i,j}_2$, ..., $CS^{i,j}_t$, AI^i_j }. $PY^{i,j}_1$ denotes the first peytham of jth line of the pallavi or anu pallavi in the ith patham P_i. Similarly, $CS^{i,j}_1$ denotes the first casual step or motif of jth line of pallavi or anu pallavi in the ith patham. AI^i_j denotes audience interpretation for jth line of pallavi/anu pallavi of ith patham. P_i. The temporal relation $B(PY^{i,j}_1) < E(PY^{i,j}_1) < ...E(PY^{i,j}_s) < B(CS^{i,j}_1) < ... < E(CS^{i,j}_t)$ may not hold. The equalities $B(AI^i_j) = B(L^i_j)$ and $E(AI^i_j) = E(L^i_j)$ hold.

- **Case-B: $L^{i,j}_k$** = {$PY^{i,j,k}_1$, $PY^{i,j,k}_2$, ... $PY^{i,j,k}_s$, $CS^{i,j,k}_1$, ..., $CS^{i,j,k}_t$, $AI^{i,j}_k$}. $PY^{i,j,k}_b$ denotes bth peytham of kth line of the jth saranam in the ith patham P_i. $AI^{i,j}_k$ is the audience interpretation of kth line of jth saranam of ith patham. Similar to *Case-A*, the temporal order may not hold for the peythams and casual steps or motifs as there is a time overlap. The equalities $B(AI^{i,j}_k) = B(L^{i,j}_k)$ and $E(AI^{i,j}_k)=E(L^{i,j}_k)$ hold.

- $PY^{i,j}_k = \{ F^{i,j,k}_{ST}, ..., F^{i,j,k}_{ET} \}$, where ST and ET denote start time and end time. $PY^{i,j}_k$ is all the frames in the interval (ST,ET) for the kth peytham of jth Line of pallavi or anu pallavi in the ith patham P_i.

- $PY^{i,j,k}_l = \{ F^{i,j,k,l}_{ST}, ..., F^{i,j,k,l}_{ET} \}$, where ST and ET denote start time and end time. $PY^{i,j,k}_l$ is all the frames in the interval (ST,ET) for the lth peytham of kth Line of jth saranam in the ith patham P_i.

- $CS^{i,j}_k = \{ F^{i,j,k}_{ST}, ..., F^{i,j,k}_{ET} \}$, where ST and ET denote start time and end time. $CS^{i,j}_k$ is all the frames in the interval (ST,ET) for the kth casual step or motif of jth Line of pallavi or anu pallavi in the ith patham P_i.

- $CS^{i,j,k}_l = \{ F^{i,j,k,l}_{ST}, ..., F^{i,j,k,l}_{ET} \}$, where ST and ET denote start time and end time. $CS^{i,j,k}_{,l}$ is all the frames in the interval (ST,ET) for the lth casual step of kth Line of jth saranam in the ith patham P_i.

- $AI^i_j = \{ M^i_j, E^i_j, T^i_j, PO^i_j \}$.Let M^i_j, E^i_j, T^i_j, and PO^i_j denote the mood, emotion, tempo and posture of a dancer of jth line of pallavi/anu pallavi in the ith patham respectively. The starting and ending times of M^i_j, E^i_j, T^i_j, and PO^i_j are same.
- $AI^{i,j}_k = \{ M^{i,j}_k, E^{i,j}_k, T^{i,j}_k, PO^{i,j}_k \}$.Let $M^{i,j}_k$, $E^{i,j}_k$, $T^{i,j}_k$, $PO^{i,j}_k$ denote the mood, emotion, tempo and posture of a dancer of kth line of jth saranam in the ith patham respectively. The starting and ending times of $M^{i,j}_k$, $E^{i,j}_k$, $T^{i,j}_k$, and $PO^{i,j}_k$ are same.

In property 1, V represents a dance video containing one or more pathams, P_1, P_2 and so on. Pathams follow a temporal order, that is, ending time of P_1 is greater than starting time of P_1. As in Property 2, each patham contains one pallavi PL^i, one anu pallavi AP^i and one or more saranams SA^i and also preserves temporal order. Each of these parts is made up of lines either L^i_j or $L^{i,j}_k$. Each line has peythams $PY^{i,j,k}$, motifs or casual steps $CS^{i,j,k}$ and either AI^i_j or $AI^{i,j}_k$ which in tern are collection of frames $F^{i,j,k}$ in the time interval (ST, ET).

3.3.2 Basic Definitions
This section provides the basic definitions for different types of attributes and other elements for the graphical model. Also, we define the various graphical notations that are required for the modeling of the video data in the next section.

Definition 1: **Video Fragment (VF).** *A Video Fragment of a video* V *represents one or more movements, which may be either* pre-existing *in the dance vocabulary or a motif* with *dynamics. Examples include* V, P, PL, AP, SA, L, PY, CS and AI *(which are defined in the previous section).*

Definition 2: **Primitive Attribute (PA).** *A Primitive Attribute of VF is an attribute which is non-empty and holds values to describe the properties of VF, whose types are* String, Normalized String or Token. *Examples are* DancerID, DanceID, PathamID etc.

Definition 3: **Reference Attribute (RA).** *A Reference Attribute of VF is an attribute whose value is a special identity to the VF so as to be referenced by the parent level VF. Examples would be* LineID, PeythamID or CasualStepID *of pallavi, anu pallavi or saranam.*

Definition 4: **Composite Attribute (CA).** *A Composite Attribute of a VF is an attribute, which holds values such as* Date, Unicode characters *or* Regular Expressions *in order to compliment the description of the properties of VF. Examples include* Costume, StartTime, EndTime *etc.*

3.3.3 The Semantic Model
Formally, the tree-structured organization of the dance steps can be modeled as a directed acyclic graph, as shown in *Figure-1*. A Video Semantics Directed Acyclic Graph (VSDAG) model is a 5-level directed acyclic graph with a set of tree nodes (*N*) and a set of arcs (*A*) connecting a child node to its parent node. There are four node types.

1. **Rectangle Node**: A rectangle node specifies any of the *VFs* defined earlier and contains *PA*, *CAs*, *RA* as well as *VFs*, with an exception that root level rectangle node cannot contain *RA*.
2. **Oval Node**: An oval node describes *PA* of a *VF* in dance video data.
3. **Parallelogram Node**: A parallelogram node specifies the reference attribute, *RA* of a *VF* in the video.
4. **Round Rectangle Node**: A round rectangle node specifies a composite attribute, *CA* of a *VF*.

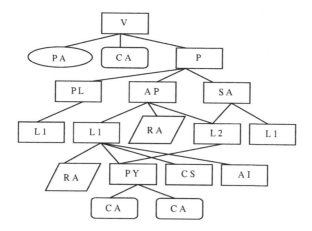

Fig. 1. The VSDAG model to describe the video semantics at different granularities

Note that a terminal node can be an oval node, parallelogram node or round rectangle node and it cannot be a rectangle node. The arcs connecting nodes represent containment behavior, that is child level nodes are part of parent level nodes. The VSDAG model elegantly represents repetition information. Let RN_1 and RN_2 be the two rectangle nodes of the same level for VF_1 and VF_2 respectively. Let RN_3 be the child level rectangle node for VF_1 to represent *PY*, *CS*, or *L*. Suppose a new rectangle node is to be created with the same behavior as RN_3 for RN_2, then it can be avoided by adding a new arc from RN_2 to RN_3. This operation simulates acyclic graph behavior efficiently.

4 Semantic Video Annotation System

The video annotation system has been designed and developed in order to annotate the video semantic content according to the VSDAG model. Using this annotation tool, previously annotated video data can also be viewed and manipulated. The video data that are extracted will be categorized as below.

- **Background data:** The basis *peythams, casual steps* or motifs extracted during earlier annotations and dancer details constitute background data. Also, it includes song information such as name, description and musician name.

- *Bibliographic data:* Metadata includes data like location, costume, date etc.
- *Patham data:* Patham data include all movements that are choreographed, comprising of *peythams* and *motifs* with *dynamics* at different data granularities from peytham or casual step to patham.
- *Audience data:* Data related to audience interpretation while viewing the dance performance such as *mood*, *tempo* of the dance, *emotions*, dance *postures* are considered as audience data.

4.1 The Order of Video Annotation

The order of video annotation is based on VSDAG model's hierarchical structure from top to bottom. Here, the background data are annotated first. Then the annotation of bibliographic data will follow. Annotaion of patham data such as pallavi, anu pallavi will be accomplished afterwards. Finally, audience interpretation of dance data will be annotated. The order of video annotation is sequential as mentioned above with the following restrictions:

- Bibliographic annotation cannot be done before the annotation of background data.
- Patham data cannot be annotated before bibliographic data has been annotated.
- Patham data and audience perception data may be annotated in any order.

The background data have been stored commonly in a relational database for facilitating future annotations and this annotation is done first. Because background data are required for annotating bibliographic, patham and audience data. For instance, dancer details are required for the annotation of bibliographic data. Similarly, available peythams of Bharathanatyam and casual steps are required for the annotation process of patham data. Audience data annotation will be done interactively with maximum originality. Note that 'Verbalization of Thought' paradigm of Protocol Analysis is fully incorporated in our patham as well as audience interpretation data annotation process.

4.2 The Video Annotation Process

This section illustrates the video annotation process as shown in *Figure-2A*. First of all, the background information such as Dancer Information, Bharathanatyam's Peytham Information and Casual Steps Information are determined through the three windows. In the Dancer Information screen, dancerId (auto generated), dancerName, address and email are extracted and stored. Peytham Information window stores all 87 available peythams of Bharathanatyam with peythamId (auto generated), name, description and usage. Similarly, casual steps with attributes such as casualStepId, name and description are determined through Casual Steps Information window.

In the second step, Bibliographic details such as danceId(auto generated), danceName, description, date of performance, location, costume(selected thru combo box), musicianName, captureRate, dancerId(auto updated) and backdrop(selected through combo box) of the dias are annotated using this screen.

The third step in the annotation process is the annotation of the patham content (Please refer *Figure-2B*). Patham is annotated by looking at the running video. Initially, the general details like *raagam* as well as *thaalam* (selected from combo box), pathamId(auto generated), name and theme are determined. Then the actual parts of the patham are annotated in the order pallavi, anu pallavi and saranams which are available as radio buttons. Pallavi has one or more Lines and each line has one or more peythams and/or casual steps. Start time and End time determines the time interval for either peytham or casual step. The button NextStep indicates the end of one step. Similarly, when NextLine button is clicked, it shows end of one line. This process is repeated for all the lines of pallavi. Next, the radio button for anu pallavi is selected and all the lines are annotated in the same order. Similarly, all the saranams will be annotated one after another.

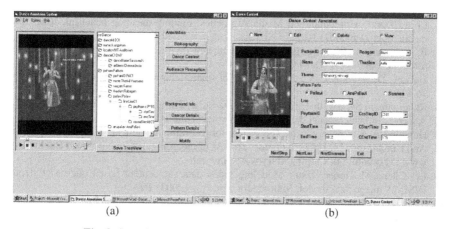

Fig. 2. Sample screen shots depicting interactive annotation

Finally, the annotation of audience perception will be carried out. The properties such as mood, feeling, tempo and posture of dancer are annotated through the combo boxes. If the intended vocabulary does not exist, then the annotator is free to verbalize his thought through the provided text boxes. The above information is extracted for every line of pallavi, anu pallavi and saranam of a patham.

Subsequent annotation of all the other pathams will follow the same order as above. The hierarchy of a patham after the annotations is displayed in a tree view and is stored in an XML compliant structure.

5   Conclusion

Nowadays, video data are widely used in all kinds of applications, thereby making understanding, modeling and indexing tasks complex. Conceptual modeling of videos involves abstraction and representation of the content by means of a suitable model. In this paper, we have focused at the extraction and representation of semantics from video, by applying *Protocol Analysis* of Cognitive Psychology.

We have proposed a conceptual model, called VSDAG model, which models the semantic content of the dance video at different granularities. This hierarchical model segments a Patham into parts such as Pallavi, Anu Pallavi and Saranams and associates several lines of Bharathanatyam steps and motifs as well as audience interpretations such as mood, tempo, dynamics, and emotions to these parts.

We have implemented a video annotation system in order to extract the expressive semantic information such as peytham, motif, mood etc and to represent the annotations generated in a tree view. The tree view is a preferred component, because our video data model is a model for semi-structured data without a schema, represented as a directed acyclic graph. The annotations depicted in a tree view, are stored in a XML compliant structure for later analysis and video data mining.

References

1. Chitra Dorai.: Computational Media Aesthetics: Finding meaning beautiful. IEEE Multimedia, (Oct-Dec 2001) 10-12
2. B.Shneiderman.: Meeting Human Needs with new digital imaging technologies. IEEE Multi Media, Vol.9.No:4 (Oct-Dec 2002) 8-14
3. Davcev, D., Trajkovic, V.: OO modeling of spatio-temporal dance data. ACM-ITP (2002) 76-81
4. Kalaimamani Saraswathy.: Bharatha Nattiya Kalai, Thirumagal Nilayam (1994)
5. A web of Indian classical dances.: www narthaki.com/index.html
6. Hutchinson, A.: Labanotation: The system for recording movement, T Art Books (1954)
7. Ann Hutchinson, G.: Dance Notation: process of recording movement Dance Books (1984)
8. www.DTD.com/index.html and www.w3.org/xml/
9. Lei Chen., M Tamer Ozsu.: Modeling video data for content based queries: Extending DISIMA image data model. Multimedia Modeling (2003) 169-189
10. Y F Day., A Khokhar., A Ghafoor.: A framework for semantic modeling of video data for content based indexing and retrieval. Vol 7(5) ACM Springer Multimedia Systems J (1999) 409-423
11. Shu Ching Chen., Mei-Ling Shyu., R L Kashyap.: ATN as a semantic model for video data. Vol.3(1), Int, J. of NIS (2000) 9-25
12. YF. Day et al.: OO conceptual modeling of video data. IEEE conf Data Engg, (1995) 401-408
13. Lei Chen., M Tamer Ozsu.: Modeling of video objects in a video database. IEEE Conf. ICME (2002) 217-221
14. M.S. Hacid., C. Decleir,J., Kouloumdjian.: A database approach for modeling and querying video data. IEEE Trans on Knowledge and Data Engineering, Vol.12(5) (2000) 729–750
15. Arun, H., Ramesh, J., Terry, E., Weymouth. (ed.): Production Model Based Digital Video Segmentation. In: Furht (1996) 111-153
16. Ben Arie et al.: Human Activity Recognition using Multi dimensional indexing. IEEE Trans on Pattern Analysis and Machine Intelligence, Vol.8. (Aug 2002) 1091-1104
17. Stephane et al.: Face tracking and realistic animations for Telecommunicant clones. IEEE Multi Media. (Jan-March 2000) 34-242
18. Yihong Gong., Lim Teck Sin., Chua Hock Chuan., Hongjiang Zhang., Masao akauchi.: Automatic Parsing of TV Soccer Programs. IEEE Conf MM Comp & Sys.(1995) 167-174
19. Lee Campbell.: Recognizing Classical Ballet Steps Using Phase SpaceConstraints. MIT Media Lab TR297 (http://www-white.media.mit.edu/cgi-bin/tr_pagemaker)
20. Ericsson, et al.: Protocol Analysis:Verbal Reports as Data. The MIT Press
21. Gaborski, RS., Vaingankar, VS., Chaoj, VS., Teradesai, AM.: VENUS: A system for novelty detection in video streams with learning. Proc. 17th Intl conf. FLAIRS, South Beach, FL (2004) PaperID #154

BioPubMiner: Machine Learning Component-Based Biomedical Information Analysis Platform

Jae-Hong Eom and Byoung-Tak Zhang

Biointelligence Lab., School of Computer Science and Engineering,
Seoul National University, Seoul 151-744, South Korea
{jheom,btzhang}@bi.snu.ac.kr

Abstract. In this paper we introduce BioPubMiner, a machine learning component-based platform for biomedical information analysis. BioPubMiner employs natural language processing techniques and machine learning based data mining techniques for mining useful biological information such as protein-protein interaction from the massive literature. The system recognizes biological terms such as gene, protein, and enzymes and extracts their interactions described in the document through natural language processing. The extracted interactions are further analyzed with a set of features of each entity that were collected from the related public database to infer more interactions from the original interactions. The performance of entity and interaction extraction was tested with selected MEDLINE abstracts. The evaluation of inference proceeded using the protein interaction data of *S.cerevisiae* (bakers yeast) from MIPS and SGD.

1 Introduction

Normally, novel scientific discoveries are based on the existing knowledge which has to be accessible and thus usable by the scientific community. In the 19th century, the spread of scientific information was still done by writing letters with new discoveries to a small number of colleagues. This job was taken over professionally by printed journals. Currently, we are on another switch into electronic media. Electronic storage with huge capacity allows the customized extraction of information from the literature and its combination with other data resources such as heterogeneous databases. Indeed, it is not only an opportunity, but also a pressing need as the volume of scientific literature is increasing immensely. Furthermore, the scientific community is growing so that even for a rather specialized field it becomes impossible to stay up-to-date just through personal contacts in that particular community. The growing amount of knowledge also increases the chance for new ideas based on the combination of solutions from different fields. And there is a necessity of accessing and integrating all scientific information to be able to judge the own progress and to get inspired by new questions and answers [1].

After the human genome sequences have been decoded, especially in biology and bioinformatics, there are more and more people devoted to this research domain and hundreds of on-line databases characterizing biological information such as sequences, structures, molecular interactions, and expression patterns [2]. Despite the prevalent topic of research, the end result of all biological experiments is a publication in the form of textbook. However, information in text form, such as MEDLINE (http://www.pubmed.gov), is a greatly underutilized source of biological information

G. Das and V.P. Gulati (Eds.): CIT 2004, LNCS 3356, pp. 11–20, 2004.

to biological researchers. Because it takes lots of time to obtain important and accurate information from this huge databases with daily increase. Thus knowledge discovery from a large collection of scientific papers is become very important for efficient biological and biomedical research. So far, a number of tools and approaches have been developed to resolve such needs. There are many systems analyzing abstracts in MEDLINE to offer bio-related information services. Suiseki [3, 4] and BioBiblioMetrics [5] focus on the protein-protein interaction extraction and visualization. MedMiner [6] utilizes external data sources such as GeneCard [7] and MEDLINE for offering structured information about specific key-words provided by the user. AbXtract [8] labels the protein function in the input text and XplorMed [9] presents the user specified information through the interaction with user. GENIES [10] discovers more complicated information such as pathways from journal abstracts. Recently, MedScan [11] employed full-sentence parsing technique for the extraction of human protein interactions from MEDLINE.

Generally, these conventional systems rely on basic natural language processing (NLP) techniques when analyzing literature data. And the efficacy of such systems heavily depends on the rules for processing raw information. Such rules have to be refined by human experts, entailing the possibility of lack of clarity and coverage. In order to overcome this problem, we used machine learning techniques in combination with natural language processing techniques to analyze the interactions among the biological entities. We also incorporated several data mining techniques for the extensive discovery, i.e., detection of the interactions which are not directly described in the text.

We have developed BioPubMiner (Biomedical Publication Mining & Analysis System) which performs efficient interaction mining of biological entities. For the evaluation of performance, literature and interaction data of the budding yeast (*S. cerevisiae*) was used as the model organism.

The paper is organized as follows. In Section 2, the major three component of BioPubMiner is described. In Section 3, we describe the methodology of the interaction inference module of BioPubMiner. In Section 4, performance evaluation of each component is given. Finally, concluding remarks and future works are given in Section 5.

2   System Description of BioPubMiner

BioPubMiner, a machine learning based text mining platform, consist of three key components: literature processing, interaction inference, and visualization component.

2.1   Literature Processing

The literature processing module is based on the NLP techniques adapted to take into account the properties of biomedical literature and extract interactions between biological entities. It includes a part-of-speech (POS) tagger, a named-entity tagger, a syntactic analyzer, and an event extractor. The POS tagger based on hidden Markov models (HMMs) was adopted for tagging biological words as well as general ones. The named-entity tagger, based on support vector machines (SVMs), recognizes the region of an entity and assigns a proper class to it. The syntactic analyzer recognizes base phrases and detects the dependency represented in them. Finally, the event extractor finds the binary relation using the syntactic information of a given sentence, co-occurrence statistics between two named entities, and pattern information of an event verb. General medical term was trained with UMLS meta-thesaurus [12] and the biological entity and its interaction was trained with GENIA corpus [13]. And the underlying NLP approach for named entity recognition is based on the system of Hwang *et al.* [14] and Lee *et al.* [15] with collaborations (More detailed descriptions of language processing component are explained in these two papers).

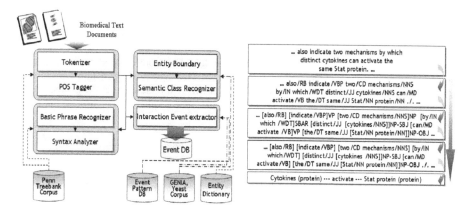

Fig. 1. The block architecture of literature processing module (left) and the example of text processing (right). The resulting event DB contains interactions between entities extracted from domain-documents. Event pattern database was constructed from the GENIA corpus

2.2   Interaction Inference

The relation inference module, which finds common features and group relations, is based on data mining and machine learning techniques. A set of features of each component of the interaction are collected from public databases such as Saccharomyces Genome Database (SGD) [16] and database of Munich Information Center for Protein Sequences (MIPS) [17] and represented as a binary feature vector. An association rule discovery algorithm (Apriori [18]) and information theory based feature filter were used to extract the appropriate common feature set of interacting biological entities. In addition, a distribution-based clustering algorithm [19] was adopted to analyze group relations. This clustering method collects group relation from the collection of document which contains various biological entities. And the clustering procedure discovers common characteristics among members of the same cluster. It also finds the features describing inter-cluster relations. BioPubMiner also provides graphical interface to select various options for the clustering and mining. Finally, the hypothetical interactions are generated for the construction of interaction network. The hypotheses correspond to the inferred generalized association rules and the procedure of association discovery is described in the Section of 'Methods.' Figure 2 describes the schematic architecture of relation inference module.

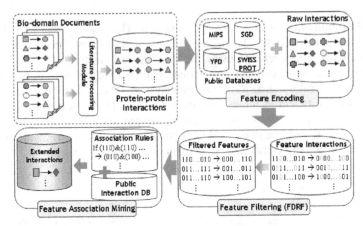

Fig. 2. The block diagram of relation inference module. For feature encoding, feature definition from public database such as SGD and MIPS are used. The raw interaction represents the
set of interactions which was constructed from previous literature processing module. The
extended interactions include original interactions and inferred interactions through the feature
association rule mining

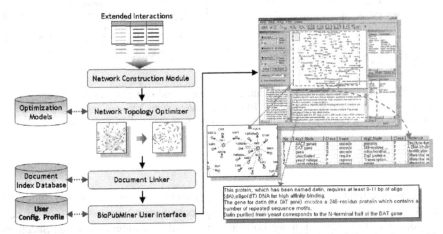

Fig. 3. The workflow diagram of the visualization module. The dashed line in the resulting
interaction graph stands for the inferred interactions

2.3 Visualization

The visualization module shows interactions among the biological entities as a network format. It also shows the documents from which the relations were extracted
and inferred. In addition, diverse additional information, such as the weight of association between biological entities could be represented. Thus the user can easily
examine the reliability of relations inferred by the system. Moreover, the visualization
module shows interaction networks with minimized complexity for comprehensibility
and can be utilized as an independent interaction network viewer with predefined
input format. Figure 3 shows the overall architecture of visualization module and its
interface.

3 Methods

In this section we describe the approaches of the relation inference module of Bio-PubMiner. Basically, the interaction inference is based on the machine learning theory to find the optimal feature sets. Additionally, association rule discovery method which is widely used in data mining field is used to find general association among the selected optimal features.

3.1 Feature Dimension Reduction by Feature Selection

The correlation between two random variables can be measured by two broad approaches, based on classical linear correlation and based on information theory. Linear correlation approaches can remove features with near zero linear correlation to the class and reduce redundancy among selected features. But, linear correlation measures may not be able to capture correlations that are not linear in nature and the calculation requires all features contain numerical values [20]. In this paper, we use an information theory-based correlation measure to overcome these drawbacks.

Each feature of data can be considered as a random variable and the uncertainty of it can be measured by *entropy*. The entropy of a variable X is defined as

$$H(X) = -\sum_i P(x_i) \log_2(P(x_i)),$$

(1)

And the entropy of X after observing values of another variable Y is defined as

$$H(X|Y) = -\sum_j P(y_j) \sum_i P(x_i|y_j) \log_2(P(x_i|y_j)),$$

(2)

where $P(y_j)$ is the prior probability of the value y_j of Y, and $P(x_i|y_j)$ is the posterior probability of X being x_i given the values of Y. The amount by which the entropy of X decreases reflects additional information about X provided by Y and is called *information gain* [21], which is given by

$$IG(X|Y) = H(X) - H(X|Y)$$

(3)

It is said that symmetry is a desired property for a measure of correlation between features and information gain [20]. However, information gain is biased in favor of features with more values and the values have to be normalized to ensure they are comparable and have the same affect. Therefore, we used the *symmetrical uncertainty* as a measure of feature correlation [22], defined as

$$SU(X,Y) = 2 \left[\frac{IG(X|Y)}{H(X) + H(Y)} \right], \quad 0 \le SU(X,Y) \le 1$$

(4)

Figure 4 shows the overall procedure of the correlation-based feature dimension reduction filter which was earlier introduced by Yu *et al.* [20], named fast correlation-based filter (FCBF). In this paper, we call this FCBC procedure as feature dimension reduction filter (FDRF) for our application. The algorithm finds a set of principal features S_{best} for the class concept. First, the procedure in Figure 4 calculates the symmetrical uncertainty (SU) values for each feature, selects relevant feature into S'_{list} based on the predefined threshold δ, and constructs an ordered list of them in descending order according to their SU values. Next, it further processes the ordered list to remove redundant features and only keeps principal ones among all the selected relevant features.

With symmetrical uncertainty as a feature association measure, we reduce the feature dimension through the feature selection. In Figure 4, the class C is divided into two classes, conditional protein class (C_C) and result protein class (C_R) of interaction. The relevance of a feature to the protein interaction (interaction class) is decided by the value of c–correlation and f–correlation, where an SU value δ is used as a threshold value. These two correlations are defined in the paper of Yu et al. [20].

Given training dataset $S = (f_1,...,f_N,C)$, where $C = C_C \cup C_R$ and User-decided threshold δ, do following procedure for each class C_C and C_R.

1. **Repeat** Step 1.1 to 1.2, for all i, $i = 1$ to N.
   1.1 **Calculate** $SU_{i,c}$ for f_i.
   1.2. **Append** f_i to S'_{list} when $SU_{i,c} \geq \delta$.
2. **Sort** S'_{list} in descending order with $SU_{i,c}$ value.
3. **Set** f_p with the first element of S'_{list}.
4. **Repeat** Step 4.1 to 4.3, for all $f_p \neq NULL$.
   4.1 **Set** f_q with the next element of f_p in S'_{list}.
   4.2 **Repeat** Step 4.2.1 to 4.2.3, for all $f_q \neq NULL$.
      4.2.1 **Set** $f'_q = f_q$.
      4.2.2 if $SU_{p,q} \geq SU_{q,c}$,
         Remove f_q from S'_{list} and **Set** f_q with the next element of f'_q in S'_{list}.
         else **Set** f_q with the next element of f_q in S'_{list}.
      4.2.3 **Set** f_q with the next element of f_q in S'_{list}
   4.3 **Set** f_p with the next element of f_p in S'_{list}.
5. **Set** $S_{best} = S'_{list}$

Output: the most informative optimal feature subset: S_{best}

Fig. 4. The procedures of feature dimension reduction filter (FDRF)

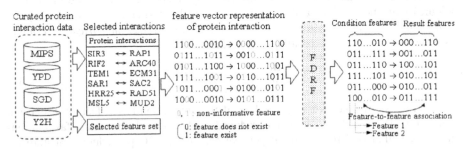

Fig. 5. Protein interaction as feature vector forms. Each interaction is represented with binary feature vector (whether the feature exists or not) and their associations. The FDRF sets those features as "don't care" (D/K) which have SU value less than given SU threshold . This is intended to consider in association mining only those features that have greater SU value than a given threshold. The features marked D/K are regarded as D/K also in association rule mining (i.e., these features are not counted in the calculation of support and confidence). These features are not shown in the vector representation of right side of Figure 5

3.2 Feature Association Mining

Entity Interaction as Feature Association

After the extraction of interaction from literature, each interaction is represented as a pair of two entities that directly binds to each other. To analyze interaction of entities with feature association, we consider each interacting entity pair as transaction of mining data. These transactions with binary vector representation are described in Figure 5. Using association rule mining, then, we extract association of features which generalize the interactions.

Association Mining

To predict protein–protein interaction with feature association, we adopt the association rule discovery data mining algorithm (so-called Apriori algorithm) proposed by Agrawal *et al.* [18]. Generally, an association rule R $(A \Rightarrow B)$ has two values, *support* and *confidence*, representing the characteristics of the association rule. Support (SP) represents the frequency of co-occurrence of all the items appearing in the rule. And confidence (CF) is the accuracy of the rule, which is calculated by dividing the SP value by the frequency of the item in conditional part of the rule.

$$SP(A \Rightarrow B) = P(A \cup B), \; CF(A \Rightarrow B) = P(B \mid A) \tag{5}$$

where $A \Rightarrow B$ represents association rule for two items (set of features) A and B in that order. Association rule can be discovered by detecting all the possible rules whose supports and confidences are larger than the user-defined threshold value called minimal support (SP_{min}) and minimal confidence (CF_{min}) respectively. Rules that satisfy both minimum support and minimum confidence threshold are taken as to be *strong*. Here we consider these strong association rules as interesting ones.

In this work, we use the same association rule mining and the scoring approach of Oyama *et al.* [23] for performance comparison with respect to the execution time.

4 Experimental Results

Performance of Literature Processing

To test the performance of entity recognition and interaction extraction of our literature processing module, we built a corpus from 1,500 randomly selected scientific abstracts from PubMed identified to contain biological entity names and interactions through manual searches. The corpus was manually analyzed for biological entities such as protein, gene, and small molecule names in addition to any interaction relationships present in each abstract within the corpus by biologist in our laboratory. Analysis of the corpus revealed 6,988 distinct references to biological entities and a total of 4,212 distinct references to interaction relationships. Performance evaluation was done over the same set of 1,500 articles, by capturing the set of entities and interactions recognized by the system and comparing this output against the manually analyzed results previously mentioned. Table 1 shows the statistics of abstract document collection for extraction performance evaluation.

Table 1. The statistics for the test document collection

# of abstracts in collection	# of biological entities	# of interactions
1,500	6,988	4,212

We measured the recall and the precision for both the ability to recognize entity names in text in addition to the ability of the system to extract interactions based on the following calculations:

$$\text{Recall} = TP / (TP + FN)$$
$$\text{Precision} = TP / (TP + FP) \tag{6}$$

where, TP (true positive) is the number of biological entities or interactions that were correctly identified by the system and were found in the corpus. FN (false negative) is the number of biological entities or interactions that the system failed to recognize in the corpus and FP (false positive) is the number of biological entities or interactions that were recognized by the system but were not found in the corpus. Performance test results of the extraction module are described in Table 2.

Table 2. The precision and recall performance of the entities and interaction extraction

Rcognition Categories	Recall	Precision
Biological entities	83.5	93.1
Interactions of entities	73.9	80.2

Performance of Inference Through Feature Selection and Association Mining

To test the performance of inference module of BioPubMiner through feature selection (reductions), we used protein–protein interaction as a metric of entity recognition and interaction extraction. The major protein pairs of the interactions are obtained from the same data source of Oyama *et al.* [23]. It includes MIPS [17], YPD and Y2H by Ito *et al.* [24] and Uetz *et al.* [25]. Additionally, we used SGD [16] to collect more lavish feature set. Table 3 shows the statistics of interaction data for each data source and the filtering result with FDRF of Figure 4.

Table 3. The statistics for the protein–protein interaction dataset

Data Source	# of interactions	# of initial features	# of filtered features
MIPS	10,641		
YPD	2,952	6,232	1,293
SGD	1,482	(total)	(total)
Y2H (Ito *et al.*)	957		
Y2H (Uetz *et al.*)	5,086		

We performed feature filtering procedure of Figure 4 as a first step of our inference method ($\delta = 0.73$) after the feature encoding with the way of Figure 5. Next, we performed association rule mining under the condition of minimal support 9 and minimal confidence 75% on the protein interaction data which have reduced features. Next, we predicted new protein–protein interaction which have not used in association training setp. The accuracy of prediction is measured whether the predicted interaction exists in the collected dataset or not. The results are measured with 10 cross-validation for more realistic evaluation.

Table 4 gives the advantage of obtained by filtering non-informative (redundant) features and the inference performance of BioPubMiner. The accuracy of interaction prediction increased about 3.4% with FDRF. And the elapsed time of FDRF based association mining, 143.27 sec, include the FDRF processing time which was 19.89 sec. The elapsed time decrease obtained by using FDRF is about 32.5%. Thus, it is of great importance to reduce number of feature of interaction data for the improvement of both accuracy and execution performance. Thus, we can guess that the information theory based feature filtering reduced a set of misleading or redundnt features of interaction data and this feature reduction eliminated wrong associations and boosted the pocessing time. And the feature association shows the promising results for inferencing implicit interaction of biological entities.

Table 4. Accuracy of the proposed method and the effect (in elapsed time) of filtering optimal informative features with FDRF. Total interactions for prediction is selected from Table 3

Prediction method (Association ming)	# of interactions			Accuracy ($|P|/|T|$)	Elapsed Time
	Total	Excluded (T)	Predicted (P)		
Without FDRF	4,628	463	423	91.4 %	212.34 sec
With FDRF	4,628	463	439	94.8 %	143.27 sec

5 Conclusions

In this paper, we presented a component-based biomedical text analysis platform, BioPubMiner, which screens the interaction data from literature abstracts through natural language analysis, performs inferences based on machine learning and data mining techniques, and visualizes interaction networks with appropriate links to the evidence article. To reveal more comprehensive interaction information, we employed both the data mining approach with optimal feature selection method in addition to the conventional natural language processing techniques. The main two component of the proposed system (literature processing and interaction inference) achieved some improvement. From the result of Table 4, it is also suggested that with smaller granularity of interaction (i.e., not protein, but a set of features of proteins) we could achieve further detailed investigation of the protein–protein interaction. Thus we can say that the proposed method is a somewhat suitable approach for an efficient analysis of interactive entity pair which has many features as a back-end module of the general literature mining and for the experimentally produced interaction data with moderate false positive ratios.

However, current public interaction data produced by such as high-throughput methods (e.g. Y2H) have many false positives. And several interactions of these false positives are corrected by recent researches through reinvestigation with new experimental approaches. Thus, study on the new method for resolving these problems related to false positive screening further remain as future works.

Acknowledgements

This research was supported by the Korean Ministry of Science and Technology under the NRL Program and the Systems Biology Program. The RIACT at Seoul National University provided research facilities for this study.

References

1. Andrade, M.,A., *et al.*: Automated extraction of information in molecular biology. *FEBS Letters* **476** (2000) 12-17.
2. Chiang, J.,H., *et al.*: GIS: a biomedical text-mining system for gene information discovery. *Bioinformatics* **20**(1) (2004) 120-21.
3. Suiseki. http://www.pdg.cnb.uam.es/suiseki/index.html.
4. Blaschke, C., *et al.*: Automatic extraction of biological information from scientific text: protein-protein interactions. In *Proceedings of ISMB'99* (1999) 60-67.
5. BioBiblioMetrics. http://www.bmm.icnet.uk/~stapleyb/biobib/.
6. Tanabe, L., *et al.*: MedMiner: an internet text-mining tool for biomedical information, with application to gene expression profiling. *BioTechniques* **27** (1999) 1210-17.
7. Safran, M., *et al.*: Human gene-centric databases at the Weizmann institute of science: GeneCards, UDB, CroW 21 and HORDE. *Nucleic Acids Res.* **31**(1) (2003) 142-46.
8. Andrade, M.A., *et al.*: Automatic extraction of keywords from scientific text: application to the knowledge domain of protein families. *Bioinformatics* **14**(7) (1998) 600-07.
9. Perez-Iratxeta, C., *et al.*: XplorMed: a tool for exploring MEDLINE abstracts. *Trends Biochem. Sci.* **26** (2001) 573-75.
10. Friedman, C., *et al.*: GENIS: a natural-language processing system for the extraction of molecular pathways from journal articles. *Bioinformatics* **17**(Suppl.1) (2001) S74-S82.
11. Daraselia, N., *et al.*: Extracting human protein interactions from MEDLINE using a full-sentence parser. *Bioinformatics* **20**(5) (2004) 604-11.
12. Humphreys, B. L., *et al.*: The Unified Medical Language System: an informatics research collaboration. *J. American Medical Informatics Association* **5** (1998) 1-11.
13. Kim J.D., *et al.*: GENIA corpus - semantically annotated corpus for bio-textmining. *Bioinformatics* **19**(Suppl 1) (2003) i180-182.
14. Hwang, Y.S., *et al.*: Weighted Probabilistic Sum Model based on Decision Tree Decomposition for Text Chunking, *J. Computer Processing of Oriental Languages* **16**(1) (2003) 1-20.
15. Lee, K.J., *et al.*: Two-Phase Biomedical NE Recognition based on SVMs. In *Proceedings of ACL'03 Workshop on Natural Language Processing in Biomedicine* (2003) 33-40.
16. Christie, K.R., *et al.*: Saccharomyces Genome Database (SGD) provides tools to identify and analyze sequences from Saccharomyces cerevisiae and related sequences from other organisms. *Nucleic Acids Res.* **32**(1) (2004) D311-14.
17. Mewes, H.W., *et al.*: MIPS: analysis and annotation of proteins from whole genomes. *Nucleic Acids Res.* **32**(1) (2004) D41-44.
18. Agrawal, R., *et al.*: Mining association rules between sets of items in large databases. In *Proceedings of ACM SIGMOD'93* (1993) 207-16.
19. Slonim, N., *et al.*: Document clustering using word clusters via the information bottleneck method. In *Proceedings of SIGIR'2000* (2000) 208-15.
20. Yu, L., *et al.*: Feature selection for high dimensional data: a fast correlation-based filter solution. In *Proceeding of ICML'03* (2003) 856-63.
21. Quinlan, J.: C4.5: Programs for machine learning. *Morgan Kaufmann* (1993).
22. Press, W.H., et al.: Numerical recipes in C. *Cambridge University Press* (1988).
23. Oyama, T., *et al.*: Extraction of knowledge on protein–protein interaction by association rule discovery. *Bioinformatics* **18** (2002) 705-14.
24. Ito, T., *et al.*: A comprehensive two-hybrid analysis to explore the yeast protein interactome. *Proc. Natl Acad. Sci. USA* **98** (2001) 4569-74.
25. Uetz, P., *et al.*: A comprehensive analysis of protein-protein interactions in Saccharomyces cerevisiae. *Nature* **403** (2000) 623-27.

A Linear Time Algorithm
for Constructing Tree 4-Spanner in 2-Trees

B.S. Panda and Anita Das

Computer Science and Application Group
Department of Mathematics
Indian Institute of Technology Delhi
Hauz Khas, New Delhi 110 016, India
bspanda@maths.iitd.ernet.in, mar02003@ccsun50.iitd.ernet.in

Abstract. A spanning tree T of a graph G is said to be a **tree t-spanner** if the distance between any two vertices in T is at most t times their distance in G. A graph that has a tree t-spanner is called a **tree t-spanner admissible graph**. It has been shown in [3] that the problem of recognizing whether a graph admits a tree t-spanner is NP-complete for t 4. In this paper, we present a linear time algorithm for constructing a tree 4-spanner in a tree 4-spanner admissible 2-tree.

Keywords: Tree Spanner, Distance in Graphs, Graph Algorithms, 2-trees.

1 Introduction

A spanning subgraph H of a graph G is called a t-**spanner** if the distance between every pair of vertices in H is at most t times their distance in G. For a t-spanner H of G, the term t is called the **stretch factor** and $|E(H)|$, the number of edges in H, is called the **size** of the spanner. A t-spanner H of G is called a tree t-**spanner** if H is a tree. The notion of t-spanner was introduced by Peleg and Ullman [21] in connection with the design of synchronizers in distributed systems. Spanners are useful in many areas such as communication networks, message routing, data analysis, motion planning, computational geometry, image processing, network design, and phylogenetic analysis (see [1,2,3,9,11,16,21,25]). The study of graph spanners has attracted many researchers and is currently an active area of research (see [5-10,13,18,23,25,26]). The goal behind the notion of spanners is to find a sparse spanner H of a given graph G such that the distance between every pair of vertices in H is relatively close to the corresponding distance in the original graph G. Therefore, one of the fundamental problems in the study of spanners is to find a minimum t-spanner, i.e., a t-spanner having minimum number of edges, for every fixed integer $t \geq 1$. Unfortunately, the problem of finding a minimum t-spanner is NP-Hard for $t = 2$ [21,25] and for $t \geq 3$ [8,26]. For a minimum t-spanner H of G, $|E(H)| \geq |V(G)| - 1$ with equality holding if and only if H is a tree t-spanner, where $|V(G)|$ is the number of vertices of G. The problem of determining whether an arbitrary graph admits a tree t-spanner has been studied in detail, as summarized below.

G. Das and V.P. Gulati (Eds.): CIT 2004, LNCS 3356, pp. 21–30, 2004.

Cai and Corneil [10] have shown that for a given graph G, the problem of deciding whether G has tree t-spanner is NP-Complete for any fixed $t \geq 4$ and is linearly solvable for $t = 1, 2$. The status of the case $t = 3$ is still open for arbitrary graphs.

Before proceeding further, let us define k-trees. Let $G[S], S \subseteq V$, be the induced subgraph of $G = (V, E)$ on S. A subset $C \subseteq V$ is said to be a **clique** if $G[C]$ is a maximal complete subgraph of G. A clique C is called a k-clique if $|C| = k$. A 3-clique is called a **triangle**. A graph G is called a k-**tree** if it can be obtained by the following recursive rules.

- Start with any k-clique as the basis graph. A k-clique is a k-tree.
- To any k-tree H add a new vertex and make it adjacent to a k-clique of H, thus forming a $(k + 1)$-clique.

An edge e of a 2-tree is called a forced edge if it appears in every tree 4-spanner of G. It has been shown in [20] that a 2-tree admits a tree 4-spanner if and only if it does not contain a triangle having all forced edges. Furthermore, it has been shown in [20] that a tree 4-spanner admissible 2-tree can be recognized in linear time. A 2-tree G, as seen from the definition, consists of $|V(G)| - 2$ triangles. Given a tree 4-spanner admissible 2-tree G, we employ a D-$search$ (a search similar to the classical breadth-first search or BFS but differs from BFS in that the next element to explore is the element most recently added to the list of unexplored elements) to search the triangles of G. Using this search, we explore all the triangles and keep on adding some edges of the triangles using certain rules to construct a spanning tree of G. We show that this tree is indeed a tree 4-spanner of G.

The rest of the paper is organized as follows. Section 2 presents some pertinent definitions and results. Section 3 presents an algorithm for constructing a tree 4-spanner of a tree 4-spanner admissible 2-tree. The proof of correctness of the algorithm is presented in this section. Section 4 presents the complexity analysis of the proposed algorithm. Finally, Section 5 concludes the paper.

2   Preliminaries

For a graph $G = (V, E)$, let $N_G(v) = \{w \in V | vw \in E\}$ be the set of neighbors of v. If $G[N_G(v)]$, the induced subgraph of G on $N_G(v)$, is a complete subgraph of G, then v is called a **simplicial vertex** of G. An ordering $\alpha = (v_1, v_2, \ldots, v_n)$ is called a **perfect elimination ordering** (PEO) of G if v_i is a simplicial vertex of $G[\{v_i, v_{i+1}, \ldots, v_n\}]$ for all i, $1 \leq i \leq n$. Let $d_G(v)$ denote the **degree** of v in G. Let $d_G(u, v)$ denote the **distance** from u to v in G. Unless otherwise stated the graph G is assumed to be connected. A triangle $\{a, b, c\}$ is said to be **simplicial triangle** if one of its vertices is simplicial. An edge of a simplicial triangle is called **simplicial** if it is incident on a simplicial vertex of the triangle. A triangle is said to be **interior** if all of its edges are shared by at least two triangles. A triangle is said to be **double interior** if the triangle is interior and two of its adjacent triangles on different edges are interior. A triangle is said to be **triple interior** if the triangle is interior and its adjacent triangles on each of the three edges are also interior. A graph is said to be **chordal** if every cycle in it of length at least four has a chord. It is well known that a graph is chordal iff it has a PEO (see [13]). Since k-trees are a subclass of chordal graphs, every k-tree has a PEO. A 2-tree is said to be a **minimal triple interior** (respectively, **double or single interior**) 2-tree if it contains a triple interior (respectively, double or single interior) triangle but none of its proper subgraph contains a triple interior (respectively, double interior or single interior) triangle. Figure 1 illustrates a minimal interior, a minimal double interior and a minimal triple interior 2-tree.

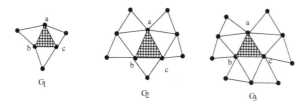

The shaded triangle {a,b,c} is an interior, a double interior, and a triple interior tringle in G_1, G_2 and G_3, respectively.

Fig. 1. Minimal interior, minimal double interior, and minimal triple interior 2-tree.

Let Δ be a triangle of a minimal triple interior 2-tree. Δ is called an outer triangle if it contains a simplicial vertex. It is called an innermost triangle if it is triple interior. Δ is called inner triangle if it is neither innermost nor outer triangle. The **multiplicity**, $M(e)$, of an edge e is defined to be the number of triangles containing e.

For a triangle, Δ, with three edges e_1, e_2, and e_3 we say that Δ is one-side developing with respect to e_1 if either $M(e_2) = 1$ and $M(e_3) > 1$, or $M(e_3) = 1$ and $M(e_2) > 1$. Suppose $M(e_2) = 1$ and $M(e_3) > 1$. In this case, e_3 is said to be a developing edge of Δ with respect to e_1. The triangle Δ is said to be double-side developing with respect to e_1 if $M(e_2) > 1$ and $M(e_3) > 1$. In this case, e_2 and e_3 are said to be developing edges of Δ with respect to e_1.

Let H be a spanning subgraph of G. Since the distance $d_H(x, y) \leq t \times d_G(x, y)$ for every $x, y \in V(G)$ if and only if $d_H(x, y) \leq t$ for every edge $xy \in E(G)$, we have the following useful lemma.

Lemma 2.1: A spanning subgraph H of G is a t-spanner if and only if $d_H(x, y) \leq t$ for every edge $xy \in E(G)$.

In view of Lemma 2.1, in the rest of the paper we assume that a spanning subgraph H (or a spanning tree T) of G is a t-spanner (or tree t-spanner) if $d_H(x, y) \leq t$ (or $d_T(x, y) \leq t$) for every edge $xy \in E(G)$.

Let G be a tree 4-spanner admissible 2-tree. An edge e of G is said to be a **forced edge** if it belongs to every tree 4-spanner of G. An edge which is common to two triple interior triangles is called a **strong edge**.

Strong edges are shown to be forced in [20]. Due to page constraint, proofs of the results cited from [20] are omitted.

Lemma 2.2 [20]: Every strong edge of a tree 4-spanner admissible 2-tree is a forced edge.

A triangle in a 2-tree is called a 1-**layer triple interior triangle**, if all the triangles which are developed on its three edges are triple interior.

Since all the edges of a 1-layer triple interior triangle are strong edges, and hence forced edges by Lemma 2.2, the following corollary follows.

Corollary 2.3: Let G be a 2-tree containing a 1-layer triple interior triangle. Then G can not have a tree 4-spanner.

A triangle having two strong edges is called a **semi-strong triangle**. Let $\{a, b, c\}$ be a semi-strong triangle having strong edges ab and bc. The triangle $\{x, a, c\}$ is called **dependent on the triangle** $\{a, b, c\}$. Suppose $\{x, a, c\}$ is dependent on $\{a, b, c\}$ and ax is an edge of a double interior triangle. Then the edge ax is called a **semi-strong edge**. The motivation behind introducing the concept of semi-strong edge is that semi-strong edges are also forced edges.

It has been shown in [20] that semi-strong edges are forced edges.

Lemma 2.4 [20]: Every semi-strong edge of a tree 4-spanner admissible 2-tree is a forced edge.

We have seen earlier that if a 2-tree G has a 1-layer triple interior triangle, then it can not have a tree 4-spanner. A 2-tree may contain triangle consisting of forced edges that is not a 1-layer triple interior triangle. The following figure contains a 2-tree which does not have any 1-layer triple interior triangle but it has a triangle consisting of semi-strong edges. So, the graph does not admit a tree 4-spanner.

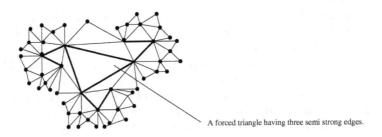

A forced triangle having three semi strong edges.

A 2–tree in which thick edges are strong edges.

Fig. 2. A 2-tree without any 1-layer triple interior triangle that has a triangle containing forced edges.

A triangle is said to be **strong triangle** if each of its edge is a strong edge or a semi strong edge. The following theorem characterizes tree 4-spanner admissible 2-trees.

Theorem 2.5 (Characterization Theorem) [20]: A 2-tree G admits a tree 4-spanner if and only if it does not contain a strong triangle as an induced subgraph.

3 Algorithm and Proof of Correctness

In this section, we present an algorithm to construct a tree 4-spanner of a tree 4-spanner admissible 2-tree G.

The algorithm maintains a stack of edges, the current edge and a triangle containing the current edge as the current triangle. In every iteration, the stack is popped and the popped edge is made the current edge, and an unmarked triangle containing the current edge is made the current triangle. Based on the current edge and the current triangle, the algorithm pushes one or more edges to the stack. The algorithm also maintains two arrays, namely CUR and NUM to maintain the information of the triangles of G. $CUR[\ ] = 1$ if the triangle is made current triangle at some iteration of the algorithm. Otherwise $CUR[\ ] = 0$. $NUM[\ ]$ represents the number when the triangle was marked. The information stored in these arrays will be used for the proof of correctness of the algorithm. The exact rules for pushing the edges in to the stack are given in the following algorithm.

Algorithm Tree 4-Spanner Construction
Input: A tree 4-spanner admissible 2-tree G;
Output: A tree T which is a tree 4-spanner of G;
1. Find all the triangles of G;
2. $T =\ $;
    $S =\ $;
    $CUR[\Delta] = NUM[\Delta] = 0$ for all triangles of G;
    count $= 1$;
    Let ab be a simplicial edges of G;
    $push(S, ab)$;
3. while$(S =\ )$
    {
    CE=Pop(S);
    $T = T\ \{CE\}$;
    while(there is any unmarked triangle say Δ, containing CE)
        {
        CT $= \Delta$; CUR$[\Delta] = 1$; NUM$[\Delta]=$ count++;
        Let the edges of Δ be CE,e and f;
        case I: if(CT is one sided developing w.r.t CE)
            Let CT be developing on e;
            if(there is an unmarked triangle $\Delta' = \{e, g, h\}$ such that
                    g and h are forced edges)
        {
        $T = T\ \{g, h\}$;
        $push(S, g); push(S, h)$;
        $mark\Delta$; CUR$[\Delta'] = 0$; NUM$[\Delta']=$count++;
        $COVER(CT, e)$;
        }
        else if(the triangle containing e or f is a triple interior
            triangle(let e) and two of the other edges are strong)
        {
        $T = T\ \{e\}$;

```
    push(S, e);
    COVER(CT, f);
    }
    else
    {
    T = T   {e};
    push(S, e);
```

Case II: if(CT is double side developing on e and f w.r.t CE)
if(either e or f is a forced edge)

```
    {
    wlg, let e be a forced edge;
    T = T   {e};
    push(S, e);
    COVER(CT, f);
    else
    {
    T = T   {e};
    push(S, e);
    COVER(CT, f);
    }
```

Case III: if CT is zero-sided developing

```
    {
    T = T   {e};
    push(S, e);
    }
    }
```

Procedure COVER (CT, e)

```
    {
    for each one side developing triangle Δ = CT containing e
    {
    Let the edges of the triangle be e,x and y such that Δ is developed on x;
    T = T   {x};
    push(S, x); MarkΔ;
    CUR[Δ] = 0;NUM[Δ] = count++;
    }
    for each zero side developing triangle Δ = CT containing x
    {
    Let the edges of the triangle be e, x and y;
    T = T   {x};
    push(S, x); MarkΔ;
    CUR[Δ] = 0;NUM[Δ] = count++;
    }
    }
```

Next, we prove that **algorithm Tree 4-spanner Construction** correctly constructs a tree 4-spanner of a tree 4-spanner admissible 2-tree. We do this by first showing that T, which is constructed by this algorithm, is a spanning tree of G, and then we will show that this is a tree 4-spanner of G.

Theorem 3.1: Algorithm tree 4-spanner Construction produces a spanning tree T of G.

Proof: The proof is by induction on i, where i is the iteration number. The **Algorithm tree 4-spanner construction** consists of several iterations. In each iteration, a triangle is made current triangle, and based on whether it is one side developing, two side developing or zero side developing, certain edges are marked. Let T_i be the graph formed by the set of edges selected on or before ith iteration, and S_i be the set of vertices spanned by the triangles which are marked on or before ith iteration.

Claim: T_i is a spanning tree of $G[S_i]$ for each i.

Assume that the set of edges included in T by the end of $(i-1)^{th}$ iteration is a spanning tree of the set of vertices spanned by the set of triangles which are marked on or before (i-1)th iteration.

Let $CT = \{CE, e, f\}$ be the current triangle and CE be the current edge in ith iteration. Edges are added to T based on whether CT is one sided or two sided or zero sided developing.

Case I: CT is zero sided developing.
In this case only e is added to T. So it is easy to see that T_i is a spanning tree of $G[S_i]$.

Case II: CT is developing one side on e.
In this case only one edge e is added, if there is no triangle $\{e, g, h\}$ containing two strong edges g and h. In this case clearly our claim is true. Suppose there, is a triangle $\{e, g, h\}$ such that, where g and h are strong edges. In such a situation g and h are both added to T and CT and $\{e, g, h\}$ are both marked. Moreover, for all one sided developing triangles $\{e, x, y\}$ on x, the edge x is added and the triangle $\{e, x, y\}$ is marked and for all zero sided developing triangles $\{e, x_1, y_1\}$, x_1 is added to T and $\{e, x_1, y_1\}$ is marked. So T_i forms a spanning tree of $G[S_i]$

Case III: CT is two sided developing.
Assume one of the edges e or f is a forced edge. Wlg let e is a forced edge. In this case e is added to T and CT is marked. Also for all one side developing triangles $\{f, g, h\}$ on g and for all zero side developing triangles $\{f, g, h\}$, the edge g is added to T, and all such triangles are marked. So by this construction it is easy to see that T_i is a spanning tree of $G[S_i]$.

If CT is two sided developing and any of the edge f or g is an edge of a triple interior triangle, whose other two edges are not forced, then e is added to T and CT is marked. Also for all one side developing triangles $\{f, g, h\}$ on g and for all zero side developing triangles $\{f, g, h\}$, the edge g is added to T, and all such triangles are marked. In this case also, we get T_i to be a spanning tree of $G[S_i]$.

Now, assume that neither e nor f is a forced edge. In this case as well, e is added to T and for all one side developing triangles $\{f, g, h\}$ on g, the edge g is added and $\{e, f, g\}$ is marked, and for all zero side developing triangles $\{f, g_1, h_1\}$ the edge g_1 is added to T, and all such triangles are marked. So T_i is a spanning tree of $G[S_i]$ by induction property in this case.

So, our claim is true. Hence T is a spanning tree of G.

Next, we show that T is a tree 4-spanner of G.

Theorem 3.2: Let G be a tree 4-spanner admissible 2-tree. Then algorithm tree 4-spanner construction successfully constructs a tree 4-spanner of G.

Proof: Let T be the graph produced by the algorithm. So by theorem 3.1, T is a spanning tree of G. Let $e \in G$ and $e = xy$. If $e \in T$, then $d_T(x, y) = 1$ and there is nothing to prove. So suppose that $e \notin T$. Let Δ be the triangle containing e such that $NUM[\Delta]$ is minimum.

Case I: $CUR[\Delta] = 1$

Let $\Delta = \{CE, e, f\}$. Since $e \notin T$, $e = CE$ because CE is the current edge when the triangle Δ was current. Now if Δ is one sided developing(let on f), then f is added to T, so $d_T(x, y) = 2$. If Δ is one sided developing (let on f), then f is added to T, if in the developed triangle $\{f, g, h\}$, g and h are not forced. If g and h are forced edges then g and h will be included in T not f. In first case $d_T(x, y) = 2$ and in second case $d_T(x, y) \leq 4$. If one of g or h is forced, then by the construction f and that forced edge will be taken in T. So in that case also $d_T(x, y) \leq 4$. If Δ is both sided developing, then $d_T(x, y) = 2$ as f is added to T in this case. So $d_T(x, y) \leq 4$ if $CUR[\Delta] = 1$.

Case II: $CUR[\Delta] = 0$.

Let Δ_1 be the current triangle when δ was marked. So Δ_1 was either one side developing or two sided developing. In either case it can be shown using the arguments employed above that $d_T(x, y) \leq 4$.

So T is a tree 4-spanner of G.

Theorem 3.3: Algorithm tree 4-spanner construction correctly constructs a tree 4-spanner of a tree 4-spanner admissible 2-tree.

4   Complexity Analysis

Assume that the input graph G which is a 2-tree is given in adjacency list representation. First we will do some preprocessing and compute certain information which will make the implementation of the above algorithm easy.

First we have to find all the triangles of G. Since, cliques in chordal graphs can be found in O(m+n) time [11], and cliques in 2-tree(which is a chordal graph) are triangles, all the triangles of the 2-tree can be found in O(m+n) time. Scan the adjacency list and find a numbering of the edges of G. Modify the adjacency list of G such that for each $v \in V$, $L(v)$, the adjacency list of v, contains an adjacent vertex, say, w, edge number of the edge vw as obtained in the previous step, and a pointer to the next cell. This step takes O(m+n) time. Next number all the triangles of G and construct an array TN of pointers such that $TN[i]$ contains the list of the edges of the triangle having number i. This takes $O(m + n)$ time. Construct an array A of pointers such that A[i] contains the list of triangles containing the edge having number i. This can done as follows. From the list of triangles, construct a list of order pair by replacing a triangle, say Δ, by (e, Δ), (f, Δ), (g, Δ), where e, f, and g are the edges of Δ. Now, sort this list in non-decreasing order on the first component. All the triangles containing an edge appear consecutively on this list. Since each edge has a unique number, bucket sort can be used to sort the above list. So this takes $O(m+n)$ time. Now from this sorted list, the array A can be constructed in $O(m+n)$ time. Now, from the lists TN and A, we can construct an array N such that N[i] = 1 if the triangle having number i is interior,else N[i] =0. This takes $O(m+n)$ time.

From the array N, we will construct two arrays D and TP. The array D, such that D[i] = 1 if the triangle having number i is a double interior triangle. This can be done as follows. First scan the array A. If A[i] =1, find out the edges of the triangle i. Then find out the triangles other than i which contains the edges of the ith triangle. If any two triangles having these edges have the value in A 1, then the triangle having number i is an double interior triangle and D[i] = 1 , else D[i]=0. If the triangles containing the edges of the triangle having number i have the A value 1, then the triangle is a triple interior triangle and TP[i] = 1, else TP[i] = 0. Clearly these steps take $O(m+n)$ time.

Now, we show that **Algorithm Tree 4-spanner Construction** can be implemented in $O(m+n)$ time. Algorithm Tree 4-spanner Construction starts by selecting a simplicial edge. This can be done by selecting an edge e with A[e] = 1. This takes $O(m + n)$ time. Next, the algorithm marks the triangle containing the edge e. Whether the current triangle develops in one direction or in two directions can be tested by checking the array A for the edges of the triangle. The edge number of the edges can be found by scanning the appropriate list of the modified adjacency list of G obtained above. Again a triangle is two side developing or one side developing or zero side developing can be tested in $O(m+n)$ time for all triangles. Also it is easy to see that other operations of the algorithm tree 4-spanner construction takes $O(m+n)$ time. By the above discussion and by theorem 3.4, we have the following theorem.

Theorem 4.1: Tree 4-spanner in tree 4-spanner admissible 2-tree can be constructed in linear time.

5   Conclusion

In this paper, we have presented a linear time algorithm for constructing a tree 4-spanner in a tree 4-spanner admissible 2-tree.

References

1. I. Althöfer, G. Das, D. Dobkin, D. Joseph, and J. Soares, On Sparse Spanner of Weighted Graphs, Discrete Comput.Geom. 9 (1993), 81-100.
2. J. P. Barthélemy and A. Guénoche, Trees and Proximity Representations, Wiley, New Yark, 1991.
3. S. Bhatt, F. Chung, F. Leighton, and A. Rosenberg, Optimal Simulation of Tree Machines, in Proc. 27th IEEE Foundations of Computer Science, Toronto, 1986, pp. 274-282.

4. H. L. Bodlaender: A Linear-Time Algorithm for Finding Tree-Decompositions of Small Treewidth. SIAM J. Comput. 25(6) 1305-1317 (1996)
5. A. Brandstadt, V. Chepoi, and F. Dragan, Distance approximating trees for chordal and dually chordal graphs, Journal of Algorithms, 30 (1999) 166-184.
6. L. Cai and D.G. Corneil, Tree Spanners: an Overview, Congressus Numerantium 88 (1992), 65-76.
7. L. Cai and J. M. Keil, Degree-Bounded Spanners, Parallel Processing Letters, 3(1993), 457-468.
8. L. Cai and J. M. Keil, Spanners in Graphs of Bounded Degree, Networks, 24(1994),187-194.
9. L. Cai, NP-completeness of Minimum Spanner Problems, Disc. Appl. Math., 48 (1994), 187-194.
10. L. Cai and D.G.Corneil, Tree Spanners, SIAM J. Discrete Math. 8 (1995) 359-387.
11. L. P. Chew, There Are Planar Graphs Almost As Good As the Complete Graph, J. Comput. Syst. Sci. 39 (1989), 205-219
12. B. Courcelle, Recognizability and Second-Order Definability for Sets of Finite Graphs, Information and Computation. 85 (1990) 12- 75.
13. S. P. Fekete and J. Kremner, Tree Spanners in Planar Graphs, Discrete Applied Mathematics, 108 (2001) 85-103.
14. M. C. Golumbic, Algorithmic Graph Theory and Perfect Graphs. (Academic Press, New York, 1980).
15. A. L. Liestman and T. C. Schermer, Grid Spanners, Networks, 23 (2) (1993) 123-133.
16. A. L. Liestman and T. C. Shermer, Additive Graph Spanner, Networks, 23 (1993), 343-364.
17. M. S. Madanlal, G. Venkatesan, and C. P. Rangan, Tree 3-spanners on Interval, Permutation and Regular Bipartite Graphs, Infor. Proc. Lett. 59 (1996) 97-102.
18. G. Narasimhan, B. Chandra, D. Gautam, and J. Soares, New Sparseness Results on Graph Spanners, in Proc. 8th Annual ACM Symposium on Computational Geometry (1992) 192-201.
19. B. S. Panda and S. K. Das, A Linear Time Algorithm for Finding Tree 3-Spanner on 2-Trees, Proceedings of 2nd IFIP Interntional Conference on Theoretical Computer Science (TCS-2002), (Eds. R. Baeza-Yates, U. Montanari and N. Santoro), Kluwer Academic Pub, pp. 292-309, 2002.
20. B.S. Panda and Anita Das, A linear time algorithm for finding Tree 4-spanner in 2-trees, Manuscript, Dept. of Mathematics, Indian Institute of Technology Delhi, 2004, page1-19.
21. D. Peleg and J. D. Ullman, An Optimal Synchronizer for the Hypercube, Proceedings of the 6th ACM Symposium on principles of Distributed computing, Vancouver (1987) 77-85.
22. D. Peleg and E. Upfal, A Trade Off Between Space and Efficiency for Routing Tables, Proceedings of the 20th ACM Symposium on Theory of Computing, Chicago (1988), 43-52.
23. D. Peleg and A. A. Schäffer, Graph spanners. J. Graph Theory 13 (1989) 99-116.
24. P. H. A. Sneath and R. R. Sokal, Numerical Taxonomy, San Francisco, 1973.
25. D. L. Swofford and G. J. Olsen, Phylogeny reconstruction, in (D.M.Hills and C. Moritz, eds.), Molecular Systematics, pp. 411-501, Sinauer Associates, Sunderland, MA, 1990.
26. G. Venkatesan, U. Rotics, M. Madanlal, J.A. Makowsky, and C. P. Rangan, Restrictions of Minimum Spanner Problems, Information and computation, 136(2)(1997)143-164.

Task Scheduling Algorithm for Interconnection Constrained Network of Heterogeneous Processors

E. Ilavarasan, P. Thambidurai, and N. Punithavathi

Department of Computer Science & Engineering and Information Technology
Pondicherry Engineering College
Pondicherry-605014, India

Abstract. Efficient scheduling of parallel programs represented by a-cyclic directed graph (DAG), with or without duplication, is one of the most challenging NP-complete problems in parallel and distributed systems. Because of its key importance, this problem has been extensively studied and various heuristics algorithms have been proposed. However, most of the available algorithms are designed under the assumption of unbounded availability of fully connected processors and lie in high complexity range. In this paper, we propose a new task scheduling algorithm, namely, Highly Communicating and Dependant Based Task Scheduling (HCDBTS) algorithm for scheduling DAG structured applications onto interconnection constrained network of heterogeneous processors. Our objective is to develop an efficient scheduling algorithm that will deliver a good schedule i.e., minimize the completion time of the application and still work with limited number of interconnection constrained processors. We compared the performance of HCDBTS algorithm against the Heterogeneous Earliest Finish Time (HEFT) and the Heterogeneous Critical Node First (HCNF) algorithms by simulation. Our extensive simulation studies based on both randomly generated task graphs and the task graphs of some real applications such as Fast Fourier Transformations, Gaussian Elimination, LU Decomposition and Laplace Transformation, reveal that our scheduling algorithm significantly surpass HEFT and HCNF in schedule length and speedup ratio.

1 Introduction

Heterogeneous computing (HC) system is a suite of geographically distributed processors interconnected by high-speed networks, thereby promising high speed processing of computationally intensive applications with diverse computing needs. HC is emerging as a cost-effective solution to high-performance computing as opposed to expensive parallel processors and it is envisioned that such a computing system will enable users around the globe to execute their applications on the most suitable computing resources. In order to take the advantages of HC system, an application is first split into coarse-grained communicating tasks, which are represented by an edge-weighted directed a-cyclic graph (DAG), and then, a scheduling algorithm is used to assign the tasks of the application to the best suited processors. Since both the performance of a particular application and utilization of system resources heavily depend on how application is scheduled, deploying an efficient scheduling algorithm is crucial. Task scheduling can be performed at compile-time or at run-time. When the characteristics of an application, which includes execution times of tasks on different processors, the data size of the communication between tasks, and the task dependencies are known a priori, it is represented with a static model.

G. Das and V.P. Gulati (Eds.): CIT 2004, LNCS 3356, pp. 31–39, 2004.

The objective of the scheduling is to map tasks onto the best-suited processors and order their executions so that task-precedence requirements are satisfied and a minimum overall completion time is obtained. Static scheduling, except for a few highly simplified cases, is an NP-complete problem [1,2]. Thus, heuristic approaches are generally sought to tackle the problem.

Because of its key importance on performance, the task-scheduling problem in general has been extensively studied and various heuristics were proposed in the literature [3-19]. These heuristics are classified into a variety of categories such as, list-scheduling algorithms [10,11], clustering algorithms [6,16], duplication-based algorithms [3,5,7,17] and guided random search methods [4,9] these heuristics are mainly for systems with fully connected homogeneous processors.

The task-scheduling problem has also been studied by a few research groups for the heterogeneous systems and several heuristics algorithms such as Levelized Duplication Based Scheduling (LDBS) [5], Hybrid Re-Mapper [12], Mapping Heuristics (MH) [14], Heterogeneous Earliest Finish Time First (HEFT) [15], Fast Critical Path (FCP) [17] and Fast Load Balancing (FLB) [17], Task Duplication Scheduling (TDS-1) [18] and Heterogeneous Critical Node First (HCNF) [19] for scheduling a-cyclic task graphs on heterogeneous systems. All these algorithms were proposed for fully interconnected networks of heterogeneous processors. No results have so for been reported, as far we know, for scheduling algorithms with interconnection constrained networks of heterogeneous processor. The objective of the work is to develop an efficient scheduling algorithm that will deliver a good schedule i.e., minimize the completion time of an application and still work with limited number of interconnection constrained processors.

In this paper, we propose a new static scheduling algorithm namely, HCDBTS algorithm for interconnection constrained heterogeneous processors. We compared the performance of HCDBTS algorithm against the HEFT and HCNF algorithms using simulation results. Our extensive simulation studies based on both randomly generated task graphs and the task graphs of some real applications such as Fast Fourier Transformations, Gaussian Elimination, LU Decomposition and Laplace Transformation, reveal that our scheduling algorithm significantly surpass HEFT and HCNF in schedule length and speedup. Schedule length ratio is the ratio of the parallel time to the sum of weights of the critical path tasks on the fastest processor. Speed up is the ratio of the sequential execution time to the parallel execution time.

The rest of the paper is organized as follows: In the next section, we define the problem and the related terminology. In Section 3 we present the related work in scheduling for heterogeneous systems, Section 4 introduces our HCDBTS algorithm and Section 5 provides experimental results. Finally Section 6 concludes the paper with some final remarks and summarizing comments.

2   Task Scheduling Problem

A scheduling system model consists of an application, a target computing environment, and performance criteria for scheduling. An application is represented by a directed acyclic graph, $G = (T, E)$, where T is the set of t tasks and E is the set of e edges between the tasks (processors and machines terms are interchangeably used in the paper). Each edge$(i,j) \in$ E represents the precedence constraint such that task t_i

should complete its execution before task t_j starts. *Data* $_{k,i}$ is the amount of data required to be transmitted from task t_k to t_i. In a given task graph, a task without any parents is called an *entry task* and a task without any child is called an *exit task*.

The target machine architecture is represented as a three-tuple P={M, [L$_{ij}$], [h$_{ij}$]}; M={m$_1$, m$_2$,.., m$_p$} is a set of p heterogeneous machines; [Lij] is p x p matrix describing interconnection network topology with a 1/0 indicating the presence/ absence of a direct link between m_i and m_j; and [h$_{ij}$] is a p x p matrix giving minimum distance in number of hops between machines m_i and m_j. The bandwidth (data transfer rate) of the links between different machines in a heterogeneous system may be different depending on the kind of the network. The data transfer rate is represented by a p x p matrix, R$_{pxp}$. The estimated computation time (ECT) of a task t_i on machine m_j is denoted as ECT$_{i,j}$, where $0 \leq i < n$ and $0 \leq j < p$. The ECT value of a task may be different on different machines depending on the machine's computational capability. We have considered, Grid and Hypercube machine architectures for comparison of our algorithm with HEFT and HCNF algorithms with the modification in processor selection phase. For static task scheduling, the ECT value for each task-machine pair is assumed to be available a priori. A random task graph and its estimated computation time on three different machines is shown in Fig. 1. and Fig. 2.

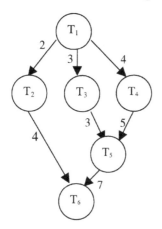

	M$_1$	M$_2$	M$_3$
T$_1$	8	10	11
T$_2$	10	11	13
T$_3$	7	8	10
T$_4$	14	16	17
T$_5$	6	8	9
T$_6$	11	12	13

Fig. 1. A Random Task Graph   **Fig. 2.** ECT of the Task on M$_1$, M$_2$ and M$_3$

We make the following assumptions:

- Task executions of a given application to be non-preemptive.
- Task execution can start only after all the data have been received from its predecessor's tasks.
- All machines and inter-machine networks are available for exclusive use of the application program. Communication cost is zero, when two task t_i, t_k are assigned to the same machine, otherwise data have to be transferred from the machine on which task t_i is assigned to the machine on which task t_k is assigned. This data transfer incurs the communication cost given by Eq.(1).

$$C_{i,k} = \frac{data_{i,k}}{R[M[i], M[k]]} \qquad (1)$$

where R[M(i),M(k)] represents bandwidth of the link between the machines onto which tasks t_i and t_k have been assigned.

Let $EST(t_i, m_j)$ and $EFT(t_i, m_j)$ are the earliest execution start time and earliest execution finish time of task t_i on machine m_j, respectively. For the entry task t_{entry}, $EST(t_{entry}, m_j) = 0$, and for the other tasks in the graph, the EFT and EST values are computed recursively, starting from the entry task, as shown in (2) and (3), respectively. In order to compute the EST of a task t_i, all immediate predecessor tasks of t_i must have been scheduled.

$$EST(t_i, m_j) = \max\left\{ avail[j], \max_{t_m \in pred(t_i)}\left\{AFT(t_m) + C_{m,i} \times h_{kj} \right\}\right\} \tag{2}$$

$$EFT(t_i, m_j) = ECT_{i,j} + EST(t_i, m_j) \tag{3}$$

where $pred(t_i)$ is the set of immediate predecessor tasks of task t_i and $avail[j]$ is the earliest time at which processor m_j is ready for task execution. If t_k is the last assigned task on processor m_j, then $avail[j]$, is the time that processor m_j completed the execution of the task t_k and it is ready to execute another task when we have a noninsertion-based scheduling policy. The inner max block in the EST equation returns the ready time, i.e., the time when all data needed by t_i has arrived at m_j.

After a task t_i is scheduled on a machine m_j, the earliest start time and the earliest finish time of t_i on machine m_j is equal to the actual start time $AST(t_i)$ and the actual finish time $AFT(t_i)$, of task, respectively. After all tasks in a graph are scheduled, the schedule length (i.e. the overall completion time) will be the actual finish time of the exit task t_{exit}. Finally the schedule length is defined as

$$makespan = \max\{AFT(t_{exit})\} \tag{4}$$

The objective function of the task-scheduling problem is to determine the assignment of tasks of an application to machines such that its schedule length is minimized.

3   Related Works

This section presents the reported task-scheduling algorithm that supports heterogeneous processors.

3.1   Heterogeneous Earliest Finish Time (HEFT)

The HEFT is an application scheduling algorithm for bounded number of heterogeneous processors, which has two phases: task prioritizing phase for computing priorities of all the tasks and, processor selection phase for selecting the tasks in the order of their priorities and scheduling each selected tasks on its best processor which minimizes the task's finish time. The tasks are assigned ranks (priorities) based on the following expression,

$$rank_u(n_i) = \overline{w}_i + \max_{n_j \in succ(n_i)}(\overline{c}_{i,j} + rank_u(n_j)) \tag{5}$$

where n_j is the set of immediate successors of task n_i, $\overline{c}_{i,j}$ is the average communication cost of edge(i,j) and $\overline{w}_i$ is the average computation cost of task n_i.

3.2 Heterogeneous Critical Node First (HCNF)

It is list-scheduling algorithm, which schedules task in the critical path first followed by those with the highest computation. In order to reduce the communication time, the critical immediate predecessor (CIP) is considered for duplication. The CIP gets duplicated only if it provides earliest finish time for the candidate task.

4 Proposed Algorithm

The HCDBTS Algorithm is mainly for scheduling DAG structured task graph with duplication onto inter-connection constrained network of heterogeneous machines for minimizing the schedule length. The algorithm comprises of three phases namely, task prioritization phase, processor selection phase and task assignment phase. The framework of the algorithm is shown in Fig. 3.

1. List = {set of all ready tasks}
   // Tasks Prioritizing Phase
2. Sort tasks in the list based on their average communication cost in non-increasing order. //O(T) log |T|)
3. The task with high communication cost is given highest priority. Tie if any, is broken based on number of dependent tasks (child tasks). A task with more dependent task is given preference.
   //Processor Selection Phase
4. While (List! = Φ) // O(|T|)
5. Construct Set_M = {$m_1, m_2, \ldots .m_i$} set of available processors.
   // Task Assignment phase
6. For each $m_j \in$ Set_M do O(|M|)
   6.1. Compute $EST_1(t_i, mj)$ with duplication of $CIP(t_i)$ on machine m_j.
   6.2. Compute $EST_2(t_i, m_j)$ without duplication of $CIP(t_i)$ on machine m_j.
   6.3. If $(EST_1(t_i, m_j) > EST_2(t_i, m_j))$
   > > Undo_Duplication $(CIP(t_i), mj)$.
   > > $EST(t_i, m_j) = EST_2(t_i, m_j)$.

   > Else

   > > $EST(t_i, m_j) = EST_1(t_i, m_j)$.

   > End if
7. $EFT(t_i, m_j) = EST(t_i, m_j) + ECT(t_i, m_j)$.
8. If $(EFT(t_i, m_j) < EFT(t_i, m_{j-1}))$
   > > $m_s = m_j$

   > End if
9. End for
10. Schedule t_i on to processor m_s.
11. Temp=SUCC(t_i).
12. Sort List based on their average communication cost in non-increasing order.
    //O(|T| log|T|)
13. List =List $-\{t_i\}$+Temp
14. End While

Fig. 3. Framework of the proposed HCDBTS Algorithm

In task prioritizing phase, initially, a list containing set of tasks in non-increasing order of their average communication cost is generated. A task in the list with high average communication cost receives higher priority. Tie, if any is broken based on their dependant tasks (child task). i.e, task with more dependant tasks is given preference. A candidate (high priority) task is chosen from the list for scheduling the task on suitable processor.

In processor selection phase, a set of suitable candidate processors from set (Set_M) for t_i is chosen. Set_M comprises of processors where the immediate predecessors of t_i are scheduled, plus their adjacent processors. The processors, which are more than one hop away, are left out as it provides large communication latency to the candidate task and this will no way affect the schedule length, but helps in improving the runtime of the algorithm.

In task assignment phase, task t_i is assigned to one of the processors in Set_M, which allows it to start at the earliest, using insertion based scheduling approach. The task is said to be ready for execution on processor m_j only when it receives data from all of its immediate parents, so as to meet precedence constraints. Let $d(t_i, t_m)$ denotes the time when task t_i has received the data from task $t_m \in pred(t_i)$ and defined as

$$d(t_i, t_m) = \begin{pmatrix} \min\{AFT(t_m) + C_{m,i} \times h_{kj}\} & if\ m_k != m_j \\ AFT(t_m) & otherwise \end{pmatrix} \quad (6)$$

$$\forall t_m \in pred(t_i), \forall m_k \in Set\_M$$

Here $AFT(t_m)$ denotes the actual finish time of task t_m on processor m_k and Set_M corresponds to the set of processors where task t_m is scheduled /duplicated. The hop count h_{kj} provides the distance between the processors m_k and m_j in interconnection constrained network of heterogeneous processors. The critical immediate predecessor of task t_i is defined to be

$$CIP(t_i) = \{t_m \mid DAT(t_i, m_j) = \max\{d(t_i, t_m)\}\} \quad (7)$$

where $DAT(t_i, m_j)$ denotes the data arrival time of task t_i on machine m_j. Now t_i can start execution on processor m_j either at the ready time of the processor or at a time earlier than this if a suitable scheduling slot is available on processor m_j. Before scheduling task t_i, CIP of task t_i gets duplicated, if the start time can be improved further. The time complexity of the algorithm is O ($|T| \log |T| + |T| (|M| + |T| \log |T|)$) or O ($|T|^2 \log |T|$) where $|T|$ is the number of tasks in the DAG.

5 Performance Results and Discussions

For uniformity and to draw some conclusive results, the performance of HCDBTS, HEFT and HCNF scheduling algorithms are evaluated for both arbitrary benchmark DAGs and real graphs with a limited number of interconnection constrained networks of heterogeneous processors. The performance metrics chosen for comparison are Schedule Length Ratio (SLR), Speedup and running time of the algorithms.

The simulation studies performed are grouped into three sets; 1) Executing randomly generated task graphs with a different number of tasks between 30 and 60 on a 4D Hypercube network. 2) Executing randomly generated task graphs between 30 and

60 on a 2D-Grid network with varying diameter. 3) Executing task graphs of the real applications such as Fast Fourier transformations, Gaussian Elimination, LU Decomposition and Laplace Transformation on a 3D Hypercube network.

For the first set of simulation studies, we used random task graph consists of 30, 40, 50, and 60 tasks, such that the communication to computation ratio (CCR) is 0.1, 1.0 and 10.0. Task graph of 20 numbers are used for each CCR on a 4D Hypercube network. The computation intensive applications may be modeled by assuming CCR = 0.1, whereas data intensive applications may be modeled assuming CCR = 10.0. The average schedule length ratio produced by HCDBTS, HEFT and HCNF scheduling algorithms are shown in Fig. 4, through Fig. 6. This shows that HCDBTS outperforms HEFT and HCNF.

For the second set of simulation studies, we used random task graph consists of 30, 40, 50, and 60 tasks such that the communication to computation ratio (CCR) is 0.1, 1.0 and 10.0 and 20 different task graph are used for each set on a 2D Grid by varying the diameter. The diameter denotes the maximum distance between processors in number of hops in an interconnection constrained network. The results obtained for the second set of studies are shown in Fig. 7, through Fig. 9.

For the third set of simulation studies, we used task graph of the real applications such as Fast Fourier Transformations, Gaussian Elimination, LU Decomposition and Laplace Transformation and we used 10 task graphs of each applications such that CCR = 1.0 on a 3D Hypercube. The average schedule length ratio and the average speedup ratio produced by HCDBTS are compared with HEFT and HCNF and the results are shown in Fig. 10 and Fig. 11.

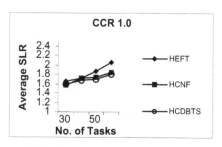

Fig. 4. Average SLR of the DAGs

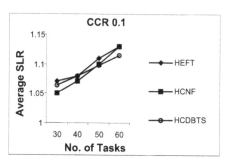

Fig. 5. Average SLR of the DAGs

6 Conclusion

In this paper, we presented a new scheduling algorithm called HCDBTS for scheduling DAG-structured applications onto interconnection constrained network of heterogeneous processors. Based on the experimental study using large set of randomly generated application graphs with various characteristics and application graphs of several real world problems, we showed that, the HCDBTS algorithm significantly outperformed HEFT and HCNF scheduling algorithms. Our future work will focus on balancing the load on each processor and scheduling of task graph onto distributed mobile computing systems.

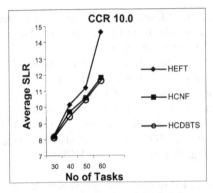

Fig. 6. Average SLR of the DAGs

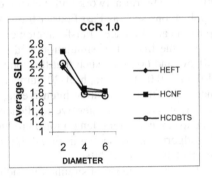

Fig. 7. With varying Diameter

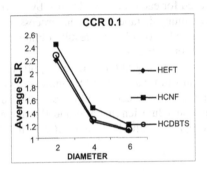

Fig. 8. With varying Diameter

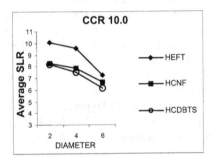

Fig. 9. With varying Diameter

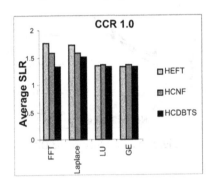

Fig. 10. Average SLR for real graphs with CCR=1.0

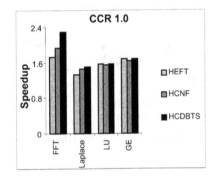

Fig. 11. Average speedup for real graphs with CCR=1.0

References

1. H.EI-Rewini, H.H. Ali, and T.G.Lewis, *"Task Scheduling in Multiprocessing Systems"*, *IEEE Trans. Comp.*, pp.27-37. Dec.1995
2. M.R.Garey and D.S. Johnson, "Computers and intractability: A Guide to the Theory of NP-Completeness", W.H. Freeman and Co. 1979.

3. I. Ahmad and Y.-K. Kwok, "On exploiting task duplication in parallel program scheduling" *IEEE Trans. Parallel and Distributed Systems*, Vol.9, No.9, pp.872-892, Sept. 1998.
4. H.Singh and A. Youssef, "Mapping and Scheduling Heterogeneous Task Graphs using Genetic Algorithms", Proceedings *of Heterogeneous Computing Workshop*, pp. 86-97, 1996.
5. Atakan Dogan and Fusun Ozguner, "LDBS: A Duplication based scheduling algorithm for heterogeneous computing systems," *ICPP'02*.
6. T.Yang and A.Gerasoulis,"DSC: Scheduling Parallel Tasks on an Unbounded Number of processors," *IEEE Trans. Parallel and Distributed Systems*, Vol.5, No.9, pp.951-967, Sept. 1994.
7. S. Darba and D.P.Agrawal, "Optimal scheduling algorithm for distributed-memory machines", *IEEE Trans. Parallel and Distributed Systems*, Vol.1, No.1, pp. 87-94, Jan. 1998.
8. M.K. Dhodhi, I.Ahmad, A. Yatama, "An integrated technique for task matching and scheduling onto Distributed heterogeneous computing systems", *Journal of parallel and distributed computing''*, Vol. 62, pp. 1338-1361, 2002.
9. E.S.H. Hou, N. Ansari, and H.Ren, "A Genetic Algorithm for Multiprocessor Scheduling,", *IEEE Trans. Parallel and Distributed Systems*, Vol.5.no.2, pp. 113-120, Feb. 1994.
10. J.-J. Hwang Y.C. Chow, F.D. Anger, and C.Y. Lee, "Scheduling Precedence graphs in systems with interprocessor communication times," *SIAM Journal on Computing*, vol. 18, pp.224-257, Apr. 1989.
11. Y.Kwok and I.Ahmed, "Dynamic Critical-Path Scheduling: An Effective Technique for Allocating Task Graphs to Multiprocessors," *IEEE Trans. Parallel and Distributed Systems*, Vol.7, No. 5, pp. 506-521, May 1996.
12. M. Maheswaran and H.J. Siegel, "A Dynamic Matching and Scheduling Algorithm for Heterogeneous Computing System", *Proceedings of Heterogeneous Computing Workshop*, pp.57-69, 1998.
13. A. Raduiescu and J.C. Arjan, "Low-cost Task Scheduling for Distributed-Memory Machines", *IEEE Trans. on Parallel and Distributed Systems*, Vol.13, No. 6, June 2002.
14. H. Topcuoglu, S.Hariri, M-Y.Wu, "Task scheduling algorithms for heterogeneous computing processors", *IPPS/SPDP Workshop on Heterogeneous computing*, pp.3-14, San Juan, Puerto Rico, Apr. 1999.
15. H.Topcuoglu, S.Hariri, M-Y.Wu, "Performance-Effective and low-complexity task scheduling for heterogeneous computing", *IEEE Trans. Parallel and Distributed Systems*, Vol. 13, No. 3, March 2002.
16. J.Liou and M.A. Palis, "An Efficient Clustering Heuristics for Scheduling DAGs on Multiprocessors", *Int'l conf. on Parallel and Distributed Processing*, 1996.
17. A.Radulescu and A.J.C. Van Gemund, "Fast and Effective Task Scheduling in Heterogeneous Systems", *Proceedings of Heterogeneous Computing*, pp.229-238, May 2000.
18. A. Ranaweera and D.P. Agrawal, " A Task Duplication based Algorithm for heterogeneous Systems," *Int'l Conference on Parallel and Distributed Processing*, pp.445-450, May 1-5, 2000.
19. Sanjeev Basker and Prashanth C.SaiRanga, "Scheduling Directed A-cyclic task graphs on heterogeneous Network of Workstations to minimize Schedule length", *Int'l Conference on Parallel Processing*, 2003.

Detecting Topology Preserving Feature Subset with SOM

Arijit Laha

Institute for Development and Research in Banking Technology
Castle Hills, Hyderabad 500 057, India
alaha@idrbt.ac.in

Abstract. Kohonen's Self-organizing Map (SOM) is one of the most popular neural network algorithms. SOM produces topology preserving map of the input data. In the current study the SOM's topology preservation property is used to identify the input features whose removal does not affect significantly the neighborhood relations among the input data points. The topology preservation property of of an SOM is measured using a quantitative index. However the same index can be slightly modified to compute topology preservation in the SOM along individual features. Thus studying the topology preservation due to each individual feature we can compare their quality with respect to their importance in affecting the neighborhood relation among input points. Experimental study is conducted with a synthetic data set, well known Iris data set and a multi-channel satellite image dataset. The results are cross verified by comparing with Sammon error of the data computed in the corresponding dimension. k-NN classification performance is also considered for the data sets.

Keywords: SOM, topology preservation, feature quality, Shammon error.

1 Introduction

The Self-organizing map (SOM) developed by Kohonen [1] is one of the most popular neural network models. The SOM implements a nonlinear *topology preserving* mapping from a higher dimensional feature space to a lower (usually 2) dimensional grid of neurons. The distribution of the weight vectors of a trained SOM approximates the distribution of the feature vectors in the training data. This property is known as *density matching*. These properties enable many researchers to use SOM successfully in various problem domains such as pattern recognition, clustering, text and image analysis, speech recognition, vector quantization [2,3], data visualization, knowledge engineering [4], etc. For a more exhaustive listing of the works using SOM visit [5].

Topology preservation refers to the property of a trained SOM that two points close to each other in the feature space are mapped to the *same node or two neighboring nodes in the lattice plane of the network*. Various attempts are made by researchers to find a quantitative measure for this property. In

G. Das and V.P. Gulati (Eds.): CIT 2004, LNCS 3356, pp. 40–48, 2004.

[6] topographic product is used, Villmann et. al [7] developed a topographic function that takes into account the data manifold also, [8] used Kendal's rank correlation coefficient to measure the topology preservation. In a recent work Su et. al [9] developed a simple and intuitive measure of topology preservation that can be easily modified to measure the topology violation when a feature subspace with one or more dimensions removed is considered. In most of the real life applications though the *absolute dimension* of the data is quite high, the *intrinsic dimension* [10] is much lower. It was observed by the researchers that the topology preservation is affected severely if the intrinsic dimension of the data is much higher than the dimension (usually 2 or 3) of the SOM lattice. This is often called dimensionality mismatch [11] and in such cases the SOM fold and twist to achieve the mapping. Consequently, the utility of the map in many applications is markedly diminished.

Large dimensionality of the data poses two kind of problems in designing systems those use the data for learning, (1) the number of parameters to learn becomes large and (2) the requisite number of training samples for good learning becomes large. Both these factors lead to rapid increase of computational load. This is called "curse of dimensionality". However, often it is found that some of the features do not contribute to the information content of the data, i.e., the information content of those features are already contained by the rest of the features. So it is highly desirable to identify the useful (for the problem at hand) features and use them for developing the system. This is known as *feature selection* [12] or *dimensionality reduction*. In other words, feature selection corresponds to compression and (possibly) improvement of the feature space by elimination, through selection or transformation, of redundant or unimportant (for the problem at hand) features.

It is shown in this paper, even though the overall topology preservation for higher dimensional data is not satisfactory, measuring the topology preservation along individual dimensions allows us to find a subset of dimensions for which the topology is better preserved. This in turn allows us to perform feature selection. This selection of features can be validated in terms of low Sammon's error [13] and/or low k-NN classification error for labeled data.

2   SOM and Topology Preservation

2.1   SOM Algorithm

SOM is formed of neurons located on a regular (usually)1D or 2D grid. Thus each neuron is identified with a index corresponding to its position in the grid (the viewing plane). Each neuron i is represented by a weight vector $\mathbf{w}_i \in \Re^p$ where p is the dimensionality of the input space. In t-th training step, a data point $\mathbf{x}$ is presented to the network. The winner node with index r is selected as

$$r = \underset{i}{arg\ min}\{\|\mathbf{x} - \mathbf{w}_{i,t-1}\|\}$$

and $\mathbf{w}_{r,t-1}$ and the other weight vectors associated with cells in the spatial neighborhood $N_t(r)$ are updated using the rule:

$$\mathbf{w}_{i,t} = \mathbf{w}_{i,t-1} + \alpha(t)h_{ri}(t)(\mathbf{x} - \mathbf{w}_{i,t-1}),$$

where $\alpha(t)$ is the learning rate and $h_{ri}(t)$ is the neighborhood kernel (usually Gaussian). The learning rate and the radius of the neighborhood kernel decreases with time. During the iterative training the SOM behaves like a flexible net that folds onto the "cloud" formed by the input data.

2.2   Quantitative Measure of Topology Preservation

The SOM transforms the patterns in feature space into the responses of nodes in one or two dimensional lattice of neurons. This transformation retains metric-topological relationship among the feature vectors. A quantitative measure of topology preservation capture the extent to which the metric-topological relationship is retained. There can be different choices constraints to be satisfied for a "perfect" topology preservation. The strongest is that for each pair of points in feature space, the distance should be equal to the distance of the mapped points. A weaker one demand that the distances should be of same order. The topographic product [6], most popular measure, is based on the weaker constraint. Su et. al [9] proposed another kind of weaker constraint and a measure based on that. They observed that if a map is topologically ordered then the weight vector of each node should be more similar to the weight vectors of its immediate neighbors (8 neighbors for a 2-D SOM) on the lattice than to the weight vectors of its non-neighbors. Their measure is designed to detect the violation of this condition. The measure is especially suitable if the SOM is used for visualizing cluster structure of the data.

The method for 2-D SOM can be formulated as follows:
Let Λ_r be the set containing the immediate 8 neighbors of node r and Ω_r denote the set containing the nodes which are not immediate neighbors of node r. Let the size of the map is $m \times n$. Consider a node $i \in \Omega_r$ and another node $i_r \in \Lambda_r$ such that

$$i_r = \underset{k \in \Lambda_r}{argmin} \|\mathbf{p}_i - \mathbf{p}_k\|,$$

where, $\mathbf{p}_i = (p_{i1}, p_{i2})$ is the position vector of the node i in the lattice plane and $\|\mathbf{p}_i - \mathbf{p}_k\|$ is the Euclidean distance between the nodes i and k. Since node r is closer to the neighboring node i_r than to i in the lattice plane, the weight vector of node r should be more similar to the weight vector of the node i_r than to the weight vector of the node i. Therefore, if the map is preserving the topology then for each node r the following relation should hold:

$$\|\mathbf{w}_i - \mathbf{w}_r\| \geq \|\mathbf{w}_{i_r} - \mathbf{w}_r\| \text{ for } 1 \leq r \leq m \times n, i_r \in \Lambda_r \text{ and } i \in \Omega_r. \qquad (1)$$

Now the quantitative measure of topology violation V is defined as:

$$V = \sum_{r=1}^{m \times n} \sum_{i \in \Theta_r} [1 - \exp^{-\|\mathbf{p}_i - \mathbf{p}_r\|^2}] \frac{\|\mathbf{w}_{i_r} - \mathbf{w}_r\| - \|\mathbf{w}_i - \mathbf{w}_r\|}{\|\mathbf{w}_{i_r} - \mathbf{w}_r\|}, \qquad (2)$$

where $\Theta_r = \{i : \|\mathbf{w}_i - \mathbf{w}_r\| < \|\mathbf{w}_{i_r} - \mathbf{w}_r\| \text{ for } i \in \Omega_r \text{ and } i_r \in \Lambda_r\}$ is the set of nodes in Ω_r those violate eq. 1 with respect to node r. The measure of violation V has the following properties:

1. $V = 0$ if $\Theta_r = \emptyset$, i.e., the topology is perfectly preserved.
2. The larger the value of V the greater is the violation.
3. If $i \in \Theta_r$ and the nodes r and i is far apart in the lattice plane, their contribution to V will be high due to the factor $(1 - \exp^{-\|\mathbf{p}_i - \mathbf{p}_r\|^2})$.

Usually, perfect topology preservation (i.e., $V = 0$) is achieved if the dimensionality matching is perfect as well as the distribution of the training data has strong similarity with the distribution of the nodes in the lattice plane, such as shown in Figure 1. Figure 1 depicts in the distribution of the weight vectors of the nodes along with the neighborhood relations on the lattice plane of a 10×10 SOM trained with 2-D data points uniformly distributed over a square. Otherwise, even though the dimensionality matches, there could be some topology violation due to existence of cluster structures and variation of density within the data. However if the dimensionality matching exists, the violations are typically small and can be attributed to the disturbances produced due to the non-uniformity of the data in unfolding of the map during training. On the other hand, for high dimensional data, when the violation is caused by dimension mismatch, the value of the topology violation for same training data increases rapidly with the size of SOM. To prevent such rapid increase of the value of V we modify the eq. 2 as follow:

$$V = \sum_{r=1}^{m \times n} \frac{1}{K_r} \sum_{i \in \Theta_r} [1 - \exp^{-\|\mathbf{p}_i - \mathbf{p}_r\|^2}] \frac{\|\mathbf{w}_{i_r} - \mathbf{w}_r\| - \|\mathbf{w}_i - \mathbf{w}_r\|}{\|\mathbf{w}_{i_r} - \mathbf{w}_r\|}, \qquad (3)$$

where $K_r = \sum_{i \in \Omega_r} [1 - \exp^{-\|\mathbf{p}_i - \mathbf{p}_r\|^2}]$ is a scaling factor that prevent quick increase of the value of V with the size of the map.

The measure of topology violation V can be easily modified to measure the topology violation for each individual feature. The condition for topology preservation along k-th feature for all node r is given by

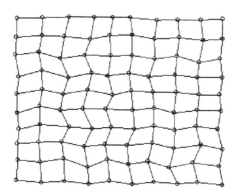

Fig. 1. Distribution of weight vectors of a 10×10 SOM trained with 2-D data points uniformly distributed over a square. The SOM preserve topology perfectly with $V = 0$.

$$| w_{ik} - w_{rk} | \geq | w_{i_r k} - w_{rk} |$$

$$\text{for } k = 1, 2, \cdots, p,\ 1 \leq r \leq m \times n, i_r \in \Lambda_r \text{ and } i \in \Omega_r. \quad (4)$$

Thus the measure of topology violation V_k along k-th feature is defined as:

$$V_k = \sum_{r=1}^{m \times n} \frac{1}{K_r} \sum_{i \in \Theta_{rk}} [1 - \exp^{-\|\mathbf{p}_i - \mathbf{p}_m\|^2}] \frac{| w_{i_r k} - w_{rk} | - | w_{ik} - w_{rk} |}{| w_{i_r k} - w_{rk} |}, \quad (5)$$

where Θ_{rk} is the set of nodes in Ω_r those violate eq. 4 with respect to node r for the k-th feature.

2.3   Feature Selection

The quantitative measure of topology preservation/violation is primarily used for adjudging the effectiveness of the SOM in applications whose performance depend crucially on topology preservation. Here we directly use the quantitative measure of topology violation for different features to assess their relative importance. The idea is rooted in the fact that the information carrying features try to stretch the map along their respective direction in a sustained and systematic manner. On the other hand, if there exist some features carrying random (comparatively) values, they produce random perturbation in the process of formation of the map, which should be reflected in higher topology violation for them. Thus a ranking of the features based on their topology violations correspond to their ranking of *quality*. Here the term "quality" is used to express the capacity of the features to retain the topological ordering of the input signals in the original feature space. The idea can be expressed as follows:

Let $\Phi_i = \{\mathbf{x}_j : \|\mathbf{x}_i - \mathbf{x}_j\| \leq \epsilon\}$ be the set of input feature vectors within a ϵ-neighborhood of $\mathbf{x}_i$ and $\Phi_{ik} = \{\mathbf{x}_j : | x_{ik} - x_{jk} | \leq \epsilon\}$ be the set of input feature vectors within a ϵ-neighborhood of $\mathbf{x}_i$ along the k-th feature. Now for two features k and l

$$V_k < V_l \Leftrightarrow | \Phi_i \cap \Phi_{ik} | > | \Phi_i \cap \Phi_{il} | . \quad (6)$$

In other words, lower value of V_k signify that for an input vector $\mathbf{x}_i$ more of its ϵ-neighbors in original space will be retained within its ϵ neighborhood if the input data is projected along the k-th feature than if the data is projected along another feature l with higher value of topology violation V_l. This interpretation has close correspondence to the well known Sammon error [13] for the projection along k-th feature defined as

$$E_k(X) = \frac{1}{\sum_{i=1}^{N} \sum_{j>i} \delta_{ij}(k)} \sum_{i=1}^{N} \sum_{j>i} \frac{(d_{ij} - \delta_{ij}(k))^2}{\delta_{ij}(k)}, \quad (7)$$

such that,

$$V_k < V_l \Leftrightarrow E_k(X) < E_l(X), \quad (8)$$

where N is the number of input data points, $d_{ij} = \|\mathbf{x}_i - \mathbf{x}_j\|$ and $\delta_{ij}(k) = | x_{ik} - x_{jk} |$.

For labeled input data similar correspondence exists between the topology violation measures and error rates of k-NN classifiers those use the data projected along individual features.

3   Experimental Results and Discussions

We present the experimental results of our study for three different data sets, **2dishes-4D**, **Iris** and **Satim-7**. All three sets are labeled. 2dishes-4D is a synthetic data with 4 features and 1500 points. In first two features the data has two well separated dish-like clusters corresponding to two classes with 500 and 1000 data points respectively. The dishes are nonoverlapping along feature 2 and have overlap along feature 1. Figure 2 shows the scatterplot of this data set along first two features. The other two features consist random numbers generated from a uniform distribution with mean 0 and variance 1. The well-known Iris data set has 4 dimensions and 150 points, 50 from each of three classes. Satim-7 is prepared by randomly selecting the 1600 feature vectors from a 7-channel satellite image. The data contains 200 points belonging to each of the 8 land cover classes. The feature vectors have 7 dimensions, each of them represents the gray value of the pixel in the image captured by corresponding channel sensor. The results are summarized in the Tables 1-3.

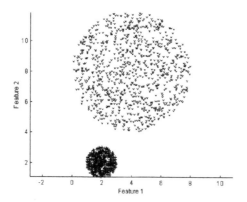

Fig. 2. Scatterplot of 2dishes-4D data along first two features.

In the results each of the reported values of V (topology violation computed *all* features using eq. 5) and V_k (topology violation computed k-th feature using eq. 7) are averages of five SOMs trained with different initializations and sequences of choice of input vectors. We also presented the results for each data sets using SOMs of two different sizes. For studying the k-NN classification performances, each data set is divided into two random partitions of equal sizes and containing same proportion of class representation. The partitions are alternately used as training and test sets and the reported results are averages of these two cases.

Table 1. Experimental results for 2dishes-4D.

Feature	Topology violation V_k		Sammon Error	k-NN Classification Performance		
k	Netsize 10×10	Netsize 15×15	$E_k(X)$	1-NN	3-NN	5-NN
All	0.05	0.09	0	100%	100%	100%
1	2.8	5.5	0.389	78.13%	78.86%	79.27%
2	3.6	5.9	0.102	100%	100%	100%
3	27.2	60.0	0.870	52.60%	56.80%	59.00%
4	27.1	60.7	0.868	56.00%	61.07%	61.20%

Table 2. Experimental results for Iris.

Feature	Topology violation V_k		Sammon Error	k-NN Classification Performance		
k	Netsize 6×6	Netsize 10×10	$E_k(X)$	1-NN	3-NN	5-NN
All	0.27	0.47	0	96.00%	96.00%	98.00%
1	2.28	5.92	0.423	60.66%	68.00%	71.00%
2	4.27	9.61	0.683	42.00%	45.33%	48.00%
3	1.27	2.65	0.078	91.33%	93.33%	93.33%
4	1.45	5.08	0.448	94.67%	94.67%	95.33%

For all three data sets the overall topology violation Vs are quite low while the V_ks are much larger (by order of 1 or 2). For the 2dishes-4D data V is quite small (0.05 and 0.09 respectively) indicating very good topology preservation and dimensionality match. This is what we expected since the features 3 and 4 are added random components to original 2-D data. This is farther reflected in the values of V_ks, with V_3 and V_4 much (almost 10 times) higher than V_1 and V_2. This is also corroborated by considerably higher Sammom errors and lower k-NN classification performances of features 3 and 4. For features 1 and 2 it can be observed that V_1 is slightly less than V_2 but the $E_1(X)$ is higher than $E_2(X)$ and classification performance of feature 2 is better than feature 1. This discrepancy can be explained from the fact that the data is non-overlapping in feature 2 (Figure 2), which accounts for lower Sammon error and better classification performance of feature 2. On the other hand, the overlap of data along feature 1 reduce the topology violation along it. This effect is demonstrated in Figure 3.

For Iris data set V_2 is largest while V_3 is the smallest value of topology violation. The Sammon errors and classification performances also support them. It is also in accord with the well-known fact among pattern recognition community that feature 3 of Iris has least discriminatory power while feature 2 has the highest.

In case of Satim-7 data there are many features having close values of V_k, however, feature 6 stands out as the highest topology violator (way above the others) with highest Sammon's error and worst k-NN classification performance. While for the other features though it is difficult to exactly corroborate the V_ks with Sammon errors and classification performances, the general fact, that low topology violation corresponds to low Sammon error and high k-NN classification performance, holds out. To explain the discrepancies observed, different data

Table 3. Experimental results for Satim-7.

Feature k	Topology violation V_k		Sammon Error $E_k(X)$	k-NN Classification Performance		
	Netsize 10 × 10	Netsize 15 × 15		1-NN	3-NN	5-NN
All	0.21	0.36	0	82.21%	82.37%	82.06%
1	4.7	8.9	0.426	30.99%	34.62%	38.87%
2	4.6	9.2	0.620	29.06%	31.12%	33.90%
3	4.5	9.3	0.467	34.01%	41.50%	44.43%
4	8.6	17.5	0.456	38.25%	42.87%	44.31%
5	4.4	9.3	0.223	43.63%	51.68%	53.06%
6	11.3	29.5	0.845	27.18%	30.06%	35.06%
7	4.2	9.9	0.488	41.18%	48.62%	53.37%

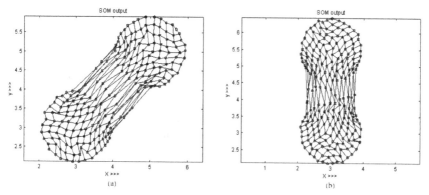

Fig. 3. 15 × 15 SOFMs for data with 2 dishes (50000 points each) of equal size. (a) Dishes are non-overlapping in both features, $V_1 = 4.34$ and $V_2 = 4.45$. (b) Dishes overlap in feature 2, $V_1 = 6.82$ and $V_2 = 3.90$.

specific properties and their effect on topology preservation need to be studied. For example, as described above, relative degrees of overlap along different features among the clusters affect the topology preservation. We have found that if the clusters overlap more along a certain feature relative to other features, topology is preserved better along that feature, while Sammon error and k-NN classification performance are adversely affected.

4   Conclusion

We propose a quantitative measure of topology violation for SOM along individual features motivated by the topology preservation(violation) measure developed by Su et. al[9]. We used the proposed measure to find the relative quality of each feature, where the term "quality" is used in context of the power of individual features to retain the topological ordering of the data points in original feature space. A correspondence is established between the topology violations and the feature-wise Sammon errors and k-NN classification errors. The experimental results in general confirm the correspondences. However, for close values of the topology violations some discrepancies are found. This can be attributed to nature of SOM algorithm which is somewhat sensitive to the initialization of the nodes as well as the sequence of training signals presented. The formation of the map is also susceptible to the peculiarities of the cluster structures in the data. To remove the discrepancy one needs deeper understanding of various factors influencing the map formation and possibly taking them into account in devising a more sophisticated measure for topology preservation. However, the experimental results strongly suggest that, there is indeed a direct relation between the topology violation along a feature and its quality. This method showed remarkable capacity of identifying especially the feature with worst quality for each of the data sets studied. The scheme can be readily be used to identify the bad features, which can be enormously useful if the developer of a pattern recognition system is constrained in the numbers of features those can be used.

References

1. T. Kohonen, "Self-Organizing Maps", *Springer Series in Information Sciences*, vol. 30, Springer, Berlin, 1995.
2. T. Kohonen, E. Oja, O. Simula, A. Visa and J. Kangas, "Engineering application of self-organizing map", *Proc. IEEE*, vol. 84, no. 10, pp. 1358-1383,1996.
3. H. Ritter and K. Schulten, "Kohonen's self-organizing maps: exploring their computational capabilities", *IEEE Int. Conf. on Neural Networks*, vol. 1, pp. 109-116, San Diego, 1988.
4. J. Himberg, J. Ahola, E. Alhoniemi, J. Vesanto and O. Simula, "The self-organizing map as a tool in knowledge engineering", *Pattern Recognition in Soft Computing Paradigm, ed. N. R. Pal*, pp. 38-65, World Scientific, Singapore, 2001.
5. http://www.cis.hut.fi/nnrc/refs/references.ps
6. H. Bauer and K. R. Pawelzik, "Quantifying the Neighborhood Preservation of Self-Organizing Feature Maps," *IEEE Trans. on Neural Networks*, vol. 3, no. 4, pp. 570-579, 1992.
7. T. Villmann, R. Der, M. Herrmann and T. M. Martinetz, "Topology preservation in self-organizing feature maps: exact definition and measurements" *IEEE Trans. on Neural Networks*, vol. 8, no. 2, pp. 256-266, 1997.
8. A. Laha and N. R. Pal, "On different variants of self-Organizing feature map and their properties", *Proceedings of the 1999 IEEE Hong Kong Symp. on Robotics and Controls*, vol. 1 pp. I-344-I-349, 1999.
9. M. C. Su, H. T. Chang and C. H. Chou, "A novel measure for quantifying the topology preservation of self-organizing feature maps", *Neural Processing Letters*, vol. 15, no. 2, pp. 137-145, 2002.
10. K. Fukunaga, *Introduction to Statistical Pattern Recognition*, Academic Press Inc., Harcourt Brace Jovanovich, Publishers, 1990.
11. H. Ritter and K. Schulten, "Convergence properties of Kohonen's topology conserving maps: Fluctuations, stability and dimension selection", *Biol. Cybern.*, vol 60, pp. 59-71, 1988.
12. N. Kwak and C. H. Choi, "Input feature selection for classification problems", *IEEE Trans. on Neural Networks*, vol. 13, no. 1, pp. 143-159, 2002.
13. J. W. Sammon, "A nonlinear mapping for data structure analysis", *IEEE Trans. Comput.*, vol 18, pp. 401-409, 1969.

Adaptive Neural Network-Based Clustering of *Yeast* Protein–Protein Interactions

Jae-Hong Eom and Byoung-Tak Zhang

Biointelligence Lab., School of Computer Science and Engineering,
Seoul National University, Seoul 151-744, South Korea
{jheom,btzhang}@bi.snu.ac.kr

Abstract. In this paper, we presents an adaptive neural network based clustering method to group protein–protein interaction data according to their functional categories for new protein interaction prediction in conjunction with information theory based feature selection. Our technique for grouping protein interaction is based on ART-1 neural network. The cluster prototype constructed with existing protein interaction data is used to predict the class of new protein interactions. The protein interaction data of *S.cerevisiae* (bakers yeast) from MIPS and SGD are used. The clustering performance was compared with traditional *k*-means clustering method in terms of cluster distance. According to the experimental results, the proposed method shows about 89.7% clustering accuracy and the feature selection filter boosted overall performances about 14.8%. Also, inter-cluster distances of cluster constructed with ART-1 based clustering method have shown high cluster quality.

1 Introduction

These days, with the advancement of genomic technology and genome-wide analysis of organisms, one of the great challenges of the post–genomic era of today is to understand how genetic information of proteins results in the predetermined action of gene products both temporally and spatially to accomplish biological functions, and how they act together to build an organism. It is known that protein–protein interactions are fundamental biochemical reactions in the organisms and play an important role since they determine the biological processes. Therefore the comprehensive description and detailed analysis of protein–protein interactions would significantly contribute to the understanding of biological phenomena and problems.

After the completion of the genome sequence of *S.cerevisiae*, budding yeast, many researchers have undertaken the functional analysis of the yeast genome comprising more than 6,300 proteins (YPD) [1] and abundant interaction data has been produced by many research groups. Thus, the demands for the effective methods to discover novel knowledge from the interaction data through the analysis of these data are more increasing than ever before.

Many attempts have been made to predict protein functions (interactions) using such data as gene expressions and protein–protein interactions. Clustering analysis of gene expression data has been used to predict functions of un-annotated proteins based on the idea that genes with similar functions are likely to be co-expressed [2, 3]. Park *et al.* [4] analyzed interactions between protein domains in terms of the interactions between structural families of evolutionarily related domains. Iossifov *et al.* [5] and Ng *et al.* [6] inferred new interaction from the existing interaction data. And there are many other approaches for analyzing and predicting protein interactions.

G. Das and V.P. Gulati (Eds.): CIT 2004, LNCS 3356, pp. 49–57, 2004.

However, many approaches to protein interaction analysis suffer from high dimensional property of the data which have more than thousand features [7].

In this paper, we propose an adaptive neural network based clustering method for clustering protein–protein interactions in the context of their feature association. We use ART-1 version of adaptive resonance theory [8] as an adaptive neural network clustering model. The ART-1 [9] is a modified version of ART [10] for clustering binary vectors. The advantage of using ART-1 algorithms to group feature abundant interaction data is that it adapts to the change in new protein interactions over various experiment data without losing information about other protein interaction data trained previously. Here, we assume protein–protein interaction of yeast as feature-to-feature association of each interacting proteins. To analyze protein–protein interactions with respect to their interaction class with their feature association, we use as many features as possible from several major databases such as MIPS and SGD [11, 12] to construct a rich feature vector for each protein interaction which is provided to the proposed clustering model. Here, we use the same approach of Rangarajan *et al.* [13] for the design of clustering model and employ the feature selection filter of Yu *et al.* [14] to reduce computational complexity and improve the overall clustering performance by eliminating non-informative features.

The remainder of this paper is organized as follows. In Section 2, we introduce the concept of the feature selection filter and the overall architecture of the clustering model with its learning algorithm. Section 3 describes the representation scheme of the protein–protein interaction for the adaptive neural network based clustering and also presents the experimental results in comparison with the conventional *k*-means clustering. Finally, concluding remarks and future works are given in Section 4.

2   Feature Dimension Reduction and Clustering

Feature Dimension Reduction by Feature Selection

Here, we consider each protein–protein interaction as the feature to feature associations. We constructed massive feature sets for each protein and interacting protein pairs from public protein description databases [11, 12, 15, 16, 17]. However, there exist also many features which have no information of their association with other proteins. Therefore, feature selection may be needed in advance of the clustering of protein–protein interactions. Especially, this feature selection is indispensable when dealing with such high dimensional (feature dimension) data.

Feature selection is the process of choosing a subset of original features so that the feature space is optimally reduced according to a certain evaluation criterion. Generally, a feature is regarded as a good feature when it is relevant to the class concept but is not redundant with other relevant features, and the correlation between two variables can be regarded as a goodness measure.

The correlation between two random variables can be measured by two broad approaches, one is based on classical linear correlation and the other is based on information theory. Linear correlation approaches (e.g., *linear correlation coefficient*, *least square regression error*, and *maximal information compression index*) have several benefits. These approaches can remove features with near zero linear correlation with the class variable and reduce redundancy among selected features. But, linear correlation measures may not be able to capture correlations that are not linear in nature and the computation requires all features are numeric-valued [14]. In this paper, we use an information theory-based correlation measure to overcome these drawbacks.

Each feature of a data can be considered as a random variable and the uncertainty of a random variable can be measured by *entropy*. The entropy of a variable X is defined as

$$H(X) = -\sum_i P(x_i)\log_2(P(x_i)),$$ (1)

And the entropy of X after observing values of another variable Y is defined as

$$H(X|Y) = -\sum_j P(y_j)\sum_i P(x_i|y_j)\log_2(P(x_i|y_j)),$$ (2)

where $P(y_j)$ is the prior probability of the value y_j of Y, and $P(x_i|y_j)$ is the posterior probability of X being x_i given the value of $Y=y_j$. The amount by which the entropy of X decreases reflects additional information about X provided by Y and is called *information gain* [18], which is given by

$$IG(X|Y) = H(X) - H(X|Y)$$ (3)

According to this measure, a feature Y is considered to be correlated more to the feature X than to the feature Z, if $IG(X|Y) > IG(Z|Y)$. It is said that symmetry is a desired property for a measure of correlation between features and information gain [14]. However, information gain is biased in favor of features with more values and the values have to be normalized to ensure they are comparable and have the same effect. Therefore, here we use the *symmetrical uncertainty* as the measure of feature correlation [14, 19], which is defined as

$$SU(X,Y) = 2\left[\frac{IG(X|Y)}{H(X)+H(Y)}\right], \quad 0 \le SU(X,Y) \le 1$$ (4)

Figure 1 shows the overall procedure of the correlation-based feature dimension reduction filter which was earlier introduced by Yu *et al.* [14], named the fast correlation-based filter (FCBF). In this paper, we call this FCBF procedure as the feature dimension reduction filter (FDRF) for our application. The algorithm finds a set of principal features S_{best} for the class concept. The procedures in Figure 1 are divided into two main parts. In the first part (Step 1 and Step 2), it calculates the symmetrical uncertainty (SU) value for each feature, selects the relevant features into S'_{list} on the basis of the predefined threshold δ, and constructs an ordered list of them in descending order according to their SU values. In the second part (Step 3 and Step 4), it further processes the ordered list to remove redundant features and only keeps principal ones among all the selected relevant features.

With symmetrical uncertainty as a feature association measure, we reduce the feature dimension through the feature selection procedure. In Figure 1, the class C is divided into two classes, the conditional protein class (C_C) and the resulting protein class (C_R) of interaction. The relevance of a feature to the protein interaction (interaction class) is decided by the value of c–correlation and f–correlation, where an SU value δ is used as a threshold value. The two correlations are defined as follows [14].

Definition 1 (c–correlation $SU_{i,c}$, f–correlation $SU_{j,i}$). Assume that a dataset S contains N $(f_1,..., f_N)$ features and a class C (C_C or C_R). Let $SU_{i,c}$ denote the SU value that measures the correlation between a feature f_i and the class C (called c–correlation). Then a subset $S' \subseteq S$ of relevant features can be decided by a threshold SU value δ, such that $\forall f_i \in S'$, $1 \leq i \leq N$, $SU_{i,c} \geq \delta$. And the pairwise correlation between all features (called f–correlation) can be defined in the same way as the c–correlation with a threshold value δ. The value of f–correlation is used to decide whether a relevant feature is redundant or not when considered with other relevant features.

Given training dataset $S = (f_1,...,f_N,C)$, where $C = C_C \cup C_R$ and
User-decided threshold δ, do following procedure for each class C_C and C_R.
1. **Repeat** Step 1.1 to 1.2, for all i, $i = 1$ to N.
   1.1 **Calculate** $SU_{i,c}$ for f_i.
   1.2. **Append** f_i to S'_{list} when $SU_{i,c} \geq \delta$.
2. **Sort** S'_{list} in descending order with $SU_{i,c}$ value.
3. **Set** f_p with the first element of S'_{list}.
4. **Repeat** Step 4.1 to 4.3, for all $f_p \neq NULL$.
   4.1 **Set** f_q with the next element of f_p in S'_{list}.
   4.2 **Repeat** Step 4.2.1 to 4.2.3, for all $f_q \neq NULL$.
      4.2.1 **Set** $f'_q = f_q$.
      4.2.2 if $SU_{p,q} \geq SU_{q,c}$,
         Remove f_q from S'_{list} and **Set** f_q with the next element of f'_q in S'_{list}.
         else **Set** f_q with the next element of f_q in S'_{list}.
      4.2.3 **Set** f_q with the next element of f_q in S'_{list}
   4.3 **Set** f_p with the next element of f_p in S'_{list}.
5. **Set** $S_{best} = S'_{list}$
Output the most informative optimal feature subset: S_{best}

Fig. 1. The procedure of the feature dimension reduction filter (FDRF)

Clustering Protein Interactions

We use ART-1 neural network for grouping the class of protein–protein interactions. In our ART-1 based clustering, each protein interaction is represented by a prototype vector that is a generalized representation of the set of features of each interacting proteins. Figure 2 presents the architecture of ART-1 based clustering model. The PPI_i stands for each protein interaction and it includes the set of features of two interacting proteins. The degree of similarity between the members of each cluster can be controlled by changing the value of the vigilance parameter. The overall procedure for clustering protein–protein interactions with the ART-1 based clustering model described in Appendix A. The basic layout of this procedure is identical with the work of Rangarajan *et al.* [13].

3 Experimental Results

Protein Interaction as Binary Feature Vector

An interaction is represented as a pair of two proteins that directly binds to each other. This protein interaction is represented by a binary feature vector of interacting proteins and their associations. Figure 3 describe this interaction representation processes. Interaction data prepared in this manner are provided to the ART-1 based clus-

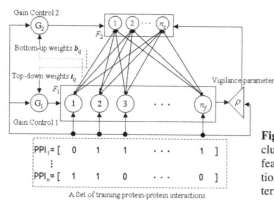

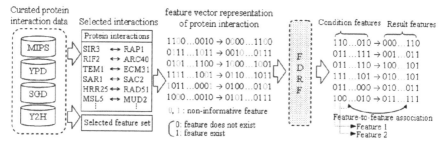

Fig. 2. The architecture of ART-1 based clustering model. PPI_i stands for the feature vector of protein–protein interaction which represents the feature characteristic of interacting proteins.

ter model to group each protein interaction class and learn the association of features which generalize the interactions. Then, the constructed cluster prototype is used to predict the classes of protein interactions presented in the test step. The class of interacting protein from MIPS [11] which is known for the most reliable curated protein interaction database in current literature is used to evaluate the clustering accuracy.

Fig. 3. Representation of protein interaction by feature vectors. Each interaction is represented as a binary feature vector (whether the feature exists or not) and their associations. The FDRF sets those features as 'don't care' which have SU value less than an SU threshold δ. This is intended to eliminate non-informative features so as to boost up the clustering performance of ART-1 based clustering model. The features marked 'don't care' are also regarded as 'don't care' in ART-1 based clustering model training. These non-informative features are not shown in the vector representation of right side of Figure 3. The resulting binary vector of interaction is provided to the ART-1 based clustering model, described in Figure 2, for model training and testing

Data Sets

Each *yeast* protein has various functions or characteristics which are called 'feature.' In this paper, set of features of each protein are collected from public genome databases [11, 12, 15, 16, 17]. We use similar features of protein interaction of Oyama *et al.* [20] which include YPD categories, EC numbers (from SWISS-PROT), SWISS-PROT/PIR keywords, PROSITE motifs, bias of the amino acids, segment cluster, and amino acid patterns. A major protein pairs of the interactions are also obtained from the same data source of Oyama *et al.* [20]. These interaction dataset include various experimental data such as YPD and Y2H by Ito *et al.* [16] and Uetz *et al.* [17]. Additionally, we used SGD to construct more abundant feature set [12].

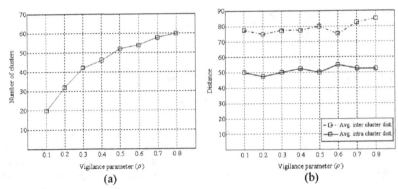

Fig. 4. The effects by the variation of vigilance parameter ρ. Figure 4(a) shows the variation of the number of cluster with the increase of vigilance parameter and Figure 4(b) shows the variation in cluster distances as the vigilance parameter ρ varies

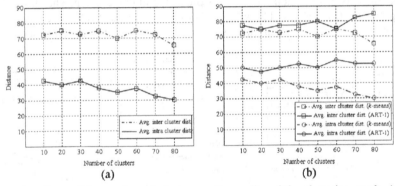

Fig. 5. The effects of the number of clusters on the quality of the clustering result. (a) The cluster distance variation of k-means cluster model. (b) The comparison of ART-1 and k-means clustering models with respect to average inter–cluster and intra–cluster distances. ART-1 based method shows good clustering qualities (all ART-1 based clustering models were trained with FDRF filtered interaction vectors)

With the constructed interaction class, we predicted the class of new protein–protein interactions. The accuracy of class prediction is measured whether the predicted class of interaction is corretly correspond to the class of MIPS. The results are measured with 10-fold cross-validation. And the quality of the clustering result is evaluated by inter– (average distance between clusters) and intra– (average distance between members of each cluster) cluster distance. The k-means method was used as a baseline clustering model. The k-means partitions a given dataset into k clusters. The same number of clusters corresponding to each variant in the results of ART-1 based model were used for performance comparison.

Results

Figure 4(a) shows the increase in the number of cluster with the increase of vigilance parameter and Figure 4(b) shows the variation in cluster distances of ART-1 based cluster model. Figure 5(a) illustrates the distance variation of k-means clustering.

Figure 5(b) compares the variation in average inter–cluster distance for the two clustering models as the number of cluster increases. Both ART-1 and k-means show distance varying at a steady rate with slight fluctuations. However, the results of ART-1 based model show quite uniform fashion compared to the result of the k-means. We can consider this uniformity of ART-1 based model indicates clustering stability, which is an important attribute of high-quality clustering models [13].

Table 1 shows the cluster prediction performance of ART-1 based model and traditional k-means model. ART-1 based model outperformed on prediction accuracy about 20% (when it trained with the interaction vectors filtered with FDRF). Thus, we can guess that the ART-1 based cluster model is very useful for the clustering of data which have many features and the proposed clustering model could be used for the analysis of protein–protein interactions. The overall prediction acuracy was improved about 14.8% by FDRF feature selection. Thus we can say that the information theory based feature selection procedure contributes to the improvement of predection acuracy and it is useful as a data preprocessing methods, especily, when we handle the data which have many features (i.e., high dimensional data).

Table 1. Result of protein interaction class prediction by k-means and ART-1 model. The ART-1 based model with FDRF filtered interaction vectors shows the best performance

Method for prototype cluster construction	Number of interactions (T)	Number of interactions predicted correctly (P)	Accuracy ($|P|/|T|$)
k-means	4,628	3,202	69.2 %
ART-1 (without FDRF)	4,628	[a] 3,466	[a] 74.9 %
ART-1 (with FDRF)	4,628	[b] 4,151	[b] 89.7 %
Diffrence	–	[a] 264 [b] 949	[a] 5.7 % [b] 20.5 %

4 Conclusions

In this paper, we presented an adaptive neural network (ART-1) based clustering method for clustering protein–protein interaction. We applied an information theory-based feature selection procedure to improve the performance of trained clustering model. The proposed method achieved the improvement of accuracy about 20%. From the experimental result of the quality of the clustering result and clustering accuracy, it is suggested that the neural network-based clustering model can be used for a more detailed investigation of the protein–protein interactions, since the proposed model can learn effectively the hidden patterns of the data which have many features.

The current public interaction data produced by a high-throughput method (e.g., Y2H) have many false positives and some of these false positives are corrected as true positives by recent researches with new modern experimental approaches. Thus, the study on the new method for adapting these changes in data set, which is related to false positive screening, remains as future works.

Acknowledgements. This research was supported by the Korean Ministry of Science and Technology under the NRL Program and the Systems Biology Program. The RIACT at Seoul National University provided research facilities for this study.

Appendix A

Input: an array of input protein interaction vectors **PPI** and vigilance parameter ρ.

1. **Initialize**
    1.1 **Set** the value of gain control G_1 and G_2,
    $$G_1, G_1 = \begin{cases} 1 \ if \ input \ PPI_I \neq 0 \ and \ output \ from \ F_2 \ Layer = 0 \\ 0 \ for \ all \ other \ cases \end{cases}$$
    1.2 **Set** all nodes in F_1 layer and F_2 layer to 0.
    1.3 **Set** all weight of top-down weight matrix, $t_{ji} = 1$.
    1.4 **Set** all weight of bottom-up weight matrix,
    $$b_{ij} = \frac{1}{n_f + 1} \quad (n_f = \text{the size of the input feature vector, here } n_f = 5{,}240).$$
    1.5 **Set** the vigilance parameter ρ (0.2 to 0.7).

2. **Repeat** Step 2.1 to 2.7, for all protein-protein interaction vector PPI_I.
    2.1 **Read** randomly chosen interaction vector
    $$PPI_I = (P_1, P_2, \cdots, P_{I=5,240}), \ where \ P_1 = 0 \ or \ 1.$$
    2.2 **Compute Input** y_j for each node in F_2, $y_j = \sum_{i=1}^{5,240} P_i \times b_{ij}$.
    2.3 **Determine** k, $y_k = \sum_{j=1}^{\text{\# of nodes in } F_2} \max(y_j)$.
    2.4 **Compute Activation,** $X_k^* = (X_1^*, X_2^*, \cdots, X_{i=5,240}^*)$ for the node k in F_1
    Where, $X_i^* = t_{ki} \times P_i \ (i = 1, \cdots, 5240)$.
    2.5 **Calculate similarity** δ, between X_i^* and PPI_I :
    $$\delta = \frac{\|X_k^*\|}{\|PPI_I\|} = \frac{\sum_{i=1}^{5,240} X_i^*}{\sum_{i=1}^{5,240} P_i}.$$
    2.6 **Update weight** of top-down weight matrix with PPI_I and node k
    If $\delta > \rho$, update top-down weight of node k, $t_{ki}(new) = t_{ki} \times P_i$ where $i = 1, \cdots, 5240$.
    2.7 **Create a new node** in F_2 layer
        2.7.1 **Create** a new node l.
        2.7.2 **Initialize** top-down weight t_{li} to the current input feature pattern.
        2.7.3 **Initialize** button-up weight for the new node l.
        $$b_{li}(new) = \frac{X_i^*}{0.5 + \sum_{i=1}^{5,240} X_i^*} \quad \text{where } i = 1 \ldots 5240.$$

The procedure of ART-1 model based clustering of protein–protein interaction. The basic procedure and the update formula are identical with the work of Rangarajan *et al.* [13].

References

1. Goffeau, A., Barrell, B.G., *et al.*: Life with 6000 genes. *Science* **274** (1996) 546–67.
2. Eisen, M.B., Spellman, P.T., *et al.*: Cluster analysis and display of genomewide expression patterns. *Proc. Natl. Acad. Sci. USA* **95** (1998) 14863-68.
3. Pavlidis, P. andWeston, J.: Gene functional classification from heterogeneous data. In *Proceedings of the 5th International Conference on Computational Molecular Biology (RECOMB-2001)* (2001) 249-55.
4. Park, J., Lappe, M., *et al.*: Mapping protein family interactions: intra-molecular and intermolecular protein family interaction repertoires in the PDB and yeast. *J. Mol. Biol.* **307** (2001) 929-39.
5. Iossifov, I., Krauthammer, M., *et al.* Probabilistic inference of molecular networks from noisy data sources. *Bioinformatics* **20**(8) (2004) 1205-13.
6. Ng, S.K., Zhang, Z., *et al.* Integrative approach for computationally inferring protein domain interactions. *Bioinformatics* **19**(8) (2003) 923-29.
7. Eom, J.-H., Chang, J.-H., *et al.*: Prediction of implicit protein–protein interaction by optimal associative feature mining. In *Proceedings of the 5th International Conference on Intelligent Data Engineering and Automated Learning (IDEAL'04)*, (2004) 85-91.
8. Carpenter, G.A. and Grossberg, S.: A massively parallel architecture for a self-organizing neural pattern recognition machine. *Computer Vision, Graphics and Image Processing* **37** (1987) 54-115.
9. Barbara, M.: ART1 and pattern clustering. In proceedings of the 1988 connectionist models summer 1988. Morgan Kaufmann (1988) 174-85.
10. Heins, L.G. and Tauritz, D.R.: Adaptive resonance theory (ART): an introduction. *Internal Report* 95-35, Dept. of Computer Science, Leiden University, Netherlands (1995) 174-85.
11. Mewes, H.W., Amid, C., *et al.*: MIPS: analysis and annotation of proteins from whole genomes. *Nucleic Acids Res.* **32**(1) (2004) D41-44.
12. Christie, K.R., Weng, S., *et al.*: Saccharomyces Genome Database (SGD) provides tools to identify and analyze sequences from Saccharomyces cerevisiae and related sequences from other organisms. *Nucleic Acids Res.* **32**(1) (2004) D311-14.
13. Rangarajan, S.K., Phoha, V.V., *et al.*: Adaptive neural network clustering of web users. *IEEE Computer* **37**(4) (2004) 34-40.
14. Yu, L. and Liu, H.: Feature selection for high dimensional data: a fast correlation-based filter solution. In *Proceedings of the 12th International Conference on Machine Learning (ICML'2003)*, (2003) 856–863.
15. Csank, C., Costanzo, M.C., *et al.*: Three yeast proteome databases: YPD, PombePD, and CalPD (MycoPathPD). *Methods Enzymol.* **350** (2002) 347-73.
16. Ito, T., Chiba, T., *et al.*: A comprehensive two-hybrid analysis to explore the yeast protein interactome. *Proc. Natl. Acad. Sci. USA* **98** (2001) 4569-4574.
17. Uetz, P., Giot, L., *et al.*: A comprehensive analysis of protein–protein interactions in Saccharomyces cerevisiae. *Nature* **403** (2000) 623-627.
18. Quinlan, J.: C4.5: Programs for machine learning. Morgan Kaufmann. (1993)
19. Press, W.H., Teukolsky, S.A, *et al.*: Numerical recipes in C. *Cambridge University Press.* (1988)
20. Oyama, T., Kitano, K., *et al.*: Extraction of knowledge on protein–protein interaction by association rule discovery. *Bioinformatics* **18** (2002) 705-14.

Design of Neuro-fuzzy Controller
Based on Dynamic Weights Updating

Abdul Hafez[1], Ahmed Alrabie[2], and Arun Agarwal[3]

[1] Department of CSE, Osmania University, Hyderabad, India
hafezsyr@ieee.org
[2] Department of Communication, University of Aleppo, Syria
a_kh_rabie@postmaster.co.uk
[3] Department of CIS, University of Hyderabad, Hyderabad, India
aruncs@uohyd.ernet.in

Abstract. Neural and fuzzy methods have been applied effectively to control system theory and system identification. This work depicts a new technique to design a real time adaptive neural controller. The learning rate of the neural controller is adjusted by fuzzy inference system. The behavior of the control signal has been generalized as the performance of the learning rate to control a DC machine. A model of DC motor was considered as the system under control. Getting a fast dynamic response, less over shoot, and little oscillations are the function control low. Simulation results have been carried at different step change in reference value and load torque.

1 Introduction

Traditional control techniques have been used in problems where systems are well defined, and have a high degree of certainty. *PID* controller is the most common widely used in successful applications. Due to the difficulties and limitation of the conventional methods like the small range of control parameters and loss of accuracy in nonlinear systems, intelligent control methods have come up as a new area of research.

Neural networks have been successfully applied to system identification and nonlinear control systems that have some uncertainty in its parameters [1]. They have been applied in designing the controller; in this case the architecture of the controller will be independent of the system under consideration. Particularly, learning algorithms are not giving a guarantee for successful convergence, and also the length of learning phase varies depending on the initial hypothesis. Present work focuses on this issue. Adaptive neural network has been proposed as a speed controller for a separately excited DC motor using on-line weights updating.

Fuzzy logic is another intelligent technique that has been applied to control theory. Many successful works have been done in the field called fuzzy control and adaptive fuzzy control [2], these works are applications like steam engine control, analysis of control algorithms, derivation of fuzzy control rules, predictive fuzzy control, and optimal fuzzy control [3]. Another work incorporates the fuzzy logic with the neural techniques, such as ANFIS [4] that is an adaptive-network-based fuzzy inference system using a hybrid learning procedure. ANFIS constructs an input-output mapping based on both human knowledge (if-then rules) and stipulated data pairs.

G. Das and V.P. Gulati (Eds.): CIT 2004, LNCS 3356, pp. 58–67, 2004.

This paper extends the work in [5] by proposing a fuzzy technique to compute the initial learning rate and the increment (and decrement) factor. A rule base was built to give the initial learning rate as an output given two inputs, the error of the motor speed and the derivative of the error. For getting a fine adjustment of the learning rate, a factor proportional to the rate of error to the reference value was addedThe remaining parts of this paper are organized as following: the second section gives brief information about the DC motor model and its specifications. Third and forth sections are showing the principle of neural networks learning algorithms, and using of fuzzy logic in control applications. Fifth section presents our proposed method. In the sixth section, simulation results were carried out to show a comparison with other techniques presented in literature.

2 The DC Motor Model

A DC motor has a natural relationship between torque T_m and current I_a, along with voltage E_m and angular speed [6]. For an ideal motor, the current required is directly proportional to the applied toque, and the speed is directly proportional to the applied voltage as

$$E_m = K_e.W \tag{1}$$
$$T_m = K_t.I_a \tag{2}$$

These relationships are normally expressed, as given under, with the assumption that the motor is ideal, this means $K_t = K_e = K$. The following are the mathematical equations of the separately excited *DC* motor:

$$E_m = K.W (t) \tag{3}$$
$$T_m = K.I_a(t) \tag{4}$$
$$E_m(t) = V_a(t) - R_a.I_a(t) - L_a[dI_a(t)/dt] \tag{5}$$
$$T_m(t) = T_L + B.W(t) + J.[dW(t)/dt]. \tag{6}$$

3 Neural Networks Learning Algorithms

The basic approach in learning is to start with an uncertain network, present a training pattern to the input layer, pass the signals through the net and determine the output values of the output layer, these outputs are compared to the target values; the difference between the two is called the error. This error or some scalar function like J is minimized when the network matches the desired output. The learning algorithms utilize step-by-step error minimization process.

Back-propagation-learning algorithm is based on gradient decent [7]. Weights W are initialized with small random values, and they are changed in a direction that will reduce the error:

$$J = \sum (Y_d - Y_a)^2 \tag{7}$$
$$\Delta W = -\eta (\partial J / \partial W) \tag{8}$$
$$W (n) = W (n - 1) + \Delta W (n - 1), \tag{9}$$

where η is the learning rate. Y_d is the desired output, and Y_a is the actual output. As described in [7], the effectiveness and convergence of the error-back-propagation learning algorithm depend significantly on the value of the learning rate η, the problem being solved, and network topology. An adaptive learning rate is used to accelerate the convergence [5]. Back propagation is used to adjust on-line the weight parameters of the neural controller based on the inverse model architecture of the system. The adaptive learning rate was proposed as a function of initial value and a term of the error $E = Y_d - Y_a$. The error E was normalized to the reference value. To make learning rate independent of the reference value, we use the following equation:

$$\eta(n) = \eta(n-1) + ne \cdot \eta_0 \tag{10}$$

where ne is the normalized error, $ne = (Y_d - Y_a)/\Delta Y_{ref}$, and η_0 is the initial learning rate determined by the fuzzy adjustment mechanism. ΔY_{ref} is the difference between previous reference value and present reference value. The inverse model technique is used to build the neural controller. Assuming that the system to be controlled can be described by

$$y(t+1) = g[y(t),\ldots, y(t-n+1), u(t),\ldots, u(t-m)], \tag{11}$$

the inverse model network should approximate the following relationship giving the most recent control input

$$u(t) = g-1[y(t+1), y(t),\ldots, y(t-n+1), u(t),\ldots, u(t-m)]. \tag{12}$$

Two-layer feed forward neural network was used to map the relationship from the output to the input of the system. This network can be used for controlling the system by substituting the output at time (t+1) by the desired output, the reference value, architecture of neural controller and the block diagram of the system identification are described in Figs. 1. More details about the identification process are in [1].

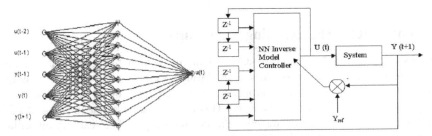

Fig. 1. The architecture of neural inverse model controller, left, and the block diagram of the system identification, right

4   Fuzzy Logic and Control

Fuzzy logic deals with systems having a degree of uncertainty by mimicking the human in thinking and acting. In fuzzy set theory, a variable has a degree of membership in a given set in the range of 0 to 1. Variable value is expressed using natural languages. When the control algorithm depends on fuzzy logic, it is called as fuzzy control; this fuzzy control algorithm includes if- then rules. The inputs to the fuzzy controller usually are chosen to be the error E and the change of error ΔE that are described as follows:

$$E(n) = Y_d(n) - Y_a(n) \tag{13}$$

$$\Delta E(n) = E(n) - E(n-1). \tag{14}$$

where $E(n)$ and E (n-1) are the error at the time (n) and (n-1) respectively, $\Delta E(n)$, the change of +error at the time (n). The control signal $U(n)$ that to be applied to the system is given as following:

$$U(n) = U(n-1) + \Delta U(n). \tag{15}$$

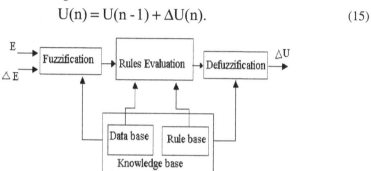

Fig. 2. Block diagram of the fuzzy inference system

Block diagram in Fig. 2 depicts the fuzzy inference system consisting of the following:

Fuzzification. The inputs determine the degree to which they belong to each of the appropriate fuzzy sets via membership functions. Inputs are always numerical values. The input variable (in this case the interval between minimum and maximum values), and the output is a fuzzy degree of membership in the qualifying linguistic set (always the interval of the degree is between 0 and 1). Our proposed technique uses forty-nine rules, and each one of the rules depends on resolving the inputs into a number of different fuzzy linguistic sets: neglrg, negmed, negsml, zero, possml, posmed, poslrg. Before the rules can be evaluated, the inputs must be fuzzified according to each of these linguistic sets, (via its membership function).

Knowledge base and rules evaluation. Knowledge base consists of a certain number of if-then rules that describes the behavior of control signal (the fuzzy controller output), and a database provides the necessary definitions of fuzzy rules and fuzzy data manipulation depending on the system inputs conditions.

Defuzzification. The input for the defuzzification process is a fuzzy set (the aggregate output fuzzy set) and the output is a single number. As much as fuzziness helps the rule evaluation during the intermediate steps, the final desired output for each variable is generally a single number. However, the aggregate of a fuzzy set encompasses a range of output values, and so must be defuzzified in order to resolve a single output value from the set. The most popular defuzzification method is the centroid calculation, which returns the center of area under the curve; this defuzzification method is also used in our technique.

5   The Proposed Technique

The proposed technique is feed forward neural network with On-line back propagation algorithm to adjust the weights and biases. The controller architecture is based on the inverse model of the system under consideration. Fuzzy adjustment mechanism has been used to adjust the learning rate. The control signal is the output of the neural controller and can be described as follows:

$$U = F(X, W). \tag{16}$$

$F(X, W)$ is the activation function at the output of the inverse model neural controller.

By adjusting the weights W, the control signal will changes as:

$$U(n) = U(n-1) + \Delta U(n) \tag{17}$$
$$= F\{X(n), W(n-1) + \Delta W(n-1)\}, \tag{18}$$
$$\Delta U > 0, \qquad \text{if } \Delta W > 0. \tag{19}$$
$$\Delta U < 0, \qquad \text{if } \Delta W < 0. \tag{20}$$

The change of weight is given by the equation

$$\Delta W = -\eta(\partial J/\partial W) = \eta E. X, \tag{21}$$

where E is the error of the output respect to the desired output $E(n) = Yd(n) - Ya(n) X$ is the input vector to the output layer. η is the learning rate. A proof of (21) is available in [7]. To get fine-tuning, by getting faster response and less overshooting, the learning rate will be changed according to the error in the output value E and the rate of change of error ΔE according to the following equation:

$$\eta(n) = \eta(n-1) + ne \cdot \eta_0. \tag{22}$$

The initial learning rate η_0 is the output of the fuzzy adjustment mechanism, and *ne* is the normalized error. A fuzzy membership functions has been built for each of the two inputs and the output. Depending on the prior knowledge about the desired behavior of the system, the range of the two inputs and the output values has been divided into seven membership functions $F_0 \in$ {*neglrg, negmed, negsml, zero, possml, posmed, poslrg*}. Plots of these member functions and the surface of the output of the fuzzy adjustment mechanism are shown in Figs. 3-4.

We can summarize the knowledge base depending on which, the fuzzy inference system was built [8]:

- If $E>0$ and $\Delta E < 0$, the response time should be reduced when E is large, and the overshoot when $E<0$, should be prevented at a time in which E is close to zero. The increment in control signal should be positive when E is still far from zero, and control signal should be zero or negative when E is close to zero.
- If $E<0$ and $\Delta E < 0$, the control signal should be decremented to prevent the overshoot.

- If $E<0$ and $\Delta E > 0$, the control signal should be incremented when E is near to zero, but should be decremented when E is still far from zero.
- If $E>0$ and $\Delta E > 0$, the control signal should be incremented to prevent the negative peak of the plant response.

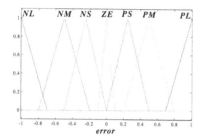 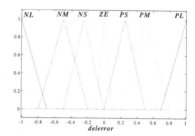

Fig. 3. Membership functions of the error left and membership functions of the change of the error right

More details about the behavior of the system especially at zero values of E and ΔE can be found in [3]. We can generalize the above rules to be applied to the process of the fuzzy adjustment mechanism, then the rule based of the fuzzy mechanism will be as described in Table 1.

When the reference value is changed from one value to another, the value of ne jumps immediately from ne = 0.0 to *ne* = 1.0. This causes suddenly increment in η; the value of this change is η_0. To prevent the learning rate value from the recursive increase according to (22), it will be reset to minimum acceptable value $\eta = 0.06$ when the error is smaller than maximum value $E_0 = 0.001$. Configuration of the neural controller with the fuzzy adjustment mechanism is described in Fig.5. and Table 1.

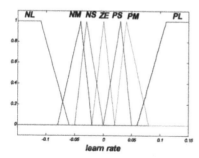 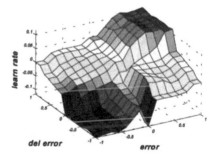

Fig. 4. Membership functions of the initial learning rate η_0, and the surface of the fuzzy adjustment mechanism output

6 Simulation Results

Model of a DC motor has been built using SIMULINK. The simulation software has been developed starting from NNCTRL toolkit available on the web. This toolkit was developed to work with Matlab 5 and later versions. Parameters of DC motor are described in the appendix.

The simulation has been carried for step change in the reference value. At starting time the initial value is zero, during the operation time the change will be negative or positive, that means to higher or lower new reference value. The response to the step function and to the change in the load torque at time t = 2 Sec with amplitude T_L= 3 N.m and The response to different reference values of the output and the change in the learning rate value are shown in figs. 6,7. The sample interval time T_s = 0.02 sec was used in the simulation process.

In direct inverse model, there is one problem relates to training the model on realistic signal. In other words the training set should be with the same characteristics as those the model is expected to work with, during the operation time. To overcome this problem, one should repeat the training recursively on new data that have been collected from new experiment. This problem will not be faced in the on-line inverse model neural controller because the on-line adjusting of the weights is enough to make the model adaptable to the character of signal. Even in specialized training in which by on-line training, the final neural model, does a fine-tuning, the model will be optimized for the reference trajectory on which the network has been already trained, and the error will not reach the smallest value.

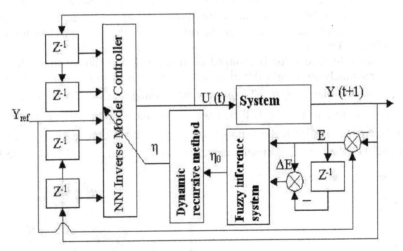

Fig. 5. Configuration of the fuzzy mechanism and neural controller

As described in [5], the learning rate is the key factor to adjust the response time and the overshooting. The performance of using fixed learning rate values is shown in fig. 8, two values of the learning rate have been used, high value and low value, in addition to the value produced with the fuzzy mechanism.

The Performance of fuzzy *PI* controller is compared with our fuzzy-neural technique in fig. 8. *PI* fuzzy controller has been built using rule base in [9].

7   Conclusion

In this paper, we have proposed an adaptive neural controller with fuzzy adjusted learning rate. On-line weights updating was used to track the reference value. Because the controller parameters are independent of the system parameters, change in sur-round conditions. Simulation results suggest that the proposed technique is better than direct inverse model controller or the fixed learning rate real-time neural controller, and is also better than the *PI* fuzzy controller. The use of fuzzy mechanism has pro-duced a good estimation of the minimum learning rate.

Table 1. The rule base matrix for the learning rate

ΔE \ E	NL	NM	NS	ZE	PS	PM	PL
PL	ZE	PS	PS	PS	PM	PL	PL
PM	NS	ZE	PS	PS	PM	PL	PL
PS	NM	NS	ZE	PS	PS	PL	PL
ZE	NL	NM	NS	ZE	PS	PM	PL
NS	NL	NL	NS	NS	ZE	PS	PM
NM	NL	NL	NM	NS	NS	ZE	PS
NL	NL	NL	NM	NM	NS	NS	ZE

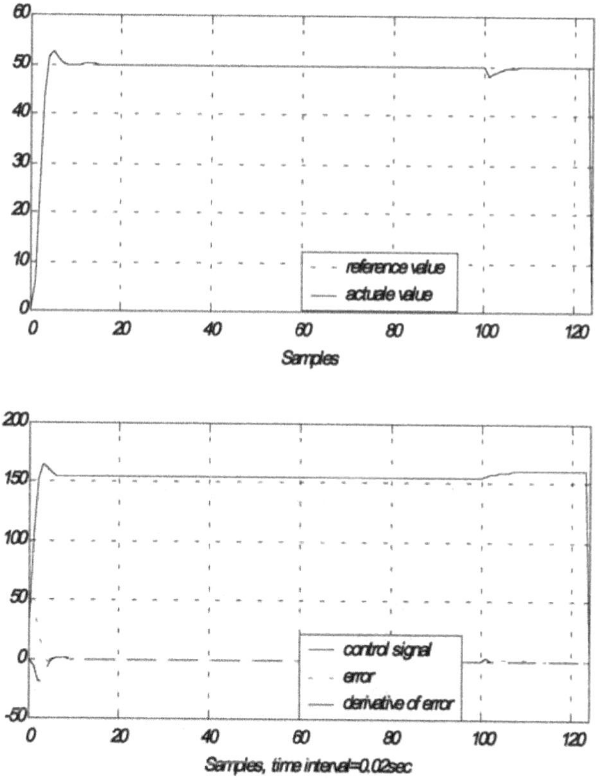

Fig. 6. The response to the speed step change at: 50 rad/sec, control, error, and change of error signals

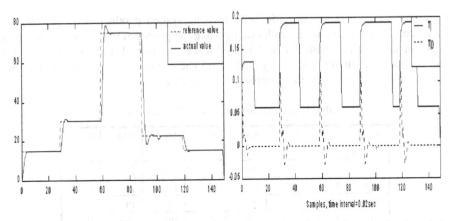

Fig. 7. The response to different values (25, 50, 75 rad/sec) of the reference signal, and the matched learning rate

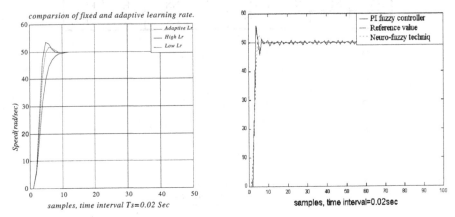

Fig. 8. Comparison of response at high, low, and adaptive learning rate, left, and Response of PI fuzzy controller comparing with our neural fuzzy technique, right

References

1. M. Norgaard, O. Ravn, N.K. Poulsen, and L.K. Hansen.: Neural Networks for Modeling and Control of Dynamic Systems: A Practitioner's Handbook. Springer-Verlag, London, U.K, 2000.
2. Fouad Mrad, and Ghassan Deeb.: Experimental comparative analysis of conventional, fuzzy logic, and adaptive fuzzy logic controllers. IEEE, Indus. App. Conf, 1999.
3. C. C. Lee.: Fuzzy logic in control systems: Fuzzy logic. IEEE Trans., Syst. Man,Cybern., vol. 20, pp. 404-435, 1990.
4. Jyh-Shing, and Roger Jang.: ANFIS: Adaptive-network-based fuzzy inference system. IEEE Trans. Syst. Man, Cybern., vol. 23, pp. 665-683, May/June, 1993.
5. A.M. Zaki, H.M. Mashaly, A. Abdel-Sattar, S. Wahsh, and S.I. Amer. Implementation of adaptive neural network real-time speed controller for dc-motor. 8th European Conference on Power Electronics and Applications, Lausanne, 1999.
6. R.L. Woods, and K.L. Lawerence. Modeling and Simulation of Dynamic Systems. Prentice Hall, New Jersy, 1997.

7. J. M. Zurada, Introduction to Artificial Neural Systems. Jaico Publishing House, India, 1994.
8. Han-Xlong, and H.B. Gatland. A new methodology for designing a fuzzy logic controller. IEEE Trans., Syst. Man, Cybern., vol. 25, pp. 505-512, March, 1995.
9. Bimal K. Bose. Fuzzy logic and neural networks in power electronic drives. IEEE Industrial Applications Magazine, pp. 57-63, May/June 2000.

Appendix

Following are the parameters of the DC motor and the extension of its terms:

E_m	the back emf of the DC motor.
T_m	the delivered torque by the motor.
$K = 2.73 \ N.m/A$	torque and back EMF constant.
$W(t)$	speed of motor.
$J = 0.026 \ Kg.m^2$	total inertia.
$B = 0.0023 \ Kg.m^2/Sec$	total damping constant.
$T_L = 3 \ N.m$	the load torque.
$R_a = 4.95 \ Ohm$	armature resistance.
$L_a = 0.06 \ H$	armature inductance.
$I_a(t)$	armature current.
$V_a(t)$	terminals armature voltage.

Interval Computing in Neural Networks: One Layer Interval Neural Networks

Raquel E. Patiño-Escarcina[1], Benjamín R. Callejas Bedregal[1], and Aarão Lyra[2]

[1] Universidade Federal do Rio Grande do Norte
Laboratório de Lógica e Inteligência Computacional LABLIC – DIMAP
59078-970 Natal, RN, Brasil
raquel@ppgsc.ufrn.br, bedregal@dimap.ufrn.br
[2] Universidade Potiguar
59056-000 Natal, RN, Brasil
aarao@unp.br

Abstract. Several applications need a guaranty of the precision of their numerical data. Important tools which allow control of the numerical errors are dealing these data as intervals. This work presents a new approach to use with *Interval Computing in Neural Networks*, studying the particular case of one layer interval neural networks, which extend Punctual One Layer Neural Networks, and try to be a solution for the problems in calculus precision error and treatment of interval data without modify it. Beyond it, seemly, interval connections between neurons permit the number of the epochs needed to converge to be lower than the needed in punctual networks without loss efficiency.

The interval computing in a one layer neural network with supervised training was tested and compared with the traditional one. Experiences show that the behavior of the interval neural network is better than the traditional one beyond of include the guarantee about the computational errors.

1 Introduction

Neural networks are powerful computational tools that can be used for classification, pattern recognition, empirical modelling and for many other applications. In real-life situations, these applications have physical quantities as data set, but it is not so easy to obtain measures that represent these physical quantities exactly. In many cases, it is extremely important to know how different the actual value of data can be from the real data. To achieve reliability, both mathematical and computationally, all quantities are represented by the smallest machine representable intervals where the physical quantities belong to the intervals. This concept was originally introduced by [13], to the field of reliable numerical computations. Later the concept of interval value has been successfully applied in regression analysis [21]; fuzzy-interval [20], [11], [18] and [10]; principal Component Analysis [6]; estimative of Power Flow and voltages of electric networks [4]; etc.

G. Das and V.P. Gulati (Eds.): CIT 2004, LNCS 3356, pp. 68–75, 2004.
© Springer-Verlag Berlin Heidelberg 2004

Artificial neural networks (ANN) are viewed as a parallel computational model, with varying degrees of complexity, comprised of densely interconnected adaptive processing units. A very important feature of these networks is their adaptive nature, where learning by example replaces traditional programming in solving problems. The computational process envisioned with artificial neural networks is as follows: an artificial neuron or processing element receives inputs from a number of other neurons or from an external stimulus. A weighted sum of these inputs constitutes the argument to an activation function or transfer function. This activation function is generally nonlinear. The resulting value of the activation function is the output of the neuron, this output gets distributed or fanned out along weighted connections to other neurons. The actual manner in which these connections are made defines the information flow in the network and is called architecture of the network. The weighted connections in these architectures play an important role, such that these network are also called connectionist models of computation. The method used to adjust the weights in the process of training the network is called the learning rule. In summary, the three essential ingredients of a computational system based on ANNs are the transfer function, the architecture, and the learning rule.

2   Interval Mathematic

Uncertainty comes as a result of incompleteness of our observations, measurements and estimations of the world. The uncertainty in the input data can be enlarged due to both rounding and truncating processes that occur in numerical computation. As a consequence the actual error presented in the final results can not be easily evaluated. In order to rigorously control and automatically handle these numerical errors was proposed to apply techniques of interval Mathematics.

The Interval Mathematic is a theory introduced by R. E. Moore [13] and T. Sunaga [19] in the latest of 50's in order to give control of errors in numeric computations in the solutions of the problems concerning real numbers, it was thought to replay questions about accuracy and efficiency.

A real interval, or only interval, is a set of all real numbers between two real numbers, the least of these real numbers is called lower bound and the greatest is called upper bound. A real interval will be denoted by $X = [\underline{x}, \overline{x}]$, where $\underline{x}$ and $\overline{x}$ are the lower and upper bounds, respectively.

In the following, lower case letters denote elements of the real numbers and capital letters to denote interval quantities and vectors. The set of all intervals will be denoted by $\mathbb{IR}$. An interval X where $\underline{x} = \overline{x}$ is called *Degenerated Interval*.

Let $A, B \in \mathbb{IR}$. The operations used in this work, are:

– The addition, defined by the equation:

$$A + B = [\underline{a}, \overline{a}] + [\underline{b}, \overline{b}] = [\underline{a} + \underline{b}, \overline{a} + \overline{b}] \tag{1}$$

– The subtraction, defined by the equation

$$A - B = A + (-B) = [(\underline{a} - \overline{b}); (\overline{a} - \underline{b})] \tag{2}$$

- The multiplication, defined by the equation:

$$A \cdot B = [\underline{a}, \overline{a}] \cdot [\underline{b}, \overline{b}] = [min\{\underline{ab}, \overline{a}\underline{b}, \underline{a}\overline{b}, \overline{ab}\}, max\{\underline{ab}, \overline{a}\underline{b}, \underline{a}\overline{b}, \overline{ab}\}] \qquad (3)$$

- The distance of the interval A until the interval B, defined by:

$$dist(A, B) = dist([\underline{a}, \overline{a}], [\underline{b}, \overline{b}]) = max\{|\underline{a} - \underline{b}|; |\overline{a} - \overline{b}|\} \qquad (4)$$

- The weight of the interval A, defined by:

$$w(A) = w([\underline{a}, \overline{a}]) = (\overline{a} - \underline{a}) \qquad (5)$$

- The sign of the interval A, defined by:

$$sign(A) = sign([\underline{a}, \overline{a}]) = (\overline{a} + \underline{a}) \qquad (6)$$

An interval A where $w(A) = 0$ is called *Symmetrical Interval*. More information about interval mathematics and applications can be found in [1], [2], [9], [14], [15] and [16].

3   Interval Computing in Neural Networks

In [17] was proposed some methods for processing interval data input in neural networks. These methods are the most basic and intuitive form to work with intervals but these not guarantee that the resultant data set represents the real data set of the problem. In [8] each interval in the input data set is a set of the possible values formed with opinion of the experts about one variable, here was used the interval mathematics to calculate the output of the network. This work is a proposal of solution to the problem of interval data but doesn't show other advantages with the interval mathematics. In [5] was proposed a neural network with interval weights but the solution isn't more simple and the network is modelled like the problem of the solution equations. These works represent the carefulness of the researchers around the importance to have algorithms can work with interval data. This approach is a contribution for solving part of the problems seen before.

A Neural Network is said to be an *Interval Neural Network* if one of its input, output and weight sets have interval values.

Interval Neural Networks (IANN) are formed by processing units called Interval Neurons. They are based on the neuron model proposed by McCulloc-Pitts. This neuron is prepared for receiving interval or real data. An Interval Neuron is formed by three functions (figure 1):

- *Normalizer Function*($\mathbb{T}$): This function analyze the input nature and normalize it in order to have only interval inputs.
- *Sum Function*(Σ): This function is the same as the sum function in the neurons of the traditional neural networks. Join in a linear way inputs with their respective synaptic weights.

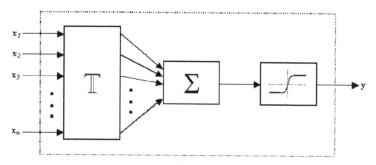

Fig. 1. Interval Neuron structure.

– *Activation Function*: This function could be any interval derivable linear function. Restrict the output to interval values between [-1 1] or [0 1].

In Interval Neural Networks, neurons are connected as they are in traditional Neural Networks. Interval Neural Networks can be classified in the same way that Punctual Neural Networks are classified.

4   A One Layer Interval Neural Network

The one layer Interval Neural Network is formed by interval neurons where the activation function is the binary threshold function of the form:

$$y = \begin{cases} + & \text{If } sign(X) > 0, X_i = [\underline{x}, \overline{x}] \in \mathbb{IR}, \\ 0 & \text{in other case.} \end{cases} \tag{7}$$

When neural networks are used as classifiers, the output set is a binary one and therefore their outputs are binaries too. Patterns are represented with 0 or 1. The output is transformed from $\mathbb{IR} \rightarrow \mathbb{R}$ by the activation function, thus, the interval space is divided by the pattern separation and each interval belongs to the pattern where the majority area of it belong.

Neurons of the one layer interval neural network are full connected with inputs, each of these connections are represented by an interval that represent at the same time the force between relationships.

4.1   Learning in the One Layer Interval Neural Network

One of the most important features of a neural network is its ability to adapt to new environments. Learning implies that a processing unit is capable of changing its input/output behavior as a result of changes in the environment. Therefore, learning algorithms are critical to the study of neural networks. Thus, the one layer interval neural network has to be trained in order to extract knowledge of a data set.

In process of the training, each neuron compute and send its output, that is going to said if the neuron is active or not. With the concepts given in section 2

Table 1. Learning algorithm for the one layer interval neural network.

Step 1	Initialize inputs weights and bias weigth
	Initialize inputs weights (W_{ij}) and bias weight θ_i with small random intervals where $size(W_{ij})$ and $size(\theta_i)$ are minimum.
Step 2	Present an input pattern $[X, d]$ to the network
	X_i is a set of input intervals that represent the pattern and d_i represent a binary vector that codifies the class of the pattern X_i. The vector $X_i = ([\underline{x}_0, \overline{x}_0], [\underline{x}_1, \overline{x}_1], ..., [\underline{x}_{n-1}, \overline{x}_{n-1}])$.
Step 3	Calculate the output of the network for the input X_i
	$$y(t) = f_n(\sum_{i=0}^{N-1} W_{ij}(t)X_i(t) - \theta_j)$$
	f_n is the interval activation function, the calculus is made by the equation 7
Step 4	Weights modification
	$W_{ij}(t+1) = W_{ij}(t) + \eta[d(t) - y(t)]X_i$, where $0 \le i \le N - 1$
	$$d(t) = \begin{cases} +1 & \text{If the input is of class A,} \\ 0 & \text{If the input is of class B.} \end{cases}$$
	η is a real value less than 1 and $d(t)$ is the desired output for the actual pattern. If the network classified it correctly, then the weights are not going to be modified.
Step 5	the total error in the neural network for the pattern i is calculated by $e = \sum_{k}^{m} = 1[d_i - y_k(t)]$, if $i = n$ (number of pattern) and $\sum_{i}^{n} e \le \epsilon$ where ϵ represent the minimum error, the algorithm finishes in other case go to Step 2

the outputs are obtained and the weights are modified in order to correct a possible error in the output. In the table 1 the algorithm for training the one layer interval neural network is presented.

5   Experiment Results

In order to analyze the influence of intervals into the neural network, let us consider a simple example: the classification of two classes. For the experiences we use five real data sets and five interval data sets. All sets have 60 patterns with 2 inputs and the testing sets have 30 patterns. Each real data set was intervalized by creating a same data set where each element will be an interval. Thus, let $Q_n = \{q_1, q_2, q_3, ..., q_n\}$, where $n = 60$ is one real data set where $q_i = \{x_1, x_2\}, x_i \in \mathbb{R}$. Let $IP_n = \{P_1, P_2, ..., P_n\}$ where $n = 60$ is one interval data set where $P_i = \{X_1, X_2\}, X_i \in \mathbb{IR}, x_i \in X_i$.

The neural network was trained one hundred times, the mean of all solutions is included in the mean of all solutions obtained with the interval neural network with same structure. If the set IP_n has symmetrical interval, the mean of all solutions of the punctual network is included in the mean of all solutions of the interval network. The straight line formed by the middle points of the weights in the interval network defines the separation of the classes. It is coincident with the straight line formed for the weights of the punctual network, because of it, the interval neural network can be considered as a generalization of the punctual neural network.

The number of epochs necessary for training this interval neural network is smaller than the number necessary for punctual neural network without loss efficiency. The interval neural networks was trained with the set Q_n and the results was successfully, of this form, again can be said that the IANN is a generalization of the punctual neural networks. The table 2 shows the results of this training experiences, there are showed results of the mean epochs number to train the interval neural network and the punctual neural network and the efficiency of the classification. We were tested with different values for the rate of learning (η) and the minimun error $\epsilon = 0$

Table 2. IANN vs. Punctual Neural Network with η variable and $\epsilon = 0$.

		$\eta = 0.2$	$\eta = 0.4$	$\eta = 0.8$
Interval	Number of Epochs	15.34	6.96	14.10
	Percentage of Efficiency	100%	100%	100%
Punctual	Number of Epochs	14.9	15.06	14.41
	Percentage of Efficiency	92%	89%	91%

The rate of learning (η) and the minimum error are the important parameters in the process of training, for this reason, they are very important for evaluating the behavior of interval neural network. The minimum error of the IANN can be very small and the neural network can converge faster than the punctual neural network with same learning rate, and the efficient of the interval neural network isn't lower. The table 3 shows the results of training both networks with different error rate and with $\eta = 0.2$ (learning rate).

New testes was did with interval neural network for four random real synthetic data sets, $Q_n^1, Q_m^2, Q_k^3, Q_l^4$ and interval asymmetric data set denoted by $IP_n^1, IP_m^2, IP_k^3, IP_l^4$. The networks were trained and tested. The table 4 shows the results of the training with $\eta = 0.2$ and $\epsilon = 0$.

With these experiences, can be concluded that the inclusion of the interval mathematics in neural networks has many advantages in addition to the control of computational errors. The interval neural network was evaluated with sev-

Table 3. IANN vs. Punctual Neural Network with ϵ variable.

		$\epsilon = 0$	$\epsilon = 1$	$\epsilon = 2$
Interval	Number of Epochs	15.34	6.61	6.70
	Percentage of efficiency	100%	100%	96%
Punctual	Number of Epochs	14.98	12.14	10.11
	Percentage of efficiency	92%	91%	85%

Table 4. IANN vs. Punctual Neural Network with some training sets.

		P_n^1 e IP_n^1	P_m^2 e IP_m^2	P_k^3 e IP_k^3	P_l^4 e IP_l^4
Interval	Number of Epochs	19.47	45.29	9.64	52.24
	% Efficiency	100%	92%	89%	100%
Punctual	Number of Epochs	173.29	46.89	11.12	54.11
	% Efficiency	100%	89%	89%	100 %

eral data sets, varying training parameters and the number of epochs is smaller than the punctual network, the efficiency was good and better. It can be very important when dealing with real problems. The results of this research are very encouraging for applying interval mathematic to other models of the neural networks.

6   Conclusions

Other works was developed in this area [3], [5], [8], [17] but they are solutions to problems about the interval data like input data for the neural network. This paper propose the inclusion of interval mathematics in the structure of the neural network and shows that the performance of the neural network with interval mathematics is better. It proposes a modification in the neurons but the structure of the network wasn't modified with this form, the network is very simple and the process is natural.

In conclusion, this paper proposes a new model of neural network that generalize the traditional neural network and has new and better characteristics, the process of interval data. This approach guarantee an exact and efficient computation process and find a satisfactory and better solution.

References

1. Alefeld, G., Herzberger, J.:Inroduction to interval computations. Academic Press, New York, (1983)
2. Alefeld, G., Mayer, G.: Interval analysis – theory and applications. Journal of Computational and Applied Mathematics **121** (2000) 421-464
3. Baker, M.R., Patil, R.B.: Universal approximation theorem for interval neural networks. Reliable Computing **4** (1998) 235-239
4. Barboza, L.V., Dimuro G. P., Reiser R.H.S.: Power Flow with load Uncertainty. TEMA-Tendências em Matemática Aplicada e Computacional **5** (2004-1) 27-36
5. Beheshti, M., Berrached, A., Korvin, A.D., Hu, C., Sirisaengtaksin, O.: On Interval Weighted Three-Layer Neural Networks. In The 31st Annual Simulation Symposium, (1998) 188-195
6. Bock, H. H., Diday, E.: Analysis of Simbolic Data. Exploratory methods for extracting statistical information from complex data. Springer verlag, (2000).
7. Hayes B.: A lucid Interval. American Science **91** (2003-6) 484-488
8. Ishibuchi., H., Nii, M.: Interval-Arithmetic-Based Neural Networks. In: Bunke, H., Kande, A., (Eds.): Hybrid Methods in Pattern Recognition, Series in Machine Perception and Artificial Intelligence **47** (2001)

9. Kearfott, R.B., Kreinovich V.: Applications of Interval Computations. Kluwer Academic Publisher (1996)

10. Kohout, L.J., Kim, E.: Characterization of Interval Fuzzy Logic Systems of Connectives by Group Transformation . Reliable Computing **10** (2004) 299-334

11. Kreinovich, V., Scott, F., Ginzburg,L., Schulte, H., Barry, M.R., Nguyen, H.T.: From Interval Methods of Representing Uncertainty to a General Description of Uncertainty. In: Hrushikesha Mohanty and Chitta Baral (eds.): Trends in Information Technology. Proceedings of the International Conference on Information Technology CIT'99, Bhubaneswar, India, Tata McGraw-Hill, New Delhi (2000) 161-166

12. McCulloch, W.S., Pitts, W.: A logical calculus of the ideas immanent in nervous activity. Bulletin of Mathematical Biophysics **5** (1943) 115-133

13. Moore R.E.: Automatic error analysis. in digital computation, Technical Report LMSD-48421, Lockheed Aircraft Corporation, Missiles and Space Division, Sunnyvale-CA, january (1959)

14. Moore R.E.: Interval Arithmetic and Automatic Error Analysis in Digital Computing. Ph.D. Thesis, Stanford University, Stanford-CA, (1962)

15. Moore, R.E.: Interval Analysis. Prentice Hall, New Jersey, (1966)

16. Moore, R.E.: Methods and Applications of Interval Analysis. SIAM, Philadelphia, (1979)

17. Rossi, F., Conan-Guez, B.: Multilayer Perceptron on Interval Data. In: Classification, Clustering, and Data Analysis (IFCS 2002); abstracts. Cracow, Poland: Springer, (2002). 427-434, http://apiacoa.org/publications/2002/ifcs02.pdf.

18. Silveira, M.M.M.T., Bedregal, B.R.C.: A Method of Inference and Defuzzification Fuzzy Interval. In: The 2001 Artificial Intelligence and Application. Marbella-Spanish, September (2001)

19. Sunaga, T.: Theory of an Interval Algebra and its Applications to Numerical Analysis. RAAG Memoirs 2 (1958) 29-46

20. Turksen, I. B.:Interval value fuzzy sets based on normal form. Fuzzy Sets and Systems **20** (1986) 191-210

21. Voschinin, A. P., Dyvak N. P. ; Simoff S. J. Interval Methods: Theory and Application in the Design of Experiments, Data Analysis and Fittin. In: Letzky, E. K., (Ed.): Design of Experiments and Data Analysis: New Trends and Results, Antal Publishing Co., Moscow, (1993)

Design and Deployment of IP Virtual Private Networks: A Case Study

Chittaranjan Hota[1] and G. Raghurama[2]

[1] Computer Science and Information Systems Department, IPC,
Birla Institute of Technology and Science, Pilani, Rajasthan, 333031, India
c_hota@bits-pilani.ac.in
[2] Electrical and Electronics Engineering Department, APU,
Birla Institute of Technology and Science, Pilani, Rajasthan, 333031, India
graghu@bits-pilani.ac.in

Abstract. Private networks carry vital and sensitive business communications between employees, customers, and enterprise partners across widely dispersed geographic area. All users of these private networks want to access data and resources as if they were located at the same physical site in the enterprise. To complement classical corporate wide area network infrastructures, IP Virtual Private Networks have been gaining ground, with the capability of offering cost-effective, secure, and private-network like services. IP VPNs also guarantee high revenues to the Service Providers. Deploying VPNs, especially in a large-scale environment, needs a large amount of planning. In this paper we propose a layered framework for building an IP VPN that can be used to cater to the needs of various users of the enterprise. We have considered a hypothetical case study. We have discussed the design issues and a possible implementation scenario. We have also surveyed few future technologies related to VPNs that could provide additional value-added services to VPN users that are in their early stages of becoming products.

1 Motivation and Challenges

Today's enterprises have many needs that can vary due to their size and physical infrastructure. Single locations, multiple locations, mobile workers, telecommuters etc. These enterprises all have one thing in common though i.e. they need to securely connect all of their workforce locations internally with each other and with the outside world. Normally, leased lines establish a private network connecting campuses or branch offices of an enterprise over a traditional WAN. As the lines are dedicated, security and bandwidth guarantees are ensured. But, as the corporate business environment has changed over past years, the above traditional hub and spoke WAN design is facing challenges like adding a new site can be slow and difficult, meshing is costly, off-net connectivity with remote users and extranet partners is expensive and difficult to manage, adding IP services is costly, and international connections can be very expensive. Hence, traditional networks will not meet these demands. The Internet revolution and rise of public networking has dramatically altered the networking requirements and opportunities of the enterprise. The deployment of new IP applications and the availability of ubiquitous Internet connectivity promise to facilitate the exchange of critical information both within the enterprise and throughout its sphere of influence. As a result, in recent years there has been a considerable amount of interest in offering Virtual Private Network services over the Internet that has be-

G. Das and V.P. Gulati (Eds.): CIT 2004, LNCS 3356, pp. 76–86, 2004.
© Springer-Verlag Berlin Heidelberg 2004

come a low cost backbone. It is "virtual" in the sense that it logically shares the physical links. It is "private" in the sense that it isolates traffic using tunneling and encryption. The VPN hype will continue in the years to come, due to the rising desire for economical, reliable, and secure communications [7]. Cahners In-Stat Group estimated that VPN services would hold a $23.7 billion share of the total $104.4 billion worldwide IP service revenues in 2005. Several key technologies are employed by VPNs as shown in the Figure 1. These technologies can be described as below:

Tunneling: It is defined as encapsulation of data packets (the original, or inner packet) into another one (the encapsulating, or outer packet). Here, the inner packet is opaque to the network over which the outer packet is routed. Tunneling can be used to transport multiple protocols over a network based on some other protocol, or it can be used to hide source and destination addresses of the original packet. Examples of layer 2 tunneling protocols are PPTP, L2F, and L2TP, and IPSec is a well-accepted layer 3 tunneling protocol.

Authentication: Before any secure communication can begin, one network system must ensure that the other one is the intended correspondent. When a VPN tunnel is established, the two end points must authenticate each other. PAP, CHAP, and PKI are some of the authentication protocols that can be used.

Access Control: After authentication, the communication entities can decide whether to allow the communication session to continue or to reject the session. In case of VPNs, it allows authorized access to resources. ACLs and Capability Lists are few of the access control mechanisms that can be employed.

Data Security: As VPNs use a shared medium to transport private traffic, it is possible for the data to be intercepted and even altered by others during its transit over the shared infrastructure. So, having strong encryption algorithms and well-conceived keys help to ensure that the integrity of the data cannot be compromised and also to make it opaque to interceptors. Public Key encryption algorithms, Digital Signatures, and Message Authentication codes are few of the technologies in this area.

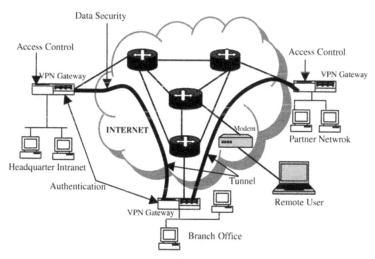

Fig. 1. Key Technologies of Virtual Private Networks

As an enterprise, if you plan to deploy an IP VPN as a replacement to your private networking, detailed planning and well thought out migration strategy is essential. We have considered our university (BITS) as an enterprise and proposed the design and deployment of IP VPN for its' users.

BITS network (NEURON) has several different users situated at different locations all over the world including remote access, extranet and intranet users. At Pilani, BITS has a campus wide Intranet. The LAN is based on CISCO catalyst switches, multimode and single mode fiber segments, and UTP segments. The default gateway is a CISCO 3600 router that connects BITS LAN to the Internet with a 2 Mbps-leased line. A Firewall protects the Intranet from unauthorized outside access. The security mechanism currently enforced by few of the applications (like Virtual University) is based on authentication and authorization mechanisms implemented at application layer only. But as the hackers now days find new methods to break the security cover, a VPN solution could be the best that does not compromise the security at any level. The different types of applications that can be run with this new solution are:

- Off-Campus Programs like Virtual University, Collaborative Programs, etc.
- Admission Tests conducted at predefined locations all over India
- Placement Tests conducted for Practice School students
- Student Welfare Division Operations
- E-Commerce applications with Extranet Partners

But the problems in providing an IP VPN solution could be seen at different levels like Planning, Implementation, and Management. In this paper we have tried to analyze a viable solution addressing the above issues and challenges meeting the objectives. The VPN solution that we are looking for could be accomplished in two different ways. One is by the Corporate itself (Enterprise-Managed Solution) and the other way is by outsourcing to a third party (Service-Provider Managed solution). In the former one, enterprises manage their own VPN-enabled customer premises equipment. In the later one, the VPN management complexity is shifted to provider edge devices. In this work, we have considered the former one.

2 VPN Gateways

VPN gateways act as endpoints for tunnels. An outbound IP packet from the private network arriving on the private interface is passed through to the public interface, where it is examined as per the outbound policy rules to determine whether it should be tunneled, sent without modification or dropped. An inbound packet arriving on a public interface will be decapsulated and examined against the inbound policy rules.

2.1 VPN Gateway Functions

The gateway should implement four basic functions like Tunneling, Authentication, Access Control, Data Integrity and Confidentiality. These functionalities of VPN gateways vary with respect to the type of user it is supporting like Remote, Intranet, and Extranet. In addition to the above categories of functionality, these gateways might have basic packet routing and forwarding capabilities, and also some basic firewall capabilities. As the routing protocols are not necessarily secure, gateways do not rely on them but rather rely on statically configured routes. Even if the VPN gateway is not processing the routing information, it should be able to relay routing exchanges to its next hop routers. VPN gateway might also implement various firewall functions, NAT being perhaps the most common. NAT allows two privately addressed sites to share the same private address space. These gateways might also implement packet filtering to further restrict the traffic going into and coming out of the tunnel. VPN gateways also can perform another set of advanced functions like Quality of Service support for Network Applications, Redundant Failover, Hardware Acceleration, and Load Balancing capabilities for mission critical applications. Certain applications like voice over IP might require strict latency and jitter control so that the quality of the voice signal is acceptable. But QoS is a network wide consideration, i.e. for a VPN tunnel to have QoS, every hop and link along the tunnel path must have QoS support. But for a VPN gateway to have QoS support, we can assume that it has the capability of classifying and marking the offered traffic based on the type of the service quality the traffic should receive, and the capability of performing QoS negotiation with the network routers in the Internet infrastructure. For supporting mission critical applications, Gateway should have redundant failover capabilities or even better two or more VPN gateways should share the load of the VPN traffic simultaneously. Redundant failover can be implemented by two gateways communicating with a Hello protocol as in OSPF, and if one is failed, other should take over the connection. The encryption operation is computationally intensive and repetitive that takes lot of processor cycles. So, this work could be off loaded to hardware. This is essential for network speeds of T3 (45 Mbps).

2.2 Interaction with Firewalls

Firewalls prohibit entry and exit of unauthorized traffic into and from the intranet. The various mechanisms that can be employed for this are packet filtering, through stateful inspection, and using an application level proxy. Firewalls do not consider the security of the traffic after it leaves the corporate private network, but VPN gateways allow legitimate traffic into the private network and also ensure that traffic is still secure after it leaves the private network. We can have the following arrangements where firewalls and gateways can complement with each other as their functions overlap in many ways.

2.2.1 Gateway and Firewall in Parallel

Here, traffic going through the VPN gateway and firewall are separated; VPN traffic goes through the gateway and all other goes through the firewall. These two do not interfere with each other. The WAN side router needs to have a routing table entry for the gateway only, but the LAN side router must separate the traffic destined to a VPN tunnel from all other based on the destination address of the IP packets. This scenario is as shown below.

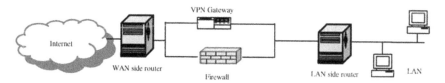

2.2.2 Gateway and Firewall in Series

There could be two ways of arranging these. VPN gateway is on LAN side and the firewall is on the WAN side, or the other way around. In the first case, specific rules must be installed in the firewall to allow VPN traffic to pass through. It is as good as opening a hole through the firewall; any tunneled traffic or tunnel creation message should be permitted access. As the tunneled packets are opaque, allowing them to pass through the firewall weakens the protection. Although the firewall cannot screen the tunneled traffic, it can establish rules for which type of tunnels are legitimate. All the traffic that crosses the firewall is also processed by gateway. VPN packets get right treatment where non-VPN ones are simply passed through. Here access control policies are enforced by the firewall. In the later case, VPN gateway can also perform some access control on non-VPN traffic. As no tunnels penetrate past the gateway, all the traffic is in the clear and the firewall can apply policy rules. Figures below depict different scenarios.

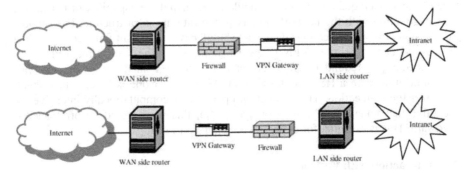

3 VPN Design Issues

Surely firewalls are not the only devices that interact with the gateway at the network perimeter. Other devices like routers, DNS servers, Authentication servers etc. do interact as well. Apart from the central security issues, issues like topology, addressing & routing, quality of service, scalability, and resiliency could also be considered.

Topology: Following types could be thought of. A full mesh allows any site to directly talk to any other. But the designing is complex and it does not scale well. In hub and spoke one could be a central hub and spoke sites do interact indirectly through the hub. In a partial mesh, only selected sites are directly connected and others indirectly. As the hub and spoke had a single routing bottleneck, partial mesh one is preferred.

Addressing & Routing: When packets traverse through the Internet, private IP addresses must be hidden which can be achieved through the use of NAT. A registered IP address is required at the public interface of the VPN gateway to route encapsulated packets. Static routes are built up into the VPN gateway and neighboring routers to forward encrypted and clear text packets.

Quality of Service: When QoS is required, packets must be classified, marked, and processed according to the QoS policy. VPN gateway can classify and provide QoS guarantees to the IP packet by examining the Differentiated Service Code Point (DSCP) field of IP header.

Scalability: Topology plays a role in making a VPN scalable one. Other factors that can influence this could be load balancing, the number of concurrent tunnels, and rapid bandwidth provisioning. In Intranet VPN, amount of bandwidth is the major concern, where as in Remote access VPN, both the number of simultaneous tunnels and the amount of bandwidth required are of major concern.

Resiliency: Security in VPNs is taken care by tunneling, cryptographic algorithms, and integration with firewalls. But what about the connectivity? How effective is the VPN solution, if it goes down? Resiliency of the VPN is defined as the ability of the VPN to continue despite part of the system being unavailable due to component fault or attack. VPN vendors can meet this challenge by providing any of the following solutions:

- Compute Redundant Physical Paths to reduce dependency on a single Service Provider.
- Support component or device redundancy to eliminate a single point of failure.
- Share state and VPN state to maintain both the session and VPN connection in the case of a failure.
- Automatically establish a new route without manual intervention. This can be achieved by employing any dynamic routing strategy.
- Provide multiple overlay paths or redundant VPN tunnels from one point to another.
- Achieve VPN connection failover quickly.

By combining all these above resiliency components, we can achieve a truly fault tolerant solution or optimal resiliency. Few exmaples are given below:

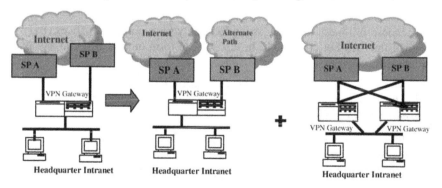

4 VPN Solution Scenario

Let us assume that the following are the details of the internal networks and servers:

BITS, Pilani Headquarters

Internal Networks	10.0.1.0 / 24
	10.0.2.0 / 24
	10.0.3.0 / 24
Entrance Exam Network	4.0.4.10 / 24
Placement Test Server	4.0.3.10
Business Partner Server	4.0.5.10
E-Mail Server	4.0.6.10
SAP Server (SWD & PS)	4.0.7.10
VoD (Virtual University)	4.0.8.10

BITS, Dubai Branch Office

Internal Network	10.0.4.0 / 24

BITS, Goa Branch Office

Internal Network	10.0.5.0 / 24

Business Partner Network

Partner 1, Bangalore	170.1.0.0 / 24
Partner 2, Hyderabad	172.1.0.0 / 24

Here, we want to develop a VPN solution for the above scenario. Let, authentication between all gateways is to be performed via digital certificates and authentication between remote users and VPN gateway is to be done via RADIUS authentication. We are also assuming that the whole solution is an Enterprise-Managed Solution.

Following are the steps to achieve this.

Step 1: Getting Internet Connectivity from ISP.

Let us assume that the above networks have Internet connectivity as given below:

Pilani, Dubai and Goa	:	T1 (1.5Mbps)
Partner 1 and Partner 2	:	T3 (45 Mbps)

Step 2: Select a specific VPN gateway for each location: Based on the performance level required at each location like bandwidth, throughput, and the number of remote users supported, decide upon the VPN gateway (7100, 3600, etc.) i.e. high end or low-end gateways are required. Let we have all 7100 series routers.

Step 3: Decide upon the topology.

Let us choose full-mesh topology as we have only three corporate offices (BITS), so managing this will not cost much. In this we can form tunnels between any pair of locations directly.

Step 4: Decide upon the Intranet, Remote User, and Extranet VPN functions and also whether to combine these in the same VPN gateway for each location.

a) Intranet VPN: Let the requirements be described as follows:

- All private traffic must be encrypted using 3DES
- All the subnets should communicate with each other
- Digital Certificates should be used for authentication between VPN gateways.

IPSec with IKE are the probable choices for the first requirement. We will use IP-Sec's ESP in tunnel mode to fully encapsulate the intrasite IP addresses (4 or 10) into publicly addressed packets, so that the original net 10 or 4 addresses are preserved. Partners IP addresses do not need full encapsulation, as they are routable through the Internet. For the third requirement we will use PKI support, and also the digital certificate functions in IKE.

b) Remote Access VPN: As the remote access client do not have a permanent IP (every time a new IP will be assigned to him, by his ISP), the VPN gateway must provide the remote user an IP address that can be easily routed within the corporate network. So, the address assignment must be under the control of VPN gateway. Also, VPN gateway should pass information regarding other corporate servers like DNS, WINS etc. to the remote users without which he cannot communicate with the corporate network. Let the requirements be described as:

- All private traffic must be encrypted using 3DES
- Users 1, 2, and 3 can access all the subnets at the corporate office, where as users 4, and 5 can access only the Entrance exam server (4.0.4.10)
- All users must access corporate intranet and the public Internet simultaneously
- Remote access users can use digital certificates or RADIUS to authenticate themselves with the VPN gateway.

All the above requirements define which functions are to be implemented in the VPN gateway, and which in the VPN client side. For the first requirement, we can use ESP and IKE. For the second requirement, group users so that access control rules can be applied to each group. The third requirement states that access be permitted to both public Internet and private intranet. For the fourth requirement, VPN gateway should support multiple authentication mechanisms.

c) Extranet VPN: These requirements will almost be similar to that of Intranet VPN scenario. The difference is that two companies and not just one are involved in the VPN configuration and policies. The gateway should provide fine-grain access control on the VPN traffic that can be achieved say by establishing restrictions at the level of applications on a specific host.

Step 5: Fix up the location of Gateway and Firewall. Let both are in parallel at all the locations.

Step 6: Decide upon the redundant failover gateways and load balancers. Let we do not have these features at present.

Step 7: Configure the CA (certification authority) server and an X.500 directory server at the corporate headquarter (BITS, Pilani) that should be accessible by all VPN gateways using digital certificates for authentication. Configure also a RADIUS server that should be accessible to the Gateway serving the Remote access users.

Step 8: Configure all the four VPN gateways as described below:

BITS, Pilani Gateway:
Four site-to-site VPN tunnels

- (10.0.1.0 / 24, 10.0.2.0 / 24, 10.0.3.0 / 24) < == > (10.0.4.0/24) serving all IP traffic

- (10.0.1.0 / 24, 10.0.2.0 / 24, 10.0.3.0 / 24) < == > (10.0.5.0/24) serving all IP traffic
- (4.0.5.10) < == > (170.1.0.0 / 24) serving Web traffic only
- (4.0.5.10) < == > (172.1.0.0 / 24) serving Web traffic only

Five User Groups

- Entrance exam user group: can access only the subnet 4.0.4.10 / 24
- Placement exam user groups: can access only the server 4.0.3.10
- PS students group: can access the SAP server 4.0.7.10 and 4.0.3.10
- Distance Learning Students group: can access VoD server 4.0.8.10
- Email user group: can access 4.0.6.10

All these users are assigned addresses from the address pool, and care should be taken to see that these addresses do not overlap with any address within the corporate network.

BITS, Dubai Gateway:
Two site-to-site VPN tunnels

- (10.0.4.0 / 24) < == > (10.0.1.0 / 24, 10.0.2.0 / 24, 10.0.3.0 / 24) serving all IP traffic
- (10.0.4.0 / 24) < == > (10.0.5.0 / 24) serving all IP traffic

BITS, Goa Gateway:
Two site-to-site VPN tunnels

- (10.0.5.0 / 24) < == > (10.0.1.0 / 24, 10.0.2.0 / 24, 10.0.3.0/24) serving all IP traffic
- (10.0.5.0 / 24) < == > (10.0.4.0 / 24) serving all IP traffic

Partner 1, Bangalore Gateway:
One site-to-site VPN tunnel

- (170.1.0.0 / 24) < == > (4.0.5.10) serving Web traffic only

Partner 2, Hyderabad Gateway:
One site-to-site VPN tunnel

- (172.1.0.0 / 24) < == > (4.0.5.10) serving Web traffic only

After the configurations are applied to the VPN gateways, it is time to implement the VPN and verify that all the components are working as designed. The proposed hypothetical VPN design is given in Figure 2.

5   Conclusion

In the rapidly expanding world of business communications and services, IP VPNs are in the earlier stages of adoption among enterprises and service providers. However, by enabling large numbers of enterprises with high value services in a cost effective manner for both the enterprise and service provider their success will only increase over time. Here, we have presented a framework for deploying IP VPN as Customer Premises Equipment based solution. We have identified distinct layers and describe major decision points within each layer. We have proposed a hypothetical VPN solution and tested also our design by building a test bed with the available

VPN hardware and software. We identified the design goals and proposed ways to achieve those. Each different VPN solution has its' own strengths, weaknesses, and vulnerabilities and it is anticipated that no single VPN solution will be sufficient enough but instead a diversity of choices will continue to emerge. We expect that our design and solution will help the Implementers.

Now days many parties collaborate between themselves over the Internet using many available multicast applications like, video conferencing, whiteboard sessions, distance learning, multimedia video and audio broadcasts etc. Future VPN research directions would include MPLS VPNs towards this objective. MPLS together with its signaling protocols, either RSVP-TE (Resource Reservation Protocol-Traffic Engineering) or CR-LDP (Constraint Based Routing using the LDP) is the important mechanism for enabling QoS in IP VPNs. We have future plans to address these issues in IP VPNs.

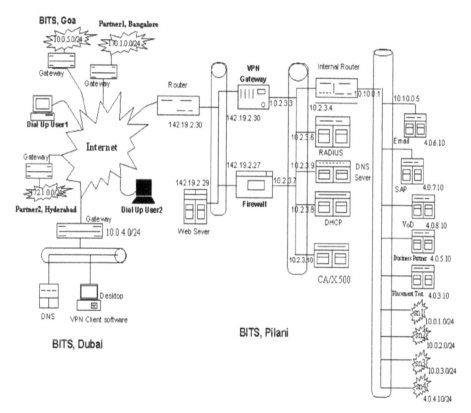

Fig. 2. Proposed Design

References

1. B.Fox and B. Gleeson, "Virtual Private Network Identifier", RFC 2685, Sept, 1999.
2. David McDysan, VPN Applications Guide, John Wiley & Sons, Inc.
3. Carlton R. Davis, IPSec Securing VPNs, Tata McGraw-Hill.
4. A. Quiggle, Implementing CISCO VPNs, McGraw-Hill.

5. Bruce Perlmutter, Virtual Private Networks: A View from Trenches, The Prentice Hall PTR

6. A. Kumar, R. Rastogi, A. Silberchatz, "Algorithms for Provisioning VPNs in the Hose Model", IEEE/ ACM Transactions on Networking, August 2002

7. J. Zeng, and N. Ansari, "Toward IP Virtual Private Network Quality of Service: A Service Provider Perspective," IEEE Communications Magazine, April 2003.

8. Patton, B. Smith, D. Doss, and W. Yurcik, "A Layered Framework for Deploying High Assurance VPNs," in proceedings of HASE 2000.

9. R. Maresca, Arienzo, M. Esposito, Romano, G. Ventre, "An Active Network approach to Virtual Private Networks," IEEE International Symposium on Computers and Communications, Taormina, Italy, July 2002.

10. P. Korzeniowski, " VPNs become Key Part of Enterprise Networks," Business Communications Review, March 2000, pp. 28-32.

11. N. Duffield, P. Goyal, Greenberg, Mishra, and Ramakrishnan, " A Flexible Model for Resource Management in Virtual Private Networks," ACM Comp. Comm. Rev., Vol 29, No 4, pp. 95-108.

12. C. Hota, and G. Raghurama, "A Heuristic Algorithm for QoS Path Computation in VPNs," International Conference on Information Technology, Bhubaneswar, India, December 2003.

13. C. Hota, and G. Raghurama, "Building Virtual Private Networks to Support Mobile VPN Users in a Group with Quality of Service Guarantees," International Conference on Electronic Business, NUS, Singapore, December 2003.

14. Juttner, Szabo, and Szentesi, "On Bandwidth Efficiency of the Hose Resource Management Model in VPNs," IEEE INFOCOM 2003.

15. Steven Brown, Implementing Virtual Private Networks, Tata McGraw-Hill, 2000.

QoS Driven Online Multicast Routing Algorithm

R. Manoharan, P. Thambidurai, and S. Pradhiba

Department of Computer Science & Engineering and Information Technology
Pondicherry Engineering College, Pondicherry - 605014, India
rmanoharan@yahoo.com

Abstract. Recent work on multicast routing algorithms in the Internet has introduced new notions of building online multicast tree without a priori knowledge of the future requests. Most of the online multicast routing algorithms aimed to satisfy more number of requests by preserving bandwidth on frequently used links and generate long-hop multicast trees by compromising the hop length. In this paper, we propose an online multicast routing algorithm, wherein rerouting of multicast session is incorporated instead of preserving bandwidth on frequently used links in order to satisfy more number of requests. This enables individual request to have different treatments based on their delay tolerance subject to policy restrictions. Our work focuses on classifying the requests into three classes namely Class-I, Class-II and Class-III and providing the maximum, the best possible and if possible service level in terms of bandwidth and end-to-end delay bound to efficiently utilize the network resources and accepting more user requests. Extensive simulations show that our algorithm provides service level guarantee to the three classes of requests, out performs the existing algorithms in terms of call acceptance ratio and improves the resource utilization.

1 Introduction

Multicasting is an effective mechanism for group communication, as it typically requires less total bandwidth than separately sending unicast messages to all the members [1]. Multicast services have been increasingly used by various applications to transport real-time audio video and data dissemination for news, entertainment, distance learning, etc. The QoS requirements of these continuous media applications prompt the necessity for QoS driven multicast routing [2][5]. Generally in QoS driven multicast routing the main problem is setting up bandwidth guaranteed multicast sessions in a network where the user request arrive one after other with future demands unknown. An online routing is required to fulfill the request arriving dynamically with the required level of bandwidth and delay factors.

There is an upsurge to develop QoS models with service differentiation for group applications in order to better utilize the network resources. Instead of treating all multicast requests coming to any network in the same way, different priorities for requests have been assigned based on the application's QoS requirements. Some applications require speedy delivery of data, while some might require a guaranteed delivery of data, and still others might just want a guarantee that at least some of the receivers be accommodated in the network. Multimedia applications involving real-time audio and real-time video transmissions require strict QoS constraints (end-to-end delay bound, bandwidth availability) to be met by the network. Whereas applica-

G. Das and V.P. Gulati (Eds.): CIT 2004, LNCS 3356, pp. 87–96, 2004.

tions like News feeds, lectures require a guaranteed delivery of data to all the receivers but time delays are tolerable. Another class of applications just requires the presence of one or two group members to keep the group going. A typical example would be offline content transfer applications that neither requires a guaranteed bandwidth nor a fast delivery of data.

The proposed algorithm is an online multicast routing algorithm, which provides both bandwidth and delay (in terms of the hop length) guarantees apart from accommodating more number of requests as possible. In our algorithm, for a new request in the network, first the shortest-path multicast tree is constructed that ensures the best possible tree in terms of delay under the given conditions. Then bandwidth for this request is allocated along the constructed shortest-path tree. In order to satisfy more number of requests, whenever a particular request cannot be allocated due to non-availability of bandwidth in the shortest-path tree, a search for an alternate path is made in the network. Depending on the class of the request either the new request or the existing one is routed along this alternate path. In general the alternate path is used to reroute low priority applications, freeing the bandwidth in the shortest path so as to accommodate high priority applications. This approach increases the bandwidth utilization and accepts more multicast requests.

The related work in the areas of QoS multicast routing, the proposed algorithm and the simulation work along with the results are discussed in the subsequent sections of the paper.

2   Critical Review of Existing

Online multicast routing algorithms with bandwidth guarantees have been proposed in literature [7], [8]. The algorithm identifies critical links and avoids the usage of these links in order to accommodate more number of requests that arrive dynamically in the network. The algorithm specified in [7] might choose a wastefully long path, although more direct path with the required bandwidth exists. Hence the trees generated may not be shortest path trees. Also this algorithm is computationally intensive.

In order to provide QoS for multicasting lot of work has been done on finding the alternate path for satisfying the user requests, such protocols or algorithms does not accommodate more number of requests [8]. Alternate path algorithms have been proposed in which a user experiencing degraded service can initiate an alternate path for receiving the transmitted packets [8]. The main focus of such algorithms remains on providing QoS to the users and does not provide any assurance for satisfying more number of requests.

Most existing research on QoS guaranteed multicast routing focuses on either delay/bandwidth-constrained multicast routing or on satisfying more number of requests [4], [11]. Therefore multicast routing algorithms, which satisfy both the constraints, need to be developed. The proposed algorithm aims at providing QoS and satisfying more number of requests.

3   Proposed Algorithm

Generally multicast routing algorithm constructs a multicast tree and reserves bandwidth along the tree. When there is not enough bandwidth on a link in the tree, the algorithm rejects the request even there is abundant of bandwidth on other paths lead to the receiver. In order to overcome such shortcomings, alternate path techniques were proposed which would utilize these alternate paths in order to satisfy the request. But one drawback with this alternate path approach was that the trees generated were long-hop trees because they by-pass the links which fall on the shortest path tree. Though this method makes efficient use of the bandwidth it generates undesirable long-hop trees which do not prove to be suitable for time critical applications. Hence we have suggested a small change in this alternate path approach. This new approach makes use of the alternate paths available in the network and also makes wiser decisions as to which class of request needs to be rerouted along the alternate path. In our approach different priorities are set to the requests and different services will be provided to the requests based on the priority. Thus applications, which have a very high time constraint (Class-I), are always guaranteed a shortest path tree. Other applications with lower priorities (Class-II and Class-III) are provided the shortest-path tree when there are enough resources in the network. When there is a lack of resources in the network then they are given the minimum service agreed for each class.

3.1 The Algorithm

The proposed algorithm works on the assumption that routing requests comes from applications with varied delay tolerance and the requests are classified into three different classes. Once a request arrives the first step is to construct the Minimum-Hop multicast tree and the next step is to route the request along this tree i.e. reserve bandwidth for the tree. If there is no bandwidth on any link in the tree then a search is started to find an alternate path and the request is routed along the alternate path. If no such alternate path is found then the request is rejected.

Multicast routing request arrives one by one in the network and is defined by (s, R, b, c, m) where s – source, R – set of receivers, b – bandwidth, c – class of the request and m – minimum number of receivers for class-III request. The general form of the algorithm is given in this section.

In the algorithm the *Search_AltPath* uses the Local Search technique [9][10], which tries to search for neighboring on-tree nodes by flooding REQ messages and connects using RES messages. The procedure terminates unsuccessfully, if the node does not receive any replies before the expiration of a TTL value. A PROPE message is sent to the receiver for which the alternate path is to be found and the receiver that receives the PROPE message starts of a Local Search Process to find an alternate path to any on-tree node.

```
/* R = { set of receivers };S = Source; B = Bandwidth re-
quirement; C = Class of request;  M = Minimum number of
receivers that should remain on the tree; P = set of
nodes along the path; L = Number of receivers in set R
i.e. n(R) */

While ( R <> {} )
{       P = Compute_ShortestPath (S, R_{i = 0 to L})
        // P = { S, n1, n2, n3.....R_i }
```

```
    n = 0
    while ( P(n+1) <> 0 )
    {
      Result = Allocate ( P(n), P(n+1))
    If ( Result == Failure )
            P_alt=Search_AltPath(S, R_i, P(n), P(n+1))
              If ( P_alt = {}) then
                  Write "Cannot Allocate"
              Otherwise
                  P = P_alt
                  break
              End if
      End if
    }
}
```

Once the *Search_AltPath* algorithm searches an alternate path, the path has to be installed for two possible cases. First, when a class-II or class-III request has found an alternate path for a receiver, which was not accommodated in the tree because of insufficient bandwidth on a link. The node selects the best Candidate according to the dynamic QoS metrics collected by the RES messages and sends a JOIN messge to the on-tree node, which has the best resources and establishes routing state along the path. For the second possibility, a search is invoked to find out an alternate path for an existing class-II or class-III receiver, which is using the link on which, bandwidth for a class-I request cannot be allocated. In that case, the new node selects the best Candidate according to the dynamic QoS metrics collected by the RES messages. Then the node sends JOIN message to the on-tree node, which has the best quality, establishes routing state along the path. When the chosen on-tree node receives the JOIN message, it starts transmitting data packets on the newly set-up path towards the receiver. The receiver then sends a REMOVE message to the on-tree node that was previously attached for relinquishing the resources. Then the freed up resources are used for the new Class-I request.

The algorithm varies for Class-I, Class-II and Class-III application requests. When routing a class-III request, the main focus is to accommodate many receivers from the set of receivers. At the time of making the request the minimum percentage of receivers, which have to remain on the tree, is negotiated. When allocating the request, if there is no bandwidth on a particular link then, a search is made for an alternate path and request is routed along this path. Otherwise the network rejects the request if it is not able to satisfy the minimum agreed number of receivers.

When routing a class-II request if there is no bandwidth on a particular link then, a search is made for an alternate path which bypasses this link. If such an alternate path exists then the request is routed along this path otherwise a class-III application currently using the link is chosen and the receiver that obtains data through this link is cut-off from the tree. Then this freed up bandwidth is used for the class-II request.

When routing a class-I request, if there is no bandwidth on a particular link in the tree then, a search is made for a class-II or a class-III application, which is already using this link. The summation of the bandwidth of the class-II or class-III request and the remaining bandwidth in the network must be equal or greater than the bandwidth requirement of the class-I request being allocated. Such an application is chosen and data through this link is redirected along an alternate path. Then this freed up bandwidth is used for the class-I application. When there is no alternate-path bypassing the congested link then a class-III application currently using the link is chosen and the receiver that obtains data through this link is cut-off from the tree. Then this freed up bandwidth is used for the class-I request. This class-III receiver is removed only if the number of remaining class-III receivers in the tree does not fall below a certain percentage as negotiated earlier. If any of the case does not arise then the class-I request is rejected. Thus we are not only able to accommodate the new request but also provide the desired QoS for the class-I request without degrading the service provided for the existing users.

3.2 Examples

Typical scenarios encountered during the routing of multicast requests are illustrated with examples.

Scenario 1: A class-III request arrives, and there is no bandwidth on the shortest-path tree generated.

   We have taken a snapshot of the requests, which are arriving at a network to illustrate the first case. We assume the residual bandwidth on all the links to be 10 units before routing the two requests quoted below.

Table 1. Request arriving in the network

Source	Receivers	Bandwidth	Class	Parameter M
3	1, 0, 8, 7	6	1	-
10	1, 0, 4, 9	5	3	2

Explanation: When the first request in the Table 1 arrives, the shortest-path tree for the source 3 and its set of receivers {1, 0, 8, 7} is generated and a bandwidth of 6 units is allocated along the path. When the next class-III request arrives the bandwidth on the link 1-0 (which falls in the shortest path of the request) is not sufficient to allocate the request. As the request is a class-III request an alternate-path is found which bypasses this link i.e. 1-0 and the shortest such alternate path available is the path 10-12, 12-2, 2-0. The class-III request is then routed along this path.

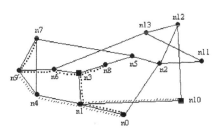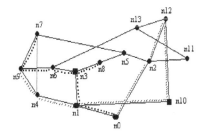

Fig. 1. Shows the shortest-path tree for the requests

Fig. 2. Shows the rerouted path the requests second class-III request takes due to lack of bandwidth on link 1-0

Figure 1 shows the shortest-path trees, which the requests would have taken, if there was enough bandwidth on the link. Figure 2 shows the rerouted path allocated for the class-III request, which arrives later and the shortest-path tree allocated for the class-I request.

Scenario 2: A class-II request arrives, and there is no bandwidth on the shortest-path tree generated.

We assume the residual bandwidth on all the links to be 10 units before routing the two requests quoted below.

Table 2. Request arriving in the network

Source	Receivers	Bandwidth	Class	Parameter M
3	1, 0, 8, 7	6	3	3
10	1, 0, 4, 9	5	2	-

Explanation: When the first class-III request arrives, the shortest-path tree for the source 3 and its set of receivers {1, 0, 8, 7} is generated and a bandwidth of 6 units is allocated along the path. For the next class-II request, there is no sufficient bandwidth on the link 1-0 which falls in the shortest-path tree. As the request is a class-II request we search for an alternate-path, which bypasses this link. No such alternate path is available with the following bandwidth requirements. Hence we search for other class-III applications, which use this link. And in this example it happens to be the class-III request just allocated. Now an alternate path has to be searched by the receiver of the class-III request which uses this link i.e. node n0. This search also becomes unsuccessful due to lack of bandwidth. Thus the only left option is to remove the class-III receiver using this link. Before doing this, the number of remaining class-III receiver is checked to see if it falls below 3. As it does not fall below the discussed level the receiver is cut-off.

Figure 3 shows the shortest-path trees, which the requests would have taken, if there was enough bandwidth on the link. Figure 4 shows the class-III receiver cut-off from the multicast tree and the shortest-path tree allocated for the class-II request.

Scenario 3: A class-I request arrives, and there is no bandwidth on the shortest-path tree generated.

We assume the residual bandwidth on all the links to be 10 units before routing the two requests quoted in order in Table 3.

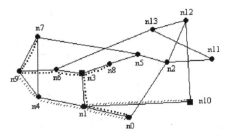 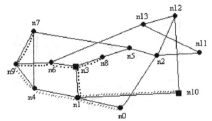

Fig. 3. Shortest path tree for the requests

Fig. 4. Shows the Class-III receiver cut off from the tree and the multicast tree of the Class-II request

Table 3. Showing Requests that arrive in the network

Source	Receivers	Bandwidth	Class	Parameter M
3	0, 5,11,12,13	6	2	-
9	0, 5, 6, 7	5	1	-

Explanation: When the first class-II request arrives, the shortest-path tree for the source 3 and its set of receivers {0, 5, 11, 12, 13} is generated and a bandwidth of 6 units is allocated along the path. For the next class-I request, there is no sufficient bandwidth on the link 1-0 which falls in the shortest-path tree. As the request is a class-I request we search for other class-II or class-III applications, which use this link. And in this example it happens to be the class-II request just allocated. Now an alternate path has to be searched by the receiver of the class-II request which uses this link i.e. node n0.

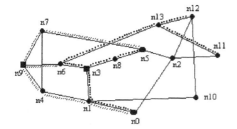
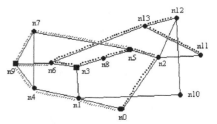

Fig. 5. Shows the shortest path tree for the requests

Fig. 6. Shows the rerouted path the first Class-II request takes due to lack of bandwidth on link 1-0

Node n0 floods an ALT-REQ message in the neighborhood. On receiving this message node n1 and node n11 respond back with their ALT-RES message. Node n0 then selects the best route from among the responses. In this case it rejects the message from node n1 because the path from node n1 traverses the congested link 0-1, instead it sends an ALT-JOIN message to node n2 (0-2, 2-5). Then it sends a REMOVE message to node n1 to which it was previously connected. Node n1 propagates this message until the source node is reached. Once the class-II request is rerouted along this path new alternate path, the freed up bandwidth is used to allocate the class-I request.

Figure 5 shows the shortest-path trees, which the requests would have taken, if there was enough bandwidth on the links. Figure 6 shows the rerouted path allocated for the class-II request, which arrives first and the shortest-path tree allocated for the class-I request, which arrives later.

4 Simulation

The proposed work was simulated and each simulation experiment was run with 2000 requests made to the network. In our simulation, network graphs were generated randomly. The number of nodes in the network, taken for the simulation was varied from 14–30 and the average degree of the graphs ranged from 3–6. The bandwidth on all links in the network was assumed to be uniform. The receivers and the source nodes, which make multicast session requests, were generated randomly. The number of receivers generated in each request varies from 30% to 70% of the total nodes in the network. The reserved bandwidth on a link reflects the network load; hence higher reserved bandwidths indicate higher network loads. The network performance measures of interest are the request rejection ratio and delay bound. A request is accepted if a path connecting the source and the destination and also satisfying the bandwidth requirement is found. The two algorithms taken for comparison are the Minimum-Hop Tree Algorithm (MHT) and the Maximum Multicast Flow Algorithm (MNF).

4.1 Simulation Results

The results obtained from the simulation are compared with the Minimum-Hop tree algorithm. Various simulation experiments were conducted for different traffic characteristics and network parameters, which are described below.

The graph in Figure 7 shows the number of requests rejected by our algorithm which is drastically less compared to the other two algorithms. When the network load increases as the number of requests increases and after a point of time the network starts rejecting new requests. This is the case with all the three algorithms. But the difference lies in how many requests are rejected even at peak time. The other algorithms allocate bandwidth along the shortest-path tree computed and when there is no bandwidth on any one of the links then the request is rejected. But our algorithm searches for alternate paths through which the request can be routed. Hence it can satisfy more number of requests and thus outperforms the MNF algorithm [7] and the MHT algorithm.

The other graphs show the improvement in request rejections for three classes of applications. The new algorithm outperforms in all the cases compared to MHT algorithm. Our algorithm also produces shorter path trees with less number of hops for all class-I requests compared to MNF algorithm. Hence the delay characteristics are better for all the class-I requests in the new algorithm.

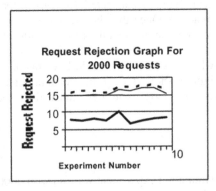

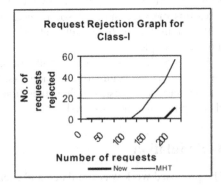

Fig. 7. Request rejection graph showing the requests made and the number of requests rejected in 10 different runs

Fig. 8. Class-I receivers rejection graph showing the number of class-I requests rejected in MHT and new algorithm

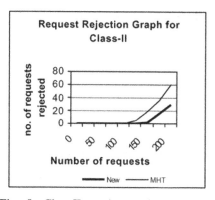

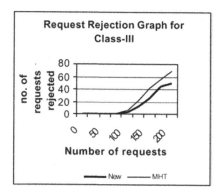

Fig. 9. Class-II receivers rejection graph showing the number of class-II requests rejected in MHT and new algorithm

Fig. 10. Class-III receivers rejection graph showing the number of class-III requests rejected in MHT and new algorithm

5 Conclusion

A QoS driven online multicast routing algorithm with bandwidth and delay guarantees using alternate path routing based on the shortest path algorithm is presented. The algorithm focusing on the service level differentiation namely Class-I, Class-II and Class-III based on delay, bandwidth requirements of applications that demand multicasting and accommodating as many future demands without priori knowledge. The algorithm chooses an alternate path when there is no sufficient bandwidth on the links in the shortest path tree. If the request happens to be a class-I request then space is created for this request by freeing any class-II or class-III applications already using the link and allocating an alternate path for the class-II or class-III receiver. Thus the algorithm provides the guaranteed service to the class-I application without affecting the service of the already existing users. The simulation results obtained showed significant improvement in resource utilization and the number of requests satisfied was significantly larger than that satisfied by the Minimum Hop Tree algorithm.

References

1. L. Sahasrabuddhe and B. Mukherjee, Multicast Routing Algorithms and Protocols: A Tutorial, IEEE Network, Jan./Feb 2000
2. Aaron Striegel and G. Manimaran, A Survey of QoS Multicasting Issues, IEEE Communications Magazine, June 2002
3. Liming Wei, Deborah Estrin, The Trade-offs of Multicast Trees and Algorithms, in Proceedings of the 1994 International Conference on Computer Communications and Networks, pp. 17-24, 1994
4. A. Fei and M. Gerla, Receiver-initiated multicasting with multiple QoS constraints, Proceedings, IEEE INFOCOM, 2000
5. Bin Wang and Jennifer C. Hou, Multicast Routing and it QoS Extension: Problems, Algorithms, and Protocols, IEEE Network, vol. 14, no. 1, pp. 22 -- 36, Jan/Feb 2000

6. S. Chen and K. Nahrstedt, An overview of quality-of-service routing for the next generation high-speed networks: Problems and solutions, IEEE Network, Special Issue on Transmission and Distribution of DigitalVideo, Nov./Dec. 1998
7. Murali Kodialam, T. V. Lakshman, and Sudipta Sengupta, Online Multicast Routing With
   Bandwidth Guarantees: A New Approach Using Multicast Network Flow, IEEE/ACM
   Transactions On Networking, Vol. 11, No. 4, August 2003
8. Daniel Zappala, Alternate Path Routing for Multicasting, IEEE/ACM Transactions on Networking, Vol. 12, No. 1, Feb 2004
9. M. Faloutsos, A. Banerjea, and R. Pankaj, QoSMIC: Quality of service sensitive multicast
   Internet protocol, in Proceedings, ACM SIGCOMM, Sep. 1998
10. Shigang Chen, Klara Nahrstedt, and Yuval Shavitt, A QoS-Aware Multicast Routing Pro-
    tocol, IEEE JSAC, vol.18, no.12, Dec. 2000
11. R. N. Rouskas, and I. Baldine, Multicast Routing with End-to-End Delay and Delay Varia-
    tion Constraints, IEEE JSAC, pp.346-56, Apr. 1997

Software Radio Implementation of a Smart Antenna System on Digital Signal Processors for cdma2000

Kerem Kucuk[1], Mustafa Karakoc[1], and Adnan Kavak[2]

[1] Kocaeli University, Electronics and Computer Education Department, 41300 Izmit, Turkey
{kkucuk,mkarakoc}@kou.edu.tr
[2] Kocaeli University, Computer Engineering Department, 41040 Izmit, Turkey
akavak@kou.edu.tr

Abstract. This paper presents a software defined radio (SDR) implementation based on programmable digital signal processors (DSP) for smart antenna systems (SAS). We evaluate adaptive beamforming algorithms, namely non-blind-type least mean square (LMS) and blind-type constant modulus (CM) using TI TMS320C6000 high performance DSPs for cdma2000 reverse link. Adaptive beamformers are implemented using TI code composer studio (CCS) that includes assembly language and C code development tools. Performance variation of these sofware radio beamformers in terms of weight computation time and received SINR are compared for different C6000 development boards (TMS320C6701 EVM, TMS320C6711 DSK, and TMS320C6713 DSK) and array topologies under varying multipath propagation conditions. Results show that while antenna array and algorithm type are important for the SINR performance, DSP type becomes important for the weight computation time.

1 Introduction

Software defined radio (SDR) is often described as a radio whose functionality is defined in software [1]. SDR uses programmable digital devices to perform the signal processing necessary to transmit and receive baseband information at radio frequency. This technology offers greater flexibility and potentially longer product life, since the radio can be upgraded very cost effectively with software. Smart antenna systems (SAS) [2] are considered to be prominent technology for CDMA based 3G systems, which provide significant capacity increase and performance enhancement at the base station. These antenna systems employ adaptive beamforming algorithms in order to recognize and track the desired user while suppressing the interference. SAS employs an antenna array that uses the spatial domain to improve link performance and enable other value-added services. It consists of both the software and the hardware objects associated with the additional processing capability. SDR implementation of adaptive algorithms on programmable chips, which are digital signal processors (DSP) and field programmable gate arrays (FPGA), will play a key role in the integration of SASs into 3G base station [3], [4]. Small computational load and high signal-to-interference plus noise ratio (SINR) are desired parameters that enable the SDR implementation of an adaptive beamformer [5], [6].

Our objective in this paper is to find out answers to the following questions, 1) how feasible is the DSP-based software radio implementation of adaptive beamforming algorithms for cdma2000 reverse link? and 2) how the performances of these algorithms are affected by different DSP and antenna topology under varying channel

G. Das and V.P. Gulati (Eds.): CIT 2004, LNCS 3356, pp. 97–106, 2004.

propagation conditions? For this intention, we demostrate DSP implementation of least mean square (LMS) and constant modulus (CM) adaptive algorithms for cdma2000 system [7] on Texas Instruments (TI) TMS320C6000 high performance floating point DSP platform (TMS320C6701 EVM, TMS320C6711 DSK, and TMS320C6713 DSK) [8]. We statistically compare the performance variation of these algorithms in terms of beamformer weight vector computation time (cycle time) and received SINR when uniform linear array (ULA) and uniform circular array (UCA) antenna configurations are involved. We consider changing multipath fading and angle spread conditions. Both LMS and CM algorithms employ gradient-based, iterative approach in obtaining optimum weight vector [9]. In the most widely used non-blind type LMS algorithm [10], a training signal, i.e., reverse link pilot signal in cdma2000 system, which is known to both the transmitter and receiver is utilized. However, the blind type CM algorithm [11] avoids the requirement of a training sequence and utilizes the constant envelope property of the transmitted CDMA signal.

DSP emulations are performed in the following steps: Received data in cdma2000 reverse link format is generated as described in Section II and saved in a data file of a PC. In the signal modeling, a wireless vector channel that has one direct path and one multipath component for the desired signal, a multiple access interference (MAI) signal, and an additive white Gaussian noise (AWGN) signal is considered. The adaptive algorithms are coded, compiled, and finally loaded in a memory of the DSP boards by means of code composer studio (CCS) code generation tools. By accepting the data generated in the PC as the input and executing the adaptive algorithm, the DSP processor computes the beamforming weight vector.

The remainder of the paper is organized as follows. Signal model received at the antenna array is described in Section II. TI TMS320C6000 floating point DSPs used in this paper are briefly introduced in Section III. Implementation method and simulation system are given in Section IV. Weight computation time and received SINR results are presented in Section V, and finally the paper is concluded in Section VI.

2   Received Signal Model

The cdma2000 [7] reverse link baseband signal model in radio configuration 1 (RC1) is used in our simulations [9]. The signal s(t) is exposed to multipath propagation environment, which induces complex path attenuation, $\alpha_l = \beta_l e^{j\phi_l}$ and time delay τ_l to each multipath signal as depicted in Figure 1. The signal received by M element antenna array at the base station can be expressed as,

$$x(t) = \sum_{\ell=1}^{L} \alpha_\ell \, s(t - \tau_\ell) a(\theta_\ell) + i(t) + n(t) \tag{1}$$

where i(t) is the multiple access interference (MAI) which is given by

$$i(t) = \sum_{q=1}^{N-1} \sum_{\ell=1}^{L_q} \alpha_{q,\ell} \, s(t - \tau_{q,\ell}) a(\theta_{q,\ell}) \tag{2}$$

and n(t) is the Mx1 complex-valued additive spatially white Gaussian noise vector, $a(\theta_l)$ is the Mx1 array response vector of the multipath impinging from DOA θ_l. The array output is multiplied by a complex weight vector **w** which is determined according to aforementioned beamforming algorithms to result, and results in

$$z(t) = \mathbf{w}^H(t)\,\mathbf{x}(t) \qquad (3)$$

where H denotes complex conjugation and transpose (Hermitian) operation. Here, we note that the signal **x**(t) is generated in a PC using Matlab and loaded to the DSP memory. Computation of weight vector **w** is performed on the DSP.

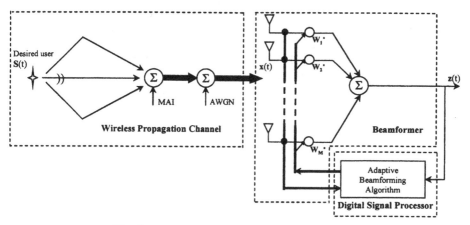

Fig. 1. Received signal model at an antenna array

3 DSP Architectures

The Texas Instruments TMS320C67x high performance floating point DSPs [12] were chosen for the implementation of CM and LMS adaptive beamformers. We used TMS320C6701 DSP based EVM (Evaluation Module), TMS320C6711 DSP based DSK (DSP Starter Kit), TMS320C6713 DSP based DSK. TMS320C67x DSPs use high-performance, advanced VelociTI very-long-instruction-word (VLIW) architecture which enables multichannel and multifunction processing. The C67x processor consists of three main parts: CPU, peripherals, and memory. Eight functional units operate in parallel, with two similar sets of the four functional units. The functional units communicate using a cross path between two register files, each of which contains 16 registers with 32-bit-wide. The 256-bit-wide program memory fetches eight 32-bit instructions every single cycle. The C6701 EVM uses the PLL clock generator interface to support four clock rates. We used OSC Bx4 clock rate up to 133 MHz. The C6701 EVM includes a peripheral component interconnect (PCI) interface that enables host access to the onboard joint test action group (JTAG) controller, DSP host port interface (HPI), and board control/status registers [13]. Operating at 150 MHz, the C6711 delivers up to 1200 million instructions per second (MIPS) and 600 million floating-point operations per second (MFLOPS). The C6711 DSK communicates a PC via parallel port interface [14]. The C6713 DSP operates at 225 MHz and delivers up to 1350 MFLOPS, 1800 MIPS with dual fixed-/floating-point multipliers up to 450 million multiply-accumulate operations per second (MMACS). The kit uses universal serial bus (USB) communications for true plug-and-play functionality [15].

C6701 DSP has 128 KB, C6711 DSP has 72 KB and C6713 DSP has 264 KB on-chip memory. The C6701 EVM has 256 KB SBSRAM and 8 MB SDRAM. The C6711 DSK has 16 MB external SDRAM and 128 KB external flash. The C6713 DSK has 512 flash and 8 MB SDRAM.

4 Implementation Method and Simulation System

Figure 2 shows the configuration of defined hardware structure of the system. The system consists of a PC and the DSP boards (C6701 EVM, C6711 DSK, or C6713 DSK boards). The key part of a SAS, which is the computation of beamformer weight vector is implemented on the DSP board. The PC is used for received data generation and post-processing of the beamformer performance.

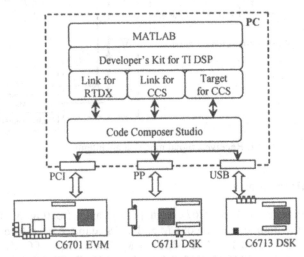

Fig. 2. Configuration of defined hardware structure of the system

Since the code requires square root and division operations, a fixed point implementation was not feasible. Therefore, we decided to implement the algorithms on the floating point DSPs. The adaptive algorithms were implemented in C code generation tools and assembly language development tools, compiled, and loaded in a memory of the DSP boards by means of CCS. The CCS includes tools for code generation, such as a C compiler, an assembler, and a linker [16]. In assembly, to calculate square root and division, we selected RSQRSP instruction that can be used as a seed value for an algorithm to compute the reciprocal square root to greater accuracy [17]. DSPs have very stringent memory requirements, so we have to decide where to allocate the memory for each code based on the size of the data. We have estimated that the data sizes for the implementation do not fit on-chip memory and hence, have to be placed in external SRAM.

The assembly and C programs include subroutines which were used for matrix vector multiplication. These subroutines were used TI's floating point assembly benchmarks [18]. Some portion of the assembly and C codes which calculate weight vectors in an iterative manner are given in Table 1 through Table 4 for the adaptive algorithms. The cdma2000 RC1 signal model is used to generate the signal transmitted by a mobile and received by an antenna array. The antenna array topology is 5-element ULA or UCA. The received signals are transferred into the DSP boards by using Matlab link and CCS development tools.

Table 1. Assembly code of weight vector computation via LMS algorithm

```
Loop        LDW     .D2    *B12++[1],B4
            LDW     .D2    *B11++[1],B1
            LDW     .D1    *A12++[1],A4
            LDW     .D1    *A11++[1],A1
            MPYSP   .M2    B4,B5,B6
            MPYSP   .M1    A4,A5,A6
            SUBSP   .L2X   B6,A6,B6
            MPYSP   .M2    B6,B3,B8
            ADDSP   .L2    B8,B1,B8
            STW     .D2    B8,*B11[4]
            MPYSP   .M2X   B4,A5,B6
            MPYSP   .M1X   A4,B5,A6
            ADDSP   .L1X   A6,B6,A6
            MPYSP   .M1X   A6,B3,A6
            ADDSP   .L1    A6,A1,A6
            STW     .D1    A6,*A11[4]
            SUB     .S2    B0,1,B0
[B0]        B       .S2    Loop
```
NOP hasn't shown in this table

Table 2. C code of weight vector computation via LMS algorithm

```
for(i=0;i<5;i++)  {
    *(WRP+5)=(*WRP)+((*XRP)*(*ERP)-(*XSP)*(*ESP))*(*mu);
    *(WSP+5)=(*WSP)+((*XRP)*(*ESP)+(*XSP)*(*ERP))*(*mu);
    WRP=WRP+1;WSP=WSP+1;XRP=XRP+1;XSP=XSP+1;
    }
```

Table 3. Assembly code of weight vector computation via CM algorithm

```
Loop        LDW     .D1    *A1++[1],A5
            LDW     .D2    *B1++[1],B5
            LDW     .D1    *A2++[1],A6
            LDW     .D2    *B2++[1],B6
            MPYSP   .M1X   A6,B3,A7
            MPYSP   .M2    B6,B3,B7
            MPYSP   .M2X   B8,A11,A12
            MPYSP   .M1    A5,A8,A9
            MPYSP   .M2X   B5,A10,A13
            SUBSP   .L1    A9,A13,A9
            MPYSP   .M1    A5,A10,A13
            MPYSP   .M2X   B5,A8,A14
            ADDSP   .L1    A13,A14,A13
            MPYSP   .M1    A9,A12,A9
            SUBSP   .L1    A7,A9,A7
            STW     .D1    A7,*A2[4]
            MPYSP   .M1    A13,A12,A9
            SUBSP   .L2X   B7,A9,B7
            STW     .D2    B7,*B2[4];
            SUB     .S2    B0,1,B0
[B0]        B       .S2    Loop
```
NOP hasn't shown in this table

Table 4. C code of weight vector computation via CM algorithm

```
for(i=0;i<5;i++) {
    *(WRP+5)=0.99*(*WRP)-0.01*(*ERP)*((*XRP)*XRRR-
        (*XSP)*XSSS);
    *(WSP+5)=0.99*(*WSP)-0.01*(*ERP)*((*XRP)*XSSS+
        (*XSP)*XRRR);
    WRP=WRP+1;WSP=WSP+1;XRP=XRP+1;XSP=XSP+1;
}
```

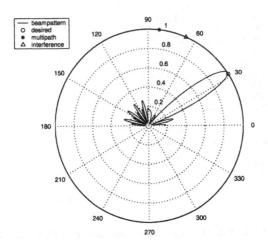

Fig. 3. An example of a spatial spectrum obtained via LMS algorithm implementation on C6711 DSK for the ULA configuration

The DSP processor executes the adaptive algorithm and then sends the computed weight vector and algorithm convergence time information back to the PC. In this way, SASs are spread beampattern direction of desired user by computed weight vectors as shown Figure 3.

We perform Monte Carlo simulations (100 runs) in order to assess the variation of algorithm convergence time and received SINR performances of adaptive beamformers under varying multipath conditions for the given DSP processors (C6701, C6711, and C6713), algorithms (LMS, CM), and array topologies (ULA, UCA). We consider a simple wireless propagation channel that consists of a direct path and a multipath components for the desired signal and an interference signal. Relavant paramaters in each simulation run are set as follows: DOA of the desired signal's direct path is set to 32°. Multipath and interference signal DOAs are selected randomly drawn from uniform distribution. The amplitude and phase components of multipath fading parameters are represented by Rayleigh and uniform random variables, respectively. Number of signal samples is 1000, step size parameter in the LMS algorithm and weight factor in the CM algorithm are choosen 0.01 and 0.99, respectively. Convergence criteria for the algorithms are determined from the norm of the weight error vector between consecutive weight vector samples, which has to be less than 0.001 and is given by,

$$\|\Delta w\| = \|w(t+1) - w(t)\|. \tag{4}$$

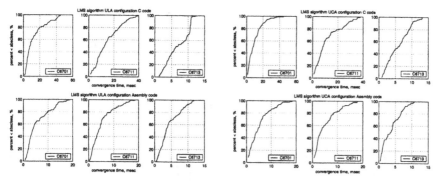

Fig. 4. Cumulative distribution of convergence time of LMS for ULA when using different DSPs

Fig. 5. Cumulative distribution of convergence time of LMS for UCA when using different DSPs

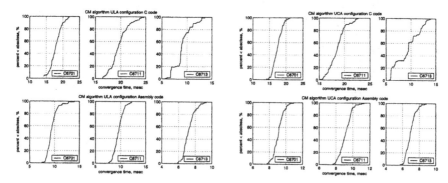

Fig. 6. Cumulative distribution of convergence time of CM for ULA when using different DSPs

Fig. 7. Cumulative distribution of convergence time of CM for UCA when using different DSPs

5 Results

From the simulations, we obtained the statistics of convergence time and received SINR. Figures 4 through 7 show the cumulative distributions of the convergence time of the algorithms that were implemented using either C or assembly codes on the DSP processors for the 5-element ULA and UCA configurations. As depicted in Figures, C6713 DSP results in the fastest weight computation time within less than approximately 5 ms at 50 percentile values at the maximum in all antenna-algorithm types for assembly. In addition, C code implementation C6713 DSP has reasonable time approximately 7ms at 50 percentile. The mean values (50 percentiles) and deviations for the convergence times which are compiled from cumulative distributions are tabulated in Table 5 and Table 6. By close inspection of the cumulative distribution plots, we see that convergence time behavior is predominanty characterized by the algorithm type and code implementation type rather than the DSP and antenna configuration. As expected, LMS is faster than CM in the computation of weight vectors for the same array type. However, the spread of convergence time for the CM algorithm is smaller when compared to the LMS algorithm, indicating that CM is less sensitive to changing multipath fading and angle spread conditions in the propagation channel. For the same algorithm and same processor type, using ULA or UCA topology does not affect the convergence time performance much.

Table 5. Statistics of convergence time (ms) and received SINR (dB) for the assembly code implementation of beamformers

		DSP	LMS		CM	
			ULA	UCA	ULA	UCA
Convergence time (ms)	Mean	C6701	5,84	5,30	9,54	9,12
		C6711	5,32	5,22	9,61	9,13
		C6713	4,47	3,85	7,25	6,98
	Std.	C6701	4,66	4,20	1,07	0,61
		C6711	4,32	4,48	0,94	0,70
		C6713	3,06	2,87	0,69	0,59
		DSP	LMS		CMA	
			ULA	UCA	ULA	UCA
SINR (dB)	Mean	C6701	5,92	6,15	3,08	6,17
		C6711	5,96	6,15	3,32	6,17
		C6713	5,88	6,14	3,02	6,17
	Std.	C6701	0,63	0,03	2,08	0,03
		C6711	0,41	0,03	2,20	0,03
		C6713	0,63	0,03	1,78	0,03

Table 6. Statistics of convergence time (ms) and received SINR (dB) for the C code implementation of beamformers

		DSP	LMS		CM	
			ULA	UCA	ULA	UCA
Convergence time (ms)	Mean	C6701	13,36	10,19	17,92	17,45
		C6711	14,86	11,83	19,72	18,58
		C6713	6,92	5,82	9,19	9,32
	Std.	C6701	11,89	8,54	1,74	1,43
		C6711	9,82	9,93	1,78	1,62
		C6713	3,40	3,39	1,73	2,44
		DSP	LMS		CM	
			ULA	UCA	ULA	UCA
SINR (dB)	Mean	C6701	5,83	6,15	3,30	6,17
		C6711	5,81	6,15	2,99	6,16
		C6713	5,80	6,15	2,85	6,08
	Std.	C6701	0,91	0,03	2,01	0,03
		C6711	0,83	0,03	2,05	0,03
		C6713	1,02	0,03	2,15	0,10

Regarding beamformer SINR performances, the mean values and standard deviations of SINR distributions are also presented in Table 5 and Table 6. SINR output of the beamformer is independent of DSP processor type as seen from Figures 8 and 9. Both algorithms result in almost the same SINR values in the UCA configuration. However, when ULA is considered, SINR performance of the LMS algorithm is considerably larger (appr. 3 dB differences at 50%) than that the CM algorithm. When different antenna configurations are considered for the same algorithm type, UCA leads to higher SINR values. In addition, SINR performance in the UCA topology is less affected by the channel variation as obvious from its smaller standard deviations.

6   Conclusions

We have demonstared the software radio implementation of a smart antenna system (SAS) on floating point digital signal processors (DSP) for cdma2000 reverse link channel. Performance evaluation of the implemented algorithms is observed in terms of weight computation time and received SINR for different array topologies (ULA or UCA), DSPs (C6713, C6711, and C6701), and code generation tools (assembly or C) under varying multipath fading conditions. When we consider SINR as the performance criteria, the algorithm type and antenna configuration plays significant role than the DSP type and implementation method. On the other hand, if weight computation time is considered to be a crucial parameter, C6713 DSP has the best performance for all antenna configurations and algorithm types. It seems possible that

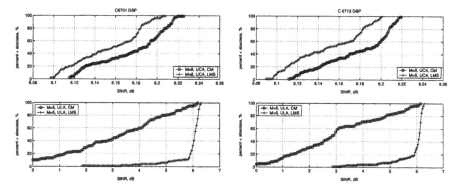

Fig. 8. Cumulative distributions of received SINR for the beamformer implementation on C6701 DSP

Fig. 9. Cumulative distribution of received SINR for the beamformer implementation on C6713 DSP

software radio implementation of LMS and CM algorithms are feasible only by using C6713 DSP since it can achieve the convergence time in less than 5 ms with assembly and 7 ms with C, which are reasonably smaller than 10 ms frame interval of cdma2000 system. We however note that these convergence time values are sensitive to algorithm parameters and multipath conditions.

Acknowledgement

This research was supported by TUBITAK (Scientific and Technical Research Council of Turkey) under contract EEEAG/102E015.

References

1. Burns, P.: Software defined radio for 3G. Artec House MA (2002) 221-237.
2. Rappaport T. S., Liberti, J. C.: Smart Antennas for Wireless Communication. Prentice Hall NJ (1999).
3. Im H., Choi S.: Implementation of a smart antenna test-bed. IEEE AP-S International Symposium & URSI Radio Science Meeting, (2000) 83-88.
4. Choi S., Lee, Y., Hirasawa, K.: Real-time design of a smart antenna system utilizing a modified conjugate gradient method for CDMA-Based Mobile Communications. IEEE, VTC'97, 1 (1997) 183-187.
5. Park J. J., Oh H. S., Kyeong M. G.: Real-time implementation of MMSE adaptive beamformer using modified systolic array. Proc VTC 2001-spring, 1 (2001) 180-184.
6. Jeon S. S., Wang Y., Qian Y., Itoh T.: A Novel Smart Antenna System Implementation for Broadband Wireless Communication. IEEE Trans. on Antennas and Propagation, 50(5) (2002) 600-606.
7. TIA/EIA Interim Standard, Physical Layer Standard for cdma2000 spread spectrum systems, TIA/EIA/S-2000-2.
8. Dahnoun N.: DSP Implementation using the TMS320C6000 DSP Platform. Prentice Hall NJ (2000).

9. Karakoc, M., Kavak, A.: Evaluation of Smart Antenna Algorithms for cdma2000 reverse link. Lecture Notes in Computer Science, Vol. 3042. Springer-Verlag, Berlin Heidelberg New York (2004) 1360-1365.
10. Godara L.: Application of antenna arrays to mobile communications, Part II: beamforming and direction-of-arrival considerations. Proceedings of the IEEE, 85(8) (1997) 1195-1245.
11. Veen, A. J., Paulraj, A.: An analytical constant modulus algorithm. IEEE Trans. of Signal Proc., 44(5) (1996) 1136-1155.
12. Texas Instruments: TMS320C6000 Technical Brief. TX (1999).
13. Texas Instruments: TMS320C6701 Evaluation Module Technical Reference. TX (1998).
14. Texas Instruments: TMS320C6711 Floating-Point DSPs. TX (2002).
15. Spectrum Digital: TMS320C6713 DSK Technical Reference. TX (2003).
16. Texas Instruments: Code Composer Studio Getting Started Guide. TX (2001).
17. Texas Instruments: TMS320C6000 CPU and Instruction Set Reference Guide. TX (2002).
18. Texas Instruments C67x DSP Benchmarks.
    http://www.ti.com/sc/docs/products/dsp/c6000/67bench.htm.

An Efficient Cost Effective Location Management Scheme Based on Velocity Vector Information of Mobile Unit

Subrata Nandi and Manish K. Raushan

Department of Computer Science and Engineering, National Institute of Technology,
Durgapur (DU) PIN-713209, WB, India
sn_nitdgp@yahoo.co.in, sn_comp@nitdgp.ac.in,
manish_raushan@indiatimes.com

Abstract. In cellular mobile networks total location management cost (update + paging) is to be minimized. Previous studies suggest that velocity vector (speed and direction) of a mobile unit (MU) can be used to design optimal strategies. But the schemes use complex velocity estimation techniques and requires explicit announcement of velocity profile during an update. We propose a novel velocity based location management scheme in which explicit announcement of velocity by MU is not required during an update as mobile switching centre (MSC) stores and adjusts velocity profile of MU intelligently. Location of MU can be predicted using the profile of MU stored in the MSC during the paging process. The proposed scheme can be implemented using directional Cell Identification Codes which requires no extra signaling overhead. Simulation shows that our scheme performs far better than existing schemes.

1 Introduction

The service area (SA) of a cellular mobile system is divided into smaller areas of hexagonal shape, called cells. Each cell is served by a base station (BS) within its area. BS is connected to the mobile switching center (MSC) which, in turn, is connected to the public switched telephone network (PSTN). A mobile unit (MU) communicates with another unit via a BS.

Location management is the problem of tracking down a mobile user (MU) in the SA area, which includes two basic activities: location update and terminal paging. In location update a message is sent by the MU that informs the network about its new location, and paging is a search process conducted by the network, to find the MU's location when a connection to the user (for an incoming call) is requested. There is a clear trade-off between the cost of update and cost of paging and the goal is to minimize the combined cost. This motivates the design of efficient location management schemes that are cost effective and also easy to implement.

The different location management schemes are reviewed in [1]. There are two basic kinds of location management schemes: static and dynamic. In this paper we focus on dynamic ones, which can be further classified in two types predictive and non-predictive. The dynamic non-predictive category uses time-based [4], movement-based [5] and distance-based [6] update schemes. In the predictive category, update schemes based only on speed information of MU is proposed in [9] where the paging

G. Das and V.P. Gulati (Eds.): CIT 2004, LNCS 3356, pp. 107–116, 2004.
© Springer-Verlag Berlin Heidelberg 2004

area can be estimated as a circular strip. Lee and Hwang [8] suggested that combining the direction information along with speed could further reduce the paging area. Here user location can be predicted more precisely by the MSC, which can significantly reduce the paging cost. Thus, an optimal paging scheme is an outcome of an efficient update scheme. It is also observed that the predictive schemes exhibits lower location management cost than the non-predictive schemes. Moreover, velocity (speed and direction combined) information can be the best criteria for location update in designing cost effective location management schemes.

Updates are triggered by the MU, therefore estimation of the MU speed and movement direction with low overhead is a real challenge. Instead of calculating the actual speed [13] of an MU, speed can be defined as a ratio of distance to time with respect to the LUC as suggested in [8]. But distance computation is a non-trivial issue, as it requires knowledge of SA layout. The speed-adaptive location management scheme proposed in [10] uses an enhanced look-up table, which is a modification of dynamic look-up table suggested in [11]. Another approach referred in [8] uses direction information along with speed, which is an improvement of the basic velocity paging [7]. The scheme requires additional record of length N to be added to the visitor location register (VLR) database. Thus it is observed that in addition to new cell-id most of the predictive schemes also requires explicit announcement of some topology related information during each update.

A novel technique to compute both distance and directional information of the movement of MU has been proposed in [3]. The technique encodes each cell with a 4-bit locally unique distance cell identification code referred as CIC-DIS but it works only for uniform 2-D arrangement of hexagonal cells. We proposed direction based cell identification code in [12] referred as CIC-DIR, which is an extension of CIC-DIS and is applicable to any arbitrary 2-D arrangement of hexagonal cells. The procedure to compute distance and direction using CIC-DIR [12] incurs low implementation overhead and can be embedded within the MU.

The objective of this paper is to propose a novel update scheme based on velocity vector (speed and direction combined) information of MU with low implementation overhead. In the proposed scheme, updates are triggered if either speed or direction changes or if even though speed and direction remains unchanged but distance traversed by MU with respect to last update exceeds some distance threshold. Update also takes place if MU stays in a cell for sufficient long duration. Optimal threshold values are determined through simulation runs. These values are estimated offline and are known to both MU and MSC, therefore no explicit announcement of velocity by MU is required during an update. The MSC intelligently modifies the velocity profile of a MU after an update. During the paging process the location of MU is predicted by the MSC and minimal set of cells to be paged is computed. It is found that the scheme optimizes overall location management cost for all categories of users with wide range of mobility behaviors. The proposed scheme can be implemented using CIC-DIR.

The structure of the paper is as follows: In section 2 we explain the CIC-DIR coding technique. Computation of distance and direction using CIC-DIR code is briefly explained in section 3. Section 4 presents the details of the proposed location management strategy with suitable illustration. Simulation results are in Section 5. Summary and conclusion are given in Section 6.

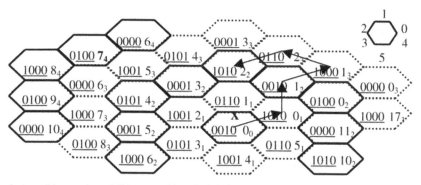

Fig. 1. An arbitrary shaped SA area with cells labeled with 4-bit directional codes (underlined) assigned by CIC-DIR along with numbering convention used to explain distance computation. Sample moves of an MU after an update at cell X is shown by arrows. A possible numbering convention of sides of a cell used to identify direction of movement is shown in top-right

2   The Directional Cell Identification Coding (CIC-DIR) Scheme

The directional cell identification coding scheme (CIC-DIR) [12] which is an extension to the approach used in CIC-DIS [3] is explained here. A small SA consisting of hexagonal cells is considered in Fig.1. Arbitrary 2-D arrangement of cells is assumed. Each cell is assigned a locally unique 4-bit code (two for each dimension) such that no two neighboring cells can have the same code as shown in Fig 1. The tile in the ith row and j^{th} column will have the code [i%3 j%3]. Consider that the six sides of a hexagonal cell are numbered from 0 to 5 in anticlockwise direction as depicted in Fig. 1. The BS continuously broadcast through the downlink control channel in GSM a sequence of eight 4-bit codes according to the following rule. The 1st code contains the CIC of the cell to which the BS belongs. Next six codes contain CIC of its six neighbors in a certain order, which is to be followed by all BSs. The 7th code is a special code 1111 (used only to delimit the sequence). BS of cell X will broadcast a CIC sequence 0010 1010 0110 1001 0101 1001 0110 1111 which will be repeated instead of sequence 0010 0010 0010 0010 0010 0010 0010 0010. Whenever the MU moves to another cell first it synchronizes with respect to the new sequence by identifying the delimiter code 1111. The MU then checks the relative position of the CIC stored in memory say x, (where 0<=x<=5) within the new sequence. Thus x can be identified as the side or direction through which transition took place. This information can be used to calculate the distance of MU in cell units and relative direction with respect to the LUC.

3   Computation of Distance and Direction Using CIC-DIR

Computation of distance and direction of a MU using CIC-DIR [12] is explained briefly. Distance is measured in terms of number of cells it is far from the LUC. The cells surrounding the LUC are considered to be organized in several concentric rings with the LUC at the center. A sample SA is shown in Fig. 1 with X as the LUC. To explain the procedure, a numbering convention shown in Fig. 1 is used which distinguishes different cells surrounding the LUC. For example, according to the convention the 4th cell in the 2nd ring is identified by a number 4_2 with respect to the LUC X. Whenever a MU crosses a cell boundary and enters a new cell it identifies the side x through which transition took place with respect to the last cell, using CIC-DIR. Distance is computed each time a MU moves to a new cell. All cells in a particular ring are equidistant from the LUC. Therefore, it is obvious that the distance value will be same as the ring number to which the new cell belongs.

It is observed that the total set of cells C_{tot} in each ring can be divided in two subsets C_{222} and C_{321}. The six sides in each cell can be divided in three subsets S^+, S^- and S^0 transition through which causes distance value to be incremented by one, decremented by one and remain unchanged respectively. Cells belonging to subset C_{222} will have two side members each in S^+, S^- and S^0, whereas cells belonging to subset C_{321} will have three side members in S^+, one in S^- and two in S^0 out of total six sides. If N_R is the number of the Nth cell in R^{th} ring, it is observed that in the Rth ring C_{321} contains total six cells satisfying condition ((N%R) equals 0) and C_{222} contains remaining cells i.e. (C_{tot} - C_{321}). Whenever the MU moves to a new cell distance is computed. It uses the previous cell number N_R (as a tuple [N,R]) and side of the previous cell through which MU has moved as input to calculate the new cell number. The new [N,R] value is stored in the MU. After each update [N,R] value is set to [0,0]. Distance is same as the ring number R of the current cell. Moves are counted with respect to the last update. Conditions derived to check if the input side belongs to S^+, S^- or S^0 are presented below. The following notations are used:

[N_i,R_i] – identifies the Nth cell in the Rth ring where the MU resides after its ith move.
s_{i+1} – side of the cell [N_i,R_i] through which transition took place in the ($i+1)^{th}$ move.
Let, $Q_i = N_i/R_i$

If (N_i%R_i equals 0), i.e. previous cell belongs to C_{321} then

- s_{i+1} belongs to S^+ if s_{i+1} is equal to ((Q+5)%6) or ((Q+6)%6) or ((Q+7)%6)
- s_{i+1} belongs to S^- if s_{i+1} is equal to ((Q+3)%6)
- s_{i+1} belongs to S^0 if s_{i+1} is equal to ((Q+2)%6) or ((Q+4)%6)

If (N_i%R_i not equals 0), i.e. previous cell belongs to C_{222} then

- s_{i+1} belongs to S^+ if s_{i+1} is equal to ((Q+6)%6) or ((Q+7)%6)
- s_{i+1} belongs to S^- if s_{i+1} is equal to ((Q+3)%6) or ((Q+5)%6)
- s_{i+1} belongs to S^0 if s_{i+1} is equal to ((Q+2)%6) or ((Q+4)%6)

The new ring number R_{i+1} which represents the distance value, will be incremented, decremented or remain unchanged depending on whether s_{i+1} belongs to S^+, S^- and S^0 respectively. N_{i+1} will be calculated easily after each move.

Consider a set of moves made by a MU after an update at cell X as shown in Fig. 1. Initially, after the update at cell X tuple value is reset to [0,0] and stored in MU which implies initial distance value is zero. Initial direction is assumed to be along side 0. After 1st move s_1 is 1 and s_1 belongs S^+ resulting new tuple [0,1]. Next four consecutive moves is through sides 1, 0, 2 and 3 where the sides belongs to S^+, S^+, S^0 and S^- respectively computed from the conditions stated above. The new cell tuple values are calculated from the previous ones as [1,2], [1,3], [2,3] and [2,2] respectively which shows the distance value after the 4th move is 3. Thus direction and distance computation using CIC-DIR is efficient as it is simple and requires low memory in the MU.

4   The Update and Paging Scheme Based on Velocity Vector Information

We propose a velocity vector based efficient and cost effective location management scheme. The update process is explained first. Here both MU and MSC stores the necessary information such as last known cell-id, distance, direction, time elapsed since last update in order to take part in a location update process. MU modifies the information as and when required and takes decision when to update. The MSC stores the MU profile information and modifies it if required after an update. The MSC also determines the paging area based on stored MU profile whenever a call arrives. The roles played by the MU and the MSC during an update are explained below.

Following notations regarding the proposed location management policy are common to both MU and the MSC:

Speed change = δs and direction change threshold = δd,

Distance threshold = D cells and dwell time threshold = T units.

MU do not have to know details of SA layout. It uses cell numbering temporarily assigned for distance computation as explained in section 3 and stores the following values:

Previous cell number tuple = $[N_{old}, R_{old}]$

Previous direction = MUd_{old} and previous speed = MUs_{old}

Previous Distance = MUD_{prev}, time elapsed = $MUt_{elapsed}$ and dwell time= T_{dwell}

MU increments $MUt_{elapsed}$ and T_{dwell} every time unit. After every move the MU identifies the side number (s) through which transition took place using CIC-DIR and performs the following:

- Computes new cell number $[N_{new}, R_{new}]$ using the technique explained in section 3.
- Sets $MUD_{prev} = R_{new}$. Computes new direction MUd_{new} from s.
- Computes new speed value $MUs_{new} = MUD_{prev} / MUt_{elapsed}$.
- Triggers update based on the following conditions:
  1. If speed changes by $\pm\delta s$ i.e. $| MUs_{new} - MUs_{old}| = \delta s$.
  2. Direction of its movement changes by $\pm\delta d$ i.e $| MUd_{new} - MUd_{prev} | = \delta d$.
  3. Neither its speed nor its direction changes but distance traversed by the MU with respect to LUC exceeds D cells.
  4. Neither its speed nor its direction changes but MU stays in a cell for sufficiently long duration i.e. $(T_{dwell} > T)$. It means that MU may have reached the destination of its trip therefore effective speed will be zero.
- If update is triggered, sets $[N_{old}, R_{old}]=[0,0]$, $MUD_{prev}=0$ and $MUt_{elapsed} = 0$, $MUd_{old} = MUd_{new}$ which is intuitive.
- Sets $T_{dwell} = 0$ after each move.

MSC uses the globally unique cell-id to identify cells. It is assumed to have the knowledge of the entire SA layout therefore it can compute the distance between any two given cells. MSC is required to store the following values corresponding to each MU it is serving:

Cell-id of the LUC= C_{old} and time elapsed since last update= $MSCt_{elapsed}$

Previous direction = $MSCd_{old}$ and previous speed = $MSCs_{old}$

MSC increments $MSCt_{elapsed}$ in every time unit. After an update from a MU, MSC receives the new cell-id C_{new} and performs the following:

- Compute the distance between C_{old} and C_{new}.. Let it be D' .
- Compute new direction of movement $MSCd_{new}$ from the information regarding location of C_{new} with respect to C_{old}. Let difference $MSCd_{diff} = (MSCd_{new} - MSCd_{old})$.
- Check if ($MSCt_{elapsed} > T$), MSC concludes that update is due to condition 4. Therefore $MSCs_{new} = 0$ and $MSCd_{new} = MSCd_{old}$.
- Check if (($MSCs_{old}* MSCt_{elapsed}$)> D'), MSC concludes that update is due to condition 1. Therefore $MSCs_{new} = MSCs_{old} +ð$ s.
- Check if (($MSCs_{old}* MSCt_{elapsed}$)< D'), MSC concludes that update due to condition 1. Therefore $MSCs_{new} = MSCs_{old} -ð$ s..
- Check if ($MSCd_{diff} > ðd$), MSC concludes that update is due to condition 2. Modify $MSCd_{new}$ accordingly.
- Check if ($MSCd_{diff} < ðd$), MSC concludes that update due to condition 2. Modify $MSCd_{new}$ accordingly.
- Otherwise, the MSC concludes that the update is due to condition 3. Therefore $MSCs_{new} = MSCs_{old}$ and $MSCd_{new} = MSCd_{old}$.
- Set $MSCt_{elapsed} = 0$.

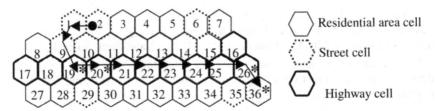

Fig. 2. Illustrates a sample service area showing cells with global cell-id and a MU trip from Cell 2 to Cell 36. Trip consists of 11 moves and '*' denotes cells where updates takes place

Whenever a MU performs registration i.e. update after it is switched on, both MU and MSC sets the above parameters to initially agreed values i.e. $[N_{old}, R_{old}]=[0,0]$ (as explained in section 3, $MUd_{old}= MSCd_{old}= 0$, $MUs_{old}= MSCs_{old}= 8$ cells/hr(say), $MUD_{prev}= 0$, $MUt_{elapsed}= MSCt_{elapsed}= 0$. The values of ðs, ðd, D and T can be determined by simulation experiments such that it optimizes both number of updates and paging area. These are agreed upon values and known to both MU and MSC. Therefore, no explicit announcement of velocity by MU is required during an update. The MSC can intelligently modify the MU's velocity profile after an update.

During the multi step paging process, MSC first predicts intelligently the location of MU at a distance $R=MSCt_{elapsed}* MSCs_{old}$ from LUC. The angular strip of cells bounded by solid lines are paged as shown by the Fig. 3, here $ðr= MSCt_{elapsed} *ðs$ The angle subtended by the strip at LUC is $2*ðd$. Paging then starts with cells along the arc at distance R and spreads both outward and inward in each step with respect to LUC.

Consider the sample service area in Fig. 2 with hexagonal cells. Cells having highways are in bold, cells having streets are in dotted notation. Cells are labeled using globally unique cell-id (assigned by the administrator) to be used by the MSC. Consider a MU, which makes a set of moves from cell 2 to cell 36. The first two moves are on streets next 8 moves are on highways and last one move is on street. Update

Update takes place at the cells labeled with '*' according to the velocity vector strategy. Optimal threshold values used in this example are $\delta s= 1.0$ cell/hr, $\delta d= 1$, $D= 5$ and $T= 1000$ units. Table 1 shows how parameters stored in MU changes during each move and when update decisions are taken. It is assumed that at time t MU performs an update and starts its trip from cell 2 to cell 36. Initially assumed values are shown in Table 1. After every update the change of parameters stored in MSC for the particular MU is shown in Table 2. Number of updates here is 4, which may be equal to or greater than the number of updates made in the simple distance-based (with threshold= 3) scheme. But the overall cost will always be less using velocity vector update scheme, as it will reduce the paging cost drastically.

Table 1. Illustrates moves of a MU with details of values stored and update decisions taken by MU using velocity vector update scheme. Speed is measured as cells/hr and time in secs

Number of the Move (Time)	Previous Cell [N_{old}, R_{old}]	Previous Speed, Direction ($MUs_{old,}$ MUd_{old})	New Cell [N_{new}, R_{new}]	New Speed, Direction (MUs_{new}, MUd_{ne})	New Dist-ance MUD_{new}	Update Y/N ? (Reason for update)
1st (t)	[0,0]	9,2 Assume	[2,1]	(9, 2)	1	N
2nd (t+400)	[2,1]	(9, 2)	[5,2]	(9, 3)	2	N
3rd (t+800)	[5,2]	(9, 2)	[6,2]	(9, 4)	2	Y (Direction)
4th (t+1200)	[0,0]	(9, 4)	[5,1]	(10, 5)	1	Y (Speed)
5th (t+1500)	[0,0]	(10, 5)	[5,1]	(10, 5)	1	N
6th (t+1800)	[5,1]	(10, 5)	[10,2]	(10, 5)	2	N
7th (t+2100)	[10,2]	(10, 5)	[15,3]	(10, 5)	3	N
8th (t+2400)	[15,3]	(10, 5)	[20,4]	(10, 5)	4	N
9^{th}(t+2700)	[20,4]	(10, 5)	[25,5]	(10, 5)	5	N
10th (t+3000)	[25,5]	(10, 5)	[30,6]	(10, 5)	6	Y (Distance)
11th (t+3300)	[0,0]	(10, 5)	[4,0]	(10, 4)	1	N
No move (t+3600)	[4,0]	(10, 4)	[4,0]	($\sim 0,4$)	1	Y (Dwell Time)

Table 2. Illustrates how the MSC keeps track of the velocity profile of an MU after every update. Here $\delta s= 1$ cell/hr and $\delta d=2$. Speed is measured as cells/hr and time in secs

Time during update	Cell-id C_{new} (globally unique) received by MSC due to update	Reason for Update	Updated Speed $MSCs_{new}$	Updated Direction $MSCd_{new}$
t	2	---	9	2
t+800	20	Direction changes	9	$2+\delta d=4$
t+1200	21	Speed changes	$9+\delta s= 10$	4
t+3000	27	Distance Exceeds	10	4
t+3600	37	Dwell time exceeds	0	4

5   Simulation Model and Results

A realistic simulation environment has been used to compare the proposed velocity vector-based (VVB) strategy with time-based (TB), movement-based (MB), simple

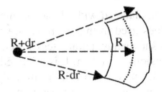

Fig. 3. Solid lines bound the paging area. The dot represents last updated cell position

distance-based (DB) and distance direction-based (DDB) schemes. Circular city area model [2] has been used to model the SA of radius 100 Km which consists of hexagonal cells (radius 2 km each). Users population consists of three categories (high mobility [30%], low mobility [10%] and commuters [60%]). The total time of simulation is from 8:00 AM to 8:00 PM, which is divided into rush hours in morning (8:00 AM – 10:30 AM) and evening (5:30 PM – 8:00 PM) and busy hours (11:30 AM – 4:30 PM). Mobility of users is simulated using behavior based directional mobility model. Commuters move from residence to office in morning and come back home in evening. High mobility users generate random destinations and normally move all through the day and low mobility users occasionally generate trips to destinations close to their residence. Trips are generated based on the time of the day and the category of the user. Average speed of MU typically ranges on the highways from 10-16 cells/hr and on streets 2-8 cells/hr depending on mode of transport (bus, taxi/car etc.) selected by the MU. Call generation follows Poisson distribution with mean 4 -5 call/hr/MU in busy hours and 1-2 call/hr/MU in rush hours. Call duration follows exponential distribution.

Optimal threshold values used for the comparison of the different strategies are as follows: Time threshold in time–based scheme $T^*=1000$ sec. Movement threshold in movement-based scheme $M^* = 2$ cells. Distance threshold in simple distance-based scheme $D^* = 3$ cells. Optimal distance threshold for velocity vector-based scheme is found to be $D = 5$ cells from several simulation runs, which shows that larger distance threshold value can be selected here compared to simple distance-based scheme. The Dwell time threshold for velocity vector scheme is $T= 1000$ sec, direction and speed respectively $\delta d= 2$ and $\delta s= 1.0$ cell/hr. The overall cost has been evaluated as $Cost_{total} = Cost_{paging} + a * Cost_{LU}$ where $a = 5$, assuming one updating cost is equivalent to five times a paging cost. The graph in Fig. 4, 5 & 6 shows the performance of different schemes as a plot of paging, update and total cost respectively verses time of day (in hours). Though update cost for velocity and distance-direction based are nearly equal as shown in Fig. 5, Fig. 4 shows paging cost is significantly low for velocity vector scheme. Therefore, with respect to total cost the velocity vector scheme performs best which is reflected in Fig. 6.

6   Summary and Concluding Remarks

The proposed velocity vector based location management scheme has several advantages. Explicit announcement of velocity profile is not required during an update therefore no extra bandwidth is consumed. Efficient implementation of the update scheme using the CIC-DIR shows that implementation overhead in terms of storage requirement and computational complexity is very low in MU. Location update cost is

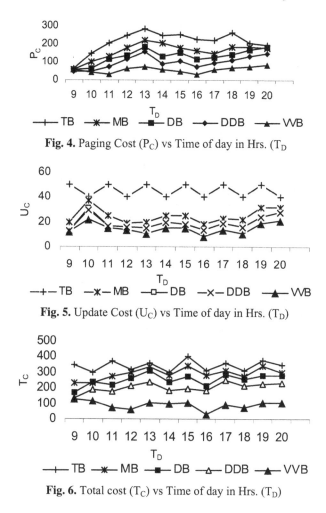

Fig. 4. Paging Cost (P_C) vs Time of day in Hrs. (T_D

Fig. 5. Update Cost (U_C) vs Time of day in Hrs. (T_D)

Fig. 6. Total cost (T_C) vs Time of day in Hrs. (T_D)

less than other schemes in most of the time of the day. Sometimes it is equal or marginally higher than the distance based scheme. But paging cost is significantly less with respect to all other schemes as the MSC can use predictive paging strategy. Therefore total cost is less in all situations. The scheme works well throughout the day especially in busy hours when call rate is high. It works well for all categories of users with a wide range of mobility patterns.

References

1. DasBit, S., Mitra, S.: Challenges of computing in mobile cellular environment—a survey, Elsevier Computer Communications 26 (2003) 2090–2105
2. Markoulidakis, J. G. et. at.: Mobility Modeling in Third-Generation Mobile Communications Systems, IEEE Personal Communications, p. 41-56, August 1997
3. Naor, Z., Levy, H.: Cell Identification Codes for Tracking Mobile Users, 0-7803-5417-6/99 IEEE 1999

4. Rose, C., Yates R.: minimizing the average cost of paging and registration: A timer-based method, WirelessNetworks, vol. 2, no. 2, p. 109-116, June 1996
5. Akyildiz, I.F., Ho, J.S.M.: Movement-based location update and selective paging for PCS Networks, IEEE/ACM Transactions on Networking, vol. 4, No. 4, p. 629-638, August '96
6. Abutaleb, A., Li, V.O.K.: Location update optimization in personal communication systems, Wireless Networks, vol. 3, no. 3, p. 205-216, 1997
7. Wan, G., Lin, E.: A Dynamic Paging Scheme for Wireless Communication Systems, Proceedings of the ACM/IEEE International Conference on Mobile Computing and Networking, MOBICOM 1997, p. 195-203
8. Lee, B.K., Hwang, C.S.: A Predictive Paging Scheme Based on the Movement Direction of a Mobile Host, IEEE Vehicular Technology Conference, VTC '99, p. 2158-62, 1999
9. Hwang, S-Hee, et. at.: An Adaptive Location Management Scheme Using The Velocity of Mobile Nodes, 0-7803-7700-1/03/ © 2003 IEEE
10. Wang, Z., Zhang, J.: A Speed-Adaptive Location Management Scheme, Proceedings of the Ninth International Conference on Parallel and Distributed Systems (ICPADS'02)1521-9097/02 © 2002 IEEE
11. Naor, Z.: Tracking Mobile Users with Uncertain Parameters, MobiCom 2000, Boston, MA, August 2000, pp. 110-119
12. Nandi, S., Manish, M., K.: An Efficient Implementation of Distance-based Update Scheme Using Directional Cell Identification Codes. International Workshop in Distributed Computing, IWDC 2004, ISI, Kolkata, India, (Accepted as poster paper)
13. Hellebrandt, M., et. al.: Estimating Position and Velocity of Mobiles in a Cellular Radio Network. IEEE Transactions on Vehicular Technology, Vol. 46, No.1, February 1997

Integrated Computation, Communication and Control: Towards Next Revolution in Information Technology

Feng Xia, Zhi Wang, and Youxian Sun

National Laboratory of Industrial Control Technology,
Institute of Modern Control Engineering
Zhejiang University, Hangzhou 310027, China
{fxia,wangzhi,yxsun}@iipc.zju.edu.cn

Abstract. There is a strong trend in modern industrial systems to integrate computation, communication, and control theories into networked control systems (NCSs). This is anticipated to be the next wave in the information technology revolution. From a control perspective, the interdisciplinary relationship between computation, communication and control is illustrated through control loop timing analysis of NCSs. Critical issues in the emerging field of integrated computation, communication and control (ICCC) are discussed. Since it is difficult to analytically quantify the impacts of computation and communication constraints on the quality of control (QoC), a simulation-based approach is proposed. A numerical example of networked DC motor control is utilized in simulations, with different scheduling schemes and communication protocols employed. Results and analysis give valuable suggests for improving the control performance of NCSs which feature the integration of control with computation and communication.

1 Introduction

With advances in the information technologies of communication, computation and control, a successful implementation of real-time control systems requires a good understanding of not only control theory but also computation and communication theories. It is witnessed [1,2] that the integration of these fields will provide new capabilities. For instance, integration of computation and communication has resulted in the Internet, which provides us the ability to exchange information in the form of email or to share useful resources.

From a control perspective, we observe the trends of integrating computation, communication and control in the field of information technology. Already today networked control systems (NCSs) play an important role in real-time control, and they have attracted much attention from both academia and industry. A networked control system [3,4] is an integration of sensors, controllers, actuators and communication network of certain local field and is used to provide data transmission between devices in order that users of different sites in this location can realize resource sharing and coordinating manipulation. The primary advantages of a networked control system include flexible design, simple and fast implementation, ease of diagnosis and maintenance, and increased agility. The change of communication architecture from point-to-point to common-bus, however, introduces different forms of communication time delay between sensors, actuators, and controllers. The characteristics of this time delay could be constant, bounded, or random, mainly depending on the different

G. Das and V.P. Gulati (Eds.): CIT 2004, LNCS 3356, pp. 117–125, 2004.

features of the employed communication protocol. Particularly, most NCSs are embedded systems that built upon embedded microprocessors. These systems are often subject to hard economic constraints, which in turn give rise to resource constraints on the computing platform level, e.g., limited CPU time and communication bandwidth. In reality this is true in spite of the fast development of computing hardware [5,6]. Furthermore, several tasks may exist in the same microprocessor. And hence, the CPU time constitutes a shared resource that the tasks compete for, just as the network bandwidth for interconnected nodes.

In the context of resource constraints, integrating communication, computation and control into networked control systems is anticipated to be the next phase of the information technology revolution. It is well-known in control systems that time delays can degrade a system's performance and even cause system unstable. In order to guarantee good Quality of Control (QoC), it is necessary to effectively deal with resource constraints using a more holistic approach. The success of this approach involves the confluence of control with computation and communication. The computation theory intended for attacking CPU time constraint covers different real-time scheduling schemes, such as Rate Monotonic (RM) and Earliest Deadline First (EDF) [7]. Different communication protocols including CAN (Controller Area Network) and Ethernet may render different impact on control performance [8].

In this paper, we examine the integration of control with computation and communication, in the context of NCSs and from a perspective of real-time control. Control loop timing analysis of NCS shows the underlying principle of interaction between real-time scheduling, communication protocols and QoC. Trends and issues in the emerging field of integrated computation, communication and control (ICCC) are discussed. Since it is difficult to analytically quantify the impacts of real-time scheduling schemes and network protocols on control performance, we follow a simulation-based approach [6] to analyze the QoC of NCSs with resource constraints. A numerical example of NCS with DC motor problem is utilized in our simulations, where different scheduling schemes and communication protocols are employed. Considering several scenarios with: 1) only computation constraint, 2) only communication constraint, and 3) both computation and communication constraints, we show the impacts of computation and communication constraints with different scheduling schemes and communication protocols on the QoC of NCS. Simulation results and analysis give valuable suggests for the design of NCS which features the integration of computation, communication and control.

The rest of this paper is structured as follows. Section 2 illustrates the interaction between scheduling, communication and real-time control in NCS through control loop timing analysis. Section 3 gives emerging issues in the field of integrated computation, communication and control. The simulation-based approach to analyze the impacts of computation and communication constraints on control performance is illustrated in Section 4. The QoCs based on different scheduling schemes and communication protocols are presented. This paper concludes with Section 5.

2   Integrating Computation, Communication and Control in NCS

In this section, we illustrate, from a control perspective, the interdisciplinary relationship between computation, communication and control through control loop timing analysis of a networked control system. Although typical characteristics of NCS timing problems involve both control delay and jitter, we only focus on control delay in this paper. The reasons for this include: 1) control delay is the primary aspect of NCS timing problems that affect control performance, and 2) the components of control delay can sufficiently explain the relationship between computation, communication and control.

In the control context, a networked control system is typically implemented by a set of computational devices (sensors, actuators, controllers, etc) that run one or several tasks, which communicate data across a field level communication network (fieldbus). Due to data transmissions and controller processing, the control delay of certain control loop includes not only the execution time of controller algorithm and the AD/DA conversion delays, but also the delays associated to the communication network. That is, the control delay [3,6,9] contains both computation delay and communication delay, and will then be:

$$\tau_k = \tau_{sc}^{\ k} + \tau_c^{\ k} + \tau_{ca}^{\ k} \tag{1}$$

where $\tau_c^{\ k}$ is the computation delay. $\tau_{sc}^{\ k}$ and $\tau_{ca}^{\ k}$ are sensor-to-controller delay and controller-to-actuator delay. In (1), the processing delay of sensor has been included into $\tau_{sc}^{\ k}$, while the processing delay of actuator into $\tau_{ca}^{\ k}$, since they are relatively constant and small.

In general, the variation of $\tau_c^{\ k}$ is not substantial compared to $\tau_{sc}^{\ k}$ and $\tau_{ca}^{\ k}$ if the controller is designed properly. Therefore, this delay is insignificant in many control techniques. However, in case of implementation upon embedded microprocessor with limited CPU time, the computation delay can be dramatically large. It is cannot still be neglected, and should be treated separately. When designing a networked control system, engineers must reduce this computation delay as much as possible, e.g., by employing certain real-time scheduling schemes in computation community, in order that the resulting QoC is improved. Thus the employed scheduling scheme greatly affects the magnitude of computation delay, which in turn impacts the QoC. In this sense, the integration of computation and control will come to effectively schedule the limited CPU time, in a manner of minimizing the computation delay.

The communication delay, i.e. $\tau_{sc}^{\ k}$ and $\tau_{ca}^{\ k}$, includes both the medium access and the message transmission delays. While the message transmission delay is approximately constant, the medium access delay is highly variable as it depends on network characteristics such as communication protocols and available bandwidth [3]. Several fieldbus protocols have been proposed for constructing NCSs, including CAN, Ethernet, and token bus like Profibus. These communication protocols hold different features such as MAC sublayer protocol, packet size, and typical data rate, etc. With a token bus, the variation of $\tau_{sc}^{\ k}$ and $\tau_{ca}^{\ k}$ can be periodic and deterministic. While in random access networks such as CAN and Ethernet, $\tau_{sc}^{\ k}$ and $\tau_{ca}^{\ k}$ become stochastic processes. That is, CAN and Ethernet may significantly affect the communication delay and the QoC can be impacted. When developing control systems over these protocols, this impact must be well understood.

3 Emerging Issues in ICCC

As mentioned above, this paper is intended to examine the integration of control with computation and communication from a control perspective. Since the primary objective of NCS design is to efficiently use the limited communication and computation capacity while maintaining good control performance, the timing analysis in Section 2 naturally leads to two research directions: 1) integrated control and real-time scheduling, and 2) integrated communication and control.

From a historical perspective, the control community and real-time scheduling community have normally been separated [5,10]. This separation has allowed the control community to focus on its own problem domain without worrying about how scheduling is being done, and it has released the scheduling community from the need to understand what impact scheduling has on the stability and performance of the plant under control. However the separated development of control and scheduling theories has led to a lack of mutual understanding between the fields. In order to effectively cope with computation constraints in NCSs, control and real-time issues should be discussed from the point of view of integration. In recent years, a number of research efforts have been devoted to control and scheduling codesign of real-time control systems. A state-of-the-art on this field can be found in [10].

In the field of integrated communication and control [11], the interaction of between control performance and real-time communication theory must be examined in order to effectively use the communication resources and minimize delays in the design process. A proper communication protocol is necessary to guarantee the network Quality of Service (QoS), whereas advanced controller design is desirable to guarantee the QoC. Because of the integral link between network and control in a NCS, it is important to consider network and control parameters simultaneously to assure both network QoS and QoC. Many works have been conducted on ways to minimize the influence of communication on the QoC of the NCS. For instance, the impact of network architecture on control performance in NCS was discussed in [8] and design considerations related to QoC and network QoS are provided.

Besides the above-mentioned two issues, a more challenging one is to improve control performance by the way of fully integrating computation and communication theories. In NCSs where the microprocessor holds high computing speed and large memory size while the communication bandwidth is limited, is it possible to trade computation for communication in order to minimize the effect of communication delay on system performance and enhance the utilization of computing resources? A feasible approach is to reduce communication by employing state estimators [12]. By using the estimated values instead of true value at every node, a significant savings in the required bandwidth is achieved. At the same time, the problem of how to trade increased communication demands for decreased computation when there is only computation constraint still lacks investigation. In order to develop effective methods for this issue, the interaction between computation and communication and their synthetic effect on control performance should be thoroughly identified.

Another important issue still missing is the accompanying theoretical confluence of computation, communication and control communities. With the integration of control with computation and communication involved in the technological development of NCS, there is a further convergence of theories [2] at a more integrated view of system theory. As far as we know, little work has been reported on this issue to date.

4 Simulation Based Analysis

4.1 Modeling Overview and Simulation Setup

In the NCS model (see Fig. 1) [13] employed for simulations, the time-driven sensor samples the process periodically and sends the samples to the controller over the network. Upon receiving a sample, the controller computes a control signal that is sent to the actuator, where it is subsequently actuated. The threads executing in the controller and actuator nodes are both event-driven. In order to obtain computation constraint, there is an interfering task that may execute in the controller node. A disturbance node with high priority is also introduced to generate communication constraint. The main reasons behind the choice of this model are that: 1) it is in existence in many fields as a typical networked control system, 2) the system components are enough to examine the impacts of computation and communication constraints on control performance, and 3) it can be easily complexified e.g. by extending it with more nodes or adding dependencies across control loops.

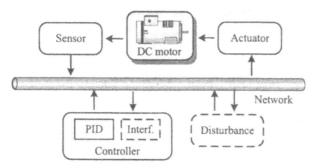

Fig. 1. The NCS setup employed for simulations

We consider networked PID control of a DC servo motor. The goal of the control is to make the servo position $y(t)$ follow the reference position $r(t)$ as closely as possible. Let the servo model be discribed by the transfer functions:

$$G(s) = \frac{980}{s^2 + 20s} \tag{2}$$

The employed PID controller is implemented [6,13] as follows.

$$P(t) = K_P(r(t) - y(t)),$$

$$I(t) = I(t - h) + \frac{K_P h}{T_I}(r(t) - y(t)),$$

$$D(t) = \frac{T_D}{Nh + T_D} D(t - h) + \frac{NK_P T_D}{Nh + T_D}(y(t - h) - y(t)), \tag{3}$$

$$u(t) = P(t) + I(t) + D(t).$$

The corresponding parameters are $K_P=0.9$, $T_I=0.1$, $T_D=0.007$ and $N=10$. A sampling period of $h=6$ms is chosen. Default network is assumed to be of CAN-type with a data rate of 500Kbps. All simulations are made using Matlab/Simulink based on the TrueTime toolbox [13].

4.2 QoC with Computation Constraint

In this subsection, we observe the impact of computation constraint on the system performance. The RM and EDF scheduling schemes are, respectively, utilized to schedule the CPU in the controller node, where an interfering task is introduced. Due to the competition from interfering task, the CPU time dedicated to execute the PID algorithm becomes limited. Let h_i be the sampling period of the interfering task. It is evident that the computation constraint will be more serious as h_i decreases. Therefore, we adjust the value of h_i to achieve different limitation on the CPU time for control.

With the RM scheduling scheme employed, the system responses are given in Fig.2, with different values for h_i. In scenarios holding that $h_i>4$ms, the control system performs pretty well, and the QoC is almost unaffected by the interfering task. Because the CPU time constraint is nonsignificant in these situations, the PID control task can be guaranteed schedulable. This is especially true when h_i is larger than the control period, since the control task will hold higher priority according to the principle of RM. With h_i increasing, the impact of computation constraint on QoC gradually becomes clear. The network control system becomes unstable when h_i is set to be 3.1ms, although the QoC is satisfactory when $h_i=3.2$ms. Similarly, Fig.3 shows the system performance when the EDF scheduling scheme is employed. Satisfactory control performance can be achieved given that $h_i>3.2$ms in the EDF context. The system still remains stable when $h_i=3.1$ms, and the output response is not bounded as h_i decreases to 3.0ms. Other than comparing the effectiveness of RM and EDF, we attempt to examine the impact of computation constraint on control system performance. As we can see from Fig.2 and 3, the QoC of networked control system can be dramatically affected by computation constraint in a way that this constraint may result in long computation delay, and different real-time scheduling schemes may result in different system performance even under the same constraint.

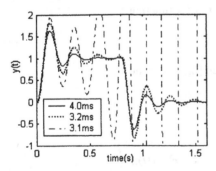
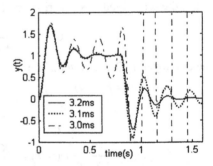

Fig. 2. System responses when CPU is scheduled by RM, with different h_i

Fig. 3. System responses when CPU is scheduled by EDF, with different h_i

4.3 QoC with Communication Constraint

In order to observe the impact of communication constraint on QoC, the interfering task inside the controller node is removed, getting rid of the effect of CPU constraint. Two popular communication protocols, namely CAN and Ethernet, are involved in this subsection. The bandwidths of CAN and Ethernet are set to be their typical data rates, i.e. 500K and 1M bps, respectively. Interfering traffic with highest-priority will be generated by the disturbance node, which periodically sends certain data (with 10 bytes for CAN and 46 bytes for Ethernet as default sizes) to itself via the network. The expected fraction of the network bandwidth occupied by this node can be specified to reflect the constraint of communication bandwidth. Let r_o denote the ratio (in percentage) of this fraction to the total network bandwidth. Hence the communication constraint will be more serious with bigger r_o value. Note that the value of r_o differs from the runtime bandwidth occupational ratio of the disturbance node, depending on the features of the underlying communication protocol. In the context of CAN bus, the r_o value may be used to represent the runtime bandwidth occupation of the interfering traffic. However, this is not the case for Ethernet. To comply with the MAC sublayer protocol of Ethernet, the disturbance node also needs to compete for communication bandwidth although it holds the highest priority. Therefore, the actual bandwidth occupational ratio of the interfering traffic must be lower than the value of r_o, when Ethernet is used.

Fig.4 presents the system performance with CAN as the communication protocol. Because the amount of data flow in the control loop is relatively small, the system shows satisfactory QoC even when the interfering traffic occupys up to 80% of the communication bandwidth. When the r_o value climbs to 90%, the system will become unstable, due to long communication delay caused by waiting for network access. In the context of Ethernet, we find that the QoC remains acceptable even when the r_o value is set to be 99.99%. This is mainly because the actual bandwidth occupational ratio of the interfering traffic is remarkably lower than the value of r_o, and the control loop always holds chances to access the Ethernet. In order to examine how different communication constraints impact QoC, we adjust the data size in the interfering traffic, while setting r_o=99%. As shown in Fig.5, the system performance almost remains unaffected with a data size smaller than 65 bytes. When the data size reaches 66 bytes, the system goes unstable. The reason behind this involves that the actual

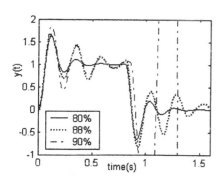

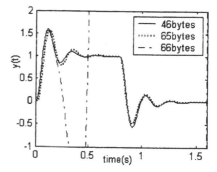

Fig. 4. System responses over CAN, with different r_o values

Fig. 5. System responses over Ethernet, with different interfering data sizes

bandwidth occupation of the interfering traffic is strongly enhanced with larger data size, thus increasing the communication delay in the control loop.

4.4 QoC with Computation and Communication Constraints

In this subsection, we focus on the integrated impact of CPU computation and network communication constraints on QoC. Both the interfering task and the disturbance node are introduced. The limited CPU is scheduled by EDF, and the network is of CAN-type. The values of h_i and r_o are selected as the basic factors that affect the resulting QoC, and will be adjusted to achieve different computation and communication constraints. The generally used performance criteria IAE [14] is employed to measure the QoC, which is given by

$$IAE = \sum_{k=0}^{K} |y(kh) - r(kh)| \times h \qquad (4)$$

where K is the final time of the evaluation period in discrete time.

In Fig.6, QoCs have been evaluated with IAE values for different h_i and r_o. As we can see, the control performance can be greatly affected by both computation and communication constraints. Serious constraints may cause the system unstable, which is represented with an infinite IAE value. When the impact of a certain constraint significantly outweighs another, there may exist approaches to improving QoC in the sense of reducing IAE. These approaches involve achieving a tradeoff between computation constraint and communication constraint through proper combination of advanced technologies from computation and communication communities.

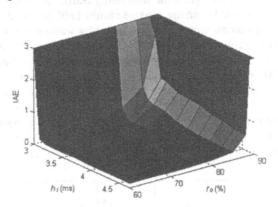

Fig. 6. IAE values as QoC, with different h_i and r_o

5 Conclusions

It is envisioned that the fields of communication, computation and control will converge. As can be seen from NCS, this convergence tends to provide new capabilities. In this paper, we observe the trends of integration of control with computation and communication, from a control perspective. Issues in this emerging field are discussed. The interaction between computation, communication and control is examined and analyzed, using a simulation-based approach. Some useful suggestions for improving the overall system performance are also described.

Due to the high complexity of the interdisciplinary relationship between computation, communication and control theories, many works require to be done. Our future efforts in this field will focus on design methodology for NCS, tradeoff between computation and communication constraints, and control-oriented scheduling schemes.

Acknowledgement

This work is supported by National Natural Science Foundation of China (NSFC 60084001, 60203030, 60304018), National Basic Research Program of China (2002CB312200) and Advance Research Program of France-China (PRA SI03-02).

References

1. Scott Graham and P. R. Kumar, "The Convergence of Control, Communication, and Computation", pp.458–475, Lecture Notes in Computer Science, Volume 2775, Springer-Verlag, Heidelberg, 2003
2. Scott Graham, Girish Baliga and P. R. Kumar, "Issues in the convergence of control with communication and computing: Proliferation, architecture, design, services, and middleware", to appear in *Proceedings of the 43rd IEEE Conference on Decision and Control*, Bahamas, Dec. 2004
3. Mo-Yuen Chow and Yodyium Tipsuwan. "Network-Based Control Systems: A Tutorial", in *Proc. of The 27th Annual Conf. of the IEEE Industrial Electronics Society*, 2001, 1594-1602
4. Linda G. Bushnell. "Networks and control" (Guest editorial), *IEEE Control System Magazine* (Special section), vol. 21, no.1, pp. 22-23, February 2001.
5. Karl-Erik Årzén, Anton Cervin, Dan Henriksson. "Resource-Constrained Embedded Control Systems: Possibilities and Research Issues", in *Proc. of CERTS'03 – Co-design of Embedded Real-Time Systems Workshop*, Porto, Portugal, July 2003.
6. Feng Xia, Zhi Wang, and Youxian Sun. "Simulation Based Performance Analysis of Networked Control Systems with Resource Constraints", to appear in *Proc. of the 30th Annual Conference of the IEEE Industrial Electronics Society*, Busan, Korea, Nov. 2004
7. C. Liu and J. Layland. "Scheduling Algorithms for Multiprogramming in a Hard Real-Time Environment", *J.ACM*, 20, 46-61. 1973
8. Feng-Li Lian, "Analysis, Design, Modeling, and Control of Networked Control Systems," Ph.D. dissertation, University of Michigan, 2001.
9. B. Wittenmark, J. Nilsson, and M. Torngren. "Timing problems in real-time control systems". In *Proceedings of American Control Conference*, pp: 2000-2004, 1995.
10. K-E. Årzen, et al. "Integrated Control and Scheduling". Research report ISSN 0820-5316. Dept. Automatic Control, Lund Institute of Technology, 1999
11. Y. Halevi and A. Ray, "Integrated communication and control systems: Part I – Analysis," *J. Dynamic Syst., Measure. Contr.*, vol. 110, pp. 367-373, Dec. 1988.
12. J. K. Yook, D. M. Tilbury, and N. R. Soparkar. "Trading Computation for Bandwidth: Reducing Communication in Distributed Control Systems Using State Estimators", *IEEE Trans. on control systems technology*, Vol.10, No. 4, July 2002, 503-518
13. Anton Cervin, et al. "How Does Control Timing Affect Performance?", *IEEE Control Systems Magazine*, 23:3, pp. 16–30, June 2003
14. Feng Xia, Zhi Wang and Youxian Sun. "Design and Evaluation of Event-driven Networked Real-time Control Systems with IEC Function Blocks", to appear in *Proc. of IEEE International Conf. on Systems, Man and Cybernetics*, Hague, Netherlands, Oct. 2004

Designing Mobile Distributed Virtual Memory System

Susmit Bagchi

Department of Computer and Information Science
Norwegian University of Science and Technology
Trondheim, Norway
susmit@idi.ntnu.no

Abstract. Due to the enhancement of wireless communication bandwidth, reliability and services offered by WWW, the high-end mobile applications are becoming reality. However, the operating systems supporting mobile devices and the stationary servers are not completely capable to handle the challenges of mobile computing paradigm. The battery-powered mobile devices are constrained in computational resources. The novel concept of mobile distributed virtual memory (MDVM) extends the server CPU and memory resources to the mobile clients over the mobile communication interface in order to support resource-demanding high-end mobile applications. This paper describes the design architecture of various components of MDVM system.

Keywords: Mobile computing, Operating Systems, Distributed Computing.

1 Introduction

Although the realization of high-end mobile applications such as, m-commerce, SES [6] and virtual organization [7] are becoming promising, the mobile computing paradigm is restricted by the battery power and hardware resource limitation of mobile devices [11] and the limitation of wireless communication bandwidth along with reliability [10]. Because of these restrictions, mobile computers limit the nature of user applications [2][10]. The existing operating systems supporting mobile devices and the stationary servers offer very little support to the mobile computation paradigm [1][3]. The trends in future technological advancements indicate that the wireless communication bandwidth and reliability will be enhanced [6]. Researchers argue that the resource-thin mobile computers should utilize remote server based resources in order to support mobile applications [4][5] and an example is the remote memory architecture [8]. The concept of mobile distributed virtual memory (MDVM) enables the mobile clients exploiting server resources using mobile communication network [13]. The MDVM system allows mobile clients to utilize server CPU and memory for the data cache and process execution purposes [13]. The prior works on remote paging to realize distributed virtual memory (DVM) aim to utilize the high-speed network for paging rather than the local disk space assuming static network topology. Such assumptions are not applicable to MDVM system. Unlike the monolithic kernel-based MDVM system, the DVM system designs base on the user-space pager server of microkernel architecture. Researchers have focused on modifying the kernel of operating system to handle the challenges of mobile computing in an efficient manner [12]. The MDVM design considers the monolithic kernel of a general-purpose operating system. The monolithic kernel architecture offers enhanced performance as com-

G. Das and V.P. Gulati (Eds.): CIT 2004, LNCS 3356, pp. 126–136, 2004.

pared to the microkernel by reducing context switch frequency, TLB misses and instruction count [15]. This paper presents the design of MDVM system components considering Linux kernel 2.4.22. The paper is organized as followings. Section 2 describes the MDVM system concept. Section 3 presents the design components of the MDVM system. Section 4 and 5 state the background work and conclusion respectively.

2   Concept of MDVM System

The MDVM design concept extends the CPU resource and memory resource of servers to the mobile clients using wireless communication network interface [13]. The mobile clients can use server memory and CPU resources to achieve the functionalities such as, **memory space for large data cache, virtual memory space** and **CPU for processes execution** [13]. The conceptual view of the MDVM design architecture is illustrated in Figure 1. From the view of mobile client, MDVM is the remote virtual memory space accessible from anywhere in the mobile communication network and such memory can migrate from cell to cell in order to save communication bandwidth, time and cost.

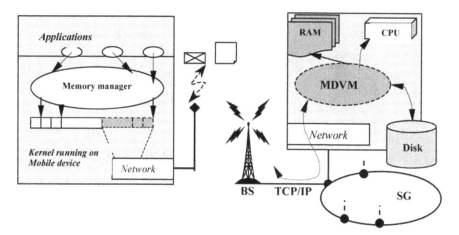

Fig. 1. MDVM Interacting with Other Resources in Kernel and Mobile Client

3   MDVM System Design

In each cell of mobile communication system, a group of servers will be offering resources to the mobile clients in the cell. The servers in the cells are connected by TCP/IP wired network and form server-group (SG). The MDVM is a software system residing within the monolithic kernel and involves no special hardware. Placement of MDVM subsystem in the monolithic kernel is shown in Figure 2. The mobile clients may need small amount of data access such as a byte or they may need to access larger chunk of data such as multiple pages. This requires MDVM system having capability of byte addressing and page addressing. A byte is considered as 8bit data and the memory page size is typically considered as 4KB. The MDVM system servers consider the page size of 4KB because the maximum transmission unit (MTU) of the packets over TCP/IP Ethernet link is in the order of 1.5KB. The larger the page size, the more are the fragmentation and joining of packets at source and destination respectively. This will lead to the increased network traffic, bandwidth saturation and computation overhead at source and destination. The MDVM system architecture is composed of two subsystems namely MDVM-Server (MS) and MDVM-Stub (MC) as illustrated in Figure 3.

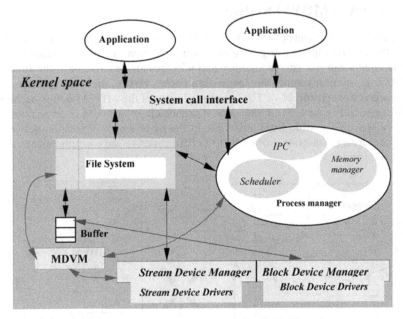

Fig. 2. MDVM System within a Monolithic Kernel

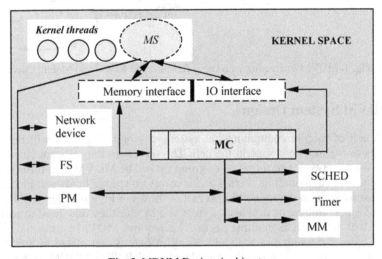

Fig. 3. MDVM Design Architecture

The required functions performed by MDVM system can be broadly classified as: **1. Server operations:** The server operations are comprised of networking activities, accepting and serving the requests from mobile clients, cache swapping and cache replication; **2. Stub operations:** The set of stub operations includes estimation of resource-load, memory allocation, memory management and providing system services. The job of MS is to handle the server operations and the job of the MC is to handle the relatively lower level stub operations. The MC subsystem is the entry point of MDVM system. Once MC is loaded into the kernel, it launches the MS subsystem as another component. The MS and MC both execute in the kernel address space. There exist two interfaces between MC and MS namely **IO interface** and **Memory interface**. The IO interface is used to realize packet based command-reply operations between MS and MC. The memory interface is used to perform memory management related operations. The server operations of MS subsystem require it to interact with network device, process manager and the local file system. The network device interface is needed in order to perform the activities requiring network communication interface. The examples of such functions are to form server group, cache replication, memory migration and to communicate to the mobile clients. The file system (FS) interface is utilized by the MS subsystem in order to perform cache page swapping on the local disk space based on the state of mobile clients and page access patterns. The interface to the process manager (PM) is required to start a process as requested by the mobile clients. The set of kernel subsystems utilized by MC is comprised of memory manager (MM), timer (Timer), scheduler (SCHED) and the PM. The interface to the virtual memory manager of the kernel is required because MC subsystem needs to estimate and manage the page frames in order to support the memory requests from MS. The memory management operations performed by MC include memory-load estimation, page allocation/ de-allocation, page locking and page fault handling. The MC subsystem utilizes timer interface in order to estimate the memory-load of the system periodically and to decide about further allocation of memory to the mobile clients. The process manager and scheduler interfaces are required in order to support the low-level process execution monitoring and controlling activities.

3.1 Components of MDVM-Server

The set of jobs performed by MS subsystem consists of: *1. Accepting requests from mobile clients; 2. Allocating virtual memory address space for the data cache of the mobile client; 3. Start a process execution if requested by the mobile clients; 4. Manage the cache page swapping in order to reduce memory-load and to enhance memory utilization in the system; 5. Replicate the cache pages on remote disk as a fault tolerance mechanism; 6. Ring membership management and participating in other activities in the ring, for example, leader election, sending status update to the leader and performing memory-migration between the two MDVM servers residing in two different SGs etc.* Based on these activities, the internal components of MS subsystem can be subdivided as: *1. Memory manager block of MS subsystem; 2. Process executor block of MS subsystem; 3. Communicator block of MS subsystem; 4. Command IO processor block of MS subsystem.* The internal organization of MS subsystem is illustrated in Figure 4. The jobs of the memory manager of MS are to allocate cache memory to the mobile clients, maintaining cache replication, migration and to use swapping actions in order to free virtual address spaces occupied by inactive mobile clients and migrated pages. The virtual memory (VM) allocator of memory manager uses the memory interface offered by MDVM-Stub (MC). The VM allocator of memory manager of MS subsystem allocates an empty virtual address space for every mobile client on the reception of a request for the data cache. Later, the memory interface is used to map the page frames allocated by MC subsystem.

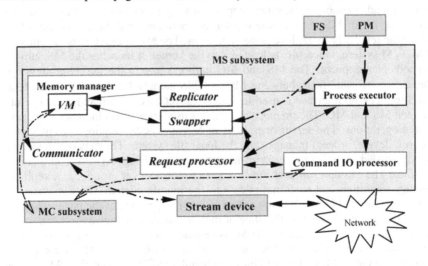

Fig. 4. Internal Components of MS Subsystem

The MC subsystem measures the memory-load on the MDVM-Server periodically and decides whether to allocate page frames further or not. In order to improve the performance such as response time, the page frames are locked into the main memory by MC subsystem. However, a mobile client may get disconnected from network for long time, may migrate to another cell or may go to doze mode. The cache pages allocated to such mobile clients need to be swapped to local disk to free the memory not used at present time by the inactive mobile clients. The MS component employs a cache swapper to perform such job. The swap files maintained by MS subsystem are different from normal swap space maintained by virtual memory manager of the kernel. This is because the lifetime of a swap space is dependent on the continuity of activity of the server without any shutdown or crash. On the face of normal or abnormal shutdown, the data in swap area becomes stale. But, the swap files maintained by MS need not to become completely stale as it contains the valid data cache for mobile clients. The replicator of the memory manager of MS subsystem uses the communicator block of MS to send cache pages to the leader of the SG and to implement memory migration. The replicator block takes the page frames mapped in the virtual address space allocated to the mobile clients and sends them to the leader of SG to store on the disk. This is a measure against the server crash and to improve the data cache availability to the mobile clients. The replicator maintains the cache consistency by periodically updating the replicated remote pages or by updating remote pages on every event of the change in data cache. The design choice for consistency model depends on the policy employed for the data consistency management. The replicator of MS subsystem can send the pages to another MDVM server residing in another SG as a mechanism for memory migration. The operation of memory migration is functionally similar to replication. However, the differences are that the memory migration is a receiver-initiated process and the receiver MDVM server resides in another SG. It is the job of the receiver MDVM server to decide upon time-to-migrate-pages based on the pattern and the frequency of mobility of a client. The communicator block of the architecture of MS is responsible for handling all kinds of network communication. The communicator operates on the TCP/IP protocol stack. The size of the messages may vary from a few bytes to a page size of 4KB. The process executor block of MS subsystem handles the jobs related to the starting of processes, handling the state of the execution of processes and to store the result of the execution of processes submitted by the mobile clients. The process executor collaborates with memory manager of MS subsystem in order to maintain the client-wise information related to the data cache and the requested processes. This is needed when the data cache migrates from one SG to another SG due to the mobility of clients. The process executor and the memory managers of MS subsystem maintain the logical integrity between the data cache and process execution space allocated to a mobile client.

3.2 Components of MDVM-Stub

The second component of MDVM system architecture is the MDVM-Stub (MC). The jobs performed by MC subsystem include: *1. Resource estimation and allocation; 2. Memory management; 3. Command processing and system services.* The components of MC subsystem are illustrated in Figure 5.

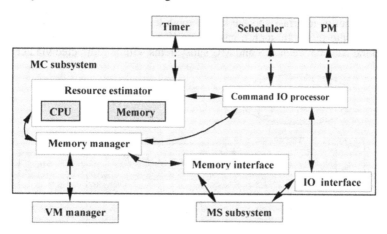

Fig. 5. Internal Components of MC Subsystem

The data cache allocation for mobile clients is done in the physical memory. The MC subsystem locks the page frames in RAM while allocating the data cache for mobile clients in order to avoid cache page swap made by virtual memory manager of the kernel. The execution space is resident in the virtual address space of the system and is controlled by the virtual memory manager of the kernel. However, because of the page locking, the memory-pressure on the kernel changes over time. The MC subsystem uses the resource estimator to periodically estimate the total available memory resource in the system to avoid steep increase of memory-load leading to thrashing. Accordingly, the CPU-load estimation is equally important, otherwise too much multiprocessing would lead to thrashing. The job of the command IO processor involves the processing of commands sent by MS subsystem and returning the results or sending commands to MS subsystem. The functions of the memory manager block of MC subsystem are to allocate/de-allocate/lock the page frames and to allow MS subsystem to utilize the allocated page frames for the data cache of mobile clients. The memory manager block uses the memory-load information supplied by resource estimator before performing frame allocation. In order to allocate/ de-allocate page frames to MS subsystem, the memory interface is used by the memory manager of MC. The functions of command IO processor of MC subsystem are to process the commands sent by MS subsystem and to send a command to MS subsystem. The command-reply communication uses the packet based IO and uses IO interface between MS and MC subsystems. The scheduler and process manager interfaces and the kernel data structures are used by MC subsystem in order to collect process-wise resource consumption data, state of execution and to control the process execution by manipulating the scheduling parameters.

3.3 MDVM System Interfaces

The interfaces in between MC and MS subsystems are named as command IO interface (CII) and memory interface (MMI). The Linux operating system is chosen to experimentally build up the MDVM system because it is the open source monolithic kernel. In order to support CII and MMI in the kernel, a distinct mechanism is required supporting the existing kernel architecture. The kernels of the operating systems offer a set of interfaces to the kernel modules, which can be exploited to design the MDVM interfaces. In such a case, the CII and MMI of MDVM system will be split and the calls between MS and MC subsystems will be redirected via kernel.

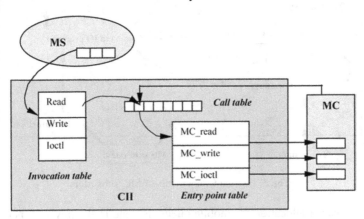

Fig. 6. The Command IO Interface

3.3.1 Command IO Interface

The command IO interface (CII) is designed to carry out command packet based IO between MS and MC subsystem. The CII design architecture is shown in Figure 6. The MS subsystem maintains a command invocation table in order to invoke a command by passing the command packet containing the command, the parameters and buffer space to hold the result. The set of main operations includes Read, Write and IO_Control. The Read operation executed by MS subsystem will read the command execution result from MC subsystem or it will get a command from MC to execute. Similarly, the Write operation will write a command to MC subsystem by MS subsystem or will output the result of a command executed by MS. The design of MS is such that, being a continuously running kernel thread, it will periodically poll the MC subsystem by Read operation to get any command from MC. The MS can send a command to MC subsystem any time through the Write operation. Linux kernel maintains a call-table holding the map to the actual function table containing the method entry points. Hence, when MS subsystem will invoke any method, the kernel of the operating system will redirect it to the appropriate entry point. The method entry points are registered by MC subsystem in the kernel call-table in the beginning. As the MC subsystem is the starting point of MDVM system, the MC component registers the method entry points with the kernel to allow it to redirect the calls from MS.

3.3.2 Memory Management Interface

The memory management interface (MMI) between MC and MS subsystems is used to handle the paged virtual memory for the data cache allocation to the mobile clients. The MC subsystem registers the page fault handling routine into the kernel in order to handle page faults made by kernel thread MS. Initially, an empty virtual address space is allocated by MS subsystem for the data cache of mobile clients. Kernel invokes the page fault handler of MC when MS incurs page faults. In response, the MC subsystem maps a set of page frames within the virtual address space allocated by MS for a mobile client. The MMI design architecture is illustrated in Figure 7. Similarly, when MS subsystem releases a virtual address space, the MC subsystem consequently deallocates the page frames mapped in the corresponding virtual address space by using MMI. On doing such un-mapping, the MC subsystem may or may not release the allocated page frames to the kernel based on the memory-load on the system. If the memory-load on the system is not high, the allocated pages remain locked in RAM for future use. Otherwise, if the memory-load on the server is high then the page frames are unlocked and released immediately.

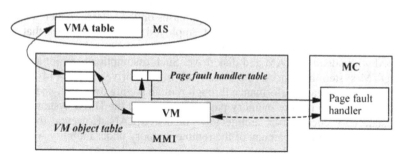

Fig. 7. The Memory Management Interface

3.3.3 Command Packet Structure

The command based IO between MC and MS employs a command packet based interface. All the commands and the results of the execution of a command are packed in the command packet structure (CPS). The design architecture of command packet structure is illustrated in Figure 8a and the reply packet structure (RPS) is illustrated in Figure 8b. The CPS structure contains a numeric number telling the job queue number (JQN), the command to execute (CMD), Param_Offset value indicating the offset in the packet from the beginning where the parameter values start in the buffer and the Param_Length indicating the total length of the buffer containing the parameters. Likewise, the RPS containing the result of the execution of a command stores the result in the buffer and adjusts the Result_Buffer_Length and Result_Offset parameters accordingly. The CII is used between MS and MC subsystems to send and receive the CPS and RPS. The data copy between the two memory areas containing CPS and RPS does not incur heavy penalty in terms of performance because MS and MC subsystems reside in the kernel address space. There is no need to copy the memory area between the user space and the kernel space.

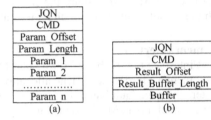

Fig. 8. The Command Packet and Reply Packet Structures

4 Related Work

Prior works have addressed the issues in operating system related to mobility in the area of file systems [16-18], data management [19][11][20][21] and network-layer routing protocols addressing schemes and packet filtering [22-24]. Other works include issues related to caching and file system [16][18][25][26] and mobile communication system [27-29]. The existing DVM system [30] does not provide an easy way to dynamically use and share DVM resources preserving transparency, adaptability and extensibility. The DVM system becomes non-scalable under the condition of mobility of clients. The DVM system design bases on the external pager-server in the microkernel. The remote paging concept employed in DVM assumes that network bandwidth is high and network topology is static and both the clients/servers are equipped with adequate RAM and disk drive. Such assumptions are not applicable in the MDVM system design. As the bandwidth of disk drives is low [14], the aim of DVM system is to gain performance through remote paging over high-speed network. The majority of the remote memory paging system and the DVM system [30] target to the stationary client-server architectures on wired LAN. However, the issues related to the location transparency of the remote memory under mobility, virtual memory management under dynamic memory-pressure and virtual memory migration among servers are not investigated. The concept of MDVM extending the server resources to the mobile clients did not get much attention. It is important to make operating system kernel "mobility aware" to tackle challenges of mobile computing.

5 Conclusions

The MDVM system is intended to meet the resource constraints of the mobile devices by extending server resources to the mobile clients over wireless communication network. This paper describes the design architecture and components of the MDVM system. The designing of MDVM in monolithic kernel will provide user transparency, performance, greater control on system resources and required system services. The required subsystems of a monolithic kernel in order to design MDVM as a software module are outlined. The Linux operating system is chosen for building experimental prototype of MDVM system because it is a monolithic kernel, free source and comparable to other commercial operating systems in terms of efficiency.

References

1. Black A., Inouye J., System Support for Mobility, ACM SIGOPS, Ireland, 1996.
2. Duchamp D., Issues in Wireless Mobile Computing, 3rd Workshop on Workstation OS, 1992.
3. Bolosky W. et. al., OS Direction for the Next Millennium, Microsoft Research, Redmond.
4. Forman G., Zahorjan J., The Challenges of Mobile Computing, UW CSE TR#93-11-03, 1994.
5. Marsh B. et. al., Systems Issues in Mobile Computing, MITL-TR-50-93, Princeton, 1993.
6. Nadia M., Kin Y., Designing Wireless Enterprise Applications on Mobile Devices, ICITA 2002.
7. MOWAHS, IDI, NTNU, 2003, www.mowahs.com.
8. Shigemori Y. et. al., A proposal of a Memory Management Architecture for Mobile Computing Environment, IEEE DEXA, 2000.
9. Weiser M., Some Computer Issues in Ubiquitous Computing, ACM Communications, 1993.
10. Pitoura E. et. al., Dealing with Mobility: Issues and Research Challenges, TR-CSD-93-070, 1993.
11. Badrinath R. et. al., Impact of Mobility on Distributed Computations, ACM OS Review, 1993.
12. Bender M. et. al., Unix for Nomads: Making Unix Support Mobile Computing, USENIX, Mobile & Location-Independent Computing Symposium, 1993.
13. Susmit B., Mads N., On the Concept of Mobile Distributed Virtual Memory System, IEEE DSN, International Conference on Dependable Systems and Networks, Italy, 2004.
14. Schilit B., Duchamp D., Adaptive Remote Paging for Mobile Computers, TR-CUCS-004-91, Columbia University, February 1991.
15. Chen B., The Impact of Software Structure and Policy on CPU and Memory System Performance, PhD Thesis, CMU-CS-94-145, 1994.
16. Tait D. et. al., Detection and Exploitation of File Working Sets, TR-CUCS-050-90, Columbia, 1990.
17. Kistler J., Satyanarayanan M., Disconnected Operation in the Coda File System, ACM Transactions on Computer Systems, February, 1992.
18. Tait D. et. al., Service Interface and Replica Management Algorithm for Mobile File System Clients, 1st International Conference on Parallel and Distributed Information Systems, 1991.
19. Badrinath R., Tomasz I., Replication and Mobility, In Proc. Of 2nd IEEE Workshop on Management of Replicated Data, November 1992, pp. 9-12.
20. Alonso R., Korth H., Database System Issues in Nomadic Computing, MITL, December 1992.
21. Tomasz I., Badrinath R., Querying in Highly Mobile Distributed Environments, In 8th International Conference on Very Large Databases, 1992, pp. 41-52.
22. Ioannidis J., Duchamp D., Maguire G., IP-Based Protocols for Mobile Internetworking, ACM SIGCOMM, September 1991, pp. 235-245.

23. Wada H. et. al., Mobile Computing Environment Based on Internet Packet Forwarding, In Winter USENIX, January, 1993.
24. Zenel B., Duchamp D., Intelligent Communication Filtering for Limited Bandwidth Environments, IEEE 5th Workshop on HotOS-V, May 1995.
25. Mummert L. et. al., Variable Granularity Cache Coherence, Operating Systems Review, 28(1), 1994, pp. 55-60.
26. Mummert L., Exploiting Weak Connectivity in a Distributed File System, PhD Thesis, 1996.
27. Lin C., An Architecture for a Campus-Sized Wireless Mobile Network, PhD Thesis, 1996.
28. Lee J., Routing and Multicasting Strategies in Wireless Mobile Ad Hoc Network, PhD thesis, 2000.
29. Akyol B., An Architecture for a Future Wireless ATM Network, PhD Thesis, June 1997.
30. Khalidi Y. et. al., The Spring Virtual Memory System, Sun Microsystem Lab., TR-SMLI-93-9, February 1993.

Efficient Grid Location Update Scheme for Mobile Ad Hoc Networks

Khaled Ahmed Abood Omer and D.K. Lobiyal

School of Computer and Systems Sciences, Jawaharlal Nehru University,
New Delhi 110067, India
kaa0301@students.jnu.ac.in, dkl@mail.jnu.ac.in

Abstract. Location update schemes are vital for the success of position-based routing in mobile ad hoc networks. However, efficient location update schemes have been focus of research for scalability of ad hoc networks. Therefore, researchers have proposed various location update schemes. Grid Location Service has been one of the commonly referred location update scheme in the literature. In this paper, we propose an efficient grid location update scheme that outperforms the Grid Location Service scheme. We use the concept of Rings of squares for location updates and selective query mechanism for destination query. The simulation results show that our proposed grid location update scheme has better percentage of successful queries with smaller location update cost for updating the location servers. Our proposed location update scheme also performs location updates faster than the GLS scheme.

Keywords: Location update, Grid Location Service, Rings, Selective Query, New Grid scheme.

1 Introduction

Mobile Ad Hoc networks (MANET) are a set of autonomous wireless mobile nodes that do not require a pre-established infrastructure. Each node in the network acts both as a router and an end system. These nodes cooperate with each other to forward message without specific user administration or configuration. Various routing algorithms have been proposed for MANET to take care of the challenges posed for message forwarding due to frequent changes in topology. Many of these routing algorithms use information about the physical location (position) of the participating nodes [4, 7]. These algorithms are known as Position based routing algorithms.

Position based routing algorithms assume that each node knows its physical location using Global Positioning System (GPS) [5]. A node in the network maintains database of location information of other nodes. Such a node is referred to as location database server. Efficient location update schemes [6] are needed for maintaining up to date information in the location servers. These schemes should replicate location information to minimize database servers' failures and network partitioning [1]. Location update schemes should distribute location information inside the network in a dynamic, scalable, secure and fair way. Distribution of

G. Das and V.P. Gulati (Eds.): CIT 2004, LNCS 3356, pp. 137–146, 2004.

location information should also involve minimum communication overheads in updating and retrieving of the information.

In this paper, we have proposed a new Grid Location Update scheme. Further, we have conducted experiments for Grid Location Service and compared its performance with our proposed scheme for a common network scenario.

Next section describes previous research work done in the area of location update schemes. In section 3, details of proposed new grid location update scheme are explained. Section 4 discusses, the metrics used for performance evaluation with their significance. The simulation environment and experimentation details are given in section 5. Results of the research are discussed and presented in section 6. The last section concludes the work with its findings.

2   Previous Work

In the literature, Home agent, Quorum based, Grid Location Service, and Doubling Circles [6] are the four most referred location update schemes. In this section we give overview of Grid location Service update scheme.

Li, Jannotti, De Couto, Karger, and Morris described a new distributed location database service called Grid Location Service (GLS) [2]. In this scheme, they divide the network area into a hierarchy of squares. In this hierarchy, n-order squares contain exactly four (n-1)-order squares. Each node maintains a location database of all other nodes within the local first-order square. Therefore, each node periodically broadcasts its location information within the local first-order square to update the location database. For other order squares, each node selects a small set of nodes as its location database servers with ID's closest and greater than the ID of the node. A node transmits its current location information using geographic forwarding algorithm to update location servers in all order squares.

A node sends its new location information to the location servers in different order squares based on the criteria mentioned above. A node can direct a location query to a node with the ID nearest to the ID of the destination node in its local order square. If this query fails, the node continues the search until the highest order squares are queried.

A node updates its order-i servers after each node movement of a distance $2^{i-2}d$. For example, a node updates its order-2 location servers every time it moves a particular threshold distance d since last update.

3   Proposed Grid Location Update Scheme

In GLS scheme, location updates are performed on location servers distributed from first- order square to n^{th} order square. Updating and querying location information to/from Location servers in higher order squares involve more delay. This delay in high mobile network may adversely affect the network in maintaining up to date location information and in term of consumption of battery power. Further, the stringent condition used for selecting a location server (i.e.

the server must have an ID least and greater than the ID of the node) results in more update failures. This is due to the non-availability of location servers since at times the condition for selecting a server may not be satisfied for few nodes. Also in GLS scheme, queries involve high flooding when the search is performed in higher order squares since there is large zone with more number of nodes to be examined. When the search is performed in the highest order square, entire network gets flooded. This can be considered as one of major drawback of GLS. Therefore, we proposed a new grid scheme to overcome the drawbacks of GLS scheme.

Our proposed new Grid location update scheme is a distributed location update scheme. In this scheme, we assume that the network area is partitioned into squares of same size. We introduce the concept of Rings from cellular networks. As shown in figure 1, rings of squares surround each square. The innermost ring consists of one square only referred as Center Square or Ring 0. Ring 0 is surrounded immediately by Ring 1, Ring 1 is in turn surrounded immediately by Ring 2, and so on.

A node with its new location information updates its location servers as follows. A square that a node visits currently is considered as Ring 0. Therefore, this node updates all the nodes in Ring 0. In Ring 1, only one location server per square is updated, i.e. there are 8 locations servers in Ring 1. In Ring 2, only 4 location servers are updated, such as one server in one square in south direction, another server in a square in north direction, another server in a square in east direction, and one server in west direction. Similarly, in the Ring 3, and 4 updates are performed in the same manner as in Ring 2. This is shown in figure 1.

In this scheme, we have used distance based triggering strategy for initiating an update [1]. In this strategy, a moving node triggers a location update when a threshold distance is traveled. In our scheme, the distance moved is measured in terms of number of Rings. Therefore, a moving node triggers an update when it crosses the boundary of any ring. When a moving node crosses the boundary of a Ring i, only location servers in rings 0, 1,..., i are updated, for example if Ring 4 is crossed, then location servers in rings 0, 1, 2, 3, and 4 are updated.

We use selective query for a destination node. A query for a destination node is forwarded from the source to location servers located within the same square where source node is located or Ring 0 for the source. In case a query fails, the source forwards the search to location servers in Ring 2. This process continues until the servers in Ring n (n=4 in our case) have been queried.

4   Performance Metrics

Several update scheme independent metrics are proposed for analyzing the performance of location update schemes. We use the following quantitative metrics for performance evaluation of network simulated in our experiments. Percentage of successful updates is defined as the number of successful updates divided by the total attempts of updates. It shows the ability of an update scheme to provide up to date location information to be used for efficient routing. An update scheme with higher percentage of successful updates provides most recent loca-

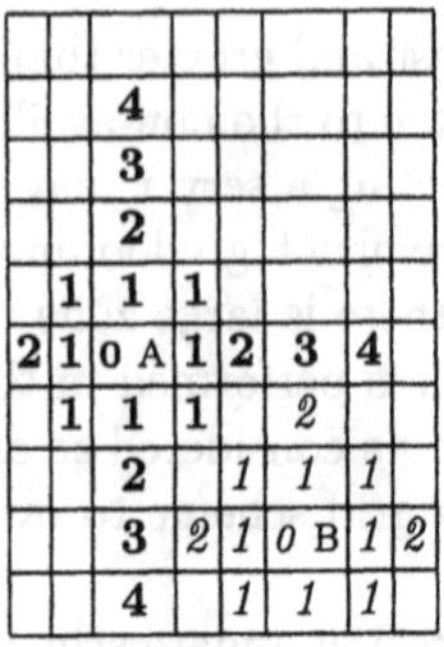

	4						
	3						
	2						
1	**1**	**1**					
2	**1**	**0** A	**1**	**2**	**3**	**4**	
1	**1**	**1**		*2*			
	2		*1*	*1*	*1*		
	3	*2*	*1*	*0* B	*1*	*2*	
	4		*1*	*1*	*1*		

Fig. 1. shows the structure of rings for New Grid scheme. Node A updates its new location servers' in rings 0, 1, 2, 3, and 4 (in bold) after crossing the boundaries of Ring 4 of its old position. Node B queries for node A in the Rings 0, 1,2 or 3 (in italic).

tion information of the nodes. Location update cost is defined as the number of update messages that participates in originating and forwarding successful updates per node per clock tick. A scheme having lower location update cost efficiently uses the scarce resources of the network such as battery power, bandwidth, etc. Destination query cost is defined as the number of messages that participates in originating and forwarding successful queries per node per clock tick. A scheme having lower destination query cost efficiently uses the scarce resources of the network such as battery power, bandwidth, etc. Average hop count is defined as the total number of hop count divided by successful updates. It is approximately the time needed to update the location servers, and signifies the end-to-end delay involved for a given successful update. A network with lower average hop count may transmit the location update messages faster. Percentage of successful queries is defined as the number of successful queries divided by total attempts of queries. It shows the ability of a scheme to reach a destination successfully. An update scheme with higher percentage of successful queries is considered as an efficient update scheme.

5   Simulation and Experiments

We have developed our own programs in C++ programming language to simulate the proposed work using discrete event simulation technique. Both the location update schemes are implemented according to the scheme descriptions given in section 2 and section 3.

5.1   Simulation

In our simulation, a random unit graph is used to represent the network, such that each node has equal transmission range R. For each graph, n nodes are randomly distributed in the deployment region (square region), such that all nodes are allowed to move only within this deployment region. Therefore, n nodes select their x and y coordinates at random from a given interval [a, b]. The number of nodes distributed per unit area is constant. Here nodes are uniformly distributed keeping the density constant. Transmission range of a node is also considered constant.

Each node moves using a random waypoint mobility model [2]. A node selects a random destination as its new position. Then this node moves at a constant speed from its old position to the new position along the line joining these positions. When the node reaches the destination, it selects a new destination and starts moving toward it immediately. In the simulations we consider zero pause time for each node.

The Geographic Distance Routing (GEDIR) is a greedy algorithm [8], has been used for forwarding update message and destination search messages. Both the schemes use GEDIR for searching and updating the location servers.

As in [3], no link layer details are modeled here. We assume that links are collision and contention free and all transmitted messages are correctly received. Thus each node is assumed to have an infinite-buffer and use store-and-forward queuing technique.

5.2   Experiments

GLS scheme has considered the length of the first order square side equal to the transmission range (i.e. 250 meters). The threshold value of distance for GLS triggering update is set 200 meters for the second order square, 400 meters for the third order square. Thus for each order we are doubling the distance of previous threshold value.

In our proposed new grid scheme, we have also considered all squares in the rings have their side equal to the transmission range (i.e. 250 meters). Where as the threshold value of distance for triggering update is determined in terms of rings.

As described in simulation, the mobility model considered for movement of the nodes is random waypoint model with zero pause time. We have fixed the speed of nodes to 10 meters per second (simulation clock tick). An experiment is conducted for 1200 seconds and it is repeated for 20 runs.

We have chosen the implementation parameters same as those used in GLS scheme [2]. The density of 0.0001 nodes per square kilometer, and the transmission range of 250 meters are used for experimentation. The number of nodes n in the network is varying as 100, 200, 300, 400, 500, and 600 nodes.

For the query phase, we examined 500 source-destination pairs selected randomly, where each pair takes one second to perform the query. We start the first queries after 500 seconds have passed to allow the network to be stable.

6   Results and Discussions

In this section, the results of the experiments measured in terms of the performance metrics discussed in section 4 are analyzed. For better understanding of these results graphs have been plotted and explained.

In figure 2, the cost of successful location updates is shown. Here, we can see that our proposed scheme outperforms GLS scheme by consuming smaller network resources for updating the location servers compared to that of GLS scheme. But for 600 nodes GLS scheme has slightly smaller update cost due to the reduction in successful updates of GLS scheme caused by scattering of servers. In GLS the location servers are scattered in different squares of the network (specially for higher order squares), where as in the new grid scheme the servers are available in the surrounding rings.

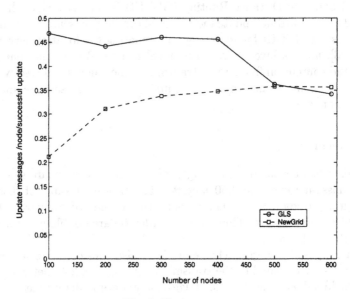

Fig. 2. Update cost.

Figure 3 gives percentage of successful updates. In general, as the number of nodes in the network increases, the successful updates remain almost same. It describes that the proposed scheme has better successful updates than GLS. This is because, in GLS scheme a node has only one location server for each square of the three squares of order-i square with ID of the server be the least and greater than that of the node. The probability of finding this server in GLS scheme is less than that of finding servers for the proposed scheme.

Figure 4 gives the percentage of successful queries. In general, as the number of nodes in the network increases, the successful queries decrease for GLS whereas it remains almost the same for our proposed scheme. It shows that GLS has smaller successful queries than the proposed scheme. This is because, in GLS scheme a node has one location server for each square of the three squares of order-i square.

Our proposed grid scheme outperforms GLS scheme, even if a back off in case of failure is considered for GLS scheme. The result of GLS scheme with using back off is also shown which almost replicates that of the original GLS scheme [2].

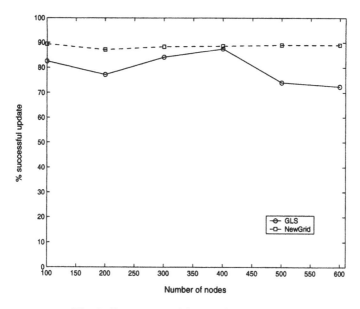

Fig. 3. Percentage of Successful Updates.

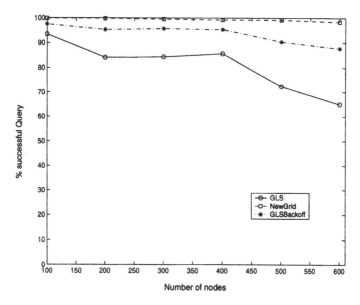

Fig. 4. Percentage of successful queries.

The cost of successful queries in the proposed scheme is slightly more than that of GLS scheme as shown in figure 5. But we believe that this is acceptable since we have high percentage of successful queries in our scheme compared to the GLS scheme.

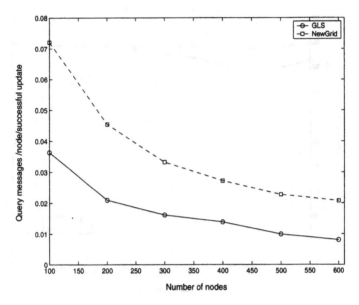

Fig. 5. Query Cost.

Also the proposed scheme is faster in updating its location servers than GLS scheme. Figure 6 illustrates the average hop count for the two schemes. In general, as the number of nodes in the network increases, average hop count increases. However, the hop count for new Grid scheme is minimum and maximum for GLS scheme. This is because in GLS scheme, location servers are scattered in different squares of the network, where as in the new grid scheme the servers are available in the surrounding rings. Also in GLS scheme, the successful updates are smaller than that in our proposed scheme.

We have investigated the impact of varying speed on the performance of these schemes. It is clear that a network with high speeds results in high location updates that consume the scarce resources of the network more. From figure 7 we can notice that location update cost of our proposed scheme is much less than that of GLS scheme for increasing speed. At the same time, we can see that the successful queries of our scheme are high compared to that of GLS scheme. This is achieved at small update cost of our scheme as shown in figure 8 therefore, our scheme is superior to GLS.

7   Conclusion

In this paper, we have introduced an efficient new Grid location update scheme. We have also conducted a performance study of GLS location update scheme with our new Grid location update scheme. Simulations are run for different scenarios based on density-based approach. According to the results and discussion above, we found that the new Grid scheme outperforms GLS scheme in terms of successful updates, location update cost, and hop counts. Also our scheme

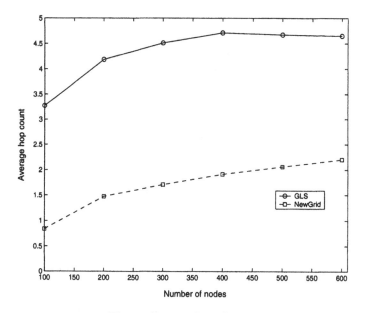

Fig. 6. Average Hop Count.

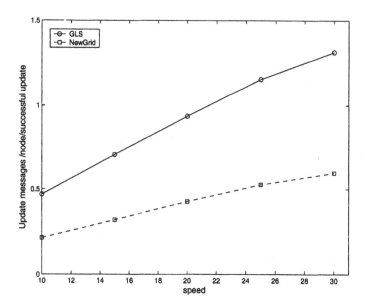

Fig. 7. Location Update Cost vs. Speed.

performs better than GLS scheme in terms of location update cost as the speed
of the nodes increases. Finally, for the successful queries, the proposed scheme
also outperforms the GLS scheme. Therefore, we believe that our proposed grid
location update scheme is more scalable compared to GLS scheme for large Ad
Hoc networks.

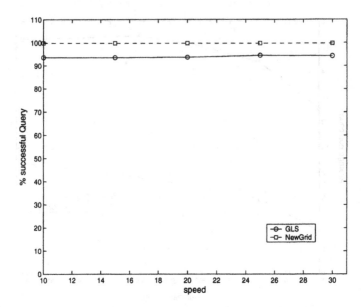

Fig. 8. Percentage of Successful Query vs. Speed.

References

1. G. Karumanchi and S. Muralidharan and R. Prakash: Information dissemination in partitionable mobile ad hoc networks, in Proc. of IEEE Symp. On Reliable Distributed Systems, Lausanne, Oct. 1999
2. J. Li and J. Jannotti and D.S.J. De Couto and D.R. Karger and R. Morris: A scalable location service for geographic ad hoc routing, in Proc. of MOBICOM 2000, pp.120-130
3. K.N. Amouris and S. Papavassiliou and M.Li: A position based multi-zone routing protocol for wide area mobile ad-hoc networks, in Proc. of 49th IEEE Vehicular Technology Conference, 1999, pp.1365-1369
4. M. Mauve and J. Widmer and and H. Hartenstein: A survey on Position-Based Routing in Mobile Ad Hoc Networks, IEEE Network, November/December 2001, pp.30-39
5. NAVSTAR GPS operation:http://tycho.usno.navy.mil/gpsinfo.htm, 1999
6. Stojmenovic I.: Location updates for efficient routing in ad hoc wireless networks, In: Stojmenovic I. (Eds.): Handbook of Wireless Networks and Mobile Computing, Wiley, 2002, pp.451-471
7. Stojmenovic: Position-Based routing in ad hoc networks, IEEE Communication Magazine, July 2002, pp.128-134
8. X. Lin and Stojmenovic I.: Geographic Distance Routing in ad hoc wireless networks, Technical report TR-98-10, SITE, University of Ottawa,1998

Power Optimization in Mobile Networks Using Genetic Algorithm to Guarantee QoS

Ahmed H. Salem and Anup Kumar

Department of Computer Engineering and Computer Science, Speed Scientific School
University of Louisville, Louisville, KY 40292
asalem@faculty.sullivan.edu, AK@louisville.edu

Abstract. The increasing technological developments made in the area of mobile communications enable users to gain access to a wide variety of services. These developments have led researchers to address the issue of Quality of Service (QoS) based connectivity for mobile network users. It is important to design a control algorithm that can quickly manage and determine the minimum required signal power that achieves a certain data rate, to guarantee QoS. In this paper, we introduce a new algorithm to determine the minimum required signal power to guarantee a specific data rate for a user. This approach is based on using a genetic algorithm to estimate the shadow and fading coefficients that correspond to the maximum interference at different points in the base station's domain. The estimated parameters at different point in the domain of the base station indicate that the proposed algorithm is both fast and accurate so it can be used in real-time applications.

1 Introduction

Today's world of computing and business mobility tends to be led by the increased use of mobile computers, PDA's, notebooks and cellular phones. The existing wireless networks use different algorithms to control power capacity, and balancing QoS over the networks [1-6], [10-13]. These algorithms utilize the power and interference ratios by using network management tools to control channel assignment and segmentation. The algorithms proposed for power distribution and energy consumption [7-10], [12], [20], required a priori knowledge of the path gains on all the radio links. In these researches [9],[10], [12], [20], a distributed, power-controlled algorithm was proposed that used only the measured C/I ratio on the active links (instead of the path gains) to adjust the powers and achieve C/I balancing, where (C) is the signal power of the carrier and (I) is the amount of interference to the power signal. The models in [9], [10], [12], [20] incorporate peak signal power constraints that affects other receivers in the neighborhood. In power management researches [9], [10], [12], [20], the optimal transmitted power level is established by a set of quality-of-service (QoS) constraints; the functional form of optimal transmitted power is given by some function of signal to interference ratio which did not take fading into account, and by the levels of interference in the channel. Also, it assumed that the interference is independent of the transmitted power at the transmitter end. In these approaches, fading was not considered, and it is assumed that an infinite stream of data is waiting to be transmitted. An implicit assumption is made that the transmitter is intelligent and somehow has the information regarding the level of interference at the receiver end. Finally, most power researches consider basic multiple access protocols from an energy-optimal standpoint for their solutions [6], [9-12], [20].

G. Das and V.P. Gulati (Eds.): CIT 2004, LNCS 3356, pp. 147–159, 2004.
© Springer-Verlag Berlin Heidelberg 2004

This paper proposes an adaptive power control model that adjusts the transmitted power based on the surrounding interference level around the user. This interference level could be different from different users. This paper introduces a segmentation-based approach for calculating the interference coefficients (λ path loss coefficient and η shadowing coefficient that causes fading), for a set of users in a given covered region. This paper uses the genetic algorithm for power calculation and optimization with respect to fading and noise ratios that affect the wireless domain. The proposed power optimization model is applicable to different mobile network architectures (TDMA, CDMA, W-CDMA, GSM, EGSM and 3GSM).

In order to build our model the following components were developed:

- Modeling the required transmitted power and deducing the relation between the transmitted power and data rates. In this section, we calculate the probability power density function for average and minimum power to maintain the targeted data rate with interference taken into consideration.
- Estimation of gain and the fading coefficients to calculate the worst normalized interference possible in a covered domain.
- Computation of the path loss and shadow coefficients using the genetic algorithm. In this section, we use the genetic algorithm to calculate the worst possible interference in the covered domain.
- Consumption of actual power needed to guarantee data rates. This section is discussed in the results and discussion.

2 Transmission Power Model

Consider a single network node attempting to send information to another node at a particular rate, while minimizing energy consumption. Its communication channel is subject to time-varying interference. If the received signal power is (p) during a time slot (t), with a received normalized interference power (ψ), then the successful reception of the data occurs with probability s(ψ, p), and failure occurs with probability e(ψ, p) = 1− s(ψ, p). Success or failure is denoted by χt = 1 or 0, respectively, at discrete time t. unless otherwise noted, we shall equate the transmitted and received power as (p), i.e. "normalized," so the desired link has gain 1. The SIR (signal Interference Ratio) at the receiver is denoted by γ = (p/ ψ), assuming that the normalized interference power ψ > 0. The normalized interference power is assumed to be based on the fading coefficient. The fading coefficient represents the path loss coefficient (λ) and shadowing coefficient (η), which covers all the interference in the covered domain which also affect the transmitter power; it is modeled as a stationary, ergodic stochastic process where{ Ψt: t = 1, 2, 3,...,n}. Table 1 shows a summary of all the symbols which are used throughout our model proof.

Since our goal is to seek a rule for p = p(ψ) which minimizes energy consumption subject to maintaining a transmission rate f $\geq$ r for some fixed r (the expected data rate), the assumption is as follows: 0< r < 1 where the quantity f is defined by [9], [12], [20].

$$ f = \lim_{n \to \infty} \sum_{t=1}^{n} \chi_t $$

Table 1. Summary of all symbols which are used through this paper

Symbol	Description
p	The received signal power during a time slot
ψ	normalized interference power
Ψ	is the over all normalized interference power over the communication session with respect to the over all round cycle time (t)
$S(\psi, p)$	probability successful reception of the data
$E(\psi, p)$	$e(\psi, p) = 1- s(\psi, p)$ probability failure occurs
s	Instantaneous transmission rate the probability function.
$E(\chi t)$	Expected value
χt	Is used to denoted success (= 1) of failure (= 0)
γ	$\gamma = (p/\psi)$: the normalized signal to interference ratio
$P(\psi)$	Is the actual transmitted power
f	Actual data transmission rate
r	Target data transmission rate
μ	LaGrange multiplier

Since the $(\lim_{n \to \infty} \sum_{i=1}^{n} \,)$ is the expected value of χ which is $E_{(\chi t\ )}$ we could say [9], [12], [20]

$$E\ (\chi_i) = \lim_{n \to \infty} \sum_{i=1}^{n} \chi_i$$

So we could say $\acute{r} = E_{(\chi t\ )}$, and also since the limit is the summation of all the probabilities of successful and failure reception of the data [9],[12], [20].

$$\acute{r} = E(\chi_i) = E(S(\psi, P_{(\psi)})) = \int_0^\infty S(\psi, P_{(\psi)}) \ dp_{(\psi \le \Psi)} \tag{1}$$

We need to optimize equation (1) with respect to the actual transmitted power P(ψ) in order to guarantee the actual transmitted data rate. Therefore, to optimize the equation (1), we need to know the following: (1) the parametric form of the of P(ψ) and (2) the probability of successful reception of the data s(ψ, p). P(ψ) is the actual transmitted power with respect to the normalized interference power and is uniformly distributed over the covered domain. Therefore, the density of P(ψ) can be expressed as follows:

$$P(\psi) = 1/\Psi \ \text{for} \ 0 \le \psi \le \Psi$$

Where ψ is the normalized interference and it represents linear density in the covering domain. To find S(ψ, P(ψ)), we will base the assumption on the most common used modulation in mobile networks, which is NC-FSK-fade and DPSK from NC-FSK fade. Using this assumption, the relation between probability of error and the signal to interference ratio γ is [9], [12], [20] can be stated as follows:

$$e = \frac{1}{\gamma + 1}$$

since $e(\psi, p) = 1- s(\psi, p)$ then [9], [12], [21]

$$S(\psi, P) = 1 - e(\psi, P)$$

$$= 1 - \frac{1}{\gamma + 1} = \frac{\gamma + 1 - 1}{\gamma + 1} = \frac{\gamma}{\gamma + 1}$$

and since $\gamma = (p/\psi)$ then

$$S(\psi, P(\psi)) = \frac{\left(\dfrac{P(\psi)}{\psi}\right)}{\left(\dfrac{P(\psi)}{\psi}\right) + 1} = \frac{P(\psi)}{P(\psi) + \psi}$$

Now, by optimizing equation (1), we find that

$$\int_0^\infty S(\psi, P(\psi))\, dp(\psi \leq \Psi) \geq r \tag{2}$$

$$\min P \int S(\psi, P(\psi))\quad dp(\psi \leq \Psi) \tag{3}$$

Equation (2) is optimized by the LaGrange multiplier; therefore:

$$I(y(x)) = \int F(x, y)\,dx \tag{4}$$

$$G(x, y) = 0 \text{ or Constant} \tag{5}$$

From Equation (4) and (5), the LaGrange function will be:

$$L(x, y, \lambda) = F(x, y) - \mu G(x, y)$$

where μ is the LaGrange multiplier by applying equation (4) with equation (3)

$$I(y_{(x)}) = \int F(x, y)\,dx \equiv \min P \int S(\psi, P(\psi))\quad dp(\psi \leq \Psi)$$

And by combining equation (5) with equation (2), the LaGrange will be:

$$G(x, y) = 0 \text{ or Constant} \equiv \int_0^\infty S(\psi, P(\psi))\quad dp(\psi \leq \Psi) \geq r$$

Then:

$$F = P(\psi) - \mu \frac{P(\psi)}{P(\psi) + \psi} \tag{6}$$

And since μ is the Lagrange Multilayer that needs to be found, therefore

$$\frac{\partial F}{\partial P(\psi)} = 0 \rightarrow 1 - \omega \frac{P(\psi) + \psi - P(\psi)}{(P(\psi) + \psi)^2}$$

$$1 = \frac{\omega \psi}{(P(\psi) + \psi)^2} \rightarrow P(\psi) = \sqrt{\omega \psi} - \psi$$

μ will be estimated based on the interference in order to be calculated, which would bring 2 cases: Case 1: $\mu \leq I$ and Case 2: $\mu \geq \Psi$

Case 1: $\mu \leq \Psi$

$$\int_0^\mu S(\psi, P(\psi))\, dp(\psi \leq \Psi) \geq r$$

$$\int_0^\mu \frac{P(\psi)}{P(\psi) + \psi}\, dp(\psi \leq \Psi) \leq r$$

Since

$$P(\psi \leq \Psi) = \frac{\psi}{\Psi}$$

then

$$dP(\psi \leq \Psi) = \frac{1}{\Psi} d\psi$$

$$\int_0^\mu \frac{\sqrt{\mu \psi} - \psi}{\sqrt{\mu \psi} - \psi + \psi} * \frac{1}{\Psi} di = r$$

$$\frac{1}{\Psi}\int_0^\mu \frac{\sqrt{\mu\,\psi}-\psi}{\sqrt{\mu\,\psi}}\,d\psi = r \Rightarrow \frac{1}{\Psi}\int_0^\mu \left(1 - \frac{\sqrt{\psi}}{\sqrt{\mu}}\right)d\psi = r$$

$$\psi - \frac{2}{3}*\frac{\psi^{3/2}}{\sqrt{\mu}}\,\Big|_0^\mu = r\Psi \Rightarrow \mu - \frac{2}{3}*\frac{\mu^{3/2}}{\mu^{1/2}} = r\Psi$$

$$\mu - \frac{2}{3}\mu = r\Psi \Rightarrow \frac{1}{3}\mu = r\Psi$$

Therefore:

$$\mu = 3r\Psi \quad \text{for all } r \le \frac{1}{3} \tag{7}$$

Case 2: $\mu > \Psi$

$$\int_0^\Psi \frac{\sqrt{\omega\,\psi}-i\psi}{\sqrt{\omega\,\psi}-\psi+\psi}*\frac{1}{\Psi}\,d\psi = r$$

$$\frac{1}{\Psi}\int_0^\Psi \frac{\sqrt{\omega\,\psi}-\psi}{\sqrt{\omega\,\psi}}\,d\psi = r \Rightarrow \frac{1}{\Psi}\int_0^\Psi \left(1 - \frac{\sqrt{\psi}}{\sqrt{\omega}}\right)d\psi = r$$

$$\frac{1}{\Psi}\int_0^I (1 - \frac{\sqrt{\psi}}{\sqrt{\mu}})\,di = r \Rightarrow \frac{1}{\Psi}\left(i - \frac{\tfrac{3}{2}\psi^{3/2}}{\sqrt{\mu}}\right)\Big|_0^\Psi = r$$

$$\frac{1}{\Psi}\left(I - \frac{\tfrac{3}{2}\Psi^{3/2}}{\sqrt{\mu}}\right) = r \Rightarrow 1 - \frac{3}{2}\frac{\Psi^{1/2}}{\mu^{1/2}} = r$$

$$1 - r = \frac{3}{2}\frac{\Psi^{1/2}}{\mu^{1/2}} \Rightarrow \frac{9}{4}(1-r) = \frac{\Psi}{\mu}$$

Therefore:

$$\mu = \frac{4\Psi}{9(1-r)} \quad \text{for all } r > \frac{1}{3} \tag{8}$$

Finally:

$$P(\psi) = \begin{cases} \sqrt{3\psi\,r\psi}-\psi & \text{if } r \le \frac{1}{3} \text{ and } \psi \le 3\psi\,r \\[2mm] 0 & \text{if } r \le \frac{1}{3} \text{ and } \psi > 3\psi\,r \\[2mm] \left(\frac{2\sqrt{3\psi\,\psi}}{3(1-r)} - \psi\right) & r > \frac{1}{3} \end{cases} \tag{9}$$

$$E[p] = \begin{cases} \frac{3}{2}\psi\,r^2 & r \le \frac{1}{3} \\[2mm] \psi\left(\frac{4/9}{1-r} - \frac{1}{2}\right) & r > \frac{1}{3} \end{cases} \tag{10}$$

3 Estimation of Gain and Fading Coefficients

Figure 1 shows a cell that is covering an area starting at point X and ending at point Y. It is clear that the channel signal power that is being transmitted from the base station (BS) to the mobile device (MD) varies from one point to another. Let us also say that within segment A (line of site), which is a point inside the domain covered by the cell, the channel signal power is greater than at segment C, due to environmental interference. The signal power at segment D would be very weak; for example, a roof or tree may block, scatter, or deflect part of the transmitted signal power, causing the signal to lose power as shown in Figure 1.

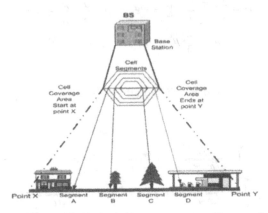

Fig. 1. Different physical interferences over a cell covered area

From Figure 1, it can be seen that the amount of interference changes from point (A) to (B) to point (C), depending on the distance between the sender and the receiver and the effect of attributes and terrain of the domain; thus, the signal power changes from one location to another, depending on the distance between the transmitter, the receiver, and the landscape. This interference is caused due to path loss of the transmitted signal and different noise levels in the area (landscape). It is quite difficult to determine the noise in the existing environment; therefore, we would use a simple radio channel model that would help us gather the noise information in a domain without knowing the details of the environment. The model is based on the Bello and Turin model, which states that all radio channels are a set of signals that have amplitude and phase [13], [14], [16].

Base stations communicate with mobile devices through a set of channels designed with up-link and down-link capabilities. The mobile unit communicates with the base station through the up-link, and the base station communicates with the mobile unit through the down-link. These channel links are configured as radio channels; thus, the interference could change and vary from one channel to another since the description of these channels is in terms of amplitude and phase. Thus, the change in any amplitude or phase could cause either high or low changes in phase and amplitude. This is known as the "fading effect." The fading effect depends on large scale variations or low scale variations, and both depend on two factors:

1. Path loss coefficient: characterizes the rapid fluctuations of the received signal strength over short travel distances (a few wavelengths) or short time duration (in the order of seconds). In general we could say the amount of noise that the signal will suffer from the surroundings with respect to the distance will increase.

2. Shadowing coefficient: signal reflection and scattering is a good example for shadowing coefficient. Suppose a signal is transmitted from the base station (BS) to a mobile device (MD), and during transmission, the signal hits a surface or a sudden surface appears in the line of transmission. Part of the signal will be reflected, and the other part will be scattered. The mobile device might receive the

scattered signal before the reflected signal over different time slots. This is signal interference.

Therefore, the path loss and shadowing coefficient affects the transmission and are related by the given equation [13], [14], [16].

$$P_r / P_t = d^{-\lambda} 10^{-\eta/10} \tag{11}$$

Where: P_r: Received power

P_t: Transmitted power.

d: Distance between transmitter and receiver.

λ: Path loss coefficient for the indoor environment and its range from 1 to 6.5 in value [16-19].

η: Shadowing coefficient in dB is a random variable of zero, meaning that it takes a random range value from 1 to16 dB [16-19].

We have defined the gain (g) to be the received power signal over the transmitted power signal, i.e. $g = (P_r/P_t)$. Based on the Bello and Turin model [13],[14],[16], the gain is given by the following equation:

$$g = d^{-\lambda} 10^{-\eta/10} \tag{12}$$

By using the Gain (g) and (ψ) Normalized Interference Power in our model, the gain (P_r/P_t) will be equal to one for ideal transmission and reception. What this means is that Normalized Interference Power (ψ) is affected by two main parameters: the shadowing coefficient (η) and the path loss coefficient (λ). [These affect the signal to interference ratio (P_r/I)]. Also, we will deduce the relation between (P_r/I), the shadowing coefficient (η), and the path loss coefficient (λ). The genetic algorithm will be used to determine the optimum values of the shadowing coefficient(η) and the path loss coefficient(λ) in order to minimize the gain (worst case) at deferent points in the covered domain. Further, we will show the relationship between P_{min} (minimum transmitted power signal) and the interference at certain data rates using the probability density function $P(\psi)$. Hence, we will be able to use this relation to calculate the minimum required power at different points in the covered area by the base station to guarantee the required data rate which will enhance the QoS. Gain is affected by the path loss and the shadow coefficient as follows:

$$P_r / P_t = d^{-\lambda} 10^{-\eta/10} \tag{13}$$

Since the power received is the amount of transmitted power reduced by the amount of interference, then:

$$P_r = P_t - I \tag{14}$$

Divide both sides by P_t then:

$$P_r / P_t = 1 - I / P_t \tag{15}$$

Since $\psi = I/P_t$, by substituting I/P_t for ψ in we get the following equation:

$$\psi = 1 - P_r / P_t \tag{16}$$

Since $g = P_r/P_t$ then:

$$\psi = 1 - g \tag{17}$$

Therefore the normalized interference is:

$$\psi = 1 - d^{-\lambda} 10^{-\eta/10} \tag{18}$$

Now, the problem lies in finding the value of the normalized interference (ψ). In the next section, we will use a multi path and the fading effect to calculate the interference over the base station domain by building a table for all interferences using Genetic Algorithm.

4 Computation of Normalized Interference Using the Genetic Algorithm

Genetic algorithms perform multi-directional searches by maintaining a population of potential solutions – encouraging the exchange of information between search directions. The population undergoes an evolutionary process through which relatively good solutions are reproduced, while relatively bad solutions die. To distinguish between these solutions, an objective function is used which plays the role of an environment [15]. A genetic algorithm that yields good results in many practical problems is composed of three operators.

1. Reproduction: Reproduction is the process in which individual strings are copied according to their objective function values. The reproduction operators may be implemented in algorithmic form in a number of ways [15]. In our proposed model, we used a "roulette wheel" based approach, where each current string in the population has a roulette wheel slot size in proportion to its fitness value, which is calculated in equation 20. We need to get the maximum values for (λ) and (η) to minimize the gain (g), which will maximize the normalized interference (Ψ). This will allow us to calculate the minimum required signal power for a specific data rate (r) in equations 9 and 10. So, we find that the fitness function for the normalized interference (Ψ) is:

$$\psi = 1 - g \tag{19}$$
$$Fitness = 1 - d^{-\lambda} 10^{-\eta/10} \tag{20}$$

2. Crossover: Crossover may proceed in two steps. First, members of the newly-reproduced strings in the mating pool are mated at random. Second, each pair of the strings undergoes crossover [15]. In our model, we use the chromosome of length 60 bit, the first 30 starting from bit number 1 and ending at bit 30 for path loss coefficient (λ), and the last 30 bit starting from bit no 31 and ending at 60 for the shadowing coefficient (η). We apply crossover with a probability equal to 90%.

3. Mutation: Mutation operators play a secondary role in the GA [15]. Usually, we use mutation operators in order to insert new information in each reproduced generation.

Figure 2 shows the flowchart of the genetic algorithm model that has been developed to find the shadowing coefficient (η), and the path loss coefficient (λ) minimizes gain (Pr/Pt) and maximizes the normalized interference (Ψ) at different points in the covered area at the base station.

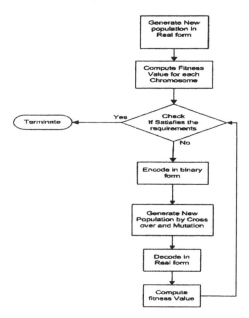

Fig. 2. Flowchart of Genetic Algorithm

5 Results and Discussion

This section discusses the results obtained from the model implemented using Matlab. We also compared our results with the models given in [9], [12], [20]. The genetic algorithm has been used to find the shadowing coefficient (η) and the path loss coefficient (λ) that minimizes gain (Pr/Pt) and maximizes the normalized interference (worst case) at different points in the covered area at the base station. Table (1) shows the optimum values of the shadowing coefficient (η) and path loss coefficient (λ) that promote maximum gain (pr/pt) and minimize normalized interference (Ψ) at different points in the covered area at the base station. It is clear from table (1) that the further away from the base station the mobile device moves, the gain decreases and the interference (Ψ) increases.

In order to teach the base station to transmit the minimum power needed to guarantee a specific data rate, we used the genetic algorithm to estimate the worst cases of interference at different points in the domain covered by the base station. By increasing the values of (λ) and (η) to minimize the gain (Pr/Pt) in order to increase the normalized (Ψ) interference, we were able to calculate the minimum level of transmitted power needed to guarantee successful transmission of information over a certain channel.

In the models given in [9], [12], [20], the measurement of transmitted power was not controlled based on the estimated interference values but on selected random power signal value with constant value of signal interference ratio, or by constant power and variable interference ratio. The disadvantage of these models is that they cannot calculate the interference power signal at each point covered by the base station. However, in our model, we can calculate the worst interference power signal at

Table 2. Results of Gain, and Normalized Interference at different points

Distance	λ	η	Gain (Pr/Pt)	Normalized interference (Ψ)
2	4.8118	14.4849	1	0
10	1.5628	15.6275	1	0
100	1.0001	15.9994	0.398	0.602
200	1.0001	15.953	0.1969	0.8031
300	1.004	15.9268	0.1276	0.8724
400	1.0023	15.8593	0.0954	0.046
500	1.0005	15.8888	0.0774	0.9226
600	1	15.9875	0.06620	0.9338
700	1.0002	15.9913	0.0567	0.9433
800	1.0001	15.9912	0.0496	0.9504
900	1	15.9978	0.0442	0.9558
1000	1.00009708969	15.994133	0.039730	0.9602
1500	1.00013985181	15.989147	0.026447	0.9736
2000	1.00002995662	15.989843	0.015989	0.9841
2500	1.00003596686	15.995563	0.015903	0.9841
3000	1.00025278435	15.995914	0.013230	0.9868
3500	1.00005919958	15.995610	0.011357	0.9886
4000	1.00009007305	15.999887	0.009944	0.9901
4500	1.00000716745	15.997155	0.008840	0.9912
5000	1.00024049395	15.998415	0.007942	0.9920

each point in the domain covered by the base station as shown in table 1. By using this information, we can calculate the minimum required power to guarantee the required data rate at a certain interference power signal, using equation 9. This equation represents the relation between the minimum required power versus the data rate and interference power signal at any time slot (t). Figure 3 shows the minimum required power levels at various interference ratios (Pr/Pt) at certain data rates. Furthermore, in Figure 3 we draw the relation between the interference power and the minimum required transmitted power at a certain data rate (data rate is constant). It is clear that, as the interference increases, the minimum required transmittal power is increased.

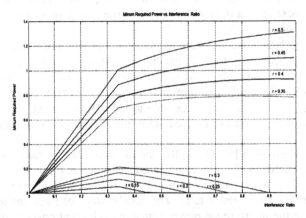

Fig. 3. Minimum Required Power at various interference ratios

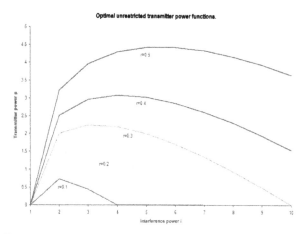

Fig. 4. The Power at various interference ratios [9], [12], [20]

To compare the results of our model with the approaches given in [9], [12], [20], we have redrawn the relation between the transmitted power, data rate, and interference power signal from [9], [12], [20] in Figure 4. It is clear from Figure 3 and 4 that if we need to keep the transmitted data rate less than or equal to 0.3 or (30%) our proposed model can achieve this goal, transmitting with less power and with the same required data rate; thus, the model can be seen as an improvement upon what is achieved in [9], [12], [20]. Suppose that we need to transmit a data rate (r) equal to 0.5 or (50%). Our proposed model can achieve that by transmitting power less than 1.3; otherwise, the algorithm proposed in [9], [12], [20] needs 4.5 to transmit the required data rate (r). From this comparison, we conclude that the proposed algorithm can guarantee the required data rate with less transmitted power and without previous knowledge about the interference, which guarantees QoS. Figure 5 is intended to show the relation between average transmitted power versus data rate (r) at certain normalized interference (Ψ) levels. As the interference increases (Ψ), the minimum required transmitted power is increased at a certain data rate. For example, when using multimedia applications (such as time sensitive applications, i.e. video), the required data rate (r) must be greater than or equal to 0.64 or (64%). So if the normalized interference (Ψ) is equal to 0.25, the minimum required transmitted power is less than 0.5 Watts; and if $\Psi = 1$ (worst case), the required average transmittal power to guarantee a data rate of 0.64 is less than 1 Watt (0 dB).

6   Conclusion and Future Work

In this paper, we introduced a new approach to determine the minimum required signal power to guarantee a specific required data rate. In the proposed approach, we use the genetic algorithm to estimate the shadow and fading coefficients that correspond to the maximum interference at different points in the base station's domain; thus, this newly-gained information will enhance the QoS by optimizing the transmitted power signal. The estimated parameters at different point in the domain of the base station indicate that the proposed algorithm is accurate and fast, so it can be used

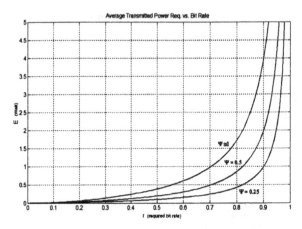

Fig. 5. Average Power Transmitted in Watt versus Data rate at different Normalized Interference

in real time applications. Also, our comparison results show that the proposed algorithm can achieve QoS with minimum transmitted power. In order to use the proposed approach, first we must know the covered area dimensions and the distance between the mobile device and base station. With this in mind, our future work is to use artificial neural networks (ANN) in order to effectively calculate the required power signal level needed between the base station and the mobile device.

References

1. Deepak Ayyagari, Anthony Ephremides, Power Control for Link Quality Protection in Cellular DS-CDMA Networks with Integrated (Packet and Circuit) Services" pp.97, 2000.
2. I. Badira and A. Elhakeem, a radio-link protocol analysis of integrated CDMA networks: A Comparison with TDMA, in : IEEE International Conference on Universal Personal Communications Record Vol. (1996)pp.7-11.
3. S.K. Das, R. Jayaram, Kakani, and Sanjoy K. Sen, A call admission and control scheme for quality-of –service (QoS) provisioning in next generation wireless networks, Wireless Networks 6 (2000) 17-30
4. S. A. Grandhi, R., Vijayan, D.J. Goodman, and J. Zander, "Centralized power control in cellular radio systems," IEEE Transactions on Vecicular Technology vol. 42, pp. 466-468, November 1993.
5. P.W Baier, P Jung and A. Klein, Taking the challenge of multiple access for third-generation cellular mobile radio systems- a European view, IEEE Communications Magazine 34(2) February 1996) 82-89.
6. David J. Goodman "Trends in Cellular and Cordless Communications" IEEE Communications Magazine, pp. 31-40, June 1991
7. J.B Adersen, J.S, Rappaport, S. Yosnida, propagation Measurements and Models for wireless, Communications Channels, IEEE Communication Magazine, January 1995, Vol 43 N4:42-9
8. S. A. Grandhi, R. Vijayan, and D. J. Goodman, "Distributed power control in cellular radio systems" IEEE Transactions on Communications, vol. 42, pp, 226-228, February/ March/April 1994.

9. J. M. Rulnick and N. Bambos, "Mobile Power Management for Maximum Battery Life in Wireless Communication Networks," Proc. IEEE INFOCOM '96, 1996, vol. 2, pp. 443-450.

10. M. Zorzi and R. Rao, "Energy-Constrained Error Control for Wireless Channels," IEEE Personal Communications, Dec. 1997, pp. 27-33.

11. 3rd Generation Partnership Project (3GPP), Technical Specification group core Network "Gateway Location Register (GLR)- Stage 2" Technical Report 3GTS 23.119 version 1.0.0, GPP,1999.

12. John M. Rulnick and Nicholas Bambos, Mobile Power management for wireless communication networks, Wireless Networks 3 (1997) 3-14.

13. J.B Adersen, J.S, Rappaport, S. Yosnida, propagation Measurements and Models for wireless, Communications Channels, IEEE Communication Magazine, January 1995, Vol 43 N4:42-9

14. Bello. PO.; Atroposcatter channel model IEEE transactions on communication, Technology, April 1968, Vol- 17,pp. 130-137

15. David E. Golderg "Genetic Algorithm", Addison-Wesley publishing company, January 1989

16. H. Hashemi, The indoor radio Propagation Channels Proceeding of the IEEE, July 1993 Vol 81 N7:943-68

17. My. T.T.le " A Global QoS Management for Wireless Networks" Doctor of Philosophy thesis University of California at Berkeley 1996

18. D. Yetes, A framework for uplink power control in cellular radio systems, IEEE Journal on Selected area in Communications 13(7) (September 1995) 1341-1347.

19. W. Tschrik, Effect of transmission power control on the co-channel interference in cellular radio networks, Elektrotechnik und Informationstechik 106(5) 1989) 194-196.

20. John M. Rulnick and Nicholas Bambos, Power-induced time division on asynchronous channels, Wireless Networks 5 (1999) 71-80 pp.1-2

Associativity Based Mobility-Adaptive K-Clustering in Mobile Ad-Hoc Networks

C. Jayakumar[1] and C. Chellappan[2]

[1] Research Associate, Department of Computer Science and Engineering, Anna University,
600025 Chennai, India
jayakumar@cs.annauniv.edu
[2] Director, Ramanujan Computer Center, Anna University, 600025 Chennai, India
drcc@annauniv.edu

Abstract. In this paper we propose Clustering technique provides a solution to support QoS in ad hoc networks. For the effective functioning of cluster based routing algorithms, the clusters must be long-lived and stable. The proposed scheme considers the spatial and temporal stability of the nodes. The node elected as the clusterhead is such that it has maximum associativity as well as satisfies a minimum connectivity requirement. Effective work has been done for Cluster Reorganization. Cluster Head Re-election is periodically done so that the cluster head is centered in a cluster. Cluster management will be effective, since the cluster heads are elected based on various parameters like processing capabilities, speed of the node, number of neighbor nodes and associativity with the neighbor nodes. Though overhead is incurred initially due to cluster setup, cluster maintenance will be easier in the long run. Ultimately routing efficiency will increase due to long-lived clusters and reduced control packets.

1 Introduction

An ad hoc network is made up of mobile nodes with wireless interfaces, which communicate with each other over multihop paths, in the absence of any fixed infrastructure. Each mobile node in the network also acts as a router for the network traffic. Of late, there has been a need to support QoS and security in ad hoc networks owing to their varied usage scenarios and convergence of different applications traffic. Ad hoc routing protocols can be divided into two broad categories, namely table-driven routing protocols [2, 3, 4] and on-demand routing protocols [5, 6,12]. Cluster based routing is a mixture of pro- active and reactive algorithms. In this paper we introduce a protocol for the formation and management of clustered ad hoc networks.

2 Clustering in MANET

In clustered network architecture, the whole network is divided into self-managed groups of nodes called *clusters*. The clusters can contain a special node, called the clusterhead, which routes the packets destined outside of the cluster. This, although creates a bottleneck at the clusterheads, reduces the number of control packets needed, because only the clusterheads have to be informed about changes outside the cluster. Clusters can be either distinct or overlapping. In the latter case the neighbor-

G. Das and V.P. Gulati (Eds.): CIT 2004, LNCS 3356, pp. 160–168, 2004.

ing clusters can have a common node, referred to as gateways [13]. Examples of Cluster based routing algorithms are the ZRP (Zone Routing Protocol) [9, 10] and CBRP (Cluster Based Routing Protocol) [1, 7].

For the effective functioning of cluster based routing algorithms the size and the membership of the clusters must be chosen carefully. The most important requirement is to keep clusters as stable as possible, because dynamic membership changes need more communication between the clusters in order to provide up-to-date membership information.

2.1 Previous Works

In most of the methods proposed in the literature [1, 7] for routing in hierarchical (clustered) networks, much thought has not been given for the selection of the cluster head. For instance [1] selects cluster head based on the node identifier (Least ID clustering algorithm). Though this could reduce initial computational overhead in determining the cluster head, later a lot of network bandwidth is consumed for intra-cluster routing. The cluster head elected by this method need not be centrally located in the cluster. The result is that those nodes that are farther away from the cluster head have to route their packets across more hops than those in the proximity of the cluster head. Given that the nodes are uniformly distributed across the cluster the average number of hops for the cluster head to reach the nodes increases.

The concept of associativity (relative stability of nodes) was used to get long-lived routes in routing in [8]. Long-lived clusters also reduce the probability that a packet will be routed to the previous cluster of the addressed node, thus reducing the delay and overhead. Although for stability [11] reasons larger clusters are desirable, larger clusters put a heavy burden on cluster heads, and hinders the efficient communication within the cluster. Associativity of the nodes had not been considered while [1] determined the cluster head. As a result the cluster head selected need not be the best in terms of spatial stability. This is not trivial since the movement of cluster head results in dismantling of the entire cluster, which in turn results in additional overhead of cluster formation. The proposed algorithm uses associativity as a metric in the selection of the cluster head so that the temporal stability of the cluster and hence the bandwidth utilization, which is a crucial factor in ad hoc networks, are increased.

The main goal of this protocol is to form clusters in such a way that the cluster is stable over a long period of time. The node elected as the clusterhead (CH) is such that it has maximum associativity as well as satisfies a minimum connectivity requirement.

3 Associativity-Based Mobility-Adaptive K-Clustering

The proposed scheme considers the Spatial and Temporal stability of the nodes. *Cluster Management* will be effective, since the Cluster heads are elected based on various parameters like processing capabilities, speed of the node movement, number of neighbor nodes and associativity with the neighbor nodes. Due to the *Cluster Reorganization* and *Cluster Head Re-election*, the clusters will become stable, cluster heads will be centered and *Cluster deformations* will be reduced. In the long run, the clusters will be long lived. Ultimately Routing efficiency will increase due to reduction of control packets.

For the convenience of discussion about the design, we first define the different parameters.

K – diameter of the cluster i.e. the number of nodes from one end to other end
    MAX_WAIT_TIME- maximum waiting time a node can wait during the random waiting of the cluster initialization process.

Status of the node- indicates whether the node is Undecided, Cluster member or Cluster Head.

Associativity Ticks (AT) – every node maintain AT field for the neighboring nodes. When a new neighbor is found, its AT is set to 0. Periodically all nodes will announce their presence to their neighbors thorough Hello packets. Whenever a hello packet is received from a neighbor, its AT is incremented .If it is not received within the stipulated time, its AT is decremented and the valid field is set to 0.When the AT become zero, the entry will be deleted.

Weight (WT) of the node – it is calculated based on the node's capabilities. Some of the parameters used for calculating weights are speed of movement of the node, Number of neighboring nodes, Sum of AT of the neighboring nodes, node processing speed, memory capacity etc.

CH Factor – it is calculated from weight, number of neighbors, Sum of AT by giving calculated percentage of weights to each other.

Number of Neighboring nodes (NN)- total number of adjacent nodes.

MIN_NN- minimum NN required becoming a cluster head.

3.1 Hello Packet Exchange

A node will periodically broadcast Hello packets to its neighbors every HELLO_
INTERVAL time. The Hello packet format is given below

NODE_ID	STATUS	NODE_WEIGHT	CLUSTER_ID	CLUSTER_HEAD_WEIGHT	NO_OF_HOPS

A node on receiving Hello packet will update its own Neighbor table. The neighbor table data structure contains

STATUS	CLUSTER_ID	WEIGHT	CLUSTER_HEAD_WEIGHT	AT_OF_NODE

If an entry is already present in the table for the node which sent the Hello packet, the entry is updated and the AT corresponding to that node is incremented. If it is not present, a new entry is created with the required information from the Hello packet with AT set to 1. The node will start a timeout for receiving the next Hello packet If a node doesn't receive Hello packet within the HELLO_INTERVAL and a random threshold value, it will decrement the AT corresponding to that node and invalidate that entry. If the AT becomes zero, that entry will be deleted from the Neighbor table.

3.2 Cluster Initialization

Cluster Initialization occurs as shown in the figure 3.1. The colored nodes are the initiators. All the nodes, which are in Undecided state, start waiting for a random of MAX_WAIT_TIME. The node, which first wakes up, will become the initiator. The initiator will broadcast Cluster Control Claim (CCC) packet with hop count set to K/2 and start a timer set to CCC_WAIT_TIME. If a node receives a CCC packet from an initiator, it will check first if it has already sent any CCC packet or Cluster Control Reply (CCR) packet to other initiator. The information present in the CCC packets are

INIATOR_ID	HOP_COUNT	ROUTE

where route will contain the route from initiator to the node. If so it will discard the CCC packet. Otherwise the node will copy the initiator id and the route. After that it will reply to the Initiator by CCR packet using the reverse of the route obtained from the CCC packet. The format for CCR packet is

NODE_ID	WEIGHT	SUM_AT	NN	ROUTE

where route will contain reverse of the route field in the CCC packet. The node will decrement the hop count. If the hop count becomes zero, it will discard the CCC packet. Otherwise it will broadcast the CCC packet to its neighbors by updating the route information. After sending CCR packet it will wait for some interval to receive the Cluster Head Indication (CHI) packet. The node, which received the CCC packet, will reply back to the Initiator by CCR packet, which contains the necessary information for electing the cluster head. The information like weight, sum of AT and number of neighbors are all calculated using the Neighbor table. The route information is obtained from the CCC packet. The initiator will accept the CCR packets, which arrive within the CCC_WAIT_TIME, other packets will be discarded. Once a CCR packet is received, the information contained in the packet is copied into the Initiator table. The information stored in the initiator table are

NODE_ID	NODE_WEIGHT	NN

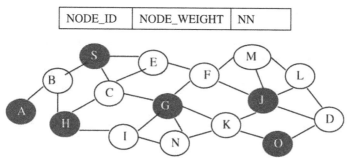

Fig. 3.1. Cluster Initiators

3.3 Cluster Head Election

In the figure 3.2 colored nodes indicates the cluster head and also its members. When CCC_WAIT_TIME expires, the Initiator will start the cluster head election process. The node has the Maximum CH Factor and NN greater than MIN_NN is elected as Cluster Head. If the initiator itself is the newly elected cluster head, it will broadcast CHI packet to all the members of the cluster. If other node is elected as cluster head, the initiator will send TC packet to that node and will wait for the CHB packet to come.

The information present in TC packet are

INIATOR_ID	CLUSTER_HEAD_ID	MEMBER_NODE_ID	ROUTE

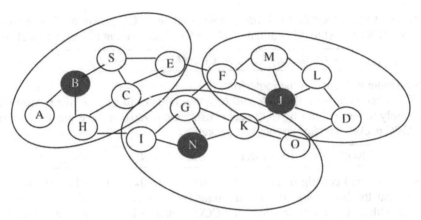

Fig. 3.2. Clusters with cluster heads

where route is used to unicast this packet to new Cluster Head. The node, which received the TC packet, will update its status to Cluster Head and will send CHI packet to all the members of the cluster and will start the necessary events for the cluster head. The information present in the CHI packet are

INIATOR_ID	CLUSTER_HEAD_ID	NO_OF_HOPS	CHB SEQUENCE NUMBER

3.4 Cluster Head and Member Assertion

A node on receiving CHI packet will check whether it is any old CHI packet by checking the CHI sequence number. If it is old, it will discard that packet. Otherwise the node will update the Cluster Head information if it is the correct intended CHI packet and will wait for the CHB packet. The information present in the CHB packet are

CLUSTER_ID	WEIGHT	NO_OF_HOPS	ROUTE	CHB SEQUENCE NUMBER

The Cluster Head after sending CHI packet will start sending CHB packet periodically every CHB_INTERVAL time. A node on receiving CHB packet will check for the sequence number. It will discard the packet if it is old. If it is the intended CHB packet, it will update the Cluster Head information and will send Member beacon (MB) packet to the Cluster Head. The MB Packets contains

NODE_ID	WEIGHT	SUM-AT

The node will start a timeout to receive the next CHB packet. If a member node doesn't receive CHB packet for the CHB_INTERVAL and some random threshold value, it will check for any adjacent nodes to join with any other cluster. If it could, it will join with the chosen cluster. Otherwise it will start the cluster formation process again. Cluster Member nodes will send MB packet in response to CHB packet. The necessary information in the packet is calculated from the Neighbor table. The Cluster Head on receiving MB packet from a member node will update the Cluster Head table with the information from the MB packet and will set a timeout for receiving the next

MB packet from that member node. If the cluster head doesn't receive an MB packet from a member, it will delete the entry corresponding to that member from the Cluster head table. Cluster Head table contain information about ID, Sum of AT, Weight of the member nodes, Number of hops, Sum of AT of the neighboring nodes of the member node which belong to cluster. It will also update the Adjacency Cluster table accordingly by removing the node. Adjacency Cluster table contains information about the neighbor cluster id and the list of the gateway nodes, which are adjacent to this neighbor cluster.

3.5 Cluster Reorganization

Every node will check for Cluster reorganization every REORGANIZATION_ INTERVAL period of time. The factors that are considered for reorganization are Number of hops with other clusters, Weight of the other cluster heads and Associativity ticks with the neighboring nodes of other clusters. Once a node has decided to join with some other cluster, it will join by updating the cluster head information and will start the Cluster Reorganization timer.

The Advantage of Cluster reorganization is that the cluster will rearrange themselves according to the spatial and temporal stability of nodes in the network and hence the clusters formed will be long lived. Cluster deformation will be very much smaller compared to other clustering algorithms and hence the routing overhead will be minimized due to reduction is the number of maintenance packets required for handling such deformation.

3.6 Mobility Adaptive Maintenance

When a new node joins the cluster, it will receive the CHB packet from the Cluster Head. In response to that it will send MB packet and therefore it now has become a member of the cluster. The cluster head accordingly updates the information in the Cluster Head table and the Adjacency Cluster Table. When a node moves away from a cluster, the MB timeout for that node will occur, since the Cluster head cannot receive any MB packets from that node. Hence it will delete the corresponding entries receive any MB packets from that node. Hence it will delete the corresponding entries from the Cluster head table and the Adjacency Cluster table. When the Cluster Head itself moves away, all the nodes in the cluster cannot receive the CHB packet from the cluster head. Hence timeout occurs in all the member nodes. They will try to join with other clusters. If possible they will join. Otherwise, they will start the cluster initialization process

3.7 Cluster Head Re-election

Every REELECTION_INTERVAL of time, the cluster head will check for electing a new cluster head. The eligibility criteria are as follows.

- Number of Neighbors > MIN_NN
- Sum of AT of this cluster > sum of AT nodes in other cluster
- Sum of AT > sum of AT of current cluster head

The node will try to elect a new cluster head. If not possible, it will remain as the cluster head and will schedule the Re-election again after REELCTION_INTERVAL. New cluster Head is elected by calculating REFACTOR (Re-election Factor) which is a weighted percentage of weight, Number of Neighbors, Sum of AT, and Sum of AT of this cluster. The Cluster head is informed by sending Take control change (TCC) packet. The information stored in the TCC packet are

OLD_CLUSTER_ID	NEW_CLUSTER_ID	ROUTE

On Receiving TCC packet, the member node will update its status to cluster Head and will send Cluster Head Change (CHC) packet to all its member. On Receiving CHC packet, the member nodes will update the new cluster head information and will wait for the CHB from the new Cluster head. The advantage of Cluster head Re-election is the cluster head is made to be centered in the cluster as for as possible, so that it can manage a number of nodes effectively. Combined with Cluster Reorganization, it makes way for clusters to be long lived with minimum deformations.

4   Simulation and Results

The algorithm was implemented using version 2.26 of ns2 tool set. Clustering setup and maintenance has to be added to the network simulator code for simulation. For the simulations of the algorithms, all the required data structures, packet formats, messages and packet receiving and transmitting functions are added to network simulator. Necessary handlers for scheduling the packet transmission and timeouts have been added to the network simulator.

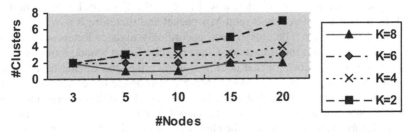

Fig. 4.1. Number of clusters vs. number of nodes for different K

The figure 4.1 represents the number of clusters formed for different values of diameter (K) for different number of nodes (N) in the system. From the graph one can find that when K=2 the total number of clusters formed is high when compared to others. This indicates that as K increases the number of cluster formed will decrease and will help in maintaining the clustering at ease.

The figure 4.2 gives the details of the cluster changes with time, keeping the number of nodes in the system same and the diameter of the cluster same. One can infer that when it is compared to the Distributed Mobility-Adaptive Clustering (DMAC) Algorithm, the proposed algorithm shows better performance by keeping the number of cluster changes minimal.

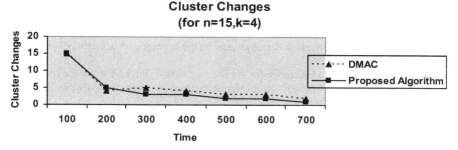

Fig. 4.2. Cluster changes with time

5 Conclusion

When compared with other clustering schemes, though the initial cluster setup cost is high, cluster maintenance becomes very much easier in the long run since the clusters are long-lived. Cluster deformations are greatly reduced due to Cluster Reorganization and Cluster Head Re-election since they result in stable clusters. The node elected as clusterhead has maximum associativity as well as satisfies a minimum connectivity requirement. Cluster Management is effective in our approach by improving the cluster stability and thereby reducing the overhead of exchange of control packets.

References

1. P. Krishna, Mainak Chatterjee, Nitin H. Vaidya, Dhiraj K. Pradhan, "A Cluster-based Approach for Routing in Ad-Hoc Networks", Proc .of 2nd Symposium on Mobile and Location-Independent Computing 1995,1-10.
2. M. Royer and C-K. Toh, "A Review of Current Routing Protocols for Ad-Hoc Mobile Wireless Networks", IEE Personal Communications, Vol. 6, Issue. 2, pp.46-55, 1999.
3. R. Sivakumar, P. Sinha and V. Bharghavan, "CEDAR: A Core-Extraction Distributed Ad hoc Routing algorithm", IEEE Journal on selected areas in communication, Vol 17, No. 8, August 1999.
4. Zygmunt J. Haas and Marc R. Pearlman," The Routing Algorithm for the Reconfigurable Wireless Networks", Proceedings of the 6th IEEE International Conference on Universal Personal Communications '97,1997, 12-16.
5. David B. Johnson, Davis A. Maltz," The Dynamic Source Routing Protocol for Mobile Ad Hoc Networks", IETF Draft, April 2003.
6. Charles E. Perkins, Elizabeth M. Royer and Samir R. Das, "Ad Hoc On Demand Distance Vector (AODV) Routing", IETF draft, Oct 1999.
7. M. Jiang, J. Li and Y.C. Toy," Cluster-Based Routing Protocol", IETF draft, August 1999.
8. Chai-Keong Toh," A novel distributed routing protocol to support Ad-Hoc mobile computing", Proceeding of IEEE Fifteenth Annual International Phoenix Conference on Computers and Communications, 1996, pp.480-486
9. Z. J. Haas, M. R. Pearlman, P. Samar, "The Interzone Routing Protocol (IERP) for Ad Hoc Networks", IETF draft, June 2001.
10. Z. J. Haas, M. R. Pearlman, and P. Samar, "The zone routing protocol (ZRP) for ad hoc networks", IETF draft, July 2002.

11. Rohit Dube, Cynthia D. Rais, Kuang-Yeh Wang, Satish K. Tripathi," Signal Stability based Adaptive Routing for Ad-Hoc Mobile Networks", IEEE Personal Communications, February 1997.
12. C.K.Toh," Long-lived Ad-Hoc Routing based on the concept of Associativity", IETF Draft, March 1999.
13. Basagni S," Distributed Clustering for Ad Hoc Networks", Proceedings of the International Symposium on Parallel Architectures, Algorithms, and Networks (I-SPAN'99), IEEE Computer Society, pp.310-315, Australia, June 23-25,1999.

Self-organized Security Architecture for MANET

Panneer Pandi Gnana Durai and Ranjani Parthasarathy

School of Computer Science Engineering
CEG Anna University, Chennai-25
gpanneerpandi@sify.com, rp@annauniv.edu

Abstract. An ad hoc Network is a new generation of network offering unrestricted mobility without any underlying infrastructure. In this kind of network, all the nodes share the responsibility of network formation and management. Fundamental characteristics of an ad hoc network, such as open medium, dynamic topology, dynamic cooperation and constrained capabilities lead to vulnerabilities. Unlike wired network, an ad hoc network does not have a clear line of defense, and every node must be prepared for encounters with an adversary. This paper proposes a three-layer security architecture for ad hoc networks, that provides self-organized distributed security, and authenticated, security aware routing. The first layer in the design performs the operation of a certification server such as issuing, renewal and revocation of certificate using the principle of secret sharing and threshold cryptography. Each certificate issued by this layer has a certain period of validity. Nodes should renew their tokens before expiration. Each node also accumulates its credit whenever it renews the token. The second layer provides authenticated and security aware routing using the token issued by the layer 1. Layer 3 consists of a modified version of reverse labeling restriction protocol that effectively handles internal attacks. This model has been simulated and is found to provide security with negligible overhead.

Keywords: Wireless and mobile computing, communication networks and sensor networks.

1 Introduction

The history of ad hoc network can be traced back to 1972 and the DoD sponsored Packet Radio Network (PRNET) which evolved into Survivable Adaptive Radio Networks (SURAN) program in early 1980s [1]. The goal of this program was to provide packet switched networking to mobile battlefield elements in an infrastructure less environments (Soldiers, tanks, aircraft, etc., forming the nodes in the network). In recent years, ad hoc wireless networking has found applications in military, sensor networks, commercial and educational environments, emergency rescue missions, home networks of personal devices, and instantaneous classroom/conference room applications.

Ad hoc network is vulnerable [2] to various kinds of attacks, ranging from passive eavesdropping to active denial of service attack (DoS). Passive attacks typically involve unauthorized listening to the transmitted packets. That is, the attacker does not disrupt the operation of a routing protocol but only attempts to discover valuable information by listening to or observing the traffic. Active attacks attempt to improperly modify data, gain authentication, or procure authorization by inserting false packets. The attacks may either be targeted at data packets or at routing packets. In

G. Das and V.P. Gulati (Eds.): CIT 2004, LNCS 3356, pp. 169–179, 2004.

this paper the focus is on routing packets. Active attacks under this category include black hole attack, routing table overflow, rushing attack, and denial of service attack [9].

In black hole attack, the malicious node uses the routing protocol to advertise itself as having the shortest path to nodes whose packets it wants to intercept. It can choose to drop the packets to perform a denial-of-service attack, or alternatively use its place on the route as the first step in a man-in-the-middle attack.

In a routing table overflow attack, the attacker attempts to create routes to nonexistent nodes. This is specifically used with proactive routing algorithms which attempt to discover routing information even before they are needed.

Rushing attack is targeted against on-demand routing protocols that use duplicate suppression at each node. Attacker disseminates route request quickly throughout the network suppressing any later legitimate route requests, which nodes drop due to duplicate suppression.

In denial of service attack, a malicious node hijacks network bandwidth. Adversaries may issue DoS attacks from various layers of the network stack, ranging from physical layer -interfering and jamming, network layer, transport layer – TCP flooding and SYN flooding, to numerous attacks in the application layer.

In addition to this, forging routing packets, information disclosure, tampering and blackmail attacks also come under active attacks.

In order to secure ad hoc networks against these attacks several researches have provided cryptography based security solutions. However, these solutions have certain limitations either in terms of the attacks that they thwart, or in being too restrictive. This paper proposes a practical three-tier security architecture that attempts to handle all of the attacks except the rushing attack mentioned above. The paper is organized as follows.

Section 2 presents an overview of other security solutions that have been proposed, and highlights their limitations. It also provides the perspective in which the proposed security model has been conceived. Section 3 describes this model. Section 4 presents the details of the simulation of this model using the GloMoSim [15] simulator, and the results. Section 5 concludes the paper.

2 Related Work

Given below are the security mechanisms that have been put forth by various researches for securing ad hoc networks. To provide robust and ubiquitous security for ad hoc networks [4, 5], Luo, Kong et al, distribute the authentication services into each individual node's locality to ensure maximal service availability and robustness. In this architecture, each node carries a certificate signed with secret key (SK), well known Public key (PK) is used for certificate verification. Nodes without valid certificates are treated as adversaries and denied access to any network resources such as packet forwarding and routing. When a mobile node moves to a new location, it exchanges certificates with its new neighbors. Authenticated neighboring nodes help each other forward and route packets. They also monitor each other to detect possible misbehaviors and break-ins. Specific monitoring mechanisms are left to each individual node's choice. Here this token is used for authentication purposes only, and it has no provision to identify the well behaving nodes.

In the work proposed by Hao, Yang et al [3] a unified network-layer security solution, which protects both routing and packet forwarding functionalities in the context of the AODV protocol is used. A self-organized approach is used by exploiting full-localized design, without assuming any a priori trust or secret association between nodes.

Ariadne is another secure on demand routing protocol for ad hoc networks proposed by Johnson et al [11] which prevents attackers or compromised nodes from tampering with uncompromised routes consisting of uncompromised nodes, and also prevents a large number of Denial-of-Service attacks. This scheme requires a centralized certification server, which is not always possible in a dynamic topology.

Security-Aware ad hoc Routing SAR [12] proposes a new routing technique that incorporates security attributes as parameters into ad hoc route discovery. SAR enables the use of security as a negotiable metric to improve the relevance of the routes discovered by ad hoc routing protocols. It uses a two-tier classification of routing protocol security metrics, and proposes a framework to measure and enforce security attributes on ad hoc routing paths. This framework enables applications to adapt their behavior according to the level of protection available on communicating nodes in an ad hoc network. This design requires a key hierarchy and separate metrics for providing SAR, which leads to computation and message overhead in low power devices.

A method to avoid sequence number attacks has been suggested by Bhargava et al [13]. Baruch awerbuch et al [14] propose an on-demand routing protocol for ad hoc Wireless networks that provides resilience to Byzantine failures caused by individual or colluding nodes. Their adaptive probing technique detects a malicious link after log n faults have occurred, where n is the length of the path. These links are then avoided by multiplicatively increasing their weights and by using an on-demand route discovery protocol. This solution identifies the malicious links instead of malicious nodes.

Viewed in this context, this paper proposes a three- tier security architecture that handles internal, as well as external attacks and provides authenticated and security aware routing without key hierarchy and separate metrics. This design uses the token to authenticate the nodes in the network. This is similar to the design discussed in [3, 4, 5], but it has a provision to identify the well behaving nodes from its token, and rewards such nodes. This design provides authenticated and security aware routing as discussed in design [11, 12], but without any key hierarchy, extra metrics, and a centralized certificate server. This design also finds the malicious nodes instead of malicious links. This is achieved by using the modified reverse labeling restriction protocol to thwart sequence number modification attack in the network layer. The details of this architecture are given in the following section.

3 Proposed Security Architecture

The objective of this model is to provide security in a collaborative, self-organized manner, both reactive and proactive. It should provide tolerance to compromised nodes, have the ability to detect and remove adversaries from network, and handle routing misbehaviors. This design uses the concept of secret sharing [6] and threshold cryptography [7]. Hence key management is handled in a distributed, cooperative manner. In this design, each node has a signed token in order to participate in the network operations. This token has a certain period of validity. Each node in the network renews its token before it expires. The period of the validity of a node's token is dependent on how long it has stayed and behaved well in the network. A metric called credit is used to identify the well behaving node. A well-behaving node accumulates its credits and renews its token less and less frequently. Whenever a node sends or forwards any packet (Control or Data), it appends its token with the packet. Intermediate nodes verify the signature of previous nodes. If the message is not from a legitimate neighbor, they drop the packet. Further, this credit also helps to provide an optional security aware routing. In security aware routing only nodes having a credit above the specified level can participate in the route recovery, path maintenance, and packet forwarding. Thus the addition of the credit field (which is not present in the token used in [3]), helps to provide an additional level of security by identifying veteran (secured) nodes.In addition to this it also uses an intrusion detection scheme called modified reverse labeling restriction protocol to handle internal attacks. This scheme is used to exactly identify the malicious node.

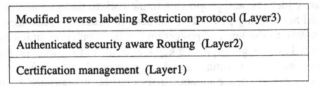

| Modified reverse labeling Restriction protocol (Layer3) |
| Authenticated security aware Routing (Layer2) |
| Certification management (Layer1) |

Fig. 1. Architecture of the proposed model

In essence, this security solution exploits collaboration among local nodes to protect the network layer without completely trusting any individual node. Thus this design provides distributed, self-organized security. It also provides authenticated and security aware routing with less message and computation overhead. This architecture is shown in figure 1. It consists of three layers. Layer 1, which does certificate management, provides the first wall of security. It handles the external attacks. The core functions of this layer are issuing new tokens, renewing existing tokens, expiration timer management, and partial signature generation. Layer 2 provides the second level of security that consists of authenticated and security aware routing. It overcomes almost all routing update misbehaviors. Layer 3 implements Modified Reverse labeling restriction Protocol.

3.1 Layer 1

This layer uses the principle of secret sharing [6] and threshold cryptography [7]. Each node in the network should have a token to communicate in the network. A token consists of five fields, namely, node Id, signing time, expiration time, credit and a reserved field for future use. The format of the token is given in figure 2.

| Node id | Signing time | Expiration time | Credit | Reserved |

Fig. 2. Token format

Node Id: This value is assumed to be unique and used to identify each device in the network uniquely (It may be derived from Medium Access Layer (MAC) address).

Signing time: It is the time when the new nodes get the token, or an already existing node renews its token.

Expiration time: This time indicates the time at which the validity of the token expires. Before this time the node should renew its token.

Credit: This value indicates how long a node acts well in the network. Whenever a node renews its token this value is incremented. It is also used as a security metric in this design. A dealer issues this token at the bootstrapping phase. After that any combination of k members where k is the threshold can provide the token. In the bootstrapping phase, the dealer node generates a global public key (PK) – private key (SK) pair using the RSA algorithm [7]. For K nodes this will take a secret polynomial f (x) of order k −1, and encrypt the token and generate the secret share [4,5] for k nodes and distribute it. The dealer quits the network once the bootstrapping phase is over. After the bootstrapping phase, each node in the network has an encrypted token, global public key (PK), which is used for token verification and a secret share (sk_i). This secret share is used later to sign a token for new nodes, which join the network, and for token renewal of neighboring nodes.

When a new node comes into the network it broadcasts a token request. The neighbor node verifies the token request and gives a partially signed token (token signed by its secret share) and partial secret share. The new node collects minimum k such partial tokens and secret shares to generate a complete token and its own secret share using the k–bounded offsetting coalition algorithm [4, 5].

Also, the nodes in the network should renew their token before they expire. The token renewal process is similar to a new token issue process except for credit management and verification of period of validity. The new sign out time, and credit is calculated from the previous token as follows.

New sign out time=New sign in time + (old sign out time −old sign in time +T_0). New credit=old credit +1.

Where To is period of validity of the fresh token. Whenever the node renews its token, the period of validity is increased by T0, and the credit is increased by one. In a nutshell this layer takes care of certificate management, which is used to authenticate the nodes in the network. This certificate is used by the layer2 for providing authenticated, security aware routing, and by layer3 to handle internal attacks.

3.2 Layer 2

This layer uses the token for providing routing security. It consists of two modules, Authenticated routing, and Security aware routing.

3.2.1 Authenticated Routing

After bootstrapping phase each node in the network has a token to communicate in the network. When a node starts the route request process, it should append its certificate with the route request. The intermediate nodes should verify the validity of the token before doing the normal operation (relaying route request, or sending reply). In the reverse direction also, the same process is applicable. By verification of certificate before processing the request, denial of service attack, routing loops, partition of network, and external attacks are overcome.

3.2.2 Security Aware Routing

In this architecture well behaving nodes have higher credits than other nodes. If a node wants a secure path rather than an optimal path, it should specify the credit level required to participate in routing and packet forwarding. If the intermediate node satisfies the credit level, it participates in the communication (forwarding) else it drops the packet. The intermediate nodes verify the previous node's credit level from the token. If the previous node had not satisfied the security level it drops the node from the route list. Thus only nodes, which have a credit value equal to or higher than the requested credit can form a route. This can be better understood with an example. Consider the scenario given in figure3. Nodes N1, N3, N4, N6 have a credit of 4, N5 has a credit of 6, and N2 has a credit of 2.If the node N1 needs a path from N1 to N6 with a credit of 4, it takes the path N1-N3-N4-N5-N6. Even though N1-N2-N6 is optimal it will not take the path as N2 has only 2 credits. N5 has a credit of 6 so it can take part in the communication.

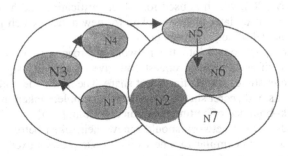

Fig. 3. Security aware routing

3.3 Layer 3 – Modified Reverse Labeling Restriction Protocol

This is an extension of the reverse labeling restriction protocol [13]. The purpose of using this protocol is to avoid false destination sequence attacks. In such attacks, a malicious node may send a route reply indicating that it has a latest route to the destination. In the reverse labeling restriction protocol [13], which handles these types of attacks, every host maintains a blacklist to record suspicious hosts. Suspicious hosts can be released from the blacklist or put there permanently. The destination host will broadcast an INVALID packet with its signature when it finds that the system is under attack on sequence. The packet carries the host's identification, current sequence, new sequence, and its own blacklist. Every host receiving this packet will examine its route entry to the destination host. If the sequence number is larger than the current sequence in INVALID packet, the presence of an attack is noted. The next hop to the destination will be added to this host's blacklist. In this scheme, legitimate nodes between the source and the malicious nodes are unnecessarily punished as blacklisted nodes. Sometimes a legitimate node may also be put in the permanent black list, which is unfair.

The proposed modification aims at this unfairness. This modification helps to exactly identify the node, which does the sequence number modification attack. In this design, once the sender receives the INVALID message from the destination, it decrypts the certificate, which comes with the route reply, and finds the malicious node (the node which sent the route reply without having the latest route). It sends an alert message to all nodes that the specified node is a malicious node and puts it in the token revocation list. Similarly if a node transmits a number of route request(beyond a threshold value), it is considered as a symptom of a compromised and hence, the node is blacklisted.

Table 1. Attacks handled

Type of Attack	Handled by
Denial of Service attack:	L1, L2
Impersonation	L1, L2
Tampering	L1, L2
Internal Attack	L1, L2, L3
External Attack	L1, L2

3.4 Security Analysis

A summary of the security attacks handled by this design is given in table 1, and an explanation of how it is handled is given below.

3.4.1 External Attacks
These are attacks by nodes that are not part of the network (ie, they do not have a token).

Denial of Service. Before processing the request the routing protocol in the layer 2, verifies the token that comes with the request using the public key. By dropping the invalid requests (i.e., requests with invalid tokens), it thwarts the DoS attack discussed in section 1.

Tampering. In this scheme the presence of a valid token is required to make any modifications to the routing information. Thus tampering routing table attacks by external attackers are handled.

Impersonation. The token contains the encrypted form of node id. Due to uniqueness of node id impersonation is avoided.

3.4.2 Internal Attacks
This kind of attacks may come from the compromised node, or from a misbehaving internal node. In such cases, when a node sends unnecessary request with a valid token, the layer 3 modified reverse labeling restriction protocol identifies the misbehaving node and puts it in the black list. The requests which, come from the nodes in the blacklist are dropped by neighbors. Thus the malicious internal as well as compromised nodes are removed from the network.

4 Simulation and Results

The proposed scheme has been implemented and simulated using the GloMoSim [15] simulator. Layer 1 operation such as bootstrapping phase, new member inclusion and token renewal are implemented in the application layer and the authenticated routing, security aware routing are implemented in the ad hoc on demand distance vector (AODV) routing protocol. The message format for route request, route reply, and route error have been modified as shown in figure 4,5,6 respectively. These messages have some common fields and some fields specific to the message type (request, reply or error). These fields are explained in table 2.

To test the effectiveness of the proposed security model, two issues have been studied- one is the tolerance to attacks and the other is the effect on performance. Performance Analysis, to analyze the performance, the delay introduced in the network to send the first packet (delay introduced due to certificate processing) and the average end-to-end delay   are measured for AODV and authenticated AODV (with the security architecture). Table 3 gives the result for authenticated AODV and table 4 gives the result for AODV. The simulation has been carried out using the following parameters.

Packet Type	Hop Count
Source Address	Source Sequence Number
Destination Address	Destination Sequence Number
Last Address	Broadcast ID
Certificate	Credit

Fig. 4. Route request message format

Packet Type	Hop Count
Source Address	Life Time
Destination Address	Destination Sequence Number
Certificate	Credit

Fig. 5. Route reply message format

Type	Destination count
Unreachable Destination IP Address (1)	
Unreachable Destination Sequence Number (1)	
Additional Unreachable Destination IP Addresses (if needed)	
Additional Unreachable Destination Sequence Numbers (if needed)	
Certificate	

Fig. 6. Route error message format

Value of k has been varied from 3 to 6 and the implementation has been tested. The result shown are for k=3. From the tables 3 and 4 and graphs shown in figure 7 and 8, it can be seen that even though the delay introduced for the first packet is slightly higher for authenticated AODV, the average end-to-end delay for authenticated AODV varies by 0.2 to 1 milliseconds, which is not significant. Thus it can be seen that there is very little performance degradation. Similarly there is negligible degradation in the packet delivery ratio as seen from figure 9. However as seen in figure 10, there is a slight reduction in throughput due to the overhead involved in the processing.

Table 2. Fields in routing messages

Packet type	Indicates the type of packet .It is 0, 1, or 2 for route request, route reply, and route error respectively – Common to all.
Hop count	The number of hops from the source IP Address to the node handling the request or reply – common to all.
Broadcast ID	A sequence number uniquely identifying the particular route request when taken in conjunction with the source node's IP address.
Certificate	Signed token of the node, which is sending or relaying the route request – common to all
Destination sequence number	The last sequence number received in the past by the source for any route towards that destination –common to all.
Destination Address	The IP address of the destination for which a route is desired –common to all – used in route request.
Credit	Indicates the credit level required to participate in security aware routing – common to all.
Last Address	Address of the immediate predecessor node, which handles the packet previously –used in route request message.
Source sequence number	Sequence number of the node sending route request –used in route request message.
Lifetime	Period of validity of the reply- used in route reply message.
Destination count	The number of unreachable destinations included in the message (should be at least 1) –used in route error message.
Unreachable Destination IP Address	The IP address of the destination, which has become unreachable due to a link break –used in route error message.
Unreachable destination Sequence Number.	The last known sequence number, incremented by one, of the destination listed in the previous Unreachable Destination IP Address field –used in route error message.

Simulation area	(600,600) meters
Mobility Model	Random –Waypoint
Node placement	Random
Pause time	30 seconds
No of nodes	10-50
Speed	0 –10 meter per second
Frequency	2.4GHz.
To	seconds

4.1 Malicious Packet Identification

To study the effectiveness of the security provided, some malicious nodes are introduced in the network at random, which send route requests at random to the network. It is verified that the packets from malicious nodes are identified and dropped as required. Table 3 gives the observation regarding malicious node identification. It indicates that the network identifies all the malicious packets from the malicious nodes. This has been tried for various scenarios.

5 Conclusion

This paper has presented a self-organizing security architecture with authenticated and security aware routing for ad hoc networks. This architecture has been imple-

Table 3. Malicious packet identification

No of malicious packets introduced	No of malicious packets captured
6	6
12	12
30	30
36	36

Table 4. Observation for AODV

No of Nodes	Delay for First Packet (Second)	Average End to end Delay (Second)
10	0.02865	0.004321
20	0.15575	0.005413
30	0.187577	0.006349
40	0.05885	0.00614

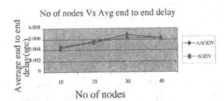

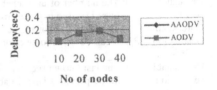

Fig. 7. Numbers of nodes Vs end-to-end delay

Fig. 8. Numbers of nodes Vs Average end-to-end delay

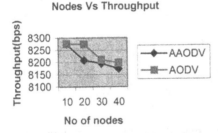

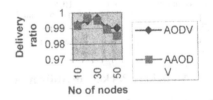

Fig. 9. Number of nodes Vs Packet delivery ratio

Fig. 10. Number of nodes Vs throughput

mented and simulated using the GloMoSim simulator. The results of the simulation show that this design achieves its goal at the cost of a negligible delay in the network.

References

1. Ram Ramanathan and Jason Redi BBN Technologies, "A brief overview of ad hoc networks challenges and directions", IEEE communication magazine may 2002 pp 20-22.

2. L. Zhou and Z. J. Haas, "Securing Ad Hoc Networks," IEEE Network, vol. 13, no. 6, Nov.– Dec. 1999, pp. 24–30.
3. Hao Yang, Xiaoqiao Meng, Songwu Lu, "Self-organized network-layer security in mobile ad hoc networks", Proceedings of the ACM workshop on Wireless security September 2002,Pp 11-20.
4. Haiku Luo, Jiejun Kong, Petros Zerfos, Songwu Lu and Lixia Zhang, "Self-securing Ad-Hoc Wireless Networks", IEEE ISCC (IEEE Symposium on Computers and Communications) 2002, Italy, July 2002.
5. Haiku Luo, Jiejun Kong, Petros Zerfos, Songwu Lu, Lixia Zhang et al "Providing Robust and Ubiquitous Security Support for Mobile Ad-Hoc Networks", in Proc. IEEE ICNP, pp 251--260, 2001.
6. Adi Shamir "How to Share a Secret", Communications of the ACM, 22(11): 612-613, 1979.
7. Ivan B. Damgard and Maciej Koprowski. "Practical threshold RSA signatures without a trusted dealer", Research Series RS-00-30, BRICS, Department of Computer Science, University of Aarhus, November 2000. Pp 14.
8. Y. Zhang, W. Lee, "Intrusion Detection in Wireless Ad-Hoc Networks," Proceedings of the Sixth ACM International Conference on Mobile Networking and Computing, Boston, August 2000 (Mobicom 2000).
9. Wei Li, P.Agarwal "Routing Security in Wireless Ad hoc network", IEEE communication magazine (October 2002), pp 70-75.
10. B. Dahill, B. Levine, E. Royer, and C. Shields, "A secure routing protocol for ad hoc net works," Technical Report UM-CS-2001-037, Electrical Engineering and Computer Science, University of Michigan, August 2001.
11. Y. C. Hu, A. Perrig, and D. B. Johnson "Ariadne: A secure on-demand routing protocol for ad hoc networks". In Proceedings of the Eighth ACM International Conference on Mobile Computing and Networking Mobicom2002.
12. Seung Yi, Prasad Naldurg, Robin Kravets seungyi et al "A Security-Aware Routing Protocol for Wireless Hoc Networks" Proceedings of the 2001 ACM International Symposium on Mobile ad hoc networking & computing pp 299 – 302.
13. Bharat Bhargava, "Intruder Identification in Ad Hoc Networks" CERIAS Security Center and Department of Computer Sciences Purdue University, research proposal 2002.
14. Baruch Awerbuch, David Holmer, Cristina NitaRotaru and Herbert Rubens "An On Demand Secure Routing Protocol Resilient Byzantine Failures", Department of Computer Science Johns Hopkins University Proceedings of the ACM workshop on Wireless security 2002, Atlanta, pp 21-30.
15. http://pcl.cs.ucla.edu/projects/glomosim.

Clock Synchronization
in IEEE 802.11 Ad Hoc Networks

S.S. Thakur, S. Nandi, D. Goswami, and R. Bhattarcharjee

Indian Institute of Technology, Guwahati
Guwahati-781039, India
{sst,sukumar,dgoswami,ratnajit}@iitg.ernet.in

Abstract. In an Independent Basic Service set (IBSS), of IEEE 802.11 standards, it is important that all stations are synchronized to a common clock. When the number of stations in an IBSS is very small, there is a negligible probability that stations may go out of synchronization. More the stations, higher is the probability of getting out of synchronization. Thus, the current IEEE 802.11's synchronization mechanism does not scale; it cannot support a large-scale ad hoc network. To alleviate the synchronization problem, "Adaptive Time Synchronization Procedure" (ATSP) is proposed [1]. ATSP is scalable up to 300 nodes. As the number of nodes increases beyond 300 again synchronization become problem. In this paper, we modify ATSP to further increase the scalability of IEEE 802.11 ad hoc networks. The modified algorithm divides nodes in priority levels depending on their clock speed. This algorithm allows nodes only with highest priority to contend for beacon transmission. Reduction in beacon contention increases scalability of IBSS.

1 Introduction

Due to the widespread availability of inexpensive hardware and its relatively stable and complete protocol definition, the IEEE 802.11 standards [3] is the default choice for use in ad hoc networking research. Standard supports two operating modes; one in infrastructure mode and the other in ad hoc mode. For infrastructure operating mode, a station serves as the access point and responsible for buffering and forwarding traffic to stations in its basic service set (BSS). When the infrastructure does not exist or does not work, the ad hoc mode is useful. An ad-hoc mode of IEEE 802.11 is called an Independent Basic Service Set (IBSS), in which all of the stations are within each other's transmission range.

Performance analysis of IEEE 802.11 wireless LAN has been reported in [6, 2, 9, 13]. Reference [6] evaluates the performance of the Distributed Coordination Function (DCF) of IEEE 802.11 standards and proposes an adaptive contention window protocol to replace the exponential backoff protocol. In [2] and [13], the saturation throughput of DCF is analyzed using different techniques. The effect of network size and traffic patterns on the capacity of ad hoc wireless networks is examined in [9], where the locality of traffic is shown to be a key factor of scalability of ad hoc networks.

G. Das and V.P. Gulati (Eds.): CIT 2004, LNCS 3356, pp. 180–189, 2004.
© Springer-Verlag Berlin Heidelberg 2004

Most of the works are focused on the IEEE 802.11 MAC protocol. Scalability issue is addressed only in [1]. Our paper is extending the work done in [1] on the scalability issue of IEEE 802.11 ad hoc networks. Envision that in a classroom or in an auditorium, more than 100 students turn on their laptops to form an IBSS. Will the ad hoc network work properly? This question is not trivial. In [1] scalability of IEEE 802.11 ad hoc networks from the viewpoint of clock synchronization is analyzed. Our paper modifies ATSP proposed in [1] to further increase the scalability of IEEE 802.11 ad hoc networks.

Clock synchronization in an IBSS is needed for power management and synchronization of frequency hopping. In power management each station uses its clock to determine the beginning and the end of the ad hoc traffic indication (ATIM) window. In Frequency Hopping Spread Spectrum (FHSS), each station determines when to "hop" to a new channel according to its timer. Due to beacon contention, the stations may fail to successfully transmit beacon frames [1]. As a result, some stations in the IBSS may become so out of synchronization with others that power management or FHSS can not work properly. To alleviate the asynchronism problem and increase the scalability of IEEE 802.11 based ad hoc networks, we have proposed the simple algorithm and shown its performance.

2   Clock Synchronization

This section reviews the Timing Synchronization Function (TSF) as specified in the IEEE 802.11 specifications [3], and comments on a few related clock synchronization algorithms.

2.1   The TSF of IEEE 802.11

According to the IEEE 802.11 specifications [3], the TSF in an IBSS shall be implemented via a distributed algorithm that shall be performed by all of the members of the IBSS. Each station in an IBSS shall adopt the timing received from any beacon or probe response that has a TSF value later than its own TSF timer.

Each station maintain a TSF timer with modulus 2^{64} counting in increments of microseconds (μs). Stations expect to receive beacons at a nominal rate. Stations periodically exchanging timing information through beacon frames, which contains a timestamp among other parameters, achieve clock or timing synchronization. Each station in an IBSS shall adopt the timing received from any beacon that has a TSF time value (the timestamp) later than its own TSF timer. All stations in the IBSS adopt a common value, *aBeaconPeriod*, which defines the length of beacon intervals or periods. This value, established by the station that initiates the IBSS, defines a series of Target Beacon Transmission Times (TBTTs) exactly *aBeaconPeriod* time units apart. Beacon generation in an IBSS is distributed; all stations in the IBSS participate in the process. At each TBTT, each station.

Table 1. Beacon generation window and slot time.

	FHSS	DSSS	Infrared
aCWmin	15	31	63
aSlotTime	$50\mu s$	$20\mu s$	$8\mu s$

1. Calculates a random delay uniformly distributed in the range between zero and $2.aCWmin.aSlotTime$. (The '$aCWmin$' and '$aSlotTime$' parameters are specified in Table 1)
2. If a beacon arrives before the random delay timer has expired, the station cancels the pending beacon transmission and the remaining random delay.
3. The station waits for the period of the random delay.
4. When the random delay timer expires, the station transmits a beacon with a timestamp equal to the value of the station's TSF timer.
5. Upon receiving a beacon, a station sets its TSF timer to the timestamp of the beacon if the value of the timestamp is later than the station's TSF timer. (It is important to note that clocks only move forward and never backward.)

Thus, as illustrated in Figure 1, at the beginning of each beacon interval, there is a beacon generation window consisting of $W + 1$ slots each of length $aSlotTime$, where $W = 2.aCWmin$. Each station is scheduled to transmit a beacon at the beginning of one of the slots. For FHSS, the beacon size is at least 550 bits. Therefore, for the data rate of 1Mbps the beacon length is 11 slots. The beacon length is 7 slots if the data rate is 2Mbps.

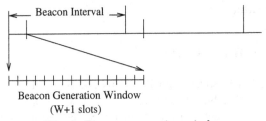

Beacon Generation Window
(W+1 slots)

Fig. 1. Beacon generation window.

2.2 Asynchronism

Clock synchronization is important for power management in both DSSS and FHSS as well as for the synchronization of hopping sequence in FHSS. If the clocks of two stations are so badly out of synchronization that either power management or FHSS cannot work properly, the two stations are said to be out of synchronization. If there are pairs of stations out of synchronization in an IBSS, the network is said to be in hazardous asynchronism. In this subsection, we will discuss the types of asynchronism. Let Δ be the maximum clock difference tolerable by power management and FHSS.

Two clocks are out of synchronization if their times are different by more than Δ. Two stations are out of synchronization if their clocks are out of synchronization. Assume that the clocks in an IBSS are all different in speed (or accuracy). Thus, there is a unique fastest station, whose clock is fastest in the system. We are particularly interested in two conditions of asynchronism.

Fastest-Station Asynchronism: This refers to a situation where the clock of the fastest station is ahead of the clocks of all other stations by more than Δ units of time. Fastest-station asynchronism may occur in an IBSS because under the IEEE 802.11 timing synchronization function, stations can only set their timers forward and never backward. Slower clocks synchronize with faster clocks, but faster clocks do not synchronize themselves with slower clocks. Thus, if the fastest station fails to transmit beacons for too many beacon intervals, its clock will be ahead of all other clocks by more than Δ.

Global Asynchronism: Given a value k between one and one hundred, k percent global asynchronism (or simply k percent asynchronism) refers to the situation that at least k percent of the $\frac{n(n-1)}{2}$ pairs of stations are out of synchronization

2.3   Related Work

Different synchronization method called reference broadcast synchronization (RBS) is presented in [11] for broadcast networks, especially for wireless ad hoc networks. A reference broadcast or beacon does not contain an explicit timestamp; instead, receivers use its arrival time as a point of reference for comparing their clocks. RBS uses nontrivial statistics methods such as regression to estimate the phase offset and clock skew of any two nodes.

Mills [10] proposes a Network Time Protocol (NTP) to synchronize clocks and coordinate time distribution in the Internet system. NTP cannot be used for sparse ad hoc networks, which can be partitioned. To deal with partitioning in sparse ad hoc networks, a time synchronism algorithm is proposed in [12].

Work on scalability issue of IEEE 802.11 ad hoc networks is done in [1]. It pointed out the clock asynchronism problem faced by a large-scale IBSS and have proposed a simple scheme to fix it. Analysis of asynchronism and analysis of beacon contention is also done in [1]. In [1] adaptive timing synchronization procedure (ATSP) is proposed to solve the scalability issue of IEEE 802.11 ad hoc networks. ATSP does not solve the scalability issue completely; there are some problems with ATSP that are mentioned below.

1. In ATSP the fastest station is, to some extent, in charge of timing synchronization. If the fastest station leaves the IBSS because of mobility or other reasons, the second fastest node become the fastest. $I(i)$ is assigned to each station i that range between 1 and I_{max} (maximum value of $I(i)$). Before failure of the fastest node all the stations have their $I(i)$ set to I_{max}. According to ATSP the $I(i)$ is decreased by one in every I_{max} beacon interval, it takes at most I_{max}^2 beacon interval for second fastest node to take control. It may lead to asynchronization.

2. ATSP is scalable up to 300 nodes. As the number of nodes increases beyond 300 global asynchronism and fastest node asynchronism again become a problem. As the fastest node fails, all the nodes that are satisfying the

condition will contend for beacon transmission. As the number of nodes is more so good number nodes will satisfy the condition and contend for beacon transmission, this will lead to collision. The main problem is contention after failure of the fastest node. We need priority for beacon transmission among the nodes based on clock speed to solve the problem of contention.

3   Modified Adaptive Time Synchronization Procedure(MATSP)

In this paper, we have modified ATSP to alleviates the problems of ATSP mentioned in earlier section. The proposed algorithm in this paper, consider how to reduce beacon contention by dividing nodes in several priority levels based on their clock speed. Faster nodes should have higher priority for beacon transmission than slower nodes. Nodes should change the priority level dynamically depending upon the received timestamp. Following variables are used in the algorithm, their definitions are noted below.

$I(i)$ – We assign to each station i an integer $I(i)$ that determines how often each station shall participate in beacon contention. That is station i contend for beacon transmission once in every $I(i)$ beacon periods. Therefore, smaller the value of $I(i)$, higher the station's chance of beacon transmission. Let the maximum possible value of $I(i)$ be I_{max}.

$P(i)$ – We calculate the priority value $P(i)$ for each station i. Priority value is calculated in each beacon interval using time stamp received and timer value of node. Detail procedure of priority calculation will be described later.

$C(i)$ – Let $C(i)$ be a counter at station i that counts number of beacon intervals since last synchronization.

Algorithm MATSP

1. As a station joins the IBSS, it will receive beacon frame and set its timer. For each station i, let $I(i)$ be random number between 1 and I_{max}. Let $C(i) := 1$ and $P(i) := 0$.
2. In each beacon interval every station participates in beacon contention if $P(i) = 0$ and $C(i)$ mod $I(i) = 0$.
3. Whenever station i receives a beacon with a timing value later than its own, the station sets its timer to this value, increases $I(i)$ by 1 if $I(i) < I_{max}$, calculates the value of $P(i)$ and sets $C(i) := 0$.
4. If station i does not receive any beacon frame with timing value later than its own for I_{max} consecutive beacon interval it decrements $I(i)$ by 1 if $I(i)>1$, it also decrements $P(i)$ by 1 if $P(i) > 0$ and sets $C(i) := 0$.
5. At the end of a beacon interval, each station increases its $C(i)$ by 1.

3.1   Silent Feature of MATSP

This subsection explains the working of algorithm.

Transmission of Beacon by Fastest Station: Second step in algorithm allows only those nodes to contend for beacon transmission, who lies in highest priority level and satisfy the condition $C(i) \bmod I(i) = 0$. Here division in priority levels reduces the contention for beacon transmission.

New Station Successfully Transmit Beacon: Nodes change their priority value dynamically depending on received timestamp. Every time a new node successfully transmit beacon new priority value is assigned to other nodes. Procedure for the priority $P(i)$ calculation is given below.

Procedure for $P(i)$ Calculation

In IEEE 802.11, specification requires clock accuracy to be within $\pm 0.01\%$. Assume that the values of clock accuracy of the n stations are uniformly distributed over the range $[-0.01\%, 0.01\%]$. In the worst case, two clocks satisfying the 802.11 requirement may differ by 0.02%. For the length of a beacon interval, T=0.1s, two clocks with a difference of d in accuracy will drift away from each other by $d * T$, and in worst case, two clocks satisfying the 802.11 requirement may differ by $0.02\% * 0.1s = 20\mu s$.

We can divide the nodes in m priority level, by calculating difference between time stamp received and their timer value. If the clock is synchronized then the worst case difference will be $20\mu s$. Let us divide all the nodes in 0 to 9 priority levels. Nodes having difference between 0 to $2\mu s$ with timestamp received have 0 priority value and those having difference between 18 to $20\mu s$ difference have 9 priority value. Detailed $P(i)$ calculation procedure is described below.

Let $T(i)$ be the timer value of each station i and T_r is received timestamp value. We calculate the difference between T_r and $T(i)$

1. Calculate $D(i) = T_r - T(i)$.
2. Set priority value of each node $P(i) := [D(i)/C(i)]/[20/m]$.

The maximum clock drift in one beacon interval being $20\mu s$. If the clocks are synchronized in every beacon interval then $D(i)$ will range from 0 to $20\mu s$. If the clocks are not synchronized in every beacon interval then $D(i)$ is accumulated clock drift and $C(i)$ keeps a count of the number of intervals from last successful reception of beacon. We have used $C(i)$ in expression since the priority levels are to be decided on the basis of clock drift in one beacon interval. The division by $20/m$ in the above expression enables us to divide nodes into a maximum of m priority levels. That is, the nodes differing by more than $20/m\mu s$ will be lying in different priority levels. In this way all the nodes are divided in m priority levels that range in $[0, m-1]$.

Newly Joined Fastest Station Competing for Synchronization: If newly joined station don't receives timestamp later than its own, it assume that it is the fastest station at that moment. So it should contend for beacon transmission and take over the control of clock synchronization. This case has been taken care in step four of the algorithm by reducing $P(i)$ and $I(i)$ values. In turn the fastest node will take over control of clock synchronization.

Once the clocks have been synchronized, the fastest station will not receive a timing value greater than its own; its $I(i) - value$ will gradually decrease to

1 and stay there. The other stations will gradually increase their $I(i) - value$ until they reach I_{max}. Define a stable state to be one in which the fastest station $I(i) - value$ has reached 1 and the other stations have reached I_{max}. Once the IBSS reaches a stable state, the fastest station has a very high probability of successfully sending a beacon and thereby synchronizing all the other stations.

4   Simulation Setup

To verify performance and demonstrate the scalability of our proposed algorithm, we have developed a simulation program in C. The simulator follows the protocol details of beacon generation and contention. The parameters are specified in Table 2.

The value of $aBeaconPeriod$ is set to 0.1s as recommended by the IEEE 802.11 specification. According to the IEEE 802.11 specification the time allocated for the physical layer (PHY) to hop from one frequency to another frequency in FHSS is $224\mu s$. This value gives an upper bound on Δ, the maximum tolerable clock drift; for if the clocks of two stations are $224\mu s$ apart, the faster station may have hopped to the new frequency and started transmitting while the slower station is still listening to the old frequency and therefore, missing the frame. The station that starts IBSS sets the values of I_{max} and number of priority levels.

Global Asynchronism

Given a value k between one and one hundred, k percent global asynchronism refers to the situation that at least k percent of the $n(n-1)/2$ pairs of stations are out of synchronization. The IEEE 802.11 specification requires clock accuracy to be within $\pm 0.01\%$. In the worst case, two clock satisfying the 802.11 requirement may differ by 0.02%. Assume that the values of clock accuracy of the n stations are uniformly distributed over the range $[-0.01\%, 0.01\%]$. Out of the $n(n-1)$ pairs of stations, at least $n^2/8$ pairs, or more than 25 percent, are different by at least d=0.01% in their clock accuracy. Thus, a condition of d-global asynchronism with d=0.01% will result in a condition of 25% global asynchronism in which 25 percent of links may experience frame losses due to asyschronism.

Table 2. Simulation Setup.

Parameter	Value
Beacon generation window (W)	30 slots
Beacon length	7 slots
Propagation delay	$1\mu s$
aBeaconPeriod	0.1s
Clock accuracy	$\pm 0.01\%$
Δ	$224\mu s$
I_{max}	10
Priority Levels	20

For the length of a beacon interval, $T = 0.1s$, two clocks with difference of d in accuracy will drift away from each other by $d \cdot T = 0.01\% \cdot 0.1s = 10\mu s$. Thus, with $\Delta = 224\mu s$, $d = 0.01\%$ and $T = 0.1s$, we have $\tau = \lceil \frac{\delta}{d \cdot T} \rceil = 23$. If no beacon is successfully sent in 23 consecutive beacon intervals then it result in condition of 25% global asynchronism.

In our simulation, the inter-asynchronism time is measured in two ways. First, we count the number of consecutive beacon intervals during which no beacons are successfully sent. When this number exceeds $\tau = 23$, we record an event of asynchronism. Second, way we count the number of pairs of stations which are out of synchronization. Whenever there are more than 25 percent of pairs out of synchronization, we record an incident of global asynchronism.

Fastest-Node Asynchronism

Assume that the clock of the fastest station is faster in speed(or accuracy) than the clocks of the second fastest station by d, where $d = 0.003\%$. In the simulation, we let the fastest clock and the second fastest clock differ in accuracy by d, while the other clocks are uniformly distributed in the range of $[-0.01\%, \rho_2]$ where ρ_2 is the accuracy of the second fastest clock. We compare the timing value of the fastest station with that of other stations. Whenever the fastest node is out of sysnchronization will all other stations, we record an incident of asysnchronism.

Next, we examine fastest-node asynchronism by simulation assuring that all the clocks are uniformly distributed in accuracy between -0.01% and $+0.01\%$. Again we follow the same procedure. We compare the timing value of the fastest station with that of other stations. Whenever the fastest node is out of syschronization will all other stations, we record an incident of asynchronism. We tested the performance of our algorithm in static IBSS and dynamic IBSS.

4.1   Static IBSS

For global asynchronism, we adopted $d = 0.01\%$ and $\tau = 23$ (maximum number of consecutive interval in which no beacon is sent) and chose 10 for I_{max} and 20 priority levels. For diffrent values of $n \le 1500$, we ran simulation for 20 times. Not a single incident of global asynchronism was observed. We also ran simulation for fastest-station asynchronism, with $d = 0.003\%$ and with completely randomized clocks, and once again observed not a single case of asynchronism.

4.2   Dynamic IBSS

We evaluated the performance of our algorithm for dynamic IBSS. In our algorithm the fastest station is, to some extent, in charge of timing synchronization. Should the fastest station leave the IBSS because of mobility or other reasons, the second fastest node will become the fastest. Now the restabilization is done and finally the second fastest station will take control. Restabilization does not mean asynchronism. In order to understand the probability of asynchronism in the process of restabilization, we let the fastest station leave and return to the IBSS once every six minutes. That is, it alternately leaves the IBSS for three minutes and returns for next three minutes. We ran the simulation for different values of $n \leq 1000$.

As expected, no asynchronism was caused by a fastest node joining the IBSS. Not a single instance of asynchronism was observed for different values of $n \leq 900$ for 100 rounds of restabilization. The algorithm is behaving nicely up to 900 nodes. When simulation is run with 1000 and 1100 nodes sometime its running without any single instance of asynchronism. But sometime during restabilization global asynchronism occurs and that asynchronism continues till the end of simulation. We can say that the algorithm is behaving nicely up to 900 nodes in dynamic IBSS with 20 priority levels.

5   Comparison with ATSP

In this section comparison of our proposed algorithm with ATSP is reported.

1. *If the fastest node fails* – In ATSP, if the fastest node fails all nodes contend for beacon transmission. As there is no priority among the nodes in ATSP, so there will be high contention for beacon transmission. Proposed algorithm divides the nodes in m priority levels. This will reduce the contention by m times. we can say this algorithm converge m time faster than ATSP. If the fastest node fails, only nodes having highest priority (lowest priority value) will contend for beacon transmission. The second fastest node have higher priority than other nodes, it will take the control of beacon transmission in at most $2 * I_{max}$ beacon interval. So we can say that proposed algorithm converges very fast as compared to ATSP.

2. *Scalability* – ATSP is not scalable for more than 300 nodes because of higher contention. Proposed algorithm divide the nodes in m priority level and this division of nodes in m priority level will reduce the contention to $1/m$. Since contention is reduced so it will increase the scalability of IBSS. This algorithm can easily support 1000 nodes in an IBSS. If we take more priority level scalability of IBSS will be more. We can set number of priority level depending upon the number of nodes in IBSS. Due to limited bandwidth of IEEE 802.11 ad hoc networks and the limit of MAC protocol, this much scalability is more then sufficient to IBSS.

6   Conclusion

In [1] clock synchronization in IBSS is addressed and they have proposed ATSP that is able to synchronize 300 nodes. We have identified problems exist in ATSP and modified ATSP to solve the problems. We have increased the scalability of IBSS by introducing dynamic priority among the nodes for beacon contention. As the number of nodes in IBSS increases, contention for beacon transmission also increases. In the proposed algorithm we divide the nodes in priority levels depending on their clock speed. Now nodes with highest priority will only contend for beacon transmission. Reduction in beacon contention will increase scalability of IBSS. So the algorithm proposed in this paper solves asynchronism problems faced by large-scale IBSS more effectively.

References

1. Huang, L., Lai, T. H.: On the Scalability of IEEE 802.11 Ad Hoc Networks. In MOBIHOC (2002) 173-182.
2. Bianchi, G.: Performance analysis of the IEEE 802.11 distributed coordination function. In IEEE Journal on Selected Areas in Communications. Vol. 18. 3(2000) 535-547.
3. – Wireless LAN Medium Access Control (MAC) and Physical Layer (PHY) specification. In IEEE Standard 802.11 (1999).
4. Stemm, M., Gauthier, P., Harada, D., Katz, R. H.: Reducing power consumption of network interfaces in hand-held devices. In 3rd International Workshop on Mobile Multimedia Communications (1996).
5. Lamport, L.: Time, clocks and the ordering of events in distributed systems. Communications of the ACM. Vol. 21. 7(1978) 558-565.
6. Bianchi, G., Fratta, L., Oliveri, M.: Performance evaluation and enhancement of the CSNA/CA MAC protocol for 802.11 wireless LANs. In PIMRC (1996) 392-396.
7. –: Higher-Speed Physical Layer Extension in the 2.4 GHz Band. In IEEE Std 802.11bi (1999).
8. Ebert, J. P., Burns, B., Wolisz, A.: A trace-based approach for determining the energy consumption of a WLAN network interface. In European Wireless (2002) 230-236.
9. Li, J., Blake, C., Couto, D. S. J. D., Lee, H. I., Morris, R.: Capacity of ad hoc wireless networks. In 7th ACM International Conference on Mobile Computing and Networking (2001).
10. Mills, D. L.: Internet time synchronization: the network time protocol. In Global States and Time in Distributed Systems. IEEE Computer Society Press (1994).
11. Elson, J., Girod, L., Estrin, D.: Fine-grained network time synchronization using reference broadcasts. In the Fifth Symposium on Operating Systems Design and Implementation (2002).
12. Romer, K., Zurich, E.: Time synchronization in ad hoc networks. In Proceedings of MobiHoc (2001).
13. Tay, Y. C., Chua, K. C.: A capacity analysis for the IEEE 802.11 MAC protocol. ACM/Baltzer Wireless Networks. Vol. 7. 2(2001) 159-171.

Internet Banking – A Layered Approach to Security

D.P. Dube and S. Ramanarayanan

Institute for Development and Research in Banking Technology (IDRBT),
Castle Hills, Road # 1, Masab Tank,
Hyderabad – 500 057, Andhra Pradesh, India.
{dpdube,srnarayanan}@idrbt.ac.in

Abstract. The advent and popularity of the Internet presented the banking industry with both a challenge and an opportunity to utilise this medium. Although internet banking offered customers the comfort of accessing their accounts from any place, there has been fear of exploitation of the inherent weakness in the technology. The opportunity was there to "take the bank to the customers' place" while the challenge lay in changing the mindset of the customers to begin to 'trust' and accept this system. The task was to ensure translation of the unquantifiable trust to a more palpable security to the system. This scenario, combined with the basic flow of the Internet banking system, has made us propose a holistic approach to security. Each layer of the Internet Banking has its own risks that can be mitigated through the use of the suggested control mechanisms thereby enabling defence-in-depth, thus prompting the concept of a layered approach to security.

Keywords: Internet Banking, trust, security, layered approach.

1 Introduction

The early stages of the last decade heralded the arrival of the Internet [1] as a public domain – as an avenue of information dissemination, a medium for interaction between people of geographic diversities and a world-wide broadcasting facility. The Internet was found to be easy to use and, slowly but surely, the world quickly lapped up all that it had to offer. The banking industry also found ample potential in the Internet and decided to leverage its business by utilising the Internet as one of its delivery channels. In the initial stages of its inception, though it was fraught with some amount of risk, the banking industry wanted to utilise the reach and capabilities of the Internet.

Internet Banking [2] started in two modes – a non-transactional [2] mode wherein the bank utilised the Internet as a medium of advertisement about its services and the transactional [2] mode wherein the bank allowed its customers to use the Internet to check details pertaining to their account viz. account balance, statements, enquiries and even transfer of funds and payment of bills. Though both the modes are susceptible to risk, the transactional mode of Internet Banking, referred to as online banking, was more prone to risk due to the heterogeneous architecture, the involvement of various components and the involvement of the finances of the bank and its customers.

G. Das and V.P. Gulati (Eds.): CIT 2004, LNCS 3356, pp. 190–197, 2004.

2 Problem

The operational structure of the Internet banking system changed the way in which banking was traditionally done. With no requirement of any geographically stationary teller and a brick-and-mortar building in the Internet banking system, the 'trust' relationship that a customer enjoyed with the bank and its officials seemed lost. Moreover, the absence of inherent security in the Internet coupled with the growing threat to Internet from attackers, viruses etc. raised a valid doubt in the minds of the customers over the security of the Internet Banking system.

3 Motivation and Methodology

The Central bank of our country, the Reserve Bank of India, had thrown open the doors to the various banks in the country to offer Internet Banking, to its customers, circa 1999. With various private and tech-savvy banks taking the lead in this area, the legacy banks were now being virtually pushed to offer this service. These banks too realised that the 'trust' that their customers reposed in them through the traditional mode of banking would now change. The challenge lay in translating the palpable trust in the brick-and-mortar way of banking to a similar level of trust in the internet banking mode. All these factors, combined with our knowledge that not much work has been done in this area, have motivated us in endeavouring to create a similar level of trust in the Internet banking scenario. And we realised that to replicate the trust into the internet banking system we needed to create a sense of security in this delivery channel thereby enabling the customers to trust the system. To this end, the methodology that we decided to adopt was to utilise the various layers (components) of the Internet banking system and add security, by mitigating the risks involved, to each layer and hence create a holistically secure system. The driving force behind the choosing of this methodology was the working of the OSI 'layers' in ensuring a 'well-connected' network.

4 Schematic Flow of Internet Banking

Steps

1. Client requesting for the web page of the bank offering Internet Banking.
2. The request passes through the Internet to the firewall of the bank located in the Data centre.
3. Depending upon the type of request and the configuration in the firewall, the request is passed   on to the web server or the request is dropped.
4 & 5. The web server displays the web page containing the application interface and the control passes to the Internet banking application server.
6. The details entered by the customer are sent to the Internet Banking database for verification and subsequent action.
7, 8 & 9. Data is transferred from the Centralised database to the Internet Banking database through the middleware.
10. The verification result and the transaction result are passed onto the Internet Banking application server.
11,12 & 13. The details are given to the web server to be displayed to the customer.

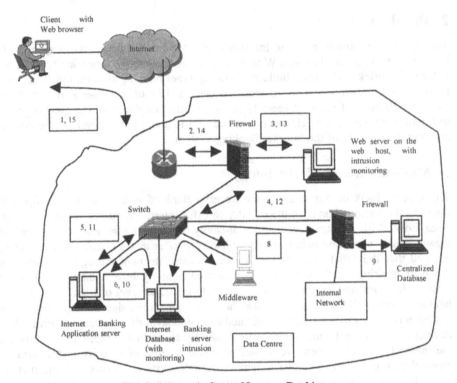

Fig. 1. Schematic flow of Internet Banking

14 & 15. The web server displays the results of the transaction on the web browser of the customer.

Steps to be followed to complete one transaction, say, a balance enquiry, are:

1-2-3-4-5-6-10-11-12-13-14-15.

In case the transaction requires real-time connectivity, say, payment of bills, the control is transferred from the Internet Banking database to the Central database. The steps to be followed to complete this transaction are:

1-2-3-4-5-6-7-8-9-10-11-12-13-14-15.

5   A Layered Approach to Security

The fact that each financial transaction has to traverse different layers of the Internet before it can reach its final conclusion, has prompted a layered approach [3, 4] to the security of such a transaction; wherein each layer adds a level of security and in this process also helps the succeeding layer determine the security mechanisms that it needs to incorporate to build a holistic secure system of Internet Banking. Also the layers function as a complement to the other preceding and succeeding layers in providing a secure system – if one layer fails, then the next layer does a cover-up. (i.e.) if security is breached in one layer, then the other layers in the system can stop the attack and/or limit the damages that may occur. While this functioning of the layers in a complementary fashion aids in the security of the system, it should also be noted that total security in one layer doesn't guarantee the same level of security in its preceding or succeeding layers. Starting with the web browser at the client's end to the management of the bank offering this service, each layer is elaborated below, along with the risks associated with that particular layer and the control measures that need to be adopted to reduce the risk to a minimum.

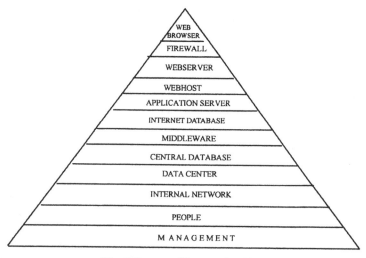

Fig. 2. Layers of Internet Banking

As can be observed from the above diagram, the web browser is the starting point of the layers and can be said to be the tip of the security triangle with the management of the bank being the foundation.

5.1 Web Browser

The web browser [5] is a software application located on the client system that is used to locate and display web pages.

Risks: The misuse of information provided by the end-user, active content (example: applets etc.) that can crash the system or breach the user's privacy, cookies that can cause annoyance.

Controls: Proper security settings in the browser based on the web content zone, non-disclosure of personal information unless warranted, robust-logon process and controlling cookies.

5.2 Perimeter Access Control (Firewall)

A firewall [5] is a system or group of systems that enforces an access control policy between a trusted network and an untrusted network.

Risks: The access control methodology – whether a firewall starts with a 'deny all' policy first or 'permit all' first, the attack on the firewall itself resulting in the failure or malfunction of the firewall and the inappropriate framing of the access control policy itself.

Controls: The primary control is to frame an access control policy that takes into consideration the various factors like the methodology to be used – use the 'deny all' first methodology to start with and later 'permit' based on requirement, the inbound and outbound access to be permitted, the type of firewall – use stateful inspection firewall; and the need for people with valid experience and expertise to configure the firewall. The firewall should be 'self-monitoring' and should prevent itself from being attacked; or in the least should be able to alert the administrator in any such event.

5.3 Web Server

The web server [5] is a software application that is used to deliver web pages to a web browser, when requested for that particular web page.

Risks: Inherent weaknesses in the web server software itself, improper configuration, unnecessary open 'ports' and/or 'services', lack of authentication; and lack of access control.

Controls: A proper policy that specifies the requirement in terms of necessary services and ports; proper configuration of the web server in terms of the policy defined; removing unnecessary information and default pages from the web server; ensuring PKI-enabled server side certificate for authenticating itself to the customer; ensuring access control to each service, directory, the administrator password and the physical system per se; session encryption; appropriate utilisation of the 'get' and 'post' operations; ensure content management and change management; ensure availability of the web server in terms of processors and memory; ensure proper 'patching' after due testing of patches; enabling auditing/logging and monitoring.

5.4 Web Host (with Intrusion Monitoring)

It is the system on which the web server software is loaded – the operating system. This web host [5] is also loaded with intrusion monitoring software.

Risks: Unknown and unnecessary services in the operating system, access control of the system and the capacity planning of the web host.

Controls: Plan carefully to ensure sufficient amount of CPU, memory and disk storage for the expected usage; monitor system resources; ensure redundancy and availability of system resources; ensure physical and logical security; and ensure auditing/logging and monitoring. The intrusion monitoring software detects any attempts to attack the web host and/or web server and alerts the administrator to such attempts; to enable the administrator to take proper action on the alerts.

5.5 Internet Banking Application Server

It is a program, residing on a system, that handles all application (Internet Banking, in this case) operations between the end-users' and the back-end database.

Risks: Security of the operating system, access control for the server and the application, application specific risks.

Controls: The application specific risks need to be taken care of at the time of design of the application, while at the same time ensuring that it is properly configured in the server. All controls specified for the web host is valid in this case too. Ensure proper access control – both physical and logical for the system. Ensure sufficient redundancy and availability in terms of clustering and/or load balancing.

5.6 Internet Banking Database (with Intrusion Monitoring)

It is the system on which all the details of the Internet Banking customers are stored. It is also loaded with intrusion monitoring software to monitor the activity on the system and the database. This database gets its data from the centralised banking database through a middleware. All transactions which do not require online access to the central database are handled by this database server.

Risks: The customer details are classified as very sensitive and tampering with this database can cause a huge loss – quantitative and qualitative, to the bank; access control for the server and the database.

Controls: Apart from applying all the controls specified for the web host, ensure proper access control – both physical and logical for the system. Access to the database files should be allowed only through the application. Ensure sufficient redundancy and availability in terms of clustering and/or load balancing.

5.7 Middleware

The middleware [5] is software that connects otherwise separate applications. It is used to transfer data from the central database to the Internet banking database.

Risks: Availability is a major risk. If the middleware is not available, transfer cannot take place; also, a 'slow' middleware cannot guarantee availability. Access to the middleware is also a risk.

Controls: Apart from ensuring proper access control – both physical and logical for the system, there should also be sufficient redundancy built into the system to ensure availability of the resource.

5.8 Database (with Intrusion Monitoring)

It is the centralised location of data pertaining to all the customers of the bank and other data pertaining to the bank.

The risks and controls associated with the central database are similar to the Internet Banking database. In addition to those controls, the bank should also ensure that proper back up of the database is taken; while also planning for contingencies like earthquake etc. by investing in a Disaster Recovery Site.

5.9 Data Centre

The data centre is the facility where the entire banking system viz. the servers, databases etc are housed.

Risks: Physical security of the centre and the equipment it houses.

Controls: A physical security monitoring system should be in place to monitor all the entry/exit points. Access should be controlled through one/two factor mechanisms and backed up with logs/registers. Environmental conditions in the centre should be maintained as stipulated in the policies and procedures.

5.10 Internal Network

It is the network which hosts the systems used by the bank staff for the monitoring and maintenance of all the servers, databases and systems of the bank.

Risks: Improper network design for hosting each system can cause unwanted traffic; traffic to the systems for management purposes can eat up bandwidth.

Controls: The network should be properly designed so as to optimally utilise the bandwidth available – place the web server on a separate sub-network connected to the firewall, the database and application servers placed on a separate sub-network in the internal network. Also, the path between the internal systems and the servers and databases should be secure when doing content management.

5.11 People

This layer is basically the administrators and operators of each and every system, server or database.

Risks: Insufficient exposure to technology and their requirements during installation and maintenance; random application of patches and updates.

Controls: Ensuring the compliance to policies and procedures during administration and management; auditing of the people, processes and the systems; encouraging knowledge up gradation activities and educating them on the evils of 'social engineering'. The most important control that we can suggest is *'to do the right things in the right way at the right time'*.

5.12 Management

This includes all the different types of management including the bank top management. The primary responsibility of the bank management is to lend support to the implementation of the Internet banking system as a delivery channel of the bank; support the framing, implementation and compliance to all the policies and the procedures relating to the entire Internet banking system.

6 Conclusion

When the control of a transaction traverses through the layers, it can be seen that the lacunae or weakness in one layer is made up for, by the next layer. For example, if the web server has some unnecessary service open and some attacker tries to enter the Internet banking system through that service, then the intrusion monitoring software in the web host will alert the administrator to some anomalous activity happening in the web host, enabling the administrator to take suitable corrective action thereby ensuring that the system remains secure. Also, total security in one layer will not guarantee the total security of the entire Internet Banking system. For example, let the web server be totally secure. Now, this does not guarantee that the application server and the application is secure because any misconfiguration of the application could leave gaping holes through which the application server could be compromised thereby exposing the entire system to other threats. These lead us to the conclusion that a layered approach to security will give a secure credence to the Internet banking system and thus ensure the trust in this delivery channel that we had originally set out to achieve.

References

1. Leiner, B.M., Cerf, V.G., Clark, D.D., Kahn, R.E., Kleinrock, L., Lynch, D.C., Postel, J., Roberts, L.G., Wolff, S.: International Society: All history about internet, available at http://www.isoc.org/internet/history/brief.shtml
2. Mittal, S.R., Srinivasan, M.R., Sarda, N.L., Bhojani, S.H., Sobti, R., Ganapathy, K.R., Ghaisas, D., Nair, R., Shettigar, K.M., Kothari, M.P.: Report on Internet Banking, RBI, June 2001, available at http://www.rbi.org.in
3. Loro, L.: Defense in Depth – A Layered Approach Network Security, February 2003. Available at http://www.2000trainers.com/article.aspx?articleID=217&page=1
4. Watson, P.: Computer Security Education and Information Security Training, SANS Institute. Available at http://www.sans.org/resources/idfaq/layered_defense.php
5. Online Computer dictionary for computer and Internet terms and definitions, Webopedia. Available at http://www.webopedia.com

On Reduction of Bootstrapping Information Using Digital Multisignature

Sadybakasov Ulanbek[1,*], Ashutosh Saxena[2], and Atul Negi[3]

[1] Sebat Educational Institution,
Prospect Chui 219/6, Bishkek, 720001, Kyrgyzstan
ulanbek@sebat.edu.kg
[2] Institute for Development and Research in Banking Technology, IDRBT,
Castle Hills, Masab Tank, Hyderabad, (A.P.) 500 057, India
asaxena@idrbt.ac.in
[3] Department of CIS, University of Hyderabad,
Gachibowli, Hyderabad (A.P.) 500 046, India
atulcs@uohyd.ernet.in

Abstract. The bootstrapping of security mechanisms for large-scale information systems is an important and critical exercise. Several Trusted Third Parties (TTPs) are being setup world wide for establishing authenticity. They primarily use Hardware Security Module (HSM), tamper proof device, for signing the user's certificates. In order to have Disaster Recovery Process (DRP) in place, cloning of these bootstrapping tamper proof HSMs is desirable. For this, one needs to have a set of effective protocols such that any certificate issued by the original or by the cloned HSM can be distinguished and any misuse be avoided.
In this work, we present a set of protocols, which are enhancements to the existing scheme proposed in [1], by incorporating digital multisignature so that the bootstrapping information size and the cost of certificate verification is reduced.

Keywords: public key infrastructure (PKI), HSM, multisignature

1 Introduction

The fast development of worldwide distributed information systems and communication networks (e.g. the World Wide Web on the Internet) and their use for electronic commerce leads to security problems whose solution becomes increasingly important as the use of these systems grows [2]. While for some small-scale systems security can perhaps be viewed simply as a desirable feature, integral security is a mandatory requirement for any large-scale information system to be merely operational, and for security-critical systems to be acceptable to its users.

The article by Maurer et al [3] illustrates in a simple manner several interesting aspects of distributed system security: the minimal requirements and

---

* This work was carried out when the author was pursuing M. Tech. degree in Computer Science at University of Hyderbad, Hyderabad (A.P.), India.

G. Das and V.P. Gulati (Eds.): CIT 2004, LNCS 3356, pp. 198–204, 2004.

trust relations necessary for achieving a secure channel between two entities in a distributed system, the timing constraints on the involved communication channels, the duality between authenticity and confidentiality, and the distinguishing features between secret-key and public-key cryptography. They also propose a black-box view of cryptographic primitives, showing that a digital signature scheme can be interpreted as the dual of a symmetric cryptosystem and a public-key cryptosystem can be interpreted as the dual of a message authentication code.

Cryptographic primitives and trust relations are both interpreted as transformations for channel security properties, and a cryptographic protocol can be viewed as a sequence of such transformations of both types. A protocol thus makes it possible to transform a set of secure channels established during an initial setup phase, together with a set of insecure channels available during operation of the system, into the set of secure channels specified by the security requirements. They emphasize the trust, which is another fundamental ingredient for distributed systems security.

Rueppel's approach [4] illustrates the importance of confidentiality and authenticity as basic security goals but does not address trust as a fundamental ingredient of security bootstrapping in distributed system. In contrast, Rangan [5] addresses trust relations between users and authentication servers in a model that is based on logic of belief.

The paper is organized as follows. In section 2, we introduce certain notations and motivate the scheme. Section 3 describes our scheme. In section 4 we describe how certificates are generated and verified using our approach.

2 Preliminaries

2.1 Background

Cryptosystems are information systems that use cryptography and suitable key-management infrastructures (KMI). KMIs are primarily concerned with storing trees or forests (collections of trees) of keys. KMIs must necessarily assume the confidentiality and integrity properties of some keys, called *critical keys*, in the trees or forests before the confidentiality and integrity properties of other keys can be deduced using suitable cryptographic mechanisms. The confidentiality and integrity properties of the critical keys must be maintained using *out-of-band* security techniques, which are usually some form of physical security. Cryptography is not, and cannot be, concerned with the protection of these properties of the critical keys.

PKIs (Public Key Infrastructure) are a specialised form of KMI [6]. PKIs are interested in the provision of integrity services for a collection of public values, which includes a public key. The critical keys in PKIs are called *root keys* or *root public keys*. The integrity properties of the root public keys are an assumption, which cannot be cryptographically verified. Similarly, the confidentiality properties of the root private keys are also an assumption. Depending on the type of the PKI, there may be one or more root public keys. For the sake of clarity and without loss of generality, in this work we will assume a PKI with the following structure.

Root Public Key (Level 0): there exists a single root public key, which is used for authorising the public keys of certificate issuers;

Certificate Issuer Public Keys (Level 1): there exists a set of certificate-issuer public keys which are used for authorising the public keys of users; and,

User Public Keys (Level 2): there exists a set of user public keys, which are used for confidentiality and integrity mechanisms.

The verification actions in the traditional PKI are as follows.

Verification Action 1: The first integrity verification is signature verification whether a certificate was issued by a certificate issuer or not.

Verification Action 2: The second integrity verification is that of a certificate path validation, which is a sequence of signature verification operations, to verify if the certificate issuer is authorised to issue certificates.

Note that the root certificate issuer authorises itself to authorise other certificate issuers. That is, the certificate for the root public key is a *self-signed* certificate, which can be verified using the same key.

The proposed model extends the functionality of traditional PKI by including an additional integrity verification mechanism as follows.

Verification Action 3: An integrity verification mechanism verifies if the instance of a black-box, which was involved in certificate generation, was authorised.

We can call the 1st and the 2nd verifications as a *vertical verification*. The 3rd one can be treated as a *horizontal verification*.

2.2   Motivation

Following the notation of section 2.4 of [1] we suggest that B_r is a set of signature tuples and not a single value. This does not constrain the possibility of using multisignature systems to reduce the size of the information contained in B_r. This is because the specification does not constrain the possible relationships between various instances of signature generation functions that could be used to implement $Sig_{x_i}()$. The $Sig_{x_i}()$ is a signing process on message M using x as a private key. Such a design for the signature algorithm is an open problem.

This open problem motivated us to present a set of protocols to enhance the proposed scheme(s) of [1], by incorporating digital multisignature so that the bootstrapping information size and the cost of certificate verification is reduced.

Referring to [7], the digital signature is now well known as a means of replacing written signatures in electronic communications. In many applications a document may need to be signed by more than one party. When a signature depends on more than one person we call it a *multisignature*.

Bootstrap Operation of [1] is depicted in Fig. 1 using graph notation where we assume the root level (level 0) has three HSMs (black-boxes). By arrow we mean certificate generation process.

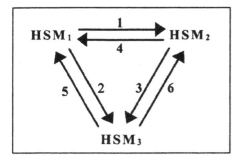

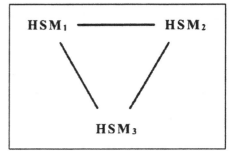

Fig. 1. The bootstrap operation of [1] by using graph notation.

Fig. 2. The result after applying digital multisignature.

By applying digital multisignature we can get the following graph.

In general, we can express the bootstrap operation of [1] as $B_o = H(H - 1)$. Where B_o is the number of bootstrap operations, and H is the number of HSMs. In our work the number of bootstrap operations is the number of involved HSMs. As it is clear we reduced the exchanges due to adopting multisignature.

2.3   The RSA Signature Scheme

Throughout the paper we use the RSA [8] signature scheme so we briefly revise it. This section may be skipped by those readers who know it.

The RSA [8], the most popular scheme, works in the following manner. One, e.g., a key distribution centre, computes n as the product of two primes p and q

$$n = p * q \ . \tag{1}$$

These primes are very large, "random" primes. Although n is made public, the factors p and q must be secret. Note that if $n = p * q$ then

$$\phi(n) = (p - 1) * (q - 1) \ . \tag{2}$$

The key distributor picks up the integer d to be a large, random integer, which is relatively prime to $\phi(n)$. That is, checks that d satisfies

$$\gcd(d, \phi(n)) = 1 \tag{3}$$

("gcd" means "greatest common divisor")

and computes public key e such that

$$e * d \equiv 1 \bmod \phi(n) \tag{4}$$

using the extended Euclidean algorithm. The distributor transmits the private (secret) key d to the sender and publishes the public key (e, n). To sign a message M, the sender computes

$$S = M^d \bmod n \ . \tag{5}$$

To verify the signature, the receiver computes

$$S^e \equiv M^{e*d} \equiv M \bmod n \ . \tag{6}$$

3   Scheme Description

In our work we adapt the RSA signature scheme [8] to enable multisignatures to be easily implemented by groups of users such that signature verification will require only a single RSA transformation.

Our scheme must possess the property (2) of [8]. If a message M is first deciphered by decryption procedure D and then enciphered by encryption procedure E, M is the result. Formally,

$$E(D(M)) = M \ . \tag{7}$$

We use the scheme proposed in section 5 of [7]. The scheme is as follows.

$$(d_1 + d_2 + ... + d_t) * e \equiv 1 \bmod \phi(n) \tag{8}$$

where $d_1 + d_2 + ... + d_t$ are the private keys of all black-boxes (which are either production black-boxes or back-up black-boxes) and the e is the public key.

Each black-box i takes the message M and signs it by

$$S_i = \mathrm{M}^{d_i} \bmod n \ . \tag{9}$$

The signed copies are then multiplied by central authority to form

$$S = S_1 * S_2 * ... * S_t \bmod n \ . \tag{10}$$

The message M can be recovered as following

$$\begin{aligned} S^e \bmod n &= (S_1 * S_2 * ... * S_t)^e \bmod n \\ &= \mathrm{M}^{[(d_1 + d_2 + ... + d_t)*e]} \bmod n \\ &= \mathrm{M} \ . \end{aligned} \tag{11}$$

4   Certificate Generation and Verification

In this section, we describe how certificate generation and verification proceeds using our scheme.

1. Certificate Generation for Root Public Key. Suppose that there are three black-boxes in level 0. To certify each other we need collaboration of two to certify one. To do that, firstly we should create

$$\begin{aligned} (d_2 + d_3) * e_1 &\equiv 1 \bmod \phi(n) \\ (d_1 + d_3) * e_2 &\equiv 1 \bmod \phi(n) \\ (d_1 + d_2) * e_3 &\equiv 1 \bmod \phi(n) \ . \end{aligned}$$

The certificate generation for the first black-box is as follows

$$\begin{aligned} S_2 &= \mathrm{M}^{d_2} \bmod n \\ S_3 &= \mathrm{M}^{d_3} \bmod n \ . \end{aligned}$$

The central authority combines S_2 and S_3 as per (10) to form

$$S_{r_1} = S_2 * S_3 \bmod n \ .$$

The certificates for the second and the third black-boxes can be generated consequently.

Note that the black-boxes are either production black-boxes or back-up black-boxes.

2. Certificate Generation for the Certificate Issuer Public Key. Suppose we have five black-boxes in level 1. The three black-boxes, which are in level 0, create

$$(d_1 + d_2 + d_3) * e \equiv 1 \bmod \phi(n) \ .$$

For the first black-box in level 1, the certificate generation is as follows

$$S_1 = \mathrm{M}^{d_1} \bmod n$$
$$S_2 = \mathrm{M}^{d_2} \bmod n$$
$$S_3 = \mathrm{M}^{d_3} \bmod n \ .$$

Similarly, we have $S_{c_1} = S_1 * S_2 * S_3 \bmod n$ as per (10). The certificates for other black-boxes in level 1 can be generated consequently.

3. Verification of Certificate for the Root Public Key (Horizontal Verification). In this stage, we verify whether the instance of a black-box, which was involved in certificate generation, was authorised or not. To verify S_{r_1} we should possess e_1. The verification process is as follows

$$\begin{aligned}
S_{r_1}^{e_1} \bmod n &= (S_2 * S_3)^{e_1} \bmod n \\
&= \mathrm{M}^{[(d_2+d_3)*e_1]} \bmod n \\
&= \mathrm{M} \ .
\end{aligned}$$

To verify S_{r_2} we need e_2 and so on. As mentioned in section 2.1, this verification process is called as a *horizontal verification*. By horizontal we mean that a verification process takes place in root level where black-boxes verify each other.

4. Verification of Certificate Issuer Public Key (Vertical Verification). To verify at this stage, we need only e. The verification process of S_{c_1} is as follows

$$\begin{aligned}
S_{c_1}^{e} \bmod n &= (S_1 * S_2 * S_3)^e \bmod n \\
&= \mathrm{M}^{[(d_1+d_2+d_3)*e]} \bmod n \\
&= \mathrm{M} \ .
\end{aligned}$$

The verification of others can be done as above, only by using e.

Without loss of generality, we considered three black-boxes at level 0 and five at level 1. In the obvious way, the system above can be extended to enable any number of black-boxes to take part in.

5   Conclusion

In this work, we have investigated the important problem of bootstrapping in PKI. We proposed a scheme, which involves digital multisignature that reduces the bootstrapping information size and the cost of certificate verification. In our work, the root level is transparent for both certificate issuers and for users. The scheme also avoids any misuse of HSMs (black-boxes).

In our scheme the set of black-boxes who co-sign is fixed. This can lead to a problem when some of black-boxes are out of order. The model can further be enhanced by incorporating threshold signature schemes to overcome the problem.

References

1. Kapali Viswanathan and Ashutosh Saxena. "Towards Logically and Physically Secure Public-Key Infrastructures", 3rd International Conference on Cryptography in India, INDOCRYPT2002, December 2002, Springer-Verlag Lecture Notes in Computer Science.
2. R. Ganesan and R. Sandhu, Securing Cyberspace, Communications of the ACM, Vol. 37, No. 11, 1994, pp. 29-31.
3. Ueli M. Maurer and Pierre E. Schmid. A calculus for security bootstrapping in distributed systems. Journal of Computer Security, 4(1):55-80, 1996.
4. R.A. Rueppel, A formal approach to security architectures, Advances in Cryptology - EURO-CRYPT '91, Lecture Notes in Computer Science, Vol. 547, pp. 387-398, Berlin: Springer-Verlag, 1991.
5. P.V. Rangan, An axiomatic theory of trust in secure communication protocols, Computers & Security, Vol. 11, 1992, pp. 163-172.
6. Ashutosh Saxena, PKI: Concepts, Design and Deployment, Tata McGraw Hill Ltd, ISBN 0-07-053463-2, 2004.
7. Colin Boyd. Digital multisignatures. In Henry J. Beker and F. C. Piper, editors, Cryptography and Coding – 1986, Oxford Science Publications, pages 241-246. Clarendon Press, Oxford, 1989.
8. Ronald L. Rivest, Adi Shamir, and Leonard M. Adleman. A method for obtaining digital signatures and public-key cryptosystems. Communications of the ACM, 21(2):120-126, 1978.

SpamNet –
Spam Detection Using PCA and Neural Networks

Abhimanyu Lad

B.Tech. (I.T.) 4th year student
Indian Institute of Information Technology, Allahabad
Deoghat, Jhalwa, Allahabad, India
abhimanyulad@iiita.ac.in

Abstract. This paper describes SpamNet – a spam detection program, which uses a combination of heuristic rules and mail content analysis to detect and filter out even the most cleverly written spam mails from the user's mail box, using a feed-forward neural network. SpamNet is able to adapt itself to changing mail patterns of the user. We demonstrate the power of Principal Component Analysis to improve the performance and efficiency of the spam detection process, and compare it with directly using words as features for classification. Emphasis is laid on the effect of domain specific preprocessing on the error rates of the classifier.

1 Introduction

'Spam' refers to unsolicited e-mail, generally sent in bulk for advertisement. A typical user gets around 10-50 spam mails a day [6], and even careful users can get signed up on unwanted mailing lists. Spam is undesirable because it eats up resources like disk space and user time. Thus we find it worth the effort to design a domain specific classifier for accurately weeding out spam from a user's mailbox.

The nature of spam emails received differs among users, and spam content can also vary with time[6]. The ability to adapt the classification mechanism to the evolving mind of the spammer is one of the prime concerns of any anti-spam software.

This paper introduces SpamNET – a program which uses a combination of heuristic rules, Principal Component Analysis and Neural Networks to produce an accurate spam detection system which is able to adapt to the changing trends of mails received by the user. It re-trains its network every 7 days to discover new patterns in the user's mailbox. SpamNET is a user level program, i.e. it runs as part of the user's mail client rather than sitting on the mail server providing general services to it's users. This allows SpamNET to make more generous use of the user's processing power, rather than being constrained by scalability issues that are inherent to applications running on a server.

The rest of the paper is organized as follows. In section II, we describe the existing state-of-the-art in spam detection. In section III, we describe the architecture of SpamNET in detail. Section IV shows the results obtained by our classifier, and Section V describes the conclusion drawn by us.

G. Das and V.P. Gulati (Eds.): CIT 2004, LNCS 3356, pp. 205–213, 2004.

2 Previous Work

A General Techniques

The stone age of spam detection was marked by the use of simple keyword filters – if a given term was present in the mail's headers or in the body, the message was marked as spam. This method has been found to be non scalable as each potential spam term has to be manually added to the system. Thus no appreciable time was saved on the part of the user [2]. There are several spam filters available today [1]. The most common of them can be categorized as follows:

User defined filters: They allow creation of rules of the form – "If _____ field contains _____, move it to _____ folder." Adding filter rules to combat each new kind of spam mail is often impossible.

Header filters: These analyze the headers to detect whether the headers are forged. But many spam mails have valid headers and therefore such filters are bound to fail for a large number of spam mails.

Content filters: These scan the body of the email message and use the presence, absence and frequency of words to determine whether the message is spam or not. Content based filtering has been found to be most effective for spam detection.

Two well established techniques – Bayesian classification and Neural Networks have been widely applied to the problem of classifying mails as spam or non-spam.

B Bayesian Classification

Bayesian classification has been found be an effective technique which makes use of prior knowledge about the 'training' samples to make intelligent decisions about 'unseen' or 'test' samples. Moreover, it is able to mathematically assign to each mail a probability of being spam.

One of the earliest reports on the use of Bayesian classification for spam filtering is [3] where Pantel and Lin describe the SpamCop program. They were able to achieve 92% detection rate and 1.16% rate of misclassifying non-spam mails. A message is classified as spam if

$P(\text{Spam}|M) > P(\text{Non-Spam}|M)$.

Also, they assume the conditional independence of attributes in a message.

Bayesian classification and its application to spam classification has been described in [8]. Better detection rates have been reported by incorporating domain specific knowledge into the Bayesian classifier [4].

C Neural Networks

Neural Networks are able to discover rules which otherwise are difficult for humans to describe or even comprehend. They not only provide an easy way to model complex relationships between input and output, but also provide adaptability and learning ability implicitly.

Various types of neural networks have been tried to classify mails as spam or non-spam. [6] describes a mass of fully connected neurons used for classifying emails. It uses no layers and no formal structure. Every neuron in the system has have access to all the inputs to the network and the outputs from every other neuron. The network is able to control the window of input it wishes to read next. Experiments show that preprocessing and choice of features is more important towards the performance of classification than the architecture of the neural network itself.

3 SpamNet

A Architecture

SpamNET categorizes emails using a Neural Network. The feed forward neural network is trained using the backpropagation algorithm. It uses a single hidden layer with 10 neurons. The 'tansig' transfer function is used both for the hidden and output layer.

The neural network takes input from the Extractor module which extracts words (e.g. free, hi, meeting, presentation, assignment etc.) as well as concepts (e.g. CONTAINS_INVISIBLE_TEXT) from the mails. While concepts are directly fed to the neural network in a quantified form, words appearing in the mail are first converted to a feature vector using a volatile vocabulary, then passed on to the PCA module before supplying it to the Neural Network. The neural network gives an output between -1 and 1. While an output of 1 represents an almost certain spam mail, -1 represents an almost certain non-spam mail. The 'concepts' provide an additional level of detection ability apart from the vocabulary based approach.

After every 7 days, SpamNET re-trains itself to capture the varying trends of the user's incoming mail. In training mode, the extractor module constructs a vocabulary of all words appearing in the mails, then creates a term document matrix (which depicts the frequency of occurrence of words in different mails) and the PCA module finds the optimal representation of this feature space by computing the eigenvectors for the term document matrix. Then the neural network is trained using the transformed feature vectors. In the testing mode, the transformed vector is used as input to the neural network, which then classifies the mail as spam or non-spam.

SpamNet also has a "short circuit" path to the output which directly classifies the mail as spam or non-spam without going through the usual path mentioned above. E.g. mails coming from addresses to which the user has replied or has composed a mail to in the past invoke this "short circuit" path and are thus are unconditionally marked as non-spam.

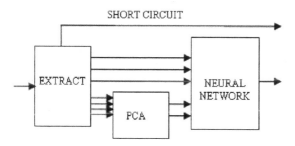

Fig. 1. Architecture of SpamNET

B Preprocessing: Extractor Module

The Extractor module is responsible for converting a mail into a form that is useful to the classifier.

The module extracts two kinds of information from the email – 1) Words 2) Concepts. The Extract module is HTML and CSS aware, and is case sensitive. Moreover, it prefers to read the HTML version of the mail when multiple MIME formats are available in the received mail. The extractor parses the message according to the following rules, and also makes note of various abnormalities, as mentioned below:

1. Invisible text is detected. This includes:

   a. Text of zero size.
   b. Text in background color or with a foreground color very close to that of the background.
   c. Text between HTML tags which will not be shown by the email client.

   Such text is meant to confuse the spam detector. E.g. a clever spammer may put in some non-spam words e.g. conference, meeting, urgent or may be even pick up the latest story on Yahoo! News and enclose it between appropriate tags such that it is invisible to the user but will be picked up by the spam detection program and used for making a decision about the mail. Presence of invisible text in the mail triggers the short-circuit path and the email is immediately marked as spam.

2. Symbols such as *, #, % etc. are stripped if they occur between alphabetic letters. Thus v*i*a#g#r#a gets converted to viagra. Even spaces occurring between single letters (except valid single letters like 'a' and 'I') are detected and stripped off. At the same time, the extractor module makes note of special punctuations like "!!!", before stripping them off.

3. Empty tags e.g. <b></b> which appear between otherwise non-delimited text are ignored and the surrounding pieces of text joined together. Thus V<b></b>iagra gets converted to Viagra.

4. Currency values like. $100,000,000 and $2 million are detected & noted.

Removal of Stop Words

Words like articles, prepositions, conjunctions, common verbs (e.g. 'know', 'see', 'do', 'be'), auxiliary verbs, adjectives (e.g. 'big', 'late', 'high'), and pronouns are removed, leaving only content words likely to have some meaning. This process condenses the vocabulary and thus reduces the computational cost of further processing on it.

Stemming

The words are passed through a stemmer which reduces multiple instances of a single word to the root word. E.g. flying and flied are reduced to fly. This stemming step is found to bias the classifier towards reducing false positives (non-spam mails being marked as spam) as well as improve the learning ability of the classifier in general. This behavior can be explained as follows. Suppose "paint" happens to a non-spam word for a particular user, then "painting", "painted" and "painter" should automatically become "non-spam" words without requiring explicit training with all such variants of a single word. This will essentially protect new non-spam mails containing such variants of a non-spam word against getting classified as spam. On the other hand, spam words like "viagra", "rich" usually occur in the same form in all spam mails and even their variants would not usually occur in non-spam mails. Therefore non-spam mails getting classified as spam due to stemming is very rare as compared to the other way round.

The Term-Document Matrix (TDM)

The Term Document Matrix M stores information about the frequency of occurrence of words in each mail. Words are listed on the vertical axis, and mails on the horizontal axis. Mi,j represents the frequency of ith word in the jth mail. This information helps in building the set of active and dormant features, which is explained in the section on Volatile Vocabulary. The feature vectors representing individual mails are column vectors in the term document matrix. These vectors are normalized so that classification is not affected by the length of the documents.

Feature Selection

(Difference of Means Method)

We use the frequency of certain words in the mails as inputs to the PCA module, which then feeds a transformed feature vector to the neural network. These words are chosen according to their ability to distinguish between the two classes of mails we are interested in, i.e. spam and non-spam. It must be appreciated that such words may vary from user to user. e.g although presence of words like "Viagra" is almost certainly enough to classify mails as spam, the same might not be true for "free", if the user deals with free software. Therefore these words must be chosen according to the specific user.

One technique used to find such discriminatory words is the difference of means method. For each feature, the difference in means of that feature in the "spam mails" class and that in "non-spam mails" class is calculated. Features having higher differences are potentially better attributes for distinguishing samples into the two classes.

Volatile Vocabulary

This part of the Extractor module is responsible for learning the user profile and adapting to the changing patterns of mails received by the user. When the extractor is working in training mode, it creates a combined vocabulary of all the words that appear in the spam and non-spam mails. This vocabulary is not only large but also contains words which play no important role in classification. In fact, a proper selection of features can actually improve the classifying and generalizing ability of the classifier. For choosing such words which have high discriminating power for the classification problem at hand, we use the difference of means method described above. Words whose difference of means for the two classes is greater than 1/7th of the highest difference of means are marked as active i.e. they will be used as features for classifying new mails. Words which do not satisfy this criterion are either too unique to help in future classification, or they are words which appear in almost equally in both spam and non-spam mails and hence are too common to help in classification. Instead of deleting these words, they are marked as dormant – since they may become active in the future. E.g. if the user joins a new mailing list that deals with Linux, initially the word "Linux" will be added to the vocabulary but marked as dormant. Over the time, the user will receive more mails from the list which will cause the word "Linux" to contribute heavily to the non-spam class, and hence eventually become an active word. Words that stay in the dormant list for more than 28 days (i.e. four training cycles) are removed, which prevents the vocabulary from growing infinitely large.

When in testing mode, the extractor module finds words in the message which can fall into one of the three categories – active, passive or dormant. Only the active words are used to construct the feature vector. It must be pointed out that the size of the vocabulary does not necessarily increase with time, since words like "free" may start appearing in non-spam mails when the user joins a free software mailing list, and eventually the word "free" will lose its discriminatory power and hence get removed.

C PCA Module

PCA is a useful statistical dimensionality reduction technique that has found application in fields such as face recognition and image compression, and is a common technique for finding patterns in data of high dimension. An introduction to PCA can be found in [5].

The feature vectors constructed in the previous step are used to compute the eigenvectors using Singular Value Decomposition. The top two eigenvectors are selected (having the greatest eigenvalues) which are then used to transform input vectors to the reduced vector space.

The features that make up the input vector can be strongly correlated with each other. It is generally desirable to find or reduce the feature set to one that is minimal but sufficient. This can be done by judicious elimination or by the Principle Components Analysis (PCA) reduction technique amongst others. PCA can be used to reduce the feature vector dimension while retaining most of the information by constructing a linear transformation matrix. The transformation matrix is made up of the most significant eigenvectors of the covariance matrix.

Upon experimentation, it was found that using more than two dimensions (i.e. the first two eigenvectors arranged according the their eigenvalues) reduced the distinctiveness of the clusters and hence the performance of the classifier.

The reduction in the dimensionality causes a reduction in the number of inputs to the neural network which makes it more efficient. Another implication of using PCA is that the number of inputs to the neural network is made independent of the current size of the vocabulary. The number of words in the vocabulary may increase or decrease, but it will always result in only two inputs to the neural network, since we are using only the first two eigenvectors.

The use of PCA as a preprocessing step not only improves efficiency, but has also shown a consistent decrease in the error rate of the classifier. We also tried the difference of means method to select the top 35 (highest difference in means) out of a set of 403 attributes, but applying PCA to reduce the 403 dimension space to a two dimensional space was found to be invariably better at detecting new spam mails than using the 35 dimension space. Moreover, the performance of the classifier when PCA is used is found to be fairly stable against changes in size as well as nature of the vocabulary. On the other hand, when only the difference of means method is used without PCA, the error rate of the classifier varies drastically when the number of features is changed.

D "Short Circuit" Rules

Apart from using the presence or absence of words as criteria for making a decision, we find that the use of domain specific information can greatly decrease the error rate – especially the false negatives (spam mails being marked as non-spam), caused by cleverly crafted spam mails.

The presence or absence of certain features immediately ascertains whether a mail is spam or not. In such cases, a decision can be made directly i.e. by completely by-passing the PCA and neural network modules. We call these domain dependent heuristics as short circuit rules.

E.g. If a mail appears to come from a person whom the user has replied to or composed a mail to in the past, then the mail is considered to be non-spam. However, if the user replies to a mail that was marked with a spamness value of greater than .8, the user is warned and asked whether the reply-to address should be marked as a non-spam address.

The Extractor module can detect obfuscated words e.g. v*i*a*g*r*a. If the obfuscated word happens to be on the active list in the vocabulary and having a higher mean frequency of occurrence in spam samples than non-spam samples, the mail is immediately categorized as spam. This scheme works very well for detecting spam mails since non-spam mails will almost never have obfuscated words, especially words that are known to appear in spam mails. Such a scheme also prevents mail from a friend containing "M-A-I-L-M-E" to be classified as spam due to a short circuit rule.

Presence of invisible text, as mentioned in the section of Extractor Module, also triggers the short-circuit and the mail is immediately marked as spam.

E Neural Network Inputs

The neural network used by us has 6 inputs. While two of these connect to the output of the PCA module, the rest 4 capture outputs of the following heuristic criteria:

1) Number of strong punctuators, e.g. "!!!"
2) Percentage of capital words found in the mail.
3) Number of currency values found.
4) Percentage of colored text in the mail.

4 Results

The SpamNET program was trained using a spam database available on the Internet [7]. Mails, especially non-spam, were obtained from the mailing list of the third year I.T. students at our institute. The system was trained using 100 spam and 100 non-spam mails, and tested using 200 spam and non-spam mails each.

Fig. 2 shows the output of the neural network for 200 spam (red) and 200 non-spam (blue) mails. 2 spam and 2 non-spam mails were misclassified. Moreover, 1 spam mail and 1 non-spam mail can be seen to be on the verge of misclassification.

False Negatives

Mail 1 is a mail from SCazzz@aol.com which goes as "I am looking for a friend named…". It does not appear to contain any spam like words. Mail 2 is a mail from

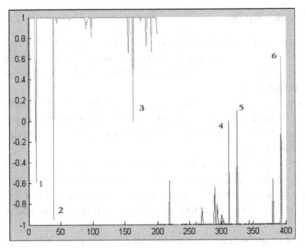

Fig. 2. Neural Network output

careerm@netexecutive.com and posed as a recruitment consultant. Although it mentioned a "large database of recruiters" which would indicate it is a spam, but terms like 'database' (and other terms found in that mail like 'resume', 'internet' etc) are usually discussed on our mailing list, and thus did not help in classifying the mail as spam. Mail 3 had many words in capitals, but almost all were innocent looking and thus it was difficult for the classifier to decide on the nature of the mail.

False Positives
Mail 4 and 5 were ACM newsletters which contained repeated references to 'business' and also contained the phrase "casualty-free". Moreover, the ACM mails made repeated use of FONT tags, while almost all non-spam mails used for training were plain text. Mail 6 described SCO's suit against IBM. It repeatedly talked of phrases like '$3 billion suit', '$5 million per quarter', 'Linux....free in its basic form' which the classifier found too tempting to ignore.

Table 1 describes detection rates obtained under various configurations.

Table 1. Average error rates obtained by multiple cross-validations over a set of 291 spam and 317 non-spam mails

Eigenvectors (PCA)	Stop wordlist used	Stemming used	Case sensitivity	Size of vocabulary	False Negatives	False Positives
2	Y	Y	Y	403	1.5%	1.3%
3	Y	Y	Y	403	2.0%	2.0%
4	Y	Y	Y	403	2.1%	2.0%
2	N	Y	Y	403	1.8%	1.2%
2	Y	N	Y	403	3.0%	4.0%
2	Y	Y	N	530	1.5%	1.5%

5 Conclusion

The traditional methods of filtering which looked for particular words and phrases have given way to more intelligent filtering techniques like Bayesian classifiers and

Neural Networks. Although Bayesian classification has been reported to provide over 99% accuracy for spam detection, neural networks have shown good potential for adaptive spam detectors. Irrespective of the classifier used, the preprocessing step has a profound effect on the performance of the classifier. Domain specific preprocessing which takes into the account the structure of the email together with the ability to handle mail headers and HTML content is found to have a positive effect on the classifier performance. Moreover, the use of dimensionality reduction has been experimentally found to hold a promising alternative to manually selecting good features for the classifier.

We are motivated by the misclassifications obtained by us to try the potential of semantic analysis to capture the context in which a word is used. The word 'database', when used with 'email', e.g. 'Email Database', or 'Database of Emails' should have a higher contribution towards classifying the mail as spam, than the individual occurrence of 'database' as well as 'email'.

References

1. 'White Papers – Spam Tutorial' – VicomSoft.
   http://www.spambolt.com/anti_spam_faq/ email_spam_filter.html
2. Sivanadyan, Detecting spam using Neural Networks.
   http://www.cae.wisc.edu/~ece539/project/f03/sivanadyan.pdf
3. Patrick Pantel and Dekang Lin. ``SpamCop—A Spam Classification & Organization Program.'' Proceedings of AAAI-98 Workshop on Learning for Text Categorization.
4. Paul Graham, at the 2003 Spam Conference http://www.paulgraham.com/better.html
5. Lindsay I Smith. A tutorial on Principal Components Analysis
   http://www.cs.otago.ac.nz/cosc453/student_tutorials/principal_components.pdf
6. Martin, Spam Filtering Using Neural Networks
   http://web.umr.edu/~bmartin/378Project/report.html
7. The Great Spam Archive (Online spam database) http://www.annexia.org/spam/
8. Androutsopoulos, I. Koutsias, J., Chandrinos, K. V., Paliouras, G., and Spyropoulos, C. D. An Evaluation of Naïve Bayesian Anti-Spam Filtering. In Proceedings of Workshop on Machine Learning in the New Information Age, 11th European Conference on Machine Learning, Barcelona, 2000.

TCP Based Denial-of-Service Attacks to Edge Network: Analysis and Detection

V. Anil Kumar[1] and Dorgham Sisalem[2]

[1] CSIR Centre for Mathematical Modelling and Computer Simulation, India
anil@cmmacs.ernet.in
[2] Fraunhofer Institute for Open Communication Systems, Germany
sisalem@fokus.fhg.de

Abstract. Congestion control algorithms in TCP are designed for a co-operative environment with the assumption that the end hosts voluntarily participate in the congestion control process. The steady growth of malicious activities such as Denial-of-Service attacks (DoS) reveals that the Internet no longer remains as a network of only trusted entities. We focus on a special class of DoS attacks targeted to edge networks by exploiting the vulnerabilities of TCP congestion control to duplicate and optimistic acknowledgement spoofing. We analyse two DoS attack scenarios namely pulse and sustained attack arising from two different behaviours of the attacker. Our results show that such attacks are feasible and also reveal the negative impact of the attacks on the target. We present a method for detecting such attacks by passively monitoring the traffic of the targeted network. The detection is achieved by differentiating malicious streams of duplicate and optimistic acknowledgments from normal acknowledgments. ...

1 Introduction

End-to-end congestion control is the primary mechanism used in today's Internet to control the transmission behaviour of communication systems. A major shortfall of the congestion control in TCP is that it is voluntary in nature and end-system's participation in it cannot be guaranteed. There could be various motivations behind the end-systems not voluntarily participating in the congestion control process. For example, a greedy web client can reduce the file download time by violating the congestion control [1]. On the other hand, a server implementation could attempt to serve its clients faster than the standard implementation. While such misbehaviours can cause unfairness among competing flows, a more dangerous consequence of violating congestion control is Denial-of-Service (DoS) attacks. The focus of this paper is on the analysis and detection of special type of DoS attacks targeted at edge networks connected to the Internet. Unlike conventional DoS attacks where external sources are used to flood the targeted network, these attacks exploit the transmission power of an internal machine in the target to flood its own network without compromising the machine. We show through simulation that an attacker by acting as a TCP client can setup a connection with a server and remotely control the server's transmission rate to generate flood traffic of desired pattern.

We analyse, two DoS attack scenarios caused by two different behaviours of the attacker, the subsequent flood patterns generated and the impact of these floods on the

G. Das and V.P. Gulati (Eds.): CIT 2004, LNCS 3356, pp. 214–223, 2004.
© Springer-Verlag Berlin Heidelberg 2004

Internet access router of the targeted network. In the first case the attacker forces the server to generate periodic flood of ON-OFF patterns. This is called periodic pulse attack and its main victim is outbound TCP flows from the targeted network. The periodic flood fills the router buffer and enforces high packet loss to TCP flows traversing the router so that the flows will experience frequent timeouts and severe throughput degradation. In the second case, we study the scenario where the server is forced to generate sustained flood which can fill and maintain the router buffer for a longer period. We call this as sustained attack and it can affect both TCP and non-TCP flows.

Finally we present our intrusion detection approach to detect maliciously crafted duplicate and optimistic ACKs which are used to generate the flood. A common characteristic of both the attack is that the buffer occupancy of the router increases abruptly and this feature is used in our detection system. We define a minimum threshold RTT (Round Trip Time) for outgoing packets in such a way that under normal conditions a packet cannot be acknowledged before the defined RTT period elapses. The threshold RTT is computed as a function of the instantaneous buffer occupancy of the router, and attacks are detected whenever the observed RTT falls below the threshold.

In this paper, the term attack flow denotes the TCP flow setup by the attacker, the terms sender or server denotes the end-point of the attack flow on the internal machine, and the term attacker or receiver or client denotes the end-point of the attack flow on the attacker's machine. Further, the term edge or targeted router is used to refer the Internet access router of the targeted network and the term ISP router is used to refer the router at the Internet Service Provider of the targeted network. We use Reno as the reference TCP model to analyse and simulate the attacks.

2 Congestion Control and Retransmission Policy in TCP

Congestion Control in TCP consists of four intertwined algorithms, slow start, congestion avoidance, fast retransmit and fast recovery, which are covered in detail elsewhere [2][3][4]. The sender maintains a state variable called congestion window (cwnd), which is the sender side limit on the number of packets it can transmit before it receives an ACK. As the sender receives ACKs, it modifies the cwnd using one of the algorithms mentioned above. The transmission criteria of the sender is that whenever the cwnd is less than the receiver advertised window (rwnd) and more than the number of packets outstanding in the network, the sender sends new packets until the cwnd becomes equal to the number of outstanding packets.

In [1] the authors show that the congestion control is vulnerable to duplicate and optimistic ACK spoofing. Duplicate ACK spoofing represents the situation where the receiver sends large number of ACKs to the same packet and compels the sender to respond with new data packets. In optimistic ACK spoofing, the receiver sends ACKs to packets which are sent by the sender but have not yet reached the receiver. In this paper, a combination of optimistic and duplicate ACK spoofing is used to force the sender to generate the DoS flood. Next, we explain why flood with ON-OFF pattern is effective in attacking TCP flows.

TCP flows suffer major performance degradation whenever packet loss recovery is achieved through retransmission timeout (RTO) [5][6][7]. Though fast retransmission and fast recovery algorithms are intended to recover from packet loss before RTO expires, there are three situations under which this does not happen. First, if cwnd is less than four and a packet loss occurs, the sender cannot receive three duplicate ACKs and the recovery algorithms will not be triggered. Second, if a retransmitted packet is lost, the sender has to wait till the RTO expires before transmitting the lost packet again. Third, when multiple packets are lost within a window of packets, the recovery algorithms are not often successful even if they are triggered [8]. In pulse attack, DoS pulses with high intensity and short duration impose one of the above conditions to normal TCP flows and compel them to undergo RTO based recovery process periodically.

3   Description of Attacks

3.1   Pulse Attack

Consider multiple TCP flows with RTO 1 second (minimum recommended value) sharing a bottleneck router. If the router is bombarded with a short duration high intensity burst which can instantly fill the router buffer and maintain the filled status for some duration, say t, all TCP flows with RTT less than t are likely to experience packet loss leading to timeout [9]. The flows will resume transmission again after 1 second and if the burst frequency is also 1 second, they will again experience timeout and the process will continue as per TCP's retransmission policy. In [9] the authors demonstrate the inability of TCP flows to co-exist with such high intensity periodic bursty traffic.

We next explain how an internal server on the targeted network can be turned to a flood source without compromising it. The attacker as a genuine client establishes a TCP connection with the server. After receiving a data packet, the attacker sends a large number of duplicate ACKs forcing the server to perform a fast retransmit and then enter into fast recovery. In fast recovery, as soon as the cwnd exceeds the number of outstanding packets, the server starts to respond with data packets which act as the DoS flood. The number of duplicate ACKs should be of the order of the buffer size of the targeted router. Receiver window is the only upper limit on the number of packets that the server transmits in fast recovery, and the attacker can enhance this limit by advertising high window size while establishing the connection. The filled queue has to be maintained for the desired duration to enforce packet loss to normal TCP flows. This is possible only if new packets are added to the buffer at the same rate as packets are dequeued. The attacker does this by shifting the attack flow from the fast recovery to the congestion avoidance mode by sending optimistic ACKs. For this, the attacker has to estimate the number of packets that the server has sent in fast recovery. This is explained below with the help of an example.

Consider the case where the server, after establishing the connection, sets the cwnd to 2 and sends packet number 1 and 2. The attacker, after receiving both the packets, sends ACK to packet 1 and then sends 50 duplicate ACKs to packet 1. When the server receives ACK to 1, its cwnd becomes 3 and after receiving the 3rd duplicate ACK cwnd becomes 5, [max(cwnd/2, 2) + 3]. The 50th duplicate ACK will inflate the cwnd to 52 and this means the server now has 52 unacknowledged packets in the network. Using this information the attacker can send optimistic ACK and clear the server's account on the number of outstanding packets. Optimistic ACKs are continued to maintain the queue for the desired duration. For example, if the targeted link is of 1 Mbps speed and the attacker's aim is to maintain the queue for 120 ms, it has to send 10 optimistic ACKs at a rate of one ACK in each 12 ms. This is because the ACKs will trigger at least one packet of size 1500 bytes in each 12 ms which is the time required for the router to dequeue 1500 bytes through 1 Mbps link. After sending sufficient number of ACKs, the attacker abruptly stops ACKs and this will force the attack flow to timeout. Note that the normal flows through the router are also likely to experience a timeout around the same time. The transmission process of attack and normal flows will resume after one second and the attacker repeats the whole process as soon as it sees a packet from the server.

3.2 Sustained Attack

In this attack, the attacker by modifying its ACK generation policy generates a sustained flood which can affect all traffic of the targeted system. The attacker first spoofs sufficient number of duplicate ACKs so that the resulting flood will instantly fill the router buffer and then spoofs optimistic ACKs to maintain the buffer in the filled status. Unlike pulse attack, here the attacker continues to generate optimistic ACKs as long as it desires to continue the attack.

4 Simulation

The attacks are simulated in network simulator [10] version 2 using the topology shown in figure 1. Nodes S1-S3 are the sender nodes to which TCP senders are attached and nodes D1-D3 are the destination nodes to which TCP receivers are attached. R1 and R2 are the routers configured with drop-tail queues and their queue size is limited to 50 packets. The packet and window sizes used are 1500 bytes and 64 packets respectively. Reno TCP is used as the sender and TCP sink without delayed ACK is used as the TCP receiver. In order to generate the attack flow, the ACK generation strategy of TCP sink is modified and no modification is done to the TCP sender.

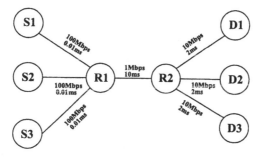

Fig. 1. Simulation setup

4.1 Pulse Attack

The attack is simulated using three TCP flows. Three normal TCP flows, one to each S-D pair, are attached to the nodes and the simulation is run for 30 seconds. The three middle plots in figure 2 show the time verses packet sequence plot of the flows when all the three are normal flows. Next the receiver at D1 is replaced with the attack flow, which generates 50 continuous duplicate ACKs and then 20 optimistic ACKs at a rate of one in each 12 ms period. The uppermost plot gives the sequence plot of the attack flow and the two lowermost plots represent the sequence plot of the normal flows in presence of the attack flow. Whenever the attack flow generates the pulse, timeout is imposed on normal flows and this causes throughput degradation to normal flows. While the maximum no. of packets transmitted by the normal flows in absence of the attack flow is about 750, this has come down to 300 in presence of the attack flow. Figures 3a, 3b and 3c show the transmission pattern of the attacker, that of the sender at S1 and the queue occupancy of the router R1 respectively. A noteworthy observation in the plot is that though the ideal period to cause maximum damage is 1 second, it is difficult for the attacker to achieve this. This is because once the flood generation is started the attacker sends optimistic ACKs and the RTO timer starts only after the optimistic ACKs are stopped. Once the optimistic ACK stops, the sender's retransmission starts after one second and the flood will again be restarted only after one RTT from the retransmission time. This is clear from figure 3b where the flood has a period of about 1.3 second, which is the sum of RTO, duration for which optimistic ACKs are sent and one RTT.

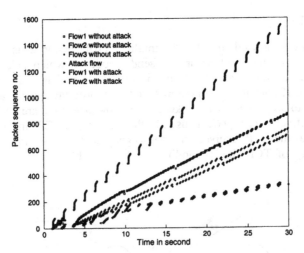

Fig. 2. Sequence no. verses time of TCP flows in presence and absence of the attack

4.2 Sustained Attack

The sustained attack is simulated using the same topology given in figure 1. Two normal TCP flows are attached to S2-D2 and S3-D3 pairs and the attack flow is attached to S1-D1 pair. The attacker first generates 50 duplicate ACKs and then generates continuous optimistic ACKs at a rate of one in each 12 ms for 30 sec. duration. Figures 4a, 4b and 4c show the transmission pattern of the attacker, that of the sender and the queue occupancy of the router R1. The buffer occupancy of the router remains at its maximum throughout the attack.

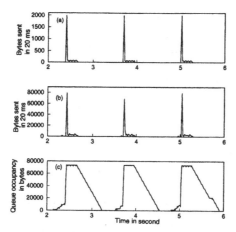

Fig. 3. (a) Transmission pattern of the attacker, (b) Transmission (flood) pattern of the sender and (c) Queue occupancy of the targeted router during pulse attack

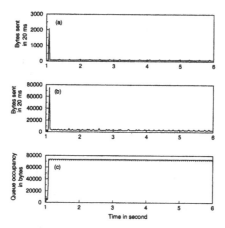

Fig. 4. (a) Transmission pattern of the attacker, (b) Transmission (flood) pattern of the sender and (c) Queue occupancy of the targeted router during sustained attack

5 Detection

A common characteristic of both the attacks is that the output queue occupancy of the WAN interface of the edge router increases suddenly and stays at a high value during the attack. This, of course, cannot be taken as an exclusive signature of attacks because the bursty Internet traffic can also frequently fill and maintain the router queue. However, if the queue is occupied by genuine packets, the queuing delay caused by buffering the packets will be reflected in the RTT of the packets, where as in the case of attacks, the attacker generates ACKs at high rate before it actually receives the data packets. In fact, for launching an effective DoS attack the ACKs should be generated in such a way that the rate of the resulting flood is of the order of the bandwidth of the targeted network. In such situations, the router queue occupancy increases, but the

RTT of malicious packets will be independent of the queue size. We use this characteristic of the attack flows to distinguish them from the normal flows.

The monitor (detection system) computes and maintains the instantaneous queue occupancy, *Qinst,* of the output interface of the router as in the case of routers with FIFO queue management. For each outbound TCP packet, the monitor computes a minimum threshold RTT, called *RTTmin-thresh,* as a function of *Qinst. RTTmin-thresh* is defined as the sum of various finite delays introduced to the packet as explained below: 1) Queuing delay at the edge router. This is a function of the number of bytes in the queue when the packet reaches there. 2) Transmission time of the packet at the link. If B is the bandwidth in bytes/second, the transmission time for a packet of length L bytes is L/B. 3) Bi-directional propagation delay of the point-to-point link between the edge router and the ISP router, 2Xp, where p is the one direction propagation delay. 4) Transmission time of the ACK packet at the ISP side of the link.

By considering the default size of 40 bytes for ACK packets, the *RTTmin-thresh* is computed as follows:

$$RTTmin\text{-}thresh = (Qinst + L + 40) \text{ X } (1/B) + 2p \ . \tag{1}$$

If the observed RTT of the packet falls below the value computed using equation (1) then we conclude that it belongs to a malicious flow.

The RTT in equation (1) is only a lower bound. The observed value depends on the delay and congestion in the rest of the path that the packet has to travel and its value could be much higher than that in equation (1). The bottom line is that during normal operation, the observed RTT cannot be less than the *RTTmin-thresh.* To obtain the actual RTT, the monitor records the time at which the TCP packet is transmitted. When the monitor receives an ACK, the time is again recorded and the difference in these two is the observed RTT.

5.1 Detection of Malicious Duplicate Acknowledgments

Detecting malicious duplicate ACKs is difficult because the exact number of duplicate ACKs expected during fast recovery cannot be quantified. This is because, if a retransmitted packet is lost, the sender is likely to receive large number of duplicate ACKs. This is shown in figure 5. As soon as the sender receives 3 duplicate ACKs (A1, A2, A3), it retransmits the lost packet (P1) and begins fast recovery. Additional duplicate ACKs (A4, A5) cause the sender to transmit new packets (P2, P3). Suppose the retransmitted packet (P1) is lost and at the same time P2 and P3 are successful in reaching the receiver. Since P1 is lost, P2 and P3 are treated as out of order packets and the receiver generates duplicate ACKs (A6 and A7) and this duplicate ACKs will again cause the sender to send new packets (P4 and P5). This cyclic process will be terminated either when P1 is retransmitted again (after RTO expiry) or when the number of outstanding packets exceeds the rwnd. So the challenge is to differentiate duplicate ACK stream triggered due to retransmission loss from those maliciously generated by the attacker. Next we explain our algorithm to distinguish between these two types of duplicate ACKs.

When the monitor detects the first duplicate ACK, it computes the maximum number of duplicate ACKs expected (max-dupack) under the assumption that the retransmission, if happens, will not be lost. The monitor records the RTTthresh and time of

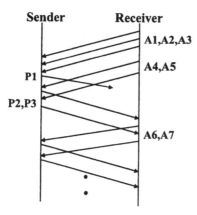

Fig. 5. Duplicate ACK stream due to retransmission packet loss

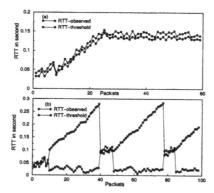

Fig. 6. (a) Threshold and observed RTT when duplicate ACKs are generated due to retransmission loss and (b) Threshold and observed RTT for malicious duplicate ACK

all the packets transmitted in fast recovery. If the number of duplicate ACKs exceeds the max-dupack, additional dupACKs are marked suspicious and indexed sequentially starting with one (the first dupACK which exceeds max-dupack as 1, the second as 2 and so on). If the suspicious dupacks are the result of a retransmission packet loss, the first marked suspicious ACK will be generated by the first packet sent in fast recovery and the second suspicious ACK by the second packet sent in fast recovery and so on. These suspicious ACKs are used to compute the observed RTT for packets sent in fast recovery and if the observed RTT falls below its threshold value, the suspicious ACKs are identified as malicious ACKs. The algorithm is simulated in two different scenarios using the topology shown in figure 1. The first simulation depicts the case where duplicate ACKs are generated due to retransmission packet loss. A single TCP flow is set up between node S2 and D2 and the router R2 is modified to drop packet with sequence number 26 and its retransmission. Figure 6a shows the threshold and observed RTT of packets transmitted. Packet number 26 is actually the first packet transmitted in fast recovery and packet no. 27 is the second and so on. Observed RTTs of these packets are always greater than the threshold RTT.

Figure 6b shows the simulation result where the duplicate ACKs are generated by the attacker. While receiving packets 1 to 9 the attacker behaves as a normal receiver and acknowledges up to and including packet 9. The observed RTT for these packets are greater than the threshold RTT. The attacker then changes its behaviour and generates duplicate ACKs for 9 and the sender begins fast recovery. Packets 10 to 40 are sent in fast recovery in response to the malicious duplicate ACKs. All these packets have observed RTT less than the threshold RTT. The attacker then repeats the process.

5.2 Detection of Malicious Optimistic Acknowledgements

Figure 7 shows the observed and threshold RTT verses time plotted during an attack in which the attacker first sends duplicate ACKs to fill the router buffer and then continuously generates optimistic ACKs at a rate of one in each 12 ms. An important observation is that though the observed RTT is less than the threshold RTT during the initial phase of the attack (so the attack can be detected), the observed RTT increases with time. This is because the sender is in congestion avoidance phase in which the cwnd and hence the number of outstanding packets increases in response to the optimistic ACKs.

6 Conclusion

In this paper, we have explored the possibility of a class of Denial-of-Service attacks where an internal machine in the targeted network is exploited as the flood source without compromising the machine. We studied two different behaviours of the attacker which result in two disastrous flood patterns. Through simulation, we have evaluated the potential negative impacts of these attacks on the targeted system. We have also proposed an Intrusion Detection System to detect the attacks by passively monitoring the targeted network.

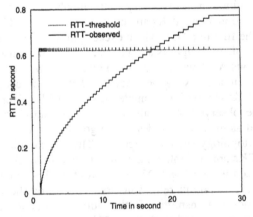

Fig. 7. Threshold and observed RTT for optimistic ACKs

References

1. S. Savage, N. Cardwell, D. Wetherall, T. Anderson: TCP congestion control with Misbehaving receiver. Computer Communication Review, 29(5), pp.71-78, October 1999
2. V. Jacobson: Congestion avoidance and control. In proceedings of SIGCOMM, page 314-329, 1988
3. V. Jacobson: Modified TCP congestion Avoidance Algorithm. Technical report LBL, April 1990
4. M. Allman, V. Paxson, W. Stevens: TCP Congestion Control. RFC 2581, April 1999
5. H. Balakrishnan, V. N. Padmanabhan, S. Seshan, M. Stemm, R. H. Katz: TCP Behavior of a Busy Internet Server: Analysis and Improvements. In Proceedings of IEEE Infocom, March 1999
6. M. Allman, H. Balakrishnan, S. Floyd: Enhancing TCP's Loss Recovery Using Limited Transmit. RFC 3042, January 2001
7. V. Paxson, M. Allman: Computing TCP's Retransmission Timer. RFC 2988, November 2000
8. K. Fall, S. Floyd: Simulation based Comparison of Tahoe, Reno, and SACK TCP. Computer communication Review, July 1996
9. A. Kuzmanovic, E.W. Knighty: Low-Rate TCP-Targeted Denial of Service Attacks. In proceedings of ACM SIGCOMM, August 2003
10. Network simulator version 2: http://www.isi.edu/nsnam/ns

Network Intrusion Detection
Using Wavelet Analysis

Sanjay Rawat[1,2] and Challa S. Sastry[1]

[1] AI Lab, Dept. of Computer and Information Sciences
University of Hyderabad, Hyderabad-500046, India
challa_sastry@lycos.com
[2] IDRBT
Castle Hills, Road No. 1
Masab Tank, Hyderabad-500057, India
sanjayr@idrbt.ac.in

Abstract. The inherent presence of self-similarity in network (LAN, Internet) traffic motivates the applicability of wavelets in the study of 'burstiness' features of them. Inspired by the methods that use the self-similarity property of a data network traffic as normal behaviour and any deviation from it as the anomalous behaviour, we propose a method for anomaly based network intrusion detection. Making use of the relations present among the wavelet coefficients of a self-similar function in a different way, our method determines the possible presence of not only an anomaly, but also its location in the data. We provide the empirical results on KDD data set to justify our approach.

Keywords: Network traffic, Intrusion detection, Burstiness, Wavelets, Hurst parameter, Energy plot, Self-similarity.

1 Introduction

As more and more data are being stored on computers and sensitive information is flowing through the public networks, the computer security has become the prime focus of industry and academics. Various techniques such as cryptography, bio-authentication, firewalls and intrusion detection systems are being employed to ensure the security of information. Intrusion detection systems (IDS) has been the active area of research for more than one decade due to the increasing rate of attacks. There are two techniques to build an IDS: Misuse-based IDS which works on the signatures of the known attacks and thus can not capture new attacks. The other one is anomaly-based IDS that learns the normal behavior of the system (users or computer networks or programs) and any deviation in this behavior is considered as a probable attack. Intrusion detection systems based on later technique are able to detect new attacks. Based on the data being analyzed by the IDS to detect intrusion, there are host-based IDS (HIDS) and network-based IDS (NIDS). HIDS collects data from the system, it is protecting, while NIDS collects data from the network in the form of packets. Due to the

G. Das and V.P. Gulati (Eds.): CIT 2004, LNCS 3356, pp. 224–232, 2004.

nature of the problems of the IDS, in the research area of IDS, data mining and machine learning techniques have found wide spread use [14].

It has been observed that the network traffic is self-similar in nature. It is pointed out in [7] that the self-similarity of network traffic distributions can often be accounted for by a mixture of the actions of a number of individual users and hardware and software behaviors at their originating hosts, multiplexed into an interconnection network. It can be seen that traffic related to attacks, especially DoS attacks, is bursty in nature. Traffic that is burst on many or all time scales can be described statistically using the notion of self-similarity. Self-similarity is the property that is associated with fractal-objects whose structure is unchanged on different scales.

In view of its multiscale framework and localization aspects, the wavelet technique is capable of being used for the analysis of scaling and local "burstiness" features of a function. In the recent literature on wavelet based IDS, the wavelet analysis has been used to both describe and analyze the data network traffics. Besides, it has been used to characterize network related problems like congestion, device failure etc [4]. The basic philosophy in wavelet based IDS is that the self-similarity is prevalent in the network traffic under normal condition and therefore can be considered as signature for normal behavior. The loss of self-similarity, signifying a possible attack, can be taken as the deviation from the normal behavior.

Although the method presented herein is inspired by the method promoted in [10], yet it uses the relations present among the wavelet coefficients of self-similar functions in a different way to detect not only the deviation in the data from self-similarity, but also the locations at which the anomalies occur.

The rest of the paper is organized as follows. In section 2, we discuss the basic concepts of self-similarity and wavelet analysis. In the subsequent section, we consider proposing a method for the detection of anomaly using wavelets. In section 4, we discuss some of the existing results dealing with similar applications. While in section 5, we present our experimental setup and results.

2   Self-similarity and Wavelet Analysis

In this section, we present the definition of self-similarity and the basic concepts of wavelets. Formally we can define self-similarity as follows [10]:

Definition: A process or function $\{f(t) : t \in (-\infty, \infty)\}$ is said to be self-similar with self-similarity parameter H, if and only if $c^{-H} f(ct) = f(t)$, $\forall$ $c > 0$ and $t \in (-\infty, \infty)$.

It has been studied that, for a self-similar function f, the Hurst parameter H lies in $(0.5, 1)$ and any deviation from this signifies the presence of anomaly in the data. As in [1, 10], we make use of Hurst parameter (H) to establish the presence of self-similarity in the traffic. From now on, we consider f to be a finite variance self-similar process with the self-similarity parameter $H \in (0.5, 1)$. In mathematical terms, we, however, treat the function f as being a compactly supported self-similar L^2 function.

A wavelet is a "little wave" that is both localized and oscillatory. The representation of a function in terms of wavelet basis functions, generated by dyadic scaling and integer translates of the wavelet, involves low frequency block containing the "identity" of the function and several high frequency blocks containing the visually important features or "flavours" (such as edges or lines).

There is a class of discrete wavelet transforms (DWT), called multiresolution approximations of L^2, that can be implemented using an extremely efficient algorithms [9].

A framework through which compactly supported, orthogonal (biorthogonal) sufficiently regular and real wavelets are constructed is called *multiresolution analysis* (MRA) [9]. An MRA consists of a ladder of closed spaces $\{V_j\}_{j \in Z}$ in $L^2[(-\infty, \infty)]$ satisfying the following properties

1). $V_j \subset V_{j+1}$ for all $j \in Z$.
2). $f(.) \in V_j \iff f(2.) \in V_{j+1}$.
3). $\cup_{j \in Z} V_j$ is dense in L^2.
4). $\cap_{j \in Z} V_j$ is empty set.
5). There exists a function $\phi \in V_0$ such that $\{\phi(.-n)\}_{n \in Z}$ forms an orthonormal basis for V_0.

The V_j spaces can be considered as different approximation spaces and the function ϕ that generates the MRA is called scaling function. An example for ϕ is $\chi_{[0,1)}$, called Haar scaling function. The detail-spaces W_j defined by $W_j = V_{j+1} \ominus V_j$ constitute a disjoint partition for L^2, i.e,

$$L^2 = V_J \bigoplus \left[\bigoplus_{j \geq J} W_j\right] = \bigoplus_{j \in Z} W_j, \tag{1}$$

for any integer J. The function ψ, called the wavelet function, generates [9] the detail-spaces W_j. Finally, a function $f \in L^2$ has the following wavelet representation

$$f = \sum_{k \in Z} c_{J,k} \phi_{J,k} + \sum_{j \geq J; k} d_{j,k} \psi_{j,k} = \sum_{j,k \in Z} d_{j,k} \psi_{j,k}. \tag{2}$$

In (2), $\psi_{j,k}(t) = 2^{\frac{j}{2}} \psi(2^j t - k)$, $c_{J,k} = \langle f, \phi_{J,k} \rangle$ and $d_{j,k} = \langle f, \psi_{j,k} \rangle$ with $\langle ., . \rangle$ being the standard L^2 - innerproduct operation. Ingrid Daubechies [9] has given a procedure for the construction of compactly supported, sufficiently regular and orthonormal wavelets.

3   Application of Wavelets to IDS

In this section, using the properties of wavelet bases and self-similar functions, we present our methodology for the detection of anomaly in the data.

The coefficients in the wavelet representation of a self-similar function satisfy the following simple relation: for any integers j, m, n such that $j = m + n$, we have

$$d_{j,k} = 2^{\frac{j}{2}} \int_{-\infty}^{\infty} f(t)\psi(2^j t - k)dt$$

$$= 2^{\frac{j}{2}} \int_{-\infty}^{\infty} f(2^{-n}t)\psi(2^m t - k)2^{-n}dt$$

$$= 2^{\frac{j}{2}}2^{-nH-n} \int_{-\infty}^{\infty} f(t)\psi(2^m t - k)dt \tag{3}$$

$$= 2^{\frac{-n(2H+1)}{2}} d_{m,k}.$$

Taking $m = 0$ and computing the energy E_j, at j^{th} scale, of wavelet coefficients, we get

$$E_j := \frac{1}{N_j} \sum_k |d_{j,k}|^2$$

$$= \frac{2^{-j(2H+1)}}{N_j} \sum_k |d_{0,k}|^2 = 2^{-j(2H+1)} E_0 \tag{4}$$

In the above equation, N_j represents the number of wavelet coefficients at scale j. From (3), it may be noted that N_j is same at all levels. Consequently, the Hurst parameter H can be computed using

$$H = \frac{1}{2}\left[log_2\left(\frac{E_0}{E_j}\right) - 1\right] \tag{5}$$

In [10], the plots of logarithm of energies at various levels have been considered. The scales for over which the plots are straight lines are determined to identify the scale interval over which the self-similarity holds. The presence of intrusion into the data is found by analyzing the deviation from the line behavior of energy plots at the determined scales.

As the energy computed is global in nature in the sense that the location and the 'strength' of anomaly are hidden by the averaging taken in (4), we present in this work another way of using (3) for the determination of possible presence of anomaly in the data. Instead of taking energy, using (3), we compute H directly from

$$H = \frac{1}{2}\left[\frac{2}{n}log_2\left(\frac{d_{m,k}}{d_{m+n,k}}\right) - 1\right]. \tag{6}$$

The Hurst parameter H computed for different m, n and k, reveal not only the scale interval over which H falls in the desired range, but also the time instances where H goes out of range at the scales of self-similarity of f in the event of presence of anomaly in the data. We believe that this observation helps us detect not only the presence of anomaly in the data, but also the location of it.

Though the precise mathematical relation shown in (3) ensures one-to-one relation between the coefficients at all pairs of levels of self-similarity, more often than not, it does not match with what we see in practice. The reason for this is: in actual computations, when dealing with compactly supported wavelet basis functions, we use finite number of coefficients at every (finite) level and as we increase the level, number of coefficients involved becomes doubled. Consequently different levels have different number of coefficients. In view of it, taking ratios of coefficients of two levels as shown in (6) is seemingly unjustified. To get rid of this problem, in our simulation work, we use $f \star \overline{\psi}_j(2^{-j}k)$ to compute $d_{j,k}$ (with $\overline{\psi}_j(x)$ being $2^j\psi(-2^jx)$). At every level j, we collect appropriate coefficients from $f \star \overline{\psi}_j$ and then take the ratios as shown in (6). Leaving it aside, after computing $f \star \overline{\psi}_j$ at different j and treating them as coefficients, we take ratios of them at different j. Although it has no justification, we observe that both the approaches give similar results.

4   Related Work

Various data mining and machine learning techniques have been applied to anomaly-based intrusion detection systems. Lee et al [14][15] have shown the applicability of various data mining methods for IDS. A team at University of Minnesota has applied clustering based method to NIDS [13]. Their approach is based on the rare class classification and local outlier factor.

The recent work of William and Marlin [2] shows that DARPA'98 data set shows self-similarity, but within a certain interval of time i.e. from 8 am to 6 pm. The periodogram method is used to estimate the Hurst parameter H. If the value of H falls within the interval (0.5 and 1.0), the process (traffic) is self-similar. The methodology involves the plotting of periodogram for each two-hour period of each attack-free day in the DARPA data. The hurst parameter is estimated from each plot by performing a least square fit to the lowest 10% of the frequencies to determine the behavior of the spectral energy as it approaches the origin. The main importance of this study is the observation that other methods which use temporal distribution for their model, should concentrate only on the data between 8 am to 6pm of each day.

In another work by Nash and Ragsdale [17], the self-similarity of the network traffic is used to propose the generation of network traffic for IDS evaluation. They observe that it is difficult to produce the traffic that includes large number of intrusions and more than this, it is also difficult to analyze such a huge traffic for sign of intrusions. Self-similarity is used to reproduce traffic, which is closer to real traffic. Also the wavelet coefficients are used to decompress the data for analysis. Hurst parameter is used to demonstrate the self-similarity. Mandelbrot's method is used to estimate Hurst parameter.

The study by Gilbert [10] discusses the theoretical and implementation issues of wavelet-based scaling analysis for network traffic. As a network traffic, packet per second and user-requested-page per session are considered for demonstration of self-similarity. Energy-plots and partition function are calculated using the wavelet coefficients. A straight line indicates the presence of self-similarity.

On the similar lines, Huang et al [11] propose the use of energy plot to analyze the network in terms of RTT (round trip time)and RTO (retransmission timeout). A tool named as WIND has been built to analyze the packets collected from tcpdump tool. TCP/IP packets can be analyzed across different time periods and across part of traffic destined to different subnets by exploiting the built-in scale-localization ability of wavelets.

In [4], the use of wavelet coefficients is proposed to analyse various network related anomalies. These anomalies are grouped into three categories: Network Operation Anomalies which include network device outages and change in traffic due to configurational changes; Flash Crowd Anomalies which include traffic due to some software release or external interest in some specific web site and Network Abuse Anomalies which include DoS or scans.

5   KDDcup'99 Data Set and Experimental Setup

In 1998, DARPA, together with Lincoln Laboratory at MIT, released the DARPA 1998 data set [8] for the evaluation of IDS. The data set consists of seven weeks of training and two weeks of testing data. There are a total of 38 attacks in training and testing data. The processed version of DARPA data, containing only the network data (Tcpdump data), is termed as KDD data set [12]. There are approximately 5 million records in training set and 0.3 million records in the testing set. Each of these records is described with 41 attributes, wherein 34 are numeric and 7 are symbolic. This set of attributes includes general TCP features like bytes/sec, flags, duration etc and derived features like the-same-host features and the-same-service features. A detailed description of these features can be found in [14]. It has been observed [2] that the DARPA data exhibit self-similarity within certain interval of time. As KDD data set is derived from DARPA data set, out of curiosity, we choose KDD data set for our experimentation. Recently, it is shown by Sabhnani and Serpen [18] that KDD data set is not suitable for misuse-based IDS as the distribution of attacks in training and testing data is not same. The portion of new attacks, in the R2L and U2R categories, in testing data is more than the known attacks. Therefore any misuse-based IDS will show poor detection rate. Ours is an anomaly-based approach, consequently the choice of this data set is not affected by the short-comings of KDD set as pointed out in [18]. We test our approach on the 10% of the KDD set, which is provided with the full set. This set consists of almost all the attacks present in DARPA data set with a total of 4,94,020 records. Out of these records, there are 97,277 normal records in the data set which we have considered in the beginning part of the data by sorting out the data suitably.

We have carried out our simulation work using nearly symmetric orthonormal wavelet ('sym6') of MATLAB package. Using (6), we have computed the Hurst parameter H at different levels. The H values computed, remaining close to 0.8 and hence falling in the interval $(0.5, 1)$, reveal that self-similarity of the data is present between the levels 1 and 4. In Fig. 1, we have displayed the gradient of H values at the levels 3, 4 to demonstrate how H changes within a given level. Our motive behind taking gradient of H values is to notice the abrupt changes in H as it may signify the presence of anomaly in the data. To show this concept empirically, we choose the Neptune attack from the KDD data set, which is a DoS attack sending large number of SYN packets to target host to exhaust its buffer. As this attack never establishes the session, many bytes become almost zero in each connection attempt. Column 2 of KDD set indicates this feature.

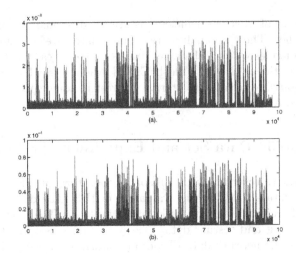

Fig. 1. The changes in H values of the normal data.

Under normal condition, the behavior of column 2 in terms of H is shown in Fig. 1. It can be seen that the changes in H are of very small order.

To test the detection ability of our approach, we introduce many sessions of Neptune attack in the end of the data. The H-gradient plot of this data is shown in Fig. 2.

It is clearly visible, in Fig. 2, that the variation in H corresponding to the anomalous data, (i.e., in the right half of the Fig. 2), is almost zero. However, the actual values of H go out of the desired range. This is happening because, as explained above, for a long period of time, the attacker is just sending SYN packets without establishing the connection, resulting in similar values for H at

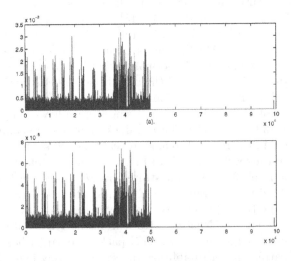

Fig. 2. The changes in H values in the presence of Neptune attack.

all levels of significance (hence the changes in H values are almost zero). We also carry out the similar experiments with smurf attack, present in the KDD data set. Under this attack, the victim receives a large number of ICMP reply (echo) within a short period of time. This hampers the performance of victim to respond it properly to other requests from genuine senders. This activity is captured in the KDD set in the column "count", which counts the number of connections to the same host as the current connection in the past two seconds. Due to the pausity of space, we are not showing the results in figure.

On the basis of above experiment, it can be inferred that the proposed approach is capable of detecting the attacks wherein the burstiness is present in the traffic.

6 Conclusion

The present work proposes a wavelet based algorithm for the detection of anomaly in the network data. The main feature of the work is to analyse the anomaly present in the data along with its location. Although our method is working well in the cases that we have considered, yet more extensive experimental work is further required to establish the wide applicability of our method.

Acknowledgement

The authors are thankful to Prof. Arun K. Pujari, University of Hyderabad and Prof. V. P. Gulati, Director, IDRBT for their support and encouragement. The second author is thankful to the National Board for Higher Mathematics (NBHM), India, for its financial support (Grant No.FNO: 40/7/2002-R & D II/1124).

References

1. Abry P., Veitch D.: Wavelet Analysis of Long-Range Dependent Traffic. IEEE trans. Inform. Theory. 44(1998) 2-15
2. Allen W. H., Marin G. A.: On the Self-Similarity of Synthetic Traffic for the Evaluation of intrusion Detection Systems. In: Proc. of the IEEE/IPSJ International Symposium on Applications and the Internet (SAINT), Orlando, FL. (2003) 242-248
3. Bace R., Mell P.: NIST Special Publication on Intrusion Detection System. SP800-31, NIST, Gaithersburg, MD (2001)
4. Barford P., Plonka D.: Characteristics of Network Traffic Flow Anomalies. In: Proc of ACM SIGCOMM Internet Measurement Workshop IMW (2001)
5. Beran J.: Statistics for Long-Memory Processes. Chapman and Hall, New York (1994)
6. Cabrera J., Ravichandran B., Mehra R.: Statistical Traffic Modeling for Network Intrusion Detection. In: Proc of the 8th IEEE Symposium on Modeling, Analysis and simulation of Computers and Telecommunications, San Francisco, California. (2000) 466-475

7. Crovella M., Bestavros A.: Self-Similarity in World Wide Web Traffic: Evidence and Possible Causes. IEEE-ACM Transactions on Networking. Vol 5(6) (1997)
8. DARPA 1998 data set,
   http://www.ll.mit.edu/IST/ideval/data/1998/1998_data_index.html
9. Daubechies I.: Ten lectures on wavelets. CBMS-NSF Series in Appl. Math, No.61. SIAM Philadelphia (1992)
10. Gilbert A. C.: Multiscale Analysis and Data Networks. Applied and Computational Harmonic Analysis. 10 (2001) 185-202
11. Huang P., Feldmann A., Willinger W.: A Non-intrusive, wavelet-basesd Approach to Detect Network Performance Problems. In: Proc of the First ACM SIGCOMM Workshop on Internet Measurement IMW'01, San Francisco, California, USA. (2001) 213-227
12. KDD 1999 data set, http://kdd.ics.uci.edu/databases/kddcup99/kddcup99.html
13. Lazarevic A., Ertoz L., Kumar V., Ozgur A., Srivastava J.: A Comparative Study of Anomaly Detection Schemes in Network Intrusion Detection. In: Proc of Third SIAM Conference on Data Mining, San Francisco (2003)
14. Lee W., Stolfo Salvatore J.: Data Mining Approaches for Intrusion Detection. In: Proceedings of the 7th USENIX Security Symposium (SECURITY-98), Usenix Association, January 26-29. (1998) 79-94
15. Lee W., Stolfo S., Mok K.: Mining in a Data-flow Environment: Experience in Network Intrusion Detection. In: Proc of the 5th ACM SIGKDD International Conference on Knowledge Discovery & Data Mining (KDD '99), San Diego, CA. (1999) 114-124
16. Leland W., Taqqu M. S., Willinger W., Wilson D. V.: On the Self-similar Nature of Ethernet Traffic (extended version). IEEE/ACM Transactions on Networking. Vol. 2 (1994) 1-15
17. Nash D., Ragsdale D.: Simulation of Self-Similarity in Network utilization Patterns as as Precursor to Automated Testing of Intrusion Detection Systems. IEEE Transactions on Systems, Man and Cybernetics, Part A: Systems and human, vol. 31(4) (2001) 327-331
18. Sabhnani M., Serpen G.: On Failure of Machine Learning Algorithm for Detecting Misuse in KDD Intrusion Detection Dataset. To appear in Journal of Intelligent Data Analysis (2004)

Building a Secure
and Highly Scalable Data Distribution System

Shivakant Mishra

Department of Computer Science
University of Colorado, Campus Box 0430
Boulder, CO 80309-0430, USA
mishras@cs.colorado.edu

Abstract. This paper describes the design, implementation, and performance evaluation of MykilDDS, a secure and highly scalable data distribution system over the Internet. MykilDDS facilitates a secure distribution of data over the Internet to a significantly large number of clients. It integrates IP multicast with Mykil group key management system. Important advantages of MykilDDS include security, high scalability, differentiated quality of service for data distribution, high availability, and support for user mobility and smaller, hand-held devices. A prototype of MykilDDS has been implemented. The paper describes this implementation and reports on the performance measured from this implementation.

1 Introduction

Internet is increasingly being used for a multitude of critical as well as non-critical applications. One class of these applications is data dissemination from one or a small number of servers to a significantly large number of clients. Examples include pay-per-view programs, video-on-demand services, frequent stock quote updates, software patches and updates, and advertising. Some common requirements of these applications include security, high scalability, high availability, fault tolerance, and support for smaller, hand-held devices. For example, a video-on-demand service requires that only pre-registered clients are able to watch a video program being broadcast. A popular pay-per-view program can have a very large number of subscribers, sometimes in excess of 100,000. Clients who have paid for a particular pay-per-view service must be able to watch the program being broadcast in near real time, despite temporary problems in communication network or intermediate routers. Finally, subscribers to a stock quote service must be able to receive the latest quotes on their smaller, hand-held devices.

The current Internet technology, namely IP multicast, is insufficient to satisfy all the requirements of these applications. IP multicast provides only a best-effort multicasting support without any security guarantees. Any process connected to the Internet can send a message to an IP multicast group or receive messages multicast with in an IP multicast group without any restrictions. There is no

G. Das and V.P. Gulati (Eds.): CIT 2004, LNCS 3356, pp. 233–242, 2004.

support for controlling the membership of a multicast group, or maintaining the authenticity, integrity or confidentiality of multicast information. In fact, a majority of current Internet routers do not support IP multicast because of this lack of security support.

In this paper, we propose a data distribution system called MykilDDS. This system provides a secure distribution of data over the Internet to a large number of clients. MykilDDS integrates IP multicast with Mykil group key management system [2, 3] to build a data distribution system that has six important features. First, it is designed for a network such as the Internet, where IP multicast is enabled only in smaller subnets that are under a single administrative control. Second, it provides support for a secure distribution of data, and ensures that only pre-authorized clients are able to decrypt this data. The system provides an elaborate framework for new clients to register in an efficient manner, and a key management system to manage the cryptographic keys used for data distribution. Third, MykilDDS is scalable in terms of the number of clients it can support. It provides an acceptable performance for a group of more than 100,000 clients with frequent membership changes. Fourth, MykilDDS provides a differentiated quality of service for data distribution. In particular, it allows clients with different computing and bandwidth capabilities to receive the multicast data. Fifth, MykilDDS provides support for high availability and fault tolerance. Pre-registered clients can receive the data being distributed, despite communication failures, router malfunctions, or server failures. Finally, MykilDDS allows clients to access a data distribution system using small devices such as PDAs or cell phones that have limited resources, such as memory, CPU cycles or communication bandwidth.

The rest of this paper is organized as follows. The next section, Section 2 describes the design of MykilDDS. Section 3 describes the implementation and performance evaluation of MykilDDS. Finally, Section 4 discusses future work and concludes the paper.

2   MykilDDS: Design

Because of lack security support in IP multicast, there are only a few routers in the Internet that allow multicast traffic to flow through them. Instead, IP multicast is mainly used in smaller subnets that are under a single administrative control, e.g. a network with in a university, a government organization, or an industry. Based on this current Internet organization, MykilDDS divides the entire network interconnecting the clients into smaller units called *areas*. This is shown in Figure 1. Each area corresponds to a single autonomous unit, with in which IP multicast may be enabled. Each area is represented by a special node called *area controller*. An area controller maintains the membership of an area, manages the cryptographic keys used in the area, and facilitates data propagation. All areas are logically connected to one another to form a tree-like hierarchy, with the root containing the data distribution source. In Figure 1, area 0 is the root, areas 1, 2, and 3 are its children, and area 4 is a child of area 1, while area 5 is a child of area 2.

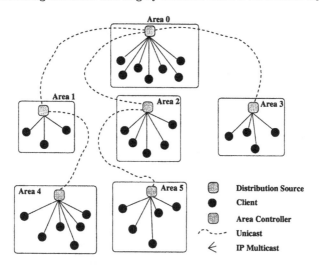

Fig. 1. Architectural Overview of MykilDDS.

2.1   Data Dissemination

To accommodate security, each area controller maintains an area key for its area. This key is shared among all clients with in the area, and is used for encryption/decryption using an appropriate symmetric-key cryptographic algorithm such as AES [1]. In addition, an area key of an area is also known to the area controller of all children areas. So, in Figure 1, area key of area 0 is known to the area controller of area 0, all clients in area 0, and area controllers of areas 1, 2, and 3. Similarly, area key of area 1 is known to the area controller of area 1, all clients in area 1, and area controller of area 4. Management of area keys is done using Mykil key management system that is described in the next subsection.

While there is no common cryptographic key shared by all clients, data distribution in MykilDDS avoids encrypting the data being distributed multiple times. We explain data dissemination in MykilDDS using the organization shown in Figure 1. When the source needs to distribute some data $\mathbf{D}$, it first generates a random key K_r, encrypts $\mathbf{D}$ using K_r ($E_{K_r}(\mathbf{D})$), and encrypts K_r using K_{a0} ($E_{K_{a0}}(K_r)$), where K_{a0} is the area key of area 0. It disseminates $\{E_{K_r}(\mathbf{D}); E_{K_{a0}}(K_r)\}$ to its clients in area 0 using IP multicast, and to the area controllers of its children areas (i.e. areas 1, 2 and 3) using an appropriate unicast protocol, e.g. TCP.

When a client in area 0 receives this message, it first retrieves K_r by decrypting $E_{K_{a0}}(K_r)$ (recall that all clients in an area share the area key of their area), and then decrypts $E_{K_r}(\mathbf{D})$. When an area controller of an area (e.g. area 1) receives this message, it first retrieves K_r by decrypting $E_{K_{a0}}(K_r)$ (recall that area controllers of all children areas share the area key of their parent area). It then re-encrypts K_r using K_{a1} ($E_{K_{a1}}(K_r)$), where K_{a1} is the area key of area 1. The area controller then disseminates $\{E_{K_r}(\mathbf{D}); E_{K_{a1}}(K_r)\}$ to its clients in area 1 using IP multicast, and to the area controllers of its children areas (i.e.

area 4) using an appropriate unicast protocol, e.g. TCP. This process continues until the data has been disseminated to all clients.

There are four important points to note here. First, the data dissemination process makes use of IP multicast, whenever available. Considering that IP multicast results in saving network bandwidth, this is a desirable feature. Second, security of multicast data is achieved without requiring a common cryptographic key among all clients. This is very important from scalability point of view. Whenever a new client joins in or an existing client leaves, only the area key of a single area has to be changed. Not requiring a common key among all clients is useful from security point of view as well. A key compromise requires a change in the area key of a single area affecting the clients of a single area, as opposed to all clients. Third, as the data moves from one area to another, only the random key K_r needs to be decrypted and re-encrypted. Considering that an area key is typically small (128 or 256 bits), this is quite efficient when compared to the alternative of decryption and re-encryption of the entire data as it moves from one area to another. Finally, an advantage of using a random key to encrypt the data being disseminated is that long-term keys such as area keys are not exposed much. The random key chosen to disseminate the data is different every time a new data is disseminated.

2.2   Group and Key Management

The secure data dissemination is made possible by organizing the clients into areas, maintaining a different area key for each area, and ensuring that the data is not decrypted/re-encrypted as it moves from one area to the next. The next requirement in the design of MykilDDS is how are various keys managed and how is the membership of the group (registered clients) maintained. Again, IP multicast does not provide any support for doing this. We have incorporated Mykil key management system [2, 3] in MykilDDS to address these issues.

Mykil is built on top of IP multicast to implement a *secure multicast group*. A secure multicast group is a multicast group in which members register and authenticate themselves with a designated registration authority, receive a set of *cryptographic key(s)*, and use these keys to encrypt the multicast data that they send and decrypt the multicast data that they receive. More specifically, support for secure multicast consists of three components: a *registration server*, a *key management server*, and a *key distribution protocol*. Figure 2 illustrates the relationship among these components, and the steps followed when a new member joins a multicast group. A registration server authenticates and registers a user that intends to join a secure multicast group based on the appropriate credentials, e.g. valid credit card information, age, etc. A successful registration results in the user receiving a set of secret keys (and perhaps some other information). A registered user contacts a key management server using the key(s) and other materials obtained from the registration server. A key management server manages a set of cryptographic keys used for various purposes in a secure multicast group, e.g. one or more *group key(s)* that is (are) used to encrypt and decrypt multicast data. It stores these keys, updates them when certain events

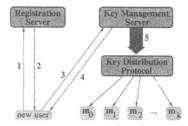

Fig. 2. Secure Multicast Components.

occur, and distributes them to the group members using a key distribution protocol. The process of updating the cryptographic keys, and distributing them to the group members is called a *rekeying* operation. Rekeying is required in secure multicast to ensure that only the *current* group members can send encrypted multicast data, and decrypt the received multicast data.

Mykil combines two hierarchy schemes – key-based hierarchy and group-based hierarchy in such a way that the good features of the two schemes are preserved and the limitations of the two schemes are eliminated. In particular, Mykil is based on Iolus[4] and LKH[5]. It uses the idea of group-based hierarchy of Iolus to divide a multicast group into several smaller subgroups called *areas* with a designated area controller (AC) for each area. There is a separate *area key* for each area. Different areas are linked with one another to form a tree structure, with ACs providing the links – an AC of an area A is also a member of another area B (area B is A's parent in the tree-structure organization). A group member belongs to exactly one area. Like LKH, Mykil builds a tree-structured hierarchy of cryptographic keys called *auxiliary-key tree* with in each area to facilitate key distribution to the area members. The area controller of an area maintains the auxiliary-key tree of that area, and each member of this area is associated with a different leaf of this auxiliary-key tree. An example of the organization of group members in Mykil is shown in Figure 3.

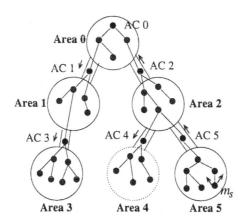

Fig. 3. Organization of group members in Mykil.

2.3   Combining Data Dissemination with Mykil

As can be seen, the organization of clients in MykilDDS is very similar to the organization of group members in Mykil. We did this on purpose, so that we can easily integrate Mykil in MykilDDS. The Mykil key management system has been combined with data dissemination mechanism to build a complete secure data distribution system. There is a one-to-one relationship between the source of data distribution and the area controller of the root area. Also, there is a one-to-one relationship between the area controllers of the mykil key management system and the data dissemination system. We combine these entities that have a one-to-one relationship to form MykilDDS. This combination provides bandwidth saving as well as possible communication failure between the two entities. In Mykil, bandwidth and computation requirements for rekeying at an area controller are low. So a single server can easily accommodate both the key management and data dissemination functionalities.

A drawback of such a combination is that it introduces a single point of failure. However, since MykilDDS is a distributed system based on Mykil, clients can recover from failure by joining other areas (See [3] for details). Furthermore, if the two entities are placed on different servers, failure of either server will result in interruption in data distribution. So, merging the two entities actually simplifies the design and maintains the same level of robustness.

An important advantage of combing the two entities is the short interval for rekeying action. In the absence of a short rekeying interval, the following scenario can arise. A Mykil area controller sends a rekeying message changing the area key from K_1 to K_2. A little later the data dissemination area controller of the same area sends some data encrypted using K_2. It is indeed possible that some clients may receive the data before receiving the rekeying message. In such a case, those clients will realize that they have not received a new rekeying message and send a request to the Mykil area controller. This can actually overload the area controller. One way to prevent such a scenario is to have short rekeying interval. Combining of two centers avoids synchronization between them and can thus achieve key update event in shortest time.

Another important advantage of merging the key management and data dissemination functionalities is that data dissemination can be efficiently done at multiple levels with different quality of services. In multimedia dissemination systems, it's normal to have a heterogeneous communication network involved. For example, in Stanley Cup finals, some users might watch from home with T1 connection enjoying high quality picture, while others might watch from their PDA with 128 K wireless connection. The data distribution system must take into account these different requirements of the users. The grouping of clients into smaller areas facilitates providing such a differentiated quality of service. We can group all users with low-bandwidth network connection in the same area under the same area controller, and provide them a lower quality picture. Furthermore, we can use lighter encryption (shorter encryption keys) for such areas to account for poor computing capabilities of the the users. MykilDDS provides this differentiated form of quality of service.

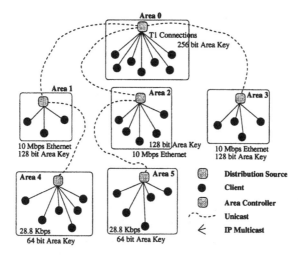

Fig. 4. Differentiated Quality of Service in MykilDDS.

In MykilDDS (See Figure 4), data is always encrypted by a single random key irrespective of the fact that clients with different capabilities belong to different areas. The length of this random key can vary depending on the criticality of the data being disseminated. If the content is something that people like to watch live, like Stanley Cup, the key size can be very short, because the contents lose their value after the game. The random key is then encrypted by the area key shared between area controller and the area members. As we can see, key for 28.4 K group is shortest, while it is longest for T1 group.

When data travels from one area to another with the same network bandwidth capabilities, there is no need for decrypting/re-encrypting data at the area controllers. Only the random key is decrypted/re-encrypted, which is significantly cheaper then decrypting/re-encrypt the entire data. However, when the data travels from one area of higher bandwidth capability to another area of lower bandwidth capability, there is a need to decrypt the data at the area controller. The area controller needs to decrypt the data, change it to lower data rate (poor quality), encrypt it, and then send it to the area controller of the area with lower bandwidth capability.

An important advantage of MykilDDS is that the distribution source needs to disseminate the data only at the highest quality of service. It is the area controllers in the network that adjust the quality of service depending on the type area being serviced. Providing this type of differentiated quality of service in MykilDDS requires that the areas be connected to one another in a specific order. In particular, it is required that the child area C_A of an area A must have either the same or lower quality of service requirements that the quality of service requirements of area A. For example, an area with bandwidth capability of 256 K can be a child of another area with bandwidth capability of 256 K or higher. However, it cannot be a child of an area with bandwidth capability lower than 256 K.

3   Implementation and Performance

To evaluate MykilDDS, we have implemented it on a network of Linux workstations, and simulated it in NS2 network simulator. OpenSSL libraries for cryptography has been used. We have used RSA_public_encrypt and RSA_private_decrypt
for encryption and decryption, and RSA_sign and RSA_verify for digital signatures and signature verification. We used 2048 bit RSA keys in the join protocol
of Mykil, and 128 and 256 bit symmetric keys for area keys. We measured two
parameters: scalability and dissemination time.

3.1   Scalability

To evaluate the scalability of MykilDDS, we simulated it in NS2 network simulator. We already had the code for simulating Mykil in NS2. To test the scalability
of MykilDDS, we measured the time it takes for a new client to join the dissemination service and an existing client to leave the dissemination service. Recall
that when a new client joins a service or an existing client leaves the service,
the keys of all the clients of an area have to be updated. In addition, the auxiliary key tree of that area is updated. Table 1 shows the time it takes for a
new client to join a MykilDDS data dissemination service that is comprised of
100,000 clients. To show the importance of organizing the clients into smaller
areas, the join time and leave time are shown for four different organizations of
these 100,000 clients: (1) one area comprised of 100,000 clients; (2) 10 areas, with
each area comprised of 10,000 clients; (3) 50 areas, with each area comprised of
2,000 clients; and (4) 100 areas, with each area comprised of 1,000 clients.

We make two important observations from this table. First, there is a clear
advantage in organizing clients into multiple areas. In general, the join time
decreases with increase in the number of areas. The reason for this is that the
number clients whose keys have to be changed decreases with increase in the
number of areas. The second observation is that the join time is quite reasonable
when the number of clients in an area is less than 2,000 (50 and 100 areas in
Table 1). This shows that MykilDDS does provide scalable solution for secure
data dissemination.

3.2   Dissemination Time

To determine the data dissemination time in MykilDDS, we implemented it on
a network (LAN) of Linux workstations. Again, we already had the code of

Table 1. Join Time and Leave Time in MykilDDS (Total 100,000 clients).

Number of Areas	Join Time	Leave Time
1	2.76 minutes	2.83 minutes
10	36.2 seconds	38.5 seconds
50	8.4 seconds	8.7 seconds
100	4.7 seconds	4.75 seconds

Mykil key management system that runs on a network of Linux workstations. We experimented with a group of 100 clients that were organized into 10 different areas; each area contained 10 clients. The hierarchy comprised of three levels: a single root area at the top level with three child areas in the next level. Each of these child areas had two child areas in the lowest level.

In our experiments, we varied two parameters: size of data being distributed and the bandwidth capabilities of the areas. We experimented with distribution of file sizes of 2 MB, 10 MB, and 100 MB. For the bandwidth capabilities, we experimented with two cases. In case 1, all areas had the same capability, while in case 2, the top level area had the highest bandwidth capability, the three area in the middle level had medium bandwidth capability, and six areas in the lowest level had the lowest bandwidth capability. The size of a file was reduced by half (poorer quality) as it was transferred from top level to the middle level, or from middle level to the lowest level.

Table 2. Time required to distribute data (Total 100 clients).

File Size	Case 1	Case 2
2 MB	2.7 seconds	1.31 seconds
10 MB	11.5 seconds	7.92 seconds
100 MB	118.2 seconds	85.93 seconds

Table 2 shows the time it takes to distribute the data to all 100 clients. We make three important observations from this figure. First, the time to distribute data naturally increases with increase in file size. Second, this time is shorter when there are areas of multiple capabilities. The reason for this is that the actual file size being transmitted in the areas in lower levels is smaller (cut down by half at each level). Also, the size of area key in the top level is 256 bits, while it is 128 bits in the lower levels. While all the computers used in our experiments had the same capability, this result shows that MykilDDS allows data distribution requiring lower computing/bandwidth capabilities in some clients. Finally, we see that time to distribute data is again quite reasonable.

4   Conclusions

This paper describes the design, implementation, and performance evaluation of MykilDDS, which is a secure and highly scalable data distribution system over the Internet. MykilDDS facilitates a secure distribution of data over the Internet to a significantly large number of clients. It organizes clients into smaller areas and ensures that a differentiated quality of service can be provided to clients in different areas. It integrates IP multicast with Mykil group key management system. A prototype implementation of MykilDDS shows that it provides a scalable solution for data distribution and can support as many as 100,000 clients. In addition, the implementation shows that MykilDDS can be used for providing differentiated quality of service supporting clients with varied computing and bandwidth capabilities.

There are two areas in which we are focusing out future research in MykilDDS. First, we plan to experiment with a real-world application comprised of audio-video distribution using Realtime Networks and RealPlayer (See *http://www.real.com/*). Second, we plan to experiment with deploying MykilDDS in a wide-area network setting. The current testing of data distribution time was done in a LAN setting, while the scalability testing was done in a simulator.

References

1. AES: advanced encryption standard. URL: http://csrc.nist.gov/encryption/aes/.
2. J.-H. Huang and S. Mishra. Mykil: A Highly Scalable and Efficient Key Distribution Protocol for Large Group Multicast. In *IEEE 2003 Global Communications Conference (GlobeCom 2003)*, San Francisco, CA, December 2003.
3. J.-H. Huang and S. Mishra. Support for Mobility and Fault Tolerance in Mykil. In *The International Conference on Dependable Systems and Networks (DSN 2004)*, Florence, Italy, June 2004.
4. S. Mittra. Iolus: A framework for scalable secure multicasting. In *Proceedings of the ACM SIGCOMM'97*, September 1997.
5. C. Wong, M. Gouda, and S. Lam. Secure group communication using key graphs. In *Proceedings of the ACM SIGCOMM'98*, October 1998.

Performance of Distributed Optimistic Concurrency Control in Real-Time Databases

Jan Lindström

University of Helsinki, Department of Computer Science
P.O. Box 26 (Teollisuuskatu 23), FIN-00014 University of Helsinki, Finland
`jan.lindstrom@cs.Helsinki.FI`

Abstract. Concurrency control is one of the main issues in the studies of real-time database systems. In this paper different distributed concurrency control methods are studied and evaluated in real-time system environment. Because optimistic concurrency control is promising candidate for real-time database systems, distributed optimistic concurrency control methods are discussed more detailed way. We propose a new distributed optimistic concurrency control method, demonstrate that proposed method produces a correct results and proposed method is evaluated and tested in prototype implementation of real-time database system for telecommunications. ...

1 Introduction

Numerous real-word applications contain time-constrained access to data as well as access to data that has temporal validity. For example consider telephone switching system, network management, navigation systems, stock trading, and command and control systems. Moreover consider the following tasks within these environments: looking up the "800 directory", obstacle detection and avoidance, radar tracking and recognition of objects. All of these contains gathering data from the environment, processing of information in the context of information obtained in the past, and contributing *timely* response. Another characteristic of these examples is that they contain processing both temporal data, which loses its validity after a certain time intervals, as well as historical data.

Traditional databases, hereafter referred as databases, deal with persistent data. Transactions access this data while maintaining its consistency. The goal of transaction and query processing in databases is to get a good throughput or response time. In contrast, *real-time systems*, can also deal with temporal data, i.e., data that becomes outdated after a certain time. Due to the temporal character of the data and the response-time requirements forced by the environment, task in real-time systems have time constraints, e.g., periods or deadlines. The important difference is that the goal of real-time systems is to meet the time constraints of the tasks.

Concurrency control is one of the main issues in the studies of real-time database systems. With a strict consistency requirement defined by serializability [4],

G. Das and V.P. Gulati (Eds.): CIT 2004, LNCS 3356, pp. 243–252, 2004.

most real-time concurrency control schemes considered in the literature are based on two-phase locking (2PL) [6]. 2PL has been studied extensively in traditional database systems and is being widely used in commercial databases. In recent years, various real-time concurrency control protocols have been proposed for single-site RTDBS by modifying 2PL (e.g. [10, 1, 14]).

However, 2PL has some inherent problems such as the possibility of deadlocks as well as long and unpredictable blocking times. These problems appear to be serious in real-time transaction processing since real-time transactions need to meet their timing constraints, in addition to consistency requirements [17].

Optimistic concurrency control protocols [11, 7] have the nice properties of being non-blocking and deadlock-free. These properties make them especially attractive for real-time database systems. Because conflict resolution between the transactions is delayed until a transaction is near to its completion, there will be more information available in making the conflict resolution. Although optimistic approaches have been shown to be better than locking protocols for RTDBSs [9, 8], they have the problem of unnecessary restarts and heavy restart overhead. This is due to the late conflict detection, that increases the restart overhead since some near-to-complete transactions have to be restarted. Therefore in recent years numerous optimistic concurrency control algorithms have been proposed for real-time databases (e.g. [5, 12, 13]).

Telecommunication is an example of an application area, which has database requirements that require a real-time database or at least time-cognizant database. A telecommunication database, especially one designed for IN services [2], must support access times less than 50 milliseconds. Most database requests are simple reads, which access few items and return some value based on the content in the database.

This paper is organized as follows. Different distributed concurrency control techniques proposed in literature are presented in Section 2. We will propose a new distributed optimistic concurrency control method which is presented in Section 3. Evaluation of the proposed method is presented in Section 4. Finally, Section 5 concludes this study.

2   Distributed Concurrency Control Techniques

In this section we present basic concurrency control techniques and some results of their complexity. Thus we present different distributed schedulers. There are three basic schedulers which allow transactions to execute safely concurrently [3]:

1. Locking methods
2. Timestamp methods
3. Optimistic methods.

These methods have been mainly developed for centralized DBMS and then extended for the distributed case.

2.1   Distributed Optimistic Method

Optimistic Concurrency Control (OCC) [7, 11] is based on the assumption that a conflict is rare, and that it is more efficient to allow transactions to proceed without delays to ensure serializability. When a transaction wishes to commit, a check is performed to determine whether conflict has occurred. There are three phases to an optimistic concurrency control protocol:

- *Read phase:* The transaction reads the values of all data items it needs from the database and stores them in local variables. Updates are applied to a local copy of the data and announced to database system by operation named *pre-write*.
- *Validation phase:* The validation phase ensures that all the committed transactions have executed in a serializable fashion. For read-only transaction, this consists of checking that the data values read are still the current values for the corresponding data items. For a transaction that contains updates, validation consists of determining whether the current transaction leaves the database in a consistent state, with serializability maintained.
- *Write phase:* This follows the successful validation phase for update transactions. During the write phase, all changes made by the transaction are permanently stored into the database.

There are several ways to extend optimistic method to distributed case. One of the easiest is to use tickets. Others are based on optimistic locking, hybrid methods and backward validation.

Concurrency control method requires certain information in order to find and resolve conflicts. This information must be gathered from the data and from the transactions. This information is read and manipulated when some transaction arrives into system, validates or commits.

Every data item in the real-time database consists the current state of object (i.e. current value stored in that data item), and two timestamps. These timestamps represent when this data item was last committed transaction accessed. These timestamp are used in concurrency control method to ensure that transaction reads only from committed transactions and write after latest committed write.

There are certain problems that arise when using optimistic concurrency methods in distributed systems [18]. It is essential that the validation and the write phases are in one critical section. These operations do not need to be executed in one phase. It is sufficient to guarantee, that no other validating transaction uses same data items before earlier validated transaction has wrote them.

- **Problem 1:** *Preserving the atomicity of validating and write phases* [18]. One has to find a mechanism to guarantee that the validate-write critical section is atomic also for global transactions.
- **Problem 2:** *The validation of subtransactions is made purely on local basis* [18]. In the global validation phase, we are interested only in the order

between global transactions. However, the order between distributed transactions may result from indirect conflicts, which are not visible to the global serializability mechanism. Used method must be able to detect also these indirect conflicts. These indirect conflicts are caused by local transactions which access same data items as global transactions.

- **Problem 3:** *Conflicts that are not detectable at the validation phase.* Transaction may be non-existent in the system, active or validated. A conflict is always detected between two active transactions. Combining the phases of two transactions we can find three different combinations of states which describe different conflict detection situations.
  1. Both transactions are active during the first validation.
  2. Both transaction were active at the same time, but the conflict occurred after the first validation. This case means that remaining active transaction made read or prewrite operation to data item after validation of the other transaction.
  3. Transactions execute serially. Because serial execution is correct, this case is not a problem.

Because optimistic concurrency control is main research area of this paper we will present more detailed discussion in the next section.

3   Proposed Distributed Optimistic Concurrency Control Method

In this section we propose a new distributed optimistic concurrency control method DOCC-DATI (Distributed Optimistic Concurrency Control with Dynamic Adjustment of the Serialization order using Timestamp Intervals). This method is based OCC-DATI protocol [16]. We have added new features to OCC-DATI to achieve distributed serializability and to solve problems of the distributed optimistic concurrency control methods presented in section 2. Commit protocol is based on 2PC, but 3PC could be also used.

Every site contains directory where all objects are located. Additionally, every site contains data structures for keeping transaction and object information. Transaction data structure contains information of transactions identification, execution phase, read and write sets, and other administration information. These data structures are used to maintain information on operations of the transaction and to find out what operations transaction has executed, which transactions have performed operation on this data item and so on.

In the read phase if a transaction reads an object which is in the local node then only necessary bookkeeping to the data structures is done and the object is returned to the transaction. Firstly, transaction requesting the read operation must be active and not aborted. Secondly, requested data item must not be marked as an validating object. Thirdly, if object is not located in the local node, distributed read operation is requested in the objects home node. This node is found from the object directory. A *subtransaction* whith the same identification is created in the remote site. An identical bookkeeping is done in the remote site as in local site. Requested object is returned to requesting site and the object is returned to the transaction.

In the read phase if a transaction writes an object which is in the local node then a *prewrite* operation is executed and only necessary bookkeeping is done to the data structures. Firstly, transaction requesting the prewrite operation must be active and not aborted. Secondly, requested data item must not be marked as an validating or preparing object. Thirdly, if object is not located in the local node, a distributed prewrite operation is requested in the objects home node. This node is found from the object directory. A *subtransaction* is created in remote site which has same identity as a requesting transaction. The identical bookkeeping is done in remote site as in transactions local site. Requested object is returned to requesting site and to the requested transaction.

In the validation phase if the transaction is local transaction, then only local validation is executed. On the other hand, if the validating transaction is global transaction, then global validation have to be done. First, a coordinator is selected to coordinate commit protocol (2PL used here).

Coordinator will be the node where first operation of a distributed transaction arrived. Coordinator sends a PREPARE message to all nodes where validating transaction have operations. Every participating site executes local validation and returns the result of the validation to coordinator. In same time, coordinator also executes local validation. If validation is successful, then participant sends YES message to coordinator. Otherwise participant sends ABORT message. If all participants (coordinator included) voted YES, then the coordinator sends COMMIT message to all participants. Otherwise the coordinator sends ABORT message. If no vote arrives from participant in predefined time, then vote is ABORT (presumed abort). This predefined time can be the same as transactions deadline.

Local validation consists iterating all objects accessed by the transaction, finding conflicting operation, and resolving conflicts. The adjustment of timestamp intervals iterates through the read set (RS) and write set (WS) of the validating transaction. First is checked that the validating transaction has read from committed transactions. This is done by checking the object's read and write timestamp. These values are fetched when the read and/or write to the current object was made. Then the set of active conflicting transactions is iterated. When access has been made to the same objects both in the validating transaction and in the active transaction, the temporal time interval of the active transaction is adjusted. Thus deferred dynamic adjustment of the serialization order is used (for more information see [16]).

In local validation a new check is needed for distributed objects. This is because state of the distributed object can be changed between last operation of the validation transaction and the validation phase by some other concurrently executing transaction. If it is, validating transaction must be restarted. This restart could be unnecessary, but it is required to ensure distributed serializability. This new check must be done to all read-write transactions, even if transaction is not writing to the distributed object. This is because, transaction is creating a new value based on old value read from database.

Time intervals of all conflicting active transactions are adjusted after the validating transaction is guaranteed to commit. If the validating transaction is aborted no adjustments are done. Non-serializable execution is detected when the timestamp interval of an active transaction becomes empty. If the timestamp interval is empty the transaction is restarted.

If the validating transaction has read a data item, then the validating transaction read must be after latest committed write to this data item. If the validating transaction has announced intention to write (prewrite) a data item, then the validating transaction read must be after latest committed write an read to this data item. If there is active transaction which is announced intention to write (prewrite) to same data item which the validating transaction has read, then the active transactions write must be after the validating transaction. Therefore, the active transaction is forward adjusted in case of read-write conflict. If there is active transaction which has read the same data item which the validating transaction will write, then the active transactions read must be before the validating transaction. Therefore, the active transaction is backward adjusted in case of write-read conflict. If there is active transaction which is announced intention to write (prewrite) to same data item which the validating transaction will write, then the active transactions write must be after the validating transaction. Therefore, the active transaction is forward adjusted in case of write-write conflict.

If local transaction validation is successful or global transaction commit is successful in all participant sites, then final commit operation is executed. For all objects in the validating transactions write set a validate bookmark is requested. Then current read and write timestamps of accessed objects are updated and changes to the database are committed.

Finally, we present solution to all problems of distributed optimistic concurrency control method that were presented in section 2.

- **Problem 1:** Preserving the atomicity of validating and write phases [18].
  Solution: In the beginning of the validation phase PREPARE bookmark is set to all data items updated by the validating transaction in the data structures of the concurrency controller. Other transactions are allowed to read data items marked by PREPARE bookmarks but not update them. If another transaction enters in the validation phase and requests PREPARE bookmark for data item already marked with PREPARE bookmark, then this validating transaction is restarted. When the prepare section is finished, the node sends it's answer to the coordinator. Then the coordinator sends COMMIT-message (or ABORT-message in which case all bookmarks are released), which can be considered as global validate. VALIDATE bookmarks are set to data items updated by the validating transaction in the data structures of the concurrency controller. Reads to these data items are not allowed. The VALIDATE bookmarks are released after the transaction is written the data item to the database.

- **Problem 2:** The validation of subtransactions is made purely on local basis [18].
  Solution: In global validation first local validation is done by checking all active transactions. Therefore, also indirect conflicts are detected.
- **Problem 3:** Conflicts that are not detectable at the validation phase.

Example 1 *Consider transactions T_1 and T_2 and history H_1. Transaction T_1 is started in the node S_1 and transaction T_2 is started in the node S_2.*

$$T_1 : r_1[X]\ w_1[Y]$$
$$T_2 : r_2[Y]\ w_2[X]$$
$$H_1 : r_1[X]\ r_2[Y]\ w_1[Y]\ w_2[X]\ c_1\ c_2$$

When executing c_1 operation on both nodes proposed algorithm will see serializable history. But order of the distributed transactions is not same in all nodes. In the node S_1 order is $T_1 \rightarrow T_2$ and in the node S_2 order is $T_2 \rightarrow T_1$. Therefore, distributed serialization graph has cycle. This case cannot be found using OCC-DATI with 2PC, because 2PC is only an agreement algorithm. But this case can be find, if current state of the data items are used. OCC-DATI uses state of data item which was stored in the data item when read or write operation was executed. In the proposed method an extra check is done if the transactions is distributed and updated some data item. All data items are rechecked using current state of the data item. Therefore, in example the transaction T_1 is committed and the transaction T_2 is aborted. The transaction T_2 is aborted because state of the data item Y has been changed. Therefore, proposed method provides solution to problem 3. □

Solution: In distributed update transactions use current state of the data items.

4   Evaluation

The prototype system used in evaluations is based on the *Real-Time Object-Oriented Database Architecture for Intelligent Networks* (RODAIN) [15] specification. RODAIN Database Nodes that form one RODAIN Database Cluster are real-time, highly-available, main-memory database servers. They support concurrently running real-time transactions using an optimistic concurrency control protocol with deferred write policy. They can also execute non-real-time transactions at the same time on the database. Real-time transactions are scheduled based on their type, priority, mission criticality, or time criticality. All data in the database is stored in the main-memory database. Data modification operations are logged to the disk for persistence.

In order to increase the availability of the database each Rodain Database Node consists of two identical co-operative units. One of the units acts as the Database Primary Unit and the other one, Database Mirror Unit, is mirroring the Primary Unit. Whenever necessary, that is when a failure occurs, the Primary and the Mirror Units can switch their roles.

The database server was running on an Intel Pentium 450 MHz processor with 256 MB of main memory. A similar computer was used for the client. The computers were connected using a dedicated network, the speed of which was controlled by changing the hub connecting the computers. To avoid unnecessary collisions, there was no other network traffic while the measurements were performed.

Used database is based on a GSM model and transactions are simple trasactions accessing Home Location Register (HLR) and Visitor Location Register (VLR). Database size is 30000 items. The used transactions and they ratios are presented in table 1.

Table 1. Transactions used in the evaluation.

Transaction	type	ratio
GetSubscriber (HLR)	local read	70 %
GetSubscriber (VLR)	remote read	20 %
UpdateSubscriber	remote write	10 %

All time measurements were performed on the client computer using the gettimeofday function, which provides the time in microseconds. The client sends the requests following a given plan, which describes the request type and the time when the request is to be sent. When the request is about to be sent the current time is collected and when the reply arrives the time difference is calculated.

Linux provides static priorities for time-critical applications. These are always scheduled before the normal time-sharing applications. The scheduling policy chosen was Round-robin (SCHED_RR) using the scheduler function sched_set scheduler. The database was also avoiding swapping by locking all the processes pages in the memory using mlockall function. The swap causes long unpredictable delays, because occasionally some pages are sent and retrieved from the disk. Because in our experiment environment our database system was the only application running no swapping occurred during the tests.

With low arrival rate the system can serve all requests within the deadlines. The single highest response time with 600 transactions per second is nearly 35 milliseconds (see Figure 1(a). A moderate arrival rate, 1000 tps (see figure 1(b)), which was usable in many precious tests here creates occasional situations, when the response time temporarily is higher than the 50 milliseconds. The transaction are treated similar in the measurements, because the service sequence does threat the differently. In the overload situation (arrival rate 1600 tps, see Figure 1(c)), the system is capable of serving most requests still within the 50 milliseconds. Unfortunately, there is no trend to predict which requests are served fast enough. Only a bit less than 20% (3400 requests out of the studies 20000) of all requests have response times over the 50 milliseconds. All kinds of requests belong to this 'over the deadline' group. The ratios of the served requests in this group are similar to the ratios of the original requests in the whole set.

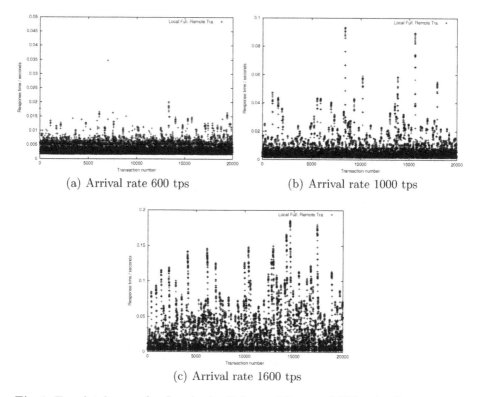

(a) Arrival rate 600 tps

(b) Arrival rate 1000 tps

(c) Arrival rate 1600 tps

Fig. 1. Two database nodes. Local using Primary, Mirror and SSS units. Remote using only Transient unit.

5   Conclusion

In this paper we have reviewed different distributed concurrency control techniques. Study have focused on distributed optimistic concurrency control methods, because optimistic concurrency control has been shown to be applicable to real-time database systems.

Our study has shown that there is no distributed optimistic concurrency control method, which is clearly suitable for real-time database system whitout modification. Therefore, a new distributed optimistic concurrency control method is proposed. Proposed method should be evaluated with some well known and widely used method. Therefore, we have selected 2PL-HP as reference method. With 2PL-HP we will use the 2PC method. We will in near future implement a simulation model for testing proposed method against 2PL-HP with 2PC.

References

1. D. Agrawal, A. E. Abbadi, and R. Jeffers. Using delayed commitment in locking protocols for real-time databases. In *Proceedings of the 1992 ACM SIGMOD International Conference on Management of Data*, pages 104–113. ACM Press, 1992.

2. I. Ahn. Database issues in telecommunications network management. *ACM SIG-MOD Record*, 23(2):37–43, June 1994.

3. D. Bell and J. Grimson. *Distributed Database System*. Addison-Wesley, 1992.

4. P. A. Bernstein, V. Hadzilacos, and N. Goodman. *Concurrency Control and Recovery in Database Systems*. Addison-Wesley, 1987.

5. A. Datta, I. R. Viguier, S. H Son, and V. Kumar. A study of priority cognizance in conflict resolution for firm real time database systems. In *Proceedings of the Second International Workshop on Real-Time Databases: Issues and Applications*, pages 167–180. Kluwer Academic Publishers, 1997.

6. K. P. Eswaran, J. N. Gray, R. A. Lorie, and I. L. Traiger. The notions of consistency and predicate locks in a database system. *Communications of the ACM*, 19(11):624–633, November 1976.

7. T. Härder. Observations on optimistic concurrency control schemes. *Information Systems*, 9(2):111–120, 1984.

8. J. R. Haritsa, M. J. Carey, and M. Livny. Dynamic real-time optimistic concurrency control. In *Proceedings of the 11th IEEE Real-Time Systems Symposium*, pages 94–103. IEEE Computer Society Press, 1990.

9. J. R. Haritsa, M. J. Carey, and M. Livny. On being optimistic about real-time constraints. In *Proceedings of the 9th ACM Symposium on Principles of Database Systems*, pages 331–343. ACM Press, 1990.

10. S.-L. Hung and K.-Y. Lam. Locking protocols for concurrency control in real-time database systems. *ACM SIGMOD Record*, 21(4):22–27, December 1992.

11. H. T. Kung and J. T. Robinson. On optimistic methods for concurrency control. *ACM Transactions on Database Systems*, 6(2):213–226, June 1981.

12. K.-W. Lam, K.-Y. Lam, and S. Hung. An efficient real-time optimistic concurrency control protocol. In *Proceedings of the First International Workshop on Active and Real-Time Database Systems*, pages 209–225. Springer, 1995.

13. K.-W. Lam, K.-Y. Lam, and S. Hung. Real-time optimistic concurrency control protocol with dynamic adjustment of serialization order. In *Proceedings of the IEEE Real-Time Technology and Application Symposium*, pages 174–179. IEEE Computer Society Press, 1995.

14. K.-Y. Lam, S.-L. Hung, and S. H. Son. On using real-time static locking protocols for distributed real-time databases. *The Journal of Real-Time Systems*, 13(2):141–166, September 1997.

15. J. Lindström, T. Niklander, P. Porkka, and K. Raatikainen. A distributed real-time main-memory database for telecommunication. In *Databases in Telecommunications*, Lecture Notes in Computer Science, vol 1819, pages 158–173, 1999.

16. J. Lindström and K. Raatikainen. Dynamic adjustment of serialization order using timestamp intervals in real-time databases. In *Proceedings of the 6th International Conference on Real-Time Computing Systems and Applications*, pages 13–20. IEEE Computer Society Press, 1999.

17. K. Ramamritham. Real-time databases. *Distributed and Parallel Databases*, 1:199–226, April 1993.

18. G. Schlageter. Problems of optimistic concurrency control in distributed database systems. *ACM SIGMOD Record*, 13(3):62–66, April 1982.

An Extension to ER Model for Top-Down Semantic Modeling of Databases of Applications

S.K. Jain[1,*], M.M. Gore[2], and Gulab Singh[2]

[1] CSE Department, National Institute of Technology, Hamirpur HP 177005 India
skj@recham.ernet.in
[2] CSE Department, M N National Institute of Technology, Allahabad 211004 India
mmgore@ieee.org, gulab_s15@hotmail.com

Abstract. An extension to ER (Entity Relationship) model for semantic modeling of databases in top down manner is presented. The model proposes a new entity type called *composite entity type* and a table based meta construct called *tabletype relationship*. A composite entity type models composite entities, whereas a tabletype relationship is shorthand and represents a number of relationship types. The concept of composite entity type is abstract, helps in semantic modeling, and is not required in implementation. A composite entity type along with tabletype relationship captures semantics of the database of an application at a higher level of abstraction and provides a top down semantic modeling approach in flavor of ER model.

Keywords: Semantic model, ER model, Top down model, Database design.

1 Introduction

The ER model [1] is widely accepted conceptual model for database design among practitioners. The model has been extended by a number of researchers to capture semantics of specific application domains. Popularity of the ER model has projected itself as a base model for representing various application domains semantically. In this article, we propose an extension to ER model to include a new entity type called *composite entity type* and a table based meta construct called *tabletype relationship*. When a composite entity type is used with the tabletype relationship, ER model develops capability of capturing semantics of the database of an application at a higher level of abstraction. The extended ER model becomes able to describe relationship semantics of composite entities at both molecular and part levels in a comprehensive and manageable manner. The proposed extension helps database designer to manage semantic complexity of large applications in the beginning of semantic modeling of their databases. It also offers an opportunity to database designer to stay at one level of abstraction at a time. At any stage of conceptual modeling, the designer can keep himself at molecular level of relationship semantics of composite entity types by suspending to consider part level relationships temporarily. This encourages the database designer to model database of an application directly at a higher level of abstraction, which is more understandable and natural. The top down semantic modeling methodology, described in this article, produces ER schema in clustered form naturally. An example, exhibiting utility of the proposed extension, is also discussed in the article.

---

* PhD candidate with MNNIT Allahabad.

G. Das and V.P. Gulati (Eds.): CIT 2004, LNCS 3356, pp. 253–262, 2004.

Table 1. Explanation of terminology used in the article

	Terms	Explanation
1	Entity	An abstract or physical object.
2	Entity type	A set of similar type entities.
3	Atomic entity	An entity that does not contain any other entity.
4	Atomic entity type	A set of similar type atomic entities.
5	Molecular/ Composite/ Complex entity	An entity that contains other entities.
6	Molecular entity type	A set of similar type molecular entities.
7	Composite entity type	
8	Complex entity type	
9	Part/Constituent entity/object	An entity that is part of some other entity. Here, other entities are molecular entities.
10	Part entity/object type	A set of similar type part entities.
11	Constituent entity/object type	
12	Dominant entity	An entity that identifies other entities on behalf of it.
13	Dominant entity type	A set of similar type dominant entities.
14	Relationship	Association between two or more entities.
15	Relationship type	A set of similar type relationships.
16	Type of relationship	One-to-one, one-to-many or many-to-many.
17	Instance level	When explanation refers to individual entities.
18	Class level	When explanation refers to sets.
19	Atomic level	When explanation of a relationship type includes part entity types of a composite entity type and an atomic entity type.
		When explanation of a relationship type includes part entity types of two different composite entity types.
		When explanation/description includes only atomic entity types.
20	Molecular level	When explanation of a relationship type includes at least one composite/molecular/complex entity type.
21	Higher level of abstraction	When description of a database schema is made using fewer numbers of entity and relationship types than that of actual numbers of entity and relationship types present.
22	Top down semantic modeling	Continuous process of refining composite entity types into their equivalent relationship structures until atomic level relationship structure of each composite entity type is obtained.
23	Intra-molecular relationships	Described by relationship type among part entity types within a specific molecular entity type. IM shows it in Fig. 1.
24	Inter-molecular relationships	Described by relationship type between two or more molecular entity types. ITM shows it in Fig. 1.
25	Molecular-atomic relationships	Described by relationship type between a molecular entity type and an atomic entity type. MA shows it in Fig. 1.
26	Part-atomic relationships	Described by relationship type between a part entity type of a molecular entity type and an atomic entity type. PA shows it in Fig. 1.
27	Part-part relationships	Described by relationship type between part entity types of two or more molecular entity types. PP shows it in Fig. 1.
28	Inter-atomic relationships	Described by relationship type between two or more atomic entity types. IA shows it in Fig. 1.

2 Motivation

We have devised a methodology for ER schema compression/abstraction [2]. The methodology uses purely syntactic criterion based on use of tables for schema abstraction. This success intuitively appealed us to use tables judiciously somewhere in database modeling process. Present work uses tables to extend ER model such that the extended model captures semantics of the database of an application in top down manner.

3 Proposed Extension to ER Model

Table 1 describes terminology used in the article. Fig. 1 exhibits structure of relationship types of the entity types present inside a molecular entity type and outside with other molecular and atomic entity types. Acronyms used in Fig. 1 are described in Table 1 from serial no. 23 to 28. We extend ER model to include a new entity type called *composite entity type* and a table based meta construct called *tabletype relationship*. A composite entity type models composite entities at a higher level of abstraction such that an ER diagram exhibits its detail separately. Tabletype relationship is a meta construct that replaces a number of relationship types in schema diagram by itself and mentions them in a table separately. The name of tabletype relationship in schema diagram refers to this table, where details are mentioned. The notation for composite entity type and tabletype relationship is shown in Fig. 2. A tabletype relationship exhibits relationship types between an atomic entity type and part entity types of a composite entity type as shown in Fig 3. In Fig. 1, relationship PA exhibits the same. A tabletype relationship can also represent relationship types between part entity types of two different composite entity types as shown in Fig. 4. The same is also shown by relationship PP in Fig. 1. Therefore, any application that consists of atomic entities, composite entities, and relationships among them can be modeled at a higher level of abstraction using composite entity types, tabletype relationships, and other constructs of ER model as shown in Fig. 5.

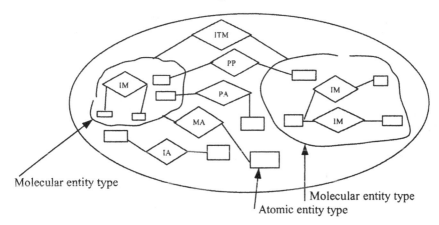

Fig. 1. Relationship types present in schema of the database of an application

(Composite entity type)   (Tabletype relationship)

Fig. 2. Notation for composite entity type and tabletype relationship

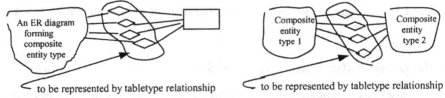

to be represented by tabletype relationship   to be represented by tabletype relationship

Fig. 3. Relationship types between part entity types of a composite entity type and an atomic entity type

Fig. 4. Relationship types between part entity types of two composite entity types

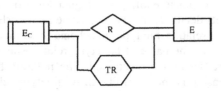

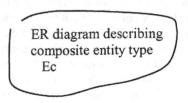

Fig. 5. Database schema prepared using composite entity type and tabletype relationship

Fig. 6. ER diagram describing composite entity type Ec

In Fig. 5, relationship type R captures relationship semantics between a composite entity type E_C and an atomic entity type E at molecular level, whereas tabletype relationship TR captures relationship semantics between constituent entity types of composite entity type E_C and an atomic entity type E. Here, constituent entity types may further be made of composite entity types. Fig. 6 represents ER diagram describing composite entity type E_C shown in Fig. 5. Table 2 describes details of tabletype relationship TR shown in Fig. 5. The first column of Table 2 includes the names of those part entity types of composite entity type E_C that participate in relationships with atomic entity type E. The names of relationship types from entity type E to part entity types mentioned in column 1 are written in column 2. The third column of the table describes type of relationship, i.e., one-to-one, one-to-many or many-to-many from entity type E to part entity types mentioned in column 1. The fourth column of the table represents names of attributes of relationship types mentioned in column 2. Complete interpretation of Fig. 5 is made along with Fig. 6 and Table 2, where details of E_C and TR are mentioned. Since Table 2 describes details of tabletype relationship TR, it is named as Table TR. In fact, E_C is one entity type present in ER diagram (Fig. 6) such that other constituent entity types are identified on behalf of it. It is just like dominant entity type in Fig. 6. Therefore, in Fig. 5, E_C should have same value domains for key and other attributes as one entity type in ER diagram (Fig. 6) has. If tabletype relationship exhibits relationship types between part entity types of two different composite entity types, the format of table for tabletype relationship will be as shown by Table 3. Table 4, named as "Remaining Relationships Table", is used to describe (1) relationship types between entity types that are not in immediate level of refinement in the hierarchy of top down modeling; and (2) relationship types between part entity types of two composite entity types that belong to two different ER diagrams.

Table 2. Table used to describe tabletype relationship TR

Table TR

1	2	3	4
Names of part entity types of composite entity type E_c that participate in relationship types mentioned in column 2 with atomic entity type E	Names of relationship types from entity type E to part entity types mentioned in column 1	Type of relationship	Attributes of relationship types mentioned in column 2
–	–	–	–
–	–	–	–

Table 3. Table to describe tabletype relationship, when part entity types belong to two different composite entity types

1	2	3	4	5
From	To	Names of relationship types from part entity type of CE1 to part entity type of CE2 as mentioned in column 1 and 2	Type of relationship	Attributes of relationship types mentioned in column 3
Names of part entity types of composite entity type CE1	Names of part entity types of composite entity type CE2			
–	–	–	–	
–	–	–	–	

Table 4. Table to describe relationship types, which could not be represented by tabletype relationships

Remaining Relationship Table

1	2	3	4	5	6	7	8	9
	From			To		Names of relationship types from part entity types mentioned in column 1 to part entity types mentioned in column 4	Type of Relationship	Attributes of relationship types mentioned in column 7
Names of part/comp osite entity types	Name of immediate composite entity type if present	Figure No. or Page No. for reference	Names of part/comp osite entity types	Name of immediate composite entity type if present	Figure No. or Page No. for reference			

4 Modeling Methodology

The proposed model captures semantics of more general form of a composite entity which we state as "any part of application domain that makes a meaningful unit can be treated as a composite entity at higher level of abstraction". We suggest following steps for semantic modeling of databases of applications:

1. Identify atomic entity types and composite entity types in the application at highest or reasonable higher level of abstraction. Here, highest or reasonable higher level may be decided based on the argument of "seven, plus or minus two" [3]; that is, on average schema should have seven items (sum of numbers of entity types, relationship types, and tabletype relationships).
2. Prepare detailed ER diagram for each composite entity type.
3. Identify atomic and molecular level relationship types in the application, and assign semantic names to tabletype relationships.
4. Prepare details of each tabletype relationship.
5. If there is any composite entity type in detailed ER diagrams of composite entity types as identified in step 1, refine composite entity types using step 2 to 4 till atomic level description of each composite entity type is obtained.

6. Examine the need of "Remaining Relationships Table"; if yes, prepare its detail.
7. Review design.

5 An Example

This section explains an example of applying our proposed semantic modeling methodology. Here, we shall use notation for ER diagrams as used by Korth & Silberschatz in [4]. In [4], cardinality constraint uses *Look Across* notation; cardinality between an entity and relationship types is represented by either a directed line (arrow) for one-side or an undirected line for many-side. Now, we model our institute semantically. In ER diagrams, we shall not exhibit attributes of entity types because of clarity in expressiveness. We shall also not mention names of most of the relationship types because of limitation of space. We describe modeling activities in steps as follows:

1. We model institute at a very high level of abstraction using two composite entity types, three atomic entity types, and relationship types among them. Fig. 7 represents its ER diagram.
2. We refine composite entity types named Building and People, shown in Fig. 7, into their relationship structures. Fig. 8 and 9 represent detailed ER diagrams of these composite entity types.
3. We prepare Table 5 to describe details of tabletype relationship named "People related to" shown in Fig. 7. At the first column of the table, the part entity types that are of composite entity type have been distinguished by adding C in brackets along with their names. We have not shown names of relationship types at third column and names of attributes at fifth column in the table due to clarity in expressiveness.
4. We further refine composite entity types named Department, Hostel, "Staff Quarter Block", and "Shopping Center" shown in Fig. 8 and exhibit them by individual ER diagrams in Fig. 10, 11, 12, and 13. Here, we are not showing attributes of entities and names of relationships due to clarity in expressiveness.
5. We make "Remaining Relationships Table" to represent relationship types between entity types (1) which are not in immediate level of refinement in the hierarchy of top down modeling; (2) that belong to two composite entity types, whose details are shown in two different ER diagrams. Table 6 represents "Remaining Relationships Table". Sub columns in Table 6 contain reference information for entity types participating in relationships.

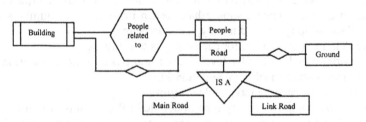

Fig. 7. Schema diagram of the example

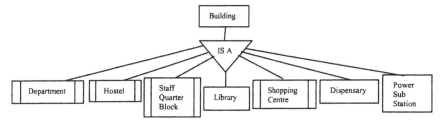

Fig. 8. ER diagram describing composite entity type Building shown in Fig. 7

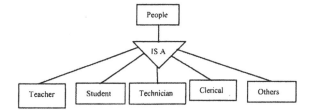

Fig. 9. ER diagram describing composite entity type People shown in Fig. 7

Table 5. Table describing details of tabletype relationship named "People related to" shown in Fig.7

People related to

1	2	3	4	5
From	People	Names of relationship types	Type of	Attributes of
Names of part entity types of composite entity type Building	Names of part entity types of composite entity type People	from part entity type of composite entity type Building to part entity type of composite entity type People as mentioned in column 1 and 2	relation-ship	relationship types mentioned in column 3
Department (C)	Teacher	-	1-to-n	-
Department (C)	Student	-	1-to-n	-
Department (C)	Technician	-	1-to-n	-
Department (C)	Clerical	-	1-to-n	-
Hostel (C)	Student	-	1-to-n	-
Hostel (C)	Clerical	-	1-to-n	-
Staff Quarter Block (C)	Teacher	-	1-to-n	-
Staff Quarter Block (C)	Others	-	1-to-n	-
Library	Others	-	1-to-n	-
Shopping Center (C)	Others	-	1-to-n	-
Dispensary	Others	-	1-to-n	-
Power Sub Station	Others		1-to-n	

6   Analysis of Proposed Extension and Related Work

The lack of semantics in relational model has compelled database researchers to develop ER model for representing databases in better understandable form. A good model should support modeling constructs required to represent semantics of application domain as close as possible to reality with least possible efforts, and this argument appears true in case of ER model. Type constructs (entity type and relationship type) of ER model directly capture semantics of entities and relationships among

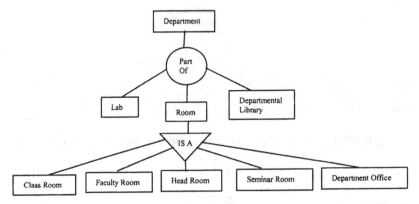

Fig. 10. ER diagram describing composite entity type Department shown in Fig. 8

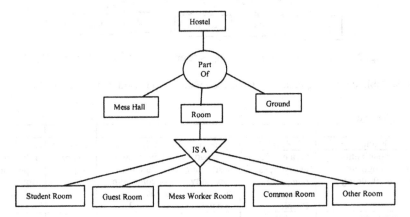

Fig. 11. ER diagram describing composite entity type Hostel shown in Fig. 8

Fig. 12. ER diagram describing composite entity type "Staff Quarter Block" shown in Fig.8

Fig. 13. ER diagram describing composite entity type "Shopping Center" shown in Fig.8

them, as they occur naturally in real world. When number of entities in application domain becomes too large, people used to combine them in meaningful units for better comprehension, communication, and documentation. Intuitively, this reasoning supports considering composite entities to occur naturally at a higher level of abstraction from standpoint of human understanding. Therefore, any model that has modeling construct to represent composite type entities will certainly ease modeling effort. The inclusion of aggregation and generalization/specialization in EER and OO models also appears valid based on this principle. Modeling concepts of composite entities are already well known in semantic modeling [5], particularly in CAD/CAM, engi-

Table 6. Table describing relationship types (1) which are not in immediate level of refinement in the hierarchy of top down modeling; (2) between part entity types of two composite entity types that belong to two different ER diagrams

Remaining Relationship Table

S N	1	2	3	4	5	6	7	8	9
	From			To			Names of relationship types from part entity types mentioned in column 1 to part entity types mentioned in column 4	Type of Relationship	Attributes of Relationship types mentioned in column 7
	Names of part / composite entity types	Name of immediate composite entity type if present	Figure No. for reference	Names of part / composite entity types	Name of immediate composite entity type if present	Figure No. for reference			
1	Faculty Room	Department	10	Teacher	People	9	-	1-to-1	-
2	Head Room	Department	10	Teacher	People	9	-	1-to-1	-
3	Lab	Department	10	Techni- cian	People	9	-	n-to-1	-
4	Departmen- tal Library	Department	10	Clerical	People	9	-	1-to-1	-
5	Student Room	Hostel	11	Student	People	9		1-to-n	-
6	Quarter	Staff Quarter Block	12	People	People	9		1-to-1	
7	Shop	Shopping Centre	13	Others	People	9		1-to-1	
-	-	-		-	-				

neering applications, VLSI design, geometric modeling etc. A composite entity is an atomic object at higher level, whereas at lower level it is not printable and exhibited by relationship structure that composes it. A composite entity is constructed using aggregation/composition relationship construct. The relationship structure of a composite entity type may also include association and generalization/specialization relationship constructs. In this article, the proposed composite entity type is a type definition. The use of composite entity type with table-based meta construct eases modeling effort and provides top down semantic modeling methodology for databases in flavor of ER model.

To our best knowledge, UML (Unified Modeling Language) is only available modeling language, which supports composite object type using composite class. The concept of top-down modeling is well known in software engineering in general, but the same is not addressed for semantic modeling of databases except [6]. In comparison to work described in [6], our model (1) captures semantics of the database of an application in top down manner, even if related entities belong to non-adjacent levels of refinement in hierarchy; (2) represents atomic and molecular level relationship semantics in one schema; (3) has inbuilt, natural clustering of entire schema in pieces; (4) up to some extend steps 2, 3, and 4 of the modeling methodology can be carried out in parallel. Up to some extend, our model can also be compared with Higher-order Entity-Relationship Model (HERM) [7]. We believe that our proposed model is superior to HERM since it preserves distinction between entity and relationship types; whereas HERM treats entity types as 0-order relationship types. At present, our model has limitation as it addresses only binary relationships. The present work can be extended to address issue of higher order relationships.

7 Conclusion

In present paper, we have proposed an extension to ER model to capture semantics of databases of applications in top down manner. The model proposes a new entity type called *composite entity type* and a table based meta construct called *tabletype relationship*. Traditionally, large database applications are modeled using EER or OO model, and bottom up clustering methodologies are applied to make database schema maintainable, comprehensible, and documental. Our proposed model has natural solution for clustering of schema and automatically generates resultant schema in manageable, comprehensive, and documental form. In our opinion, proposed top down modeling methodology in flavor of widely used ER model will certainly ease modeling process of large and complex databases e.g. database for keeping details of a building or town in architectural engineering. The model can also use readymade schema constructs from library of schemas instead of starting modeling activities for the database of an application from scratch.

References

1. Chen P P "The Entity Relationship Model- Towards a Unified View of Data" Transactions on Database Systems, Vol. 1, No. 1, 1976, pp 9-36.
2. Jain S K, Singh G, Gore M M 'Entity Relationship Schema Compression Technique Based on Use of Tables' 6th International Conference on Information Technology CIT 2003, Dec 22-25, 2003 at Bhubaneshwar India, pp 455-460.
3. Miller George A "The Magical Number Seven, Plus or Minus Two: Some Limits on Our Capacity for Processing Information" The Psychological Review, 1956, Vol. 63, pp 81-97.
4. Korth H and Silberschatz A "Database System Concepts" 2ed., McGraw Hill, 1991.
5. Batory D S, Kim Won "Modeling Concepts for VLSI CAD Objects" ACM Transactions on Database Systems, Vol. 10, No. 3, Sept 1985, pp 322-346.
6. Troyer Olga De, Janssen Rene "On Modularity for Conceptual Data Models and the Consequences for Subtyping, Inheritance & Overriding" Proceedings of ICDE, 1993, pp 678-685.
7. Thalheim Bernhard "Entity-Relationship Modeling Foundations of Database Technology" Springer, 2000.

Overlaying Multiple Maps Efficiently

Ravindranath Jampani, Risivardhan Thonangi, and Prosenjit Gupta

International Institute of Information Technology,
Gachibowli, Hyderabad 500019, India
{ravi,rishi}@students.iiit.net, pgupta@iiit.net
http://www.iiit.net

Abstract. Spatial data is often represented as layers of thematic maps. User queries often necessiate overlay operations involving these maps. Map overlay is an extensively used operation in GIS. Typical two-map overlay involves operations on a large number of polygons of each map. Many applications require overlay of more than two maps. This operation, called multiple map overlay is executed as a sequence of binary map overlay operations. The complexity of the multiple map overlay is dependent on the order in which the individual binary overlay operations are performed. In this paper, we consider the problem of determining good order in which to overlay a set of maps and propose efficient algorithms for the same.

1 Introduction

In geographical information systems (GIS), thematic maps emphasize one or more selected topics e.g. land utilization, population density etc. Thematic maps are generally represented by chlropleth maps, which separate areas of different properties by boundaries e.g. forests, lakes, roads, agriculturally used areas. In this paper we assume that such maps are modeled by a vector representation.

The *map overlay* operation is a building block for various analysis operations in GIS. A typical two-map overlay involves unions and intersections of large number of polygons of each map. Its running time depends not only on the size of the input i.e. the total number of edges of the polygons in the two maps but also on the number of pairwise intersections of such edges. In many applications, there is a need for overlaying more than two maps. This operation, called *multiple map overlay* is executed as a sequence of binary map overlay operations. The complexity of the multiple map overlay is dependent on the number of maps, their sizes, and the order in which the individual binary overlay operations are performed. For a given problem instance consisting of a sequence of maps to be overlaid, the cost of the overlay operation is different for different orders in which the overlay operations are performed. In this paper we address the problem of finding a good order in which to perform a series of overlay operations.

This problem was studied by Yost and Skelton [35] for raster GIS. Dorenbeck and Egenhofer [12] addressed the formalization of operations on regular tesselations and investigated two approaches for the problem: (i) elimination of equivalent subexpressions by using the properties of the overlay operation; (ii)

G. Das and V.P. Gulati (Eds.): CIT 2004, LNCS 3356, pp. 263–272, 2004.

integration of several overlay operations into a single one. In this paper we assume that the maps are modeled by a vector representation and to the best of our knowledge this is the first such work. Vector based approaches being less memory intensive, are better suited for dealing with large data sizes.

As discussed in [12], an overlay operation over multiple layers results in a new layer which, in turn, may be used as an argument in another overlay operation. Frequently, many overlay operations are combined this way to perform a more complex operation. The sophisticated algorithms and data structures for the efficient implementation of a single overlay operation provide little or no support for improving the processing of a series of overlays [12].

In Section 2, we review the related problem of spatial join in spatial databases and earlier work done in the area of join selectivity estimation. In Section 3, we discuss the algorithms for segment intersection reporting and counting from the computational geometry literature. In Section 4, we present an algorithm for determining a good order for performing a series of overlays. We provide some alternative strategies in Section 5. We conclude in Section 6 with directions for future research.

2 Spatial Joins

The map overlay operation is a special case of the more general *spatial join* operation in spatial databases. It is one of the most important type of query processing in spatial databases and geographic information systems. The spatial join operation selects, from two relations, all object pairs that satisfy a given set of spatial predicates. Since it is an expensive operation, a lot of effort has gone into making it efficient. A commonly used predicate is the intersection join. For an interesction join, two objects constitute a result pair if they intersect each other. Intersection joins are commonly used in map overlays. Given a sequence of such intersection joins to be formed, it becomes imperative to draw an efficient *query execution plan*. The cost of such a query execution plan depends directly on the sizes of the intermediate results generated. Thus one of the main goals in generating such a plan is to select an order such that the sizes of the intermediate results generated renders the overall query processing optimal. The crux of the problem in generating an optimal query plan for such a *multiway join* is the fact that we cannot actually perform the joins to know the costs.

2.1 Join Selectivity Estimation

We need to have a way of estimating the sizes of the intermediate results to enable us to choose an optimal order for the execution of the 2-way joins. This problem is known as the *join selectivity estimation*. The problem of determining the optimal order of overlaying multiple maps requires a solution to the problem of estimating the complexity of a single overlay operation which is a special case of a more general problem of join selectivity estimation. In this section, we review various techniques for join selectivity estimation.

Selectivity estimation techniques can be broadly classified into three categories: parametric, sampling and histograms [1]. Parametric techniques make some assumptions about the dataset and present convenient closed form formulae which can be used for estimation at little cost. Aref and Samet [2] assume the data to be uniformly distributed in the two datasets to be joined. Belussi and Faloutsos [5] assume the data items to exhibit fractal behavior. In [13] Faloutsos et al. assume that the datasets obey a power law. Since real data sets may not follow the desired properties, parametric techniques have very little applicability. Furthermore some approaches work with point datasets only.

Sampling based techniques try to infer information from the given dataset to predict query selectivity. This is achieved by actually performing the query on a small selection of the dataset called the sample and then using the results to extrapolate the selectivity for the entire dataset. Though sampling techniques have been used in selectivity estimation in conventional databases, their usability in spatial databases is less explored. In [27] Olken and Rotem explored techniques for obtaining random sample points of the query results. Vassilakopoulos and Manolopoulos [34] study the problem of obtaining approximate answers to aggregate queries using random sampling algorithms. An et al. [1] studied three well-known sampling techniques to estimate the selectivity of spatial joins.

Histogram-based techniques keep certain information for different regions in auxiliary data structures called histograms which can be queried to find out the selectivity whenever a join query is given. For intersection joins, significant techniques include the histogram based approaches of An et al. [1] and Mamoulis and Papadias [24]. The technique proposed by An et al. [1] is based on the observation that the intersection of two rectangles always results in four intersection points. Hence selectivity can be estimated by counting the intersection points and dividing by four. The technique of Mamoulis and Papadias divides the space into grid cells and stores three parameters for polygons which overlap a grid cell. The selectivity is then estimated by computing a simple function of these three parameters.

3 The Segment Intersection Problem

One of the most time-consuming steps in the map overlay processing is *line-breaking*, which we can abstract as the segment intersection problem: Given a set of n line segments in the plane, determine which k pairs intersect. A brute force algorithm that checks each pair of segments for intersection, can be implemented in $O(n)$ space and $O(n^2)$ time. Bentley and Ottman [6] gave a practical output-sensitive algorithm that runs in $O(n)$ space and $O((n + k) \log n)$ time. Chazelle and Edelsbrunner [8] improved the running time to $O(n \log n + k)$. But their algorithm takes $O(n + k)$ space. Mulmuley [25] gave a randomized algorithm which takes $O(n + k)$ space and expected $O(n \log n + k)$ running time. Clarkson and Shor [11] gave another randomized algorithm with the same running time as that of Mulmuley but whose space requirement is $O(n)$. Balaban [3] gave an optimal deterministic algorithm that runs in $O(n)$ space and $O(n \log n + k)$ time. The algorithms for Mulmuley, Clarkson and Shor and Balaban all work for curves. Simpler algorithms are possible for the red-blue segment intersection problem, which is of relevance in map overlay. Here we are given two sets of segments red and blue such that no two segments from the same set intersect each other. This problem was solved in $O(n \log n + k)$ time and $O(n)$ storage by Mairson and Stolfi [23] before the general problem was solved optimally. Other optimal red-blue intersection algorithms were given by Chazelle et al. [9] and Palazzi and Snoeyink [28]. If the two sets of segments form connected subdivisions, then the overlay can be done in $O(n + k)$ time as has been shown by Finke and Hinrichs [14]. Mairson and Stolfi [23] gave a solution to the red-blue counting problem in $O(n \log n + \sqrt{(nk)})$ time and $O(n)$ space. Palazzi and Snoeyink's solution to the counting problem takes $O(n)$ space and $O(n \log n)$ time. Since the cost of a single map overlay operation involving two maps is significantly dependent on the cost of finding the red-blue segment intersection, the solution to the red-blue counting problem solves the selectivity estimation problem in this case with 100% accuracy.

4   The Maxcut Heuristic

As mentioned in Section 3, one of the most time-consuming steps in the map overlay processing is line-breaking, which we can abstract as the segment intersection problem. In this section, we will design a heuristic for the problem of determining an optimal order of overlaying a given set of maps. For the purpose of the heuristic, we define the cost of overlaying two maps M_1 and M_2 consisting of n_1 and n_2 segments respectively as:

$$COST(M_1, M_2) = n \log n + k$$

where $n = n_1 + n_2$ and k is the number of intersections involving a segment from M_1 with a segment from M_2. As an example consider three maps A, B and C. We can overlay any two of the maps say X and Y and overlay the result with the remaining map Z where X, Y, Z take values from $\{A, B, C\}$. Since the overlay operation is commutative, there are three possibilities to consider, based on the choice of the third map. If we perform a red-blue segment intersection operation with a set of n_1 red segments and a set of n_2 blue segments, and there are k red-blue intersections, we have a total of $n_1 + n_2 + k$ segments after the intersection. Thus if the first two maps have a large number of intersections, the resultant map has a large number of segments. This in turn will increase the cost of the second overlay operation. Thus it is better to perform overlays involving maps with fewer intersections early on and those involving larger number of intersections later. This is the intuition behind the maxcut heuristic we propose below.

4.1   The Maxcut Problem

Given an undirected graph $G = (V, E)$ and $|V| = n$ and $|E| = e$, a cut is a set of all edges of E with one end in a nonempty proper subset X of V, and the other end in $\overline{X} = V - X$. Given arbitrary weights associated with edges, the weight of a cut $C \subset E$ is the sum of the weights of the edges in C. The *maximum cut* problem is to find a cut of maximum cardinality (or weight in general). The Maxcut problem even in its simplest form (with all edge weights set to 1) is NP-complete [16] on general graphs. Hence the effort in research has concentrated on development of approximate algorithms with good performance ratios. Sahni and Gonzalez [30] proposed an $O(n + e)$ algorithm with a performance ratio of $1/2$. Haglin and Venkatesan [18] proposed an approximation algorithm which runs in time $O(e \log e)$ and has a performance ratio of $1/2 + 1/(2n)$. A simpler algorithm with the same performance ration but a running time of $O(n+e)$ was proposed by Cho et al. [10]. Goemans and Wiiliamson [17] gave a randomized approximation algorithm with an approximation ratio of 0.87856.

4.2   The Algorithm

We consider the following problem, which we denote as the Map Overlay Ordering Problem (MOO):

Problem 1. Given a set $M = M_1, M_2, \ldots, M_m$ of m planar maps find an optimal order for overlaying the maps.

Given a set of maps M, we create a graph $G = (V, E)$ where $|V| = |M| = m$ and each node v_i in V represents a map M_i. G is a complete graph with edges between every pair of vertices. The weight of edge $(v_i, v_j) = COST(M_i, M_j)$. The cost can be computed by running the algorithm of Palazzi and Snoeyink [28] to count the number of red-blue intersections between segments of map M_i with those of map M_j. We compute the Maxcut on G and partition V into sets X and $V - X$ based on the cut. We recursively invoke the algorithm on X and $V - X$. The recursion terminates if the vertex set under consideration has one or two nodes.

Algorithm A {

    1. Construct a complete graph $G = (V, E)$.
        Each vertex $v \in V$ represents a map $M(v)$.
    2. For each edge $e = (u, v) \in E$,
        compute edge weights of G by running the algorithm
        of Palazzi and Snoeyink on the two maps $M(u)$ and $M(v)$.
    3. Invoke $MaxCutOverlay(V, E)$

}

4.3   Complexity Analysis

The space complexity of the above algorithm is $O(m^2 + n)$, for m maps with a total of n segments, assuming the binary overlay operation takes $O(n)$ space. In the above algorithm, the maxcut algorithm takes $O(V + E) = O(m^2)$ time for m maps. The algorithm is invoked $O(m)$ times leading to a total of $O(m^3)$ overhead due to the maxcut. Add to this the construction of the complete graph with $O(m^2)$ edges and the computation of their edge weights. This process takes

Algorithm MaxCutOverlay (V, E) {

1. If $|V| = 1$, let $V = \{v_i\}$.
   Return M_i.
2. Else If $|V| = 2$, let $V = \{v_i, v_j\}$.
   Compute the overlay of
   maps M_i and M_j and return the resultant map.
3. Else run the Maxcut algorithm of Cho et al. to partition
   V into sets X and $V - X$.
4. $M1 = MaxCutOverlay(X, E)$;
5. $M2 = MaxCutOverlay(V - X, E)$;
6. Compute the overlay of $M1$ and $M2$ and return the
   resultant map.

}

$O(m^2 n \log n)$ time in the worst case. Hence the total overhead is $O(m^2 n \log n)$. If we assume m to be a constant, this is $O(n \log n)$.

Let us compare this with the total time where we simply do the overlays one after another in the order $M_1, M_2 \ldots, M_i$. Let the number of segments in map M_i be n_i. Let k_i denote the total number of segment intersections resulting from overlaying map M_{i+1} with the map resulting from the overlay operation on $\{M_1, M_2, \ldots, M_i\}$. Noting that j intersections create j new segments, the total number of segments in the map resulting from the overlay operation on $\{M_1, M_2, \ldots, M_i\}$ is

$$O(\sum_{r=1}^{r=i} n_r + \sum_{r=1}^{r=i-1} k_r)$$

Hence the complexity of the ith overlay operation is

$$O((\sum_{r=1}^{i+1} n_r + \sum_{r=1}^{i-1} k_r) * \log(\sum_{r=1}^{i+1} n_r + \sum_{r=1}^{i-1} k_r) + k_i$$

The worst case complexity of the whole multiple overlay step would then be $O(m(n+k)\log(n+k))$. If we assume m to be a constant, this is $O((n+k)\log(n+k))$. Since m the number of maps is typically small and k the number of intersections can be fairly large ($O(n^2)$ in the worst-case), the above analysis shows why it may not hurt to invest the time overhead for finding out a good order in which to do the overlay, rather than perform the overlays in some arbitrary order.

5   Alternative Approaches

The $O(m^2 n \log n)$ overhead in Algorithm A in Section 4 above may be too much to spare in situations where n is large. The bottleneck is the selectivity estimation step which uses the $O(n \log n)$ segment intersection counting algorithm. In this section, we consider alternative approaches to circumvent this problem.

5.1   Histogram-Based Methods

The $O(n \log n)$ segment intersection counting algorithm has the advantage that it 'estimates' selectivity with 100% accuracy; we get an exact count of the number of segment intersections. If we are willing to sacrifice on this accuracy, we can reduce the time overhead for finding a good overlay order. We can replace the selectivity estimation step in the algorithm A in Section 4.2 with any of the popular histogram-based methods suggested in [1], [24] or [32]. When building a histogram for region objects, an object may be counted multiple times if it spans across several buckets. Conventional histograms suffer from this drawback. Sun et al. [32] showed how to use Euler Histograms to circumvent this problem. We propose a method to circumvent this problem while using any of the histogram-based methods.

The idea is to use a Quad-CIF tree [22], to improve histogram based selectivity estimation. Quad-CIF tree is a quad tree in which each polygon is stored at the lowest level of the tree at which it is fully enclosed by the cell at that level. This causes larger polygons to be stored in a single cell at a higher level. In a Quad-CIF tree each cell stores pointers to the polygons which are enclosed by that cell. For a histogram based on Quad-CIF tree, in each cell, instead of the pointers, we store the summary information of polygons which are completely enclosed by that cell and are not completely enclosed by a cell at lower level. This alleviates the multiple counts problem for large polygons which span multiple cells. It should be noted that some smaller polygons needs to be stored at higher level if they fall on the boundary between two large cells. Sevcik et al. [31] showed that for uniformly distributed minimum bounding rectanges (of the polygons) the number of small rectangles which fall over such boundaries is small.

In normal grid based histograms, calculation of number of intersections requires matching grids located at same position. For calculating number of intersections using two quad CIF-tree Histograms, a cell at a level i in first histogram should be matched with cell at level i and all its parent cells in the second histogram. During the estimation, if we do a depth first traversal over both the quad CIF tree Histograms, and maintain cells in the current path in the main memory, each cell needs to be accessed only once from secondary memory.

5.2   A Greedy Approach to Schedule Overlays

We can use a histogram-based selectivity estimation along with a greedy algorithm for choosing the order of overlays. We start with a set of m maps. We build a weighted graph G as in Section 4.2 whose vertices represent the maps and edges represent cost of intersections of segments of the two maps represented by the vertices concerned. We pick the edge (u, v) with the minimum cost and perform an overlay operation between the corresponding maps. Next we merge the vertices u and v. For any vertex w the cost of the new edge between w and the new vertex is the sum of the costs of the edges (u, w) and (v, w). Hence each update can be done in $O(m)$ time. The rationale behind this algorithm is the same as for that in Section 4.2: we defer more expensive overlays so as not to increase the problem sizes of the intermediate overlays early on in the overlay schedule.

6   Conclusions

In this paper, we have considered the problem of selecting a good order in which to perform a sequence of map overlay operations and have proposed some solutions. Compared to prior work on the problem which assumed raster or regular tesselations as underlying models, in this paper we assume that the input maps are modeled by the more space efficient vector representation.

Future research can be conducted in several different areas. Firstly, we intend to conduct experimental studies on these approaches in the context of performing overlays on large datasets. Becker et al. [4] show how well known main-memory algorithms from computational geometry can help to perform map overlay and spatial overlap join in a GIS. They showed how the algorithms of Nievergelt and Preparata [26] and a modified version of the algorithm of Chan [7] can be extended to cope with massive real-world data sets. We would like to conduct similar studies for the multiple map overlay problem.

Secondly, on the theoretical front, note that the problem of determining a good order for performing overlays can be decomposed into two stages: (i) finding a suitable linear ordering of the maps and (ii) finding an optimal sequence of binary overlays subject to the given order. If we model the maps as vertices of a graph with edge weights as in Section 4, the first problem is a variant of the optimal linear arrangement problem [15], a well-studied NP-complete problem for which heuristics are known. The second is similar to the matrix chain product problem [19, 20] which is amenable to an efficient dynamic programming solution. Using these results to design an efficient algorithm for the map overlay ordering problem is also something that needs to be investigated.

Thirdly, we need to look at optimizing the overlay order based on other cost functions than what is considered in Section 4, to better reflect the complexity of the overlays.

Finally, we believe our method is fairly general to be useful in applications other than GIS. For instance the typical description of a VLSI layout is the geometrical description of masks. Layout analysis and verification [33] involves the testing of a layout to see if it satisfies design and layout rules. The layout is represented as a collection of polygons for each mask layer. One of the crucial steps in layout verification is the computation of *boolean masks* which involve the unions and intersections of large number of polygons of each layer. When multiple layers are intersected, finding a good order in which to perform the intersections will be useful.

References

1. An, N., Yang, Z.-Y., Sivasubramaniam, A.: Selectivity estimation for spatial joins. *Proceedings, International Conference on Data Engineering* (2001) 368–375.
2. Aref, W., Samet, H.: A cost model for query optimization using R-Trees. *Proceedings, ACM GIS*, (1994) 60–67.
3. Balaban, I.J. An optimal algorithm for finding segment intersections. *Proceedings, 11th Annual ACM Symposium on Computational Geometry*, (1995) 211–219.

4. Becker, L., Giesen, A., Hinrichs, K.H., Vahrenhold, J.: Algorithms for performing polygonal map overlay and spatial join on massive data sets. *Proceedings, International Symposium on Spatial Databases* (1999) 270–285.
5. Belussi, A., Faloutsos, C.: Self-spatial join selectivity estimation using fractal concepts. *ACM Transactions on Information Systems*, 16(2) (1998) 161–201.
6. Bentley, J.L., Ottmann, T.A.: Algorithms for reporting and counting geometric intersections. *IEEE Transactions on Computers*, **C-28** (1979) 643–647.
7. Chan, T.: A simple trapezoid sweep algorithm for reporting red/blue segment intersections. *Proceedings, 6th Canadian Conference on Computational Geometry* (1994) 263–268.
8. Chazelle, B., and Edelsbrunner, H.: An optimal algorithm for intersecting line segments in the plane. *Proceedings, 29th Annual IEEE Symposium on Foundations of Computer Science*, (1988) 590–600.
9. Chazelle, B., Edelsbrunner, H., Guibas, L., Sharir, M.: Algorithms for bichromatic line segment problems and polyhedral terrains. *Report UIUC DCS-R-90-1578, Department of Computer Science, University of Illinois, Urbana, IL* (1989).
10. Cho, J.D., Raje, S., Sarrafzadeh, M.: Fast Approximation Algorithms on Maxcut, k-Coloring, and k-Color Ordering for VLSI Applications. *IEEE Transactions on Computers* **47(11)** (1998) 1253–1256.
11. Clarkson, K.L., Shor, P.: Applications of random sampling in computational geometry II. *Discrete Computational Geometry*, **4** (1989) 387–421.
12. Dorenbeck, C., Egenhofer, M.J.: Algebraic optimization of combined operations. *Proceedings, 10th Auto-Carto* (1991) 296–312.
13. Faloutsos, C., Seeger, B., Traina, A., Traina, C.: Spatial join selectivity using power laws. *Proceedings, ACM SIGMOD* (2000) 177-188.
14. Finke, U., Hinrichs, K.: Overlaying simply connected planar subdivisions in linear time. *Proceedings, 11th Annual ACM Symposium on Computational Geometry*, (1995) 119–126.
15. Garey, M.R., Johnson, D.S.: Computers and Intractibility: A guide to the theory of NP-Completeness. *W.H. Freeman* (1979).
16. Garey, M.R., Johnson, D.S., Stickmeyer, L.: Some simplified NP-complete graph problems. *Theoretical Computer Science* **1** (1976) 237–267.
17. Goemans, M.X., Williamson, D.P.: Improved approximation algorithms for maximum cut and satisfiability problems using semidefinite programming. *Proceedings, ACM STOC* (1994) 422-431.
18. Haglin, D.J., Venkatesan, S.M.: Approximation and intractability results for the maximum cut problem and its variants. *IEEE Transactions on Computers* **40(1)** (1991) 110–113.
19. Hu, T.C., Shing, M.T.: Computation of matrix chain products, Part I. *SIAM Journal on Computing* **11(2)** (1982) 362–373.
20. Hu, T.C., Shing, M.T.: Computation of matrix chain products, Part II. *SIAM Journal on Computing* **13(2)** (1984) 228–251.
21. Kriegel, H.-P., Brinkhoff, T., Schneider, R.: An efficient map overlay algorithm based on spatial access methods and computational geometry. *Geographic Database Management Systems*, G. Gambosi, M. Scholl, H.-W. Six (eds.), Springer Verlag, (1992) 194–211.
22. Kedem, G.: The quad-CIF tree: A data structure for hierarchical on-line algorithms. *Proceedings, ACM IEEE Design Automation Conference* (1982) 352–357.
23. Mairson, H.G., Stolfi, J.: Reporting and counting intesrections between two sets of line segments. *Theoretical Foundations of Computer Graphics and CAD*, R.A. Earnshaw ed., Springer-Verlag (1987) 307–325.

24. Mamoulis, N., Papadias, D.: Selectivity estimation for complex spatial queries. *Proceedings 7th International Symposium on Spatial and Temporal Databases* (2001) 155–174.
25. Mulmuley, M.: A fast planar partition algorithm I. *Proceedings, 29th Annual IEEE Symposium on Foundations of Computer Science*, (1988) 580–589.
26. Nievergelt, J., Preparata, F.P.: Plane-sweep algorithms for intersecting geometric figures. *Communications of the ACM*, **25(10)** (1982) 739–747.
27. Olken, F., Rotem, D.: Sampling from spatial databases. *Proceedings, International Conference on Data Engineering* (1993) 199–208.
28. Palazzi, L., Snoeyink, J.: Counting and reporting red/blue segment intersections. *3rd Workshop on Algorithms and Data Structures, Springer-Verlag Lecture Notes on Computer Science*, Volume 709 (1993).
29. Papadias, D., Mamoulis, N., Theodoridis, Y.: Processing and optimization of multiway spatial joins using R-trees*Proceedings, ACM Symposium on Principles of Database Systems*, (1999) 44–55.
30. Sahni, S., Gonzalez, T.F.: P-Complete Approximation. *Journal of the ACM* **23** (1976) 555–565.
31. Sevcik, K.C., Koudas, N.: "Filter trees for Managing Spatial Data Over a Range of Size Granularities", *Proceedings, 22nd VLDB Conference* 1996.
32. Sun, C., Agrawal, D., El Abbadi, A.: Selectivity estimation for spatial joins with geometric selections. *Proceedings, International Conference on Extending Database Technology*, (2002) 609–626.
33. Szymanski, T.G., van Wyk, C.J.: Layout Analysis and Verification, in *Physical Design Automation of VLSI Systems*, B. Preas and M. Lorenzetti eds., Benjamin/Cummins (1988), 347–407.
34. Vassilakopoulos, M., Manolopoulos, Y.: On sampling region data. *DKE* **22(3)** (1997) 309–318.
35. Yost, M., Skelton, B.: Programming Language Technology for Raster GIS Modeling. *Proceedings, GIS/LIS* **1** (1990) 319-327.

Relational Schema Evolution
for Program Independency*

Young-Gook Ra

Department of Electrical and Computer Engineering, University of Seoul, Korea
ygra@uos.ac.kr

Abstract. The database schema is assumed to be stable enough to remain valid even as the modeled environment changes. However, in practice, data models are not nearly as stable as commonly assumed by the
database designers. Even though a rich set of schema change operations is
provided in current database systems, the users suffer from the problem
that schema change usually impacts existing application programs that
have been written against the schema. In this paper, we are exploring
the possible solutions to overcome this problem of impacts on the application programs. We believe that for continued support of the existing
programs on the old schema, the old schema should continue to allow
updates and queries, as before. Furthermore, its associated data has to
be kept up-to-date. We call this the program independency property of
schema change tools. For this property, we devise so-called program independency schema evolution (PISE) methodology. For each of the set of
schema change operations in the relational schemas, the overview of the
additional code blocks due to the PISE compliance is presented in order
to prove the comprehensiveness and soundness of our PISE methodology.

Keywords: schema evolution, program independency, database view,
relational database, data model, schema version, database schema,
capacity-augmenting schema change, type mismatch, shared database

1 Introduction

Database designers construct a schema with the goal of accurately reflecting
the environment modeled by the database system. The resulting schema is assumed to be stable enough to remain valid even as the modeled environment
changes. However, in practice, data models are not nearly as stable as commonly
assumed by the database designers. Schema changes may include the simple ad-
dition/deletion of relation or of an attribute, or the decomposition of a complex
relation into several simpler relations, to just name a few. It would relieve much
of a database administrator' work if these changes were automatically handled
by a dedicated software tool, especially if this tool's functionality would include
the verification of integrity constraints and the translation of the stored database
structured accordingly to the old schema into the structure of the new schema.
Indeed many such tools and methodologies have been proposed [1, 2].

---

* This work was supported by the University of Seoul, in 2003.

G. Das and V.P. Gulati (Eds.): CIT 2004, LNCS 3356, pp. 273–281, 2004.

Even though a rich set of schema change operations is provided in current database systems, there still remains the more serious problem that schema change usually impacts existing application programs that have been written against the schema. Hence, in current DBMSs, schema updates are more restricted by their impact on existing programs rather than by the power of the supported schema change language. This problem could be partially solved using some schema version systems [3], because they maintain old schema versions and thus allow existing programs to still run against the old versions while new programs can be developed on the desired new schema version. However, in schema version systems, old schema versions are only accessible in consultation mode. This means that old programs would access obsolete data through their schema.

We believe that for continued support of the existing programs on the old schema, the old schema should continue to allow updates and queries, as before. Furthermore, its associated data has to be kept up-to-date. We call this the program independency property of schema change tools. Precisely speaking, an update on tuple values of a schema version (VS2) is visible to another schema version (VS1) if the update values are key values of VS1. If the values are non-key values of VS1, then the update is visible to VS1 as long as the update causes different non-key values of which key values are the same within a version or among versions. If the non-key value update is not propagated to VS1, the values are set to null in VS1.

There are research works that recognized the importance of the program independency property in schema updates in order to continually support existing application programs and they provide solutions [4–6]. Put simply, they basically use procedures to resolve the type mismatch of different versions: they require that such procedures are provided by the users for each occurrence of a schema change. The view approach also has been advocated by several researchers [7, 8] as an alternative solution approach for the resolution of the type match problem. The idea is that database views are to provide multiple perspectives of instances, each of which corresponds to a specific schema version. The view approach has advantages over the procedural one that the views are to provide the difference perspectives, update on derived perspectives are well investigated, and the performance of generating derived perspectives can easily be optimized.

However, Tresch and Sholl [8] have observed that the view based solutions can't support the full range of schema changes. literature [1]. In particular, view mechanisms, being defined to correspond to a stored named query [9], cannot simulate capacity-augmenting schema changes. Bertino [7] and our earlier work [10] have proposed to extend views that can add more schema components in order to assure that the capacity-augmenting changes can be simulated using views. However, our experiments have shown that this is a hard to achieve in a truly efficient manner. We are proposing a more practical solution in this paper. Our approach is neither confined to non-capacity-augmenting changes nor requires a capacity-augmenting view mechanism. This alternative solution, which is called the program independency Schema Evolution (PISE) methodology, is based on the following simple idea. For a non-capacity-augmenting schema change operation we simply derive a view schema intended by the operation and for a capacity-augmenting schema change operation we propose that (1) schema is directly modified for the additional capacity required by the operation, (2) the original schema is reconstructed as a view based on the modified schema, and (3) the target schema is generated as a view also based on the modified schema.

The next section explains overall of our approach. In the next section, we discuss related works. In the next PISE section, we present schema evolution operators with the illustration of algorithms that achieves the program independency of the operators. In the final section, our work is concluded with a future work.

2   Overview of Our Approach

The PISE methodology assumes that all schemas, through which either interactive human users or application programs interact, are actually views derived from one underlying base schema B as shown in Figure 1 (a). Suppose the existing program *Prog1* runs against the *VS1* schema and the program *Prog2* is being developed and requires new database services. For the new database services, the database administrator initiates the schema transformation *T* on *VS1* with the expectation that *VS1* would be transformed into the target schema *VS2*. Instead, the desired target schema would be created as a view *VS2* with a newer version number as shown in Figure 1 (a). The PISE methodology that generates this desired schema as a view for both capacity-augmenting and non-capacity-augmenting cases consists of three steps. Each of these steps is detailed in the following.

We first augment the underlying base schema B by the amount of capacity necessary to generate the desired target schema. In case *T* is non-capacity-augmenting, this step is skipped. This is called the base-schema-change step. In Figure 1 (b), the base schema *B* is in-place changed into *B'* by this step, i.e., *B* disappears. Then we generate the desired target schema (*VS2*) using a view derivation over the enhanced base schema *B'* as shown in Figure 1 (c). This step is referred to as the target-view-derivation step. Note that the user schema VS1 may become invalid because its source schema *B* no longer exists, i.e., it has been modified by the previous step. Lastly, we reconstruct the original base schema B as a view defined over the modified base schema *B'* as shown in Figure 1 (d). This preserves the source schema of the old user schema *VS1*, namely, the original base schema B. Hence, *VS1* now becomes valid again. This is called the original-base-schema-restoration step. This step is again skipped in case *T* is non-capacity-augmenting, because the base schema has not been changed to begin with for this case. In Figure 1 (d), we can see that the new program *Prog2* can now be developed on its desired new schema version *VS2*, while the old program *Prog1* still continues to run against the same schema VS1 despite the schema transformation *T*.

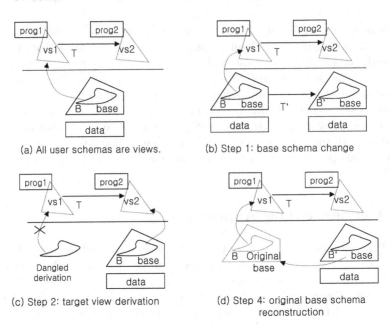

(a) All user schemas are views.

(b) Step 1: base schema change

(c) Step 2: target view derivation

(d) Step 4: original base schema reconstruction

Fig. 1. Overview of our approach.

3   Related Work

The schema change approaches are classified into four categories. The first category corresponds to in-place schema change systems that support the conventional notion of schema change, i.e., in-place changing the shared base schema and propagating the schema change to the instance level. The second category corresponds to schema version systems that support the conventional notion of versioning, i.e., the old schema is stored with its snapshot of the database only for consultation purpose. The third category is named procedural program independent schema change systems that support the notion of program independency, i.e., the application programs on the old schema are continuously supported despite the schema changes, but resolve any type of mismatch between the instances and a schema version by procedures written by a programming language. The fourth category is named view-based schema change systems that also support the program independency notion, but the distinction is that the type mismatch is resolved by implementing each schema version as a view of the underlying base schema while the mismatch is resolved by user/pre-defined procedures in the third category systems. Because our interest is on the program independency of the schema change, we focus on the third and fourth categories of the systems.

The procedural program independent systems include the encore system [4], CLOSQL [6], and Clamen [12]. The encore system allows instances of different type version to be accessed by providing exception handlers for the properties that the types of the instances do not contain. The CLOSQL proposes that update/backdate functions are provided (either by the user or predefined for some operations) for each attribute which convert the instances from the format in which the instance is stored to the format that an application program expects. In Clamen's scheme, an instance is physically represented as a disjoint union of all versions, while in Zdonik's, an instance is physically represented as an interface type, which is a minimal cover of all versions.

View-based program independent schema change systems include Tresch and Scholl [8], Bertino [7], and Thomas and Shneiderman [13]. Tresch and Scholl advocate views as a suitable mechanism for simulating schema evolution and also state that schema evolution can be simulated using views if the evolution is not capacity-augmenting. Bertino presents a view mechanism and indicates that it can be utilized to simulate schema evolution. Thomas and Shneiderman propose that an old schema is implemented as a network sub-schema. However, the old schema can no longer be changed because this system only supports in-place schema change operators and the old schema is not a base schema but a derived one.

4   Schema Change Operators Using PISE

Our PISE approach covers a comprehensive set of schema change operations that have been proposed in [1]. The set we have investigated includes change-name, add-attribute, delete-attribute, promote-key, demote-key, decompose, compose, partition, merge, export, import, extract, and import-dependency. Out of the operators, the add-attribute, promote-key, decompose, export, and extract operators are capacity-augmenting and the rest are non-capacity-augmenting. As for an representative example, the extract operation is explained. The syntax and semantics of the extract operator are presented and the algorithm that changes the source base schema, derive the target view, and reconstruct the original base schema is illustrated. Besides, for the extract operator, we show that the generated schema has the same behavior as that of a base schema for update operations and the PISE implementation of the extract operation satisfies the program independency principle.

The syntax of the extract operation is *"extract(rel, R(a_1, a_2, ..., a_m, b_1, b_2, ..., b_n)"*. The semantics is to extract non-key attributes a_1, a_2, ..., a_m, b_1, b_2, ..., b_n from the relation *rel* and forms a new relation R. The relation *rel* is decreased by the attributes b_1, b_2, ..., b_n.

Theorem 1. The extract operation is capacity-augmenting.

Proof: This operation divide the relation *rel* into the two relations *newRel* and R and there could be instances that belong to either of the two relations but not to the relation *rel*. Those could be instances of the relation R that do not share the a_1, a_2, ..., a_m attribute values with the instances of the *newRel* or the instances of the relation *newRel* that do not share the a_1, a_2, ..., a_m attribute values with the instances of the R.

PISE Implementation. By the PISE methodology, all the relations are defined from the source relations as views. For example, as seen in Figure 2, the operand

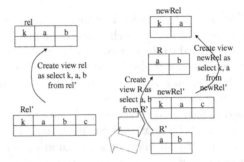

Fig. 2. The PISE implementation of the extract operation.

relation *rel* is initially defined as a view that just projects the *k, a, b* attributes from the relation *rel'*. In the first step, the source relation is physically changed to acquire the augmented schema element. For example, the source relation *rel'* as divided into the two relations *newRel* and *R'* as seen in the lower part of Figure 2. In the second step, target relations are derived from source relations. For example, the target relations *newRel* and *R* are defined as "select k, a from newRel'" and "select a, b from R'" as shown in the right part of Figure 2. In the third step, the source relations before the first step is recovered using view derivations. In the lower part of Figure 2, the dotted block arrow represents the view derivation that accomplishes the third step in this extract operation. In this example, the reconstruction is achieved by joining the *rel'* and *R'* relations based on the attribute *a*.

Theorem 2. The PISE implementation defined above in Figure 2 generates the target relations as expected by the operation semantics. In addition, the expected change also arises in the instance level.

Proof: The new relation $R(a, b)$ is extracted from the relation *rel(k, a, b)* and the relation *rel* is changed into the relation *newRel* which is decremented by the attribute *b*. By this, the expected target relations have been generated in the schema level. An instance *inst* of the operand relation *rel* has values v_k, v_a, v_b for the attributes *k, a, b*, respectively. The *inst* instance is derived from the instance *inst'* of the source relation *rel'* by projecting the *k, a, b* attributes. The real instance *inst'* has values of v_k, v_a, v_b, v_c for the attributes *k, a, b, c*, respectively, and is divided into the two tuples (v_k, v_a, v_c) and (v_a, v_b) by the above PISE 1 step and these are transformed into (v_k, v_a) and (v_a, v_b) by the target schema derivation. As a result, the operand instance *inst* = (v_k, v_a, v_b) is divided into the tuples (v_k, v_a) and (v_a, v_b) and this is the expected instance level change by this operation.

Theorem 3. The target relations generated by the above PISE implementation (Figure 2) shows the same behavior as the base relations for the insert, update, delete operations.

Proof: The insert operation into the relation *newRel* is transformed to the insert operation into the relation *newRel'*. Reversely, this appears as the instance has been inserted into the relation *newRel* because the relation *newRel* is the project of the relation *newRel'*. The same phenomena holds for the relations R and R'. The update and delete operations on the target relations are also propagated to the source relations and this reversely shows the same effect as if the operations are directly performed on the target relations.

Theorem 4. The above PISE implementation of the extract operation (Figure 2) recovers their original relation *rel* both in the schema level and in the instance level. In addition, the recovered schema exhibits the same behavior as the base schema for the insert, update, delete operations.

Proof: The proof omitted because it is similar to those of theorem 3 and 4.

Theorem 5. The above PISE implementation of the extract operation (Figure 2) assures the program independency property.

Proof: In Figure 2, let the schema before the change *VS1* and that after the change *VS2*. First we examine the scope of *VS2* tuples that are accessed from *VS1*. All tuples of the relation *newRel* of *VS2* become those of the relation *rel* of *VS1*. The tuples of the relation R are not instances of the relation *rel* and thus, all the tuples do not have to be accessed from the relation *rel* of *VS1*. Only the tuples that share the a values with the tuples of the *newRel* relation are accessed from the relation *rel*. The b values of such tuples of the relation R are determined by the k values and thus there could be no inconsistencies of b values against k values. Thus, these b values are accessed from the *rel* relation of *VS1*. In reverse, we examine the scope of *VS1* tuples that accessed from *VS2*. The tuples of the *rel* relation of *VS1* all become the instances of the *newRel* relation of *VS2*. Thus, the key attribute k values of the *rel* tuples are all accessed from the *newRel* relation of *VS2*. The a attribute values of the *rel* relation are all accessed as the values of a attribute of the R relation of *VS2*. This is true because the values of the a attribute of the relation *rel* are all the shared values between the a attribute of *newRel* and the a attribute of R. The b values of the *rel* relation of *VS1* can be non-unique against the key-attribute a values of the relation R of *VS2* and they are set to null. Thus, we have showed that the data values of *VS1* (*VS2*) are accessed from *VS2* (*VS1*) under the program independency principle.

The k value creation, deletion or the modification in the relation *rel* of *VS1* is transformed into the same operation in the source relation *newRel'* and in turn the k values for the *newRel* relation of *VS2* is created, deleted or modified. The k value creation, deletion or modification of the *newRel* relation of *VS2* is similarly propagated to *VS1*. When the a value in the *rel* relation of *VS1* is created, deleted or modified, it is transformed into the creation, deletion or the modification of the a values of both source relations *newRel'* and R' and results that both a values of the *newRel* and the R relations of *VS2* are create, deleted or modified in *VS2*. Thus, the key k value deletion or modification in *VS2* is observed from *VS1* and in reverse, the key k and a value deletion or modification in *VS1* is observed from *VS2*.

The a value creation, deletion or update in the relation R of *VS2* is transformed into the same operation in both source relations R'. This may cause that the created, deleted or the modified R' tuple do not share the a values with tuples of *newRel'* any longer and it may result that the a value change is hidden from the *a* attribute of the *rel* relation of *VS1*. The creation, deletion or modification of the *b* value in the *rel* relation of *VS1* is transformed into the same operation of the *b* value in the source relation *R'*. Then, the *b* change is seen from the *b* attribute of the relation *R* of *VS2*. The *b* value change of the *R* relation of *VS2* is similarly propagated to the corresponding *b* value of the relation *rel* of *VS1*. In summary, the nonkey value change of *VS1* (*VS2*)is propagated to *VS2* (*VS1*) as long as the integrity constraint is not violated. Thus, we have showed that the updates on *VS1* (*VS2*) are visible to *VS2* (*VS1*) under the program independency principle.

5   Conclusion and Future Work

In this paper, we present a solution to the problem of schema evolution affecting existing programs. We believe that other schemas should not be affected by a change on a given schema, even though they share a common base schema and data repository. In addition, old schemas should be preserved and kept to up to date to continue to support for existing programs. We call schema change operations that satisfy the above conditions program independent.

To demonstrate the usefulness and practicality of our PISE approach, we have chosen a comprehensive set of schema change operations, This set covers most of the schema change operations that we found in the literature [1]. Concerning the performance of the PISE system, it is closely tied to the performance of the supporting view system, because the user's schema in the PISE system is actually a view schema. Thus, further investigation is necessary to see how the conventional query optimization techniques can be used to cope with the problem of the performance degradation due to the long derivation chains that could result when the PISE system runs over time.

References

1. Ben Shneiderman and Glenn Thomas, "An architecture for automatic relational database system conversion," *ACM transactions on Database Systems*, Vol. 7, No. 2, pp. 235–257, 1982.
2. Peter McBreien and Alexandra Poulovassilis, "Schema evolution in heterogeneous database architecture, a schema transformation approach," *Conference on Advanced Information Systems Engineering*, pp. 484–499, 2002.
3. Edelweiss and Clesio Saraiva dos Santos, "Dynamic schema evolution managementusing version in temporal object-oriented databases," *International Workshop on Database and Expert Systems Application*, pp. 524–533, 2002.
4. A. H. Skarra and S. B. Zdonik, "The management of changingtypes in object-oriented databases", *Proc. 1st Conference on Object-Oriented Programming Systems, Languages, and Applications*, pp. 483–494, 1986.
5. A. Mehta, D. L. Spooner and M. Hardwick, "Resolution of type mismatches in an engineering persistent object system," *Tech. Report, Computer Science Dept., Rensselaer Polytechnic Institute*, 1993.
6. S. Monk and I. Sommerville, "Schema evolution in oodbs using class versioning," *SIGMOD RECORD*, Vol. 22, No. 3, 1993.

7. E. Bertino, "A view mechanism for object-oriented databases," 3rd *International Conference on Extending Database Technology*, pp. 136–151, 1992.
8. M. Tresch and M. H. Scholl, "Schema transformation without database reorganization," *SIGMOD RECORD*, pp. 21–27, 1992.
9. J. Ullman, "Principle of database systems and knowledge-based systems," *Computer Science Press*, Vol. 1, 1988.
10. Y. G. Ra and E. A. Rundensteiner, "A transparent schema evolution system based on object-oriented view technology," *IEEE Transactions on Knowledge and Data Engineering*, Vol. 9, No. 4, 1997.
11. W. Kim and H. Chou, "Versions of schema for OODB," *Proc.* 14th *Very large Databases Conference*, pp.149–159, 1988.
12. S. M. Clamen, "Type evolution and instance adaptation," *Technical Report CMU-CS-92-133R, Carnegie Mellon University, School of Computer Science*, 1992.
13. G. Thomas and B. Shneiderman, "Automatic database system conversion: a transformation language approach to sub-schema implementation," *IEEE Computer Software and Applications Conference*, pp. 80–88, 1980.

Reliability Enhancement in Software Testing – An Agent-Based Approach for Complex Systems

P. Dhavachelvan and G.V. Uma

School of Computer Science and Engineering,
Anna University, Chennai – 25, Tamilnadu, India
pd_chelvoume@yahoo.co.in, gvuma@annauniv.edu

Abstract. Although each paradigm have their own influence in the software engineering field with the support of their merits, researchers continue to strive for more efficient and powerful techniques. Agents are being advocated as a next generation model for engineering complex, distributed systems. Since the agent-oriented decomposition is an effective way of partitioning the problem space of complex system it has become a trend in software engineering. Although there are an increasing number of deployed agent applications, there is no systematic analysis precisely what makes the agent paradigm effective, when to use it and what type of applications can get use of it. Moreover the qualitative analysis of agent-based software engineering would not permit an objective observer to distinguish and prefer the agent-based approach from other approaches in the field of software engineering (includes software testing). Hence, the distinguishing factor cannot be just with qualitative descriptions; rather, it must be quantitative in nature. This paper therefore provides a timely summary and enhancement of agent theory in software testing, which describes an evaluation framework based on quantitative theory for adapting Agent-Oriented Software Testing (AOST) to complex systems. The multi-agent system illustrated here, is on the basis of few basic operational real-world testing techniques, as an attempt to describe how to practice agent-based software testing, which has not previously done.

Keywords: Multi agent-based, Intra-class testing, Integrated framework, Agent-based framework, Distributed frame work, Reliability enhancement.

1 Introduction

A wide range of software engineering paradigms have been recently devised (e.g. object-orientation, component ware, design patterns and software architectures) either to make the engineering process easier or to extend the complexity of applications that can feasibly be built [14-16]. Although each paradigm have their own influence in the software engineering field with the support of their merits, researchers continue to strive for more efficient and powerful techniques. Agents are being advocated as a next generation model for engineering complex, distributed systems [6]. At present, there is much debate [4][6], and little consensus, about exactly what constitutes agent-hood. Since the agents are the flexible problem solvers and their interactions are conceptualized at the knowledge level [8][10][14], agent-based approach is a both a logical and a natural evolution of a range of contemporary approaches to software engineering.

G. Das and V.P. Gulati (Eds.): CIT 2004, LNCS 3356, pp. 282–291, 2004.

In order to automate the testing processes, a set of deterministic approaches must be identified to generate test cases to test the target software to decide their correctness [14][17]. Today we still don't have a full-scale system that has achieved this goal. In general, significant amount of human intervention is still needed in testing. The degree of automation remains at the automated test script level. Some of the most challenging software testing problems relate to the sheer scale of software and application of variety of testing techniques with respect to the nature of test piece and test technique [10] [11] [12]. So, effective automation can be achieved by dividing the testing components to a maximum possible limit and maintaining by different units with high level of independency. Agent technologies facilitate the automated software testing by virtue of their high-level decomposition, independency and parallel activation. Software paradigms generally go through three main phases. Firstly, early pioneers identify a new way of doing things (based on intuition and insight). Secondly, individuals and organizations that are early adopters of leading-edge technologies recognize the potential (based on qualitative arguments) and start to build systems using the new concepts. Thirdly, the advocated concepts, and knowledge or their advantages (sometimes backed up by quantitative data), become more widespread and enter the mainstream of software engineering. At this time, agent-oriented techniques are firmly in phase two. Our proposed agent-based framework is an attempt for developing an automated software testing environment to start the movement towards phase three.

The paper is organized as follows. Section 2 discusses the evaluation framework for agent-based approach in software testing. Section 3 presents the agent-based framework for intra-class testing. Section 4 describes the timings and load scheduling in the framework. Finally, section 5 concludes our work with its significance.

2 Agent-Based Approach

2.1 Agent-Based Decomposition

Agents will need to interact with one another, either to achieve their individual objectives or to manage the dependencies that ensue from being situated in a common environment. Against the shortcomings of the distributed systems (rigidly defined interactions between computational entities and insufficient mechanisms available for representing the system's inherent organizational structure), the Adequacy and Establishment hypotheses [14] support that the Agent-oriented approaches can significantly enhance our ability to model, design and build complex, distributed systems and will succeed as a mainstream software engineering paradigm. Generally, the complexity tackling techniques are based on three important key concepts [14]:

Decomposition: For tackling the large problems, it can be divided into smaller, more manageable chunks each of which can then be dealt with in relative isolation.

Abstraction: The process of defining a simplified model of the system that emphasizes some of the details or properties, while suppressing others.

Organization: The process of identifying and managing the interrelationships between the various problem-solving components.

It is showed [14] that, the agent-oriented decomposition is an effective way of partitioning the problem space of complex system, the abstractions of the agent-oriented mindset are a natural means of modeling complex systems, and the agent-oriented philosophy for dealing with organizational relationships is appropriate for complex systems. A close relation exists between the different levels of task decomposition and the specification of the interaction between tasks. Each task is assigned to one or more agents. Agents themselves perform one more (sub) tasks, either sequentially or in parallel. [16][14]. The success of agent-oriented systems, both in terms of increased throughput and greater robustness to failure, can be attributed to a number of points. Firstly, representing the components and the machines as agents means the decision-making is much more localized. It can, therefore, be more responsive to prevailing circumstances. If, unexpected events occur, agents have the autonomy and pro-activeness to try alternatives. Secondly, because the schedules are built up dynamically through flexible interactions, they can readily be altered in the event of delays or unexpected contingencies. Thirdly, the explicitly defined relationships between the constituent parts of a composite item identify those agents that need to coordinate their actions. This, in turn, eases the scheduling task by reducing the number of items that need to be considered during decision-making.

2.2 Composition of Testing Techniques

Considerable research has gone into the development of methods for evaluating how 'good' a test set is for a given program against a given specification. Such criteria are also known as 'Test Adequacy Criteria' or simply 'Adequacy Criteria' [12] [9][10][22]. A testing technique may use one or more of these criteria to assess the adequacy of a test set for a given unit and then decide whether to stop testing this unit or to enhance the test set by constructing additional test cases needed to satisfy a criterion. The results so far encouraging and have demonstrated that the combinatorial approaches and algorithms [12][22] are indeed feasible and presents several advantages over the more traditional analysis approaches to automatic test data generation. While the test effectiveness will vary from test to test, the combinatorial approaches will results in better performance and also possible to apply variety of software reliability models that improves the overall predictability [18][19][20]. Considering the units, which are to be tested prior to integration, we have developed an enhanced model for unit testing. Because of the important role of testing in software process and product quality, an integrated model for unit testing is developed, which compromises two testing techniques – *Mutation Based Testing* and *Capability Assessment Testing*. This model provides a variety of adequacy criteria by combining these two testing techniques belong to different testing strategies. This development is motivated by the need to assess test sets for subsystems, in which come about due to the complications and huge effort with respect to time during the unit testing.

2.3 Evaluation Scheme

The proposed framework is described with its primary components in the fig. 1. Based on the key characteristics of complexity and the essential concepts and notions of agent-based paradigm, we developed a set of questions (Table 1) that reflects the complexity nature of the software in maximum possible aspects.

We used an evaluation scheme that assign three distinct values from 0 (not applicable or null significance) to 5 (highly applicable or absolutely essential) as the answers for each question at three conditions: minimum possibility (Min), most likely-hood (Most), and maximum possibility(Max) of the particular aspect/attribute that covered in that specified question. The optimal value of the particular aspect can be calculated as the weighted average of the three values for each question computed as in the eqn.(1). The eqn.(1) gives heaviest credence to the 'most likely-hood' estimate.

$$C_{W_i} = (C_{Min_i} + 2C_{Most_i} + C_{Max_i})/4 \qquad (1)$$

where $0 < i \leq n$, n is the number of complexity attributes considered in the evaluation scheme and its value is equal to sixteen in the proposed evaluation scheme. As said in the complexity theory (observation-2), the questions are generated and evaluated with respect to system and product(s). After determining the optimal level of complexity parameters, the next stage is to predict and verify the adequacy of the model for determining the optimum resultant value for complexity.

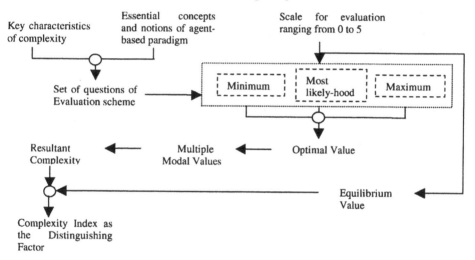

Fig. 1. Evaluation Framework

The optimum value of resultant complexity C_r can be determined by using Multi Modal approach [21] as follows.

Let $C = \{ C_{W_1}, C_{W_2}, \ldots\ldots C_{W_n} \}$ and M_i be the modal value with i^{th} highest frequency f_i. If $f_i = f_j$ for different values and $i \leq j$, then $M_i = $ maximum value of (f_i, f_j) and $M_j = $ minimum value of (f_i, f_j). Let f_{p_i} - projected frequency for M_i with respect to n and it can be calculated as

$$f_{p_i} = \frac{n}{f_t} * f_i, \qquad (2)$$

where $f_t = \sum_{k=1}^{q} f_k$, q is the modal degree of the system.

Table 1. Questions to be answered in the Evaluation Scheme

Questions Set		C_{Min_i}	C_{Most_i}	C_{Max_i}	C_{W_i}
Q1	Is the deadline of testing the product is unrealistic?				
Q2	Is the testing team for the product lack people with appropriate skills?				
Q3	Does the product need various types of testing techniques?				
Q4	Does the system need various types testing techniques?				
Q5	Is the compartmentalization is necessary for the system?				
Q6	Is it necessary to identify most error influenced (error prone) components in the product?				
Q7	Are there any possible autonomously distributed processing functions in the system?				
Q8	Is the chosen technology (some times more than one) to be changed in the system?				
Q9	Is the system needs additional techniques (components)?				
Q10	Does the system or system components qualify as the public resource center(s)?				
Q11	Does the system need high throughput?				
Q12	Does the system need multi-path inputs?				
Q13	What is the degree of strictness to apply the schedules?				
Q14	Does the system or system components need to be automated?				
Q15	Is the system size is so high?				
Q16	Can the system make the required effort distributed in nature?				

Modal Degree of System (MDS): If the system 'S' uses the multi modal approach such that the modal values as $m_1, m_2, \ldots\ldots m_q$, then the Modal Degree of the System is said to be as 'q', i.e. MDS(q), and the corresponding resultant complexity is denoted as C_{r_q}. The value of MDS varies between 1 to the no. of distinct values in the set C. The resultant complexity can be calculated as the projected mean as,

$$C_{r_q} = \frac{M_1 * f_{p_1} + M_2 * f_{p_2} \ldots\ldots\ldots Mq * f_{p_q}}{n} \tag{3}$$

The final stage is to determine the *Distinguishing Factor* as the Complexity Index. *Complexity Index (CI)* can be defined as the ratio between C_{r_q} to Equilibrium value as in the eqn. (4).

$$\text{Complexity Index } (CI) = \frac{C_{r_q}}{EV} \tag{4}$$

Equilibrium value (EV) of the evaluation scheme is defined as the median of the scale points and it is equal to 2.5 in this scheme. Here the CI is the distinguishing factor to define the necessity of agent-based approach in software testing. If CI > 1, then the agent-based approach is essential, and if CI = 1, it is recommended, else the agent based approach is not necessary.

3 Agent-Based Testing Environment

3.1 Back-Ground Information Needed

- P = { G, C, L }   : Program to be Tested.
- G = { g_1, g_2, ...g_m }   : Set of global methods in P.
- C = { c_1, c_2, ...c_n }   : Set of member functions in the test class in P.
- L = { l_1, l_2, ...l_p }   : Set of local methods in P.
- f_r = function to be tested where $f_r \in$ { G } or $f_r \in$ { C } or $f_r \in$ { L }

     'r' value is such that, $1 \le r \le N$ and $N = n + m + p$.

- T (f_r) : Test case of the function f_r generated by MBT-Agent or CAT-Agent.
- T' (f_r) : Test case of the function f_r generated by MIT-Agent.

Given input is 'P'.

1.   Define the sets of C, G, L.
2.   For each 'f_r',
  2.1.   Select the type of Mutant for 'f_r' and fix it.
  2.2.   Check, is there any function call in 'f_r'.
  2.3.   If there any function call(s) in 'f_r', submit T (f_r) to MIT-Agent. Then *goto* 2.6.
  2.4.   Else, run T (f_r).
  2.5.   Observe the output of T (f_r) and record it.
  2.6.   Repeat from 2.1 for another mutant.
3.   Repeat 2 for next f_r.
4.   Add the test report to Integrated Test Profile.

Fig. 2. Principle activities of MBT-Agent

Given input is 'P'.

1.   Define the sets of C, G, L.
2.   For each 'f_r',
  2.1. Define the test piece T_p in 'f_r'.
  2.2. Define the range of test process for 'T_p'.
  2.3. Check, is there any function call in 'f_r'.
  2.4. If there any function call in 'f_r', submit T (f_r) to MIT-Agent. Then *goto* 2.7.
  2.5.   Else, run T (f_r).
  2.6.   Observe the output of T (f_r) and record it.
  2.7. Repeat from 2.1 for another mutant.
3. Repeat 2 for next f_r.
4. Add the test report to Integrated Test Profile.

Fig. 3. Principle ativities of CAT-Agent

3.2 System Agents – Task Allocation and Implementation

A close relation exists between the different levels of task decomposition and the specification of the interaction between tasks. Each task is assigned to one or more agents. Agents themselves perform one more (sub) tasks, either sequentially or in parallel. [4][3]. For design from scratch, including the design of agents themselves, tasks distinguished within a task hierarchy can be assigned to different agents on the basis of the tasks decomposition: both *complex and primitive* tasks alike. Task allocation at this level is not *one-to-one*: in many situations the same task may be assigned to more than one agent. In other situations, agents already have certain capabilities and characteristics.

Given input is 'P' and T (f_r) from MBT-Agent or CAT-Agent.
1. Receive the T (f_r) from MBT-Agent *or* CAT-Agent with its input data specification
2. For each T (f_r),
    2.1. 2.1. Identify the subordinates and generate stubs for T (f_r), that gives T' (f_r).
    2.2. Run T' (f_r). And record the output.
3. Repeat 2 for next T' (f_r).
4. Add the test report to Integrated Test Profile.

Fig. 4. Principle activities of MIT-Agent

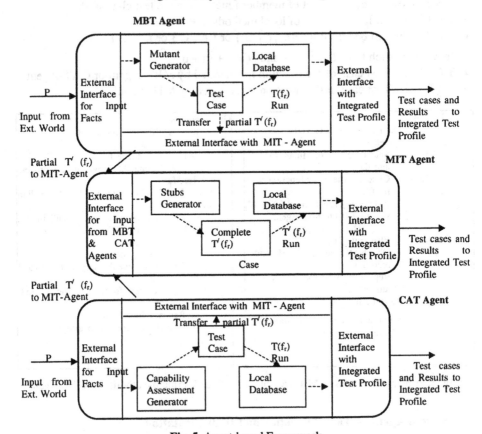

Fig. 5. Agent-based Framework

A. Mutation Based Testing (MBT) – Agent: In this framework, the mutation testing responsibilities are given to an agent *Mutation Based Testing-Agent* (MBT-Agent) such that, it has to test the functions in the sets G or C or L in an *autonomous fashion*. The algorithm in the fig. 2 depicts the principle activities of MBT-Agent.

B. Capability Assessment Testing (CAT) – Agent: In this framework, the capability assessment testing responsibilities are given to an agent *Capability Assessment Testing–Agent* (CAT-Agent) such that, it has to test the functions in the sets G or C or L in an *autonomous fashion*. The algorithm in the fig. 3 depicts the principle activities of CAT-Agent.

C. Methods Interaction Testing (MIT) – Agent: Since the interaction between a class members (methods) and program members (methods) can't be considered as unit-to-unit testing, it has to be tested in the unit test phase itself. In this framework, the method interaction testing is carried out by an agent *Method Interaction Testing–Agent* (MIT-Agent) such that, it has to test the functions in the sets G or C or L in an *interactive fashion*. Here, the global and local subordinates (program members) of a class member are treated as global and local stubs respectively. The stubs are neither with minimal functionality nor with minimal data manipulation. Since, they are the exact replicas of the actual subordinates, it will results in better performance irrespective of its overhead. The algorithm in the fig. 4 depicts the principle activities of MIT-Agent.

3.3   Interaction and Information Flow Within and Between Agents

Task control knowledge in complex and primitive tasks alike, make it possible to specify an agent's reasoning and acting patterns distributed over the hierarchy of agent components. Each component is assumed to have a discrete time scale. When and how a component will be activated is to be specified [3][4]. This most often includes the specification of at-least:

- the *interaction* required to provide the necessary input facts.
- the set of facts for which truth values are sought (target set).

Agent needs the computational apparatus to make run-time decisions about the nature and scope of their interactions. This decentralization, in turn, reduces the system's control complexity and results in a lower degree of coupling between components [6]. In the MBT-Agent, the local and global task controls are based on the Mutant specifications and Additional stubs requirements respectively. In the CAT-Agent, the local and global task controls are based on the test piece specifications and Additional stubs requirements respectively. For the task control between the agents, minimal global task control is required to initially activate all agents included in task performance. Since the input for MIT-Agent is from MBT and CAT agents, the task control in the MIT-Agent is based on the test case(s) generated either by MBT-Agent or CAT-Agent. The complete information flow structure is described in the fig. 5.

4   Experiment and Result Analysis

The test samples for the minimal version are implemented in C++ as experimental projects by two different teams. Team-1 consists of four students and headed by an academician and the Team-2 consists of four students and headed by a software developer with minimum experience. Here the time is allotted as fixed package for all testing approaches. Here the testing was carried out in three different situations. In Method-1, only capability Assessment Testing is applied for variables, loops and branching statements only. In Method-2, only Mutation Based Testing is applied for I/O statements, computational statements and assignment statements only. The Method-3 consists of both CAT and MBT techniques. The advantage of the proposed framework can be realized by analyzing the experimental values of *Time Allotted* in table 2. From the above table, the primary advantage of agent-based framework - parallel activation of different modules is realized. From the measurement of E_C, E_M, E_A and *Time Allotted* under different situations, it is observed that by applying the proposed framework, the reliability of the software can be enhanced and considerable amount of time can be saved that will be needed as the software approaches shipping without any degradation with respect to the reliability of the software.

Table 2. Test Samples and Results

Testing Attributes		Samples' type and Developers							
		Simple Game		Editor		Laboratory Experimental Pack		Medical Image Analysis Tool	
		Team1	Team2	Team1	Team2	Team1	Team2	Team1	Team2
Size in LOC		400 +	500 +	700 +	700 +	1600 +	1800 +	2500 +	2500 +
Method-1	Number of Test Cases	28	32	37	42	68	72	114	106
	Errors found (E_C)	12	8	13	8	24	11	25	11
Method-2	Number of Test Cases	30	36	42	50	62	70	96	114
	Errors found (E_M)	18	13	18	11	24	13	28	14
Method-3	Number of Test Cases	46	50	58	64	92	98	136	136
	Errors found (E_A)	23	18	23	14	36	17	42	19
Time Allotted		2 hrs	2 hrs	3 hrs	3 hrs	5 hrs	5 hrs	8 hrs	8 hrs

5 Conclusion

The compositional nature of components' architectures designed within the framework supports the exact structure requires for complete class testing. This paper has sought to justify the claim that agent-based framework has the potential to significantly improve the performance of software testing. In making this claim, a series of qualitative and quantitative measurements were exercised to highlight the significance of the proposed method. Test case generation and execution management for all agents are clearly implemented as a prototype model for further extension. The methodology proposed here rests on the idea of building a conceptual model that is incrementally refined and it can be extended from other existing models of other fields of software engineering. The arguments and results support that the agent models fit better for testing the complex software systems. This allows the system to perform better than the existing non-agent systems in the face of high throughput. The interpretations offered here concentrate on necessary, rather than sufficient conditions, so that they can be extended.

References

1. Beizer, Boris (1990), *"Software Testing Techniques"*, Van Nostrand Reinhold,1990.
2. Brazier, F.M.T. and J. Treur (1994), *"User Centered Knowledge-Based System Design: A formal Modelling Approach"*, In: L. Steels, G. Schreiber and W. Van de Velde(eds.), *"A Future for Knowledge Acquisition"*, Proceedings of the 8th European Knowledge Acquisition Workshop, EKAW-94. Springer-Verlag, Lecture Notes in Artificial Intelligence 867, pp. 283-300.
3. Bret Pettichord (2001), "Seven Steps to Test Automation Success", Version of 26, June-2001, Presented at STAR West, San Jose, November-1999.
4. C. Castefranchi (1998), " Modeling Social Action for AI Agents", Artificial Intelligence, 103(1-2), 1998, pp. 157-182.
5. Charles Petrie.(2001), *"Agent-Oriented Software Engineering"*, Springer-Verlag 2001, Lecture Notes in Artificial Intelligence, pp.58 – 76.
6. Chung, Chi-Ming and Ming-Chi Lee (1992), *"Object-Oriented Programming Testing Methodology"*, published in Proceedings of the Fourth International Conference on Software Engineering and Knowledge Engineering, IEEE Computer Society Press, 15 -20 June 1992, pp. 378 - 385.
7. Dave Kelly (1999), "Software Test Automation and the Product Life Cycle", *Mactech Magazine*, vol. 13, Issue. 10, 1999.
8. P. Faratin, C. Sierra, and N.R. Jennings (1998), "Negotiation Decision Functions for Autonomous agents", Robotics and Autonomous Systems, 24(3-4), 1998, pp. 159-182.
9. M.A. Friedman, J. Voas (1995), "Software Assessment", John Wiley & Sons, New York, 1995.
10. C. Guilfoyle, E. Warner (1994), "Intelligent Agents: The revolution in Software", Ovum Report, 1994.
11. Hetzel, William C. (1998), The Complete Guide to Software Testing, 2nd ed. Publication info: Wellesley, Mass.: QED Information Sciences, 1998. ISBN:0894352423.
12. Hong Zhu, Patrick A.V. Hall and John H.R. May (1997), *"Software Unit Test Coverage and Adequacy"*, ACM Computing Surveys, Vol.29, No. 4, December-1997, pp. 367-427.
13. N. R. Jennings and M. Wooldridge (2000), *"Agent-Oriented software Engineering"*, in : J. Bradshaw (Ed). *Handbook of Agent Technology*, AAAI/MIT Press – 2000.
14. N. R. Jennings (2000), *"On Agent-based software Engineering"*, International Journal on Artificial Intelligence, Elsevier-2000, 117, pp. 277-296.
15. N.R. Jennings (1992), "Towards a Cooperation Knowledge Level for Collaborative Problem Solving", In: Proc. 10th European Conference on Artificial Intelligence, Vienna, Austria, 1992, pp.224-228.
16. N.R. Jennings (1993), "Commitments and Conventions: The Foundations of Coordination in Multi-Agent Systems", Knowledge Engineering Review, 8(3), 1993, pp.223-250.
17. N.R. Jennings (1995), "Controlling Cooperative Problem Solving in Industrial Multi-Agents Systems", Artificial Intelligence, 75(2), 1995, pp.195-240.
18. Joe W. Duran, Simeon C. Ntafos (1984), "An Evaluation of Random Testing", *IEEE Transactions on Software Engineering*, vol. SE-10, No. 4, July-1984, pp. 438-443.
19. Jones.B.F., Sthamer.H.H., and Eyres.D.E. (1996), "Automatic Structural Testing Using Genetic Algorithms", *Software Engineering Journal-11*, 5(1996), pp. 299-306.
20. B. Korel (1996), "Automated Test Data Generation for Programs with Procedures", *Proc. ISSTA ' 96*, pp. 209-215, 1996.
21. S. Krishnamurthy, Aditya P. Mathur, and Vernon J. Rego (1996), "White-box models for the estimation of software reliability", CS Annual Report – 19, April-1996, Bell Communications Research.
22. Langevelde, I.A. Van, A.W. Philipsenand J. Treur (1992), *"Formal Specification of Compositional Architechtures"*, in B. Neumann (ed.), Proceedings of the 10th European Conference on Artificial Intelligence, ECAI'92, John Willey & Sons, Chichester, pp. 272-276.

MurO: A Multi-representation Ontology
as a Foundation of Enterprise Information Systems

Rami Rifaieh, Ahmed Arara, and Aïcha Nabila Benharkat

LIRIS- INSA Lyon, 7Avenue J.Capelle
69100 Villeurbanne-France
{rami.rifaieh,ahmed.arara,nabila.benharkat}@insa-lyon.fr

Abstract. When we deal with different information systems in an enterprise, we unfortunately deal with problems of integrating and developing systems and databases in heterogeneous, distributed environments. In the last decade, the ontologies are used in order to make understandable the data, and to be a support for system's interoperability problems. As shared common vocabulary, the ontologies play a key role in resolving partially the semantic conflicts among systems. Since, different applications of the same domain have several representations of the same real world entities; our aim is to propose MurO: a Multi-representation ontology. The latter is an ontology characterizing the concepts by a variable set of properties (static and dynamic) or attributes in several contexts and in several scales of granularity. We introduce, in this paper, the multi-representation requirements for ontologies. We develop, as well, a formalism based on Modal Description Logics for coding MurO ontologies. Then, we show its use with the ongoing EISCO (Enterprise Information System Contextual ontology) project and its relevance for answering the motivating requirements.

Introduction

Establishing an adequate communication media among various user communities and different departments can always be possible through a shared common vocabulary [20]. Thus, an informal ontology for a specific domain of interest can be used for communication in the human level. A great advantage is that ontologies can be also expressed formally in machine processable language (e.g. OIL, DAML+OIL, RDF, OWL, etc). Most of the enterprises have fairly dynamic environment and consequently information entities and relationships (taxonomies) are apt to change. Ontologies, however, can provide a formalism (such as description logics) for the multi-representation based approach to deal with taxonomies, reasoning techniques and to cope with such dynamism. A real world entity is unique but it can have several representations [3] due to various interests, purposes, or perspectives. The multi-representation ontologies [1] are defined to take into an account the notion of context or point of view during the abstraction mechanism. The paper is organized as follows. In Section 2, we informally present the MurO-Ontology concept and its usefulness for Enterprise Information Systems. We, also, discuss the motivating requirements and give a motivating example. The section 3 presents formalism to describe MurO ontology, while section 4 shows the adaptation of modal description logics to multi-representation ontology. In the Section 5, we show the application of this paradigm to an ongoing EISCO (Enterprise Information System Contextual ontology) project and

G. Das and V.P. Gulati (Eds.): CIT 2004, LNCS 3356, pp. 292–301, 2004.

its relevance for answering the motivating enterprise needs. Finally in section 6, we conclude the paper by a set of suggestions as a future work.

EIS Motivation and Requirements

EIS development is not a *plug-and-play* task; it requires a considerable endeavor to analyze and to model complex enterprises activities. Typical tasks performed include system conceptualization, systems requirements analysis, system design, specification of software requirements, detail design, software integration, testing, etc. The main perspective of improving EIS is to provide a global enterprise view over EIS with data integration, interoperability and reusability services. The reality is that many systems have overlapping models, which makes reusability being not only limited to tools but also it includes conceptual reusable models, implementation packages, and physical resources (DB, CICS transaction, etc...). There is also a lack of transparency and cooperation between existing systems within the same enterprise [14]. Therefore, there is a need for a common knowledge base over all EIS's.

The MurO-Ontology Requirements

An ontology, defined as specification of conceptualization, looks very much like a conceptual model, as it has been used for many years in designing information systems. In fact, the two are closely related, but not identical. A conceptual model relates to a particular information system, whereas an ontology is a representation of a world external to any particular system, usually shared by a community of interoperating information systems. Therefore, an ontology is an object very much like a conceptual model, and can be developed using adaptations of conceptual modeling tools like Enhanced Entity-Relationship-Attribute or UML Class diagrams.

The multi-representation problem is commonly known in the discipline of information modeling. In this paper we investigate the multi-representation problem of ontologies where a concept is seen from different perspectives. For instance, if an ontology user is only interested in information about the same concept from different contexts or points of view, then there will be no possibility to retrieve such information based on mono-representation. Multiple representations over a common space can arise in different ways such as different properties and or different taxonomies. The notion of viewpoints has been used to support the actual development process of complex systems. In this respect, a viewpoint is defined as a locally managed object, which encapsulates partial knowledge about the system and its domain.

Therefore, we consider a Multi-representation ontology as a set of context-dependent ontologies (contextual ontologies), in the sense that a set of ontologies is put together without being integrated for the purpose of global representation. Hence, Contextual ontology is an ontology that is kept locally but inter-related with other ontologies through a mapping relation between concepts.

Motivating Example

Let's consider two Information Systems used in an enterprise, Data Warehouse System (DW) and Electronic Data Interchange System (EDI). The UML models defined

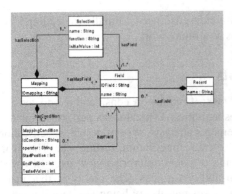

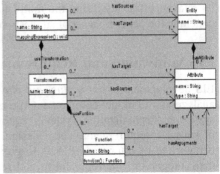

Fig. 1. A side of UML model for EDI Translator

Fig. 2. A side of UML model for DW, QETL

in *Fig.1* and *Fig.2,* gives a part of the mono-representation of each system. These systems contain concepts having the same identifier and the same meaning, such as *Mapping* in *EDI* and *Mapping* in *DW*, or different concepts but having the same structure and are semantically similar, such as *Field* in *EDI* and *Attribute* in *DW*. In this case, we can identify that the concepts *Mapping, Field,* etc. are multi-represented in these systems. In contrast to these similarities, it is difficult to provide a global querying or a knowledge sharing ability, which can help for interoperability and reusability between these systems.

The Multi-representation Ontology Approach

In the last thirty years, terminological knowledge representation systems (TKRS) have been commonly used to represent facts about an application domain [6]. Ontologies were expressed using formalism such as CG (Conceptual Graph) [17], frame logic [7], or KL-one based languages [19] (DL family), etc. Particularly, the use of DLs formalism permits to specify ontologies in machine understandable format and provides reasoning services [13]. Although DLs are very expressive and machine processable, there are still several research problems that encounter the use of DLs such as the multiple representations, dynamic information and the propagation of their changes. Such problems have direct impact on extending and exploiting further the existing families of DLs as well as the ontologies formalisms.

To multi-represented ontologies, an approach can be identified by combining the Description Logics (DL) and Modal Logics (ML). Thus, a contextual ontology can be expressed with modal logics where proposition is used to identify ontology's components and relations through Kripke's structure. In fact, this hybrid Modal DL approach takes the trump from the DL and ML. In our work, we chose to study this approach because it ties together the expressiveness of DL and the decidability over worlds of interest with modal logics.

In modal logic, the semantics of expressions or formula is defined in terms of the truth of things in different *worlds* or contexts. This contrasts with classical description logic, where things are just true or false, and not true in one context and false in another. Modal logics distinguish modes of truth. For the generalized modal logic, modes of truth are explained by referring to (abstract) worlds namely: truth in all (accessible) worlds, truth in this world, and truth in some (accessible) world.

Indexing or Stamping Mechanism

The first step, we should define a stamping mechanism that helps our approach to prefix or label the components of each ontology with operators and constructors. Informally speaking, it is a simple labeling technique where each concept C_i is known (identified) by the context S_i that it belongs to (e.g. $C_1{:}S_1$, $C_1{:}S_1 \sqcup C_2{:}S_2$, etc.). This is just a first step in the contextualizing ontology process. The similarity relationships between concepts are discussed hereafter.

Coordinating MurO-Ontology

We define in this section some bridge rules that rely a context to another using a cross mapping between a set of contextual ontologies. We can define many types of bridge rules r_{AB} such as:

- *The subsumption*: a concept A from IS_1 subsumes the concept B form IS_2 if every instance satisfying the description of B satisfies also the description of A. The extension of B is then included in A. We note that $B \subseteq A$.
- *The inclusion*: all the B instances of in IS_2 have a corresponding A instances in IS_1.
- *The identity:* a concept A from IS_1 is identical to the concept B form IS_2 if $B \subseteq A$ and $B \subseteq A$.
- *The overlapping*: a concept A from IS_1 overlaps with the concept B form IS_2 a part of the description of A and B are the same.
- *The disjunction*: when the descriptions are totally different.

Multi-representation Ontologies Formalism

As previously discussed, we use Modal Description Logics for formalizing MurO-Ontologies. Modal logic [9] is a propositional logic based language. It can be also be used as a set description language. It defines a set of worlds and the relations existing between these worlds. The minimal description language, $\mathcal{ALC}$, including full negation and disjunction, i.e. propositional calculus, is a notational variant of the propositional multi-modal logic $\mathcal{K}_{(m)}$.

Therefore, the description logic $\mathcal{ALC}$ corresponds exactly to the multi-modal logic *Km,* even though their origins are completely different. One can simply combine a description language with a suitable modal language. Thus, Modal DL is a language combining a DL language and modal logic operators. Informally, a concept corresponds to a propositional formula, and it is interpreted as the set of possible world over which the formula holds. The existential and universal quantifiers correspond to the possibility and necessity operators over different accessibility relations: $\sum C$ is interpreted as the set of all the possible worlds such that in every r-accessible world C holds; $\Diamond_r C$ is interpreted as the set of all the possible worlds such that in some r-accessible world C holds. The modal $\mathcal{ALCN}_{\mathcal{M}}$ (Modal $\mathcal{ALCN}$) language is used in this approach. Indeed, we need modal logics to enrich the semantics of our ontological models.

The Syntax and Semantics of $\mathcal{ALCN}_\mathcal{M}$

The syntax of MDL $\mathcal{ALCN}_\mathcal{M}$ consists of the classical $\mathcal{ALCN}$ constructs and the modal operators $\Box_r$ and $\Diamond_r$ known as necessity and possibility operators respectively.

The formal semantics of $\mathcal{ALCN}_\mathcal{M}$ language are interpreted by: (i) the conventional $\mathcal{ALC}$ interpretation (description logics) with Tarski's model where an interpretation is a pair $I = (\Delta^I, .^I)$, such that the set Δ^I is the interpretation domain and $.^I$ is the interpretation function that maps every concept to a subset of Δ^I and every role to a subset of $\Delta^I \times \Delta^I$. (ii) Kripke's structure stating what are the necessary relations between worlds and what are the formulas necessarily holding in some worlds. It defines where concepts are interpreted with respect to a set of worlds or contexts denoted by W. If $|W| = 1$ then our interpretation becomes the classical interpretation of Tarski-Model described in (i) above.

Having a set of contexts or worlds $W = \{w_1, ..., w_n\}$, our model of interpretation of concepts will require a kripke's structure $< W, \nabla_r, I(w)>$, where ∇_r denotes a set of accessibility binary relations between contexts and $I(w)$ is the interpretation over W.

Syntax		Semantics
$\Sigma_r C$	Necessity operator	$(\Sigma_i C)^{I(w)} = \{x \in (\Sigma C)^{I(w)} \text{ iif } \forall v \nabla w, x \in C^{I(w)}\}$
$\Diamond_r C$	Possibility operator	$(\Diamond_i C)^{I(w)} = \{x \in (\Diamond C)^{I(w)} \text{ iif } \exists v \nabla w, x \in C^{I(w)}\}$

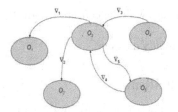

Fig. 3. Labeled oriented graph representing Kripke's structure

Fig. 4. Accessibility relations between contextual ontologies

A model of $\mathcal{ALCN}_\mathcal{M}$ based on a frame $F = <W, \nabla_0, \nabla_1, ...>$, is a pair $\mathcal{M} = <\mathcal{F}, I>$ in which I is a function association with each $w \in W$ a structure:

$I(w) = < \Delta^{I(w)}, R_0^{I(w)}, ..., C_0^{I(w)}, ..., a_0^{I(w)}, ...>$ where

$\Delta^{I(w)}$	an interpretation domain in the context $w \in W$
$R_i^{I(w)}$	set of roles that are interpreted in the context w
$C_i^{I(w)}$	set of concepts that are interpreted in the context w
$a_i^{I(w)}$	set of objects that are interpreted in the world w

Adaptation of MDL ($\mathcal{ALCN}_\mathcal{M}$) to Multi-representation Ontology

The following parameters are used as a design guide to describe the modal extension of the $\mathcal{ALCN}$ language and its adaptation for multi-representation ontology:

Set of worlds: A world is an ordinary model of the pure description language [18]. It consists of domains in which the concepts, roles names and objects names of the description component are interpreted. In our approach each world represents a contextual ontology.

Operators: The $\mathcal{ALCN}_M$ language offers operators which include $\mathcal{ALCN}$ general operators such as cardinality restriction, universal and *existential* quantification, etc. It includes also modal logics necessity operator and possibility operator respectively $\Box_i$ and $\Diamond_i$. Modal operators are applied in front of concepts to form complex ones (i.e. $\Diamond_i$ C). The number of modal operators corresponds to the number of accessibility relations identified between the worlds or ontologies. Modal operators can be applied to different kinds of well-formed expressions of the description language.

Structure: All the languages defined by contextual ontologies are interpreted with the help of the possible ontology semantics in which the accessibility relations between ontologies treat the modal operators. The set of accessibility relations defines the Kripke's structure which is in our approach a labeled directed graph see Figure.3. The accessibility relations define a set of bridges rules that enables to express the semantic similarity between world's components see Figure.4. These rules have been studied in the literature in [12] and with Schema mapping [16].

Arbitrary domain: When connecting worlds, that are ordinary models of the pure description logics language (contextual ontologies), by accessibility relations, we are facing the problem of connecting their objects. We have to distinguish between three types of domains those with constant, expanding, and varying domains. In a constant domain, we have $\Delta^{I(v)} = \Delta^{I(w)}$ for all v, w $\in$ W. In models with expanding domains $\Delta^{I(v)} \subseteq \Delta^{I(v)}$ whenever $v \; V_i \; w$ for some i. In our approach, the worlds are just arbitrary domain depending on bridge rules of the accessibility relations.

For example, we can consider a restriction for some ontology the increasing domain assumption with assumption bridge rules. Given two contexts s and t and the context t is accessible from context s. We apply the increasing domain assumption where we have $\Delta^{I(s)} \subseteq \Delta^{I(t)}$. In this case, accessible means that there are n ≥ 1 contexts $s_1, \ldots s_n$ such that $s=s_1$ and $t=s_n$ for all i ; $1 \leq i \leq$ n, there exists contextual modality such that $(s_i, s_{i+1}) \in \nabla k$. The advantage of this model is that the domain elements that have been introduced in s can also be referred to in all contexts that are accessible from s.

Finite domain: In our approach, modal description logic is used for defining multi-representation ontology which is a specification of conceptualization [17]. We deal with a finite domain. For example, the domain of employees in a company can certainly be assumed to be finite.

Rigid designators: In our approach we consider that we have rigid designators characteristic concerning objects; indeed, we talk about an object in all the worlds we will always refer to the same one. For example: when the knowledge base is talking about employees of a company, name *John Smith* should denote the same person no matter what world we consider.

In this paper, we are not concern to find out whether there exist algorithms for checking satisfiability for the proposed model $\mathcal{M}=<\mathcal{F},I>$. This issue and algorithm complexity in description logics with modal operators has been studied by [18] for several important classes of models including $\mathcal{ALC}$.

Revisited Examples

Let us consider the examples showed in Figure.1 and Figure.2. We assume that an ontological representation has been associated with each system according to the MurO-ontology requirements. Thus, we can define for each contextual ontology the relevant concepts used by the system. Let us label the concepts of EDI with e and concepts of DW by d to avoid any ambiguity and consider their ontologies O_e and O_d.

$e : Mapping$	$d : Mapping$
$e : Field$	$d : Attribute$
$e : Record$	$d : Entity$
The EDI ontology O_e	**The DW ontology O_d**

According to multi-representation ontology paradigm, these ontologies have been contextualized by defining an accessibility relation (∇i) including a set of bridges between their concepts. The relation $\nabla i = \{r_{i1}, r_{i2}, ...\}$ contains the bridge rule r_{ij} attesting that $e : Mapping \equiv d : Mapping$. Thus, the operator Σ_i applied to the concept $e{:}Mapping$ relies the objects of $e{:}Mapping$ in O_e by necessity through the accessibility relation ∇i for being identity ($\equiv$) of the concept $d{:}Mapping$ for O_d.

Related Work

In reviewing literature, we found works that deal with context, ontologies, and logics. In fact, a survey of context modeling is given in [4] that divide context approaches in: key-value models, markup scheme models, graphical models, object oriented models, logic based models, and ontology-based models. We are interested in showing ontology based models.

In [5], a framework and a concrete language C-OWL for contextualized local ontology was proposed. The definition of contextual ontology is *"to keep its contents local but they put in relation with contents of other ontologies via context mappings"* [2]. The new C-OWL language is augmented with relating (syntactically and semantically) concepts, roles, and individuals of different ontologies. The global interpretation is divided to the local interpretation and to the interpretation of the mapping rules. The local interpretation has two parts: Tarski's well-known interpretation and a hole interpretation of axiom that can be defined thought other context and which can be unsatisfiable in the first.

Another approach, the Aspect-Scale-Context information (ASC) model, has proposed ranges for the contextual information called scales [8]. The ASC model using ontologies provides an uniform way for specifying the model's core concepts as well as an arbitrary amount of sub-concepts and facts, altogether enabling contextual knowledge evaluated by ontology reasoner. This work build up the core of a non-monolithic Context Ontology Language (CoOL), which is supplemented by integration elements such as scheme extensions for web Services. All ontology based context models inherit the strengths in the field of normalization and formality from ontologies. The CONON context modeling approach in [10] is based on the same idea of ACS/CoOL approach namely to develop a context model based on ontologies because of its knowledge sharing, logic inferencing and knowledge reuse capabilities. In (CONON), an upper ontology captures general features of basic contextual entities and a collection of domain specific ontologies and their features in each sub-domain. The first order logic and description logics are used as reasoning mechanism to implement the CONON model, allowing consistency checking, and contextual reasoning. However, the ASC model and the CONON model inherently support quality meta-information and ambiguity [8]. Applicability to different existing models is limited to the type of formalism that adapts. The definition of contextual ontologies in C-OWL is identical to our perception of contextual ontologies, but the formalism suggested in this paper differs with the one suggested for C-OWL.

Towards Multi-representational Ontological Approach for EIS (EISCO Project)

The problem of multiple representations is becoming commonly known in e-commerce due to many factors such as the diversity of organizations, users, applications, abstraction mechanisms, etc. For instance, the same product needs to be marketed but each enterprise has its own representation, which varies in properties and possibly structures from other representations. This makes the development and design of ontology very difficult to accomplish. *EISCO* is a software engineering project, which is dedicated to describing a rich conceptual model based on ontologies. Hence, the ontology will be commonly used by several systems and applications within the enterprise. Sharing the same concept among several applications enforces the multiple-representation paradigm. Consequently, we need to represent each concept with different role, attributes, and instances. The *EISCO* project is actually in development. First, we aim at exploiting the formalism presented in section 3 to deal with the multi-representation problem in the context of EIS, and suggest the construction of shared ontological representation for all EIS by having in mind the two crucial issues: reusability and interoperability. Second, we work on a case study that includes scenario use and query processing to validate the proposed conceptual model and to explore its impact on re-usability and shareability of information in the enterprise [16], [15].

Our goal is first the ability of *EISCO* to provide global understanding over EIS, to support communication and global query answering by identifying relevant information sources, translating the user query into collections of sub-queries, and collating the answers. Second, *EISCO* aims at achieving information systems interoperability (intra-inter), communication between systems, and reusability.

In terms of implementation, the architecture uses ontological conceptualization of EIS in a J2EE platform and patterns as an implementation framework for reusability and interoperability. The notion bridge rules [11] are used to allow preserving the semantics locally and expressing inter-relation between concepts. The detailed description of the projects is beyond the scope of this paper.

Conclusion

In the scope of EIS with ontology development, several conceptualization and categorizations of concepts are most likely to occur, which have lead to the multiple representations problem. For this purpose, an approach of contextual ontology was proposed in this paper, where contexts are used as partitioning mechanism to the domain ontology. The contextual ontology approach is aiming at coordinating a set of context-dependent ontologies without constructing a global ontology. Thus, the problem of updating, cost, and the loss of information are avoided when bypassing the global ontology. The approach is based on well-founded theory of modal description logics to build semantically rich conceptual model that supports scalability, extensionality. Moreover, the proposed formalism of contextual ontology supports information accessibility, filtering, and reasoning services based on their contextual information. In the domain of EIS, the approach can be exploited to contribute to the existing problems of semantic interoperability, and re-usability related to multi-representations. The approach is actually applied to ongoing research project named EISCO, and a prototype based on EISCO architecture is being implemented.

References

1. A.Arara, D.Benslimane, "Multiperspectives Description of Large Domain Ontologies" In Christiansen et al. (Eds.), Proc. of FQAS'2004, June 2004, Lyon, France. Lecture Notes in Artificial Intelligence 3055 Springer 2004, pp.150-160.
2. M.Benaroch, "Specifying Local Ontologies in Support of Semantic Interoperability of Distributed Inter-organizational Applications, Lecture Notes in Computer Science, pp. (90-106), 2002.
3. D.Benslimane, A.Arara, "The multi-representation ontologies: a contextual description logics approach", in the proceeding of The 15th Conference On Advanced Information Systems Eng., Austria, 16 - 20 June, 2003, Springer-verlag.
4. T.Strang, Claudia Linnhoff-Popien, *A Context Modeling Survey*. Accepted for Workshop on Advanced Context Modelling, Reasoning and Management as part of UbiComp 2004 - The Sixth International Conference on Ubiquitous Computing, Nottingham/England, September 2004.
5. P.Bouquet, et al., " C-OWL: Contextualizing Ontologies", In Proceedings of the 2nd International Semantic Web Conference (ISWC2003), 20-23 October 2003, Sundial Resort, Sanibel Island, Florida, USA.
6. T. Catarci and M. Lenzerini. Representing and Using Interschema Knowledge in a Cooperative information Systems. International Journal of Intelligent and Cooperative Information Systems, 2(4):375-398, IEEE Computer Society Press, 1993.
7. A. Farquhar, R. Fikes, and J.P. Rice." The ontolingua server: A tool for collaborative ontology construction".Journal of Human-Computer Studies, 46:707-728, 1997.
8. Strang T., Service Interoperability in Ubiquitous Computing Environments. PhD thesis, Ludwig-Maximilians-University Munich, Oct 2003.
9. F. Giunchiglia, L. Serafini, "Multilanguage hierarchical logics, or: how we can do without modal logics", Artificial Intelligence, 65 (1994), p. 29-70
10. X Wang, et al. Ontology Based Context Modeling and Reasoning using OWL. In *Workshop Proceedings of the 2nd IEEE Conference on Pervasive Computing and Communications (PerCom2004)* (Orlando, FL, USA, March 2004), pp. 18–22.
11. Michael N. Huhns, Larry M. Stephens, "Semantic Bridging of Independent Enterprise Ontologies", ICEIMT 2002, pp. 83-90

12. P. Mitra, G.Wiederhold, and M. L. Kersten. A Graph-Oriented Model for Articulation of Ontology Interdependencies. In Intl. Conference on Extending Database Technology (EDBT), pp.86--100, 2000.

13. Hans Jurgen Ohlbach and Jana Koehler,Modal Logics, Description Logics and Arithmetic Reasoning, Journal of Artificial Intelligence, volume(109),   number (1-2), pages (1-31), 1999

14. R.Rifaieh, N.Benharkat, "A Mapping Expression Model used for a Meta-data Driven ETL tool", In proc of IEEE/ISSIPT 02, Marrakech, Morocco, 2002.

15. R.Rifaieh, N.Benharkat, "Query Based Data Warehousing Tool", in proc. of DOLAP 02, McLean, USA, 2002.

16. R.Rifaieh, N.Benharkat, "An Analysis of EDI Message Translation and Message Integration Problems", in proc. of ACS/IEEE conference, AICCSA'03, Tunisia, 2003.

17. T R Gruber. "Towards principles for the design of ontologies used for knowledge sharing". International Journal of Human-Computer Studies, 43, pp 907-928, 1995.

18. F. Wolter and M. Zakharyaschev. Satisfiability problem in description logics with modal operators. In Proceedings of the Conference on Principles of Knowledge Representation and Reasoning, pages 512–523. Moragan Kaufman, 1998.

19. W. A. Woods and J. G. Schmolze. The KL-ONE Family. *Computers Math. Applic.*, 23(2-5):133-177, 1992.

20. Uschold, M and Gruninger, M, "Ontologies: principles, methods and applications", The Knowledge Engineering Review, vol. 11, no. 2, June 1996.

A Tool to Automatically Detect Defects in C++ Programs

S. Sarala and S. Valli

Department of Computer Science and Engineering,
College of Engineering, Anna University, Chennai-25, India
saralas@cs.annauniv.edu, valli@annauniv.edu

Abstract. In this work a tool is developed to generate test cases automatically for C++ programs. This approach analyses the prototypes. When data type differs, the compiler raises a warning and implicitly converts and performs the operation. This may affect further computations in number crunching applications. So, the tool checks the data type of the actual parameters and formal parameters for a exact match. If a match doesn't occur, the tool reports this situation. This implementation is mainly focused to detect defects in the program. A defect results due to omission or mismanipulation. This work checks the correctness of the program when operator [] is overloaded. In the context of inheritance when virtual function is used, it has been observed that expected results are not achieved under certain circumstances. A test case has been developed to handle this situation and prepared to ascertain the working of template functions in the context of character input, to tackle dangling reference problem and to ascertain the working of the program, in the context of exception handling.

Keywords: Test case, Automatic Generation, Function overloading, Hybrid Inheritance, Friend Function, Virtual Function, Template Function, Dangling Reference

1 Introduction

1.1 Testing Object-Oriented Software

Software testing is an important software quality assurance activity. The objective of software testing is to uncover as many errors as possible with a minimum cost. A successful test should reveal the presence of bugs rather than proving the working of the program [5]. Object-oriented software testing has to tackle problems introduced by the features of object-oriented languages such as encapsulation, inheritance and polymorphism. The interaction between two or more objects is implicit in the code. This makes it difficult to understand object interactions and prepare test cases to test such interactions. Object-oriented testing is tedious and time consuming. Therefore, a tool support is important and necessary. This approach focuses on static testing in C++ programs. Automatic testing increases efficiency and reduces the cost of software development [3].

1.2 Developed Test Cases

This tool detects logical error in the context of runtime polymorphism. If the logical error goes unnoticed it results in execution error. The compiler issues only a warning when a function call is made without following the proper syntax. The tool checks for

G. Das and V.P. Gulati (Eds.): CIT 2004, LNCS 3356, pp. 302–314, 2004.

such a logical error. In case of inheritance, when the derived class doesn't invoke the parameterised constructor of the base class, the compiler assigns junk value to the base class members and proceeds. This is a logical error. The tool traps such defects too. Logical error occurrence is deducted by the tool when class templates and friend functions are used. The presence of logical errors results in execution error in the context of string handling. The tool has been developed to detect such defects. When writing relational conditions if assignment operator is used instead of equality operator the compiler works. Neither it reports execution error, which is also handled by the tool. Logical error in the context of hybrid inheritance is also detected by the tool. When operator [] is overloaded, the C++ compiler does not check for subscript bounds, which results in defects. The tool detects such flaws and reports to the user. When virtual function is overridden and they differ in signature the C++ compiler ignores this situation. The tool fixes this bug. In the context of template function call if the actual parameter is of type character and the value passed exceeds the length of one, the C++ compiler is not intelligent enough to trap this mistake. When the derived class object is assigned to base class object and a member function is accessed the result is not as expected under certain circumstances. The tool captures this defect caused by omission and reports the same. Dangling reference leads to execution error. The tool handles this defect. Test cases have been developed for defects encountered with exception handling.

1.3 An Overview

Section 2 discusses the existing work. Section 3 brings out the test case developed. Section 4 describes the developed algorithm to automatically generate test cases for C++ programs. Section 5 reports the working of the algorithm and the results achieved. Section 6 concludes the work.

2 Existing Work

Several literatures exist [1] [6] [8] [10-14] in the area of Object-Oriented testing. Marcio E.Delamaro et.al, [7] evaluate the feature of function overloading, operator overloading, class templates and inheritance. Y.G.Kim et.al [9] show how to generate test cases from UML state diagrams. G.Antoniol et.al [6] have uncovered operation and transfer errors in the implementation of UML state charts, with the help of mutation operators for object-oriented code. They have tackled constructors, accessors to class attributes, set operators, comparison operators, add/remove items to/from the set, item accessors and overloading of input/output stream operators. They have seeded 44 faults covering different mutation operators such as Argument Order Change (AOC), Control flow Disruption (CFD), Literal Change Operator (LCO), Language Operator Replacement (LOR), Method Parameter Order Change (POC), Scope Change Operator (SCO), Statement Swap Operator (SSO) and Variable Replacement Operator (VRO). Tse et.al [13] focus on classes with mutable objects, which is based on finite state machines. They analyse the class specifications. The test model selects a set of test data for each method of a class and the test cases are prepared by using algebraic specifications, model based specifications and finite-state machine based testing techniques. Amie L.Souter et.al [8] have tackled structural

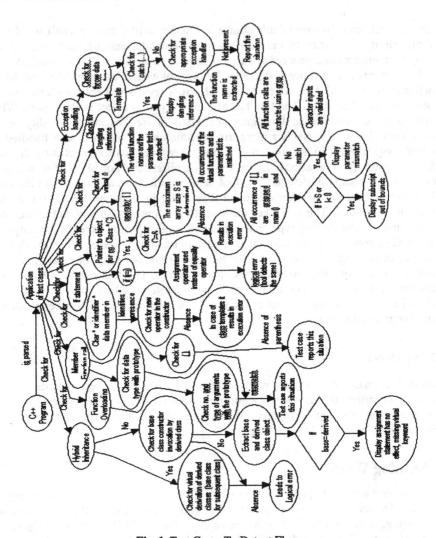

Fig. 1. Test Cases To Detect Flaws

testing of Object Oriented software with possible unknown clients and unknown information. The tool parses the source code and ensures that the member functions are working. The authors [1] discuss regression test selection technique, which is based on code based testing for C++ applications. The classes are represented by control flow graph from which test cases are selected, from an existing test suite for a new version. R.K.Doong et.al's [10] tools test Object-Oriented programs. The tool allows test case generation, test driver generation, test execution and test checking. They have exploited testing parameters and combinations of operations. Their tool automatically generates test drivers from class interface specifications. Another tool developed by the authors semiautomatically generate test cases from an algebraic specification of the class. M.J.Harrold et.al [11] tackle data flow testing for the entire class. The authors identify errors in classes, which may not have been uncovered by black box testing. John D.McGregor et.al [12] present a class testing technique that exploits the hierarchical nature of the inheritance relation to test related groups of classes. They reuse the testing information of the parent class to guide the testing of the sub-class. The authors test the base class by using both specification-based and program-based test cases. A subclass is then tested by incrementally updating the history of the parent class to reflect the differences from the parent. Only new or inherited, affected attributes and their interactions are tested.

3 Implementation

Figure 1 depicts the test cases developed for C++ programs. The number of argu-ments is counted for constructor, overloaded function and other functions. Test cases have been developed for the following Object Oriented Programming concepts, namely, Class templates, Function templates, Member functions, Inheritance, Func-tion overloading, Operator overloading, Exception handling, Runtime polymorphism, Friend function and Dangling reference. The tool is developed such that, it identifies the classes, the member functions and their signatures, default constructors, param-eterized constructors, the functions that are overloaded along with their signatures and the derived classes. The C++ program is parsed to apply the test cases. The tool checks for the presence of hybrid inheritance, as given by the first path in figure 1. If hybrid inheritance is existing, the tool checks whether the base class for subsequent class is virtually derived. If they are not virtually derived it leads to logical error. In step 2, the if part of the algorithm takes care of ensuring the hybrid inheritance is free from logical error. In the else part a test case ensures whether the derived object in-vokes the base class constructor. All the paths in fig.1 represent the other test cases given in the algorithm.

4 Algorithm

1. [Generation of test case for dynamic operator new]
   /* The lines containing '*' within class definition are extracted using grep */
   until (currentchar [i] != ' ')

      { temp[i] = currentchar [i]; i ++;   }

   if(temp=='char' or temp=='double' or temp=='int' or temp=='float' or temp==identi-fier)

      { The presence of new operator in the constructor is checked by executing grep.

        If new operator is not present it will lead to execution error. The test case reports 'missing new operator'. }

2. [Generation of test case for hybrid inheritance. Inheritance is identified by using ':'as pat-tern for grep]

   if (class name && next char==':')

      { The access specifier is skipped; The base class name is extracted as base1 Comma is skipped; The access specifier is skipped; The base class name is extracted as base2

      if (base2 != NULL)

      { In the derivation of base1 and base2 the virtual keyword is checked. If it is absent it leads to logical error. The test case reports 'missing virtual keyword' }

else
{ /* The presence of base class constructor is checked by executing grep with pattern
base1 and ( ). The output is given to wc –1 option */
If (wc –1 > 0)
then
{ /* The constructor of derived class is extracted by executing grep class name ( ) :
base is checked */
if (classname &&nextchar = ='(' &&(nextchar +1) = = ')' &&(nextchar +2) != ':') base
class constructor is not invoked. The tool reports this situation. }
[Check for object assignment in the context of inheritance]
The base and derived class objects are determined using the corresponding class name
and ; as pattern for the grep command. The base and derived object are determined as b
and d respectively.
b=d is grepped.
if (b=d) is present
display (assignment statement has no effect. Missing virtual keyword) } }
3. [Generation of test case for runtime polymorphism]
if (pointer to a class is found as in class *C)
The pattern C=& is grepped.
If it is not found, which leads to execution error and the tool displays 'address is not assigned'.
4. [Generation of test case for member functions]
/* membership operator is located */
Repeat until (currentchar [i]! = '('&& currentchar [i] != ';')
{ temp[i] = currentchar [i]; i + +;   }
if (currentchar [i] == '(')
{ The actual parameter and prototype are compared for data type match and reported as
'data type differs in function call' in case of mismatch. }
else
{ temp is checked for a possible member function call by executing grep. If a match occurs the tool reports the presence of logical error by displaying 'missing parenthesis in
function call'. }
5. [Generation of test cases for conditional operator]
if (currentchar[i]== 'i' && currentchar[i + 1]== 'f' && currentchar[i + 2]== '(')
i = i + 3;
while (currentchar[i] != '= ')   i++;
if (currentchar[i + 1]!= '=' && currentchar [i-1] != > or <)
It results in logical error. The tool reports by displaying 'usage of assignment operator instead of equality'.
6. [Generation of test case for function overloading and friend function call]
/* When the prototype is analysed friend function is identified using 'friend' as the keyword. It is stored in an array by name friend. The prototype of overloaded functions and
other member functions are stored in over and prototype array respectively. Friend function
call and overloaded function call is extracted using friend and over array respectively. */
Repeat until (currentchar [i] != '('&& currentchar [i] != ';')
{ temp[i] = currentchar [i]; i + +;   }
if (current char [i] =='(')
{The actual parameter and prototype are compared for data type match and the situation
is reported as 'data type differs in function call' in case of mismatch. }
else
{The tool reports the presence of logical error by displaying missing parenthesis in function call.}

7. [Generation of test case for operator[ ]]
   /* The lines containing operator [ ] ( ) are extracted using grep and the array size is determined as size. All calls are extracted with pattern as [ ] */
   if (subscript < 0 || subscript > size)   'subscript out of range' is displayed.
8. [Virtual function header is extracted by grepping virtual( ) as pattern]
   /* The function name and the parameter types are determined */
   All the corresponding function calls are validated for their signatures. The mismatch is displayed as 'parameter mismatch'.
9. [The actual parameters of template function are validated]
   /* The presence of template function is found using the pattern as 'template' */
   All template function calls are extracted.
   until (currentchar[i]! ='(')   i ++; i ++;
   until (currentchar[i]! =')')
   {if (currentchar[i] ==' ' ' && currentchar[i+2]!=' ' ')
       {'wrong character input in template function call' is displayed. break; }
   else
       {if(currentchar[i] = = 'a' thru 'z')
         {repeat until(currentchar[i] != ' ' || ')' || ',')
            {temp[j] = currentchar[i]; j++; i++;   }
   If type of temp is char the value is validated }   }   i++; }
10. [Test case to report dangling reference problem]
    grep class obj = obj1
    if it is found   delete obj1 is used as pattern for grep.
    If a match occurs   display 'dangling reference problem'
11. [Test case in the context of exception handling]
    Throw statements are located using grep with pattern   as throw
    until (currentchar[i]!= 'w')   i++;
    until(currentchar[i] == ' ')   i++;
    catch(...) presence is checked
    if present break;
      if(currentchar[i] == ' " ')
       {catch (char *) presence is checked
        if not present 'string exception not handled' is displayed }
       if (currentchar[i] = =' ' ')
       {catch char presence is checked
       if not present 'char exception not handled' is displayed }
       until(currentchar[i]!= '.')   i++;
       if(currentchar[i]== '.')
       {catch (float) presence is checked
       if not present 'float exception not handled' is displayed }
       if(currentchar[i] is int)
       {catch (int) presence is checked
      if not present 'int exception not handled' is displayed }
      default: 'no exception handler' is displayed

5   Working of the Algorithm

5.1   Detection of Subscript out of Bounds and Overridden Virtual Functions

When [ ] is overloaded in the context of array operations, the C++ compiler does not
validate the subscript for out of bounds in an assignment operation, which may lead to
execution error. In other circumstances junk value is returned. The test case is given

by step 7 of the algorithm. The code in Table 1 depicts a situation where an array subscript is out of bounds. There are three elements in the array. When the code displays the fourth element using overloaded operator [ ], only junk is displayed. Whereas if assignment is tried using an out of bound script, it results in execution error. So, these two instances are tackled by the test case meant for validating array subscript.

The developed test case locates the presence of overloaded operator [ ], by executing grep with the pattern as 'operator [ ] ( )'. Once it identifies that[ ] is overloaded, then identifies the maximum size of the array by grepping with pattern 'data type [ ]'. The maximum size is determined as 'size', afterwards extracts all occurrences of the call to overloaded operator[ ]. The subscript is checked with 'size' to see if it is within the bounds. If it exceeds or negative the test case displays 'subscript out of bound'. When the code in Table 1 was tested, the test case identified that 'cout << ob [4]' and 'ob [4]=44' are out of bounds. If the code in Table 1 is executed as such ob[4] will display junk and when an attempt to write into ob[4] is made it results in execution error. The developed test case detects this flaw, but would not trapped by the compiler. The next test case checks the consistency of overridden virtual functions. This test case works by extracting the virtual function by grepping with the pattern 'virtual ( )'. Then extracts the number and types of parameter(s) followed by extracting all versions of over ridden virtual function by grepping with the pattern 'function name ( )'. The test case extracts the type of parameter(s) and compares with the virtual function. If there is a deviation, it reports 'parameter mismatch'. When the code in Table 2 was subjected to the test case, which was able to detect the variation in data type of the overridden function 'vfunc' in the derived and derived2 class. On execution the code in Table 2 displays 'This is a base', which is not the intended result. The tool was successful in detecting this flaw. Step 8 of the algorithm handles this situation. The last step of the algorithm step 11 tackles the defects in the context of exception handling. The test case locates all throw statements by using 'throw' as pattern

Table 1. Array Subscript out of Bounds

```
class atype
{int a[3];
public:    atype(int i,int j,int k)
{ a[0]=i;a[1]=j;a[2]=k;  }
int &operator[] (int i)
{ return a[i]; }};
main()
{ atype ob(1,2,3);
cout << ob[4]; // junk value
ob[4] = 44; // results in execution error
return 0; }
```

Table 2. Overridden virtual function differing in parameter

```
class base
{ public:  virtual void vfunc()
{ cout << "This is a base.\n";  } };
class derived: public base
{ public:  void vfunc(int)
{ cout << "This is a derived.\n"; }};
class derived2: public base
{ public:  void vfunc(int)
{ cout << "This is a derived2.\n"; }};
main()
{ base *p,b;
derived d1; derived2 d2;
p = &b; p ->vfunc(); //base
p = &d1; p ->vfunc(); //base
p = &d2; p ->vfunc(); //base
return 0; }
```

for grep command, then greps all catch statements. It checks whether catch (...) is present by executing grep. If the catch block is not present the test case checks all the exceptions raised. Further, checks for string, float and int exceptions by looking for ' "', '.' (digit)+ respectively. Then it greps the corresponding exception handlers. If it is missing the test case displays 'exception not handled'. Other than this if there are exceptions 'no exception handler' as displayed.

When the code in Table 3 was subjected to the test case, the test case found the float exception using '.' as pattern. It looked for a float exception handler by executing grep 'catch (float)'. Since it is not present the test case displayed 'float exception not handled'. The test case identified an int exception and looked for an int handler by executing grep 'catch (int)'. Since it is present it found the next exception. The test case found a string exception when it encountered ' " '. It looked for the corresponding exception handler by looking for catch (char *). Since the handler is not present, the test case displayed 'string exception not handled'. Since, still a exception was captured by grep the default executed and reported 'exception not handled' for test () exception. When the code in Table 4 was tested, function fun was found as the template function. The parameter **a** was found to be of type char. The value was validated. Since it did not begin with, ' the test case displayed 'wrong character input function call' in template. Step 9, else part handles this situation. When the code in Table 5 was subjected to the test case, the base and derived class were detected as B and D respectively. Inheritance was identified by grepping with the pattern ':'. The base and derived objects were detected by grepping with base and derived class and ';' ; b and d were detected as base and derived objects. Then the pattern base object = derived object was grepped. Due to the presence of the pattern the test case displayed 'assignment statement has no effect. Missing virtual keyword'. Step2 of the algorithm tackles this situation.

Table 3. An Abnormal Exception Thrown

```
class test { };
class sample
{ public:
void fun1()
{ throw 99; }
void fun2( )
{ throw 3.14f ; }
void fun3( )
{ throw "error" ;    }
void fun4( )
{ throw test( ) ;  }  };
void main( )
{ try
{sample s ;
s.fun4( ) ;// execution error        }
catch ( int i )
{ cout << "strange" ; }  }
```

Table 4. Template function called with a wrong input instead of a character

```
void fun ( float a )
{ cout << "float "<< a ;  }
template <class T>
void fun ( T a )
{ cout << "all in one" << a << endl ; }
void main( )
{ char a = 10;  // prints nothing ;
fun ( a ) ;
float x = 25.09f ;  fun ( x ) ; }
```

5.2 Detection of Logical Error

When a function call is not indicated by the parenthesis, the C++ compiler does not issue any error message. It issues a warning during compilation. When such a statement is executed there is no response. The control doesn't get transferred to the function. The step 4 of the algorithm tackles this situation. In the definition of test2 method, method init is called. But the parenthesis is missing. This is given in Table 6. The tool identified the omission of parenthesis in the function call and signaled the situation. The tool compared the function name with the function prototype and found

Table 5. Code with statement which has no effect

```
class B
{ public: int i ;
B( ) { i=10; }
 void print()
{ cout << "in b"<<i; }} ;
class D : public B
{ public: int i;
D( ) { i=70; }
void print()
{ cout << "in d"<<i; }} ;
main( )
{ B b;  D d ;
 b =d; //virtual keyword missing for
 // print , no effect of b=d
 b.print();//10
 d.print();//70 }
```

Table 6. Function call with missing parenthesis

```
class CX
{ private: int x;
public: void init(int j)
{ x=j;  } };
class CY
{ public:
void test2(); };
void CY::test2()
{ CX x1;
 x1.init;// no function call takes place }
main()
{ CY y1;  y1.test2(); }
```

Table 7. Call to a friend function with missing parenthesis

```
Class a  {int a1;
public:    friend void s(a); };
s(a b) { cout << b.a1; }
void main()
{ a c; s;//omission of parenthesis in function
call}
```

Table 8. Derived Class Constructor not invoking Base Class Constructor

```
Class pet
{public:
pet() {}
pet(int i, int j)
{ food = j;
 weight = i; }
~pet() {}
protected:  int weight, food; };
class cat: public pet
{ public:
cat(): nToes('B'){}
~cat() {}
int getwt() {return weight; }
private:   int nToes; };
int main()
{ cat fluffy;
 //base class constructor is not called
cout<<fluffy.getwt();
//The compiler assigns junk values and
//gives result. It is a logical Error.}
```

that parenthesis was missing. The implementation uses grep command in UNIX to search all function calls. Once the lines containing function call is identified by executing (grep pattern file), the tool checks for parenthesis. The pattern is membership operator '.'. All function calls are validated in this aspect. When parameter type differs the compiler typecasts, issues warning and proceeds to compute. In number crunching operations this typecast may affect the result. So the tool also checks the function call with the prototype for a parameter match and indicates the mismatch if it exists to the user. The tool was subjected to a program containing a call to a friend function with missing parenthesis as in Table 7. The tool successfully detected the omission of parenthesis in the function call. Step 6 of the algorithm was able to detect the missing parenthesis in friend function call. When the code in Table 7 was executed, no function call took place and no output was produced. The tool detected this defect, which is a logical error.

Table 9. Presence of logical error in the If statement

```
int i,j;    i=8;   j=9;
if(i=j)
   cout << "here";
else
   cout << "there";
```

Table 10. Code depicting Hybrid Inheritance

```
class A
{ A() { cout << " A's constructor"; }
void print()
{ cout << "A"; } };
class B: virtual public A
{ B() { cout << "B's constructor"; }
void print()
{ cout <<"B"; } };
class C: virtual public A
{C() { cout << "C's constructor"; }
void print()
{ cout << "C"; } };
class D: virtual public B, public C
{ D() { cout << "D's constructor"; }
void print() { cout << "D"; } };
void main()
{ D obj;  obj.print();}
```

Table 11. Alternate way of Coding Hybrid Inheritance

```
class D: public B, public C
{ D() { cout << "D's constructor"; }
void print()
{ cout << "D";   } };
```

Table 12. Output for Code in Table 10 and 11

a's constructor ; b's constructor
c's constructor ; d's constructor ; D

Table 13. Code with logical error to represent hybrid inheritance

```
class B: public A   {};
class C: public A {};
class D: virtual public B, public C
{};
```

Table 14. Output produced by code in Table 13

A's constructor ; B's constructor
A's constructor ; C's constructor
D's constructor ;   D

Table 15. Omitted New operator in the constructor

```
class string
{char *str;  int len;
public: string(char *s)
{ len=strlen(s); // Omission of new //operator
for memory allocation
strcpy(str,s);    }  };
```

Table 16. Omitted New operator for String s2

```
Class test
{ char *s1, *s2;
public:    test()
{s1=new char[10]; }
void get()
{ strcpy(s1,"OOP");
   cout << s1; getch();
   strcat(s1,s2); or strcmp(s1,s2);}};
main()
{ test t;
   t.get(); }
```

Table 17. Omitted New operator in the context of templates

```
class vector
{ t* str;
public:    vector()
{ for(int i=0; i<5;i++)
 str[i]=0;  }};
void operator =(t s[])
{ for(int i=0;i<5;i++)
str[i]=s[i]; } }
main()
{ int a[5]={1,3,5,7,9};
  vector<int> v1; v1=a; }
```

Table 18. Omission of Address operator in the context of runtime polymorphism

```
class mycache
{ int table[7][24];
public: void buildtable(); };
void mycache::buildtable()
{ int i,j;
for(i=0; i<7;i++)
for(j=0; i<24;j++)
table[i][j]=0;  }
int main(void)
{ mycache *C;
C-> buildtable(); }
```

5.2.1 Detection of Logical Error when Base Class Constructor Is Not Invoked

When parameterised constructors are provided in base class, the derived class should also invoke the base class's parameterised constructor. In Table 8, the derived class constructor does not invoke base class parameterised constructor. So, when the derived object calls getwt(),its own method, it displays junk since weight is base class member. This is a logical mistake. The tool notes the number of constructors when recording the prototype. If the derived class constructor does not invoke the base class parameterised constructor the tool detects this situation and indicates the presence of logical error. The step 2 else part handles this situation. In the if statement of Table 9, a logical error is present. The output got is "here". The else part is skipped. Instead of equality operator for comparison, assignment operator is used. So, it is a logical error. The tool traps this error and reports the situation. Step 5 of the algorithm traps this situation. Once the line containing If is returned until '=' is encountered the algorithm skips the characters. If then compares the predecessor to see if it is > or < and the successor as '='. If such a match does not exist as in Table 9, the tool reports usage of 'assignment operator instead of equality'. When the hybrid inheritance in fig.2 is represented as in Table 10 and Table 11 the output is as given in Table 12 whereas, if the header is represented as in Table 13, the result is as in Table 14. It is a logical error. The tool detects such a situation and reports the same. Step 2 of the algorithm fixes this bug. When the code in Table 10 and 11 was subjected to the algorithm grep returned the lines representing inheritance. Since, class B and C has only a base class, base2 is NULL. For class D base1 is B and base2 is C. Since base2 is not NULL.

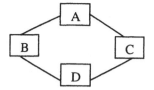

Fig. 2. Hybrid Inheritance

Class

base1: virtual and class base2: virtual is subjected to grep command as pattern. Since it is present the tool ensures that there is no logical error. When the code in Table 13 was subjected to the algorithm for class D base1 and base2 was found as B and C respectively.

Class

base1: virtual and class base2: virtual were given as pattern for grep command. It returned 0 line since the pattern was not found. So, the tool displayed 'missing virtual keyword'.

5.3 Detection of Execution Error

When strings are handled in C++ programs, under certain circumstances, execution error is encountered. If the string is of type char*, then memory should be dynamically allocated. If memory is not allocated as in Table 15, there is no means for the compiler to trap this situation. So, such programs on execution results in execution error. The tool detects such a situation. Whenever * is encountered in class, the tool checks for the new operator in the constructor. If the statement is missing the tool reports this situation. Step 1 of the algorithm handles this situation. The memory allocation operator new is omitted in the code in Table 15. The code successfully compiles. If executed it results in execution error. The tool traps this flaw. When get () in Table 16 executes, since s2 is not allotted memory and is undefined it results in execution error which is too caught by the tool. If the code in Table 17 is executed, it results in execution error. The tool detects the absence of new operator in the constructor and reports the situation. Step1 of the algorithm fixes this bug. The line t *str is returned by grep. Until ' ' is encountered the characters are stored in currentchar. In this case t is stored; t is an identifier. The presence of new operator is checked in the constructor. Since, it is not present the tool displays 'missing new operator'. In Table 18, Object C is a pointer to the class mycache. This code results in execution error, which is noted by the compiler. Step 3 of the algorithm traps this bug. Since C is a pointer to the class 'C=&' is grepped and since it is not present, the tool reports the bug 'address is not assigned'.

6   Conclusion

Automated tools can help to detect the incorrect algorithms, inferior design, efficiency issue, and coding standards. C++ programs were tested for defects. Since a class is an abstraction of the commonalities among its instances, the tool ensures that representative samples of members are tested. The ultimate aim of this tool is to reduce the defect rate for users of the class. In this work, the tool has been developed to automatically generate test cases. The tool depicts the deviation if any in the actual and formal parameter. The tool finds out the undetected bug in the context of strings and templates when new operator is missing. The tool ascertains the relational expression when equality operator is used. The tool ensures the accurate working of [ ] when overloaded. In the context of template functions the tool validates character input. The tool also checks for dangling reference problem and ascertains the working of exceptions. The tool finds out flaws not trapped by the compiler in the context of hybrid inheritance and also when derived class fails to invoke base class constructor. The tool also finds bugs in the context of runtime polymorphism, which goes unnoticed by the compiler. The tool validates all function calls pertaining to member functions, friend function, virtual function and overloaded function. The tool reports bugs not noted by the compiler and which in turn leads to logical or execution error.

References

1. G.Rothermel, M.J.Harrold and J.Dedhia, "Regression Test Selection for C++ Software", *Journal of Software Testing and Reliability*, Vol.10 (2000) 1-35
2. B.Beizer, *software-testing techniques*, Van Nostrand Reinhold, New York (1990)
3. Houman Younessi, " *Object -Oriented Defect Management of Software*", Prentice Hall, USA (2002)
4. Kit Edward, "*Software Testing in the Real World*", Addison-Wesley (1995)
5. Myers, Glenford J, "The Art of Software Testing", John-Wiley & Sons (1979)
6. G.Antoniol, L.C.Briand, M.D Penta and Y.Labiche, "A case study using the round trip strategy for state based class testing", *Technical Report*, Research Centre on Software Technology (2002) 1-10
7. Marcio E.Delamaro, Jose C.Maldonado and Aditya P.Mathur,"Interface Mutation: An Approach for Integration Testing",*IEEE Transactions on Software Engineering*, Vol-27 (2001) 228-248
8. Amie L.Souter, LL.Pollock, "A Strategy for Testing Object Oriented Software", *ACM International Symposium on Software Testing and Analysis*, Portland (2000) 49-59
9. Y.G.Kim, H.S.Hong, D.H.Bae and S.D.Cha, "Test Case Generation from UML State Diagrams", *IEE Proceedings on Software*, vol.4 (1999)
10. R.K.Doong and P.G.Frankl, "The ASTOOT approach to testing object oriented programs", *ACM Transactions on Software Engineering and Methodology*, Vol-3, (1994) 101-130
11. M.J.Harrold, and G.Rothermel, "Performing data flow testing on classes", *ACM Software Engineering Notes*, Vol-19 (1994) 154-163
12. John. D.McGregor, M.J.Harrold and K.J.Fitzpatrick, "Incremental Testing of Object Oriented class structures", *14th IEEE International Conference on Software Engineering, IEEE Computer Society*, Los Alamitos, California (1992) 68-80
13. T.H.Tse and Zhinong Xu, "Test Case Generation For Class Level Object-Oriented Testing", *Quality Process Convergence: Proceedings of 9th International software Quality Week*, California (1996) 1-12
14. B.Korel, "Automated test data generation for Programs with Procedures", *ACM International Symposium on Software Testing and Analysis*, USA(1996) 209-215

Implementation of Embedded Cores-Based Digital Devices in JBits Java Simulation Environment

Mansour H. Assaf[1], Rami S. Abielmona[1], Payam Abolghasem[1], Sunil R. Das[1,2], Emil M. Petriu[1], Voicu Groza[1], and Mehmet Sahinoglu[2]

[1] School of Information Technology and Engineering, Faculty of Engineering
University of Ottawa, Ottawa, Ontario K1N 6N5, Canada
[2] Department of Computer and Information Science
Troy State University Montgomery, Montgomery, AL 36103, USA

Abstract. This paper proposes test design architecture suitable for built-in self-testing (BIST) of embedded cores-based digital circuits by using a reconfigurable device. In the paper, a sample circuit under test (CUT) and its corresponding space compressor were realized in Java language, downloaded, and then tested at runtime in a simulation environment written in JBits.

1 Introduction

The increasing complexity and levels of integration densities in digital systems design have resulted in the need for more effective means of testing of digital systems. Today's many sophisticated systems require better and more effective methods of testing to ensure reliable operations of chips. The recent evolution from a chip-set philosophy to an embedded cores-based system-on-a-chip (SOC) in ASIC and FPGA digital design further ushered in a new dimension in the realm of digital circuit testing. Though the concept of testing has a broad applicability, finding highly efficient testing techniques that ensure correct system performance has thus assumed significant importance [1] – [15].

The conventional testing technique of digital circuits requires application of test patterns generated by a test pattern generator (TPG) to the circuit under test (CUT) and comparing the responses with known correct responses. However, for large circuits, because of higher storage requirements for the fault-free responses, the test procedure becomes rather expensive and thus alternative approaches are sought to minimize the amount of required storage. Built-in self-testing (BIST) is a design approach that provides the capability of solving many of the problems otherwise encountered in testing digital systems. It combines concepts of both built-in test (BIT) and self-test (ST) in one, termed built-in self-test (BIST). In BIST, test generation, test application, and response verification are all accomplished through built-in hardware, which allows different parts of a chip to be tested in parallel, reducing the required testing time besides eliminating the need for external test equipment. A typical BIST environment uses a TPG that sends its outputs to a circuit under test (CUT), and output streams from the CUT are fed into a test data analyzer. A fault is detected if the circuit response is different from that of the fault-free circuit. The test data analyzer is comprised of a response compaction unit (RCU), storage for the fault-free response of the CUT and a comparator.

G. Das and V.P. Gulati (Eds.): CIT 2004, LNCS 3356, pp. 315–325, 2004.

In order to reduce the amount of data represented by the fault-free and faulty CUT responses, data compression is used to create signatures from the CUT and its corresponding fault-free module. BIST techniques use pseudorandom, pseudoexhaustive, and exhaustive test patterns, or even on-chip storing of reduced test sets. The RCU can be divided into: a space compression unit and a time compression unit. In general, s responses coming out of a CUT are first fed into a space compressor, providing t output streams such that t << s. Most often, test responses are compressed into only one sequence (t = 1). Space compression brings a solution to the problem of achieving high quality built-in self-testing of complex circuits without the necessity of monitoring a large number of internal test points, thereby reducing both testing time and area overhead by merging test sequences coming from these internal test points into a single bit stream. This single bit stream of length r is next fed into a time compressor, and eventually a shorter sequence of length q, q < r, is obtained at the output.

The extra logic representing the compression circuit must be as simple as possible, to be easily embedded within the CUT, and should not introduce signal delays to affect either the test execution time or the normal functionality of the CUT. Besides, the length of the signature must be as short as possible in order to minimize the amount of memory required to store the fault-free responses.

In the subject paper, we present a JBits (JBits 2.8 by Xilinx Corporation [17]) implementation of a design test architecture and verification environment suitable for built-in self-testing (BIST) of embedded cores-based digital devices.

2 JBits Software Development Kit

JBits SDK is a development framework for Xilinx FPGAs based on the Java language. The JBits Application Programming Interface (API) provides low-level access to the configuration of resources in a Xilinx FPGA [16], [17]. Xilinx FPGAs are SRAM-based and have the ability to be configured numerous times. JBits provides a solution to support run-time reconfiguration (RTR).

RTR systems define the circuit's logic and routing just prior to, or during operation. They typically modify the circuit several times during execution of the application.

JBits provides the ability to rapidly create and modify Xilinx Virtex and XC4000 FPGA circuitry at run time by allowing direct access into the configuration bitstream.

A typical JBits program creates logic in a new bitstream, modifies the logic, and interconnects it in an existing bitstream, or performs an analysis of a bitstream.

The Xilinx Hardware Interface (XHWIF) is an API that provides a universal interface for communicating with different FPGA-based boards. The Virtex Device Simulator (Virtex DS) works on bitstreams to emulate the FPGA device in software.

The JBits API is an ideal design environment for implementing logic circuits on mainstream FPGAs, especially when the hardware is not present or a proof-of-concept is initially required.

3 Testing Architecture Environment

This section outlines the actual design and realization of the test architecture environment by hardware devices, such as FPGAs, development boards, and hardware-emulating APIs (e.g. JBits). Figure 1 introduces the system level architecture of the digital test environment for realization in hardware.

The digital testing scheme involves introducing stuck-at-0 and stuck-at-1 single faults within the CUT, and recording the corresponding outputs. The recorded outputs are then compared to predefined fault-free signatures, in order to determine if the injected faults can be detected or not.

In the following, we now briefly introduce each of our system level components.

3.1 Random Test Pattern Generator (TPG)

This system component generates pseudorandom input test patterns. The pattern generator generates sixteen bits random binary numbers. As our used CUT had three inputs, only the three least significant bits of the random numbers were selected. By implementing a 16-bit random pattern generator (Figs. 2, 3, and 4) while keeping only three bits, attempts were made to obtain a better approximation of randomly generated test patterns.

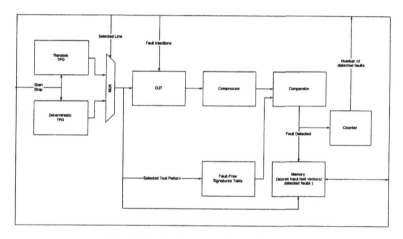

Fig. 1. The hardware testing architecture

3.2 Deterministic Test Pattern Generator (TPG)

This component generates predetermined stored test-input patterns in order.

3.3 Multiplexer

This component controls which of the TPGs (random or deterministic) is to be used to feed the input patterns to the CUT. The input select signal of the multiplexer was controlled by the user according to the desired type of generating input test patterns. The circuit diagram is shown in Fig. 5.

3.4 Compressor (Compactor)

The main functionality of this component is to reduce the number of CUT outputs, without affecting the fault detection capabilities of the CUT.

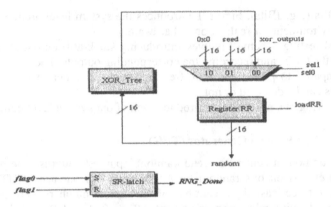

Fig. 2. A 16-bit random generator architecture

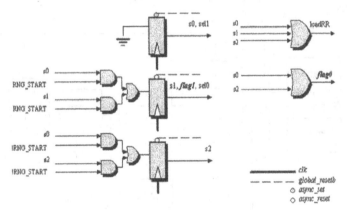

Fig. 3. Internal structure of the random generator

3.5 Fault-Free Signatures Table

This component stores the predetermined fault-free output sequences in a table.

3.6 Comparator

This component is used to compare the fault-free signature values with the actual CUT outputs. If a mismatch occurs, then the test pattern that caused that mismatch is stored in memory, along with the information of the wire where the fault injection occurred and the actual fault value (0 or 1).

3.7 Memory

This component stores the fault test patterns, fault injection locations, and fault values. It can be interrogated from outside the system by an external controller for future analysis.

3.8 Counter

This component is used to count how many faults have been detected in the system. The Counter circuit was a 5-bit full counter (Fig. 6) counting the values 00000-11111. It is needed for counting the maximum possible number of detected faults in the system. In configuration, the output of comparator was routed to the clock-enable pin of the Counter; hence, whenever a fault was detected, this pin was enabled and the number of faults could be increased by one.

3.9 Start/Stop

This input signal is used to start or stop the appropriate TPG.

3.10 Select Line

This input signal is used to select which TPG feeds the input patterns to the CUT. If this line is at a 0, then the random TPG is used, while if it is at a 1, the deterministic TPG is used.

3.11 Fault Injections

This set of input lines is used to inject faults into specific wires of the CUT and of specific values. The hardware fault injection technique is imperative in order to iteratively inject faults to every wire, and to test for both the stuck-at-0 and stuck-at-1 single line faults. For that matter, a plan was devised that is based on Fig. 7.

As we can see in the figure, every wire now has a multiplexer introduced within it, which allows us to either run the wire as such, or inject stuck-at-0 or stuck-at-1 faults.

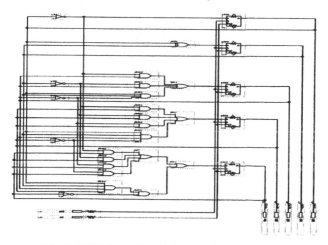

Fig. 4. XOR-three of the 16-bit random generator

If the values of the select signals of any multiplexer are at "00", then we will run the wire as such, while if the values are at "01", then we will inject a stuck-at-1 fault indicated by the logical 1 value coming into the multiplexer, and if the values are at

"10", then we will inject a stuck- at-0 fault indicated by the logical 0 value coming into the multiplexer. Finally, if the values are at "11", then we will again assume normal operation of the wire.

3.12 Selected Test Pattern

This intermediary signal is used to access the fault-free signature value stored in the table, and is itself stored in memory if it causes a detected fault condition.

3.13 Fault Detected

This intermediary signal notifies the memory controllers to store the selected test pattern, fault injection location, and value, and advises the counter to increment the number of detected faults.

3.14 Number of Detected Faults

This set of output signals designates how many faults have been detected.

4 JBits Implementation Notes

In developing our digital devices testing environment, we endeavored to define separate Java classes for each digital block. This enabled us to decrease the interdependency among different components by increasing the modularity of the final application. As the JBits implementation of a system of the size considered was considerably complex, and contained many details, increasing the modularity of the final application code not only made the development process easier in the form of debugging each component individually, but was also believed to provide a more robust way of improving the JBits implementation of each component like changing codes, adding or replacing a component, etc. Table 1 gives descriptions of those classes which have each a corresponding digital block in Fig.1.

In Table 1, the two Java classes **DigitalVerification** and **Controller** do not have explicitly matched digital blocks in Fig. 1. The Controller class was defined to contain circuitry for controlling the sequential components of various blocks such as random test pattern generator, deterministic test pattern generator, and counter. The Digital-Verification class plays the role of the host of all other blocks. It can be viewed as the circuit board that keeps and connects other blocks together. While routing the sequential and combinational parts in each block was performed inside corresponding classes, the routing among different blocks was performed in DigitalVerification class. The starting coordinates of each block inside the selected Xilinx FPGA were also addressed in this class.

5 Experimental Results

The circuit diagram of the CUT (a full-adder) without compressor is shown in Fig. 8. The "fim" blocks in this diagram indicate the locations of the fault-inject multiplexers for injecting stuck-at-0 or stuck-at-1 faults to mutually exclusive wires of the circuit.

The input test patterns were provided by the random and deterministic test pattern generators, while the CUT outputs were compressed by a space compaction circuit as shown in Fig. 9 (or they were routed directly to the comparator). The two select signals of the fault-inject multiplexers were routed to I/O pins of the board and were controlled externally. The testing of the full-adder circuit (CUT) with the proposed arrangement of the fault-inject multiplexers provided a total of 16 possible detectable single faults. Some partial results on experimentation obtained with deterministic and pseudorandom TPGs are given next.

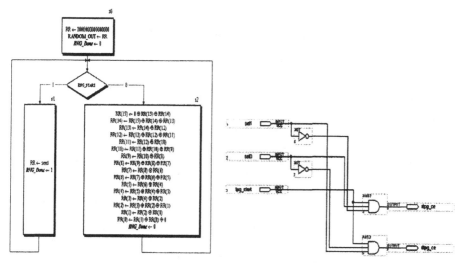

Fig. 5. Circuit diagram of TPG control component

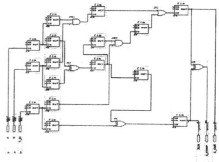

Fig. 6. Circuit diagram of the counter

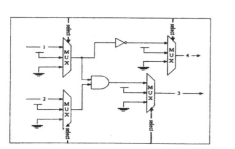

Fig. 7. The fault injection scheme in hardware

Fig. 8. CUT diagram without compressor

Fig. 9. Compressor circuit for the CUT

Table 1. Class names with their short descriptions

Class Names	Descriptions
Comparator	Implements the Comparator Circuit, which compares the output of the CUT with fault-free signatures. The comparator may change for different CUTs and compressors.
Controller	Implements a Controller Circuit, which controls the sequential blocks in the circuit such as counter and memory circuits generators.
ControlTPG	Implements a small Controlling Circuit to control test pattern generators. As an improvement, this class can be merged with Controller class.
Counter	Implements a 5-bit Full Counter to count the number of detected faults.
CUT	Implements the Circuit Under Test (CUT) block.
CUTInputMux	Implements the Multiplexer Circuit.
DeterministicTPG	Implements the Deterministic Test Pattern Generator. According to the CUT name and compressor type, the configuration of JBits object can change appropriately.
DigitalVerification	Implements a Host Class, which contains an object of all other classes to define the complete circuit. The routings between the different blocks are done in this class.
FaultCausingTPMemory	Implements the Fault Causing Injections and Fault Causing Test Patterns Memory blocks.
FaultInjectMux	Implements the Fault Inject MUX (Multiplexer), which is used to inject stuck-at-0 and stuck-at-1 faults to the CUT wires.
RandomTPG	Implements the RandomTPG (Test Pattern Generator) block.
TheoreticalResultsTable	Implements the Fault-Free Signature Table block. The implementation of this class will change according to the CUT and compressor type.

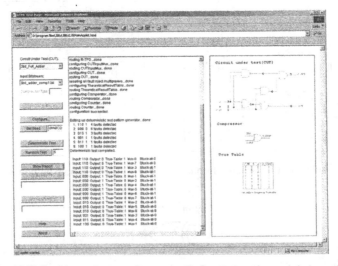

Fig. 10. Full-adder and compressor – detailed report on deterministic testing

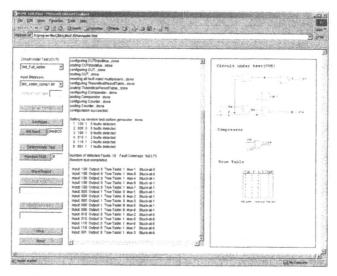

Fig. 11. Full-adder and compressor – detailed report on pseudorandom testing

5.1 Deterministic Compacted Test-Input Patterns (CUT)

Setting up Deterministic Test Pattern Generator...Done
> 1: 010 10   8 faults detected
> 2: 101 01   6 faults detected
> 3: 100 10   1 faults detected
> 4: 111 11   1 faults detected
> 5: 001 10   0 faults detected

Deterministic Test Completed
> Number of detected faults: 16
> Fault coverage: 100%

Deterministic Test Report
> Input: 010 Output: 00 True-Table: 10 Mux-2 Stuck-at-0
> Input: 010 Output: 00 True-Table: 10 Mux-5 Stuck-at-0
> Input: 010 Output: 00 True-Table: 10 Mux-8 Stuck-at-0
> Input: 010 Output: 01 True-Table: 10 Mux-1 Stuck-at-1
> Input: 010 Output: 01 True-Table: 10 Mux-3 Stuck-at-1
> Input: 010 Output: 11 True-Table: 10 Mux-4 Stuck-at-1
> Input: 010 Output: 11 True-Table: 10 Mux-6 Stuck-at-1
> Input: 010 Output: 11 True-Table: 10 Mux-7 Stuck-at-1
> Input: 101 Output: 10 True-Table: 01 Mux-1 Stuck-at-0
> Input: 101 Output: 10 True-Table: 01 Mux-3 Stuck-at-0
> Input: 101 Output: 00 True-Table: 01 Mux-6 Stuck-at-0
> Input: 101 Output: 00 True-Table: 01 Mux-7 Stuck-at-0
> Input: 101 Output: 11 True-Table: 01 Mux-2 Stuck-at-1
> Input: 101 Output: 11 True-Table: 01 Mux-8 Stuck-at-1
> Input: 100 Output: 01 True-Table: 10 Mux-5 Stuck-at-1
> Input: 111 Output: 10 True-Table: 11 Mux-4 Stuck-at-0

For portability purposes, a Java applet version of the simulator was developed. Figures 10 and 11 show, respectively, snapshots of simulation runs on full-adder (and COMPRESSOR), with detailed results for both the deterministic and pseudorandom test modes. Further results with Java applet versions of simulators could not be provided due to lack of space.

6 Conclusions

As it was shown, 16 single stuck-at logic faults were detected on the JBits implementation using the CUT in both the deterministic and pseudorandom testing modes. However, using the CUT and COMPRESSOR, though 16 stuck-at faults were detected in deterministic testing, only 15 such faults were detected in the pseudorandom testing mode.

There are many ways to ensure that the design is functioning correctly in hardware, but one of the most efficient and reliable methods is the design for testability (DFT) based on BIST approach. The current research basically extends that philosophy to realize digital circuit testing and verification in different environments while running on hardware.

References

1. Das, S. R., Ramamoorthy, C. V., Assaf, M. H., Petriu, E. M., Jone, W.-B.: Fault Tolerance in Systems Design in VLSI Using Data Compression Under Constraints of Failure Probabilities. IEEE Trans. Instrum. Meas. 50 (2001) 1725-1747
2. Bardell, P. H., McAnney, W. H., Savir, J.: Built-In Test for VLSI: Pseudorandom Techniques. Wiley Interscience, New York (1987)
3. Jone, W.-B., Das, S. R.: Space Compression Method for Built-In Self-Testing of VLSI Circuits. Int. J. Comput. Aided VLSI Des. 3 (1991) 309-322
4. Karpovsky, M., Nagvajara, P.: Optimal Robust Compression of Test Responses. IEEE Trans. Comput. C-39 (1990) 138-141
5. Lee, H. K., Ha, D. S.: On the Generation of Test Patterns for Combinational Circuits. Tech. Rep. 12-93, Dept. Elec. Eng., Virginia Polytec. Inst. and State Univ., Blacksburg, VA (1993)
6. Li, Y. K., Robinson, J. P.: Space Compression Method with Output Data Modification, IEEE Trans. Comput. Aided Des. 6 (1987) 290-294
7. McCluskey, E. J.: Built-In Self-Test Techniques. IEEE Des. Test Comput. 2 (1985) 21-28
8. Pomeranz, I., Reddy, L. N., Reddy, S. M.: COMPACTEST: A Method to Generate Compact Test Sets for Combinational Circuits. Proc. Int. Test Conf. (1991) 194-203
9. Pradhan, D. K., Gupta, S. K.: A New Framework for Designing and Analyzing BIST Techniques and Zero Aliasing Compression. IEEE Trans. Comput. C-40 (1991) 743-763
10. Reddy, S. M., Saluja, K., Karpovsky, M. G.: Data Compression Technique for Test Responses. IEEE Trans. Comput. C-37 (1988) 1151-1156
11. Saluja, K. K., Karpovsky, M.: Testing Computer Hardware Through Compression in Space and Time. Proc. Int. Test Conf. (1983) 83-88
12. Savir, J.: Reducing the MISR Size. IEEE Trans. Comput. C-45 (1996) 930-938
13. Chakrabarty, K.: Test Response Compaction for Built-In Self-Testing. Ph.D. Dissertation, Dept. Comp. Sc. Eng., Univ. Michigan, Ann Arbor, MI (1995)

14. Pouya, B. and Touba, N. A.: Synthesis of Zero-Aliasing Elementary-Tree Space Compactors. Proc. VLSI Test Symp. (1998) 70-77
15. Rajsuman, R.: System-on-a-Chip: Design and Test. Artech House, Boston, MA (2000)
16. JBits SDK: http://www.xilinx.com/products/jbits/
17. Xilinx, Inc.: The Programmable Logic Data Book (1999)

This research was supported in part by the Natural Sciences and Engineering Research Council of Canada under Grant A 4750.

Automatic Model Generation in Model Management*

Artur Boronat, Isidro Ramos, and José Á. Carsí

Department of Information Systems and Computation, Polytechnic University of Valencia,
C/Camí de Vera s/n, 46022 Valencia, Spain
{aboronat,iramos,pcarsi}@dsic.upv.es

Abstract. Model management aims at solving problems that stem from model representation and its manipulation by considering models as first-class citizens that are manipulated by means of generic operators. MOMENT is a prototype that supports generic model management using an algebraic approach within the four-layered metamodeling culture of MOF [1]. In this paper, we focus on the automatic generation of schemas that belong to different metamodels, using a term-rewriting system approach. We present the type system of the algebra that we use to represent models in the MOMENT prototype, and we describe our generic operator that automatically translates schemas between different metamodels: the operator *generate*. This algebra has been implemented using the functional language F#, which allows us to validate the correctness of our approach.

Keywords: information modeling, reverse engineering, model management, algebraic morphisms, schema generation.

1 Introduction

Nowadays, many companies are working with software products that were developed several years ago. Such applications have undergone changes to adapt to new requirements, but the lack of a specification makes this task more and more difficult. Software reverse engineering is the process that analyzes an application in an attempt to create a representation of it at a higher level of abstraction than the source code [2]. Therefore, reverse engineering is a process of design recovery. There are several CASE tools that support reverse engineering, such as Rational Rose [3], System Architect [4] or DB-Main [5]. These tools provide wizards that build a design specification of the data structure from a relational database or even wizards that detect and to organize functional services in class diagrams from the source code of the application.

Although these tools support automatic reverse engineering onto specific design methods, such as relational or object-oriented (OO for short), they do not take into account a change in the use of design methods. For instance, an application could have been developed in the early 90s following the structured paradigm and the relational model for the database. Now, the application of a reverse engineering mechanism to obtain the relational schema of the database might not be the best solution to obtain an abstract description of the application. The development company will likely use a newer paradigm to design the software. In such a case, the research field

---

* This work was supported by the Spanish Government under the National Program for Research, Development and Innovation, DYNAMICA Project TIC 2003-07804-C05-01.

G. Das and V.P. Gulati (Eds.): CIT 2004, LNCS 3356, pp. 326–335, 2004.

of model management provides advantages to improve the reverse engineering process by manipulating data models.

A model is an abstract representation of the reality that enables communication among heterogeneous stakeholders so that they can understand each other. In our approach, a model is a structure that abstracts a design artifact such as a database schema, an OO conceptual schema, an interface definition, an XML DTD, or a semantic network [6]. Model management aims at solving problems with model representation and its manipulation by considering models as first-class citizens that are manipulated by means of abstract operators. The MOMENT (MOdel manageMENT) platform is a tool that allows model representation and manipulation by means of an algebraic approach. This approach allows the automation of model manipulation tasks, which can improve a reverse engineering process such as schema or model generation.

Focusing on this point, we introduce an algebraic approach to automatically generate schemas among different metamodels within the MOMENT prototype. The paper is structured as follows: Section 2 presents related work to contextualize our schema generation approach; Section 3 offers an application example; Section 4 presents an overview of the MOMENT prototype; Section 5 explains the algebraic operator *generate* and how it works; Section 6 presents some conclusions and future work.

2 Related Work

Data reverse engineering can be treated generically from the perspective of model management. In this sense, the essentials of a model theory for generic schema management are presented in [7]. This model theory is applicable to a variety of data models such as the relational, object-oriented, and XML models, allowing model transformations by means of categorical morphisms. RONDO [8] is a tool based on this approach. It represents models by means of a graph theory and a set of high level operators that manipulate such models and mappings between them through a category theory. Models are translated into graphs by means of specific converters for each metamodel. These algebraic operators are based on imperative algorithms, such as CUPID [11]. CUPID is an algorithm for matching schemas in the RONDO tool.

In the MOMENT platform, we use the framework that is proposed in the Meta-Object Facility specification (MOF). MOF is one of the OMG family of standards for modeling distributed software architectures and systems. It defines an abstract language and a four-layered framework for specifying, constructing and managing neutral technology metamodels. A metamodel is an abstract language for some kinds of metadata. MOF defines a framework for implementing repositories that hold the metadata described by the metamodels. This framework has inspired our platform for model management although we do not use the same vocabulary to describe metamodels. In the case of MOF, the two most abstract layers offer a higher view of a specific model involving metamodel management.

3 Motivating Example

Consider a car maintenance company that has worked a long time for a large car dealership. The maintenance company has always worked with an old C application where the information is stored in a simple relational database that does not even consider integrity constraints. The car dealership has recently acquired the car maintenance company and the president has decided to migrate the old application to a new OO technology in order to improve maintenance and efficiency. Therefore, the target application will be developed by means of an OO programming language.

Suppose that a part of the original database is a table *Invoice*, as shown in Fig. 1. To obtain a class that is semantically equivalent to this table, a designer usually builds it manually, which involves high development costs since the entire initial database is taken into account. What is worse is that this process is error-prone due to the human factor.

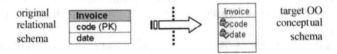

Fig. 1. Example of class generation from a relational table

4   MOMENT Overview

The MOMENT (MOdel manageMENT) platform is a tool that allows model representation and manipulation by means of an algebraic approach. We use the expressiveness of the algebra, which the platform is based on, to define and represent a model as a formal term. Operators of the algebra, also called morphisms, perform transformations over the terms of the algebra.

The MOMENT platform uses several metadata layers to describe any kind of information including new metadata types. This architecture is based on both the classical four-layer metamodeling architecture, following standards such as ISO [9] and CDIF [10], and on the more modern four-layer framework proposed in the MOF specification [1]. In our work, we structure the platform in four abstract layers:

- The M0-layer collects the examples of all the models, i.e., it holds the information that is described by a data model of the M1-layer.
- The M1-layer contains the metadata that describes data in the M0-layer and aggregates it by means of models. This layer provides services to collect examples of a reality in the lowest layer.
- The M2-layer contains the descriptions (meta-metadata) that define the structure and semantics of the metadata located at the M1-layer. This layer groups meta-metadata as metamodels. A metamodel is an "abstract language" that describes different kinds of data. The M2-layer provides services to manage models in the next lower layer.
- The M3-layer is the platform core, containing services to specify any metamodel with the same common representation mechanism. It is the most abstract layer in the platform. It contains the description of the structure and the semantics of the meta-metadata, which is located at the M2-layer. This layer provides the "abstract language" to define different kinds of metadata.

We have developed a prototype of MOMENT that runs on the .NET platform. The core of the prototype is an algebra, which provides a set of sorts and constructors to define models and a set of operators to manipulate them. To implement this algebra, we have used the F# programming [13] language for two main reasons: to bring a formal model management approach closer to an industrial programming environment, such as .NET; and to benefit from the functional programming advantages, such as independence from the control logics and a strong inference type. F# is a version of the Objective Caml programming language [12] on the .NET platform.

4.1 The MOMENT Algebra

The MOMENT algebra aims to represent models of any kind as algebraic terms in order to automate model transformation tasks in a precise, formal way. Reaching this objective implies choosing a basic specification language that permits us to describe any piece of data. We have chosen the Resource Description Language (RDF) [14] for this purpose. RDF is an emergent standard proposed by the World Wide Web Consortium (W3C) that is becoming the "de facto" standard for the Semantic Web [15]. This language provides the foundation for metadata interoperability across different web resource description communities.

This algebra offers the core services of the MOMENT platform and is used to define its four meta-layers. The algebra consists of two main elements: sorts and their operations. Such operations consist of both constructors, which allow for the definition of the structure of the platform and the representation of the models, and operators, which perform management tasks over the models defined in the platform. Four main sorts permit the definition of a model as a term:

1. *Concept*

    A concept represents an RDF resource and is identified by a URI. It defines an entity that can be described by means of properties. The constructor of this sort is expressed in F# notation as follows:

    ```
    Concept = NilConcept | Concept of (Concept * string)
    ```

    where *NilConcept* represents a null concept term; the first argument of the constructor *Concept* is a term of the sort *Concept* that represents its metaconcept in the next upper abstraction layer, and the second argument is its identifier.

2. *Property*

    To define the relationships that relate a subject element to an object element, we focus on the RDF statement structure. Such relationships are specified by means of the Property sort.

    We express the constructor of this sort in F# notation, as follows:

    ```
    Property = NilProperty
       | Property of (Property * string * Cardinality * Cardinality * Node * Concept)
    ```

    where *NilProperty* represents the null property term and the arguments of the constructor *Property* are the following elements, in order:

    - Parent property indicating its type.
    - URI that identifies the predicate of the property.
    - Minimum cardinality of the property that indicates the minimum amount of instances of the range concept, which must be related to the subject node.
    - Maximum cardinality of the property that indicates the maximum amount of instances of the range concept that can be related to the subject node.

- Subject element that receives the property. This can be a concept or another property, because a property may involve other properties.
- Object element that constitutes the value of the property. A property cannot be the object of another property for two reasons: it would make the RDF specification more difficult to understand, and it does not provide additional information.

3. *Schema*

   In our context, a schema term represents a collection of concepts and properties that describe such concepts.

4. *Level*

   A level term represents an abstraction layer in the platform. Four terms of this sort constitute the four-layer structure of the platform. The term M3-layer represents the most abstract layer in the platform and contains the MOMENT schema. This schema contains the term Concept and the term Property; the latter relates two concept terms, constituting the minimalist structure that we use to represent a model at a lower layer.

To apply our schema generation approach, we show how we can represent the relational and OO metamodels at the M2-layer, and how we can represent their schemas (also called models) at the M1-layer. We only describe the essentials of the metamodels that will be useful to present the operator *generate* in Section 5. The *Relational Metamodel* is a schema term that contains the concepts and properties that constitute the terminology to define a relational schema. *Table* and *Column* are represented by means of concept terms, which are related to each other through a property *table_column* in the relational metamodel at the M2-layer. This metamodel allows the definition of the concept *Invoice* as a table by means of the operator *new_concept*. In an identical way, the concepts *Code* and *Date* are defined as column terms, which are related to a table by means of instances of the property *table_column* defined at the M2-layer.

In a similar manner, the *OO Metamodel* is defined at the M2-layer, allowing the definition of the OO schema term that represents the OO model of the motivating example at the M1-layer.

5   Algebraic Schema Generation: The Operator *Generate*

The operator *generate* is a morphism that permits the translation of a model of a specific metamodel into a model of a different metamodel. In our case study, we generate an OO conceptual schema from a relational schema, both of which are specified by means of terms of our algebra sorts.

This morphism is defined at the M2-layer using mappings between elements of two different metamodels. These mappings are instances of the *MOMENTEquivalence* property defined at the M3-layer and indicate equivalence relationships between concepts of the two metamodels. These mappings must be defined by the user.

In the following sections, we explain the definition of equivalence mappings between elements of the two metamodels used in the motivating example. Then, we present the set of functions that define the generic morphism *generate*. Finally, we indicate the specific axioms that we have implemented in F# to support the schema generation between the relational and the OO metamodels.

5.1 Metamodel Equivalence Mappings

The metamodel equivalence mappings are instances of the *MOMENTEquivalence* property of the M3-layer. They permit the establishment of correspondences between concepts of two different metamodels indicating that they represent either a similar semantic meaning in different metamodels or model definition vocabularies.

There are two kinds of equivalence mappings:

a) Simple mappings, which define a simple correspondence between two concepts that belong to different metamodels; for instance, between a table and a class, or between a column of a table and an attribute of a class.

b) Complex mappings, which define correspondences between elements of a source metamodel and a target metamodel. These mappings relate two structures of concepts that represent a similar semantic meaning. For instance, to define an equivalence relationship between a foreign key of the relational metamodel and an aggregation of the UML metamodel, we have to relate the foreign key, the unique constraint and the not null value constraint concepts to the aggregation concept. This is because all three of these concepts of the relational metamodel provide the necessary knowledge to define an aggregation between two classes in the UML metamodel, such as the cardinalities of the aggregation.

In this paper, we focus on simple mappings, presenting a generic morphism to use at the M1-layer in the next section.

5.2 The Morphism *Generate*

To translate a schema of a source metamodel into another schema of a target metamodel, we use the morphism *generate*. This morphism is applied to a schema term of the source metamodel and defines a new schema of the target metamodel. Then, it checks all the concepts of the source schema one by one, generating the corresponding concept in the target schema in each case.

To process a concept, the operator *generate* makes use of axioms or rewriting rules. Each one of them is formed by two kinds of functions: a condition and a generation function. On the one hand, the condition function checks the properties of a concept in order to select which generation function should be applied. These conditions take into account the precedence order that exists between the concepts of a specific metamodel when this order is used to define a model. For instance, when we define a relational schema, we cannot define a column if the table that it belongs to is not defined previously. On the other hand, the generation function implies the definition of concepts and properties in the target schema by following four steps, as shown in Fig. 2:

1. The concept is reified in its metaconcept; that is, if the concept to be processed is the table *Invoice*, we obtain the metaconcept *Table* of the relational metamodel.
2. Once we know the corresponding metaconcept of the source metamodel, we query the equivalence that relates it to a concept of the target metamodel. In the case of a table of the *Relational Metamodel*, we obtain the concept *Class* of the *OO Metamodel*.
3. The operator *generate* instantiates the concept of the target metamodel, which becomes a metaconcept for its instance, i.e., the concept *Class* of the *OO meta-*

model becomes the metaconcept for its instance *OO-Invoice.* The new concept, which has been generated in the new target schema at the M1-layer, is equivalent to the original concept in step 1, through the equivalence relationship that we have defined before.

4. Finally, the operator instantiates the equivalence defined at the M2-layer between the *Metaconcept* of the source *Concept* and the *Metaconcept'* of the new generated *Concept'*. The instantiation defines a new property in the source schema at the M1-layer that has the source *Concept* as domain and the target *Concept'* as range.

The morphism *generate* is one of the MOMENT algebra operators and has been implemented in F# as part of our prototype. To automatically generate models among different metamodels, we only have to add specific rewriting rules to the operator. These axioms are applied by means of the pattern matching of the F# language to translate the source model into the target one. Focusing on simple equivalence mappings, we take into account three possible cases of rewriting rules in order to generate OO models from relational schemas: the generation of a class, the generation of an attribute when the class that contains it has been generated before, and the generation of an attribute when the class that contains it has not yet been generated.

5.2.1 Table-Class Equivalence

To take into account the translation of a table, the following condition and generation functions appear in the code of the operator:

```
| Concept(_,"Table", _) ->
        generate_r_table_2_oo_class r_schema r_concept oo_schema
```

where *generate_r_table_2_oo_class* performs the translation of the relational table into a class in the target OO schema.

When the operator processes a concept of the relational schema, it reifies the concept obtaining the metaconcept that describes the type of this concept. If the current concept is the term *Invoice* (shown in Fig. 2), its metaconcept is the term *Table* in the relational metamodel (1). The operator searches for the equivalence mapping that relates it to a concept of the OO Metamodel, obtaining the concept *Class* (2). This concept is instantiated in the new OO schema at the M1-layer (3). The identifier of the new concept is obtained from the URI that identifies the original relational table. Currently, we add the prefix *OO-* to the URI: *OO-Invoice.* Finally, the equivalence mapping *equivalence_table_class* defined at the M2-layer is instantiated in the property *equivalence_table_class_1* at the M1-layer, relating the original concept *Invoice* of the relational schema to the new generated concept *OO-Invoice* of the new OO schema (4).

5.2.2 Column-Attribute Equivalence

To translate a column of a table of a relational schema into an attribute of a class in a target OO schema, we have to take into account two situations: when the table that contains the column has already been translated and when it has not.

To deal with the first case, the following conditions and generation functions are specified in the code of the operator *generate*:

```
| Concept(_,"Column", _)
    when (validate_column_with_table r_schema r_concept oo_schema) ->
        generate_r_column_2_oo_attribute r_schema r_concept oo_schema
```

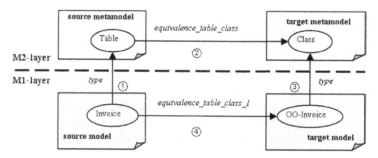

Fig. 2. Description of the rewriting process applied to a table

where the condition *validate_column_with_table* checks whether the table is translated and the generation function *generate_r_column_2_oo_attribute* translates the original column into an attribute in the target OO schema.

Fig. 3 illustrates the generation process followed in this case. Assume that we are processing the column *Code* of the table Invoice in Fig. 3. To determine whether the table *Invoice* has already been translated, the axiom finds an instance of the *table_column* property that relates the column *Invoice* to a table (1). Once we have the concept *Invoice* representing the relational table, the condition checks the existence of an instance of the property *equivalence_table_class*, which relates the table Invoice to a class in the target schema at the M1-layer (2). In this case, the generation function is applied, reifying the concept *Code* to the concept *Column* (3). Querying the equivalence mapping *equivalence_column_attribute* (4), the operator obtains the concept of the *OO Metamodel* that is equivalent to the concept *Column*, i.e., the concept *Attribute*. Then, the operator instantiates it providing an identifier, which is obtained from the original concept *Code* (5). By means of the property *equivalence_table_class_0* defined at the M1-layer, the operator obtains the class that is going to contain the recently generated attribute. By doing so, the property *class_attribute* of the OO metamodel is instantiated by relating the class *Invoice* and the attribute *Code* (6). Finally, the property *equivalence_column_attribute* is instantiated relating the original concept *Code* and the generated concept *OO-Code* (7).

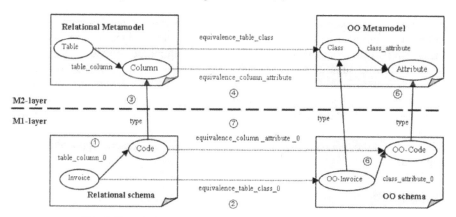

Fig. 3. Description of the rewriting process applied to column

In the second case, the axiom just checks the opposite condition of the first case, i.e., there is no class that is related to the concept *Invoice* of the relational schema by means of an equivalence mapping. Here, the generation function is a composition of the generation rule for a table and the generation rule for a column whose table has already been generated.

Equivalence mappings generated at the M1-layer are used by another operator of the MOMENT algebra, the operator *migrate*, which automatically produces a migration plan that indicates how the information of the source model at the M0-layer can be migrated to the information container of the target model. Therefore, these mappings allow us to perform data migration among models at the M0-layer.

6   Conclusions and Future Work

Reverse engineering constitutes a process that is currently present in software development companies. However, model management [6] is an emerging research field that aims at resolving data model integration and interoperability by means of generic operators. We have developed a prototype that permits the representation of models by means of the essential concepts of RDF, following the MOF metamodeling culture. For the moment, we have focused on the specification of relational schemas and object-oriented models. Model management tasks can help to improve a reverse engineering process as well as help to directly deal with the data models that are held by the applications. In this paper, we have focused on one of these tasks: schema (or model) generation.

We have presented two fundamental mainstays, which we have built our MOMENT platform on, taking into account our previous experience in the industrial project RELS [16]. A tool for the recovery of legacy systems has been built, using a term rewriting system to translate relational schemas into OO conceptual schemas and performing data migration from the legacy database to the database of the new application.

In this paper, we have considered an example of schema generation and we have presented an overview of our platform for model management taking into account the algebra used to represent and manipulate models. We have gone beyond on schema generation explaining the algebraic operator *generate* that we use to automatically generate the basic parts of a model by means of simple mappings between elements of different metamodels. Both the operator and the entire algebra have been implemented in F# [15] to be able to deal with models without the complexities that have to be taken into account in an algorithmic approach, such as in RONDO [8]. Thus, our approach is more generic and improves the scalability of the algebraic operators by simply adding axioms to the presentation of the algebra, as we have shown above.

Future work will take into account complex mappings that provide full support for generating schemas. We will also consider metamodels that are different from the relational and the OO metamodels in order to validate the generic applicability of our approach.

References

1. OMG: Meta-Object Facility Specification version 1.4. April 2002.
   http://www.omg.org/technology/documents/formal/mof.htm

2. Pressman, Roger s.: Software Engineering: A Practitioner's Approach. European Edition. McGraw-Hill, 2000.
3. Rational Software, http://www.rational.com/products/rose/
4. System Architect, http://www.popkin.com/products/sa2001/systemarchitect.htm
5. DB-Main, http://www.fundp.ac.be/recherche/unites/publications/en/2987.html
6. Bernstein, P.A., Levy, A.Y., Pottinger, R.A.: A Vision for Management of Complex Models. Microsoft Research Technical Report MSR-TR-2000-53, June 2000, (short version in SIGMOD Record 29, 4 (Dec. '00)).
7. Alagic, S. and Bernstein, P.A.: A Model Theory for Generic Schema Management. In Proceedings of DBPL'01, G. Ghelli and G. Grahne (eds), Springer-Verlag, (2001).
8. S. Melnik, E. Rahm, P. A. Bernstein: Rondo: A Programming Platform for Generic Model Management (Extended Version). Technical Report, Leipzig University, 2003. Available at http://dol.uni-leipzig.de/pub/2003-3
9. ISO/IEC 10746-1, 2, 3, 4 | ITU-T Recommendation X.901, X.902, X.903, X.904 « Open Distributed Processing - Reference Model". OMG, 1995-96.
10. CDIF Technical Committee: CDIF Framework for Modeling and Extensibility. Electronic Industries Assocaiation, EIA/IS-107, January 1994. See http://www.cdif.org/.
11. Madhavan, J., P.A. Bernstein, and E. Rahm: Generic Schema Matching using Cupid. MSR Tech. Report MSR-TR-2001-58, 2001, http://www.research.microsoft.com/pubs (short version in VLDB 2001).
12. E. Cahilloux, P. Manoury, B. Pagano: Developing Applications With Objective Caml, Éditions O'Reilly, 2000.
13. Microsoft Research F# Project. http://research.microsoft.com/projects/ilx/fsharp.aspx
14. World Wide Web Consortium, Resource Description Framework (RDF), http://www.w3.org/RDF/
15. World Wide Web Consortium, Semantic Web, http://www.w3.org/2001/sw/
16. Perez J., Anaya V., Cubel J.M., Domiguez F., Boronat A., Ramos I., Carsí J.A.: Data Reverse Engineering of Legacy Databases to Object Oriented Conceptual Schemas. SET 2002, Software Evolution Through Transformations: Towards uniform support throughout the software life-cycle, Barcelona - Spain, October 2002.

Contourlet Based Multiresolution Texture Segmentation Using Contextual Hidden Markov Models

B.S. Raghavendra and P. Subbanna Bhat

Department of Electronics & Communication Engineering
National Institute of Technology Karnataka, Surathkal-575 025, India
raghavendra_bobbi@yahoo.co.in, p_subbannabhat@yahoo.com

Abstract. In this paper, block based texture segmentation is proposed based on contourlets and the hidden Markov model (HMM). Hidden Markov model is combined with hidden Markov tree (HMT) to form HMM-HMT model that models global dependency between the blocks in addition to the local statistics within a block. The HMM-HMT model is modified to use the contourlet transform, a new extension to the wavelet transform that forms a true basis for image representations. The maximum likelihood multiresolution segmentation algorithm is used to handle several block sizes at once. Since the algorithm works on the contourlet transformed image data, it can directly segment images without the need for transforming into the space domain. The experimental results demonstrate the competitive performance of the algorithm on contourlets with that of the other methods and excellent visual performance at small block sizes. The performance is comparable with that of wavelets and is superior at small block sizes.

1 Introduction

In statistical image segmentation, it is necessary to capture both global and local statistical structure of textures. Texture segmentation is achieved using block-based modeling considering statistical dependencies between blocks. Contourlet transform is better suited for representing singularities such as edges and ridges in an image that characterize textures. The multiresolution property of contourlets makes HMM based texture segmentation [2] possible.

The de-correlation property of the contourlet transform greatly reduces the number of hidden states, hence the complexity is reduced. Here image and its contourlet coefficients are treated as random realizations from a family or distribution of signals. Coefficients are modeled either as jointly Gaussian or as non-Gaussian but independent. The HMM-HMT model [6] takes global and local dependencies between blocks and gives improved segmentation results. The HMM-HMT approach is modified for application to contourlet transform to acquire the segmentation results for several resolutions.

2 Contourlet Transform

The contourlet transform is a new extension to the wavelet transform in two dimensions using non-separable and directional filter banks. It is composed of basis images oriented at varying directions in multiple scales. With this rich set of basis images, the

G. Das and V.P. Gulati (Eds.): CIT 2004, LNCS 3356, pp. 336–343, 2004.
© Springer-Verlag Berlin Heidelberg 2004

contourlet transform can effectively capture the smooth contours in the natural texture images. Non separable multiscale representations capture the intrinsic geometrical structures in the textural images which wavelets fail to capture. Based on the two dimensional non-separable filter banks, contourlets possess multiresolution, time-frequency localization features in addition to high degree of directionality that allows one to jointly model scale, space and directional parameters of an image.

Contourlets [3] are implemented by the pyramidal directional filter bank (PDFB), which decomposes an image into directional subbands at multiple scales. PDFB is a cascade of a Laplacian pyramid and a directional filter bank. The directional filter bank decomposes images into any power of two's number of directions. Here the multiscale and directional decomposition are independent of each other. The Fig. 1 shows contourlet transform of an image, which is having four directional and three scale decompositions.

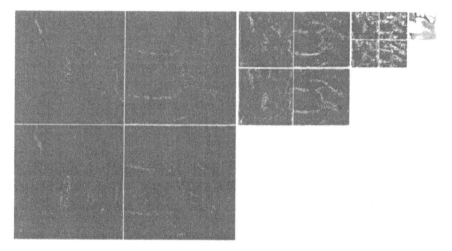

Fig. 1. Contourlet decomposition of Peppers image

The singularities such as edges in the support region affect the magnitude of contourlet coefficients. The contourlet coefficients of 2-D images are naturally arranged in the form of quad-trees. In a quad tree each node will have four children nodes. Thus image is represented as a tree after transforming it. A coefficient in a low subband (parent) can be thought of as having four descendants (children) in the next higher subband. The four descendants each also have four descendants in the next higher subband and a quad tree will emerge.

The contourlet transform picks out edge contours and represents those using coefficients. Due to the small compact support of the contourlets, edges contribute energy to a small number of coefficients. The contourlet coefficients of natural images exhibit residual dependency structure both across scale and within scale. Images have been modeled based on these dependencies. The coefficients of a 2D image are represented using quad trees and the inter-scale dependencies are captured using a hidden Markov model [5].

Fig. 2 shows the histogram of the finest subband of contourlet coefficients of an image. The distribution is characterized by a sharp peak at zero amplitude and extended tails on either sides of the peak. This implies that the contourlet transform is very sparse, as the majority of the coefficients have amplitudes close to zero. Thus the marginal distributions of natural images in the contourlet domain are highly non-Gaussian. The large/small values of contourlet coefficients tend to propagate across scale, having certain kind of persistence. The quad tree structure of contourlet transform of images is used for HMT modeling.

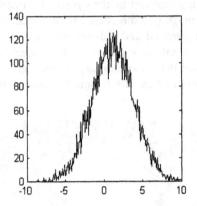

Fig. 2. Distribution of Contourlet coefficients

3   Contourlet HMT Model

The HMT model [1] is used to model the joint pdf of contourlet coefficients of an image. The HMT models the marginal pdf of each coefficient as a Gaussian mixture density with unobserved hidden states. Modeling includes two stages: modeling the marginal density of each wavelet coefficient and modeling the dependencies between the coefficients. Each coefficient c_i is associated with a set of discrete hidden states $S_i = 0,1,...,P-1$ (for P state model) which have probability mass function (pmf) $p_{S_i}(m)$. Given $S_i = m$, the pdf of the coefficient c is Gaussian with mean μ_m and variance σ_m^2. The Gaussian distribution with mean μ, variance σ^2, can be written as:

$$g(x;\mu,\sigma^2) = \frac{1}{\sigma\sqrt{2\pi}} \exp\left\{-\frac{(x-\mu)^2}{2\sigma^2}\right\} \tag{1}$$

The parameter vector of a M state Gaussian Mixture Model (GMM) is

$$\pi = \left\{ p_{S_i}(m), \mu_m, \sigma_m^2 \middle| m = 0,1,...,P-1 \right\} \tag{2}$$

The over all pdf of c is determined by the sum

$$f_C(c) = \sum_{m=0}^{M-1} p_{S_i}(m) f_{C|S_i}(c|S_i = m) \tag{3}$$

where,

$$f_{C|S_i}(c|S_i = m) = g(c;\mu_m,\sigma_m^2) \tag{4}$$

3.1 Two State Model

Consider a two state GMM, where each coefficient c_i is associated with a hidden state S_i taking value 0 and 1, depending on c_i is small or large respectively. The state variable S_i tells that, from which of the two components in the mixture model c_i is drawn. Each coefficient c_i is conditionally Gaussian given its state variable S_i. The state 0 corresponds to a low variance Gaussian with pdf $f(c_i|S_i = 0) = g(c_i; \mu_i, \sigma^2_{S_i})$ and the state 1 corresponds to a high variance Gaussian with pdf $f(c_i|S_i = 1) = g(c_i; \mu_i, \sigma^2_{L_i})$. Note that $\sigma^2_L > \sigma^2_S$. The marginal pdf is obtained by taking sum of the conditional densities as;

$$f(c_i) = p_i^S g(c_i; \mu_i, \sigma^2_{S_i}) + p_i^L g(c_i; \mu_i, \sigma^2_{L_i}) \tag{5}$$

$$p_i^S + p_i^L = 1 \tag{6}$$

where, p_i^S and p_i^L are state value pmfs for $S_i = \{0,1\}$ respectively and can be interpreted as the probability that c_i is small or large respectively. A smooth region of the image is captured by $S_i = 0$ and edge region is captured by $S_i = 1$.

Even though the contourlet transform gives uncorrelated coefficients, there exists considerable amount of high-order dependencies. Hence coefficients are statistically dependent along the branches of the tree. The expected magnitude of a contourlet coefficient is closely related to the size of its parent. This implies a type of Markovian relationship between the contourlet states [4], with the probability of a contourlet coefficient being large affected by the size of its parent. This makes the state of the children coefficients depend on the state of the parent. The dependence is modeled as Markov-I: given the state of a contourlet coefficient S_i the coefficient ancestors and descendents are independent of each other. In the HMM, these dependencies across the scale are captured using a probabilistic tree that connects the hidden state variable of each coefficient with the state variable of each of its children.

Each subband is represented with its own quad-tree; thus quad trees are assumed independent. The dependencies across the scale (between each parent and its children) form the transition probabilities between the hidden states. The Transitions among the states are governed by a set of transition probabilities. The $0 \rightarrow 0$ and $1 \rightarrow 1$ transitions have higher probabilities due to the persistence of contourlet coefficients.

The parameter $\varepsilon^{m,n}_{j,j-1} = p(S_i = m | S_{p(i)} = n)$ gives the probability that a child coefficient c_i is in a hidden state n, when its parent $c_{p(i)}$ is in state m where $p(i)$ is the parent of node i and scale $j = 1,...,J-1$ (J is the coarsest scale), $m, n = 0,1$. Each parent $\rightarrow$ child state-to-state link (transition probabilities) has a corresponding state transition matrix

$$A_i = \begin{bmatrix} p_i^{0 \rightarrow 0} & p_i^{0 \rightarrow 1} \\ p_i^{1 \rightarrow 0} & p_i^{1 \rightarrow 1} \end{bmatrix} \tag{7}$$

with $p_i^{0\to1} = 1 - p_i^{0\to0}$ and $p_i^{1\to0} = 1 - p_i^{1\to1}$. The matrix has the row sums equal to unity. The parameters $p_i^{0\to0} / p_i^{1\to1}$ are the probability that contourlet coefficient c_i is small / large given that its parent is small / large. These are the persistency probabilities. The parameters $p_i^{1\to0}$ and $p_i^{0\to1}$ are the probabilities that the state values will change from one scale to the next. To propagate the large and small coefficient values down the quad-tree it is required that, $p_i^{0\to0} > p_i^{0\to1}$ and $p_i^{1\to1} > p_i^{1\to0}$.

The HMT parameter vector is

$$\theta = \left\{ p_{S_0}(m), \varepsilon_{j,j-1}^{m,n}, \mu_{i,m}, \sigma_{i,m}^2 \middle| m, n = 0,1 \right\} \tag{8}$$

The HMM is trained to capture the contourlet domain features of the image of interest using the iterative expectation maximization (EM) algorithm.

The contoulet transform allows one to distinguish between a feature oriented at different angles by having separate subbands for features at different orientations, where as the wavelet transform combines these features into only three subbands. Thus the contourlet transform provides a greater directional selectivity than the DWT. This allows one to get richer set of models. For example, an image with features oriented at $+\alpha^0$ and another image with the same features oriented at $-\alpha^0$ will always have the same DWT HMT models but have different Contourlet HMT models. This allows one to statistically discriminate between the two images.

3.2 HMM-Contourlet HMT Texture Model

Only local statistics that reside in the block is considered in HMT based segmentation [2]. The introduction of global statistics gives HMM-HMT model providing good segmentation results. HMM is used for modeling inter dependency of blocks and HMT captures statistics inside the block. Four-neighborhood system is used taking contextual information in global dependency model.

Each of the given blocks is associated with a hidden state [6]. The state of a given block is linked to the statistics of the four surrounding blocks as shown in Fig. 3. Contourlet based multi-resolution analysis is employed for each block representative of a quad tree. The state dependent block statistics are modeled using quad tree HMTs. Each texture is characterized by multiple states in general. Distinct sets of HMTs are used to model the contourlet coefficients associated with a given state.

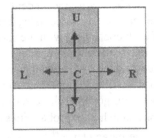

Fig. 3. Four neighborhood system

Consider M level contourlet decomposition of a textured image. The texture is devided into blocks of size $2^M x 2^M$. A hidden state is assigned to each of the blocks. For an isolated $2^M x 2^M$ block, root node is parent node and nodes at level $k = M - 1$ are the children nodes. Each of the four nodes at level $k = M - 1$ serves as parents for four distinct child nodes at level $k = M - 2$. The statistical relationship between a given parent and its associated children is modeled as a Markov process. The four quad trees are treated as statistically independent.

Two-state model is employed for each node of the tree. The associated contourlet coefficient is modeled as Gaussian. Taking median pixel value md of the texture initializes the block states. If the block mean is greater than md, the block is set to state 1. If the block mean is less than md, the block is set to state 2.

Consider a block of interest C and its four neighboring blocks sharing an edge with C. Let C_b be the contourlet coefficients associated with block b taking all four sub-bands into account, where $b = \{C, L, R, U, D\}$. The height of the subtree residing in a block of size $2^M x 2^M$ is M. The conditional likelihood of C_b can be computed from Contourlet HMT of height M. The likelihood is

$$p(C_b, b \in B) = \sum_{lC=1}^{K} \dots \sum_{lD=1}^{K} \{p(B_C, \dots, B_D) \times p(C_C) \dots p(C_D)\} \qquad (9)$$

where, K is the number of states. Assuming that, blocks not sharing a common edge are independent

$$p(B_C, \dots, B_D) = p(B_C) \times \{p(B_L|B_C)p(B_R|B_C)p(B_U|B_C)p(B_D|B_C)\} \qquad (10)$$

The dependencies between the blocks sharing the common edge are isotropic.

$$p(B_L|B_C) = p(B_R|B_C) = p(B_U|B_C) = p(B_D|B_C) \qquad (11)$$

Viterbi algorithm is used for parameter estimation in the global HMM part and EM algorithm is used in the local Contourlet HMT part. Let θ_i be the trained model parameter for each class i of textures. The likelihood of the block C to be a class i is

$$L(C|\theta_i) = \max_{lC, \dots, lD} \{p(B_C, \dots, B_D|\theta_i) \times p(C_C|B_C, \theta_i) \dots p(C_D|B_D, \theta_i)\} \qquad (12)$$

 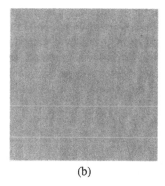

(a)   (b)

Fig. 4. Training Textures (a) Grass (b) Water

For maximum likelihood segmentation, the class label that maximizes the likelihood is assigned to the block.

$$i_{ML} = \arg\max_i L(C|\theta_i) \qquad (13)$$

The middle block C is assigned to that texture for which the associated HMM-HMT model yields the maximum likelihood. Only middle block is assigned rather than segmenting all blocks to a given texture. Each block plays the role of C thereby yielding segmentation taking contextual information of four blocks with which it has direct contact.

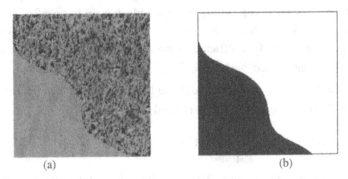

(a)   (b)

Fig. 5. (a) Image to be segmented (b) Ground Truth

4   Experimental Results

The experimental results demonstrating the performance of the HMM-Contourlet HMT texture segmentation are shown and are compared with that of HMM Wavelet HMT texture segmentation. The Haar filter is used for the wavelet-based models as well as in the contourlet transform, where it is used for both directional and multiscale decomposition. For the HMM-Contourlet HMT, training is done for each training texture shown in Fig. 4 using two-state model. The maximum block size is set to 8x8. For the three level contourlet decomposition of the texture image is performed. Thus the results are shown for the block size of 2x2, 4x4 and 8x8.

Experiments are done for symmetric two-texture image in which the ground truth is clear as shown in Fig.5. Note that, for each of the models the segmented images of different block sizes are obtained simultaneously realizing multiresolution segmentation. Fig. 6 shows segmented images using HMM-Wavelet HMT method. Fig. 7 shows segmented images using HMM-Contourlet HMT based method. The performance of the contourlet block-based segmentation is better especially at small block sizes.

5   Conclusions

The classification based on the likelihood measure of contourlet coefficients is a simple technique. Decisions made at coarser scales are satisfactory since they are based on a larger set of data but they fail as one move towards finer scales. In HMM-HMT model, inter block statistics is modeled by HMM and HMT models intra block state dependent contourlet statistics. The contourlet global dependency method gives better performance for all different resolutions. The algorithm based on the contourlets provides raw segmentation results that can be used as a front end in a more sophisticated multiscale segmentation algorithm. The average error in the contourlet based segmentation for small block size is less when compared with that for wavelet based algorithm. The experimental performance comparison shows that contourlet HMT segmentation algorithm is superior for small block sizes and gives excellent visual performance.

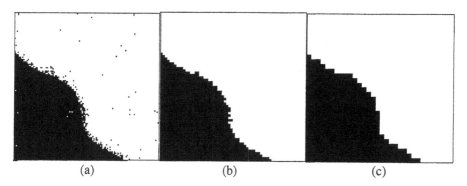

Fig. 6. Texture segmentation using HMM-Wavelet HMT method. (a) 2x2 block (b) 4x4 block (c) 8x8 block

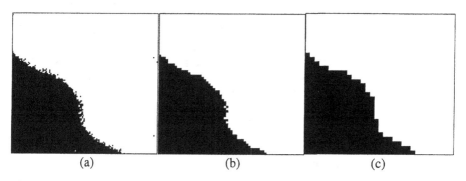

Fig. 7. Texture segmentation using HMM-Contourlet HMT method. (a) 2x2 block (b) 4x4 block (c) 8x8 block

References

1. M.S. Crouse, R.D. Nowak and R. G. Baraniuk.: Wavelet-based statistical signal processing using hidden Markov models. IEEE Trans.Signal Proc. vol. 46, No. 4, (1998) 886- 902.
2. H. Choi and R.G. Baraniuk.: Multiscale Image Segmentation Using Wavelet Domain Hidden Markov Models. IEEE Trans. Image Proc. vol. 10, no. 9, (2001) 1309-1321.
3. M.N. Do and M. Vetterli.: Contourlets: A computational Framework for Directional Multiresolution Image Representation. submitted to IEEE Tran. on Image Processing, (2003).
4. Po. Duncan D.-Y. and Do, M.N.: Directional Multiscale modeling of images using the contourlet transform. IEEE Workshop on Statistical Signal Processing 2003, (2003) 262 – 265.
5. J. Romberg, H. Choi, R.G. Baraniuk, Nick Kingsburry.: Multiscale Classification using Complex Wavelets and Hidden Markov Tree Models. Proc ICIP 2000, vol.2 (2000) 371-374.
6. J. Lu and L. Carin: HMM-based Multiresolution Image Segmentation. Proc. ICASSP 2002. vol. 4. (2002) 3357-3360.

FPGA Based Implementation
of an Invisible-Robust Image Watermarking Encoder

Saraju P. Mohanty[1], Renuka Kumara C.[2], and Sridhara Nayak[2]

[1] Dept. of Computer Science and Engineering, Univ. of North Texas,
Denton, TX 76203, USA
smohanty@cs.unt.edu
[2] Manipal Centre For Information Science, Manipal Academy of Higher Education,
Manipal – 576104, India
shridhar.n@mcis.manipal.edu

Abstract. Both encryption and digital watermarking techniques need to be incorporated in a digital rights management framework to address different aspects of content management. While encryption transforms original multimedia object into another form, digital watermarking leaves the original object intact and recognizable. The objective is to develop low power, real time, reliable and secure watermarking systems, which can be achieved through hardware implementations. In this paper, we present an FPGA based implementation of an invisible spatial domain watermarking encoder. The watermarking encoder consists of a watermark generator, watermark insertion module, and a controller. Most of the invisible watermarking algorithms available in the literature and also the algorithm implemented in this paper insert pseudorandom numbers to host data. Therefore, we focus on the structural design aspects of watermarking generator using linear feedback shift register. We synthesized the prototype watermarking encoder chip using Xilinx FPGA.

1 Introduction

Owing to the usage of Internet, concerns about protection and enforcement of intellectual property (IP) rights of the digital content involved in the transaction, are mounting. In addition, unauthorized replication and manipulation of digital content is relatively trivial and can be achieved using inexpensive tools. Issues related to ownership rights of digital content are addressed by digital rights management (DRM) systems [1, 2]. Various aspects of content management namely, content identification, storage, representation, and distribution and intellectual property rights management are highlighted in DRM. Besides, unauthorized access of digital content is being prevented by implementing encryption technologies. However, it does not prevent an authorized user from illegally replicating the decrypted content. Hence, encryption alone does not address all the IP issues related to DRM. Digital watermarking is one of the key technologies that can be used for establishing ownership rights, tracking usage, ensuring authorized access, preventing illegal replication and facilitating content authentication. Therefore, a two layer protection mechanism utilizing both watermarking and encryption is needed [3].

G. Das and V.P. Gulati (Eds.): CIT 2004, LNCS 3356, pp. 344–353, 2004.

Table 1. Watermarking Chips Proposed in Current Literature.

Research	Design Type	Watermarking	Multimedia	Domain	Chip Features
Hsiao [6]	Custom IC	Invisible-Robust	Image	Wavelet	NA
Maes [7]	FPGA board/IC	Invisible-Robust	Video	Spatial	$17/14\ kG$ Logic
Tsai [8]	Custom IC-0.35μ	Invisible-Robust	Image	DCT	$3.3V$,$50MHz$
Petitjean [9]	FPGA board	Invisible-Robust	Image	Fractal	$50MHz$
Garimella [10]	Custom IC-0.13μ	Invisible-Fragile	Image	Spatial	$1.2V$
Mathai [11]	Custom IC-0.18μ	Invisible	Video	Wavelet	$1.8V$
Tsai [12]	Custom IC	Invisible-Robust	Video	Spatial	NA
Mohanty [13]	Custom IC-0.35μ	Robust-Fragile	Image	Spatial	$3.3V$, $545MHz$
Seo [14]	FPGA board	Invisible-Robust	Image	Wavelet	$82MHz$
Mohanty [15]	Custom IC-0.35μ	Visible	Image	Spatial	$3.3V$, $292MHz$

Digital watermarking is the process of embedding data called a watermark into a multimedia object such that watermark can be detected whenever necessary for DRM. The digital watermarking system essentially consists of a watermark embedder and a watermark detector [4, 5]. The embedder inserts a watermark onto the host object and the detector detects the presence of the watermark. An entity called watermark key is also used during the process of embedding and detecting the watermark. This watermark key is unique and exhibits a one-to-one correspondence with every watermark. The key is private and known to only authorized parties, eliminating the possibility of illegal usage of digital content.

The goal is to develop low power, real time, reliable and, secure watermarking systems [16, 17]. Over the past decade, numerous watermarking algorithms have been invented and their software are available, however recently, hardware implementations are being presented in literature. We have listed most of the watermarking hardwares available in current literature in Table 1, which proves that the VLSI implementation of the watermarking algorithms is not yet significantly explored. A hardware based watermarking system can be designed on a field programmable gate array (FPGA) board, Trimedia processor board [7], or custom IC. The choice between the FPGA and cell based IC is a trade-off between cost, power, and performance [15, 18].

In this paper, we present an FPGA based implementation of an invisible-robust spatial domain watermarking encoder [19]. This algorithm is chosen as it is simple yet robust against geometric attack and is tested using Stirmark benchmark [20]. The watermarking encoder chip consists of a watermark generator, watermark insertion module, and a controller. The invisible watermarking algorithms implemented in this paper insert pseudorandom numbers to host data. Therefore, we focus on the structural design aspects of watermarking generator using linear feedback shift register (LFSR). We synthesized the prototype watermarking encoder chip in a Xilinx FPGA using VIRTEX technology which can be operated at $50MHz$ frequency.

2   Watermarking Algorithm

In this section, we describe the invisible-robust algorithm [19] chosen for VLSI implementation. Let us assume the following notations: I – original gray scale image,

W – binary or ternary watermark image, I^* – watermarked image, (i,j) – pixel location, E_1, E_2 – watermark embedding functions, D – watermark detection function, r – neighborhood radius, I_N – neighborhood image, K - digital watermark key, and α_1, α_2 – scaling constants.

The watermark insertion process consists of the following: First, the watermark W which is a ternary image having pixel values $\{0,1 \text{ or } 2\}$ is generated using the digital key K. Then, watermark insertion is performed by altering the pixels of original image using watermark embedding functions.

$$I^*(i,j) = \begin{cases} I(i,j) & \text{if } W(i,j) = 0 \\ E_1\big(I(i,j), I_N(i,j)\big) & \text{if } W(i,j) = 1 \\ E_2\big(I(i,j), I_N(i,j)\big) & \text{if } W(i,j) = 2 \end{cases} \qquad (1)$$

The encoding functions E_1 and E_2 are defined as follows.

$$\begin{aligned} E_1(I, I_N) &= (1 - \alpha_1)I_N(i,j) + \alpha_1 I(i,j) \\ E_2(I, I_N) &= (1 - \alpha_1)I_N(i,j) + \alpha_2 I(i,j) \end{aligned} \qquad (2)$$

The signs of α_1 and α_2 are used for the detection function and their actual values determine the watermark strength. The neighborhood image pixel gray value I_N is calculated as the average gray value of the neighboring pixels of the original image for a neighborhood radius r. For example, for neighborhood radius $r = 1$, it is [13]:

$$I_N(i,j) = \frac{\frac{I(i+1,j)+I(i+1,j+1)}{2} + I(i,j+1)}{2} \qquad (3)$$

The scaling $(1 - \alpha_1)$ is used to scale I_N to ensure that watermarked image gray value I^* never exceeds the maximum gray value for 8-bit image representation corresponding to pure white pixel. The neighborhood radius determines the upper bound of the watermarked pixels in an image.

The first step of detection process is the generation of watermark W using the watermark key K. Next, the watermark is extracted from the test (watermarked) image using the detection function given below, for $\alpha_1 > 0$ and $\alpha_2 < 0$.

$$W^*(i,j) = \begin{cases} 1 \text{ if } I^*(i,j) - I_N(i,j) > 0 \\ 2 \text{ if } I^*(i,j) - I_N(i,j) < 0 \end{cases} \qquad (4)$$

By comparing the original ternary watermark image W and the extracted binary watermark image W^*, the ownership can be established when the detection ratio is larger than a predefined threshold. The value of the threshold determines the minimum acceptable level of watermark detection.

3   Architectural Design of the Proposed Chip

In this section, the architecture of the invisible-robust watermarking encoder algorithm described in the previous section, is elaborated. We first provide high level description of the encoder, followed by their architectural details.

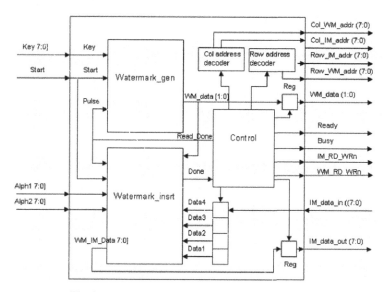

Fig. 1. Datapath and Controller for the Proposed Chip.

3.1 Datapath and Controller

The high-level view of the proposed chip is shown in Fig. 1. The encoder includes the units, such as watermark generation, watermark insertion, control, row and column address decoder, and registers. The generation unit is used to produce the watermark, and insertion unit is used to insert the watermark into the host image as per the described algorithm. The control unit controls the operation of the above two modules and the data flow in encoder. The address decoders are used to decode the memory address where the image and watermark are stored. The registers are used for buffering purpose. We assume that there are two external RAMs, one to store the original image and other to serve as a storage space for watermark data available. The watermarked image is written back to the RAM storing the original image.

3.2 Watermark Generation Unit

The ternary watermark is generated by pseudorandom sequence generator. The watermark generation unit consists of linear feedback shift register (LFSR). LFSR has a multitude of uses in digital system design and is a very crucial unit in watermark security and detection. It is a sequential shift register with combinational feedback logic around it that causes it to cycle pseudo randomly through a sequence of binary values. Therefore, we have studied the difficulties of a LFSR and have taken appropriate measures to ensure quality design [21–23]. The LFSR consists of flip-flops (FFs) as sequential elements with feedback loops. The feedback around a LFSR comes from a selected set of points called taps in the FF chain and these taps are fed back to FFs after either XORing or XNORing.

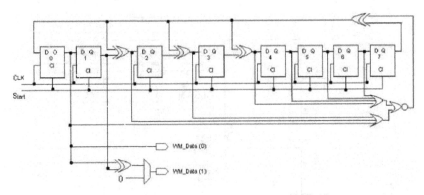

Fig. 2. Watermark Generation Unit: Linear Feedback Shift Register (LFSR).

The design aspects considered when modeling LFSRs are as follows [21–23].

- *XOR or XNOR Feed Back Gates*: The feedback path may consist of either all XOR gates or all XNOR gates; LFSR will produce same number of values with different sequence for a particular tap setting.
- *One-to-Many or Many-to-One Feedback Structure*: Both one-to-many or many-to-one feedback structures can be implemented using same number of gates. However, a one-to-many feedback structure will have a shorter worst case delay.
- *Prohibited or Lockup State*: Special care should be placed on the design aspect such that LFSR avoids the prohibited or lockup state. In the case of XOR gates, the LFSR will not sequence through the binary value when all bits are at logic zero. Similarly, for XNOR gates the LFSR will not sequence through the binary values if all bits are at logic one. Thus, the LFSR should bypass these initializations during power up.
- *Ensuring a Sequence of All 2n Values*: If taps provided for a maximal length sequence are used, the LFSR configurations described so far will sequence through $(2n - 1)$ binary values. The feedback path can be modified with extra circuitry to ensure that all $2n$ binary values are included in the sequence.

Fig. 2 shows the LFSR we designed adopting the above discussed facts. The 8-bit LFSR is modeled so as to use one-to-many feedback structure and has been modified for a $2n$ looping sequence. It calculates and holds the next value of the LFSR which is then assigned to the output signal WM_DATA after each clock edge. The NOR of all LFSR bits minus the most significant bit that is LFSR_REG (6:0) generates the extra circuitry needed for all $2n$ sequence values.

3.3 Watermarking Insertion Unit

Fig. 3(a) shows the architecture of the watermark insertion unit designed to perform the watermarking insertion. The invisible-robust watermarking involves adding or subtracting a constant times the pixel value to be watermarked to or from a constant times the neighborhood function as described in the watermark encoder function in the previous section. The four data lines provide the pixels $I(i,j)$, $I(i + 1, j)$, $I(i, j + 1)$,

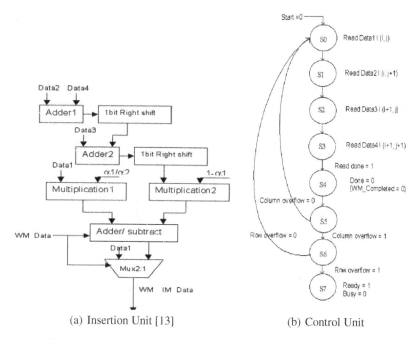

Fig. 3. Watermark Insertion Unit and Control Unit Structural Design.

and $I(i+1, j+1)$ for the row-column address pair (i, j). First, the $I(i, j+1)$ and $I(i+1, j+1)$ are given to the adder1 as input. Then, the resulting sum and carry out from adder1 are fed to the adder2 alongwith $I(i+1, j)$. The resulting sum of the adder2 is the neighborhood function value. The division by two is performed by shifting the results bit to the right by one bit, consequently discarding the rightmost bit (LSB). The scaling of the neighborhood function is achieved by multiplying it with $(1 - \alpha_1)$ using the multiplier2. At the same time, the scaling of the image pixel gray values is performed in multiplier1 by multiplying $I(i, j)$ with α_1 or α_2. The eight high order bits of the multipliers are fed to the adder/subtract unit to perform watermark insertion. Since, we are concerned only with the integer values of the pixels, the lower eight bits of the multiplier results are discarded, which represent the values after the decimal point. The output of the adder/subtract unit(watermarked image pixels) and the original image pixel values are multiplexed based on the watermark values and are driven on to signal WM_IM_Data if the watermark value is "1" or "2" as per watermark encoding function in the previous section.

3.4   The Control Unit as a Finite State Machine (FSM)

Fig. 3(b) shows the control unit implemented as FSM. Following are the control signals: Start – active high signal used to activate all the modules, Alpha1 – 8-bit input scaling constants for watermark insertion algorithm, Alpha2 – 8-bit input scaling constants for watermark insertion algorithm, Key – 8-bit Digital watermark key. Following are the output control signals: Ready – signal to indicate the insertion process is completed. Busy – signal to indicate the watermarking process is in progress.

The FSM has seven states as defined below. At each state certain events take place and the FSM moves to the next state on the next positive edge of the clock.

- S0: When the signal start is reset the control jumps to the state S0. In this state the $I(i, j)$ is read from the image RAM. The column and row addresses are registered in row_var and col_var.
- S1: The second data $I(i, j + 1)$ is read from the image RAM. In this state the column address is incremented to (Col_IM_addr = col_var + 1).
- S2: The data $I(i + 1, j)$ is read from the image RAM. The row address is increased to (row_IM_addr = row_var +1).
- S3: In this state fourth data $I(i + 1, j + 1)$ is read from the image RAM. The row address is incremented to (row_IM_addr = row_var +1). The column address is incremented to (Col_IM_addr = col_var + 1).
- S4: The signal Read_done is set, indicating that all the four pixels are read from image RAM for an address pair (i, j). The control will be in this state until done signal from the watermark insert module is set. The watermarked image pixel value and watermark pixel value are stored in respective RAM at address (i, j).
- S5: the column address is incremented (col_var = col_var + 1). In this state the control checks for the possibility of column overflow, i.e. the column address reached its right most pixel address or not. If col_var is equal to the right most address then the control moves to state S6 else to state S0.
- S6: the row address is incremented by (Row_var = Row_var + 1)and Col_var =0. In this state the control checks for row overflow, i.e. the row address reached its lower most pixel address or not. If Row_var is equal to the lower most address then the control moves to state S7, else to state S0.
- S7: In state S7, the busy signal is reset and ready signal is set indicating that the input image is watermarked.

4   Implementation, Simulation and Conclusions

The chip was modeled using VHDL and functional simulation was performed. The three modules created are watermark insertion, watermark generator, and watermark encoder. The watermark encoder is the main module which instantiates the other two components.The synthesis of the chip is carried out using Synplify Pro^{TM} tool targeting Xilinx VIRTEX-II technology with XCV50-BG256-6 target device.The simulations are done using the ModelSim. Fig. 4 shows the RTL schematic of the synthesized encoder. The timing simulation is presented in Fig. 5. From the synthesis results we provide the macro statistics and timing report of the units in Table 2. Minimum period is an indicator of the timing path from a clock to any other clock in the design. The minimum period is reported for both generation unit and encoder, whereas the critical path delay is reported for the insertion unit which is fully combinational. The cell usage indicates all the logical cells that are basic elements of the technology.

This paper presented an architecture and FPGA implementation of a watermarking encoder. Its low power high performance implementation is currently under progress.

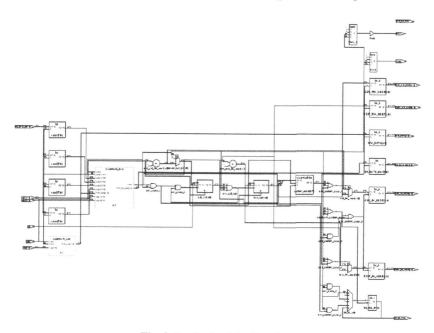

Fig. 4. Synthesis of the Encoder.

/test/start	0	
/test/clk	0	
/test/alph1	00000001	00000001
/test/alph2	00000010	00000010
/test/key	00000110	00000110
/test/im_rd_wm	1	
/test/im_data_out	UUUUUUU	00001011
/test/col_im_addr	00	10
/test/row_im_addr	00	00 00 00 01 01 01 10 10 10
/test/col_addr	00	10 10 11
/test/row_addr	00	00 00 00 01 01 01 10 10 10 11
/test/col_add	UU	UU 11
/test/row_add	UU	UU 11
/test/col_wm_addr	UU	UU 00 01 10 00 01 10 00 01 10
/test/row_wm_addr	UU	UU 00 01 10
/test/col_wm_ad	UU	UU 00 01 10 00 01 10 00 01 10 11
/test/row_wm_ad	UU	UU 00 01 10 11
/test/wm_data	UU	UU 00 01 10 01 10 01
/test/ready	0	
/test/busy	1	
/test/enable	0	
/test/wm_rd_wm	0	
/test/x	1	
/test/y	0	
/test/data_out_water	00	00 UU
/test/data_out	00000000	

Fig. 5. Simulation Waveforms of the Encoder.

Table 2. Summary of Synthesis Report.

Units	Period/Delay (ns)	Cells Usage(BELS)
Watermark Generation	4.916	43
Watermark Insertion	15.526	122
Overall Encoder	19.842	838

The disadvantage of the watermarking algorithms implemented is that the processing needs to be done pixel-by-pixel. In future, we are aiming to investigate block-by-block processing. Since DRM systems need both encryption and watermarking, we think that combining both the hardware alongwith data compression hardware would be benefi-cial. Moreover, the on-chip encryptor can be used in storing the watermarking generator key in encrypted form, thus enhancing the watermark security.

References

1. Emmanuel, S., Kankanhalli, M.S.: A Digital Rights Management Scheme for Broadcast Video. ACM-Springer Verlag Multimedia Systems Journal **8** (2003) 444–458
2. Kundur, D., Karthik, K.: Digital Fingerprinting and Encryption Principles for Digital Rights Management. Proceedings of the IEEE **52** (2004)
3. Eskicioglu, A.M., Delp, E.J.: An Overview of Multimedia Content Protection in Consumer Electronics Devices. Elsevier Signal Processing: Image Comm. **16** (2001) 681–699
4. Memon, N., Wong, P.W.: Protecting Digital Media Content. Communications of the ACM **41** (1998) 35–43
5. Mohanty, S.P.: Digital Watamerking of Images. Master's thesis, Department of Electrical Engineering, Indian Institute of Science, Bangalore, India (1999)
6. Hsiao, S.F., Tai, Y.C., Chang, K.H.: VLSI Design of an Efficient Embedded Zerotree Wavelet Coder with Function of Digital Watermarking. IEEE Transactions on Consumer Electronics **46** (2000) 628–636
7. Maes, M., Kalker, T., Linnartz, J.P.M.G., Talstra, J., Depovere, G.F.G., Haitsma, J.: Digital Watamarking for DVD Video Copyright Protection. IEEE Signal Processing Magazine **17** (2000) 47–57
8. Tsai, T.H., Lu, C.Y.: A Systems Level Design for Embedded Watermark Technique using DSC Systems. In: Proceedings of the IEEE International Workshop on Intelligent Signal Processing and Communication Systems. (2001)
9. Petitjean, G., Dugelay, J.L., Gabriele, S., Rey, C., Nicolai, J.: Towards Real-time Video Watermarking for Systems-On-Chip. In: Proceedings of the IEEE International Conference on Multimedia and Expo (Vol. 1). (2002) 597–600
10. Garimella, A., Satyanarayan, M.V.V., Kumar, R.S., Murugesh, P.S., Niranjan, U.C.: VLSI Impementation of Online Digital Watermarking Techniques with Difference Encoding for the 8-bit Gray Scale Images. In: Proc. of the Intl. Conf. on VLSI Design. (2003) 283–288
11. Mathai, N.J., Sheikholeslami, A., Kundur, D.: VLSI Implementation of a Real-Time Video Watermark Embedder and Detector. In: Proceedings of the IEEE International Symposisum on Circuits and Systems (Vol. 2). (2003) 772–775
12. Tsai, T.H., Wu, C.Y.: An Implementation of Configurable Digital Watermarking Systems in MPEG Video Encoder. In: Proc. of Intl. Conf. on Consumer Electronics. (2003) 216–217
13. Mohanty, S.P., Ranganathan, N., Namballa, R.K.: VLSI Implementation of Invisible Digital Watermarking Algorithms Towards the Developement of a Secure JPEG Encoder. In: Proceedings of the IEEE Workshop on Signal Processing Systems. (2003) 183–188

14. Seo, Y.H., Kim, D.W.: Real-Time Blind Watermarking Algorithm and its Hardware Implementation for Motion JPEG2000 Image Codec. In: Proceedings of the 1st Workshop on Embedded Systems for Real-Time Multimedia. (2003) 88–93
15. Mohanty, S.P., Rangnathan, N., Namballa, R.K.: VLSI Implementation of Visible Watermarking for a Secure Digital Still Camera Design. In: Proceedings of the 17th International Conference on VLSI Design. (2004) 1063–1068
16. Petitcolas, F.A.P., Anderson, R.J., Kuhn, M.G.: Information Hiding - A Survey. Proceedings of the IEEE **87** (1999) 1062–1078
17. Voloshynovskiy, S., Pereira, S., Pun, T., Eggers, J., Su, J.: Attacks on Digital Watermarks: Classification, Estimation-based Attacks and Benchmarks. IEEE Communications Magazine **39** (2001) 118–126
18. Mathai, N.J., Kundur, D., Sheikholeslami, A.: Hardware Implementation Perspectives of Digital Video Watermarking Algortithms. IEEE Transanctions on Signal Processing **51** (2003) 925–938
19. Tefas, A., Pitas, I.: Robust Spatial Image Watermarking Using Progressive Detection. In: Proceedings of the IEEE International Conference on Acoustics, Speech, and Signal Processing (Vol. 3). (2001) 1973–1976
20. Petitcolas, F.A.P.: Watermarking Schemes Evaluation. IEEE Signal Processing **17** (2000) 58–64
21. Nelson, V.P., Nagle, H.T., Irwin, J.D., Caroll, B.D.: Digial Logic Analysis and Design. Prentice Hall, Upper Saddle River, New Jersey, USA (1995)
22. Smith, D.J.: HDL Chip Design: A Practical Guide for Designing, Synthesizing and Simulating ASICs and FPGAs Using VHDL or Verilog. Doone Publications, USA (1998)
23. Smith, M.J.S.: Application-Specific Integrated Circuits. Addison-Wesley Publishing Company, MA 01867, USA (1997)

Multi-agent Based User Access Patterned Optimal Content Allocation Method for Federated Video Digital Libraries

R. Ponnusamy[1,2] and T.V. Gopal[1]

[1] Dept. of Computer Science & Engg., Anna University, Chennai – 600 025,
[2] Dept. of Computer Science & Engg., Anjalai Ammal Mahalingam Engg. College,
Kovilvenni – 614 403,
r_ponnusamy@hotmail.com, gopal@annauniv.edu.

Abstract. Digital Libraries are emerging technologies for content management. These contents include multi-media objects, video-objects etc. On account of storage and bandwidth costs, the content storage and delivery are the major problems. It is necessary to formulate a new method by taking into account all aspects of multimedia and video-on-demand content management. This paper describes a new method called multi-agent based user access pattern oriented optimal content allocation method for digital libraries and is concerned with various behavioural pattern of the digital library system. The content access pattern not only varies based on regional interest, subject interest, cultural interest etc. but also this pattern varies over time because of the movement of various user communities. Intelligent multi-agent based system design for dynamic content allocation has been proved as the cost-effective method when contrasted with other mathematical models for content allocation.

1 Introduction

Digital Libraries are modern social virtual institutions for information collection, preservation and dissemination. The design and development of digital library requires addressing many issues [1-6] and must be able to perform intelligent human-oriented tasks in order to make it highly sophisticated and effective. The content storage management is the one among the important issues, which decides fast and economical retrieval of information in the federated or distributed digital libraries [3], [6]. The system design and development necessitates the need for intelligent solution in order to address the above said requirements.

The delivery of large files to individual users, such as video on demand or application programs [3-6],[11],[12] to the envisioned federated web enabled video digital library network is one of the important tasks to be envisaged. The members of these libraries are scattered across the globe. Contributing to the unpredictable user requests from various regions. In order to overcome these situations a number of load balancing [7-9],[11] and server acceleration [10] approaches are used for producing good results. One approach is to replicate the information across mirrored-server architecture [11] by means of various distributed implementation methods. Later if there is a necessity a second approach has been made through increasing the bandwidth [7] capacity, requiring high bandwidth capacity as well as fast and dense server capacity.

G. Das and V.P. Gulati (Eds.): CIT 2004, LNCS 3356, pp. 354–365, 2004.

The huge rate of increase in data suggests that massive scale storage architecture is needed to be able to scale at a faster rate than the growth of processor and disks. In addition, reliance on hardware improvements alone is not sufficient to keep pace with the demand for data storage. The third approach has been proposed to reduce the bandwidth which consists in program caching [18]. The last one is more reasonable than the server replication. In this method a number of caches are distributed throughout the network, to cater to the multiple requests from its cache rather than going for individual requests. The expected competition among multimedia providers may benefit those that can provide these services at the expected quality level of service at the lowest price. For example in case of VOD, the servers can be owned or leased by the VOD providers. In either case, the providers pay for the storage of video copies in the servers and also for the use of communication links for transferring information over the network to the content consumers. The problem of the VOD providers is to manage the storage of video copies within the servers, such that the overall cost is minimised. The question is how many copies should be allocated for each video and at which server? As a consequence the researchers are motivated to focus on optimizing not only the delivery network but also electronic content allocation.

A hierarchical-architecture [12-14] for the distribution of electronic content was introduced by Nussbaumer et. al. in the year 1994. It gives high scalability. Later it has been improved as distributed algorithm by Israel Cidan et. al in the year of 2001. They also introduced the trade-off between bandwidth and storage requirements, which resulted from the placement of the content servers in the hierarchy tree. They computed the best level of the hierarchy for the server location that minimises the combined cost of communication and storage, i.e., the cost of storage within servers combined with the cost of transferring information among and between servers to end-users. This approach can not be applied in case of real network (Internet) because the requests are unpredictable. The main assumption made in the previous work is that all the requests are given precisely, and in advance, and that the network does not change. However, the requests are unpredictable in the real environment. This problem is perceived as the Partially Observable Markov Decision Problem (POMDP) i.e., problem of calculating an optimal policy in an inaccessible stochastic environment with an unknown transition model. S.H. Gray Chan has proposed modelling and Dimensioning of Hierarchical Storage System [20]. This system classifies the video-objects into two categories viz., so-popular and not-so-popular objects, according to the frequency of video-objects access. The frequently accessed so-popular objects are moved to secondary levels and less-frequently-accessed objects are stored at the root level itself. None of these methods consider user content access semantics. In this present work we have designed a multi-agent based user access pattern oriented optimal content allocation method for federated Digital Libraries. The storage, bandwidth and frequency of access are considered to be the criteria for optimal content allocation in the hierarchy tree. It considers content semantics and frequency of content access in particular region. If the frequency is very high then the content is moved to that particular region. Normally no guarantee can be given for frequency of content access. While considering the group of user accesses, the semantics of content access pattern, i.e., a particular content accessed by whom can be learned using multi-agent system. By taking the apriori information of the particular pattern for the particular period, the content is moved to the particular region.

The content access will vary according to the regional interest, subject interest, cultural interest, research interest and so on. Here a simple mathematical model without considering the content semantics of user communities will not always be the cost-effective method for content allocation in dynamic case. That is the ith object will be stored in the right locations (best level of hierarchy) for optimal delivery. But, i+1th object has newly arrived in the network. Where it has to be stored is the basic question, because the number of request for that object is unknown. Normally it is assumed to be zero. So, it will be stored in the root server. If it is accessed from the root then the total traffic in the system will increase unpredictably, when the number of requests increases. This we are doing it by means of learning the user access pattern learning. That is, what type of contents will be accessed by which region need to be identified. This is called user access patterning. After identifying i+1th object pattern, it is allocated in the same locations, if i+1th object belong to the ith object pattern.

Frances Braziner [15] has designed a dynamic electrical grid load management system for cost-effective usage of electrical production. It classifies different category of users and according to user consumption it gives different prize offer. Such a system is doing user community classification and does the negotiation between utility companies and their customers. This kind of system design need user content access pattern learning, adaptation because this access pattern will change dynamically over time. The main difference between electrical power and electronic content is that once the electrical power is produced then it ought to be used immediately. The content does not have any semantics. But the electronic content once if it is made available it can be used at any point of time and it has content semantics. In the present work for effective optimal content management, the prime criteria considered for the content allocation are bandwidth, storage, content semantics and user semantics and in addition the system design must need a dynamic adaptation. This paper considers the semantics of various content types, user communities, access patterns, locations and the relation between the user groups and the contents. In order to use the bandwidth effectively the user must move the content to the frequently accessed area. From the above observation [15] it is evident that there is a need for distributed learning, planning and dynamic adaptation model which can be implemented through the multi-agent system for solving such problems.

2   User Access Pattern Modelling

A user access pattern is instructive information that explains the essential structure of which type of contents is accessed by which regions. In this case a language region user access pattern explains how many language i requests are received from region j.

The Digital video-on-demand libraries are designed for various specific purposes such as Movie broadcasting, Tourism advertising, Virtual universities, Georeferenced Information system, etc., where in the contents are accessed across the different parts of the world. A video digital library is offering video movie services [24] to all over the world. It is offering movies of different countries in various languages. Usually the people of the respective region access these movies. That is Tamil and Hindi movies are accessed by Indians. Urdu, Afgani and Malai movies are accessed by Pakistanis, Afganis and Malaysians respectively. Even through the sectarian and regional people of the respective language movies are accessed very frequently, because of transmigration of people of specific group move from one country to another country. But, they may search for the specific movies of their own mother tongue even though they reside in a different country. Besides this, there are people who are very specific in accessing movies of certain specific actors, irrespective of their location. So, considering these factors the static policy for content storage is not applicable and hence storing the video objects (Movie object) of the respective region will not be always optimal, necessitating the need for a dynamic allocating policy.

A video browsing system [17] designed to overcome information overload, has the facility to preselect the shots of the user interest and keep it in the buffer for effective browsing. This mechanism supports interactive multimedia browsing applications by exploiting information about the expected browsing behaviour of the user, which is estimated on the basis of a rationalistic exploration strategy for the retrieval of results. It also needs a content conceptualisation. Likewise, in this present design of multi-agent system, an agent tries to fix it in every distributed server and do content conceptualisation through content analysis. The content specification is able to give the details of content language, content style, content region, etc. The agent collects the user profile while accessing the requests. Then the agent processes every user requests. After processing the request it is able to identify the region from where that particular request has come. It formulates a pattern for that type of access. It also encounts the frequency of access. That is a specific type of content which is normally be accessed by users in these regional people and group. This is called as user access pattern learning which takes a long period and changes over time. Normally the new movie objects are frequently uploaded into the system. It is necessary therefore to allocate the content in the optimal location instead of replicating it to all servers.

The user profile is collected at the first time of user request. Content profile is built at the time of up-loading the content. The content access details are collected through the user requests. Language profiles and regional profiles are collected and updated as and when they are required. All these profiles are shown in the tables 1 – 5.

3 The System Model

Sometimes the sets of servers are located in a non-hierarchical order even though the complete system is deemed to be in a hierarchical order. Therefore there is a need for a virtual hierarchical tree $T = (V, E)$ to represent the communication network, where V is the set of nodes and E is the set of directed communication links. It has been already established that the hierarchical tree approach for content management permits high-level of scalability. Each node of the tree represents the server capable of storing video-objects and the server contains the agent program. The system is assumed to have three types of nodes. These nodes are viz., Head-end, Intermediate node and a Root node. The head-ends (switches) connect all the user nodes through the client nodes. This head-end stores the video-objects, depending on the user access. It has an agent program (Head-End Accessor), which is responsible for storing the video objects in the head-end nodes and also performing user classification and content access pattern learning by analysing the user requests. It also collects the information (user profile) about the user who is accessing the object. Such types of information are forwarded to the intermediate nodes. New video objects are also up-loaded in the system through any one of these nodes, during the process loading; it collects the information (object profile) about the object. Copies of these profiles are then moved to the root- node.

Table 1. Language Profile

Language Code	Language
L001	Arabic
L002	Bulgarian
L003	Catalan
L004	Chinese
L005	Croatian
L006	Czech
L007	Danish
L008	Duch
L009	English
L010	Estonian

Table 2. Object/Content Profile

Attributes	Values
Movie Name	TITANIC
Movie Id.	M0025
Language	English
Language Id.	L009
Director Name	James Cameron
Hero Name	Leonordo DiCaptio
Heroine Name	Kate Winslet
Story Writer	James Cameron
Size	1 GB

Table 3. User Profile

Attributes	Values
User Name	James Ronold
User id.	U045
Spoken Language	English
Region	London
Region Code	R006
Address	#8, Down St., London, UK
Gender	Male

Table 4. Language Region Patterns

Language Code	Region Code	No. of Requests / Month
L009	R009	80
L009	R010	15
L009	R011	18
L009	R012	20
L009	R006	30
L005	R009	4
L005	R010	3
L005	R011	2

Table 5. Regional Profile

Region Name	Country Name	Region Code
Delhi	India	R001
Chennai	India	R002
Tokyo	Japan	R005
London	England	R006
Paris	France	R007
NewYork	U.S.A.	R008
Washington	U.S.A.	R009
Sydney	Australia	R013
Moscow	Russia	R010

The intermediate node stores an agent program and receives a user profile from the head-end and classifies users into different categories. Normally, the system (virtual tree) contains number of intermediate levels. The very first (line before the head-end) intermediate level of nodes does the user classification and also the object profile analysis. After analysing the user content frequency access over the previous period, a pattern is formed to include the probability of user access to particular language objects by combining previous access over the particular period of time in various regions. The entire user requests, object information and object copy are moved to the root server. This model is shown in the following figure 1. Here '*' indicates the content/object availability in the particular node.

The following model assumptions are made

1. While satisfying the head-end's requests for object in the network, any one of the nodes on the path from the root to head-end invariably contains the object.

2. The link capacities are sufficient to provide all types of requests for delivery of the object to all head-ends.

3. The links are bi-directional in terms of message exchange, but necessarily distributed from root node to the leaf node for providing the objects at the head-ends.

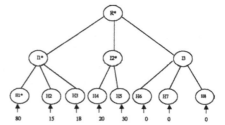

H – Head-end Node/Regional Nodes,
I – Intermediate Node,
R – Root Node

Fig. 1. Hierarchical Network Object/Content Location Model

4. A labelling process identifies each node. The agent is capable of not only identifying each node connected to all its leaf nodes but also the number of links to which the leaf nodes are linked to the root of the tree.

5. Each head-end represents the regional server located in different regions. (For example above figure .1, H1 represents region 1 (R1), H2 represents region 2 (R2) and so on.

6. The root server is initially storing the complete set of objects of all language.

7. Generally, other relevant assumptions are made for network representations, pertaining to node linking and message receipt.

4 The Multi-agent System Framework

In the Multi-Agent Framework every agent comprises of a single component are able to play various roles according to the place in which agent lives. The intelligent agent emits specialised behaviour for handling different tasks. Such behaviour can be modelled using role [21]. Since, the agent is perceived as entity with different roles. In the current design, it is performing tasks such as 1. Head-end Accessor, 2. User Access Pattern Analyser, 3. Content location Analyser, 4. Agent Replicater. 5. Content Allocator. The basic objective design of this system is capable to adapt any changing conditions that may occur in any part of the system in such a manner that every module is independent of each other as is shown in figure 2. The various roles played by the agents are

i. Head-End Accessor: This task is equipped with a browser style GUI, which is able to collect the user semantic information about the content request with the user profile (if he has not been profiled earlier) and subsequently the user is classified in a particular category. It stores this information in the local server. This is forwarded to the immediate ancestor. The location of the user is also identified by the system by fetching the IP address of the user access location. Also, it provides a provision to load the video objects in the system.

ii. User Access Pattern Analyser: This is a non-interactive component, which will analyses the different type of users and contents, according to the various attributes and put them in certain category. Based on the frequency of access in particular location the content access frequency is computed based on the type of content is assumed to be accessed in the particular region. This pattern of information is moved to the root node.

iii. Content Location Analyser: This is also a non-interactive component, which will analyses regional information and compare the best level of hierarchy location for every individual pattern. It also takes into account the parameters of storage and bandwidth, apart form the access pattern of the user. It uses a distributed algorithm as given in the section 6.

iv. Agent Replicater: This component performs the agent cloning when any one node is added, and instructs the necessary nodes to do the adjustments if any one of the components is removed.

v. Content Allocator: For every pattern, this component performs the content allocation according to the information given by content location Analyser.

5 Distributed Algorithm

In this system an agent fixes itself in every server and uses three different algorithms according to the location. The first algorithm is

Fig. 2. Agent Roles

used by the head-end, second one is used by the intermediate nodes and the root server uses the third one. The agent is able to pass the computed information to the parents. In turn each of the parent nodes also passes the required information to its entire children. This agent also passes the depth of information while cloning the new server. These algorithms compute the average request service cost for storing the particular language pattern objects in the concerned nodes.

5.1 Algorithm for Head-End Node

1. C_{ci} - Cost of moving particular language (L_j) pattern objects from the root to the Head-end node H_i.
2. S_{ci} - Storage Cost for the objects at node i, T_i - total number of requests at Head-end H_i for various objects of particular language (L_j) pattern, Set LOCATION = "UP".
3. $C_i = S_{ci} + C_{ci}$
4. Compute the average request cost at Head-end Hi (for L_j) using the following equation $C_{avg} = C_i / T_i$
5. Communicate the average cost, depth, and number of requests to the parent node.

5.2 Algorithm for Intermediate Node

1. C_{ri} - Cost of moving particular language (L_j) pattern objects from the root to the current node.

2. C_{si} - Cost of serving the particular language (L_j) objects to the Head-ends.
3. $C_{ci} = C_{ri}+C_{si}$
4. S_{ci} - Storage Cost for the particular language (L_j) objects at the ith node, Ti- the total number of requests at Node I_{ij} from its Childs for the particular language (L_j) pattern objects. Set LOCATION = "UP"
5. $C_i = S_{ci}+C_{ci}$
6. Compute the average request cost at Node I_{ij} using the following equation $C_{Avg} = C_i/T_i$
7. If any of the child's average is less than the Caver and not equal to zero then
   i. Pass the LOCATION = "HERE" to those nodes.
   ii. Drop the requests from that node, recompute the value of T_i, C_{si}, C_{Avg}
8. Communicate the average cost, depth, and number of requests to the Parent nodes.

5.3 Algorithm for Root Node

1. C_{si} - Cost of serving the particular language (L_j) pattern objects to the Head-ends.
2. $C_{ci} = C_{si}$
3. S_{ci} - Storage Cost for the particular language (L_j) pattern objects, T_i- the total number of request at root from its child for the particular language (L_j) pattern objects.
4. $C_i = S_{ci}+C_{ci}$
5. Compute the average request cost at root using the following equation $C_{Avg} = C_i/T_i$
6. If any of the child's average is less than the Caver and not equal to zero then Pass the LOCATION = "HERE" to those nodes.

Notations
C_{ci} – Communication Cost for particular patterned objects at node i, C_{ri} - Cost of moving particular patterned objects from the root to the current node i, C_{si} - Cost of serving particular patterned objects to the Head-ends from the current node i S_{ci} - Storage Cost for particular patterned objects at node i, C_i – Total Cost for particular patterned at node i,C_{Avg} – Average Total Cost/Request for particular patterned objects,T_i – Total number of requests served from node i for particular patterned objects,L_j–j^{th} Language.

The content allocator is moving all the objects of the specific language pattern to all the nodes having LOCATION information "HERE".

6 Empirical Modelling

Consider the ith object pattern; This i^{th} object pattern has C_i as the cost element for optimal storage and communication give by

$$C_i = S_{ci} + C_{ci} \qquad (1)$$

The ith object may pertain to L1, L2, L3 (L1, L2, L3... are different languages) and spread over different regions 1, 2, 3, 4... n. The first region taking x_1 number of requests for object 1, x_2 number of requests for object 2 and x_3 number of requests for object 3 and etc., under this category.

It is already known (for example) x1+x2+x3+x4 = 163 pertaining to the current (starting) month. Similarly x4+x5+x6 = 736 and x7+x8+x9+x10 = 101, totally 1000 requests for the required regions for different objects pertaining to language L1. The number of requests (x1...........xn) are random in nature and distributed over specific types of region needing L1 (language one).

It is presumed that the distribution of language L2 to various regions takes into account, the semantic aspect revealed by the requirement is indicated by $(x_1,.........,x_{10})$ for the current month. The concerned object distribution may spread over different types of region irrespective of the object in L1 (language 1) in various regions of the previous month. If the successive stage of transition from the current to the immediate successor period follows markov property, then the corresponding one step transition probability matrix is computed with the transition probability indicated by:

$$Þ_{jk} = P(x_n = k \mid x_{n-1} = j), n >= 1 \tag{2}$$

$$P = \begin{matrix} & \begin{matrix} 1, & 2, & 3, & . & \cdots\cdots & k & \cdots\cdots\cdots & n \end{matrix} \\ \begin{matrix} 1 \\ 2 \\ : \\ i \\ : \\ n \end{matrix} & \begin{pmatrix} p_{11}, & p_{12}, & p_{13}, & & p_{1k} & & ,p_{1n} \\ p_{21}, & p_{22}, & p_{23}, & & p_{2k} & & ,p_{2n} \\ & & & & & & \\ p_{i1}, & p_{i2}, & p_{i3}, & & p_{ik} & & ,p_{in} \\ & & & & & & \\ px_1, & px_2, & px_3, & & p_{xk} & & ,p_{xn} \end{pmatrix} \end{matrix} \quad ; \begin{matrix} \Sigma\Sigma\, p_{ik} = 1 \\ i \quad k \end{matrix}$$

In terms of conditional probabilistic notation, the probability distribution of the language L1 to the various regions R1, R2 ...Rn is given by

$$P (L1) = P (L1R1) + P (L1R2) + - \text{------------} +P (L1Rn),$$

Where P (L1R1) =P (R1/L1) P (L1)

$$P (L1R2) =P (R2/L1) P (L1)$$
$$P(L1Rn)=P(Rn/L1)P(L1) \quad \text{or in general}$$
$$P(Ri/L1) = P(L1Ri)/ P(L1) \text{ for i=1,2,3,.....,n}$$

In general for any language L_j we have

$$P(R_i/L_j) = P(L_jR_i)/P(L_j) \text{ for i,j} = 1,2,3, ...n \tag{3}$$

It is necessary to takes into account that the above conditional probabilities that are known already for the current month. From the given requests the content semantics of particular specific region for every given language is identified. Instead of storing all the objects in the root server for unknown future request, we are moving only the particular language objects needed to the required region. This enables us to achieve optimal content allocation.

7 Simulation Experiment Results

The system under consideration is simulated using the Java RMIServelets. It is able to pass all the user requests to the parent servers. Also, two RMI clients are developed to get the user request for object and the content uploading. These RMI clients are passing their requests to the RMIservelet server. This RMIserver agent of the video content server will automatically perform the aforesaid (as explained in Section 4) roles.

In current design the RMIserver agent process listens on a particular port. When the server receives an RMI request message, it parses the request and finds the content availability. If it is available then it will supply it from the local server otherwise it will forward the request to the parent server. In order to elicit the effective functionality; the system is designed to accept the RMI messages. This agent is also able to replicate itself, as and when the new server is installed it will automatically replicate to that server and is playing various roles as explained in above design; these roles are played in according to the location (as explained in Section 5.).

The system is tested with 20 data set collected from Internet. Simulation of such system allocates various types of movies of different languages at different regions. Especially the English language pattern is identified in five regions. There are also 4 English language video objects whose data loaded into the system. It is assumed that the storage cost is 25/object and Communication cost is 1/link for all objects irrespective of size.

Initially all the head-ends average access cost is computed using the head end algorithm. This is shown in figure 3. Later all the intermediate average cost is computed and it is compared with the head-end's average cost. This is shown in figure 4. Here the average cost of H1 is less than the I1 cost, so this pattern objects copy is moved to the node H1. Again the intermediate node I1 recompute the average cost and it is forwarded to the root. The roots average cost is computed and is compared with intermediate average cost if it is less than a copy will be moved to that node. But, it is testing whether the average value is non-zero. Here it allocates copies of object in I1 and I2, because the computed average of I1, I2 is less than the R1. The resulted request cost average is shown in figure 5 and the resulting content allocation is shown in figure 1.

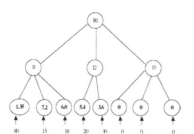 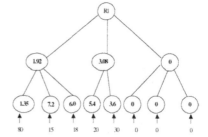

Fig. 3. Head-End's algorithm average request cost   **Fig. 4.** Intermediate Node algorithm's average request cost

In this present experiment it is found that language L009 (English) requests are occurring from the regions R009 (New York), R010 (Washington), R011 (California), R012 (Florida) and R006 (Texas). That is L009 is receiving 80 requests from region R009, 15 requests from region R010, 18 requests from region R011, 20 requests from R012 and 30 requests from R006. This is called language-region pattern. New objects (uploaded in to the network) belong to this language need to be allocated in these regions, because requests for these objects usually occur only from these regions. But, at the same time, it is necessary to compute the best level of hierarchy for these objects for optimal delivery. Likewise it is necessary to identify the sub-patterns occur within the particular language pattern. That is a particular set of movies may have similar set of attributes needs to be identified and its best location can be computed for content allocation.

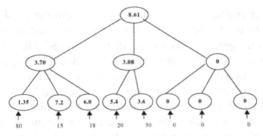

Fig. 5. Intermediate Node algorithm's recomputed average request cost and root algorithm's average cost

8 Conclusion

In this paper, an attempt is made to design and develop a multi-agent framework for optimal content allocation on federated video digital libraries. Such networks are used for specific purposes. This work has revealed that the user access pattern learning has improved the optimal content allocation effectively. This is established by means of simple simulations. The simulation does not consider the content transmission delay time. Comparing the static network model of hierarchical with dynamic multi-agent approach has been able to handle the dynamic requests. Future research may focus on incorporation of deep content conceptualisation and this may provide more optimal content allocation. This may be done by means of sub-pattern identification.

References

1. Daniel Andreson, Tao Yang, Omer Egecioglu, Oscar H. Ibarra, and Terence R. Smith, Scalability Issues for High Performance Digital Libraries on the World Wide Web, Department of Computer Science, University of California, Santa Barbara, CA93106.
2. Dieter W. Fellner, TU Braunschweig, Research Issues for Digital Libraries, http://graphics.tu-bs.de/DLResearch/Issues/df-DlresIssues010313.pdf
3. J. Frew, et. al., The Alexandria Digital Library Architecture, Int Jour. Digital Libraries (2000) 2: 259-268, Springer-Verlag 2000.
4. Cezary Mazurek et. al., "Digital Library for Multimedia Content Management", http://www.mon.poznan.pl.
5. Rama Chellappa, Digital Image and Video Libraries, http://www.wtec.org/loyola/diglibs/ob_01.htm
6. J. Leon Jhao et. al., "Data Management for Multi-User Access to Digital Video Libraries, Tech. Report, School of Business Management, The Hong Kong University of Sc. & Tech, Hong Kong, 1999.
7. Mary Y.Y. Leung, John C.S. Lui, Leana Golubchik, Use of Analytical Performance Models for system sizing and Resource Allocation in Interactive Video-on-Demand systems Employing Data Sharing, IEEE Trans. on Knowledge and Data Engineering, Vol 14, No. 3, May/June 2002.
8. Azer Bestavros et. al., Distributed Packet Rewriting and its application to scalable server architectures, In Proceedings of the 1998 Intl. Conf. On Network protocols (INCP '98), October 1998.
9. Teodoro. G, et. al., Load balancing on stateful clustered web servers. http://www.dcc.ufmg.br/~dorgival/artigos/sbac03.pdf

10. Junehwa Song, et. al., Architecture of a Web Server accelerator, Elsevier Computer Networks 38 (2002) 75 – 97.
11. Valeria Cardellini et. al., Dynamic load balancing on web-server systems, 28-39, May-June 1999, IEEE Internet Computing.
12. Israel Cidon, et. al., Optimal allocation of electronic content, Elsevier Computer Networks 40 (2002) 205-218.
13. Paul Mather, Scalable Storage for Digital Libraries, Ph.D. Report, Dept. of Computer Science, Virginia Polytechnic Institute and State University, Blauk Burg, USA, 23 Oct. 2001.
14. Damianos Gavalas et. al., Hierarchical network management: a scalable and dynamic mobile agent based approch, Elsevier Computer Networks 38 (2002) 693-711.
15. Frances Brazier et. al., Agents Negotiating for load balancing of electricity use, Proceedings of the 18th International Conference on Distributed Computing Systems, ICDCS'98, IEEE Computer Society Press, 1998.
16. Gerhard Weiss, "Multi-Agent System : A Modern Approach to Distributed Artificial Intelligence", The MIT Press, 1999.
17. Silvia Holffelder et. al., "Designing for semantic access: A Video Browsing system", GMD Report 43, German National Research Center for Information Technology, Germany.
18. J.P. Nussbaumer, B.V. Patel, F. Schaffa, J.P.G. Sterbenz, "Networking requirements for interactive video on demand", IEEE Journal on Selected Areas in Communications 13(5) 1995 (Also presented at INFOCOM 94).
19. F. Schafa, J.P. Nussbaumer, "On bandwidth and storage tradeoffs in multimedia distribution networks", Fourteenth Annual Joint Conference of the IEEE Computer and Communication Societies (Vol. 3), April 02-06, 1995.
20. S.-H. Gray Chean, Fouad A. Tobagi, "Modeling and Dimensioning Hierarchical Storage Systems for Low-Delay Video Services", IEEE Trans. on Computers, Vol 52, No. 7, July 2003.
21. Georg Gottlob, Michael Schrefl et. al., "Extending Object Oriented Systems with Roles", ACM Trans. on Info. Systems, Vol. 4, No. 3 pp 268 – 296, July 1996.
22. Jeff Nelson, "Programming Mobile Objects with Java", John Willey & Sons, Inc. 1999.
23. James Goodwill, "Developing Java Servelets: The authoritative solution", Techmedia 1999.
24. http://www.themovies.com

Optimizing Surplus Harmonics Distribution in PWM

Shiyan Hu[1] and Han Huang[2]

[1] Department of Computer and Information Science
Polytechnic University
Brooklyn, NY 11201, USA
shu@cis.poly.edu
[2] Department of Electrical and Computer Engineering
Polytechnic University
Brooklyn, NY 11201, USA
hhan@photon.poly.edu

Abstract. The goal of optimal pulse-width modulation (PWM) is to select the switching instances in such a way that a waveform with a particular characteristic is obtained and a certain criterion is minimized. The conventional method to solve the optimal PWM problem would usually lead to large content of surplus harmonics immediately following the eliminated frequency band, which may increase the filter loss and reduce the efficiency and performance of the whole controller. Meanwhile, it may increase the probability of resonance between line impedance and filter components. To overcome the shortcomings of conventional PWM methods, in this paper, we propose an algorithm for pushing the first crest of the surplus harmonics backward, ameliorating the amplitude frequency spectrum distribution of the output waveform, and thus reducing the impact of surplus harmonics.

The problem is first formulated as a constrained optimization problem and then a Quantum-inspired Evolutionary Algorithm (QEA) algorithm is applied to solve it. Other than Newton-like methods, the enhanced QEA does not need good initial values for solving the optimal PWM problem and is not stuck in local optimum. The simulation results indicate that the algorithm is robust and scalable for a variety of application requirements.

Keywords: Surplus harmonics, Constrained nonlinear optimization, Quantum-inspired Evolutionary Algorithm.

1 Introduction

The *pulse-width modulation* (or PWM in short) technique can effectively reduce the harmonics content of inverter output waveform and possesses evident merits in improving frequency, efficiency, and dynamic response speed [12]. Therefore, PWM has extensive applications and many related techniques such as [2,3] have been proposed. The *Selected Harmonics Elimination* PWM (or SHE-PWM in

G. Das and V.P. Gulati (Eds.): CIT 2004, LNCS 3356, pp. 366–375, 2004.

short) [13] is one of the optimal PWM techniques. It can generate the output waveform of higher quality through eliminating specific lower order harmonics. The basic idea is to set up the notches at the specially designated sites of PWM waveform and then the inverter alters directions many times per half-cycle to control the inverter's output waveform appropriately. Refer to Figure 1 for a three-level PWM waveform. Suppose we use two switching instances (angles) to denote every notch. Then the switching instances can be determined through solving a set of transcendental equations. There are a lot of algorithms in the literature so far (e.g., [7,1]), however, conventional methods do not give consideration for the impact by the surplus harmonics. From Figure 2 where the spectrum of an output waveform produced by the conventional PWM technique is shown, we clearly see that the first crest of the surplus harmonic (i.e., the 13th harmonic in the figure) is too high, which is unfavorable to eliminate the harmonics for the output filter and will increase the probability of resonance between line impedance and filter components and reduce the efficiency and performance of the whole controller.

In this paper, we focus on pushing the first crest of the surplus harmonics backward, at the same time ameliorating the amplitude frequency spectrum distribution of the output waveform. Since the proposed algorithm is not Newton-like, we do not need good initial values which are sometimes hard to find for the commonly-used alternatives. The algorithm can be divided into two steps: transform the original transcendental equations to a constrained optimization prob-

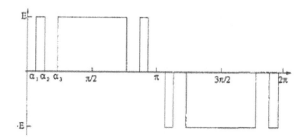

Fig. 1. A symmetric three-level PWM waveform.

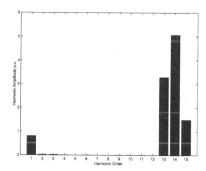

Fig. 2. The spectrum of the output waveform produced by the conventional PWM method when $n = 12$.

lem, then use an enhanced Quantum-inspired Evolutionary Algorithm (QEA) to solve it. The QEA [4] is a relatively new evolutionary computing algorithm, which is characterized by the principles of quantum computing including concepts of qubits and superposition of states. QEA can treat the balance between exploration and exploitation more easily comparing to the conventional GAs [4]. Other than the standard QEA, our QEA favors localized search which is more suitable in our case. The simulation results indicate the soundness of our method.

The rest of the paper is organized as follows: Section 2 describes the numerical transformation of PWM problem to an optimization problem. Section 3 describes the QEA for solving the optimization problem. Section 4 shows the simulation results. A summary of work is given in Section 5.

2   Numerical Transformation of the PWM Problem

As in [7], we first reduce the optimal PWM problem to a polynomial problem, which is significantly easier to handle and computationally more efficient than the original nonlinear system.

A periodical PWM waveform with n notches per half-cycle can be represented using Fourier series expansion as

$$f(t) = \sum_{n=1}^{\infty} [a_n \sin(n\omega t) + b_n \cos(n\omega t)] \tag{1}$$

where $\omega = 2\pi/T$. Owing to the property of odd quarter-wave symmetry, the coefficients of Fourier series are $b_n = 0$ for all n and

$$a_n = \begin{cases} \frac{4}{n\pi} \sum_{k=1}^{n} (-1)^{k-1} \cos(n\alpha_k) & : \quad n \quad is \quad odd \\ 0 & : \quad n \quad is \quad even \end{cases} \tag{2}$$

where $0 < \alpha_1 < \alpha_2 < \ldots \alpha_n < \pi/2$. Note that a_n is the amplitude of an n-th harmonic component of the waveform f. To set selected harmonics of a full-bridge PWM inverter output voltage to desired values, we need to solve the following set of nonlinear equations:

$$\sum_{i=1}^{n} (-1)^{i-1} \cos(k\alpha_i) = h_k \tag{3}$$

where $h_k = k\pi a_k/4E$, $k = 1, 3, 5, \ldots, 2n - 1$ and E is the inverter DC bus voltage. Let $x_i = \cos(\alpha_i)$ for odd i and $x_i = \cos(\pi - \alpha_i)$ for even i. Applying Chebyshev polynomial approximation [1], we get

$$\sum_{m=1}^{k} c_{k,m} \cdot S_{2m-1} = h_{2k-1}, 1 \le k \le n \tag{4}$$

where $S_m = \sum_{i=1}^{n} x_i^m$. From the recursion equations of Chebyshev approximation, we can get coefficients $c_{k,m}$ one by one. Hence, by setting harmonic amplitudes h in (4) to desired values, we can obtain the values of $S_{2m-1}, 1 \leq m \leq n$.
So far, equation (3) has been transformed to

$$
\left(
\begin{matrix}
x_1 + x_2 + \cdots + x_n & = & S_1 \\
x_1^3 + x_2^3 + \cdots + x_n^3 & = & S_3 \\
\cdots \\
\cdots \\
x_1^{2n-1} + x_2^{2n-1} + \cdots + x_n^{2n-1} & = & S_{2n-1}
\end{matrix}
\right)
\tag{5}
$$

Since

$$
p(x) = \prod_{i=1}^{n} (x - x_i)
\tag{6}
$$

where x_i $(1 \leq i \leq n)$ is the root of a degree-n polynomial $p(x)$. Using Taylor
series expansion, we have

$$
\frac{p'(x)}{p(x)} = \sum_{i=0}^{n} \sum_{m=0}^{\infty} \frac{x_i^m}{x^{m+1}} = \sum_{m=0}^{\infty} \frac{S_m}{x^{m+1}}.
\tag{7}
$$

Integration of (7) gives

$$
p(x) = x^n e^{\left(- \sum_{m=1}^{\infty} \frac{S_m}{m x^m}\right)}
\tag{8}
$$

Note that

$$
p(-x) = (-1)^n x^n e^{\left(- \sum_{m=1}^{\infty} \frac{(-1)^m S_m}{m x^m}\right)}
\tag{9}
$$

Then we get

$$
p(x) = (-1)^n p(-x) G(1/x)
\tag{10}
$$

Using the algorithm in [11], we have $G(x) = e^{V(x)} = \sum_{i=1}^{\infty} g_i x^i$ and $V(x) =
\sum_{i=0}^{\infty} v_i x^i$. When first n odd S_i are known, the v_i can be determined for $0 \leq i \leq
2n$: $v_{2i} = 0$ for $1 \leq i \leq n$; $v_{2i-1} = -2S_{2i-1}/(2i-1)$ for $1 \leq i \leq n$. Thus $p(x)$
can be written as a Toeplitz system through Coefficients Matching Method.

$$
\begin{bmatrix}
g_n, & \cdots, g_1 \\
& \cdots \\
& \cdots \\
g_{2n-1}, & \cdots, g_n
\end{bmatrix}
\begin{bmatrix}
(-1) p_1 \\
\cdots \\
\cdots \\
(-1)^n p_n
\end{bmatrix}
= -
\begin{bmatrix}
g_{n+1} \\
\cdots \\
\cdots \\
g_{2n}
\end{bmatrix}
\tag{11}
$$

where p_i is the i-th order coefficient in polynomial $p(x)$. From (11), we can
obtain p_i using Toeplitz Matrix algorithm. So far, we have transformed the
original transcendental nonlinear problem to a monic real-coefficient algebraic
polynomial problem $p(x) = p_n x^n + p_{n-1} x^{n-1} + \cdots + p_0 = 0$ of which all the

roots are real. Recall that we need to push down the amplitude for $(n + 1)$th harmonic, which is mathematically equivalent to

$$\begin{aligned} &\min | \sum_{i=1}^{n}(-1)^{i-1}\cos((2n + 1)\arccos x_i)| \\ &s.t. | \sum_{j=0}^{n} p_j x_i^j| < \delta, i = 1, \ldots, n \end{aligned} \tag{12}$$

where x_i is the i-th root of the monic $p(x)$ and $0 < x_1 < x_2 < x_3 < \ldots < x_n < 1$, and δ denotes the maximum tolerable error of the system.

3   Solving PWM by Quantum-Inspired Evolutionary Algorithm

The conventional numerical techniques are not effective for solving the problem (12) due to many unknown system variables and multiple local optimum. Even when applicable, they usually need good initial values. The evolutionary algorithm has been shown to have potential to overcome these limitations.

The *Quantum-inspired Evolutionary Algorithm* (QEA) [4] is a relatively new evolutionary computing algorithm, which is characterized by principles of quantum computing including concepts of qubits and superposition of states. QEA can imitate parallel computation in classical computers. Several recent results on QEA include [5, 6, 9, 8, 10]. It is worth noting that QEA simulates Quantum mechanism on classical computers and is an evolutionary algorithm but not a quantum algorithm.

As the smallest unit of information, a *qubit* is a quantum system whose states lie in a two dimensional Hilbert space. Note that a qubit can be in "1" state, "0" state or simultaneously in both (*superposition*). The state of a qubit can be represented as $|\Psi\rangle = \alpha|0\rangle + \beta|1\rangle$ where α and β specify the probability of the corresponding states, and $|\alpha|^2 + |\beta|^2 = 1$. In our implementation, a uniform deviate is compared to $|\alpha|^2$ to "observe" the state of a qubit as in [4]. The state of a qubit can be changed by unitary transformation. A *quantum gate* is a unitary transformation that acts on a fixed number of qubits. Inspired by the quantum computing, QEA uses the Q-bit representation for the probabilistic representation. An m Q-bits representation is defined as $q = [\kappa_1|\kappa_2|\ldots|\kappa_m]$ where $\kappa_i = (\alpha_i, \beta_i)^T$ and $|\alpha_i|^2 + |\beta_i|^2 = 1, i = 1, 2, \ldots, m$.

In this paper, we use the QEA for solving the optimization problem (12). Other than the standard QEA, our QEA favors localized search, which is very important since the problem (3) and (12) are highly ill-conditioned (refer to Section 4), i.e., even slight perturbation of solutions may lead to significant perturbation to the fitness value (of the target function) and thus hurt the convergence of QEA. In the new structure, we keep in the population $Q(t) \bigcup S(t)$ at generation t both the Q-bit individuals, $Q(t) = \{q_1^t, q_2^t, \ldots, q_n^t\}$ and the corresponding solutions, $S(t) = \{s_1^t, s_2^t, \ldots, s_n^t\}$, where n is the size of the population, and q_i^t is a Q-bit individual of length m:

$$q_j^t = [\kappa_{j1}^t|\kappa_{j2}^t|\ldots|\kappa_{jm}^t]. \tag{13}$$

Each Q-bit individual $q_j^t, j = 1, 2, \ldots, n$ corresponds to a solution $s_j^t, j = 1, 2, \ldots, n$ in the population, and is used for deciding whether to add or subtract a small (random) amount to s_j^t to form the new solution $s_j'^t$. By comparing s_j^t and $s_j'^t$ as well as their fitness values, we then appropriately update q_j^t (see below). After all solutions generate descendants, the best n out of the $2n$ solutions ($\{s_j^t\} \bigcup \{s_j'^t\}$) are selected to form the set of solutions $S(t+1) = \{s_j^{t+1}\}$ of the new population. Note that we also need to select those q_j^t, which correspond to s_j^{t+1}, to form $Q(t+1) = \{q_j^{t+1}\}$. If both s_j^t and $s_j'^t$ are selected, then two q_j^t's will exist in the new population. If none of s_j^t and $s_j'^t$ gets selected, nor does q_j^t. The details are elaborated as follows.

(1) In the initialization step, all α_i^0 and β_i^0, $i = 1, 2, \ldots, m$, of all q_j^0, $j = 1, 2, \ldots, n$, are initialized to $1/\sqrt{2}$, such that each $q_j^0, j = 1, 2, \ldots, n$ can represent the linear superposition of all 2^m states, namely

$$|\Psi_{q_j^0}\rangle = \frac{1}{\sqrt{2^m}}(|00\ldots0\rangle + |00\ldots1\rangle + |11\ldots1\rangle). \tag{14}$$

By the above discussion, we initialize each solution as the set of values uniformly distributed between $[0, 1]$ and then increasingly sort them. Note that we use numerical encoding for the solution.

(2) Generate new solutions $s_j'^t$ from s_j^t as described above. Note that we restrict that α, β to be positive, for avoiding the ambiguity.

(3) Update q_j^t. We apply a quantum gate, i.e., a unitary transformation $U(\Delta\theta)$ to obtain new q_j^t, namely $\kappa_{ji}^t = U(\Delta\theta)\kappa_{ji}^t$ for each κ_{ji}^t in q_j^t. The $U(\Delta\theta)$ given in [4] is

$$U(\Delta\theta) = \begin{bmatrix} \cos(\Delta\theta) & -\sin(\Delta\theta) \\ \sin(\Delta\theta) & \cos(\Delta\theta) \end{bmatrix} \tag{15}$$

where $\Delta\theta$ is defined in the Table 1. The sign of $\Delta\theta$ is not hard to decide, e.g., if $s_j'^t$ is fitter than s_j^t and $s_{ji}'^t < s_{ji}^t$, we should try to increase the possibility for decreasing s_{ji}^t. Recall that we use $|\alpha_{ji}^t|^2$ (precisely, the predicate: random$[0, 1) > |\alpha_{ji}^t|^2$) to decide whether to add a small amount to s_{ji}^t, therefore, we should increase α_{ji}^t and $\Delta\theta$ is negative.

(4) The best n out of $2n$ solutions and their corresponding Q-bit individuals are selected to form the next generation.

(5) Repeat (2)–(4) until certain condition is met.

Table 1. The lookup table for $\Delta\theta$, where $f(\cdot)$ is the fitness.

$s_{ji}^t \le s_{ji}'^t$	$f(s_j^t) \le f(s_j'^t)$	$\Delta\theta$
true	true	0.02π
false	true	-0.02π
true	false	-0.02π
false	false	0.02π

Since the solutions are only perturbed by very small values for obtaining the new solutions each time, our QEA exhibits good localized search ability. Each Q-bit individual starts from the the same value, and is successively updated to favor the specific direction for improving solution vectors. Eventually when QEA converges to the optimum, Q-bit individuals will return to the same values, namely $1/\sqrt{2}$. Since the polynomial and thus (12) are highly ill-conditioned (see below), the amount for addition and subtraction in step (2) is set to be progressively smaller every 200 iterations.

4   Simulation Results

We have performed simulations over systems of various sizes. We choose the following two systems to present our results in this paper. The first simulation is illustrative where the number of switching angles is $n = 12$, and h_1 is set to 0.8 and all other h (i.e., $h_3, h_5, \ldots, h_{23}$) are set to 0. We first compute the switching angles from (3) by the conventional PWM method. The resulting angles and spectrum are shown in Table 2 and Figure 3, respectively. We then investigate the ill-conditioned property of the nonlinear system as well as the resulting polynomials.

We perturb the above resulting angles with very small random values in $[-0.02, 0.02]$, which however leads to the significant error to the system (refer to Figure 4): evaluation of the 12th equation in (3) gives 1.04 rather than the desired 0, which greatly harms the system's reliability! The original nonlinear system is clearly ill-conditioned. We now compute the condition number of $p(x)$. The coefficients for $x^1, x^2, \ldots, x^{12}$ in the polynomial are shown in the Table 2 (the coefficient for x^0 is 0.0001). Recall that for a simple root x of the monic p of degree n, the condition number of p at x is given by

$$\chi(p, x) = \frac{\|p\| \max(1, |x|^{n-1})}{|p'(x)|}. \tag{16}$$

If p has only simple roots, then $\chi(p)$, the condition number of p, is the maximum of $\chi(p, x)$, x varying over the roots of p. Evaluating $\chi(P, x)$ at $x = 0.9809$ (corresponding to the angle 0.1955 by the conventional PWM method) already gives us the condition number larger than 10^7! The polynomial is also ill-conditioned.

We now apply the enhanced QEA method to solve the constrained optimization problem (12) where δ is set to 0.04. The resulting angles (i.e., $\cos^{-1} x$) are shown in Table 2. Then we can see from Figure 3 where the amplitude of the 13th harmonic (corresponding to h_{25}) by the enhanced QEA algorithm is 0.33 compared to 3.27 by the conventional algorithm. Therefore, the output current of 13th harmonic is largely reduced and at the same time, the energy from the reduced harmonic is optimally re-distributed to the following surplus harmonics. So the difficulty of output passive filter design is reduced and the controller's performance is enhanced.

As indicated in [1], a number of existing techniques do not perform well when n is larger than 20, due to ill condition of the systems. We therefore

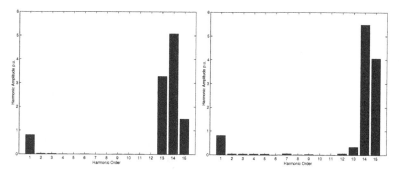

Fig. 3. The spectrum of the output waveform by the conventional PWM algorithm (left) and by the enhanced QEA algorithm when $n = 12$ (right).

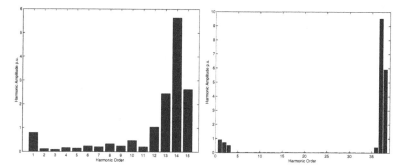

Fig. 4. The spectrum of the output waveform for randomly perturbed angles when $n = 12$ (left) and by the enhanced QEA algorithm when $n = 35$ (right).

Table 2. Resulting angles (truncated at 10^{-4}) for three cases and coefficients of the polynomial $p(x)$. "C.PWM" stands for "Conventional PWM method", "E.QEA" for "Enhanced QEA", "Rnd. Perturb." for "Randomly perturbed angles". Note that the differences due to truncation will be propagated to the final results.

Angles	1	2	3	4	5	6
C.PWM (3)	0.1955	0.2453	0.3926	0.4902	0.5926	0.7341
E.QEA (12)	0.1804	0.2314	0.3693	0.4652	0.5609	0.6998
Rnd. Pert.	0.1773	0.2270	0.3743	0.4720	0.5743	0.7158
Coeff.	-0.0116	0.2071	-1.6423	7.6863	-23.6075	50.0117
Angles	7	8	9	10	11	12
C.PWM (3)	0.7969	0.9762	1.0076	1.2168	1.2271	1.5705
E.QEA (12)	0.7615	0.9328	0.9716	1.1613	1.1803	1.5706
Rnd. Pert.	0.7786	0.9580	0.9893	1.1985	1.2088	1.5526
Coeff.	-74.6389	78.5427	-57.1569	27.4149	-7.8054	1.0000

consider the case where the number of switching angles is $n = 35$, and lower order harmonics are set to $h_1 = 0.9, h_3 = 0.7, h_5 = 0.5$ and all other h (i.e., $h_7, h_9, \ldots, h_{69}$) are set to 0. The spectrum of output waveform generated by our enhanced QEA algorithm is shown in Figure 4, where the amplitude of the 36th harmonic (corresponding to h_{71}) is 0.38, while it is 11.09 by the conventional PWM method (plot omitted). The algorithm successfully handles the highly ill-conditioned polynomials and pushes the first crest of the surplus harmonics backward.

5   Conclusions

A new robust algorithm is proposed to solve the optimal PWM problem while simultaneously ameliorating the frequency spectrum distribution of the output waveform, and thus enhance the controller's performance and reduce the diffi-culty of output passive filter design. The algorithm first transforms the nonlinear system to a constrained optimization problem, then applies the enhanced QEA method, which is more efficient than the simple QEA, to solve it. The main features of the new method are three-fold. First, the proposed method consid-ers ameliorating the frequency spectrum distribution of the output waveform of PWM, which is important but has not been addressed in the literature so far. Second, due to the power of QEA, we do not need good initial values which are sometimes hard to find for our commonly-used Newton-like alternatives. Third, the new method is robust for solving the large ill-conditioned system. Our simulation results indicate the effectiveness of the proposed method. The new technique can be applied to variable-frequency velocity modulation, static VAR compensation and other related fields.

References

1. D. Czarkowski, D.V. Chudnovsky, G.V. Chudnovsky, and I.W. Selesnick. Solving the optimal PWM problem for single-phase inverters. *IEEE Trans. Circuits and Systems*, 49(4):465–475, 2002.
2. P. Enjeti and J.F. Lindsay. Solving nonlinear equation of harmonic elimination PWM in power control. *IEE Electronic Lett.*, 23(12):656–657, 1987.
3. P. Enjeti, P.D. Ziogas, and J.F. Lindsay. Programmed PWM technique to eliminate harmonics: a critical evaluation. *IEEE Trans. Ind. Appl.*, 26(2):302–316, 1990.
4. K.-H Han and J.-H. Kim. Quantum-inspired evolutionary algorithm for a class of combinatorial optimization. *IEEE Trans. Evolutionary Computation*, 6(6):580–593, 2002.
5. K.-H Han and J.-H. Kim. On setting the parameters of qea for practical applica-tions: Some guidelines based on empirical evidence. *GECCO 2003*, pages 427–428, 2003.
6. K.-H. Han and J.-H. Kim. Quantum-inspired evolutionary algorithms with a new termination criterion, hε gate, and two phase scheme. *IEEE Transactions on Evo-lutionary Computation*, 8(2):156–169, 2004.
7. H. Huang, S. Hu, and D. Czarkowski. A novel simplex homotopic fixed-point al-gorithm for computation of optimal PWM patterns. *Proceedings of the 35th IEEE Power Electronics Specialists Conference (PESC)*, 2004.
8. J.-S Jang, K.-H Han, and J.-H. Kim. Quantum-inspired evolutionary algorithm-based face verification. *GECCO 2003*, pages 2147–2156, 2003.

9. J.-S. Jang, K.-H. Han, and J.-H. Kim. Face detection using quantum-inspired evolutionary algorithm. *Proceedings of the 2004 Congress on Evolutionary Computation, IEEE Press*, pages 2100–2106, 2004.

10. K.-H Kim, J.-Y Hwang, K.-H Han, J.-H. Kim, and K.-H Park. A quantum-inspired evolutionary computing algorithm for disk allocation method. *IEICE Transactions on Information and Systems*, E86-D(3):645–649, 2003.

11. D.E. Knuth. *The art of computer programming, vol2: Seminumerical algorithm*. Addison-Wesley, 1981.

12. H.S. Patel and R.G. Hoft. Generalized technique of harmonic elimination and voltage control in thyristor inverters: Part I harmonic eliminiation. *IEEE Trans. Ind. Appl.*, 9(3):310–317, 1973.

13. J. Sun and H. Grotstollen. Solving nonlinear equations for selective harmonic eliminated PWM using predicted initial values. *Proc. Int. Conf. Ind. Electr. Control and Instr.*, 1992.

M-BCJR Based Turbo Equalizer

Priyatam Kumar[1], R.M. Banakar[2], and B. Shankaranand[3]

[1] B.V.B.College of Engg. & Technology
Hubli-580 031, India
priyatam@bvb.edu
[2] ENC Dept., B.V.B.College of Engg. & Technology
Hubli-580 031, India
[3] National Institute of Technology Karnataka
Surathkal, Karnataka, India

Abstract. Capitalizing on the tremendous performance gains of turbo codes and the turbo decoding algorithm, turbo equalization is an iterative equalization and decoding technique that can achieve equally impressive performance gains for communication systems that send digital data over channels that require equalization, i.e. those which suffer from intersymbol interference (ISI). Turbo equalizers have been shown to be successful in mitigating the effects of inter-symbol interference introduced by partial response modems and by dispersive channels for code rates of R $>1/2$. We analyze the performance of iterative equalization and decoding (IED) using an M-BCJR equalizer. We use bit error rate (BER), frame error rate simulations and extrinsic information transfer (EXIT) charts to study and compare the performances of M-BCJR and BCJR equalizers on precoded and non-precoded channels. We predict the BER performance of IED using the M-BCJR equalizer from EXIT charts and explain the discrepancy between the observed and predicted performances.. We show that the true LLR's can be estimated if the conditional distributions of the extrinsic outputs are known and finally we design a practical estimator for computing the true LLR's from the extrinsic outputs of the M-BCJR equalizer.

1 Introduction

Graphical models for turbo codes (and low-density parity check (LDPC) codes), together with the various iterative algorithms for decoding them, have provided substantial insights into the dramatic performance improvements achievable through their use [1–4]. For an overview about graphical models we also refer to the paper by Loeliger et al. in this issue. The flurry of research in related topics over the last decade has produced a number of communications and signal processing algorithms that leverageturbo decoding approaches to provide similar gains in performance for a wide array of problems. In this paper, we discuss the turbo equalization approach to coded data transmission over intersymbol interference (ISI) channels, with an emphasis on the basic ideas and some of the practical details. The original system introduced in [8] leveraged the ideas of the turbo decoding algorithm to the related problem of equalization and decoding. We seek to provide an overview of the turbo equalization approach, with an algorithmic description and intuitive explanation of each of the steps involved in designing such a communication system.

We provide a high-level overview of turbo equalization, placing an emphasis on the concepts involved and delay a more mathematical development to subsequent

G. Das and V.P. Gulati (Eds.): CIT 2004, LNCS 3356, pp. 376–386, 2004.
© Springer-Verlag Berlin Heidelberg 2004

sections of the paper. The focus of our discussion will be the communication link depicted in Fig. 1, which contains a system configuration for a digital transmitter as part of a communication link. These basic elements are contained in most practical communication systems and are essential components of a transmitter such that turbo equalization can be used in the receiver. The role of the encoder, which is the first block in the figure, is to take the binary data sequence to be transmitted as input, and produce an output that contains not only this data, but also additional redundant information that can be used to protect the data of interest in the event of errors during transmission. There are a wide variety of practical methods for introducing such redundancy in the form of an error control code (ECC) (also referred to as forward error correction), however we will assume that a convolutional code is used for our purposes. The goal of forward error correction is to protect the data from the possibility of random single-bit errors or short bursts of errors that might occur in the data stream as a result of additive noise in the transmission or receiver errors. In order to ensure that such errors appear random and to avoid long error bursts, an interleaver is used to randomize the order of the code bits prior to transmission. This process is completely reversible, and is simply mirrored in the receiver.

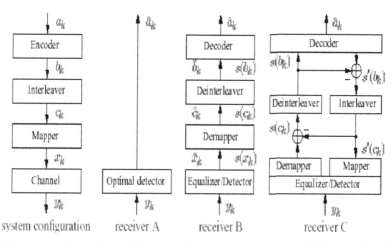

Fig. 1. System configuration and three receiver structures: the optimal detector (receiver A), one-time equalization and decoding using hard or soft decisions (receiver B), and turbo equalization (receiver C)

Finally, the permuted code bits are then converted into electrical signal levels that can be modulated either at base band or onto a carrier for transmission over a passband channel. Such modulation could take a variety of forms in such diverse applications as wired or wireless transmission, optical communications, optical data storage, magnetic recording, or even acoustic communication systems. The process of mapping binary code bits into channel symbols suitable for modulation is depicted by the mapper in Fig. 1. The traditional methods of data protection used in ECC do not work when the channel over which the data is sent introduces additional distortions, in the form of intersymbol interference. When the channel is and limited or for other reasons is dispersive in nature, then the receiver will, in general, need to compensate for the channel effects prior to employing a standard decoding algorithm for the ECC. Such methods for channel compensation are typically referred to as channel equalization. Even when the actual transmission medium is non-dispersive, often the transmit and receive filtering that takes place in a practical system gives rise to sufficient intersymbol interference that equalization becomes necessary. Given observations of the received data, the receiver now has essentially one task to complete: estimate the data that was transmitted. To do this optimally, in terms of minimizing the bit error rate (BER), the receiver must find the set of transmitted bits that are most probable, given knowledge of the complex statistical relationship between the observations and the transmitted bits. Such a receiver, as depicted in Fig. 1 as receiver A, takes into account the error control code, the interleaver, the symbol mapping, and knowledge of the channel. With so many factors involved, the resulting statistical relationship rapidly becomes difficult to manage in an efficient manner. As such, in most practical systems, receiver A is simply infeasible, as it amounts to essentially trying to fit all possible sequences of transmitted bits to the received data, a task whose complexity grows exponentially in the length of the data transmitted. The way that most practical receivers have been designed, is to first process the received observations to account for the effects of the channel and to make estimates of the transmitted channel symbols that best fit the observed data. A number of criteria for performance have been used for such equalizers, ranging from those attempting to simply invert the channel (so-called zero forcing equalizers) to linear and nonlinear equalizers based on minimizing a meansquared error (MSE) metric to even those that are symbol-error-rate (SER) optimal by maximizing the likelihood of the observations given the channel and data model. These equalization methods constitute the first step in receiver B from Fig. 1. Once the transmitted channel symbols have been estimated, they can be de-mapped into their associated code bits, de-interleaved and then decoded using a BER optimal decoder for the ECC. The most straight forward way to implement this separate equalization and decoding process is for the equalizer to make hard decisions as to which sequence of channel symbols were transmitted, and for these hard decisions to be mapped into their constituent binary code bits. These binary code bits can then be processed with the decoder for the ECC. However, the process of making hard decisions on the channel symbols actually destroys information pertaining to how likely each of the possible channel symbols might have been. This additional "soft" information can be converted into probabilities that each of the received code bits takes on the value of zero or one, which, after deinterleaving, is precisely the form of information that can be exploited by a BER optimal decoding algorithm. Many practical systems use this form of soft input error control decoding by passing soft information between an equalizer and decoding algorithm. The remarkable performance of turbo codes made it clear that the soft information need not only flow in one direction. Once the error control decoding algorithm processes the soft information, it can, in turn, generate its own soft information indicating the taken into account in the equalization process, creating a feedback loop between the equalizer and decoder, through which each of the constituent algorithms communicates its beliefs about the relative likelihood that each given bit takes on a particular value. This process is often termed "belief propagation" or "message passing" and has a number of important connections to methods in artificial intelligence, statistical inference, and graphical learning theory. The feedback loop structure described here and depicted in receiver C in Fig. 1 is essentially the process of turbo equalization. While the process of equalization and decoding through the feedback loop structure of receiver C is essentially complete, it is important to consider the effect that the soft information generated from one bit in one of the constituent algorithms (equalizer or decoder) will have on other bits in the other constituent algorithm. When processing soft information as an input to the equalizer or decoder, it is assumed that the soft information about each bit (or channel symbol) is an independent piece of information.

This enables simple, fast algorithms to be used for each of the equalizer and decoder. However, if the decoder formulates its soft information about a given bit, based on soft information provided to it from the equalizer about exactly the same bit, then the equalizer cannot consider this information to be independent of its channel observations. In effect, this would create a feedback loop in the overall process of length two – the equalizer informs the decoder about a given bit, and then the decoder simply re-informs the equalizer what it already knows. In order to avoid such short cycles in the feedback, and in hopes of avoiding local minima and limit cycle behavior in the process, when soft information is passed between constituent algorithms, such information is never formed based on the information passed into the algorithm concerning the same bit. Basically this amounts to the equalizer only telling the decoder new information about a given bit based on information it gathered from distant parts of the received signal (thanks to the interleaver). Similarly, the decoder only tells the equalizer information it gathered from distant parts of the encoded bit stream.

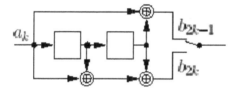

Fig. 2. Encoder of a convolutional code

As a result, the iterative equalization and decoding process can continue for many iterations before cycles are introduced, which eventually limits further improvements. This process of only passing "extrinsic information" between constituent decoders

2 Turbo Equalizer

Turbo equalizer is employed in the presence of an ISI channel to counter the effects of ISI and minimize the bit error rate (BER). It was pioneered by C. Douillard *et al.* [6] as an application of the iterative decoding principle [5], [16] and has been an object of extensive research henceforth.

2.1 Principle of Turbo Equalizer

Turbo equalizer is based on the principle of iterative decoding applied Turbo equalizer to SCCC's [17]. The receiver structure for Turbo equalizer is depicted in Figure 2.3. Both the equalizer and the decoder are SISO devices. The equalizer computes the *aposteriori* probabilities (APP's),$P(x_k = x|z_1, z_2, \ldots, z_K)$, $x. \in X$, $k = 1, 2, \ldots, K$, given K received symbols z_k, $k =1, 2,. .. ,K$ and outputs the extrinsic LLR's, $L^I(x_k)$, $k = 1, 2, ... ,$ K defined as the *a posteriori* LLR minus the *a priori* LLR. The superscript I refer to the inner SISO module *viz.*, the equalizer.

$$L^I(x_k) = In\left(\frac{P(x_k = +1/z_1, z_2,....,z_k)}{(P(x_k = -1/z_1, z_2,..., z_k))}\right) - In\left(\frac{P(x_k = +1)}{P(x_k = -1)}\right) \qquad (2.1)$$

The *a priori* LLR, $L(x_k)$, $k = 1, 2,. ... ,K$ represents the *a priori* information about the probability that $x_k . \in X$, $k = 1, 2,. ... ,K$ assumes a particular value. The APP decoder provides them. In the first equalization step, the *a priori* information, $L(x_k)$, $k = 1, 2,. .. ,K$ is not available and all values are assumed to be equally probable i.e., $L(x_k) = 0$, $\forall. k$. The *a priori* information for the decoder is obtained by deinterleaving the output extrinsic LLR's of the equalizer, $L(c_k) = \Pi^{-1}(L^I(x_k))$. Similar to the equalizer, the decoder also computes the APP's $P(c_k = c|L(c_1), L(c_2),. ..., L(c_K))$, $c\in.\{0, 1\}$ given the K code bit LLR's $L(c_k)$, $k =1, 2,. ... ,K$ and outputs the extrinsic LLR's, $L^O(c_k)$, $k = 1, 2,. ... ,K$ defined as the output LLR minus the *a priori* LLR. The superscipt O refers to the outer decoder.

$$L^O(x_k) = In\left(\frac{P(c_k = +1/L(c_1), L(c_2),...L(c_k))}{P(c_k = -1)/L(c_1), L(c_2),..., L(c_k)}\right) - In\left(\frac{P(c_k = +1)}{P(c_k = -1)}\right) \qquad (2.2)$$

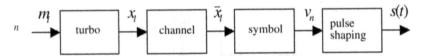

Fig. 3. Transmitter model of transmitter

The extrinsic LLR's of the decoder are interleaved to obtain the intrinsic information for the equalizer i.e.,$L(x_k)=\Pi(L^O(c_k))$, $k = 1, 2,. .. ,K$. The decoder also outputs estimates of the data bits as

$$a_k = \arg \max_{b\in(0,1)} \{P(b_k = b / L(c_1), (c_2),...., L(c_k)\} \qquad (2.3)$$

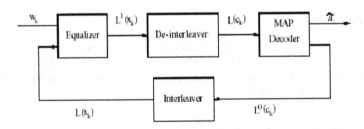

Fig. 4. Receiver model for Turbo equalizer

This process is repeated several times over a block of received symbols. The BCJR algorithm and its M-variant as used in Turbo equalizer are described in next paragraph.

3 SISO Module Based on the BCJR Algorithm

The SISO module shown in Figure 4 is a four-port device that accepts at the input the sequences of LLR's of the information bits, $\lambda^I(u)$ and the coded bits, $\lambda^I(c)$ and produces at the output sequences of *extrinsic* LLR's for the information bits, $\lambda^o(u)$ and the coded bits, $\lambda^o(c)$. It's input-output relationships and internal operations are given in subsection 3.1.

The SISO module can operate at *bit* level or *symbol* level. Quite often, the interleaver operates at *bit* level for improved performance. This necessitates the transformation of *symbol* LLR's into *bit* LLR's and *vice versa* if the SISO module is implemented at the *symbol* level (see subsection 2). Here, we describe the *symbol* level SISO module.

3.1 The Input-Output Relationships of the SISO Module

Assume that the information and code symbols are defined over a finite time index set $[1,2,\ldots,K]$. Let the operator

$$\log_j^*(a_j) \cong \log \sum_{j=1}^{J} e^{a_j} \tag{3.1}$$

From the input LLR's, $\lambda^I k(u)$ and $\lambda^I k(c)$, $k = 1, 2,\ldots,K$, the output *extrinsic* LLR's, $\lambda^o k(u)$ and $\lambda^o k(c)$ (c), $k = 1, 2,\ldots,K$ are calculated as

$$\lambda_k^o(c) = \log_{e:c_e \in c}^* \log\{\alpha_{k-1}(s_e^\alpha) + \lambda_k^I(c_e) + \beta_k(s_e^\beta)\} \tag{3.2}$$

$$\lambda_k^o(u) = \log_{e:u_e \in u}^* \log\{\alpha_{k-1}(s_e^\alpha) + \lambda_k^I(c_e) + \beta_k(s_e^\beta)\} \tag{3.3}$$

The LLR's calculated according to (3.2) and (3.3) are termed *extrinsic* due to the fact that the computation of $\lambda_k^o(u)$ does not depend on the corresponding input LLR $\lambda_k^I(u)$ and so it can be considered as an update The quantities $\alpha_k(\cdot)$ and $\beta_k(\cdot)$ in (3.2) and (3.3) are obtained through *forward* and *backward* recursions, respectively, as

$$\alpha_k = \frac{\log_{e:s_e^\beta=s}^* \{\alpha_{k-1}(s_e^\alpha) + \lambda_k^I(u_e) + \lambda_k^I(c_e)\}}{\log_S \{\log_{e:s_e^\beta=s}^* \{\alpha_{k-1}(s_e^\alpha) + \lambda_k^I(u_e) + \lambda_k^I(c_e)\}\}}, k=1,2,\ldots,K-1 \tag{3.4}$$

SISO: $\mathbf{X}^I(u) \rightarrow \boxed{} \rightarrow \mathbf{X}^o(u)$

$\mathbf{X}^I(c) \rightarrow \phantom{\boxed{xxxx}} \rightarrow \mathbf{X}^o(c)$

Fig. 5. Block diagram of SIS0 model

Fig. 6. Encoder trellis section defining notation for description of the SISO algorithm of the input LLR based on the code constraints and the information provided by all homologous symbols in the sequence except the one corresponding to the same symbol interval

$$\beta_k(s) = \left\{ \frac{\overset{*}{\log}\left\{\beta_{k+1}\left(s_e^\beta\right) + \lambda_{k+1}^I\left(u_e\right) + \lambda_{k+1}^I\left(c_e\right)\right\}}{\log\left\{\alpha_k\left(s_e^\alpha\right) + \lambda_{k+1}^I\left(u_e\right) + \lambda_{k+1}^I\left(c_e\right)\right\}} \right\}, k = 1,2,...,K-1 \tag{3.5}$$

with initial values $\alpha_o(s) = \begin{matrix} 0, & s=S0 \\ -\infty, & \text{otherwise} \end{matrix}$ $\qquad \beta_k(s) = \begin{matrix} 0, & s=S_k \\ -\infty, & \text{otherwise} \end{matrix}$

assuming that the encoder starts and ends in state 0. If the encoder ends in an unknown state, the initial values for the backward recursion are chosen as $\beta_k(s) = \alpha_k(s)$.............$\forall s$ The denominators in (3.4) and (3.5) are normalization terms which help avoid numerical problems arising out of finite precision. The $\overset{*}{\log}$ operator may be simplified

$$\overset{*}{\log}(a_j) = \max_j(a_j) + \delta(a_1, a_2,..., a_j) \tag{3.6}$$

where $\delta(a_1, a_2, ..., a_J)$ is a correction term that can be computed recursively using a single-entry lookup table [20]. This simplification significantly decreases the computational complexity of the BCJR algorithm at the expense of a slight performance degradation.

3.2 Inter-conversion Between *symbol* and *bit* Level LLR's

Inter-conversion operations between *symbol* and *bit* Level LLR's are necessitated by the presence of a bit-interleaver. These operations assume that the bits forming a symbol are independent. Suppose $\mathbf{u} = [u1, u2,..., um]$ is a symbol formed by m bits. The extrinsic LLR λ_j of the j the bit u_j within the symbol $\mathbf{u}$ is obtained as

$$\lambda_j^o(u) = \overset{*}{\underset{u:u_e=1}{\log}}\left[\lambda^0(u) + \lambda^I(u)\right] - \underset{u:u_e=0}{\log}\left[\lambda^0(u) + \lambda^I(u)\right] - \lambda_j^I(u) \tag{3.7}$$

Conversely, the extrinsic LLR of the symbol $\mathbf{u}$ is obtained from the extrinsic LLR's of its component bits u_j as

$$\lambda(u) = \sum_{j=1}^m \lambda_j u_j \tag{3.8}$$

3.3 M-BCJR Algorithm

The *M*-BCJR algorithm [7] is a reduced-complexity variant of the BCJR   algorithm
and is based on the *M*-algorithm, a reduced-search trellis decoder. The reduction in
complexity is achieved by retaining only the *M*-best paths in the forward recursion at
each time instant. In the calculation of α_k through forward recursion on α_{k-1}, only the
M largest components are used; the rest of them are set to an LLR of $-\infty$ and the corresponding states are thus declared dead. The backward recursion is executed only forward recursion. In Figure 6, we show an example of *M*-BCJR computation pattern for
M =2.

4 Performance Analysis of *M*-BCJR Equalizer

The performance of the *M*-BCJR equalizer is studied and contrasted with that of the
BCJR equalizer on a variety of ISI channels (precoded and non-precoded) with the
help of BER and FER simulations and EXIT charts [8]. The ISI channels are modeled
as convolutional codes (DTTF's) as discussed in Chapter II. In all our simulations, the
channel is assumed to be static and its coefficients f_m, $m = 0, 1,. . ., L - 1$ where L is
the length of the channel impulse response, are perfectly known. Each of the channel
coefficients has a power and is $p_m = \left| f_m^2 \right|$, $m = 0,1,..., L-1$ normalized such that

the total power $\sum_{m=0}^{L-1} p_m = 1$.

4.1 Performance of the *M*-BCJR Equalizer

In Figure 7, we show the BER and FER performance of IED for the unprecoded
channel [$\sqrt{0.45}$, $\sqrt{0.25}$, $\sqrt{0.15}$, $\sqrt{0.10}$, $\sqrt{0.05}$] with [1, 3]$_8$ as the outer code using 10 iterations and *N*=2048. The loss in performance of the *M*-BCJR equalizer as compared to
the BCJR equalizer is unexpectedly small for non-precoded ISI channels.

The BER and FER curves of the *M*=8 BCJR algorithm are almost overlapping with
those of the full BCJR which operates on the whole 16-state trellis. When *M*=4 is
used, the loss in performance is only 0.05 dB at a BER of $10^{-5.}$ For *M*=3, the loss is
0.25 dB at a BER of 10^{-4}. For *M*=2, the IED algorithm fails to evolve and does not
provide any improvement in performance with iterations. As can be seen from these
results for the above channel, we may use the *M*=4 BCJR equalizer with virtually no
performance degradation or the *M*=3 BCJR equalizer with a very small loss in performance. This is an interesting result and suggests that the complexity of the BCJR
equalizer can be reduced considerably without sacrificing its performance.

In Figure 8, we present the BER and FER simulation results over 6 iterations for
the unprecoded [0.5, 0.5, 0.5, 0.5] channel using the full BCJR and *M*=3 BCJR equalizers. An information block length of *N*=2048 was used. The full BCJR equalizer
operates on the whole trellis consisting of 8 states at each time instant. From the plots,
we observe that the performance of the *M*=3 BCJR equalizer is almost indistinguish-

able from that of the full BCJR equalizer in the region of BER=10^{-5} at reasonably high E_b/N_o. The performance of the M=3 BCJR equalizer is relatively worse at low E_b/N_o. The performance of the turbo equalizer saturates at a BER of 10^{-5} and does not improve significantly even at very high Eb/No. Such an early error floor is typical of SCC's in which the inner code is non-recursive [15]. It can be avoided by precoding the channel. The BER and FER simulation results for the precoded [0.5, 0.5, 0.5, 0.5] channel using the full BCJR, M=5 and M=3 BCJR equalizers are plotted in Figure 9. In comparison with the non-precoded channel, the M-BCJR equalizer suffers signifi-cant losses in the precoded case. The performance of the M=5 BCJR equalizer is approximately 0.25 dB worse than the BCJR algorithm at a BER of 10^{-4}. However, this difference diminishes as we progress toward smaller BER's. For M=3 BCJR, the IED hardly yields any improvement in the BER performance with increasing number of iterations. This is in stark contrast with its performance on the non-precoded chan-nel. It is also interesting to note that although the asymptotic performance on pre-coded channels is better at high E_b/N_o, the non-precoded channels offer better per-formance during the first few iterations. This behavior is a result of the fact that the initial reliability of a precoded channel is smaller than that of a non-precoded channel. However, as the iterations progress, the precoded channel outperforms the non-precoded channel. Also, there are no signs of an error floor at a BER of 10^{-5} and thus the performance may improve significantly as E_b/N_o increases.

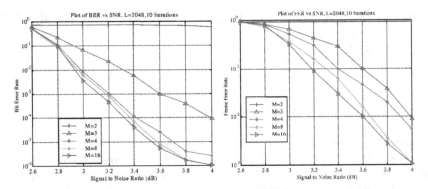

Fig. 7. BER & FER: Non-precoded [$\sqrt{0.45},\sqrt{0.25},\sqrt{0.15},\sqrt{0.10},\sqrt{0.05}$], [1, 3]$_8$

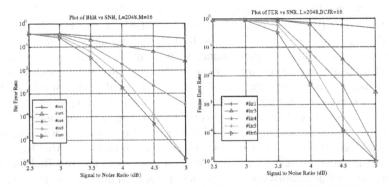

Fig. 8. Simulation results: 1.D precoded [0.5, 0.5, 0.5, 0.5], [1, 23/35]$_8$

5 Conclusion

In this paper, Turbo code was studied in detail. The simulation results show that Turbo code is a powerful error correcting coding technique in low SNR environments. It has achieved near Shannon capacity. However, there are many factors need to be considered in the Turbo code design. First, a trade-off between the BER and the number of iterations need to be made, e.g., more iteration will get lower BER, but the decoding delay is also longer. Secondly, the effect of the frame size on the BER also needs to be considered. Although the Turbo code with larger frame size has better performance, the output delay is also longer. Thirdly, the code rate is another factor that needs to be considered. The higher coding rate needs more bandwidth. From the simulation results, it is observed that the drawback of the Turbo code is its complexity and also the decoding time. Simulation results showed that the M-BCJR algorithm suffers significant losses in the case of simple convolutional decoders. This contrasting behavior of the M-BCJR algorithm in the cases of ISI channels and convolutional codes has been explained. It can be attributed to the metrics computed during the forward and backward recursions. The M-BCJR equalizer has much larger variance than in the case of a convolutional code. The larger variance of the metrics in the M-BCJR equalizer makes the algorithm less sensitive to the paths discarded.

References

1. C. Douillard, A. Picart, M. Jézéquel, P. Didier, C. Berrou, and A. Glavieux, "Iterative correction of intersymbol interference: Turbo-equalization," *Eur. Trans. Commun.*, vol. 6, pp. 507–511, Sept.–Oct. 1995.
2. M. J. Gertsman and J. L. Lodge, "Symbol-by-symbol MAP demodulation of CPM and PSK signals on Rayleigh flat-fading channels," *IEEE Trans. Commun.*, vol. 45, pp. 788–799, July 1997.
3. G. Bauch, H. Khorram, and J. Hagenauer, "Iterative equalization and decoding in mobile communications systems," in *Proc. the European Personal Mobile communications Conf.*, Bonn, Germany, Sept. 30–Oct. 2 1997,
4. M. Moher, "Decoding via cross-entropy minimization," in *Proc. IEEE Global elecommunicationsConf. 1993*, Houston, TX, Nov. 29 –Dec. 2 1993, pp. 809–813.
5. G. Bauch and V. Franz, "Iterative equalization and decoding for the GSM-system," in *Proc. IEEE 48th Vehicular Technology Conf.*, Ottawa, Canada, May 18–21, 1998.
6. C. Berrou, A. Glavieux, and P. Thitimajshima, "Near Shannon limit error-correcting coding and decoding: Turbo codes," in *Proc. Int. Conf. Communications*, Geneva, Switzerland, May 23–26, 1993 pp. 1064–1070.
7. C. Berrou and A. Glavieux, "Near optimum error-correcting coding and decoding: Turbo codes," *IEEE Trans. Commun.*, vol. 44, pp. 1261–1271, Oct. 1996.
8. D. Raphaeli and Y. Zarai, "Combined turbo equalization and turbo decoding," in *Proc. Global Telecommunications Conf. 1997*, Phoenix, AZ, Nov. 3–8, 1997, pp. 639–641.
9. T. Souvignier, A. Friedman, M.Öberg, R. E. S. P. H. Siegel, and J.Wolf, "Turbo decoding for pr4:Parallel versus serial concatenation," in *Proc. Int. Conf. communications 1999*, Vancouver, Canada, June 6–10, 1999.
10. J. Hagenauer, E. Offer, and L. Papke, "Iterative decoding of binary block and convolutional codes," *IEEE Trans. Inform. Theory*, vol. 42, pp. 429–445, Mar. 1996.
11. H. Nickl, J. Hagenauer, and F. Burkett, "Approaching Shannon's capacity limit by 0.27 dB using simple hamming codes," *IEEE Commun. Lett.*, vol. 1, pp. 130–132, Sept. 1997.

12. M. Tüchler, A. Singer, and R. Kötter, "Minimum mean squared error (MMSE) equalization using priors," *IEEE ransactions on Signal Processing*, vol. 50, pp. 673–683, March 2002.
13. A. Glavieux, C. Laot, and J. Labat, "Turbo equalization over a frequency selective channel," in *Proc. of the Intern. Symposium on Turbo codes, Brest, France*, pp. 96–102, September 1997.
14. S. Lin and J. J. Costello, *Error Control Coding*. Englewood Cliffs, New Jersey: Prentice Hall, 1983.
15. C. Weiss, C. Bettstetter, and S. Riedel, "Code construction and decoding of parallel concatenated tail-biting codes," *IEEE Trans.on Information Theory*, 2001.
16. C. Heegard and S. Wicker, *Turbo Coding*. Boston: Kluwer Academic Publishing, 1999.
17. J. Proakis and M. Salehi, *Communication Systems Engineering*. Upper Saddle River, New Jersey: Prentice Hall, 1994.

YALXP:
Yet Another Lightweight XPath Processor

R.V.R.P. Kumar and V. Radha

IDRBT, Castle Hills, Masab Tank, Hyderabad, India
rangavajhala@mtech.idrbt.ac.in, vradha@idrbt.ac.in

Abstract. Many algorithms have been proposed for processing multiple XPath Expressions such as Xfilter[5], Yfilter[6], turboXPath[13] and Xtrie[9]. But they do not deal with backward axes. XAOS[2] deals with XPath expressions with forward and backward axes (such as parent and ancestor). But XAOS deals with only one query at a time. As a result a document is parsed q times for a set of q queries, which is a significant cost in terms of time. More over, in a large-scale system, there is bound to be substantial commonality among different queries. In this paper, we present a method called YALXP, which attempts to evaluate multiple queries, with both forward and backward axes, in less number of passes exploiting commonality among the queries. Our method is built upon XAOS algorithm. Our experiments show that YALXP performs better in CPU time and memory than traditional XPath engine Xalan (ODP) – for multiple queries with single DOM construction.

1 Introduction

XPath is an underlying component of many partnering technologies of XML such as XSLT, XPointer and XForms etc. XPath, short for XML Path language, is a querying language used to select specific parts of very large XML documents in IR applications.

Little work has been done in the area of XPath processing involving backward axes. XAOS [2] deals with XPath expressions with forward and backward axes. But XAOS handles only one query at a time. As a result a document is parsed q times for a set of q queries. In case of large documents, this parsing time goes out of bounds. More over, research suggests that there is bound to be significant commonality among different queries in a large-scale system. By exploiting this commonality we can reduce a lot of processing. Lot of work has also been done in the area of multiple XPath processing such as Xfilter, Yfilter, IndexFilter [8], Xtrie and CQMC[7]. But they do not handle backward axes. In this paper we present a method called YALXP (Yet Another Lightweight XPath Processor), to evaluate multiple queries, with both forward and backward axes, in less number of passes of the document exploiting commonality among the queries. YALXP is built upon XAOS[2] algorithm. We make the following contributions in this paper.

G. Das and V.P. Gulati (Eds.): CIT 2004, LNCS 3356, pp. 387–399, 2004.
© Springer-Verlag Berlin Heidelberg 2004

1. A concise representation of a set of XPath expressions, with out loss of information, called combined x-dag, where all backward constraints in all the queries are converted into forward constraints.
2. Data structure called combined matching structure that represents all the matchings of different XPath expressions in the document.
3. Procedure to create combined x-dag.
4. Method to evaluate XPath queries using the above structures.

Section 2 gives a brief introduction to the data structures used in XAOS. Section 3 describes construction of combined x-dag, structure of combined matching structure and the query evaluation algorithm based on these structures. Section 4 presents our experimental results and we conclude with section 5.

2   Background

2.1   XAOS

XAOS, pronounced as Chaos, is an approach to evaluate XPath expressions having both forward and backward axes. Though it was originally designed for only two backward axes namely parent and ancestor, it is extensible to other backward axes. XAOS caters to only location paths of the XPath specification. This particular subset of XPath was termed as Rxp (Restricted XPath) in XAOS. XAOS works on two views of the input query namely x-tree and x-dag. X-tree is a rooted tree that has nodes, called x-nodes, corresponding to each node test in the query. Each x-node (but for the Root) has a unique incoming edge that is labeled with the relationship (such as descendant/parent etc.) it shares with the source x-node. We say that there is a matching at an element for an x-node if the name of x-node matches with that of element. There exists one output x-node in this x-tree (XAOS is extensible for multiple output nodes). The elements matching with this x-node are the output of the query.

The backward axes such as ancestor and parent in the x-tree are converted to forward axes and the resulting view is called x-dag (x-directed, acyclic, graph). At the end of every event, looking-for-set is constructed, based on x-dag, having elements likely to match with query in the next event. Matching structures are defined to store the information about the matched xml elements and the relations between different matching elements.

3   YALXP

We continue to call each XPath Expression as an Rxp (Restricted XPath), since we cater to essentially that fragment of XPath which XAOS addresses. YALXP operates on a combined view of all the input XPath expressions called combined x-dag or c-dag. Combined matching structure that represents the matching elements for c-nodes in the c-dag is built as the execution of the algorithm progresses.

YALXP can be viewed as an application built on top of an event-based xml parser such as SAX. It consumes the events sent by SAX parser and deals with them appropriately. At the end of every event we maintain a *looking-for-set* that has the set of elements expected in the next event, along with qids they are likely to match. For an element to be relevant it has to match with at least one of these items. This way, we can filter out irrelevant events. Relevant elements along with the links among them are stored in combined matching structure. YALXP uses combined x-dag to build combined matching structure. At the end of the algorithm, we emit the output matchings for different queries with the help of individual x-tree for each query. We stick to the lazy emission of output (at end document event), a concept followed by XAOS. This section describes the construction of combined x-dag, the structure of combined matching structure and complete process of query evaluation.

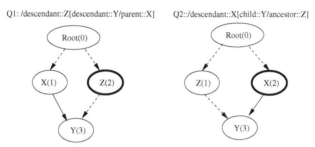

Q1: /descendant::Z[descendant::Y/parent::X]   Q2::/descendant::X[child::Y/ancestor::Z]

Fig. 1. Commonality in two queries looking different.

3.1   Combined X-dag

YALXP operates on a combined representation of the input Rxp set that is called combined x-dag or c-dag. Combined x-dag is a directed and acyclic graph that is obtained by combining individual x-dag's constructed for each Rxp in the input Rxp set. Combined x-dag is built on the premise that there exists a significant commonality among different $Rxps$ in large-scale systems. Commonality not only exists in the string form of the XPath queries. As we explain below commonality may exist in two Rxp's, which need not have any common sub-string. In figure 1, the two Rxp's do not have any commonality in the string form of the Rxp's. But after the x-dags are drawn, they look like mirror images of each other. This is the kind of commonality we are going to exploit by building combined x-dag for multiple Rxp's.

Each node in c-dag is called c-node. Each c-node represents a set of x-nodes of different queries. We define *info*, an ordered pair *(qid, x-nodeid)*, which stores the information about each x-node that a c-node represents. E.g, if a c-node has the *info (qid, x-nodeid)* with it, it means that this c-node corresponds to an x-node with id '*x-nodeid*' In the x-dag with id '*qid*'. Each edge in c-dag represents edges of different x-dags. At each edge in c-dag, we store the qids of x-dags in which the edge participates. Each edge also has a label associated with it, which is either *Descendant* or *Child*. The c-dag is constructed in such a manner that it is possible to reconstruct individual x-dags from the c-dag.

The construction of c-dag starts with the construction of individual x-dag for each Rxp. This involves construction of individual x-tree for each Rxp as explained in XAOS. X-dags for all Rxp's are built from these x-trees by translating all the backward constraints ('*ancestor*' and '*parent*') to forward constraints ('*descendant*' – represented by dotted edge and – '*child*' – represented by thick edge in fig 1) according to the rules specified by XAOS. Nodes in bold in fig 1 are the output nodes.

After this step, the c-dag is initialized to the first x-dag (corresponding to the first Rxp). Now the c-dag has a set of c-nodes and edges that correspond to x-nodes and edges of the first x-dag. At each c-node thus created, *info* (1,*x-nodeid*), where x-nodeid is x-node that the c-node represents, is registered. qid '1' is registered at each edge in the c-dag. To the Root of c-dag, *info* (*qid*,0) about Root x-node of each x-dag(*qid*) is added, since Root of c-dag matches with Root's of all the x-dags.

After this initialization process, the rest of the x-dags are added to the c-dag by traversing each x-dag in depth-first fashion. The x-node x_j whose outgoing edges and outgoing x-nodes (the x-node to which an outgoing edge leads) are going to be added to the c-dag. There are six scenarios listed as cases below in bold in which an outgoing edge and outgoing x-node can be added to c-dag. The steps with small letters under each case in the list are the operations to be performed in that case. We followed the following conventions in the list. x_k is the outgoing x-node being added. $c(qid,j)$ is the c-node corresponding to x-node with id j in x-dag for qid. We say that a c-node exists for x_k if this c-node has *info* matching with qid and k (id of x_k).

1. **If a c-node exists for x_k that is an outgoing c-node of $c(qid,j)$ and an edge with label $axis(x_j,x_k)$ exists between $c(qid,j)$ and $c(qid,k)$**
   (a) Register qid at edge between $c(qid,j)$ & $c(qid,k)$;
2. **If a c-node exists for x_k that is an outgoing c-node of $c(qid,j)$ and no edge with label $axis(x_j,x_k)$ exists between $c(qid,j)$ and $c(qid,k)$**
   (a) Let *prevnode* = $c(qid,k)$;
   (b) Remove *info* (*qid,k*) from *prevnode*;
   (c) Create a new c-node for x_k;
   (d) Add *info* to this c-node, which is $c(qid,k)$ from now on;
   (e) Add edge with label $axis(x_j,x_k)$ between $c(qid,j)$ and $c(qid,k)$ and register qid at this edge;
   (f) Add incoming edges of *prevnode* w.r.t. x-dag(*qid*), to $c(qid,k)$ and register qid at the same;
   (g) Remove qid from incoming edges of *prevnode*;
   (h) Add outgoing edges of *prevnode* w.r.t. qid, to $c(qid,k)$ and register qid at the same;
   (i) Remove qid from outgoing edges of *prevnode*;
3. **If a c-node exists for x_k that is not an outgoing c-node of $c(qid,j)$**
   (a) Add an edge with label $axis(x_j,x_k)$ between $c(qid,j)$ & $c(qid,k)$;
   (b) Register qid at this edge;

4. If no c-node exists for x_k, an outgoing c-node of $c(qid,j)$ has name equal to name of x_k and the edge between $c(qid,j)$ and this outgoing c-node has label $axis(x_j,x_k)$

   (a) Add *info* to this c-node;
   (b) Register *qid* to edge between $c(qid,j)$ and $c(qid,k)$;

5. If no c-node exists for x_k, an outgoing c-node of $c(qid,j)$ has name equal to name of x_k and the edge between $c(qid,j)$ and this outgoing c-node has label not equal to $axis(x_j,x_k)$

   (a) Add *info* to this c-node;
   (b) Add an edge with label $axis(x_j,x_k)$ between $c(qid,j)$ & $c(qid,k)$;
   (c) Register *qid* to edge between $c(qid,j)$ and $c(qid,k)$;

6. If no c-node exists for x_k and no outgoing c-node of $c(qid,j)$ has name equal to name of x_k

   (a) Create new c-node with name equal to name of x_k;
   (b) Add *info* to newly created c-node;
   (c) Add an edge with label $axis(x_j,x_k)$ between $c(qid,j)$ and $c(qid,k)$;
   (d) Register *qid* to edge between $c(qid,j)$ and $c(qid,k)$;

In cases 1,2 and 3 (where x_k was not visited in a previous traversal of x-dag), edges and x-nodes out of x_k are added in similar manner as that of x_j. In cases 4,5 and 6, there is no need to add these edges and x-nodes as they would have been added to c-dag when x_k was visited previously. It is understood that while unregistering *qid* from edges, if the edge is not left with any *qid* after removal, the edge itself is removed.

Similarly the remaining x-dags are also added to the c-dag. The resulting c-dag after this step has all the commonalities among different *Rxp*s exploited to the optimal extent (to the extent that there is no loss of information).

3.2 Combined Matching Structure

We extend the concept of matching structure of XAOS to combined matching structure in case of multiple *Rxp*'s. A combined matching structure represents the matchings for all the input *Rxp*s (i.e. for different c-nodes) at the Root of the c-dag.

We store the information of an element that matches a particular c-node C in a *matching structure*[1] represented as $\mathcal{M}_{x,i(qid's)}$ where 'x' is name and 'i' is id of the element. *qid*'s are the ids of the input *Rxp*s for which x matches. This matching structure has pointers to matching structures of elements that match with outgoing c-nodes of C. $\mathcal{M}_{Root,0(qid's)}$ represents the *Root* matching structure, where *qid*'s are the ids of the input *Rxp*s for which there is a matching at the *Root* of the c-dag. A matching structure $\mathcal{M}_{x,i(qid's)}$ is said to be a parent-matching of a matching structure $\mathcal{M}_{x',i'(qid's)}$ if x corresponds to a c-node that

---

[1] We use the term combined matching structure to denote the whole structure and matching structure to denote individual matching structure within combined matching structure.

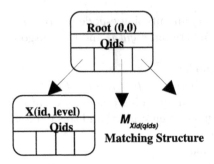

Fig. 2. Combined Matching structure.

is a parent of the c-node for which x' has matching. $\mathcal{M}_{x',i'(qid's)}$ is said to be the child-matching or sub-matching of $\mathcal{M}_{x,i(qid's)}$.

Diagrammatically, there are 3 rows in a matching structure. First row has the element name along with its id and level. Second row has the $qids$ for which the matching takes place. Third row has slots, which contain pointers to sub-matchings for the children of respective c-node in the c-dag. There is no need to store the edge information ($qids$ at these pointers) in combined matching structure (since these pointers match for the same set of queries, id's of which are present at the destination sub-matching). As the query evaluation progresses, combined matching structure is built based on c-dag.

3.3   Query Evaluation Algorithm

The query evaluation process occurs at four events namely Start document, start element, end element and end document. This process can be split into two components. One is the matching process, which occurs at all events, that filters out irrelevant events simultaneously storing relevant elements in combined matching structure. The next component is emission of the output, which occurs at end document event, using individual x-tree of each Rxp.

3.3.1   Matching Algorithm. The query evaluation at four events is described in this section. Conventions followed to explain the process are defined before algorithm *CONLFSET*.

Start Document Event
This event matches with the Root c-node. So the Root matching structure is created with all the $qids$. Looking-for-set is constructed with the help of outgoing c-nodes and outgoing edges of Root c-node.

Start Element Event
At this event, all the lfitems for which this event matches are considered for creating matching structures. A new matching structure is created, for each matched lfitem. This matching structure will have the information – element id, level and set of $qids$ for which the matching occurred. Pointers are added from the

corresponding parent matching structures to this matching structure. Looking-for-set is constructed with the help of outgoing c-nodes and outgoing edges of *curcnode*. Except for a few operations, the looking-for-set at start document and start element event is built in similar manner. This process is given in algorithm *CONLFSET*, which is self-explanatory. In *CONLFSET*, comments are given for the steps that are not necessary for start document event.

Notations Followed in *CONLFSET*

curel → current element; *level* → level of current element; *label(Co(qid))* → label of cnode; *curcnode* → The c-node for which current event matched; *Co(qid)* → Current outgoing c-node of *curcnode* w.r.t. *qid*; *Ci(qid)* → Current Incoming c-node of Co (Other than *curcnode*) w.r.t. *qid*; *Eo*→ Edge (*curcnode*, *Co(qid)*); *Ei* → Edge (*Ci(qid)*, *Co(qid)*); *Lfset* → Looking-for-set; *lfitem* → An item in Looking-for-set; *levelabove* → level above which an lfitem can be found; *lfid* → id of current lfitem; *lfname* → name of current lfitem; *lqids* → qids at *lfitem*; *qids(Eo)*→ qids registered at Eo.

Algorithm: *CONLFSET*
Input: *curcnode*
Output: Looking-for-set gets constructed

Remove lfitems with *levelabove* less than *level* from *lfset*;
    // No need of this step for start document
for each *lfitem(i)* that matched with *curel*
        // This loop is not needed for start document
    for each *Eo*
      if(one of *lqids* of *lfitem(i)* matches with *qids(Eo)*) /* Condition
          not needed for start document event */
        let *tmpqids* be a temporary array;
        for each *qid* at *Eo*
          if(there is an open and relevant element for each *Ci(qid)* of *Co(qid)*)
            if (no *lfitem* exists in *lfset* for *Co(qid)*)
              add *qid* to *tmpqids*;
            if (*tmpqids* is not empty)
              create *lfitem(lfid)* with *lfname* = *label(Co(qid))*;
              lfitem(lfid).lqids = *tmpqids*;
              if (*label(Eo)* == descendant)
                lfitem(lfid).level = "*";
                lfitem(lfid).levelabove = *level*;
              else
                lfitem(lfid).level = *level*+1;
                lfitem(lfid).levelabove = *level*;

End Element Event There is no need to construct looking-for-set at the end element event of *curel*. It is equal to the looking-for-set at the start element event of the parent of *curel*. At this event, propagation takes place at all the matching structures corresponding to *curel* w.r.t. the qids present at each matching structure.

Notations Followed in *PROPAGATE*

$mat\_str(i) \rightarrow$ Matching structure with id i corresponding to *curel*
$chmat\_str(j, mat\_str(i), qid) \rightarrow$ child matching structure with id j of $mat\_str(i)$

Algorithm: *PROPAGATE*

for each $mat\_str(i)$
    for each qid at $mat\_str(i)$
        if ($mat\_str(i)$ corresponds to a c-node that is a leaf w.r.t qid)
            $mat\_str(i).totmat(qid)$ = true;
        else
            if (there is tot_mat w.r.t qid for all $chmat\_str(j\ mat\_str(i),qid)$)
                $mat\_str(i).totmat(qid)$ = true;
            else
                $mat\_str(i).totmat(qid)$ = false;

End Document Event

There is no need to construct looking-for-set at the end document event since parsing finishes with this event. Propagation should take place at the Root matching structure w.r.t. all $qids$ in the same manner as at other end element events. After this step emission of Output takes place.

3.3.2   Emission of Output. At the end of document event, a check is done to see if total matching exists at Root matching w.r.t. all Rxp's. If total matchings exist at Root for a set of qid's, all the corresponding sub-matchings (that have total matching) should be emitted as output with the help of the individual x-tree of each qid and the combined matching structure. Consider the following scenario in emission of output. M(x1,qid) is a matching structure corresponding to x-node x1 of x-tree(qid) where x1 has an outgoing edge labeled ancestor or parent to an x-node x2. In this case, a matching structure for x2 is found as a parent matching structure of M(x1,qid).

3.3.3   Optimizations. On large documents the emission of output can take place more eagerly, after processing 500 tags or so, at the nearest end element event after which the document level becomes 1. This can be done by firing dummy events corresponding to end element of first element and end document. After this the memory held by combined matching structure (but for the Root matching structure & the matching structure corresponding to first element) can be released. The c-dag built at the start of document can be used to build combined matching structure from thereon.

The query rewriting method can be optimized to reduce the graph behavior of queries. Consider the query *descendant::X[/ancestor::Y/child::U and /parent::W]*. One can easily infer that W has to be a descendant of Y since X can have only one parent, i.e. W and hence Y has to be an ancestor to X as well as to W. This results in a tree versus a more complicated x-dag.

4   Experimental Results

We performed our experiments on Pentium IV 2.4 GHz Processor with 256MB of Main Memory running on Windows XP Professional. We implemented XAOS and YALXP in Java 1.4.1 and we use Xalan-Java 2.5 version. We used xml4j_2_0_9, developed by IBM as SAX parser.

We define commonality factor (CF) as a measure to indicate the degree of commonality among multiple queries with forward and backward axes. This factor gives some hint about the amount of reduction in the number of matching structures created and the number of traversals (both through dag and matching structures) by creating c-dag.

$$CF(N) = 1 - \frac{Tcn + Tce}{Txn + Txe}$$

where N is number of queries, Tcn is Total no of c-nodes in c-dag, Tce is Total no of edges in c-dag, Txn is Total No of x-nodes in N x-dags and Txe is Total no of edges in N x-dags.

We tested the performances of various algorithms on three sets of queries and documents generated based on three different DTDs. The three DTDs *are country.dtd*[15], *DCMDItem.dtd*[15] and *auction.dtd*[17]. Queries generated based on these DTDs had Average commonality factors for 50 queries as 0.836 for Country.dtd, 0.62 for DCMDItem.dtd and 0.33 for auction.dtd. We used the xml Database generators by Xbench[15] to generate xml documents for country and DCMDItem and Xmark[17] to generate documents for auction. We generated 1,00,000 input queries for each of the DTDs using the DTD-based XPath generator developed by Yfilter[16]. This tool generates queries with only forward axes. We rewrote these queries into the equivalent ones containing one backward axis/query. The queries are pretty lightweight, which have conjunctive predicates (joined by "*and*") and nested predicates but no *attributes* and *text()*.

In our experiments, we found that translation of backward axes to forward axes with the knowledge of DTD results in higher and consistent commonality factors among the queries. So we consulted DTD to rewrite queries. However, in the absence of DTD, rewriting proposed by XAOS can be resorted to. Also, we observed the overall time and runtime memory consumption – when N queries were executed in a single run of YALXP and when N were executed 50 at a time in multiple runs of YALXP on *country.xml*. Both factors are very high in single run. Due to this reason we executed 50 queries at a time in YALXP in all our experiments. We are working on optimizations to reduce the memory occupied by c-dag. This enables our algorithms to work more efficiently on small streaming xml documents for large number of queries.

For each DTD, we compare performances of YALXP, XALAN (ODP – One DOM Parsing – construct the DOM only once and query the same for each query individually), XAOS (OSPCN – One SAX Parsing Commonalities Not exploited) and XAOS (MSP – Multiple SAX Parsing-XAOS run in a loop for N queries) for 100 to 1,00,000 queries on small documents. On medium and large documents we present the overall times taken by YALXP and XALAN (ODP) from 100 to

500 queries only on country.dtd due to space limitation. XAOS (OSPCN) and XAOS (MSP) cannot be applied on large documents, as the main memory usage grows prohibitively large in the former and SAX parsing cost goes high in the latter. Please refer to figure 4 for graphs showing the results.

On small documents, as the commonality factor increases from 0.33 to 0.836, YALXP performs from 2 times (for 0.33 CF) to 6 times (for 0.836 CF) better than XALAN (ODP) and XAOS (MSP) in processing time. We observed that Xalan (ODP) takes longer time due to querying the DOM for each query individually coupled with the inefficiency in the searching process [2]. We also observed that as the number of queries grows, due to the parsing cost involved for each query and the traversal through all the matching structures for each query, XAOS (MSP) takes more time. By adapting the approach of XAOS for matching multiple queries, YALXP takes lesser time. The ranges of main memory used by YALXP, XAOS (MSP), XALAN (ODP) and XAOS (OSPCN) on small documents are 9-10, 27-31.5, 9-36 and 21-181M respectively for 100 to 1000 Q. We observed that, for queries with very low commonality factor of 0.33, XAOS (OSPCN) performs almost same as YALXP up to 1000 Q as shown in Fig 4.7. However, the memory consumption of XAOS (OSPCN) is far higher than that of YALXP. XAOS (OSPCN) fails to complete from 2500 queries on any document due to OS thrashing.

On medium to large documents also YALXP performs better than Xalan (ODP) as shown in figures 4.10 & 4.11. Memory used by YALXP on medium documents ranges from 19 to 21M and that by Xalan(ODP) ranges from 68 to 73M. On large documents YALXP uses from 19.5 to 21M of memory and Xalan(ODP) uses from 168 to 214M. YALXP takes constantly less memory on large documents by virtue of the optimization done, by releasing memory when the document level is 1. By this we can say that the memory taken by YALXP is proportional to only the number of elements before the second occurrence of document level being 1 and not to the total size of document. Also the emission of output is eager in case of large documents due to this optimization. In case of documents of size 25M, Xalan (ODP) fails to perform due to OS thrashing. This is due to the size of DOM representation of the whole document in memory.

5   Conclusion

We adapted the approach of XAOS for multiple queries that have forward and backward axes with the following advantages.

1. Ability to handle backward axes.
2. Evaluation of multiple queries in less number of document-order traversals.
3. Exploiting commonality among different queries with forward and backward axes thereby sharing processing and memory among different queries.

Our experiments show that YALXP performs better than Xalan(ODP) – for multiple queries with single Dom construction – in processing time. Our algorithms apply to streaming data (that are large and allow only one-pass) as well, but to limited number of queries. We are working on extending the algorithms to address more of XPath.

Acknowledgments

We would like to thank Dr. Mukund Raghavachari and Deepak Goyal for helping us understand the underpinnings of XAOS. We also thank the authors of many of the algorithms mentioned in the references for cooperating us by sharing their work.

Appendix

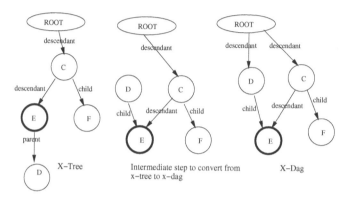

Fig. 3. Construction of x-tree & x-dag for query
"/descendant::C[child::F]/descendant::E[parent::D]"

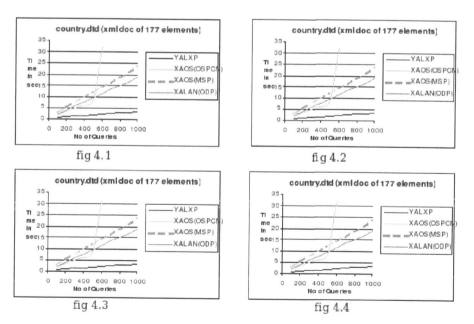

Fig. 4. Experimental Results – Comparison between CPU performances of YALXP, XAOS(OSPCN), XAOS(MSP) and Xalan(ODP)

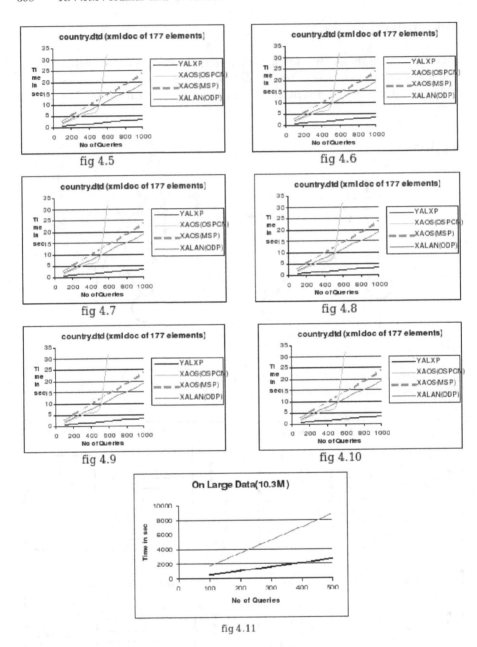

fig 4.5

fig 4.6

fig 4.7

fig 4.8

fig 4.9

fig 4.10

fig 4.11

Fig. 4. (Continued)

References

1. XML path language (XPath) version 1.0. Technical report, W3C Recommendation: http://www.w3.org/TR/xpath (1999)
2. C Barton, P Charles, D Goyal, M Raghavachari, M Fontoura, V Josifovski: Streaming XPath Processing with Forward and Backward Axes. In: Proc. of ICDE. (2003)
3. Extensible Markup Language (XML) 1.0.: www.w3.org/TR/2004/RECxml-20040204/ (2004)
4. Xalan-Java 2.5: http://xml.apache.org.
5. M. Altinel and M. Franklin: Xfilter: Efficient Filtering of XML Documents for Selective Dissemination of Information. In: Proceedings of the 26th VLDB Conference, Egypt (2000). 53–64.
6. Y Diao, M. Altinel, M. J. Franklin, Hao Zhang, P.Fischer: Yfilter: Path Sharing and Predicate Evaluation for High-Performance XMPs1L Filtering. In: ACM Transactions on Database Systems (TODS) Volume 28 , Issue 4, (December 2003) 467–516.
7. B. Ozen, O. Kilic, M. Altinel and A. Dogac: CQMC: Highly Personalized Information Delivery to Mobile Clients. In: Proceedings of the 2nd ACM International workshop on Data engineering for wireless and mobile access, (2001) 35–42.
8. N. Bruno, L. Gravano and N. Koudas, D. Srivastava: IndexFilter: Navigation-vs. Index-Based XML Multi-Query Processing. In: Proc. Of 19th International Conference on Data Engineering (2003) 139–150.
9. C.Y. Chan, P. Felber, M. Garofalakis, R Rastogi: Xtrie: Efficient filtering of XML documents with XPath expressions. In: Proc. of 18th International Conference on Data Engineering, (2002) 235–244.
10. W. Rao, Y. Chen, X. Zhang, Fanyuan ma: MTrie: A Scalable Filtering of Well-Structured XML Message Stream. In: Proceedings of Advanced Web Technologies and Applications, APWeb (2004) 246–251.
11. A. Tozawa, M. Murata: Tableau Construction of Tree Automata from Queries on Structured Documents.
12. J. Chen, D. DeWitt, F. Tian, Y.Wang: NiagaraCQ: A Scalable Continuous Query System for Internet Databases. In: Proceedings of the ACM SIGMOD international conference on Management of data, (2000) 379–390.
13. V Josifovski, M Fontoura, Attila Barta: TurboXPath: Querying XML Streams. In: The DB2, (2002).
14. Ray Whitmer: Document Object Model (DOM) Level 3 XPath Specification: http://www.w3.org/TR/DOM-Level-3-XPath.
15. XBench: A Family of Benchmarks for XML DBMSs: http://db.uwaterloo.ca/~ddbms/projects/xbench/.
16. Filtering and Transformation for High-Volume XML Message Brokering: http://www.cs.berkeley.edu/~diaoyl/yfilter/code_release.htm (2003)
17. XMark: An XML Benchmark Project: http://monetdb.cwi.nl/xml/index.html

Early Performance Modeling
for Web Based Applications

D. Evangelin Geetha, T.V. Suresh Kumar, and K. Rajani Kanth

M.S. Ramaiah Institute of Technology, 560 054 Bangalore, India
degeetha@yahoo.com, manupranu@yahoo.co.in, rajanikanth@msrit.edu

Abstract. Quality plays an important role in developing software products. In the present global economic scenario, industry is giving at most importance to the quality software products. In this context, performance, which is an important quality attribute, is no exemption. Object oriented approach has been widely used in Industry. Exploiting features of UML makes software development easy. In this paper, we present a method for the performance assessment early in the life cycle, before the design phase. We exploit features of UML based object-oriented approach. We propose an algorithm to transform requirements into Software execution model (EG), which is useful in performance assessment. The input graph for this EG, Actor-event graph (AEG), is also discussed. The model then solved and the results are presented for a case study on Web Applications.

1 Introduction

Performance is vital for software systems that perform customer-service functions, which must provide rapid response acceptable by the customers. To avoid customers waiting in queues and choose other merchants for service, timely response must be provided by the system. Real-time systems must meet critical response time requirements to prevent disasters. Timely response from management information systems is necessary to make effective use of a company's most important and costly resource: its personnel. Performance refers to system responsiveness, either the time required to respond to specific events, or number of events processed in a given time interval. For traditional information systems, performance considerations are associated with usability issues such as response time for user transactions. For 'soft' real-time systems, performance considerations relate to the ability to adequately handle the external load placed on the system. In 'hard' real-time systems, performance concerns become correctness issues; failure to meet deadlines or throughput requirements is equivalent to producing incorrect results.

The 'fix-it-later' approach is undesirable. Performance problems may be so severe that they require extensive changes to the system architecture. If these changes are made late in the development process, they can increase development costs, delay deployment, or adversely affect other desirable qualities of a design, such as understandability, maintainability, or reusability. Finally, designing for performance from the beginning produces systems that exhibit better performance than can be achieved using a 'fix-it-later' approach [7].

G. Das and V.P. Gulati (Eds.): CIT 2004, LNCS 3356, pp. 400–409, 2004.
© Springer-Verlag Berlin Heidelberg 2004

Performance is an important but often neglected aspect of software development methodologies. To construct performance models, analysts inspect, analyze and translate software specifications into models, then solve these models under different workload factors in order to diagnose performance problems and recommend design alternatives for performance improvement. This performance analysis cycle, when done properly starting at the early stages of design the developer can choose a suitable design, which meets performance objective. Early generation of performance model is therefore needed to ease the process of building quality software.

2   Related Work

Software Performance Engineering (SPE) has evolved over the past years and has been demonstrated to be effective during the development of many large systems [6]. The extensions to SPE process and its associated models for assessing distributed object-systems are discussed in [4]. Predictive performance modeling environment that enables performance measures for distributed object-oriented systems are described in [12], [13], [14]. [3] Describes the use of SPE-ED, a performance-modeling tool that supports SPE process, for early lifecycle performance evaluation of object - oriented systems. Generation of performance models and performance assessment throughout the life cycle is widely discussed in [5], [6]. The method for integrating both design and performance activity in client-server application has been discussed in [9]. Performance Analysis of internet based Software retrieval systems using Petri-nets and a comparative study has been proposed in [11]. Performance analysis using Unified Modeling Language (UML) is presented in [15], [16]. LQN performance models can be derived automatically from UML specifications using Graph Grammar Techniques [1] and XSLT [10]. The ethics of SPE to web applications during software architectural design phase is discussed in [2]. The systematic assessment of performance, early in the life cycle has been developed with OMT (Object Modeling Techniques) notation in [8]. But the paper is not mentioned the Universal Visual Modeling Language, UML notation. In this paper we explore UML notation and present general algorithms, which are useful to assess performance, early in life cycles.

3   SPE Model

This section is divided into 3 parts. In part I and part II, we describe Actor Event Graph (AEG) and Execution Graph (EG) and how a Collaboration Diagram (CoD) and Class Diagram (CD) are transformed to AEG in turn into EG. In part III, we propose an algorithm, which is developed based on algorithms in [8] to transform AEG to EG.

3.1   Actor-Event Graph

An actor-event graph is a unifying notation, whose nodes are called *actors* (a) and edges are called *events* (e). In Fig. 2 an example AEG is shown, where square boxes represent actors and arrows represent events. An actor with no incoming event is called an *initial actor* (actor x in Fig. 2) while an actor with no outgoing event is called a *final actor* (actor s in Fig. 2). An actor is an atomic set of operations, i.e. the operations executed (by a software component) with no interaction with any other actor. The detail about AEG using OMT is given in [8].

In this paper, based on the transformation rules given in [8] we transform from UML notation CoD to AEG. Each actor in Fig. 2 is labeled by an *identifier* (e.g. x inside the box) taken from the CoD, and by a *class name* (e.g. a outside the box) taken from the CD. The identifier x is the label attached to the corresponding sequence number of the arrow coming out from the corresponding atomic set of operations in the CoD (Fig. 1). Each event is labeled by a 2-ple (event name, event type). The event type can be:

- E – external event: E-type events connect actors belonging to different classes.
- I – internal event: I-type events connect actors belonging to the same class.

The following CoD's are obtained from Sequential Diagram and as such the events numbered are atomic set of operations.

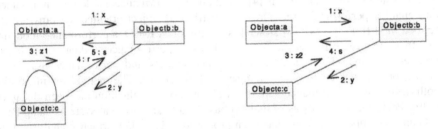

Fig. 1. Collaboration Diagrams

3.2 Execution Graph

An *execution graph* is a graph, whose *nodes* represent one (or more than one) sets of actions (actors) and *edges* represent control transfer between them. Each node is weighted by the demand-vector representing the resource usage by the node (e.g. CPU time, LAN time, WAN time, number of I/O operations, etc.). According to [6], an EG node can be of basic nodes, expanded nodes, repetition nodes, case nodes, fork-and-join and split nodes, lock-and-free nodes, share nodes. But only basic, expanded, repetition and case nodes are discussed in this paper.

The translation of AEG into EG is performed by the simple algorithm, which starts from the AEG *initial actor* (Section 3.1) and then proceeds by visiting the graph in DFS (Depth First Search) order (until the ending actor or an already visited actor is encountered) while applying the following rules:

- Every actor in the AEG is translated into a basic node of the EG eventually followed by
  - a case node, if the actor has more than one outgoing event
  - a repetition node, if the actor belongs to an AEG cycle and it is the first visited node of the cycle
- Each event in the AEG is translated into an EG edge
  - for an I type event corresponding base node contains an 'I' for an E type event corresponding base node contains an 'E'.

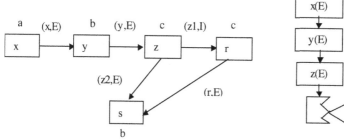

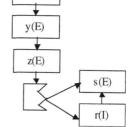

Fig. 2. Actor-Event Graph   **Fig. 3.** Execution Graph for Fig. 2

3.3 Algorithm

We develop an algorithm based on the algorithm in [8] for UML based notation.

```
// Translation of CoD and CD into AEG
Get all Collaboration Diagrams and Class Diagram
While (Collaboration Diagram exists)
Seqno :=1;
Loop
        Consider next atomic set attached to seqno on the given CoD
        If (not translated)
                Translate atomic set of operations into corresponding actor
                Denote the class name from the CD
                Generate the corresponding <a, e> pair
                If (e₁ exists) Connect e₁ to a   end if  //e₁ – last recently   generated e
                Denote e as e₁
        else
                Connect e₁ to aₚ   // aₚ – already translated actor a
        end If
        Seqno := Seqno+1;
end Loop
end While
// Translation of AEG into EG
Get the AEG initial actor and its outgoing event
While (actors in AEG exist)
Loop  // visit the AEG graph in DFS order
    Retrieve actor
    If (the actor has more than one outgoing events)
        Translate the actor into an EG case node
      else If (actor belongs to an AEG cycle, it is the first visited node of the cycle)
            Translate the actor into an EG repetition node
      else Translate the actor into an EG basic node
    end If
  Retrieve event
  Translate the event into an EG edge
        If (event type = 'E')
            Insert 'E' into the corresponding EG node
        else Insert 'I' into the corresponding EG node
        end If
        Consider next <actor, event> pair
end Loop
```

end While
// Computation of Total Processing Unit
For each scenario
  Get the number of computer resources (k)
  Get the number of software resources (m)
  Let a_j be the software resource requirements for each j software resources
  Get the amount of resource required for each request of j ($w_{i,j}$; $i=1..k, j=1..m$)
  Get service time(s_i; $i =1..k$)
  For each software component in the scenario
      Calculate the total computer resource requirement (r_i; $i =1..k$)
      Calculate the total unit of service for each k for the scenario
      Compute the total processing units for the scenario(T)
      $T :=$ sum(the total unit of service for each k for the scenario*service time)
  end For
end For

The above-mentioned algorithm is a general algorithm, through which early derivation of software performance model is possible using UML approach. In this paper,
the algorithm has been illustrated through a case study of web-based applications.

4   Case Study

Web applications use different implementation technologies than other distributed
systems. SPE model for web application is discussed in [2]. But it is developed during
the software architectural design phase. In this paper, we generate performance model
early in the life cycle, before design phase. We consider the case study discussed in
[2] and we apply the proposed algorithm for UML based notation for the same. The
case study is implemented to calculate whether the system is meeting the required
performance goal. The input data is obtained from [2] and the results are compared
with the earlier one. In this case study, we applied the algorithm (Section 3.3) to get
AEG and EG.

4.1   Description of the Case Study

A Nachtfliegen airline plans a major expansion to their modest web site to:

- Expand company information, add navigation and tabs
- Add promotions and deals to attract customers and encourage purchases
- Add functions for flight inquiry, plan an itinerary, and ticket purchase

The most important performance scenarios are: PlanItinerary and PurchaseTickets.
The performance of these scenarios is important if the web site is to meet the marketing goals to generate new revenue. If the performance is poor, users will not use the
website, and Nachtfliegen will not realize the increased revenues. Other scenarios are
also important, but they will not be addressed in the initial analysis. The PlanItinerary
requires a password for customer authentication. The PlanItinerary communicates,
through Browser, Web server, DotcomDBMS and MainframeDatabase.The CD for
the scenario is represented in Fig. 4 and CoDs are given in Fig. 5. The CoD in Fig. 5
for two cases: 5(a) for successful purchase itinerary in the first iteration, 5(b) for successful purchase itinerary in the second iteration after finding the suitable flight and

seat. For storing the itinerary without purchasing ticket, the CoD can be drawn in the similar manner.

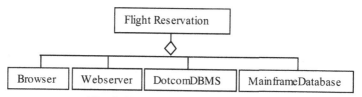

Fig. 4. Class Diagram for PlanItinerary

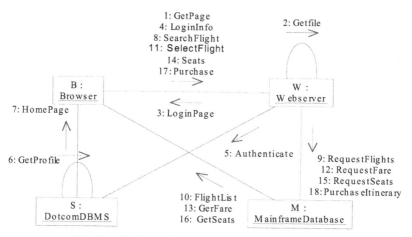

Fig. 5(a). Collaboration Diagram for Purchase Itinerary

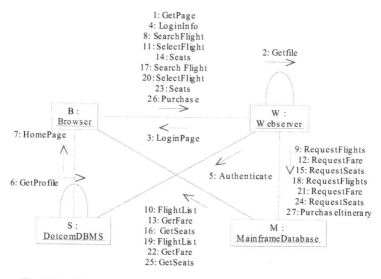

Fig. 5(b). Collaboration Diagram with iterations for Purchase Itinerary

4.2 Application of the Algorithm

This section gives a detailed description of the application of algorithm to the derivation of AEG of Fig. 6 from the CoD's in Fig. 5 and CD in Fig. 4. Then, the translation of AEG in Fig. 6 to EG is obtained as shown in Fig 7.

According to algorithm in section 3.3, all the CoD's in figures 5(a), 5(b) are orderly scanned. Fig. 6 is AEG translated from figures 5(a) and 5(b). First we consider Fig. 5(a). All the interactions are visited and translated into the corresponding <a,e> pairs. Next we consider CoD in Fig. 5(b) and interactions that are not in Fig. 5(a) translated into the corresponding <a,e> pair and attached to the current AEG. Now the actor GetSeats is connected with SearchFlight by the new event (GSn,E) and the AEG in Fig. 6 is obtained. In Fig. 6, the initial actor GetPage is considered first. By applying the algorithm, all the nodes are visited in Depth First Search order until the ending actor or an already visited actor is encountered and the EG in Fig. 7(d) is obtained. The subEGs for Login, FindFlight and Purchase are given in figures 7(a), 7(b) and 7(c) respectively.

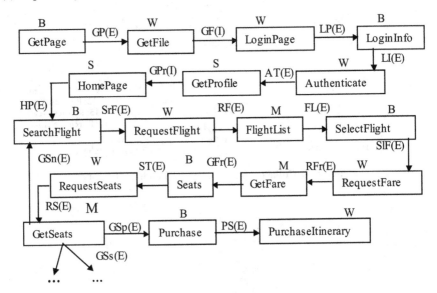

Fig. 6. Actor Event Graph for PlanItinerar

4.3 Software Execution Model

To obtain the complete performance model, the execution graph is to be integrated with the preliminary design data on the executing platform configuration, the architecture of software modules, and hardware devices with user profile and software workload. The data required for estimating software execution model are the time needed for computer resources to access Mainframe Database(DBAccess), Dotcom DBMS(LocalDB), input message(Input), the page displayed to the user(PageSize), data retrieved from the mainframe to be displayed with the page(DataSize). The results are validated using these data that are already available in [2] and algorithm given in section 3.3.

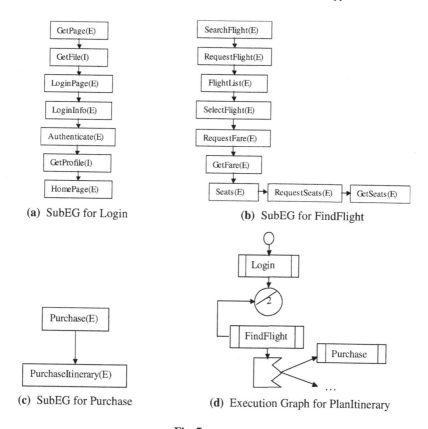

(a) SubEG for Login

(b) SubEG for FindFlight

(c) SubEG for Purchase

(d) Execution Graph for PlanItinerary

Fig. 7.

Table 1. Computer Resource Requirement for each Software Resource Requirement

Devices	CPU	Disk	INet	Delay	LAN
Service Units	Sec.	I/Os	Kbytes	Sec.	Msgs
				Software Resources	
Input (1 KB)	0.002		1		
DBAccess(1 Access)	0.0005			0.25	1
LocalDB(1 Access)	0.001	2			
PageSize(1 KB)	0.0005		1		
DataSize (1KB)	0.0005		1		
Service Time	1	0.003	0.14222	1	0.000164

First, for each software component (basic EG node), we calculate software resource requirements, a_j, for each of the j software resources. The Table 1 shows the
computer resource $w_{i,j}$, for each of the a_j requests for j^{th} software resource. The total
computer resource requirements (R_i), for login is (0.0058,8,30,0,0) and for the scenario is (0.1498,8.6,290.7,1.25,257.4). Hence, the time to process login and display

the customized homepage is 4.2 seconds. It may be noted that, the homepage is assumed to be designed using tables, instead of frames to reduce the number of requests to the WebServer. We know that 4.2 seconds is meeting the performance objective against 8 seconds. We also calculated end-to-end time for PlanItinerary, which is 42.6 seconds.

5   Conclusions

Performance model generation for UML-based object-oriented systems in early phases of the software life cycle has been introduced. A common AEG is obtained for performance model generation using UML. Calculations are done for the execution graph. Future work may be involved by automating Machine Model(MM) through simulation. Other UML diagrams like Use case may be considered for assessing performance using this approach.

References

1. Amer H, Petriu D.C: "Automatic Transformation of UML Software Specification into LQN performance Models using Graph Grammar Techniques", Carleton University, 2001.
2. Connie U. Smith and Lioyd G. Williams: "Building Responsive and Scalable Web Applications", Proceedings CMGC, December 2000.
3. Connie U. Smith and Lioyd G. Williams: "Performance Engineering Evaluation of Object Oriented Systems with SPE-ED", in LNCS (Springer Verlag 1997), 1245, pp. 135-153.
4. Connie U. Smith and Lioyd G. Williams: "Performance Engineering Models of CORBA-based distributed-object systems", Performance Engineering Services and Software Engineering Research, 1998.
5. Connie U. Smith and Murray Woodside: "Performance Validation at Early Stages of Software Development", Performance Engineering Services, Santa Fe, USA.
6. Connie U. Smith, Performance Engineering of Software Systems, Reading, MA, Addison-Wesley, 1990
7. Connie U. Smith: "Software Performance Engineering: A Case Study including Performance Comparison with Design Alternatives", IEEE Transactions on Software Engineering Vol. 19(7) July 1993.
8. Cortellessa V, Lazeolla G and Mirandola R: "Early Generation of Performance Models for Object-oriented Systems", IEE Proc.- Softw., June 2000, 147(3), pp. 67-74.
9. Daniel A. Menasce and Gomaa H: "A Method for Design and Performance Modeling of Client/Server Systems", IEEE, 2000.
10. Gordon P. Gu and Dorino C. Petriu: "XSLT Transformation from UML Models to LQN Performance Models", WOSP 2002.
11. Jose Merseguer, Javier Campos and Eduardo Mena: "Performance Analysis of Internet based Software Retrieval Systems using Petri Nets", ACM 2001.
12. Kahkipuro P: "UML based performance modeling framework for object oriented distributed systems", Proceedings of second international conference on Unified Modeling Language. October 1999, USA, (Springer Verlag, LNCS) pp. 1723.
13. Kahkipuro P: "UML-Based Performance Modeling Framework for Component-Based Distributed Systems", in R.Dumke et al. (Eds): Performance Engineering, LNCS 2047, Springer, pp.167-184, 2001.

14. Peter Utton and Gino Martin, David Akehurst and Gill Waters: "Performance Analysis of Object-oriented Designs for Distributed Systems", Technical Report, University of Kent at Canterburry.
15. Petriu D.C, Shousha C, Jalnapurkar A, "Architecture Based Performance Analysis Applied to a Telecommunication System", IEEE Transactions on Software Eng., Vol.26 (11), pp.1049-1065, November 2000.
16. Pooley R and King P: "The unified modeling language and performance engineering", IEE proc-Software, February 1999, 146(1), pp. 2-10.

An Examination of Website Quality Dimensions in Australian e-Retailing: A Confirmatory Factor Analysis Approach

Sukunesan Sinnappan[1] and Jamie Carlson[2]

[1] Uni Technology Sydney, Broadway
2007 NSW, Australia
suku@it.uts.edu.au
[2] University of Newcastle,
Callaghan 2308, NSW Australia
jamie.carlson@newcastle.edu.au

Abstract. Numerous studies have endeavored to create and develop Website quality instruments in both the information systems and marketing domains. This study contributes to further theory development and refinement of measuring Website Quality by extending previous studies in the field. It adopts a confirmatory factor analysis approach to empirically assess three Australian based e-retailing Websites across three industry groups. The study presents a parsimonious model for each industry examined, that can be used for benchmarking purposes and for future scholarly research efforts. Managerial implications are highlighted with future research directions discussed.

1 Introduction

Perceived Website quality has emerged as an issue of strategic importance for organizations to effectively communicate and transact with consumers. As the development of Internet technology continues, coupled with the intensity of online competition and a simple mouse click to select a new service provider [28], the conceptualization and measurement of Website quality has forced academics and practitioners to develop rigorous and reliable methods. Previous measurements of Website quality have been developed in business consulting and the popular press for sometime, however, these measures are ad-hoc which have not been statistically validated and tested for reliability, potentially leading to poor management decisions [35]. In academia, previous measures within the IS and e-marketing disciplines have been either conceptual in nature or limited in their analysis and methodological development. Few research efforts have produced scales capture the multi-dimensional attributes of Website quality in a rigorous and psychometrically sound way [35]. [26] supports the scarcity of research claiming that research on electronic services is in its infancy with no generally accepted theories for customer evaluations of online service offerings.

The purpose of this research is to extend previous studies by [29, 7] and further contribute to the theory advancement in assessing Website quality. The study employs confirmatory factor analysis (hereafter CFA) to assess three industry sectors in the Australian online commerce setting i.e. 1) airlines, 2) e-retail and 3) computers. The results of this study will be used to compare individual Website quality dimen-

G. Das and V.P. Gulati (Eds.): CIT 2004, LNCS 3356, pp. 410–418, 2004.

sions between each industry category, and to produce a parsimonious model for each industry. This paper is presented in three key sections. First, a review of the relevant literature is presented. In the second section, details of the methodology and results of the confirmatory factor analysis are highlighted. Thirdly, conclusions and managerial implications are discussed with directions for future research suggested.

2 Literature Review

Invariably the mechanics of Website development is based on the literatures surrounding both the information systems and marketing fields. Much of the Website implementation could be directly tied to the field of information systems while the content development is in parallel to the marketing arena. While both academic and practitioner researchers have begun to conceptualize and measure Website quality, limited attention is given to providing definitions of their theoretical domains. Two dominant theoretical models have begun to emerge from the IS and e-marketing literature to assess the quality of the Website, these include: (1) Technology Acceptance Model (TAM), and (2) Service Quality (SERVQUAL). The Technology Acceptance Model (TAM) was first conceived by [9], to explain and predict the individual's acceptance of information technology. TAM is based on the Theory of Reasoned Action (TRA), which suggest that social behavior is motivated by an individual's attitude toward carrying out that behavior [2, 13]. The TAM model posits that the actual use of a technology can be predicted by user's behavioral intention and his or her attitude towards its use, which in turn are influenced by a technology's perceived ease of use and perceived usefulness. Applications of the TAM model include e-mail, voice-mail, word processing, spreadsheets and internal company computer systems [9, 10, 11, 25]. The model has since been modified and extended within the context of the online environment [see 3, 41, 29, 31] and has also been applied within the marketing literature examining TAM as viable predictors of adoption of the Internet for retail usage [14].

Currently, there is a debate within the e-marketing literature as to whether existing measures of service quality (e.g. initially developed by [24]) apply in electronic environments. According to [32], the five SERVQUAL dimensions (reliability, responsiveness, assurance, empathy, and tangibles) are relevant and important in a Web-based environment. However, [23: 171] suggest that research is needed on whether "the definitions and relative importance of the five service quality dimensions change when customers interact with technology rather than with service personnel". Research efforts utilizing the SERVQUAL framework are beginning to emerge into the literature [see for e.g. 18, 22, 33, 39]. However, these initial research efforts suffer from the generalizability of results, with research needed to improve and refine the quality dimensions.

Previous studies now suggest that to provide value to businesses, an instrument measuring Website quality must identify in more detail the specific aspects that cause a Website to be easy to use, or useful to consumers, since this clarification of quality dimensions is conceptually important to empirically prove that some aspects of quality are more important than others in determining online consumer behavior [15, 20]. Although previous research efforts have provided valuable insight into what dimensions constitute Website quality, most instruments are either limited in the development, narrowly focused or highly domain specific to a particular sector of the Internet (e.g. bookstores, auction sites or library sites). As a result of the unique elements of the Website [17], a holistic instrument is required to effectively capture its multi-dimensional properties.

WebQual[TM] [20] has emerged into the literature as a highly reliable and valid instrument to assess the perceived quality of a Website. The WebQual[TM] instrument consists of 12 core dimensions: informational fit-to-task, tailored communications, trust; response time, ease of understanding, intuitive operations, visual appeal, innovativeness, flow/emotional appeal, consistent image, on-line completeness and relative advantage. These 12 dimensions further collapse into 4 second order latent variables: (1) Usefulness, (2) Ease-of-use, (3) Entertainment, and (4) Complimentary relationship. Goodhue and Thompson [15] and Loiacono et al [20] argue that the instrument is able to support a range of important IS and marketing studies as researchers attempt to understand what contributes to success in the electronic marketspace. The instrument is grounded in the Theory of Reasoned Action (TRA), and Technology Acceptance Model (TAM) one of the most widely cited pieces of IS research [29].

3 Methodology

To gather a sample size, the study required respondents with previous experience in the e-commerce area. The respondents for the survey were students enrolled in an e-commerce subject at a large Australian university. Since Website evaluation was a prominent topic of their syllabus, they were considered to be an ideal target population. Prior to the actual study, the students were asked to thoroughly browse five pre-selected sites[1] from three industries over a period of a month. The students were then asked to choose a Website from each of the three industries. More than two-thirds of the students selected Qantas.com.au, Dell.com.au and dStore.com.au to represent each respective industry. The survey was hosted online for one month from October to November 2002. The respondents were directed to the start page of the survey, where a set of instructions briefed each user. The questionnaires were designed to auto-check the validity of the answers before submission, which helped the survey to gather 502 valid responses. Respondents were invited to evaluate each of the sites using a 7 – point scale (1 = "Very strongly Disagree" and 7 = "Very strongly Agree").

4 Data Analysis

4.1 Survey Data in Brief

The graphical form of the summarised data is shown in Figure 1 using a radar plot. The detailed data can be found in [29]. On the whole, Dell.com.au (representing the

---

[1] The sites were dell.com.au, ibm.com.au, sony.com.au, hp.com.au, toshiba.com.au, flightcentre.com.au, qantas.com.au, virgin.com/blue, freedomair.com, travel.com.au, dstore.com.au, shopsafe.com.au, buyitsellit.com.au, shop.abc.net.au, and buyguide.com.au

computer industry) outperformed the Airline and E-retail industries. Dell.com.au was found to be strong on the constructs related to information fit-to-task, trust, response time, ease-of-understanding, and consistent image.

In order to achieve the research objectives, we carried out 3 phases of data analyses which extends previous research by [29, 7]. The first involved a reliability analysis to eliminate the weak variables for each industry. This follows a factor analysis in the second phase to uncover the salient dimensions of new constructs from the previous phase. Finally, we employed CFA to derive parsimonious models for each industry. Table 1 depicts the results from the reliability analysis using Cronbach alpha scores [8].

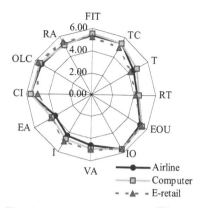

Fig. 1. Radar plot of WebQual™ constructs for each industry

As suggested by [8], items (marked with an asterisk *) were removed that were below Cronbach alpha scores of 0.7, to maintain reliable measures. As part of the second phase, the remaining items were tested using factor analysis. Factor analysis is known for identifying the core structure (variables) that is latent by summarizing the data set [16]. Table 2 shows the factor analysis score for each industry. Figures in bold denote the variance explained for each industry and dominant factors respectively. For all three data sets, Varimax rotation, Eigen value more than 1.0, with a factor loading excess of more than 0.55 was retained for significant results [16].

The results of the factor analysis in Table 2 revealed the latent dimensions that were crucial for the next phase of data analysis. The initial result suggested that the airline industry appeared to be divergent from the other two industries when all three factors are compared as posted by [29]. However, in order to derive parsimonious models for all industries a CFA was necessary. For a model to be found fit, it is recommended that certain criteria are met. It is best for a model that the Tucker-Lewis Index (TLI) [30] and the comparative fit-index (CFI) should both exceed the cut-off value of 0.90. Also the model should record the root mean square error value of approximation (RMSEA) to be either close or below 0.08 coupled with the normed chi-square (χ^2/df) value of less than 3. The model parsimony is most commonly evaluated by examining the Akaike Information Criterion (AIC). A lower AIC value indicates a better model [5, 6, 16]. Table 3 shows the initial and final results (in bold) of the CFA.

Several items that were found to be unfit and redundant were removed, this eventually lead to the elimination of certain factors from some of the models. The third factor for both the Airline and Computer models were removed (as shown in Table 4) as a consequence. This rigorous measure ensured the models are trim and parsimonious. As previously noted, the airline industry did remain different from the other two models by involving *emotional appeal* (EA), *tailored communication* (TC) and *information fit-to-task* (FIT), which reflects the importance of updated and customized information to secure customer relationships [12] and trust [4]. All industries found both *visual appeal* (VA) and *innovativeness* (I) be crucial. However, *visual appeal* (VA) was more prevalent in e-retail [29, 33], while *innovativeness* (I) was in airline

Table 1. Reliability analysis of the dimensions for each industry

Dimensions	Cronbach Alpha scores		
	Airline	Computer	E-retail
Usefulness	**0.8564**	**0.8370**	**0.8373**
FIT1	0.7407	0.6062*	0.5577*
FIT2	0.7147	0.7310	0.6491*
FIT3	0.7658	0.7126	0.6763*
TC1	0.7610	0.6996	0.7073
TC2	0.7365	0.7515	0.7067
TC3	0.7353	0.6763*	0.7121
T1	0.6659*	0.6497*	0.6203*
T2	0.5641*	0.6061*	0.5976*
T3	0.5826*	0.5332*	0.4997*
RT1	0.2805	0.1932*	0.3456*
RT2	0.4003	0.1087*	0.2987*
RT3	-0.2047	-0.0731*	-0.0675*
Ease-of-use	**0.9357**	**0.9135**	**0.9225**
EOU1	0.7621	0.7889	0.7357
EOU2	0.7818	0.7463	0.7985
EOU3	0.8077	0.7543	0.8095
IO1	0.8699	0.7351	0.8156
IO2	0.7660	0.7737	0.7738
IO3	0.8705	0.7630	0.7525
Entertainment	**0.9396**	**0.9535**	**0.9434**
VA1	0.7070	0.7714	0.7878
VA2	0.7771	0.8255	0.7670
VA3	0.7771	0.8646	0.7836
I1	0.8026	0.8362	0.8118
I2	0.8261	0.8330	0.8183
I3	0.8024	0.8647	0.8576
EA1	0.7655	0.8224	0.7888
EA2	0.7856	0.8035	0.7542
EA3	0.6883*	0.7092	0.6723*
Complementary Relationship	**0.9247**	**0.9348**	**0.8903**
CI1	0.7321	0.7969	0.5184*
CI2	0.7480	0.8010	0.5660*
CI3	0.7782	0.7700	0.4875*
OLC1	0.6565*	0.7474	0.7335
OLC2	0.7288	0.7983	0.7535
OLC3	0.7619	0.6976	0.7598
RA1	0.7295	0.8064	0.7028
RA2	0.6975	0.7490	0.6980
RA3	0.7396	0.6590*	0.5991*
Overall	**0.96**	**0.96**	**0.95**

Key: Information fit-to-task (FIT), Tailored communications (TC), Trust (T), Response time (RT), Ease-of-understanding (EOU), Intuitive Operations (IO), Visual appeal (VA), Innovativeness (I), Emotional appeal (EA), Consistent image (CI), Online completeness(OC), and Relative advantage (RA).

[29]. Both computer and e-retail industry had *online-completeness* (OLC) reflecting the need for e-commerce transactions. Only e-retail had a third factor which basically concerned *intuitive operations* (IO) and *ease of understanding* (EOU). These two items signal the significant need for simplicity in Website designs.

Table 2. Factor analysis for each industry

Industry								
Airline (**77.25%**)			Computer (**79.6%**)			E-retail (**81.1%**)		
5 factors (3 dominant & 2 weak factors)			5 factors (3 dominant & 2 weak factors)			5 factors (3 dominant & 2 weak factors)		
Factor loading score for first 3 factors								
F1(**21.2%**)	F2(**19.6%**)	F3(**17.4%**)	F1(**20.7%**)	F2(**20.2%**)	F3(**16.3%**)	F1(**20.9%**)	F2(**17.9%**)	F3(**17.9%**)
I3(.848)	TC1(.817)	IO1(.851)	I1(.847)	OLC2(.815)	EOU2(.840)	VA2(.853)	RA2(.834)	IO2(.809)
I2(.829)	FIT1(.809)	IO3(.814)	I2(.835)	OLC3(.810)	EOU3(.739)	VA3(.839)	OLC3(.823)	IO3(.805)
I1(.808)	FIT3(.807)	IO2(.721)	I3(.816)	OLC1(.722)	EOU1(.729)	VA1(.821)	OLC2(.800)	EOU3(.776)
EA2(.795)	TC3(.779)	EOU2(.720)	VA2(.778)	CI2(.719)	TC1(.644)	I1(.714)	RA1(.790)	IO1(.763)
EA1(.788)	FIT2(.776)	EOU1(.691)	VA3(.722)	CI1(.712)	FIT2(.597)	I2(.680)	OLC1(.746)	EOU2(.665)
VA3(.744)	TC2(.741)	EOU3(.676)	VA1(.714)	CI3(.687)	TC2(.594)	I3(.642)		EOU1(.622)
VA2(.742)				RA1(.655)	FIT3(.590)			
VA1(.706)				RA2(.620)				

*Use key from Table 1

Table 3. CFA models for each industry

Model Fit and Parsi-monious Measures	Airline	Computer	E-retail
χ^2/df	2.867 (**1.879**)	5.376 (**2.029**)	5.999 (**2.393**)
TLI	0.1908 (**0.9763**)	0.784 (**0.9746**)	0.7670 (**0.9482**)
CFI	0.9239 (**0.9485**)	0.8130 (**0.9851**)	0.8082 (**0.9663**)
RMSEA	0.1027 (**0.0705**)	0.1691 (**0.0802**)	0.1720 (**0.0807**)
AIC	560.47 (**127.65**)	870.73 (**90.61**)	753.97 (**172.89**)

Table 4. Parsimonious CFA model for each industry

Airline		Computer		E-retail		
F1	F2	F1	F2	F1	F2	F3
I3(.848)	TC1(.817)	I1(.847)	OLC2(.815)	VA2(.853)	OLC3(.823)	IO2(.809)
I2(.829)	FIT1(.809)	I3(.816)	OLC1(.722)	VA3(.839)	OLC2(.800)	IO3(.805)
I1(.808)	FIT3(.807)	VA2(.778)	CI2(.719)	VA1(.821)	OLC1(.746)	EOU3(.776)
EA2(.795)	TC3(.779)	VA3(.722)	CI1(.712)	I2(.680)		IO1(.763)
EA1(.788)	FIT2(.776)		CI3(.687)			EOU2(.665)
VA3(.744)	TC2(.741)					
VA2(.742)						

*Use key from Table 1

5 Conclusions, Managerial Implications and Limitations

The objective of this paper was to develop a parsimonious model using the Web-Qual™ instrument within the context of Australian online commerce across three Australian industries i.e. Airline, Computers and E-retail. Since integrating the Internet into a business's competitive strategy is now increasingly becoming a strategic imperative, organizations are continually seeking new methodologies to forge close relationships with customers. As such, WebQual™ was found in this research to be a useful website benchmarking tool of user perceptions of Website performance.

Utilizing WebQual™, respondents were able to highlight salient items deemed crucial for each industry's Website design and development practice. Consistent with previous research [5], only the airline industry has called for 'effective information', which is closely related to the trust dimension and was found to be one of the key issues in determining a Website's success. Furthermore, Dell.com.au ranked highest for the dimension of trust, which could be explained by the overall 'superiority' of the Website as seen in the radar plot. However, this could also be attributed to the strong brand awareness of Dell within Australia [1, 4]. Overall, the Australian Websites were primarily concerned with issues relating to innovativeness and visual appeal. However, differences were found across each industry category. This study also brings attention to the importance of users being an integral part of the Website design and development process. Prototypical users could play a critical role in helping to produce a high-performing Website design. This also reaffirms observations made in the usability and ergonomics literature when considering developing graphical user interface (GUI) applications.

This study extends previous studies by [29, 7] and further contributes to the theory development and application of Website quality. Even though the study was limited to Australian e-marketspace, the findings can be generalized to similar industry settings due to the nature of the market (the Web). The CFA approach has proved to increase the statistical rigor in comparison with previous studies of [29, 7] (e.g. ANOVAs and exploratory factor analysis), but nevertheless, the paper suffers from two obvious limitations. First, even though respondents of this study comprised university students who were familiar with Website evaluation, they did not represent the general Australian online population. This could have induced some degree of bias to the data. Second, the number of Websites used to represent each industry, were conveniently sampled and subjective in nature. Future selection of Websites should be based on more rigorous sampling techniques. Nonetheless, the current study does provide a substantial number of directions for future research.

6 Future Research Directions

The results of this research are limited to, and conditioned, by the context in which the empirical work was performed. Consequently, it is recommended that future research should study other industry sectors internationally to refine the WebQual[TM] dimensions to ensure larger numbers of respondents are included to avoid bias and to provide more quantitative rigor. Similarly, an interesting line of enquiry should include testing the generalisability of the WebQual[TM] instrument in a global context to capture the moderating effects of culture on perceptions of performance and importance of quality dimensions. Such research would provide fruitful information to compare and contrast the different elements that are critical to branding and Website quality in the international setting. The role of individual user differences should also be investigated to identify the impact of possible antecedents which could have an influence on Website quality perceptions. These antecedents could include prior consumer brand attitudes and awareness, level of involvement in the product category and the level of user Internet literacy. Finally, another evolving issue worth considering is the ability of 'smart' Websites which are able to cater personalized Web sessions tailor-made differently for each user. Utilizing the recent advancements in software engineering and artificial intelligence, many businesses are involved in an unprecedented race to tag, profile and serve users with different layout, color combination, unique designs to suit personality, and many other Web appealing features to acquire and retain customers.

References

1. Aaker, D.A. and Joachimsthaler, E. (2000) Brand Leadership, New York: The Free Press.
2. Ajzen, I., and Fishbein, M. (1980). Understanding Attitudes and Predicting Social Behavior. Prentice-Hall, Englewood Cliffs, NJ.
3. Atkinson, M. and Kydd, C. (1997). Individual Characteristics Associated with World Wide Web Use: An Empirical Study of Playfulness and Motivation. Database. (28)2: 53-62.
4. Barnes, S.J. and Vidgen, R.T. (2001). An Integrative Approach to the Assessment of E-Commerce Quality. Centre for Information Management Working Paper, University of Bath. Available from: http://www.webqual.co.uk/papers/webqualbookshop.pdf.
5. Bentler, P. (1990). Comparative Fit Indexes in Structural Models. Psychological Bulletin. 107: 238-246.
6. Browne, M. and Cudeck, R. (1993). Alternative Ways of Assessing Model Fit., in K. A. Bollen and J.S. Long, ed.: Testing Structural Equation Models (CA: Sage, Beverly Hills).
7. Carlson, J. and Sinnappan, S. and Voola, R. (2003). Application of the WebQualTM Instrument to Three Australian B2C Websites: Does the Relative Importance of the Dimensions of WebQual Differ Between Industries? Proceedings of the Australian and New Zealand Marketing Academy Conference. Adelaide: SA. December 2nd-4th. CD-ROM.
8. Cronbach, L.J. (1951). Coefficient Alpha and the Internal Structure Tests. Psychometrika. 16: 297-334.
9. Davis, F.D. (1989). Perceived Usefulness, Perceived Ease of Use, and User Acceptance Of Information Technology. MIS Quarterly. 13(3): 319–340.
10. Davis, F.D., Bagozzi, R.P. and Warshaw, P.R. (1989). User Acceptance Of Computer Technology: A Comparison Of Two Theoretical Models. Management Science 35(8): 982–1003.
11. Davis, F.D. and Venkatesh, V. (1996). A Critical Assessment of Potential Measurement Biases In The Technology Acceptance Model: Three Experiments. International Journal of Human Computer Studies. 45: 19–45.
12. Fingar, P., Kumar, H., and Sharma, T. (2000). Enterprise E-commerce: The Software Component Breakthrough for Business to Business Commerce. Florida, USA: Meghan-Kiffer Press.
13. Fishbein, M., and Ajzen, I. (1975). Beliefs, Attitude, Intention, and Behaviour: An Introduction to Theory and Research Addison-Wesley. Reading: MA.
14. Fenech, T. and O'Cass, A. (2001). Internet Users' Adoption of Web Retailing: User and Product Dimensions. Journal of Product and Brand Management. 10(6): 361-381.
15. Goodhue, D.L. and Thompson, R.L. (1995). Task-Technology Fit and Individual-Performance. MIS Quarterly. (19:2): 213-236.
16. Hair, F.J, Anderson, E.R., Tatham, L.R., and Black, C.W. (1998). Multivariate Data Analysis. (5 ed.). New Jersey: Prentice Hall International.
17. Hoffman, D.L. and Novak, T.P. (1996). Marketing in Hypermedia Computer-Mediated Environments: Conceptual Foundations. Journal of Marketing. 60 (Winter): 50-68.
18. Janda, S., Trocchia, P. and Gwinner, K. (2002). Consumer Perceptions of Internet Retail Service Quality. International Journal of Service Industry Management. 13(5): 412-431.
19. Lederer, A., Maupin, D.J., Sena, M.P. and Zhuang, Y. (2000). The Technology Acceptance Model and the World Wide Web. Decision Support Systems. 20: 269-282.
20. Loiacono, E.T., Watson, R.T. and Goodhue, D.L. (2002). WebQual: A Measure of Website Quality. American Marketing Association Conference Proceedings: 432-438.
21. Nunnally, J. (1978). Psychometric Theory. New York: McGraw Hill.
22. O'Neill, M., Wright, C and Fitz, F. (2002). Quality Evaluation in On-Line Service Environments: An Application of the Importance-Performance Measurement Technique. Managing Service Quality. 11(6): 402-417.

23. Parasuraman, A. and Grewal, D. (2000). The Impact of Technology on the Quality-Value-Loyalty Chain: A Research Agenda. Journal of the Academy of Marketing Science. 28(1): 168-74.
24. Parasuraman, A., Zeithaml, V.A. and Berry, L.L. (1988). SERVQUAL: A Multiple Item Scale For Measuring Consumer Perceptions Of Service Quality. Journal of Retailing. 64 (1): 12-40.
25. Phillips, L.A., Calantone, R., Lee, M.T. (1994). International Technology Adoption. Journal of Business and Industrial Marketing. 9(2): 16–28.
26. Riel, A., Liljander, V. and Jurriens, P. (2001). Exploring Consumer Evaluations of E-Services: A Portal Site. International Journal of Service Industry Management. 12(4): 359-377.
27. Shaw, M.J., Gardner, D.M. and Thomas, H. (1997). Research Opportunities in Electronic Commerce. Decision Support Systems. 21: 149-156.
28. Singh, M. (2002). E-Services and Their Impact on B2C E-commerce. Managing Service Quality. 12 (6): 434-446.
29. Sinnappan, S., Carlson, J., and Sukunesan, B. (2004). Website Quality Dimensions of Australian Internet Retailing: An Exploratory Analysis. Journal of Information Technology in Asia (Forthcoming).
30. Tucker, L.R., and Lewis, C. (1973). A Reliability Coefficient for Maximum Likelihood Factor Analysis. *Psychometrika* 38: 1-10.
31. Venkatesh, V. (2000). Determinants of Perceived Ease of Use: Integrating Control, Intrinsic Motivation, And Emotion Into The Technology Acceptance Model. Information Systems Research. 11(4): 342-365.
32. Voss, C. (2000). Developing an E-service Strategy. Business Strategy Review. 11(11).
33. Wolfinbarger M., and Gilly M. (2003). eTailQ: Dimensionalizing, measuring and predicting e-tail quality. Journal of Retailing. 79(3): 183-198.
34. Yang, Z. and Jun, M. (2002). Consumer Perception of E-Service Quality: From Internet Purchaser and Non-Purchaser Perspectives. Journal of Business Strategies. 19(1): 19-41.
35. Zeithaml, V., Parasuraman, A. and Malhotra, A. (2002). Service Quality Delivery Through Websites: A Critical Review of Extant Knowledge. Journal of the Academy of Marketing Science. 30(4): 362-375.

Aspects of Pervasive Computing for Web Based Learning

B. Ramadoss and S.R. Balasundaram

Department of Mathematics and Computer Applications
National Institute of Technology
Tiruchirappalli, 620 015 Tamil Nadu, India
{brama,blsundar}@nitt.edu

Abstract. With the emerging trends driven by advances in information technology lifelong learning has become an essential one for shaping the future of an individual in particular and the society in general[1]. The importance of computer-based learning is growing at all levels of education. The move to a learning society needs changes in personal attitudes and learning infrastructure. Web based learning generally is seen as the chance to innovative learning process. The direction is that learning can take place anywhere, at the moment when it is needed. The focus on individualizing learning process based on time, place, duration, and learning style is on the rise. Pervasive computing, with its focus on users and their tasks rather than on computing devices and technology, provides an attractive vision for the future of web based learning. This paper discusses the features of web based learning, pervasive computing and proposes a framework for use of pervasive computing in web based learning.

Keywords: Web Based Learning, Information Technology, Pervasive Computing, Learning Process, Framework.

1 Introduction

Technology has brought tremendous impact on every aspect of life today, changing the ways people work, socialize, do business, care health, communicate, inform and entertain. Same way, the information revolution has also changed the learning needs of learners, by providing new capabilities to meet the needs. The increased learning demands have begun to make an impact on the curricular, learning and performance demands on institutions, teaching professionals and students. Web based learning (henceforth known as WBL) is a major paradigm shift in the learning environment which connects remote resources and learners under a single roof, taking care of some of these demands. But most of the existing WBL systems do not take the advantage of the recent technologies to cater to the needs of anywhere, anytime, any device medium of education.

What makes this 'learning environment' possible is an emerging technology that will transform society as radically as did the introduction of steam power and the industrial revolution. This is the paradigm of the computer-based intelligent agent developing from research in distributed artificial intelligence. By integrating this new approach with recent developments in telecommunications, distributed computing, knowledge databases, language translators, and multimedia systems, a transparent 'learning environment' can be created (Boshier, 1980) to become a reality. This environment can be regarded as a pervasive learning environment, since the user interacts

G. Das and V.P. Gulati (Eds.): CIT 2004, LNCS 3356, pp. 419–425, 2004.

with visualizations and other simulacra creating an apparent 'physical' reality. Also, learners can feel that resources are reaching to their desk or palms or any unbelievable platforms.

2 Web Based Learning

The rapid rise of the Internet and corporate intranets, widely accessible and built around standard, inexpensive platforms, offers a powerful response to the change and learning needs of individuals (students, organization, teachers etc.). Web Based Learning has the ability to link resources in many different formats (text, images, sound and video), providing a very rich and powerful medium for learners.

2.1 Features of WBL

- It defines the convergence of the Internet and learning, or Internet-enabled learning.
- It uses network technologies to create, foster, deliver and facilitate learning, anytime and anywhere.
- It is a phenomenon, which provides opportunity to allow people and organizations to keep up with the rapid changes that define the Internet world.
- It constitutes a force that gives people and organizations, the competitive edge to allow them to keep ahead of the rapidly changing global economy.
- It avoids cost incurred in travel for learning.

2.2 Types of Web Based Learning [6]

A student can take a course independently, or an entire "classroom" of students can learn under the facilitation of a human instructor. Because of the independent nature of non-instructor-led training, students can learn at their own pace. Not all web based education requires human instruction, but where student-teacher interaction is concerned, it comes in two flavors: synchronous and asynchronous. Asynchronous, the more common of the two, involves modes of communication that do not require immediacy. Students may turn in assignments via email; receive class materials in the mail; may confer in groups on a BBS. Learning is self-paced, and students do not need to be online all at the same time to meet for the course.

Synchronous training, on the other hand, uses modes of communication that foster a real-time environment. Instructors and students may discuss problems in a chat forum. For a highly collaborative environment, where several students and teaching sources participate in the learning or training process, the technology expected is much more. In this environment, interactions can be seen between students and between teachers (or teaching resources).

2.2.1 Non-instructor-Led WBL

Non-instructor-led WBL can be essentially like reading a book and working independently online. It can be just as boring, too, if the designers do not use the Web tools and abilities effectively. Not everyone likes to simply read large amounts of text on screen. Many times learners are offered little or no opportunity for practical appliances of what he or she learns. In case of virtual environment, learners immerse or participate in the virtual world. They take a role within the learning environment. Use of pervasive or ubiquitous computing (discussed in detail in section 3.0), allows the learners to go to still a next level of accessing the resources at their location or device. Instead of a seeing text alone on the book, they can visualize the animation or working model of their learning objects.

2.2.2 Asynchronous WBL
In the asynchronous type, the students may feel unmotivated and disconnected from their co-participants and the course itself. Many experts stress that interaction is a key component to a successful learning model, and that several WBL systems often do not provide enough opportunity for interpersonal exchange. Pervasive computing provides enough opportunity for interpersonal exchange.

2.2.3 Synchronous WBL
Synchronous WBL systems may allow some of the interaction lacking in asynchronous training. Chat programs, teleconferencing, video conferencing help learners and resources to interact to a greater extent. With the use pervasive technology, the effect can be much more, when the dynamism increases to a higher level.

3 Pervasive Computing

Computing is no longer a discrete task bound to a desktop; network computing and mobile computing are fast becoming a part of everyday life and so is the Internet. Rather than being an infrastructure for computers and their users alone, it is now an infrastructure for everyone. Devices like *PDAs* (Personal Digital Assistants), mobile phones, offices, PCs and even home entertainment systems can access information and work together in one integrated system. The challenge is to combine these technologies into a seamless whole and on the Internet. The aim of Pervasive Computing is for computing available wherever it is needed. It distributes intelligence and connectivity to every aspect of life. So conceptually, ships, aircrafts, cars, bridges, tunnels, machines, refrigerators, door handles, lighting fixtures, shoes, hats, packaging clothing, tools, appliances, homes and even things like our coffee mugs and even the human body will be embedded with chips to connect to an infinite network of other devices. An environment can be created where the connectivity of devices is embedded in such a way that it is unobtrusive and always available. Pervasive computing, therefore, refers to the emerging trend toward numerous, easily accessible computing devices connected to an increasingly ubiquitous network infrastructure [3]. (Refer Fig.1)

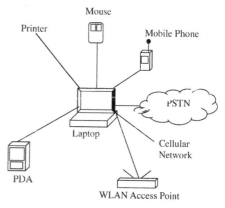

Fig. 1. Devices used in Pervasive Computing

Pervasive computing devices are not personal computers, but very tiny – even invisible – devices, either mobile or embedded in almost any type of object imaginable; all communicating through increasingly interconnected networks [5].

3.1 Subsystems of Pervasive Environment

The following is a list of subsystems involved in the Pervasive Environment.

1. Application subsystem – Virtual Machine, Device Libraries, Data Management
2. User Interface subsystem – Browsers, Multimedia support, Speech recognition, Markup languages, Script languages
3. Communications subsystem – Protocols ranging from TCP/IP, WAP to discovery protocols
4. Security subsystem – Smart cards, SSL, Firewalls etc.
5. Development subsystem – OS dependent tools, Embedded tools, Java etc.

3.2 Devices Used in Pervasive Environment

The following is a list of devices used in pervasive environment:

PDA, Consumer Service Devices, POS Terminals, Smart phone, WAP Phone, Gateways, Embedded controllers, Monitors, Screen phone, Network vehicle, Kiosk etc.

4 Features of Pervasive Computing in Web Based Learning

Pervasive Computing offers the following features for Web Based Learning:

- use of the Internet or corporate intranet
- live interaction with instructor, either through audio or text chat
- use of video, depending on bandwidth or student machines
- Web-standard content (not proprietary) which is easy to produce and change from existing presentation materials
- choice of live or "canned" archives for any-time learning
- learning occurs at users' desktops without going to special technology centers
- use of handheld devices to access information in any way

The above features are implemented through framework and agents.

4.1 Framework

A framework is a type of learning environment or system. Various frameworks are available [7] in the learning process. They are discussed in the following sections.

4.1.1 Multiple Representations of Reality

- an environment is created
- the learning task is encountered and structured within the context
- the environment may be viewed from many different perspectives
- learners enter the world and act from within it

4.1.2 Authentic Tasks
Learners experience the objects resembling real life object using handheld devices.

4.1.3 Real-World, Case-Based Context
Learners acquire new information as needed to solve the case, or learn a set of heuristics (rules first, then are presented with a problem that uses those principles). Agents (discussed later) play vital role for implementation of this kind of framework.

4.1.4 Reflective Practice
This framework provides opportunities, built right into the instructional materials, for learners to ask questions about their new learning skills.

4.1.5 Knowledge Construction
System is designed to explore the existing knowledge base and to encourage the learner to use this base as they progress through a task.

4.1.6 Collaborative Learning
Learners are placed in collaborative workgroups to solve a problem together through conversation and negotiation. Pervasive Computing supports all these frameworks [4].

4.2 Use of Agents

An agent is a software module capable of sending and receiving messages, and making intelligent decisions and performing actions based on the inherent knowledge and the information in received messages. In a convergence of activities from several disciplines, the 'multi-agent systems' technology is the most vital one seen in pervasive computing technology. Some of the important agent mechanisms deployed in pervasive computing are discussed below [2].

a) Knowledge agent – This is an expert in a specific area. This can be a tutor or any other teaching agent. This can respond to learner's queries and provide information. Also, it can link to other relevant agents or information providers.
b) Interface agent – This is an agent associated with the user interface which monitors and learns from the learner's actions and then behaves as an intelligent assistant.
c) Tutor agent – When the learner is working through any task, guidance is provided by an agent (tutor agent) to complete the task.
d) Search agent – Any requested information, say about any article or a topic is searched by roving around the web connecting various databases and devices.

4.3 Example Applications

In order to understand the potential uses of pervasive computing in WBL, we discuss below few examples

Example 1.
Consider the scenario of persons working in one place and undertaking WBL courses in a learning centre situated in another place. It may be the case where these learners

have to travel a long distance from their working site to the learning place, thereby consuming more time. To save the time, certain activities of the WBL may be taken during travel itself. For example, mini-tests, chat or email discussions with other learners, access of remote data bases of information for carrying out certain assignments etc. can be done using handheld devices. The main technical considerations relate to the ease of access implied by the use of PDAs for dissemination of information. Learners can be reached remotely, enabling access to web lectures and providing up-to-date data.

Different types of agents can be employed in this environment, like knowledge agent and search agent to act as information providers and tutor agent to assist the learners in their subject areas.

Example 2.
In the case of Geological studies, there are situations where students will be expected to go to various hilly or rocky places to identify the types of rocks, nature of soils etc. and prepare notes on the same to be submitted as a report to the instructor. A WBL learner of Geology, may use pervasive devices to capture the snapshots of these entities and then send them along with their notes using pervasive infrastructure involving laptops, cameras, sensors, and so on.

Use of knowledge agents and search agents to provide information regarding geological features of the environment will be more useful for this scenario.

Example 3.
For a course on Project Management through WBL, one of the phases of the course is developing a mini project work in organizations. While doing so, groups of students may be assigned various activities of the project work that needs coordination of features related to persons, data, resources etc. Pervasive computing helps in connecting them anytime, from any place.

With the help of interface agents, the members of the group can get proper coordination to carry out their activities.

In pervasive environments, the diversity of the devices leads to hardware adaptation problems. To simplify this, the contents should be kept in XML based form. The XML contents are then converted to the required type say HTML, WML etc.

4.4 Benefits of Pervasive Computing in WBL [3]

- inexpensive production of course materials
- live voice and interactivity across the net
- beginnings of a credible Intellectual Capital Management infrastructure
- simple technical requirements, accessible to students and instructors with limited help from professional engineering or technical staff
- simple and powerful testing/evaluation, ideal for compliance-based training needs quick to get up and running, gain organizational momentum

5 Conclusion

Pervasive computing promises a computing environment that seamlessly and ubiquitously supports learners and information providers in accomplishing their tasks and that renders the actual computing devices and technology largely invisible. Hardware and networking infrastructure to realize this vision are increasingly becoming a reality. In general, wireless communication and broadband access, coupled with the interoperability of various devices, will provide unprecedented opportunities for students whose standard gear now includes cell phones, PDAs, laptops, digital cameras, and video cameras. The interconnectivity among various devices and systems will lead to a distributed-learning model that will take formal and informal teaching and learning beyond the constraints of space, time, and media.

References

1. Self Directed Distance Learning Systems: A Eureopean level cooperation initiative, Laura Farinetti – Dipartimento di Automatica e Informatica, Politecnico di Torino, Italy, Ulrik Schroeder – Institut für Mathematik und Informatik, Pädagogische Hochschule Ludwigsburg, Germany
2. The Learning Web: A System View and an Agent-Oriented Model, Douglas H. Norrie and Brian R. Gaines, University of Calgary, Alberta, Canada T2N 1N4.
3. A System Architecture for Pervasive Computing, Robert Grimm, Tom Anderson, Brian Bershad, and David Wetherall, Department of Computer Science and Engineering, University of Washington, Seattle, {rgrimm, tom, bershad, djw}@cs.washington.
4. Buxton, W. (1995). Ubiquitous Media and the Active Office. Published in Japanese (only) as, Buxton, W. (1995). Ubiquitous Video, Nikkei Electronics, 3.27 (no. 632), 187-195.
5. http://www.ewh.ieee.org/r10/bombay/news4/Pervasive_Computing.htm
6. Continuing Education: Web-based training is one option for continuinged, by Eric Walter, from ZDNet US, 06 May 2002
7. The Web: Design for Active Learning, By Katy Campbell, Academic Technologies for Learning, katy.campbell@ualberta.ca

Author Index

Lecture Notes in Computer Science

For information about Vols. 1–3237

please contact your bookseller or Springer